Credit Card Nation

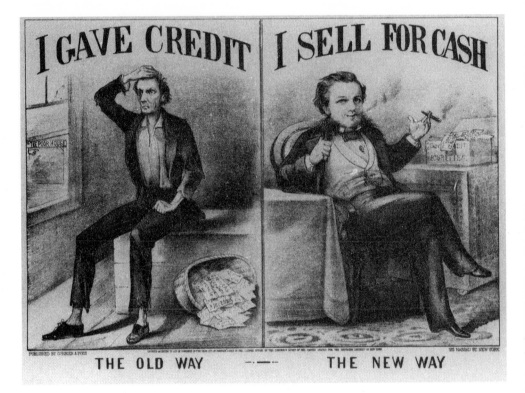

This 1870 lithograph by Currier & Ives extolls the virtues of a cash-only economy. Note that the use of credit is associated with eventual destitution: "The Poor House." The transformation of this historical ethos is one of the most profound cultural revolutions of the post–World War Two epoch. Today, the credit card industry portrays this perspective as a cultural anachronism through its ubiquitous advertising campaigns. The most striking is the 1997 "Future of Money" promotion by MasterCard that exclaims "Imagine a world without cash, without checks because today there are better ways to pay. Credit cards, debit cards, smart cards from MasterCard. The Future of Money."

Credit Card
Nation

. . .

The Consequences of
America's Addiction to Credit

. . .

Robert D. Manning

BASIC

BOOKS
A Member of the Perseus Books Group

Designed by Mark McGarry

FIRST EDITION

Library of Congress Cataloging-in-Publication Data
Manning, Robert C.
    Credit card nation : the consequences of America's addiction to credit /
    Robert C. Manning.
        p.   cm.
    Includes bibliographical references and index.
    ISBN 0-465-04366-6 (alk. paper)
    1. Credit cards—United States.   2. Consumer credit—United States.   I. Title.

HG3755.8.U6 M36   2000
332.7'65''0973—dc21
                                                                00-063101

00 01 02 03 / 10 9 8 7 6 5 4 3 2 1

For Frances Fox Piven, whose intellectual guidance and social policy activism have set the standard for a generation of scholars and social activists.

And to my only love, Anita, because I loved you before I met you, I have been in love with you since I saw you, and I will love you forever.

Contents

Acknowledgments

THE LONG AND WINDING ROAD OF THIS PROJECT has taken so many twists and turns that it would take a road map to trace its intellectual journey. The study began with an investigation into the changing nature of social inequality in the early 1980s and the impact of declining wages and job displacement on middle- and working-class families. As it became clear that consumer credit was playing an increasingly important role in the new patterns of American inequality, this uncharted social terrain became my daily research laboratory.

Over the past fifteen years, I have conducted hundreds of interviews with people from different social, cultural, and economic backgrounds from throughout the United States. I am especially indebted to those who shared their innermost feelings about this increasingly emotional topic. At Georgetown University, I am especially appreciative of the cooperation of Jennifer S. Blackshear and Jason T. Britton, who took both a personal and public advocacy position to publicize the social costs of student credit card debt. Heidi S. Hiemstra, University of Pennsylvania, offered invaluable insights and personal support in the early phases of the study.

I am immensely grateful to those who shared their personal anguish of the human cost of the roaring 1980s. Dr. Ralph David Thomas helped guide me through the turbulent world of high finance and Wall Street's "secret handshakes"; his support of the project and personal commitment to its completion were immeasurable. Thank you, compadre. In Washington, D.C., I have been most fortunate to enjoy a collegial relationship with Stephen Brobeck and the staff of Consumer Federation of America (CFA). Without his personal support and belief in the contributions of this research, the results would not have matched CFA's lofty standards or achieved the national attention that the work has since received. In terms of the latter, the most unfortunate of circumstances led Janne O'Donnell and Trish Johnson to share with me the pain of their ultimate personal loss. Their efforts to publicize the impact of student credit card debt were an inspiration to the present work.

During the most difficult stage of the project, I incurred an enormous debt to Arturo Valenzuela of Georgetown University for his help in ensuring that the institutional edifice for this study was firmly in place. Also at Georgetown, Rosa Evergreen and Liana Prieto went beyond the call of duty to bring the project to successful completion. In particular, Liana's fieldwork, which provided instructive insights that were incorporated into Chapter 7, and Rosa's dedication to completing the final polishing of the manuscript are debts that I cannot possibly repay with sufficient interest.

My editor, Vanessa Mobley, demonstrated a professional commitment to bringing this project to fruition; words cannot express the depth of my appreciation. Under the most stressful of circumstances and in the darkest of days, her stewardship enabled the hundreds of neglected voices that are the basis of this book to receive the public attention they deserve. For too many reasons to list, I thank Anita Cristina Butera for her personal and professional sacrifices in ensuring that this project was finally completed. And last, to the hundreds of people who honored the project with thousands of hours of their lives—as respondents, confidants, research assistants, and interested citizens—I thank you for discussing these personal and often intimate details of your lives and for permitting me to share them publicly. It is my hope that these efforts not only will contribute to a more democratic and public discussion of the role of bank policies in our everyday lives, but also will replace the accountant's financial tallies with more appropriate social measures of the impact of debt in American society.

r.d.m.
Washington, D.C.

Can't Leave Home Without It:

Consumer Credit and
Debt in American Society

The President of the United States: A Case History

On March 1, 1999, President Clinton was enjoying a family vacation in the scenic mountain resort of Park City, Utah. While shopping at Dolly's bookstore, the president presented his charge card and was preparing to leave with his purchase. His charge card of the rich and famous—American Express—extols the convenience of not having to worry about such mundane issues as cash or a sufficient line of credit.

To the surprise of the sales clerk, the computer rejected the charge, and he had to inform Mr. Clinton that "believe it or not, your card must have expired yesterday." The president replied, "I must have left the new one at home." The clerk then called American Express to authorize the charge to the account of "W. J. Clinton," and the request was again rejected. So much for Jerry Seinfeld's assurances that the AMEX card can solve your most pressing problems without the need for money. President Clinton then turned to the time-honored practice of the cash-deprived: He asked an aide for a personal loan and paid for his purchases with real rather than plastic money.[1]

In the United States, where the question "paper or plastic?" increasingly refers to the method of payment rather than to shopping bags, this episode highlights one of the most profound social and cultural revolutions of the post–World War II era: the ascendance of the consumer credit society, which both masks social status differences and exacerbates the widening chasm of U.S. postindustrial inequality. If even the President of the United States is thwarted in his use of the old financial standby, credit, his experience dramatically reveals the contradiction that American Express is the convenient means of payment for royalty and celebrities as well as unemployed, status-conscious college students. The ongoing technological advances of "rational" computer processing systems[2] and the economies of scale they provide imply that the credit card industry has expanded into new markets of more economically marginal members. Times have changed when the president is denied credit while an unemployed "member in good standing" is shielded from financial embarrassment by the imprimatur of a major credit card.

The tremendous expansion of the plastic economy, with a multitude of marketing themes ranging from altruistic (homebound elderly program, Chapter 9) and democratic (small business corporate programs, Chapter 8) to convenience (future of money, Chapter 4) and indolent consumption (exotic vacations or extravagant children's gifts, Chapter 5) and even frugality (rebate programs, Chapter 4), underscores the profound influence of the credit card industry among all social groups in America. The industry's promotional campaigns have historically emphasized the uniformly positive role of consumer credit in resolving problems in our daily lives: unexpected medical care, emergency airline travel, auto repairs, credit for cash-starved entrepreneurs, lost luggage, stolen wallet, expensive business dinner, money for a date, baseball game with son, family reunion expenses, season tickets with wife at the opera, new golf clubs, and even currency conversion in Europe.

The Credit Card Nation, emerging from the profound economic dislocations of U.S. industrial restructuring and the deregulation of U.S. financial services, marks its ascent from the late 1970s. It is distinguished by the rise of distinctive attitudes toward savings and debt—guided by the cultural legacy of the "cognitive connect" between household earnings and consumption decisions—that are being rapidly reshaped by the dramatic advances in computer-driven information-processing technologies and one of the most successful and innovative mass marketing campaigns of the postwar epoch.

In the process, the Credit Card Nation has greatly enhanced our quality of life over the past two decades by offering convenient methods of payment (Mobil-AMEX flash pass) and easy credit during periods of economic distress and uncertainty. Additionally, it offers low-cost and even free credit for the most economically advantaged and masks social and economic crises within the privacy of Americans' suburban castles. For instance, financial pressures that otherwise would require an explanation to family members or even bank loan officers can be temporarily concealed through the "magic of plastic." Americans appreciate this kind of financial confidentiality almost as much as they do immediate access to cash or credit. For Americans, the nonmonetary price of debt is often the most costly, since it must be repaid publicly through social obligations, reciprocity, and even shame or public embarrassment.

Plastic money may shelter Americans from the social cost of borrowing, but users may find a variety of unintended accompanying costs, aside from the annual percentage rate (APR) and penalty fees. Examples abound: the eager entrepreneur who is encumbered with costly credit card debts after the business venture goes bust; the shrewd investor whose plastic-financed e-trades yield headaches rather than a financial windfall; college students who dress for success with their university "affinity" credit cards and are then shocked when their job prospects are diminished by a poor credit report. More important, the defiant "just do it" or "just charge it" consumption culture is fracturing the "cognitive connect" forged by previous generations between work and consumption and between earnings and standard of living. Not surprisingly, consumer credit cards, together with persuasive mass marketing campaigns, have been crucial catalysts for this cognitive transformation.

As American society undergoes a fundamental shift from an economic system based on industrial production to consumer-driven postindustrial services, a fragile social balance is emerging between the new patterns of production (work) and consumption (leisure). The key question is, how can postindustrial society maintain social order if its citizens are conditioned to prefer short-term pleasure (consumption) over pain (production) or spending over saving?[3] The cross-corporate marketing of "fun"—as a commodity to be purchased and immediately enjoyed—has become a central feature of the culture of consumption and is facilitated by the widespread use of bank credit cards. This view was elegantly articulated by Benjamin Barber[4] and exemplified by advertising campaigns for the Sony-Citibank credit card. A 1998 magazine ad, featuring a professionally clad twenty-something man playing in a downtown street, rhetorically asked, "Who said hard work never killed anybody?" The answer: "Some dead guy . . . Use the new Sony Card and turn the things you buy into everything Sony . . . movies, music, electronics, games . . . The Sony Card . . . The official currency of playtime."

It is important to note, as Lendol Caldor explains in his historical study of installment credit prior to the rise of the Credit Card Nation, that the "myth of economic virtue" pervades revisionist views of credit and debt throughout American history.[5] From Mark Twain's witty satire of the lustful acquisitiveness and greedy speculation of the postbellum era in *The Gilded Age* (1873) to David Tucker's argument in *The Decline of Thrift in America* (1991) that "installment buying required a moral revolution against the Puritan ethnic,"[6] Caldor notes that "critics saw that consumer credit [as a repudiation of Puritan thrift] not only tempted people to sin, it provided the means for sinning as well." More important, Caldor explains that the extension of consumer installment credit historically served to enforce rather than undermine the moral virtue of hard work, budgeting, and saving. This leads to the assertion that increased consumer consumption has served to discourage moral laxity by rewarding strict adherence to installment contracts with additional sources of credit for financing new forms of consumption. Hence, this disciplined regimen of credit-based consumer consumption has historically helped to maintain the delicate balance between oppressive labor systems of production (work) and the social relations of consumption (leisure).[7]

Today, the ascendance of the Credit Card Nation mirrors the shifting economic balance of power of banking over industry, a trend that means financing consumption is more lucrative than traditional goods-producing industries.[8] In fact, General Electric's GE Capital (consumer credit) division generates higher profits than its core manufacturing divisions. The new easy-credit system constitutes a more serious threat to the myth of economic virtue than earlier industrial regimes. That is, in sharp contrast to Calder's historical analysis, the new ethos of consumer credit is undermining the historical balance between production (work) and consumption (leisure). For example, during the downsizing frenzy of the late 1980s and early 1990s, credit cards became the social safety net of the unemployed. This new source of unrestricted (noninstallment) credit offered workers greater bargaining power over their next form of employment; they no longer were compelled to accept the first job offer. In fact, among the many survival strategies that emerged from the layoffs of middle-class workers, including job-hunting support groups (5 O'Clock Clubs), one of the most useful was the advice to apply for as many credit cards as possible before getting a pink slip so that job seekers would have more time and financial resources for securing the best possible position after being axed (Chapter 5).

Additionally, the availability of plastic money enables many Americans to resist the labor discipline of 9-to-5 jobs by "hustling" with relatively low-cost credit, such as investing in real estate or the stock market or engaging in various forms of self-employment. It even undermines labor control by allowing people to quit intolerable jobs or leave unbearable social arrangements (residing with parents, bad marriage) by living on "other people's money" (Chapter 8). The latter is glorified in the popular bumper sticker "I pay Visa with my MasterCard." Significantly, the promotion of consumption over production features an economic logic that no longer values the moral virtue of thrift in the strictest sense. That is, access to and cost of credit reflect underlying patterns of social inequality in the United States. For example, payday loans from pawnshops or check-cashing enterprises (Chapter 7) cost over 30 times more than financing purchases on credit cards. Similarly, those who pay off their credit card charges at the end of the month receive essentially free loans—a group disdainfully referred to by bankers as "deadbeats" (Chapter 4). In short, those who need credit the most ultimately subsidize the low-cost credit of those that need it the least.

Last, the most profitable niche of the credit card market features consumers without jobs—college students. The credit card industry is aggressively marketing easy credit on campus before students can demonstrate their economic virtue. In the process, these advertising campaigns fundamentally influence the consumption tastes and corporate loyalties of young adults through cross-marketing strategies. Hence, their economic morals are being shaped by the credit card "carrot" with little knowledge of the proverbial collection "stick" because they generally lack the experience of working full-time and making installment payments (Chapter 6). Ironically, it is easier for college students to obtain credit cards while in school than after they graduate and begin an entry-level job. Not surprisingly, recent college graduates commonly refer to their credit cards as a self-deprecating entitlement: yuppie food stamps.

As a result, Americans are experiencing cognitive befuddlement that reflects an economic virtue whose moral imperatives fundamentally clash with the profit-generating motives of the credit card industry. Too much disciplinary stick leaves the credit card industry with too little profitable carrot. Hence, like the moral campaign to reduce underage alcohol consumption, the promotion of economic virtue threatens the profitable pillars of the newly deregulated financial services industry.[9] This conundrum calls for inquiry into the macroeconomic (U.S. triangle of debt) and institutional (Citibank) forces that have fundamentally shaped the Credit Card Nation. In the process, it illuminates the role of consumer credit and debt in the changing patterns of social inequality in postindustrial America.

"It's Everywhere You Want to Be"—and Preapproved, Too

After celebrating the arrival of the new millennium, American society registered another less publicized millennial milestone: almost 1.5 billion consumer credit cards. That's right, *1.5 billion cards* held by nearly 158 million cardholders. That's an average of ten credit cards per cardholder. The typical American adult has about four retail, three bank, one phone, nearly one gasoline, and a travel and entertainment (American Express, Diners Club) or a miscellaneous corporate credit card.[10]

The explosion of consumer credit cards mirrors both the growing indebtedness of American households (Chapter 2) and the tremendous success of one of the most costly, creative, and enormous mass marketing campaigns ever unleashed by corporate America. In fact, if you haven't received a "preapproved" credit card solicitation in at least a month, then you are either unpacking from a recent move, avoiding the IRS, or your mail carrier is not delivering "Dear Occupant" letters. In 1994, for example, U.S. households were bombarded with over 2.3 billion direct-mail solicitations for credit cards—a hefty 60 percent increase over the previous year. This trend continued through the end of the decade. By 1998, direct-mail solicitations peaked at 3.5 billion and then dipped by about 10 percent in 1999. Overall, about three out of four U.S. households receive these "invitations" in the mail. This means that 35–75 preapproved offers are delivered annually to each of these targeted households, depending upon their consumption activities and debt levels.[11]

Since the early 1980s, consumer credit has become the lifeblood of the U.S. economy. In fact, consumer credit cards are so important in influencing domestic economic trends (inflation, GDP, and employment) that President Carter in 1980 and President Bush in 1991 sought to regulate officially the availability and cost. Nevertheless, most Americans are unaware of the larger economic forces and institutional motivations that influence their daily attitudes toward consumption, credit, and debt. This is due to the sophisticated advertising strategies of the credit card industry, which quickly learned from early consumer research studies that "changes in [consumer attitudes] will lead to changes in the aggregate demand for consumer installment credit."[12] With slick yet familiar-sounding names such as Visa, MasterCard, American Express (Optima), Discover (Private Issue), and the hi-tech Blue card, the industry entices us with sales pitches that emphasize financial freedom and security: "Have it the way you want it with Visa," "Master the moment," "The American Express card: Your key . . . opens doors for you all over the world," "It pays to Discover," "Private Issue—the card *you* design to meet your changing [financial] needs," and "Blue [smart card] from American Express . . . a little piece of the future that got here early."

Interestingly, the standard American Express charge card promotes the economic virtue of Puritan thrift (no costly finance charges), since all purchases must be paid in full each month. Yet, at the same time, its TV commercials and billboards subliminally offer status-conscious club members the vicarious thrill of rubbing shoulders with celebrity members—many of whose profligate lifestyles are regaled in journalistic reports of the rich and famous. Not unexpectedly, the success of this marketing strategy has not been ignored by AMEX competitors. Television ads of Visa, MasterCard, and Discover have featured a wide range of celebrities, including singer Tony Bennett, politician Bob Dole, musician Elton John, basketball star Hakeem Olajuwon, football/baseball star Dion Sanders, James Bond (actor Pierce Brosnan), actor Gregory Hines, actor John Lithgow, actress Shirley MacLaine, political consultant James Carville, and writer Kurt Vonnegut, alas, no academics. Discover's Private Issue has offered personalized credit cards featuring a choice of celebrity designs by Florence Griffith Joyner, Jane Seymour, and Ringo Starr. Other cards have been tied to rock bands (KISS, Rolling Stones) or popular culture, such as the MBNA Garfield Master-Card, the Austin Powers "It's titanium, baby" Visa, and the Dilbert NextCard Visa that lets members choose their official PictureCard and titles such as Supreme Ruler or Evil Director of HR (Human Resources).[13]

If celebrities do not entice you to join their credit card club, there is marketing strategy B: appeal to emotional attachments to nonprofit charitable groups. People can support their favorite causes and organizations (colleges, sororities, environmental groups, religious associations, political causes) by joining special "affinity" credit card programs that remit monetary donations (less than 1.0 percent of annual charges) based on the volume of the member's purchases. By exploiting our social craving to establish personal identities through group association, affinity cards provide the cardholder with instant recognition. Like customized bank checks or souvenir T-shirts, consumer credit cards have become individualized billboards that convey social or political statements through pictures of virtually any activity or object of interest. These include a favorite pet (send your pet's picture to First USA), leisure activity, hobbies, professional association (American Bar Association), professional sports team (NFL), museum (Smithsonian), favorite magazine (*The Nation*), and even your city (D.C.'s Jefferson Memorial).

The most extreme version of this marketing strategy manipulates our sympathy for innocent children and the vulnerable elderly. For example, Visa with its literacy initiative, which features celebrity spokesman Danny Glover, sends a financial donation (less than 1.0 percent of member charges) to reading programs for disadvantaged children. Another Visa promotion shows a picture of a young child alone with his teddy bear; the caption entreats cardholders, "Use your Visa card and make it all better." Similarly,

Visa's "homebound elderly" program seeks to influence our spending habits by appealing to concern for indigent senior citizens. Who could not justify a credit card purchase that might benefit needy children or someone's helpless grandparents?

The industry's marketing exploits our materialistic impulses through "co-branded" credit cards with corporations that woo us with free airline travel (American Airlines), consumer products (General Electric), automobile down payments (General Motors), gasoline (Shell), telephone calls (Sprint), groceries (Giant), sports memorabilia (ESPN), and, of course, cash (Discover). Some offer special sweepstakes programs inspired by our cultural penchant to gamble and receive something for nothing. Visa's 1998 "magic of plastic" promotion registered 16,000 winners, who received free purchases when their credit card transaction was processed at a randomly selected "magic" second of the day. Likewise, Discover's 1999 "cash back bonus countdown" awarded $100 to 2,000 winners; four others received $25,000, plus a final grand prize winner $1 million during the millennium countdown at Times Square in New York City.

Another industry tactic is direct cash rebates. Among the many innovative programs is "virtual" (on-line) Principal Bank's direct deposit of as much as a 1.25 percent cash rebate (minimum of $100) of charges on its Principal Platinum Visa into a free checking account. NationsBank even offers baby boomers an opportunity to prepare for the golden years with its Start card. The latter funds a tax-deferred annuity for retirement with Metropolitan Life based on a 1 percent rebate of cardholder charges. Although these membership benefits are touted as "free rewards," the fine print will probably surprise you. The Associates National Bank Visa proclaims "up to 3 percent cash back" but only if you are a "revolver," that is, paying at least 19.9 APR. Like political freedom in any democracy, "free" in the Credit Card Nation has varying meanings and costs. Indeed, these membership benefits are paid by relatively higher finance charges and annual account fees, and a "free" airline ticket may be much more expensive than a discount fare depending on the cost of membership fees and the volume of credited charges.[14]

Even more insidious are the aggressive efforts to recruit the newest and least experienced consumers—college and, increasingly, high school and junior high school students. This is exemplified by Citibank, the largest issuer of "kiddie" cards. Its sophisticated targeting of adolescent vulnerabilities and youthful ignorance is illustrated by a 1993 advertisement: "The Citibank Classic Visa instills in students feelings of safety, security, and general wellness not unlike those experienced in the womb. Therefore it is the mother of all credit cards . . . [it offers] a sense of Identity . . . Security . . . and Autonomous Will from your newfound financial independence . . . don't be crazy . . . Call (*students don't need a job or a cosigner*)."[15] Today, student-targeted advertisements emphasize how credit cards reduce the stress of college life, contribute to social independence (especially from parents), offer conveniences for coping with modern life, enhance social status, and facilitate those special moments. This marketing equates the use of credit cards with freedom from many of the commonplace hassles as part of the normal transition to adulthood. For instance, a 1998 mass mailing by Associates National Bank Visa exclaims, "Free from parental rule at last. Now all you need is money." A 1998 Master-Card television ad discusses a first date and declares, "Dinner $40. Movie $15. Second date with the right girl: Priceless."[16]

Recent mass media campaigns reflect the rapid growth, profitability, and intensifying competition within the consumer credit industry. For instance, the three major credit card associations (Visa, MasterCard, American Express) reported less than $75 million in combined advertising expenditures during 1985. The sum climbed to $385 million for 1993–1994 (American Express, $197 million; Visa, $108.5 million; and MasterCard, $79.5 million), with almost $40 million spent by Discover.[17] A tripartite marketing blitz appeared during the 1995 National Basketball Association (NBA) Conference Finals that featured commercial breaks sponsored by Visa, Master-Card, and American Express. This credit card troika is a frequent sponsor of major sports and cultural events and institutions. For example, Visa inaugurated its 1998 Winter Olympics campaign by announcing, "Every time you make a purchase with your Visa card, Visa will make a donation to help the U.S. Olympic Team hopefuls."[18] MasterCard received international exposure with its sponsorship of the 1994 World Cup soccer games and 1998 sponsorship of the National Hockey Association; MBNA MasterCard is the primary sponsor of a major professional auto race. Visa is a leading sponsor of the National Football League and a "U.S. Team Partner" of the 2000 Summer Olympics. In comparison, American Express tends to support events that appeal to a more affluent client base, such as professional tennis, golf, and polo tournaments.

The stepchild of the credit card industry, Discover, has combined several of these marketing themes in an effort to expand its visibility and upgrade its corporate image. Not only has Discover enlisted celebrity spokesmen (John Lithgow, Gregory Hines, Kurt Vonnegut) but it has even employed a host of historical luminaries (Ben Franklin, Thomas Jefferson, Harriet Tubman) through its Smithsonian Institution affinity card program, which featured a $10 million corporate sponsorship of the Smithsonian's 150th anniversary celebration. The 1997 kickoff campaign appealed to national pride and cardholders' moral responsibility to support this national cultural institution: "It's Ben Franklin's credit card. And Harriet Tubman's. In fact, it's the credit card of just about any historic American you can name. It's the Smithsonian Card. Every time you make a purchase you'll help the Institution preserve America's past."

If preserving posterity is not sufficient motivation, the Smithsonian Discover card also appeals to economic self-interest: "Ben Franklin [said] 'A penny saved is a penny earned.' But now a penny spent can earn you free U.S. Savings Bonds . . . Save for your future, and support the Smithsonian . . . because you'll earn points toward free U.S. Savings Bonds." A $50 Series EE Savings Bond is awarded for charging $5,000. Sounds like a deal, right? But, if you charge $5,000 in a year and average a $1,000 account balance (debt), the $25 present value of the bond will have cost over $200 in finance charges. That is quite a profit for wrapping credit card interest fees in the patriotic red, white, and blue of America's national heritage. Ben Franklin would roll over in his grave if he knew his name was being used to encourage Americans to spend rather than frugally manage their budgets in order to "earn" their savings.

By the new millennium, the mass marketing campaigns of the credit card industry had successfully penetrated virtually all social and economic spheres of American society. Whether signing up national retailers like grocery store chains (Safeway), membership warehouses (Costco), and fast-food restaurants (Popeyes) or integrating corporate vending machines into proprietary credit card processing systems (1998 Coca-Cola–MasterCard joint advertising campaign), the industry made the ubiquity of consumer credit cards a testament to both technological and marketing innovations. Indeed, the term "bank" credit card is more accurately labeled "universal" consumer card. What an amazing transformation since Bank of America began marketing the precursor to Visa with its 1974 ad campaign "BankAmericard. Think of it as money." With the introduction of credit card "courtesy" checks in the early 1990s as well as easy access to cash advances through expanding systems of automated teller machines (brainchild of past Citigroup President John Reed), bank credit cards could be used to purchase anything—legal or illegal.

By Madison Avenue standards, the slogan "Visa—it's everywhere you want to be" is an understatement in the Credit Card Nation. Even so, the argument that consumer credit cards are an inevitable, technological progression of rational, modern society belies the lack of interest and even cultural resistance in other industrialized countries like Japan and in the European Union (EU). As an article on the 1998 Winter Olympics in

Nagano, Japan, explained, "Cash. The Japanese don't leave home without it. . . . [According to a 66-year-old merchant,] 'Young people can figure out how to use a credit card, but not me. I always deal in cash and I'm not going to change. . . . [Another merchant explained,] 'We did [accept credit cards] for the Olympics, but if possible I'd like to be paid in cash. . . . It's so strange; I guess Westerners don't use cash. People who speak English tend to use credit cards.'"[19]

The increasing use of exotic, international settings in credit card advertisements may reflect more the industry's desire to expand into new markets abroad than the rising demand for high-interest consumer credit. For instance, a recent Visa television advertisement introduces Sister Maria who purchases Hank Williams Jr. CDs over the Internet because of the isolation of her monastery in the Alps. It's a great advertisement for expanding the boundaries of the Internet and offers beautiful scenery for TV viewers, but it does not mirror the consumer market that Visa's member banks need to increase their profits. Similarly, a 1999 Visa ad features a group of African tribesmen joking about how to stop a charging rhinoceros. The answer— American Express, of course. For these folks, the magic of plastic is even more of a futuristic dream than the use of smart cards in the Black Hills of South Dakota. The subliminal point, however, is that consumer credit cards are expanding to the far reaches of the global village as the modern form of commercial transactions. So, get with the program—and charge.

How Consumer Debt Happens

During the 1980s, the credit card industry's marketing campaigns successfully expanded into middle-class markets, including blue- and white-collar workers who suffered unexpected employment disruptions due to corporate downsizings and recession-related layoffs. This profitable linkage with lower-income households early in the decade emboldened banks to target other nontraditional niche markets such as unemployed college students and retired senior citizens in the mid-1980s, then the working poor and the recently bankrupt with secured credit cards in the late 1980s and early 1990s. The results were impressive. The profusion of credit cards generated rapidly escalating consumer finance charges, merchant discount fees, and, of course, profits. Between 1980 and 1990, the charges of the average U.S. household jumped sharply from $885 to $3,753 per year, or more than twice as fast as disposable income, while average cardholder debt soared from $395 to $2,350. According to Lawrence M. Ausubel, in his highly acclaimed 1991 article "The Failure of Competition in the Credit Card Market," credit card issuers earned between three and five times the ordinary rate of return in banking in the period 1983–1988.[20] This extraordinary profitability intensified institutional pressures for bank deregulation that led to the Financial Services Modernization Act of 1999.

By the end of 1994, the typical American cardholder had amassed nearly $4,000 in revolving debt on a total of three or four bank credit cards with an annual interest rate of about 17 percent. While general-purpose cards (Visa, MasterCard, Discover, American Express, Diners Club) accounted for less than half (41 percent) of the $170 billion of total charges in 1980, they jumped to almost 78 percent of the $467 billion of total charges in 1990. By the end of 1994, 185 million Visa cards accounted for $271 billion in charges, 131 MasterCards for $170 billion, 42 million Discover cards for $39 billion, and 25 million American Express cards for $101 billion. In total, these 384 million credit cards were responsible for $581 billion in charges, or an average of $1,513 per account.[21]

Flush with this newfound prosperity, the credit card industry's advertising budget escalated sharply in the late 1990s. Between 1994 and 1998, it doubled from $425 million to $870 million. Although the industry spending leader remained American Express ($334 million), Visa International ($260 million) substantially narrowed the gap, followed by the credit card unit of Morgan Stanley, Dean Witter, Discover ($153 million) and Master-Card ($123 million).[22] This trend began to level off with the onset of the industry's profitability crisis beginning in 1997 due to the saturation of middle-class markets and the rise of convenience users.

Today, over 158 million cardholders have about 650 million retail credit cards, 506 million bank cards, 185 million phone cards, 107 gasoline cards, 41 million travel and entertainment cards (including American Express, Diners Club), and 66 million miscellaneous (airline, car rental) cards. Bank credit cards and travel and entertainment charge cards account for almost 80 percent of the total volume of credit card spending. At the end of 1999, Visa's 247.8 million credit cards accounted for 48.9 percent of all bank cards and $253.6 billion in U.S. receivables. MasterCard's 180.7 million cards (35.7 percent market share) and $175.1 billion in U.S. receivables are followed by Discover with 48.0 million cards (9.3 percent market share) and $38 billion in U.S. receivables and then American Express with 29.9 million cards (5.5 percent) and $23.4 billion.[23] Overall, bank credit card interest (finance charges) and fee (late, over limit) income tripled in the 1990s—from a combined $28.6 billion in 1990 to $78.0 billion in 1998.[24]

This expansion of consumer credit partially explains the tremendous increase of credit card debt, which constituted about 43 percent of the $1.4

trillion outstanding consumer (revolving and nonrevolving) debt in early 2000. From a modest $55.1 billion (15.8 percent of outstanding consumer debt) in 1980, revolving consumer (primarily bank and retail credit card) debt soared to $238.6 billion (30.2 percent of outstanding consumer debt) in 1990 and then almost doubled to $443 billion (40.4 percent of outstanding consumer debt) in 1995. Indeed, Americans amassed more credit card debt during 1995, almost $78 billion, than the cumulative total in 1980. Although the growth of credit card debt slowed substantially in the late 1990s, from $500 billion in 1996 to nearly $600 billion at the end of 1999 (42.7 percent of outstanding consumer debt),[25] the most important trend was the widening debt gap between revolvers and convenience users. This distinction is especially important for understanding the institutional dynamics (e.g., bank credit card policies) that underlie the rising cost of revolving consumer credit (climbing interest rates, fees) and their role in exacerbating postindustrial inequality by increasing the cost of credit for the lower and middle classes—a policy that essentially subsidizes the free credit of affluent groups.

For instance, at the beginning of 2000, approximately 78 million households had at least one bank credit card. Together, they had amassed a seasonally adjusted total of about $603 billion in revolving consumer debt. After the calculation is modified by compensating for delayed consumer payments and other U.S. Federal Reserve accounting adjustments, the average credit card debt for these households was about $6,648. Such a computation is a commonly used measure of aggregate consumer indebtedness, but the estimate is fundamentally flawed and increasingly inaccurate because it combines convenience users with revolvers. To the chagrin of the banking industry, the proportion of convenience users increased sharply during the economic expansion of the 1990s—from 29 percent in 1991 to about 43 percent in 2000.

A more precise estimate requires the separate examination of the approximately 33.5 million convenience households (zero credit card debt) and the nearly 44.5 million revolver households. In early 2000, revolver households averaged $11,575 in outstanding revolving debt. This is a significant increase (6.7 percent) from the average of $10,845 only one year earlier—especially considering the favorable economic conditions in the United States. And it is nearly double the aggregate household estimate ($6,648).[26] This Dickensian "Tale of Two Cities" is obscured when estimates are based only on aggregate credit card debt patterns and robust economic indicators during the prosperous 1990s. For these reasons, most Americans were shocked to learn that the nation recorded an ignominious milestone in the fall of 1998: a negative national savings rate.[27]

Although the names have changed (remember BankAmericard, Interbank Card, Midwest Bank Card, Town & Country, Everything Card?), the goals of the credit card industry remain the same: penetrate and expand into new markets, "revolve" people into debt, and thereby maximize profits. The irony is that the deluge of credit card applications, with their seductive message of simply "charge it" (the marketing precursor to Nike's mantra "Just do it"), masks the social undercurrents of financial entrapment, indebtedness, and confusion. As one professional woman confided, "I was spending money that I hadn't earned yet for things that I had already used." The central question is why? The answer requires a clearer understanding of the social causes of personal and household indebtedness as distinct from their consequences. For instance, how is the personal "problem" of debt, such as competitive consumption, distinguished from the broader societal and life-cycle trends that contribute to rising household debt, such as illness, divorce, employment disruptions, declining earnings, escalating college costs, soaring home mortgages, family emergencies, or unexpected auto and home repairs? These opposing issues are paramount in explaining skyrocketing household indebtedness in the United States.

It is important to note that the media are among the most important sources of our collective confusion and *mis*understanding of this social phenomenon. Indeed, reports in the mainstream press tend to deflect attention from the social implications of mass solicitation campaigns and omnipresent marketing by reporting on the extravagant spending sprees and compulsive shopaholic tendencies of atypical Americans. As banks embarked on marketing consumer credit cards after the 1981–1982 recession, sensationalist accounts of journalists (featuring condescending advice and a stern tone of reproval) helped to confuse public perceptions and conflate causes of debt with their deleterious consequences.

For instance, *Money* magazine profiled the spending patterns of Michael and Cynthia Proctor that led to their financial problem. According to the article, the "Proctors never asked for their first credit cards. Four of them more or less appeared pre-approved in the couple's Huntsville, Texas, mail box in the summer of 1982. [In their late 20s, the couple] made $43,000 working for the Texas Department of Corrections. Michael was also studying nights for his master's degree . . . But for all Michael's schooling, the Proctors had never learned to control debt." The story described the Proctors' three-year spending binge "'using credit cards for everything—whatever caught our fancy.'" The end came when they were unable to make the minimum payments on their nearly 60 credit accounts with an outstanding total debt of $34,500. Unlike many more typical households, which accumulated debt due to income disruptions and life-cycle crises in the 1980s, the Proctors' financially cavalier behavior eventually compelled them to "forsake restaurants and entertainment more than once a month [and] end their bimonthly shopping trips to Houston."[28] Such simple prescriptions, of course, defy the far more complex reality of the contemporary U.S. debtor society.

Similarly, the recent public attention to the growing debt and social problems associated with aggressive marketing of credit cards to college students has led to a plethora of local, regional, and national reports on the topic. From *Oprah* to *The Simpsons*, special programs have addressed the growth of student credit card debt and highlighted the large number of accounts, mushrooming debt, and repentant attitudes. Students are portrayed as informed adults who accept the legal responsibility of credit under their own volition or free will. Banks are viewed as profit maximizers that are simply developing effective marketing campaigns; after all, their "job" is to loan money and make the highest possible profit for their shareholders. This neutral framing of the role of banks in this social problem ignores the fact that credit card companies have abruptly changed their lending policies for unemployed students based on the lower risk assessment of this market niche. For example, parental cosignatures are no longer required, and banks have dramatically increased student credit lines without the traditionally required increase in income. This is because students pay their credit cards with other loans (family, federal education, private bank) and even other credit cards.

The most disturbing aspect of these media investigations is that student credit card debt is portrayed as simply a new rite of passage. Like experimenting with alcohol, credit card debt is presented as a normal part of college life and youthful inexperience. Furthermore, these stories neglect to explain that credit card marketing on college campuses, aided by corporate partnerships with college administrations, is a relatively new phenomenon that is conditioned by intense competitive consumption pressures on campus and the need to borrow large sums of money to finance a college degree. As a result, journalistic reports such as the one about "Jeff" in *Business Week* commonly frame student indebtedness as an inevitable outcome of youthful inability to curb consumption urges rather than the banks' irresponsibility in enabling him to "rack up $21,000 in debt over four years on 16 [credit] cards" even though his annual income never reached $10,000 (see Chapter 6).

The focus in the article on the student's naivete ("'When I started, my attitude was: I'll get a job after college to pay off all my debt'") ignores the active role of credit card companies in aggressively marketing Jeff more credit than he could possibly afford in college. Furthermore, these stories perpetuate the importance of individual responsibility that requires students with debt problems to hit rock bottom, as with alcohol abuse. This emphasis is significant. It suggests that individuals must experience a financial revelation that results in modification of their behavior only *after* suffering the burden of severe debt. This view justifies the costly "learning curve" for students rather than suggesting that credit card companies or financially complicit colleges should offer educational workshops on financial literacy programs *before* debt problems arise. Indeed, the article states, "[Jeff] realized he dug himself into a hole when he couldn't meet the minimum monthly payments. . . . Having educated himself on the pitfalls of credit, he now speaks to student groups on the issue." Contrary to the writer's report, Jeff attended a credit card education workshop that helped him to devise a more effective strategy for coping with his debt crisis. Only after he felt empowered with this educational intervention did he feel confident enough to discuss his debt problems with other students. In fact, Jeff laments the fact that he did not have this information earlier so that he could have made different and more informed financial decisions.[29]

Credit Card Conundrum:
The Intransigent Moral Divide Between Rich and Poor

The dominant cultural ethos toward credit and debt in American society has been shaped historically by the Puritan ethic of "economic virtue."[30] This focus on individual discipline emphasizes Calvinist values such as hard work, frugality, and self-sufficiency as signs of superior individual qualities and future otherworldly salvation. Embodied in cultural maxims such as Ben Franklin's "A penny saved is a penny earned" and Horatio Alger ragsto-riches stories, such themes have glorified individual industriousness as the hallmark of social and economic success.[31] Indeed, those who managed to save were lauded for not succumbing to the temptations of self-indulgence. For those who could not control the "sin" of impoverishment, debtors' prisons and various forms of debt peonage became their living "hell" where they repented for their improvident behavior.

During periods of economic recession, poverty was decried by more powerful groups as the consequence of lazy habits and immoral leisure activities such as drinking and gambling. Thus, Calvinist prescriptions against debt were portrayed as a moral choice—man's "free will" to choose between good (self-discipline and saving) and evil (immediate gratification and debt)—to resist the temptations (pleasurable consumption) offered by the "work of the

Devil." Significantly, the moral overtones of debt as a voluntary condition belied the influence of larger, uncontrollable factors such as an economic recession. To "save for a rainy day" mirrored the vagaries and economic
uncertainties that confronted the U.S. working class as it endured depressions,
strikes, and environmental calamities of the industrial epoch. This social context is important to an examination of how American indebtedness increased
so quickly and why the changes are so difficult to understand.

During the post–World War II era, or *Pax Americana*, the dominant position of the United States in the world economy and its soaring industrial
productivity resulted in rapidly rising wages as well as an escalating standard
of living for the American working and rising middle classes.[32] As suburban
Levittowns supplanted the urban neighborhoods of major metropolitan centers, new consumption patterns emerged: Private automobiles replaced public transportation, private lawns replaced public parks, and national retail
chains in suburban malls replaced local mom-and-pop shops in downtown
business districts. Hence, growing household income coincided with new
needs and wants as middle-class Americans assumed greater levels of installment debt for their Buick automobiles, GE washing machines, and Philco
televisions. In the process, retailing giants like Sears, J. C. Penney, and Montgomery Ward (which were displacing local shopkeepers who had offered informal lines of credit) began to expand their proprietary charge card
programs as a way of reinforcing the loyalty of their new customers. Significantly, the credit departments of corporate retailers were content simply not
to lose money on their customer accounts during this period.[33]

Until the age of inflation began in the late 1970s, the Puritan work ethic
that emphasized saving over consumption was the mainstay of the U.S.
household economy. Open a savings account at the local bank, and you were
rewarded with a new toaster or electric can opener. Pay off your home mortgage, and the ritualized burning of the loan note would follow with a joyous ceremony of family and friends. Saving even had strong nationalist
overtones. Purchasing war bonds or U.S. savings bonds was a noble act that
contributed to the preservation of freedom, democracy, and the American
Way, including the right to save even more. By the end of the 1970s, however, double-digit inflation and relatively low returns on savings began to
transform middle-class attitudes toward credit and debt. Why invest in a
passport savings account that yielded only 5 percent when inflation was
climbing above 15 percent and later even 20 percent? Why delay purchasing a new car, appliance, or furniture when inflation substantially reduced
the final cost? Most important, why accept a reduction in one's standard of
living due to declining real wages when consumer credit could obscure this

economic reality and minimize the social pain of potentially agonizing household adjustments? Indeed, how else could people cope with personal crises such as unemployment, illness, divorce, retirement, or unexpected household expenses without taking on higher levels of debt? This part of the story, which tends to be overlooked in the popular press, has been a fundamental force in erecting the social pillars of the Credit Card Nation.

Today, consumer credit has assumed an increasingly important role in the U.S. postindustrial economy and, not incidentally, has increased the power of private banks to influence macroeconomic policy. A striking feature of this trend is the growing inequality in the cost and availability of credit to different social groups. This is one of the most neglected topics in the study of U.S. consumer credit and debt, and the disparity is generally consistent with larger patterns of contemporary American inequality.[34] For instance, the "real" interest rates of consumer credit cards have soared since 1981, whereas corporate loan rates have remained intriguingly low. This is demonstrated by examining the "spread," or difference, between the banks' average cost of funds (borrowing rate from the Federal Reserve) and the interest rate banks charge their various clients (corporate [prime], small business, consumer).

Between 1981 and 1992, the spread on consumer credit cards climbed nearly tenfold—from 1.4 percent to 14.3 percent. During this same period, the spread on the corporate (prime) rate remained virtually unchanged (from 2.5 percent to 2.8 percent), while for new automobile financing it jumped from almost 1.0 to nearly 5.8 percent. As a testament to the veracity of Ausubel's "failure of competition" thesis among banks in the 1980s, the interest rates (APR) of bank credit cards have steadily increased since 1994—to an average of over 18.3 percent in 2000. Although the spread has dipped to a still robust 11.0 percent for bank credit cards in 2000, the nearly trebling of fees (late, over limit) since 1994 has compensated for the lower real lending rate and higher proportion of convenience use by cardholders. In comparison, the spread on corporate loans increased only marginally to 3.0 percent in 1999, while the auto rate fell sharply to 2.9 percent (see Figure 1.1).[35]

The historical emphasis on flawed individual attitudes and behavior underlies the emergent moral divide that defines access to consumer credit in contemporary American society. That is, the gap is widening between free or low-cost credit for more affluent convenience users (some even make money on cash rebates, free gifts, bank interest) who pay off their monthly charges (Chapter 4) and the much higher cost of credit for financially dependent revolvers who carry a monthly balance (Chapter 5). However, the latter costs are dwarfed by the financial terms of "poverty banks" in the

FIGURE 1.1 Lending Spread by Type of Loan: Corporate, Automobile, and Credit Card, 1980–1999

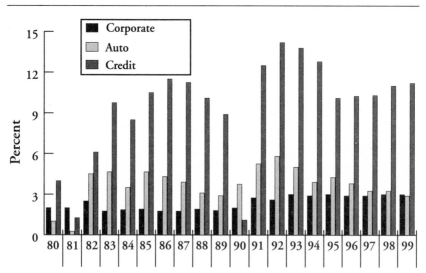

SOURCES: U.S. Federal Reserve System, *Federal Reserve Bulletins;* reported in tables 820 and 827, "Consumer Credit Outstanding and Credit Finance Rates," and "Money Market Interest Rates," *1999 Statistical Abstract of the United States* (Washington, D.C.: U.S. Government Printing Office, 2000); and CardWeb, "Rates Stand Still," June 2000, at www.cardweb.com.

credit-gouging world of finance companies, pawnshops, rent-to-own stores, cash-checking outlets, and even loan sharks (Chapter 7). These usurious alternatives at the bottom of the financial food chain feature interest rates that range from 5 percent to more than 100 percent per month. And you thought the 19.9 percent APR of a Citibank Visa was expensive![36]

The increasing cost of consumer credit by social class is exemplified by the proliferation of pawnshops and cash-checking outlets in lower-income, urban neighborhoods and, more recently, in the middle-class strip malls of suburbia. These fringe banks constitute the fastest-growing sector of the U.S. financial services industry at the same time that low-income minorities, new immigrants, and the struggling lower-middle class are finding that access to traditional banks is becoming increasingly difficult. Significantly, although major banks have been closing branches in low-income (largely minority) areas, especially following a bank merger or acquisition,[37] they still earn high profits on the poor through direct and indirect back-door arrangements such as providing corporate lines of credit (check cashing), marketing costly and low-risk secured cards (credit limit tied to a savings account), purchasing high-interest loans ("flipping"), engaging in joint ventures (Wells Fargo–Cash America), and owning stock of publicly traded fringe banks (Ace Cash Express).[38] The rapid expansion of these second-tier financial services is illustrated by the nation's largest corporate pawnshop: Cash America. It began with 4 Texas pawnshops in 1984 and grew to 178 pawnshops in seven states only seven years later. During the 1990s, Cash America continued its rapid expansion. By the end of 1995, it had 365 pawnshops and, three years later, boasted 414 domestic and 50 foreign operating locations (United Kingdom and Sweden) plus a cash checking (Mr. Payroll) subsidiary with 127 centers and a rapidly growing tire and wheel rental services (Rent-A-Tire) subsidiary.[39]

These patterns suggest that cost and availability of credit constitute a new feature of social inequality in postindustrial America. Not only are the living standards of those with access to free credit subsidized by the less affluent, but cheap credit for the upper and middle classes enables some to reap handsome profits from entrepreneurial ventures while restricting many small-business people to high-interest credit card loans and, in some cases, virtual debt peonage relationships (Chapter 8). Furthermore, the lack of credit for low-income, inner-city communities consigns most of its residents to a future of persistent poverty as small businesses starve from undercapitalization while jobs and mortgages migrate to the suburbs. Ironically, as the freewheeling world of high finance enabled corporate raiders to acquire enormous wealth through the creative use of high-yield, unsecured junk bonds, many of those who suffered the most from the merger and acquisition frenzy of the 1980s and 1990s find themselves struggling to survive on the middle-class equivalent of junk bonds: high-interest, unsecured, consumer credit card loans.

Trends in Postindustrial Inequality: What's Debt Got to Do with It?

The 1980s ushered in the massive use of credit and accumulation of debt across American society. The "decade of debt" featured the rapid growth of borrowing among all three key economic sectors: public (federal, state, local), corporate, and household. The U.S. "triangle of debt" includes the national debt (federal government), corporate borrowing (especially mergers and acquisitions), and household (installment, revolving) debt. Ironically, the greatest increase in U.S. national indebtedness was orchestrated by one of America's staunchest fiscal conservatives: Ronald Reagan. During his two presidential administrations, the cumulative total soared from $940 million to over $2.7 trillion.[40] In early 2000, the national debt was approaching $6 trillion, although politicians have promised to begin paying it down over the next decade.

The household leg of the U.S. triangle of debt must be viewed through the contemporary lens of personal life experiences that increasingly challenge the historically conditioned ethos of economic virtue. As the United States continues to grapple with the growing inequality that has accompanied the longest economic expansion in American history, social attitudes toward debt have been both reinforced and modified. For instance, we now commonly distinguish between "good" and "bad" debt, such as students confronting the sticker shock of their first major investment—college education. Similarly, those unable to contend with escalating levels of indebtedness (primarily due to illness, divorce, unemployment) are appealing to bankruptcy courts in record numbers in an attempt to restore their economic virtue and reclaim their social honor.[41] Neither personal nor corporate bankruptcy retains the stigma of shame—the Scarlet Letter of having to file for Chapter 7 or 11—suffered by past generations.

Not surprisingly, the easy access to plastic money has played an important role in how people have coped with the profound economic changes of the past two decades as well as in the escalation of personal bankruptcies (1.3 million in 1999).[42] Even so, more Americans are enjoying the free credit that banks offer to the economically virtuous members of the moral divide. But, at what cost? Indeed, a striking irony of the credit card industry's early marketing strategies is that it focused on middle- and upper-income families—bastions of the cultural ethos of economic virtue. By the late 1970s, the industry had reached an unprofitable crossroads; between 1979 and 1981, Citibank lost over $500 million on its credit card operations.[43] With the impending deregulation of consumer financial services and mounting losses in traditional lending activities (Third World loans, commercial real estate, residential mortgages), banks began shifting their attention to retail customers and developing radically new financial products (certificates of deposit, interest-bearing checking accounts). During this transition, consumer credit cards emerged as the banking industry's corporate warhorse as more resources were devoted to its consumer financial services (retail banking) operations.

The election of Ronald Reagan in 1980, with his appealing political agenda of smaller government and less intrusive federal regulations, emboldened the weakened banking sector to demand the dismantling of depression-era regulatory statutes. In addition, the Reagan administration pursued an aggressive, antiunion labor policy that contributed to the managed recession of 1981–1982 and the relatively swift reduction of double-digit inflation. In the process, the restructuring of the U.S. economy (from manufacturing to services) and the accompanying reorganization of desirable labor markets (rise of "contingent" workers) began to undermine the economic entitlements and sinecures of the American middle class. For example, real wages continued to fall, and fringe benefits, such as medical insurance, were reduced or eliminated. Signs abounded that ongoing economic change had potentially profound social consequences: Intergenerational mobility appeared to have crested, recent college graduates ("boomerang" babies) were returning home in their frustrated pursuit of employment, while not only white-collar professionals but also blue-collar craft workers encountered downward mobility following the loss of high-wage jobs to corporate mergers, downsizings, and plant closings.

For the banking industry, these events provided a fortuitous opportunity to begin penetrating and expanding into its most lucrative markets—debt-laden and anxiety-ridden middle- and working-class households (Chapter 5). Credit cards often became the best friends and financial confidants of many Americans. Credit helped to buffer the fall from the middle class, cope with unexpected emergencies, shield embarrassing economic circumstances from family and friends, and even provide the initial financing to start a small business. Of course, the advertising campaigns of this period presented a much different view of the changing role of bank credit cards.

For example, the banking industry's marketing promotions shifted from emphasizing middle-class convenience for everyday activities in the mid-1970s ("$36.75, plus tip [for dinner]. And you've got $27.88. Relax. You've Got Master Charge") and late 1970s ("Emergency Clout. You never know when it'll come in handy. Clout has the power to keep you going even when your car won't. Clout is a Master Charge card")[44] to an emphasis on new lifestyle and consumption possibilities offered by credit cards in the early 1980s ("Only Visa gives you all these ways to pay. Worldwide . . . pay in full each month—or in monthly installments—Visa gives you that choice") and mid-1980s ("From Chicago to Caracas . . . Visa. All you need" and "Master the shopping possibilities . . . [list of upscale retailers] and millions of other stores around the world, you have a convenient way to pay with MasterCard").[45]

As millions of Americans endured the social consequences of industrial restructuring—job relocations, temporary assignments, part-time employment, layoffs, buyouts (for the lucky few)—in the 1980s, the credit card industry appeared oblivious to their needs but carefully cultivated the desires of its rapidly growing lower- and middle-income members. Emphasizing financial independence and social indulgence, banks enabled cardholders to maintain the image of middle-class respectability and the material accoutrements of economic success even as they struggled simply to stay afloat. For instance, a 1980 advertisement in *Time* exulted, "You can have it the way you want it with Visa. Only Visa gives you so many ways to pay. Worldwide." With its emphasis on consumption, Visa's marketing campaigns of the mid- and late 1980s highlighted cultural sophistication, social elitism, and the accessibility of an affluent lifestyle.

By presenting examples of credit card use in luxurious and often exotic settings, Visa subliminally offered its members the vicarious experiences of being "everywhere you want to be." Advertisements in 1986 featured adventurous excursions such as "shopping north of London in George Hadfield's 18th-century farmhouse . . . [for a] meticulously restored grandfather clock" or to Lew Anfanger's Western Hat Works in downtown San Diego where "you can still buy a hat from a man whose father was a haberdasher to royalty . . . [and] will custom design a masterpiece for you." At the end of the decade, ads were promoting Visa's new "purchase security and extended protection program" that featured expensive and exquisitely designed crystal, antique statues, gilded clocks, beautiful ceramics, and carefully crafted jewelry boxes with the accompanying poem: "Lovely to look at, delightful to hold. If it breaks it's protected by Visa Gold."[46]

These marketing campaigns conjure popular stereotypes of reckless shopping sprees, impulsive consumption, and out-of-control shoppers who end up "staring into the abyss of personal bankruptcy." Images of credit card debt, moreover, provide banks with further justification to raise the financial penalty for failing to adhere to the cultural tenets of the moral divide. Although numerous journalistic accounts have highlighted the large debts of repentant consumers, they have tended either to focus on conspicuous consumption patterns or to ignore the underlying sources of indebtedness. For example, a 1991 *U.S. News & World Report* lead story on Americans' debt during the recession began with the Schartzer family (household income of $32,400) and their $24,400 consumer debt—including thousands of dollars on their credit cards. The article did not mention why this family was selected, whether it represented typical middle-class consumption patterns, or even explain the reasons for its indebtedness. There was no discussion of declining real earnings, greater household expenses, or larger patterns of economic distress. Instead, readers were left to assume that the Schartzer family was a social island of unrestrained hedonism in a Puritan sea of fiscal responsibility and to conclude that if the Schartzers inadvertently dug themselves into their financial hole, only they could overcome their behavioral sins by simply restraining their indolent lifestyle.[47] It sounds so easy.

As bank cards became available to Americans of more modest means in the 1980s, they produced more complex and conflicted societal attitudes toward credit use and worthiness. This is reflected in the concern of the middle and working classes over the "sin" of embracing credit cards as a temporary financial crutch, whereas more affluent groups perceive them as a convenience in the moneyless financial system of the plastic economy. Indeed, the old adage "the rich really aren't like us" holds true—they don't pay interest on their credit cards. Of course, many others, even people of modest economic backgrounds, can take advantage of the punitive social underpinnings of the moral divide as convenience users.

From the Weberian perspective that consumption patterns mirror the social boundaries of distinct status groups, it is understandable that affluent convenience users initially resisted bank credit cards for fear that their use would be misconstrued as a sign of financial improvidence or even worse. After all, only poor people lacked cash. The use of credit cards could imply a fall from grace and thus potential ostracism by members of one's privileged social class. Hence, the antipathy of many wealthy convenience users to the widespread acceptance of revolving credit cards was motivated by the same reasons that the struggling middle and working classes so eagerly embraced them: They obscured the widening gulf between rich and poor. By offering financial resources to lower-income groups (blue-collar workers, minorities, teenagers), credit cards could provide an entrée to a more sophisticated "style of life" that previously had been reserved to more affluent groups.

The social anxiety of higher-status groups toward the massive expansion of credit cards among the financially less worthy exemplifies the observations of Max Weber in his classic essay *Class, Status, Party:* "[A]ll groups having interests in [maintaining the existing] status order react with special sharpness precisely against the pretensions of purely economic acquisition. In most cases they react more vigorously the more they feel themselves threatened." Indeed, bank credit cards pose a serious threat to elite and middle-income lifestyle activities by failing to impose restrictive qualifying criteria as prescribed by the meritocratic ethos of the nouveau riche. Hence, the democratization of consumer credit is challenging the previously established social class order that had been carefully constructed through the earlier conspicuous consumption patterns of America's leisure class.[48]

Although the staunch defense of social class boundaries has not weakened in the United States, the personal convenience of credit cards has proved too desirable for the affluent to demur (see Chapter 4). As a result, the social anxiety of the status-conscious has spurred the creation of a hierarchical system of "preferred" or prestige cards. This "nonrational" feature of consumer credit cards serves the ostensive purpose of visibly distinguishing those who need credit from those who do not.[49] In the process, it has helped in maintaining social order during the unprecedented profusion of bank credit cards among nearly all social groups.

For instance, consider how American Express touted its Gold Card in a summer 1981 issue of *Time:* "Speak softly and carry a big stick. There is a charge card that says more about you than anything you can possibly buy with it. The Gold Card. To qualify . . . you have to be accepted by both American Express *and* a major bank." However, this elite charge card is much less convenient than the more popular bank credit cards due to the smaller number of retailers that accept it; the merchant discount fee is much higher for American Express charge cards than competing credit cards. In response, Visa and MasterCard developed high-end cards with large credit lines and special benefits for carefully selected high-income members. By 1983, *Time* was featuring advertisements for Preferred ("Citibank introduces the card to end all cards"), Premier ("all gold is not created equal"), and Gold ("the ultimate recognition from your banker") credit cards.[50] This cultivation of snob appeal, founded on the sociocultural pillars of the moral divide, is responsible for the ongoing development of new status distinctions among both credit and charge card programs.

For example, Michael Lewis describes how American Express created its own class system based on the "popular craving for an elitist symbol." Since 1966, when the standard Green spawned the more elite Gold membership, AMEX has continued to stratify its members by creating Black membership in 1984 and then Platinum in 1985. Lewis wryly speculates that a "Diamond" membership will be offered once the ranks of the Platinum card swell to the point of necessitating further social exclusivity.[51] These underlying class tensions frequently emerge in the popular culture. For instance, the introduction of the K-mart credit card led to comedian Jay Leno's barb in 1995 that "now we know why the K-mart credit card was created. So that people with Discover have someone to look down on." He offered this tongue-in-cheek marketing slogan for the card: "Don't leave your mobile home without it."

The competition for prestige cardholders intensified in the 1980s. While American Express successfully appealed to upscale business and professional households, with advertisements featuring elegant dining "for the style of your life," Visa and MasterCard also sought to expand into these markets with preferred Gold cards. In 1983, MasterCard announced, "At last. Something for the few. The ultimate recognition from your banker. A gold MasterCard card." By 1988, MasterCard was touting its credit card as "Piece by piece, the world's #1 gold card" with special member services such as medical care assistance, rental car insurance, legal help, emergency travel assistance, and cash access while on a trip. Competition for business travelers led to the Visa Business Card: "It's welcome in over six million places around the world—nearly three times more than American Express . . . cash advances . . . ten times more [locations] than American Express . . . customized monthly statements. And the option of revolving credit—a very useful business tool and something not everyone offers." Finally, with the decade of debt coming to a close, MasterCard's Christmas advertising emphasized its buyer protection program that encouraged people to "Wrap your gifts in gold. Gold MasterCard. The best gold card to master the moment."[52]

Will That Be Cash or 25 Percent Off? "Shuffling" and "Surfing" on the Rising Tide of Consumer Debt

As Americans began coping with the social and economic uncertainty of the 1989 recession, MasterCard abruptly revamped its ad campaign to reflect these public anxieties. In December 1989, MasterCard began a promotion giving members a chance to "win your MasterCard bills paid until the 21st century" up to $18,000 per year. As economic conditions worsened, MasterCard developed its Master Values campaign whereby credit cards were not simply a convenience but now offered financial savings. Major retailers with a working-class and middle-income customer base were enlisted in the discount program, including K-mart, Woolworth, Montgomery Ward, TimeLife, and Sam Goody Musicland. This "smart money" campaign of the early 1990s began with pronouncements such as "Will that be cash or 25 percent off?" and "They'll cost up to 25 percent less if you buy them with MasterCard."

The sudden emphasis on credit cards as instruments of thrift and financial responsibility contrasted sharply with the conspicuous consumption campaigns of the preceding years. A 1991 Citibank Visa promotion even proclaimed, "If you didn't pay the lowest price, we'll pay the difference. Apply for the card with Citibank price protection." Four years later, Visa's Rewards for Dining and Diversions program exclaimed, "Buy what you need, get what you want"; the campaign offered discounts for Southwest Airline tickets, Avis rental cars, Comfort Inns motel rooms, Sea World park tickets, and Red Lobster restaurant meals. As a result, the credit card industry's carefully cultivated image of the Gold Card as a status symbol of the 1980s could no longer deflect attention from its underlying role as costly financial aid for the struggling middle and working classes. This tarnished reality was sardonically expressed in a 1995 episode of Art Sansom's popular cartoon strip *The Born Loser*. One child says to his friend, "We got a Gold Credit Card in the mail today! What exactly is so special about a Gold Card anyway?" The other child replies, "That's what they send you when you run your bill up over the limit of a normal credit card."[53]

As credit card dependence increased in the mid-1990s, it created its own parlance of survival strategies, largely fueled by the banks' strategies to acquire more profitable revolvers. Among the most financially distressed, the "maxed-out" (Chapter 5), a new form of economic gamesmanship emerged whereby cash advances from one credit card are used to pay for other credit cards. This financial strategy—the credit card "shuffle"—is extolled in American popular culture and even emblazoned on many automobile bumpers, "I pay MasterCard with Visa." For others who have exhausted their credit card limits, the intensifying competition for their mature accounts has produced another popular strategy: credit card "surfing." Rather than lowering interest rates on existing accounts, banks are aggressively "poaching" into the credit card "preserves" of other banks by offering low-interest or "teaser" rates through targeted mass mailings. By accepting an introductory offer, which typically lasts from three to six months, cardholders can transfer their balance from a high- to a low-interest-rate card and save hundreds of dollars in finance charges.

Today, such creative survival strategies are temporarily stabilizing the struggling middle and working classes from the economic aftershocks of the decade of debt. They also provide people with a sense of emotional relief and cognitive denial of the extent of their financial distress by offering a debt reduction strategy that is based on the ethos of Puritan thrift. Unfortunately, the credit card industry has responded with a financial vengeance by imposing stiffer penalty fees (Fleet charges $35 for late payment) and punitive rate increases for relatively minor payment irregularities and by promoting costly "cash advance" loans.

Even cardholders with squeaky-clean payment histories are not immune to this corporate backlash. For instance, when Lizbel Lopez accepted the 8.9 percent teaser rate from Capital One Bank Visa of Richmond, she understood that the interest rate would rise to 12.9 percent at the end of 12 months. What Lopez did not know was that Capital One would punish her for increasing the balances on her other two credit cards; they totaled about $2,000. Even though she had always made the monthly payments on time, Capital One raised her interest rate to 24.9 percent. As Lopez exclaimed, "'Who would have thought that I'd get slapped on the wrist just for using the credit that was already extended to me?'"[54] More recent complaints against First USA (corporate subsidiary of Capital One Bank) inspired a 1999 *Nightline* program that examined its practice of levying late fees on customers' accounts even though their monthly statements were mailed after the computer-generated due dates.[55]

Today, the resurgent U.S. economy has led to the renewal of earlier credit card marketing themes that feature conspicuous consumption, extravagant purchases, and impulsive spending. A 1997 Visa TV advertisement features a man who forgets his wedding anniversary and immediately solves his crisis with panache (and without the help of Jerry Seinfeld) by charging an exotic vacation in Asia; a 1997 print ad for a Platinum Visa shows a middle-aged man admiring a 1961 classic Ford Thunderbird with the caption "Isn't it nice to know you could [buy it] if you wanted to!"; in a 1998 TV ad, an adoring father is able to indulge his fanciful young daughter's outlandish request—a pet elephant—with his Visa; MasterCard's 1998 "Priceless" series highlights those special occasions that are worthy of financial imprudence. In the following example, a man celebrating his wife's 50th birthday party at an expensive French restaurant is more concerned with enjoying the memorable event than paying for it. The ad promotes the "buy now, pay later" mantra but with a twist. By satisfying the social needs of others, there is less remorse over violating the tenet of Puritan thrift, since the cost is attributed to the consumption of others:

> dinner for 37, Chez Marcella: $2,416
> one happy 50th birthday card: $1.95
> one leopard-print peekaboo nightie: $45
> still being able to make her blush: priceless.
> there are some things money can't buy,
> for everything else there's MasterCard.
> Platinum MasterCard has a high spending limit
> for the things that matter.

As consumer credit cards play increasingly important roles in shaping our daily lives, the convenience of plastic often belies the nature of its high-maintenance friendship. On the one hand, the influences of consumer credit cards may be entirely positive for some groups, offer important financial assistance during specific personal and life-cycle crises for others, and provide emotional security for most in the event of an unexpected emergency. On the other hand, the idyllic world of the Credit Card Nation tends to ignore the serious social consequences of the "just charge it" society. Access to increasingly larger amounts of high-interest loans at a younger age is a prescription for serious hardship for many Americans. In fact, the changing realities of debt and their social impacts are a defining feature of the "reality bites" generation that finds itself coping with large financial encumbrances before getting married or even beginning their work careers. This experience is expressed frequently in the popular culture. For example, a young transvestite performs under the stage name of Visa de Cline. His persona reflects the common reality of his friends who are maxed out on their credit cards and fear the dreaded response of retail clerks who must decline their purchases. For them, Visa is a generational allegory of society's denial of their dreams and aspirations.

The proliferation of credit card–related stories in the media concern, bemuse, and entertain us. Each year a seasonal rite of passage includes the reprimand or suspension of college athletes for the unauthorized use of university credit cards or theft of private cards from students. High-profile celebrities get involved in embarrassing escapades, financed by cash advances or charges to their credit cards, such as tennis star Jennifer Capprioti's drug arrest in 1995. Other notable cases include CIA double-agent Aldrich Ames, whose lavish lifestyle was quickly pieced together from his Gold Master-Card account. Ames, a mega-charger, totaled over $400,000 in credit card bills on an annual salary of about $80,000 in less than three years. In March 1995, a former postal employee "struggling under a mountain of debt" including thousands of dollars in credit card bills exploded under the emotional stress and shot several people in a post office gunfight in New Jersey. In the U.S. Congress, a 1995 inquiry into the use and abuse of government-issued credit cards found that 43 House members or office staff had their government accounts canceled for being more than 120 days delinquent. The past-due accounts averaged $4,000, with one former House member owing more than $16,000.[56] The media could have coined a phrase for the potential political scandal: VisaGate.

More upbeat stories include the creative use of credit cards to finance commercial endeavors, such as the 1999 horror mockumentary *The Blair Witch Project* (Chapter 8), as well as several movies that satirize and even celebrate credit cards, including *Funny Money, Rosalie Goes Shopping, Mo' Money, The Applegates,* and TV's *The Simpsons.* Additionally, the industry's aggressive marketing campaign resulted in one of the most humorous stories of 1999. In answering the question "How young will they go?" Charter One Bank sent a credit card to three-year-old Alessandra Scalise of Rochester, New York. Her parents submitted the preapproved application with no listed income and without a Social Security number. To their shock, Ali's credit card arrived with a credit limit of $5,000—more than mom and dad had. A bizarre story was the arrest of Felix Urioste, who posed as a woman—Leasa Jensen—during his nearly four-year marriage to a Utah man. After running up credit card charges of over $40,000, he absconded from Salt Lake City. Only after Urioste's arrest on financial fraud did his husband learn that Leasa was a man. And, only in the Credit Card Nation could a young Chicago cocktail waitress achieve international notoriety over a British patron's authorization of a $10,000 tip, ostensibly to aid in her desire to attend graduate school. The charge was not honored due to an insufficient line of credit, but due to the tremendous media attention and increased volume of customers, the lounge owner promised to pay the tip himself.[57]

Although these anecdotes reflect important changes in American society, it is important to emphasize that they tend to obscure the more common reality of credit and debt in everyday life. Industry studies, in-depth interviews, and ethnographic research are used in this book to examine the larger forces shaping contemporary patterns of U.S. inequality, the institutional pressures underlying the dramatic expansion of consumer financial services, and the common experiences and perceptions of major social groups toward consumer credit and debt in their everyday lives. Unraveling the fundamental contradictions of the Credit Card Nation reveals the underlying social consequences: the moral divide whose punitive cultural ethos punishes the most financially desperate, the obfuscation of public policies that contribute to escalating debt levels, and the centrality of consumer spending to national economic prosperity at the same time that most Americans have little choice but to use plastic rather than paper money.

Ultimately, cash is becoming increasingly irrelevant in an economy of fiber-optic transmissions and computer-processed transactions. As Master-Card's 1997 advertising campaign proclaimed, "Economists predict that in the future, cash will be obsolete . . . because there are better ways to pay. Credit cards, debit cards, smart cards from MasterCard. The future of money." This technologically deterministic vision of the future is appealing, but it ignores a crucial social phenomenon. That is, the availability of credit and the cost of debt have profoundly different impacts on the various social groups of the Credit Card Nation. The first step in this analysis is to examine the major social and economic forces that profoundly shaped the decade of debt as well as the growing societal reliance on consumer credit cards.

The U.S. Triangle of Debt

Erecting the Pillars of the Debtor Society

ON DECEMBER 29, 1998, ABC's *Nightline* examined an ignominious milestone in American history: a negative national savings rate. Although the media had discussed the dramatic growth of U.S. public-sector debt and reported on corporate binge borrowing following the recent flurry of high-profile mergers and acquisitions, the impetus of this news program was the precipitous decline in the personal savings rate. As measured by percentage of U.S. disposable income, it had fallen from a high of 13.6 percent in the 1940s (nearly 24 percent during the 1942–1945 war period) to 7.6 percent in the 1950s and 1960s, then risen modestly to 8.3 percent in the 1970s and nearly 8.5 percent in the early 1980s. After the end of the 1981–1982 recession, however, the personal savings rate steadily declined—from 5.6 percent in the late 1980s to 3.7 percent in the 1990s. By the end of 1998, this trend had reached an abysmal low point: a zero savings rate for the fourth quarter and an anemic 0.5 percent for the entire year.[1] While fiscal conservatives decried the deflowering of national economic virtue, politicians and pundits debated the significance of this dubious achievement.

The most memorable feature of the *Nightline* program was the dialogue between the guests: former U.S. Secretary of Labor Robert Reich and *Harper's* Contributing Editor Vince Passaro. Secretary Reich expressed concern over the sharp decline in personal savings because this period of prosperity was "the wrong time [to get into] debt." He emphasized that "we haven't repealed the business cycle . . . What goes up must come down . . . you can't count on

things being as good as they are now." Reich supported the social-psychologi-
cal explanation that falling unemployment and rising housing prices and stock
values were contributing to "Americans having a more optimistic view . . .
that they will continue to do well," which was resulting in a greater willingness to assume higher levels of debt even though "their expectations are based
on the last few years . . . [rather than] the recession in 1991." Reich emphasized the ephemeral nature of stock market and housing appreciation to the
average American because "it's not savings in the sense that you can count on
the money being there tomorrow [in a bank]. It's [like gambling in] a casino.
It could be bad for you if—euphemistically—a [market] 'correction' occurs
[and you lose your money]." Furthermore, Reich explained that "what is rational for the individual in terms of putting some money away for a rainy day
that is sure to come may be irrational for society if everyone [saves money] at
the same time, particularly [when] the global economy is so fragile . . . [The
United States is] the locomotive of the global economy . . . if we save and stop
importing the cars and stereos from the Asian countries . . . the result would
be serious [consequences]."[2]

Vince Passaro, on the other hand, described the increasingly common
experience of unrepentant debtors caught in the economic vise of the middle-class "squeeze." With combined family earnings of over $110,000 (rank-
ing in the top 10 percent of U.S. household income), Passaro had attracted
national attention by publishing a personal essay, "Who'll Stop the Drain?
Reflections on the Art of Going Broke," in *Harper's* explaining how his family had accumulated $63,000 in consumer debt—including over $28,000
on credit cards. The most instructive aspect of the Passaros' predicament is
not the size of their annual income or the amount of their consumer debt.
Rather, as Passaro explains, the "interesting [feature] about my kind of
debt—and that of some other people according to reports—is that I have
no realistic expectations of paying it off." Passaro acknowledges that his family income "is vastly more than most Americans bring home each month."
Nevertheless, "It happens to be not enough for us."[3]

The key issue is why families like the Passaros are digging themselves into
such a deep financial hole. Are they victims of their own self-indulgence, or
unknowing "upscalers" who, according to Harvard sociologist Juliet B.
Schor, are living beyond their financial means as the ultimate social act of
competitive consumption?[4] In addressing this question, Passaro asserts that
his family is not ensnared in a materialistic web of hedonistic consumption,
as heavily indebted Americans are popularly depicted in the media. Instead,
he attributes their financial difficulties to sending his three children to private school in New York City in order "to provide [them] with even a sem-

blance of the education I had in overcrowded parochial schools on Long Island in the 1960s and 1970s."[5] Nevertheless, Passaro identifies the roots of this societal problem as "real wages remaining flat over the last two decades, an economy with two percent inflation, a culture that revolves around . . . need [for material consumption] that drives the economy . . . and people going into debt."

For Passaro, "the real problem is that people live for today and don't examine the psychological and spiritual cost of the endless cycle of increased spending. . . . Everyone's attitude toward saving is fundamentally different from a generation ago. [Americans] don't see a real purpose [in saving]."[6] As a result, the use of consumer credit by families like the Passaros constitutes a rational strategy for supplementing stagnant earnings and delaying the decline in their standard of living. In masking the inevitable "fall from grace," consumer debt has become alternatively both a friend and foe in the Credit Card Nation. This attitude is emphatically expressed by Passaro in a fit of exasperation over his family's household expenses—"good luck to the credit-card companies. That we manage to pay them at all astonishes me."[7]

The experience of the Passaros and millions of other struggling middle-class families illuminates the dangerous economic shoals that began developing in the United States early in the 1980s. During this "decade of debt," the country emerged from one of its longest economic expansions as the world's most indebted nation—a historic transformation. Examined in this chapter are the three fundamental pillars of "the indebted society": public (government), corporate (business), and consumer (private household) sectors.[8] The analysis of these trends includes (1) public tax policies that reduced government revenues and contributed to enormous federal budget deficits; (2) corporate misuse of federal tax laws that spawned merger and acquisition frenzies responsible for unprecedented levels of business debt; and (3) "fat and mean" corporate labor policies that led displaced and undercompensated workers into the alluring web of consumer credit in order to maintain or obscure their perilously fragile standard of living.[9] Together, these major economic undercurrents of American society are responsible for the emergence of the contemporary U.S. "triangle of debt" (Figure 2.1).[10]

Pax Americana: *Living the Cold War "American Dream" of Progress and Prosperity*

The Calvinist dictum "A penny saved is a penny earned," popularly attributed to Benjamin Franklin, has guided U.S. economic morality through world wars, global recessions, and even periods of national pros-

FIGURE 2.1   U.S. Triangle of Debt: Consumer, Corporate, and Federal, 2000

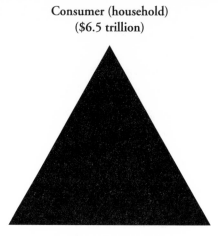

Consumer (household)
($6.5 trillion)

Corporate   Federal (national)
($4.3 trillion)   ($5.8 trillion)

SOURCES: Federal Reserve Statistical Release, "Consumer Credit," available at www.bogfrb.fed.us; Gregory Zuckerman, "U.S. Boom: Living on Borrowed Dime?" *The Wall Street Journal,* December 31, 1999, p. 1; and U.S. Bureau of the Public Debt, U.S. Department of Treasury, "The National Debt," at www.house.gov.

perity. Numerous tales of Puritan thriftiness pervade American popular culture as this precept historically has glorified personal saving over consumption. A corollary of the Protestant work ethic, fiscal conservatism is celebrated as a form of virtuous self-discipline and a sign of moral worthiness. Saving can even assume nationalist overtones during periods of political crisis—whether copper (pennies) or greenbacks. For instance, purchasing U.S. war or savings bonds was extoled as a patriotic act during World War II.

Although the rich have routinely renounced this economic "virtue," their opulent lifestyles serve the "noble" purpose of helping to demarcate social class boundaries. This sociological pattern is evident throughout American history, from the lavish Gilded Age balls of nouveau riche industrialists in their Newport, Rhode Island, mansions to the extravagant parties of Wall Street robber barons a century later in the Hamptons[11] to the popular television program *Lifestyles of the Rich and Famous.* The cultural persistence of this Puritan ethos was of more profound importance than simply to promote behavioral traits that encouraged individualism and adaptability to market-based *(homo economicus)* relations so that the most successful could escape the confines of their social class origins. Rather, this attitudinal predisposition was crucial to the fledgling nation as it generated its own sources of investment capital for financing domestic industrial expansion. Hence, promoting national frugality was the first step in establishing a self-sufficient banking system and, eventually, emancipation from the economic shackles of British colonialism.

By the early twentieth century, American society had achieved unparalleled economic growth by embracing the cultural maxim of Puritan thrift: The United States consistently exported (saved) more goods and investment capital than it imported (consumed) from other countries. With the end of World War II, the United States assumed the leadership of the free world, and the center of global power shifted from London to Washington, D.C. This new Cold War order was managed through several newly created international political institutions (United Nations), military alliances (NATO), trade organizations (GATT), and financial institutions (World Bank) that effectively mediated escalating global political tensions arising from national economic development pressures, nuclear proliferation conflicts, and national independence movements (decolonization). Together, they provided the international political infrastructure that facilitated the foreign investment (especially multinational corporations) and commercial trade that were responsible for the global prosperity of this era—the *Pax Americana*.[12] The seeds of today's ubiquitous credit dependence—public, corporate, and consumer—were sown by the very strength of the postwar U.S. economy and the attitudinal values it fostered.

Postwar Patterns of Credit and Debt: Shaping the American Dream

Although the traumatic personal experiences of the Great Depression were still vividly etched in the postwar national psyche, American society approached the challenges and opportunities of the new geopolitical order with unbridled optimism. And why not? The major international economies of England, Germany, France, Czechoslovakia, and Italy were devastated after the war, while the Soviet Union created its own insulated commercial network of Eastern bloc partners. Furthermore, not only were the industrial countries of Europe and the nascent "Asian tigers" incapable of competing with U.S. firms, but they also offered lucrative investment, capital equipment, and consumer markets for American exports. In sum, just as Elvis was crowned king of the new world of rock 'n' roll, the United States emerged from World War II as the unchallenged hegemon of the global system and enjoyed the political and economic privileges accorded its newly attained status.[13]

The postwar period, or *Pax Americana,* featured strong unions, wide-spread prosperity, and impressive saving rates among all sectors of American society. This was due to the dominance of the United States in the global economy, together with the rapid growth of U.S. labor productivity (propelled by investment in new production processes [R&D]), which produced a booming peacetime economy; unemployment plummeted from an annual average of nearly 20 percent during the 1930s to about 5 percent over the next three postwar decades.[14] The linchpin of rising incomes was the evolving bureaucratic labor system of "bread and butter" unionism. It was modeled after Henry Ford's management policies that ensured worker compliance with the strict regimen of mass-production industries. This Fordist labor regime was effectively managed through the early 1970s with financial incentives to workers, suppression of radical labor movements, and the federal government's expanded role in supervising macroeconomic growth through Keynesianism.[15]

The success of Fordism was reflected in the rapid growth of the U.S. economy and profitability of American business as well as the rising incomes of American workers. Between 1948 and 1973, average weekly earnings climbed from about $220 to about $350, while median family income more than doubled from $19,828 to almost $41,617 per year (1998 dollars). Significantly, the growth of organized labor contributed to both trends as union membership peaked at over 17 million in 1954, representing over one-third of the private, nonagricultural workforce; 65 to 75 percent of labor-organizing campaigns were successful during this decade.[16] Together, the attractive compensation packages (wages, health insurance, retirement programs) and job security of unionized, blue-collar craft workers increased domestic demand for consumer products—as well as undermined the potential strength of labor radicalism. No less significant was the entry of millions of un- and semiskilled workers into the ranks of the American middle classes through the front door of the union shop, albeit there were few women and racial or ethnic minorities.

The tremendous growth of the American middle classes reflected not only the power of organized labor but also the changing occupational structure of the U.S. economy. The decline of small-scale farming and expansion of corporate agriculture contributed to the rapid pace of urbanization as the U.S. economy began generating increasing numbers of white-collar jobs and other professional occupations—especially in the public sector. This postwar trend of occupational diversification included greater educational requirements and job professionalization.[17] As a result, federal grant and college loan programs (especially the G.I. Bill) fueled the expansion of the middle class by ensuring the affordability of postsecondary education. The latter was particularly important because the moderate cost of a university degree (underwritten with public subsidies) facilitated the upward mobility of large segments of the American working class (rural and urban) into the higher-salaried white-collar professions. Indeed, most state-supported college systems such as the City University of New York (CUNY) featured free or inexpensive tuition through the early 1970s.

With increasing household income and falling unemployment, Americans began enjoying the rewards of national prosperity. The postwar American Dream was nourished by New Deal initiatives such as the Federal Housing Administration's (FHA) and later the Veterans Administration's (VA) mortgage insurance programs. Their less stringent borrowing requirements (low down payment, extended repayment schedules of 15–20 years) made homeownership a reality for millions of aspiring middle- and working-class families, albeit along previously defined racial and social class boundaries. Between 1944 and 1950, for example, housing construction skyrocketed from 114,000 to 1.7 million single-family detached houses.

Over the next 35 years, homeownership rates steadily increased among white middle- and working-class families to a high of 65.6 percent in 1980—a crucial source of household savings and middle-class entitlements. Nevertheless, the financial sacrifices necessary for homeownership began to increase rapidly at the end of the *Pax Americana*. For instance, in the 1950s, a typical single-earner household (30-year-old male head) allocated only 14 percent of its monthly income for an average middle-class home; starter homes were priced at about twice an average family's annual income or approximately $5,000 for workers in the manufacturing sector. By the early 1970s, this proportion rose to 21 percent and, only a decade later, climbed to over 40 percent with homes costing nearly three times total household income.[18]

The rapid growth of affordable housing—especially outside of the cities—was further subsidized through the rapidly expanding networks of publicly financed highways, which doomed the more cost-efficient systems of urban-based mass transportation. The proliferation of suburban cookie-cutter bedroom communities, such as the sprawling Levittown developments in metropolitan New York, provided low-cost suburban housing that propelled the explosive demand for cars, appliances, furniture, lawn care products, and other consumer goods. Between 1950 and 1980, the population of suburbia increased by nearly 60 million people. The extension of easy credit to purchase their Cape Cods or Colonials enticed the new American middle classes to finance their rising material aspirations with "buy now, pay later" installment loans for their Buicks from General Motors, re-

frigerators from Sears, sewing machines from Singer, clothes from Montgomery Ward, and gasoline from Mobil Oil.[19]

During the 1950s and 1960s, the social acceptability of incurring higher
levels of consumer debt reflected the increasing sophistication and effectiveness of mass advertising campaigns as well as a growing confidence in the
future as mirrored in rising real wages and low unemployment.[20] Installment credit fueled the great American consumer engine; it grew from $2.6
billion in 1945 to $45.0 billion in 1960 and then to $103.9 billion in
1970.[21] Although the U.S. middle classes became increasingly dependent
upon formal sources of consumer financing—a harbinger of the future role
of the all-purpose bank card—not to be overlooked is that consumer credit
was commonly extended by small businesses through personal or family accounts, such as at the neighborhood pharmacy, local grocery, or downtown
community merchants. This significant source of financing soon disap-
peared, however. The rise of suburban malls and their corporate chain stores
in the 1970s and 1980s led to the demise of hundreds of thousands of small
retail businesses and their informal networks of consumer credit.

Laying the Foundation of the U.S. Triangle of Debt: The Political Economy of Public-Sector Indebtedness

By the early 1970s, mounting international and domestic pressures had
begun eroding the political and economic foundation of *Pax Americana*.
The negotiated settlement of the Vietnam conflict shattered the American
image of military invincibility as well as underscored the enormous economic costs and political limits of U.S. global domination. This is mirrored
in the sharp decline in the U.S. share of industrial production and international trade. Between 1950 and 1973, the largest growth in global trade was
registered by the combined Germany-France-EEC nations (15.4 percent to
30.0 percent), Japan (1.4 percent to 6.4 percent), centrally planned
economies excluding the USSR (3.1 percent to 6.4 percent), and the Middle East oil-producing states (1.4 percent to 4.2 percent); Great Britain's
share declined from 10.0 percent to 5.3 percent. Together with the collapse
of the postwar Bretton Woods financial system in the early 1970s, the
emerging features of the multicentric New World Order signaled a less
prominent role of the United States as it began negotiating power-sharing
arrangements with Germany and Japan.[22]

As suggested by these industrial production and trade statistics, two important trends were gaining momentum in the United States. First, many
U.S. corporations had already begun shifting their attention away from ex-

port markets (often preferring foreign subsidiaries in Europe and developing countries) and focusing their energies on producing and marketing for the more lucrative American consumer market. This explains the contradictory trade policies of the Reagan and Bush administrations that aggressively promoted laissez-faire principles in international forums yet restricted the entry of foreign imports by enforcing antidumping statutes and "voluntary" import restrictions. Second, with the notable exception of the military-aerospace sector, the major corporate pillars of the U.S. economy had begun redirecting their capital investment programs from goods production (especially urban manufacturing) to consumer products and services (retailing, financial services, health, recreation, information). Although profitable for these companies and their shareholders, deindustrialization profoundly impacted the U.S. occupational structure. This tremendous shift in corporate investment, which was accelerated by the oil shocks of 1973, led to the enormous growth of low-wage, unskilled, nonunion, service "McJobs" as well as the displacement of an average of one million blue-collar workers per year during the 1980s.[23]

By the end of the 1970s, the decline in U.S. global hegemony was evident in three new trends: (1) falling corporate profits; (2) sharply rising socioeconomic inequality; and (3) increasing difficulty of mediating the international and domestic tensions of the emerging post–Cold War order.[24] The Carter administration responded with a socially moderate economic program that included a tight monetary policy via the Federal Reserve (controls were even imposed briefly on consumer credit cards in 1980), expansion of military weapons and aerospace (NASA) programs, and erosion of real income through double-digit inflation and creeping federal tax brackets. Following the Reagan landslide in the 1980 election, the United States embarked on more radical domestic policies that accelerated the ongoing transformation of the economy.

The ideological underpinnings of the "Reagan Revolution" were portrayed in the mass media as linked to the inviolable cultural symbols of national pride (patriotism), personal triumph (individualism), and faith and optimism in the future (national "salvation"). Together, they underscored the resonant theme of the Reagan mantra: "Morning in America." Although the go-go 1980s brought a spectacular bubble of prosperity—based on a fragile economic edifice of a tremendous military buildup, deficit spending, and enormous influx of foreign investment—the cumulative costs and consequences of these policies transformed America into a debtor society.[25] Indeed, the costs of U.S. industrial restructuring could have been spread through a variety of belt-tightening measures: (1) a more limited role of the

U.S. government in international affairs (military, foreign aid) and more cost-effective domestic policies (aerospace, health care, public sector efficiency [S&L regulation]) as mirrored in a smaller federal budget deficit; (2) lower business profits and public subsidies (higher taxes, greater R&D investments, more workplace and environmental regulation, reduced commodity prices); and (3) diminished standard of living of U.S. households (falling income, higher taxes, less consumption, rising consumer prices, greater unemployment, fewer entitlements). In retrospect, the social and economic burdens of industrial restructuring were borne primarily by working- and middle-class households.

The first leg of the U.S. debt triangle emerged from the policies of the federal government that sought to preserve its bureaucratic self-interests by prolonging U.S. political and military global dominance at an enormous financial price. The failure to increase state revenues (particularly corporate taxes) and substantially reduce its expenditures, together with the continued inefficient growth of the public sector (e.g., fraud-riddled military procurement practices and top-heavy management of social programs), resulted in the historically unprecedented escalation of the federal deficit. This trend is summarized in Table 2.1. In 1980, President Reagan inherited a cumulative national debt of $940.5 billion and a $74 billion federal budget deficit; between 1963 and 1981, the national debt increased by a total of $632 billion. Following successive years of record budget shortfalls, the U.S. debt nearly doubled by the end of the first Reagan administration ($1.6 trillion) and nearly tripled by the end of the second ($2.72 trillion). Even with the passage of the Gramm-Rudman-Hollings deficit reduction bill, the federal budget deficit continued to climb during the Bush administration, reaching an inglorious peak of $290 billion in 1992. To cover its spending authorizations in the 1980s, the federal government borrowed approximately three-fourths of the combined net savings of all American families and businesses.[26]

In the early 1980s, the U.S. budget deficit was portrayed by the Reagan administration as a temporary "adjustment" that would "trickle" away in the wake of the "supply-side" economic recovery that it would shortly unleash. President Reagan, in his 1981 "Address to the Nation on Federal Tax Reduction Legislation," stated that "'starting next year [1982], the deficits will get smaller until in just a few years the budget can be balanced. And we hope to begin whittling at that almost $1 trillion debt that hangs over the future of our children.'" Of course, like the soundness of "voodoo economics," similar pronouncements such as "'we can . . . cut taxes, balance the budget, and build our defenses'" were merely political rhetoric grounded in the wishful thinking of think-tank pundits.[27] Instead, foreign-financed

TABLE 2.1 Growth of U.S. National Debt by Presidential Administration, 1963–1999 ($ billions)

President	Term(s)	Debt at start	Debt at end	Increase ($ billions)	Percent change per year
L. Johnson	1963–69	308.9	360.0	51.1	3.2
R. Nixon	1969–74	360.0	493.6	133.6	6.7
G. Ford	1974–77	493.6	664.9	171.2	4.1
J. Carter	1977–81	664.9	940.5	275.7	10.4
R. Reagan	1981–89	940.5	2,720.7	1,780.2	23.6
G. Bush	1989–93	2,720.7	4,188.1	1,467.4	13.5
W. Clinton	1993–99	4,188.1	5,702.3	1,514.2	5.4

SOURCE: U.S. Bureau of the Public Debt, U.S. Department of Treasury, *The Public Debt to the Penny,* at www.house.gov/istook; www.toptips.com/debtclock; and www.savingsbonds.gov/bpd.

TABLE 2.2 The U.S. Triangle of Debt: Contributions to the Net National Savings Rate, 1960–1989 (percent)

Source	1960–1969	1970–1979	1980–1989
Personal	4.7	5.5	4.7
Business	3.5	2.6	1.6
Public	–0.2	–0.9	–2.6
Federal	–0.2	–1.7	–3.6
State and local	0.0	0.8	1.0
Net National Savings Rate	8.0	7.1	3.8

SOURCE: U.S. Congressional Budget Office calculations cited in table 4 (1993), p. 4.

deficit spending became the short-term palliative pursued by federal policymakers (in the absence of a long-term industrial policy), since it entailed the least painful political consequences.

The dramatic growth of the U.S. federal deficit nearly cut the national saving rate in half for the entire decade; the federal savings rate fell steeply from –0.2 percent in the 1960s to –1.7 percent in the 1970s and to –3.6 percent in the 1980s (Table 2.2). Overall, the U.S. net national savings rate fell from 8.0 percent in the 1960s to 3.8 percent in the 1980s. This compares much less favorably with Japan (21.9 percent down to 18.2 percent), Germany (18.0 percent to 10.2 percent), France (17.7 percent to 7.8 percent), Great Britain (10.5 percent to 4.8 percent), and Canada (9.8 percent to 8.4 percent). Unlike its most successful global competitors, moreover, the United States was not dedicating its escalating federal budget to public investment in socially and commercially productive programs. For instance, while U.S. military expenditures consumed over one-fourth of the national budget in the 1980s (averaging 6 percent of gross national product [GNP]), Germany allocated only about one-eighth (about 2 percent of GNP) and Japan about one-sixteenth (1 percent of GNP) of their respective budgets to defense expenditures. Germany and Japan, in contrast, channeled much more of their public resources into major domestic reconstruction campaigns.[28]

During the 1980s, most U.S. research and development (R&D) funds were allocated to defense projects; military R&D rose over 80 percent while civilian R&D declined 3 percent. In 1990, for example, U.S. public R&D expenditures accounted for 4.8 percent of the national budget versus 4.1 percent for Germany and 2.9 percent for Japan. These figures, moreover, belie the disproportionate concentration of American R&D in military projects and thus obscure the declining long-term competitiveness of U.S. commerce (not to mention labor productivity) by the R&D-starved civilian sector.[29] Not surprisingly, America is the global leader in nearly all categories of military expenditures (controlling one-third of the world's arms trade) and is one of the few developed countries that spends more on defense than education; it ranked only eighth in per capita education expenses in the 1990s.[30]

At the end of 2000, the U.S. national debt had eclipsed $5.7 trillion. As a proportion of gross domestic product (GDP), it jumped from 32.6 percent in 1981 to 66.4 percent in 1998. In fact, interest on the national debt was the fastest-growing component of the federal budget over the past two decades. For instance, net debt interest more than doubled from $69 billion in 1981 to $152 billion in 1988 and then jumped from $203 billion in 1994 to about $234 billion in 1995—greater than the federal budget deficit of $193 billion. Although the federal deficit fell sharply, only 22.0 billion in 1997, and there was a surplus of $70 billion in 1998 (with surpluses projected through at least the next five years), this does not imply that interest payments will abruptly decline; rising interest rates in the late 1990s could result in greater debt interest expenses even if the national debt begins to decline.[31] For the 2001 national budget, the Congressional Budget Office estimates net debt interest payments at $218 billion. This constitutes 10.8 percent of the proposed $2.0 trillion federal budget, or nearly $0.11 per federal budget dollar (see Figure 2.2).[32]

FIGURE 2.2   U.S. Federal Budget: Principal Expenditures for 2001

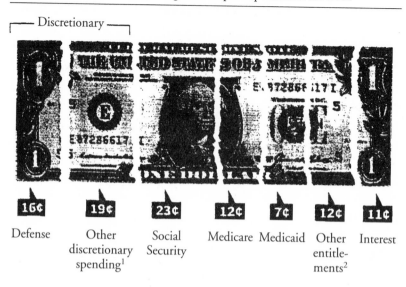

┌── Discretionary ──┐

16¢	19¢	23¢	12¢	7¢	12¢	11¢
Defense	Other discretionary spending[1]	Social Security	Medicare	Medicaid	Other entitle-ments[2]	Interest

NOTE: Spending does not include the 9 percent set aside for debt reduction.
[1]Such as education and foreign aid.
[2]Such as food stamps and farm aid.
SOURCE: Office of Management and Budget.

As the public sector's borrowing demands skyrocketed in the 1980s, the traditional sources of debt financing were being rapidly depleted. In fact, the net U.S. national savings rate plummeted sharply—to a mere 2.2 percent in the 1985–1989 period—as U.S. businesses assumed sharply higher levels of debt during the merger and acquisition frenzy. The U.S. government immediately sought to augment the nation's dwindling capital reserves by attracting unprecedented levels of foreign investment. To do so, it increased the relative rate of return on federal securities—especially to foreign investors. This strategy initially assumed the form of channeling overseas dollars (especially from countries with a favorable balance of trade with America) into liquid U.S. Treasury bonds or T-bills. Such investments were especially lucrative to foreign nationals due to the following: (1) higher interest or "coupon" rate than comparable national bonds; (2) increased value of the dollar in international markets through 1984 (currency appreciation); and (3) explicit tax exemption of profits earned by foreign investors on U.S. debt (popularly termed the "Netherlands Antilles window").[33]

The extraordinary success of the program was mirrored in the dramatic shift in global capital flows. For instance, U.S. direct foreign investment (from the United States to other countries) rose from $187.9 billion in 1979

to $373.4 billion in 1989, or a $185.5 billion increase, while foreign investment in the United States climbed from $54.3 billion to $400.8 billion, respectively, or a $346.5 billion increase. The largest creditor—Great
Britain—invested nearly twice as many dollars as Japan, followed closely by
the Netherlands and then Canada and West Germany; the United States officially became a debtor country at the end of 1985. Significantly, the vast
majority of international security transactions were government bonds rather
than corporate stocks. Between 1980 and 1989, the volume of U.S. securities transactions (government bonds and notes, corporate bonds and stocks)
by international investors rose remarkably: from $198.0 billion ($114.3 billion in government securities) to almost $4.8 trillion ($4.2 trillion in U.S.
government securities).[34]

Although these trends continued in the late 1990s, with total direct foreign investment in the United States rising to $681.6 billion in 1997 (led by
Great Britain at $129.6 billion and Japan at $12.5 billion), the "spread" between the yield on U.S. government securities and comparable bonds in the
leading investor countries declined considerably after the late 1980s. This led
foreign investors to diversify into corporate stocks, bonds, real estate, speculative investments (junk bonds), and the acquisition of U.S. corporations or expansion of foreign-owned subsidiaries.[35] The latter tactic was encouraged by
reductions in U.S. corporate taxes, the lax collection of taxes from foreign corporations by the U.S. government,[36] anti-labor policies, and the much higher
"cultural rate-of-profit" of American-based corporations.[37]

During the 1990s, the result was a spectacular increase in foreign-held
assets in the United States. From $2.386 trillion in 1990 to $3.254 trillion
in 1994, foreign-held assets jumped sharply to $5.461 trillion in 1997—an
astounding 67.8 percent increase in only three years. This trend reflects the
recent diversification of foreign investment in the United States. For instance, between 1990 and 1997, foreign-held U.S. Treasury securities rose
from $152 billion to $662 billion, while other U.S. securities holdings
climbed from $461 billion to $1.578 trillion. During this same seven-year
period, foreign-held corporate and other bonds jumped from $239 billion
to $718 billion, while corporate stock holdings rose from $222 billion to
$860 billion.[38]

At the end of 1997, foreign-controlled assets exceeded U.S. holdings
abroad by $1.224 trillion. Not unexpectedly, this investment gap was re-
flected in the dramatic increase in U.S. public debt that was foreign-held—
from 4.7 percent in 1965 to 34.0 percent in 1997. Although the federal
government reported a modest budget surplus in 2000, this does not mean
that the U.S. demand for foreign investment will decline. For instance, the

United States registered a record trade deficit of $271 billion in 1999 that required various direct and indirect forms of national borrowing.[39] As a result, the confluence of interests between the U.S. corporate sector and the federal government that crystallized in the early 1980s continued to be expressed in the national debate over a "favorable business climate." This mutual concern arose from the escalating U.S. demand for foreign capital that was necessary for stabilizing domestic lending markets and financing the national debt at moderate interest rates. Hence, by successfully attracting massive foreign investment, the U.S. state was able to pursue its political goals and bureaucratic expansion without seriously addressing such contentious issues as raising corporate taxes, streamlining the federal bureaucracy, downsizing the military, reducing aerospace subsidies, and devising a more efficient health care system.

U.S. Industrial Restructuring: Short-Term Profits and Long-Term Corporate Debt

The Reagan administration (1981–1989) immediately set the political tone of this formative phase of U.S. industrial restructuring by aggressively pursuing a probusiness agenda. This included attacking inflation, cutting corporate taxes, slashing antitrust enforcement (corporate mergers and acquisitions), reducing regulation of business and workplace conditions (OSHA), combating organized labor (remember PATCO?), supporting "defensive" corporate bankruptcies, and later expanding the monetary supply (Federal Reserve). Furthermore, as in the public sector, the real cost of corporate borrowing increased only marginally due to the enormous influx of foreign investment and the growing popularity of corporate bond offerings. This contributed to a six-year joyride of debt-induced prosperity— the casino economy—that profoundly shaped the second or corporate leg of the U.S. debt triangle.

The first objective of U.S. industrial restructuring was to reorganize corporate production and management systems in order to improve slumping profits. Under Reaganomics, corporate tax reform was argued to be crucial in this process by enabling U.S. corporations to respond more swiftly to intensifying international competition. The key assumption was that increasing corporate liquidity (essentially state-subsidized investment capital) would stimulate demand in the U.S. manufacturing sector through the massive purchase of heavy equipment and other capital goods. Hence, the Economic Recovery Tax Act of 1981 and the Tax Equity and Fiscal Responsibility Act of 1982 were enacted to increase business savings and thus encourage investment in state-of-the-art production technologies. The resulting modernization of U.S. industry, according to proponents of supply-side economic policies, would enhance labor productivity, reduce commodity prices, and therefore enable American companies to regain lost market shares (at home and abroad) through their improved competitiveness. The revitalization of these core industries, moreover, would reverberate throughout the U.S. economy as the rising wages of more productive industrial workers would stimulate household consumption and the expansion of the U.S. service sector.

As measured by share of GDP, business taxes were reduced substantially during the 1980s. From a high of 4.3 percent in 1967, then 2.7 percent in 1978, corporate income taxes fell sharply—from 2.4 percent in 1980 to a low of 1.1 percent in 1983 following the recession (1981–1982)—before stabilizing at 1.5 percent for 1984–1986. Overall, for the period 1981–1986, it is estimated that American businesses were relieved of about $100 billion in tax obligations.[40] In addition, U.S. congressional debate on corporate taxation policy revealed a shocking pattern in compliance trends. In 1990, the Internal Revenue Service (IRS) reported that of over 46,000 foreign-controlled companies, only about 38 percent paid significant taxes.

During U.S. congressional hearings in 1992, it was estimated that foreign corporations accounted for over $1 trillion in assets and $826 billion in sales and paid only $5.8 billion (0.7 percent) in taxes for 1988. This compared with $24 billion (2.9 percent) in tax payments on $823 billion in overseas sales by U.S.-controlled companies during the same year. Officials argued that this disparity not only was an unfair competitive advantage for foreign corporations and an important loss of public revenues as domestic producers were replaced by overseas competitors, but also that "American corporations are starting to learn from [foreign tax evaders]." In fact, in response to criticism of the low compliance rate of foreign corporations through legal mechanisms such as transfer pricing, the commissioner of the IRS retorted, "I would like to note that 59 percent of [all] U.S. corporations also do not pay taxes."[41]

Of course, this is nothing new. A study conducted by Citizens for Tax Justice (CTJ) compared the tax payments of 41 major "freeloader" corporations for the years 1981–1985 (following "liberal" tax reform) with 1988 (after "conservative" reform of 1986). The results are startling. These corporations reported combined profits of $44.9 billion for the five-year period and received $1.9 billion in refunds—an effective negative tax rate of –4.3 percent. As Congressman Duncan Hunter (California) astutely declared, "Taxes that used to be paid by [American companies] will now have to be paid by [all of] the working men and women of America." Similar concerns over corporate abuses of tax credits and depreciation allowances led to the Tax Reform Act of 1986; it reduced the top tax rate from 46 to 34 percent while imposing more stringent standards on corporate minimum tax, credits, shelters, and other accounting rules. As a result, corporate taxes jumped to 2.0 percent of GDP in 1988, then dropped to 1.7 percent through 1992 before rising to 1.9 percent in 1993 and then stabilizing at 2.1 percent in 1994. This trend is reflected in the 1988 taxes paid by the same corporations that comprised the 1989 CTJ study. For example, the combined tax payments of these 41 companies jumped to $4.5 billion on total profits of $16.1 billion, or an effective tax rate of 27.9 percent; only two continued to receive tax refunds. This group included such corporate behemoths as Boeing, Dow Chemical, Du Pont, General Dynamics, ITT, Merrill Lynch, Northrop, Occidental Petroleum, Pepsico, USAIR, and Walt Disney.[42]

Clearly, the Reagan administration's goal of increasing corporate liquidity for financing business restructuring strategies was successful. After-tax corporate cash flows rose from an average of 8.2 percent in the 1960s and 1970s to 8.7 percent in the 1980s. The most striking outcome of U.S. corporate tax reform in the early 1980s, however, was that results were contrary to explicitly stated expectations: U.S. corporate *dis*investment in core goods-production divisions (via accelerated depreciation allowances), *greater* corporate debt (over $2.5 trillion in 1989), and *lower* worker compensation. Furthermore, the devaluation of the dollar in 1985 (which increased the buying power of foreign investors) and growing American trade restrictions (such as "voluntary" quotas on Japanese auto imports) precipitated an unexpected influx of foreign corporations, such as Mitsubishi in Aurora, Illinois. This foreign "feeding frenzy" featured the acquisition of U.S. businesses, joint ventures with American companies, expansion of existing subsidiaries, establishment of new corporate branches, and purchase of valuable real estate. The fundamental question, as poignantly expressed by Donald L. Barlett and James B. Steele of the *Philadelphia Inquirer,* is, "What went wrong?" As Harvard economist Benjamin J. Friedman laments, "[I]increasing what business has available to invest is not the same thing as increasing what business actually invests. *Despite record internal cash flows and borrowing too, business used an unusually large part of these funds [in the 1980s] for purposes other than productive new investment.*"[43]

The statistics are unambiguous on this point. For instance, between 1982 and 1986, capital spending in the manufacturing sector grew a meager 1 percent versus 47 percent in the service industries; most of the latter is attributed to the purchase of computers and related technology. Even so, corporate borrowing assumed gargantuan proportions in this period. According to Gary Shilling, in just two years (1984–1985), new corporate debt virtually erased, in real terms, three-quarters of all the corporate equity issued from 1959 to 1983. By the end of 1987, the net worth of all U.S. nonfinancial corporations had climbed to nearly $3.4 trillion, while their cumulative obligations had spiraled to $1.9 trillion. The ratio of corporate debt to net worth thus was 56 percent—an all-time high at the time—compared with about 35 percent at the end of the 1970s. In sum, corporate debt jumped from 30 to 40 percent of GNP during the 1980s, and interest payments climbed to 28 percent of corporate cash flow in 1990—a post–World War II record.[44] So, where did all the money go?

The Postindustrial Debt Industry: Corporate Reorganization and the Lucrative "Paper Shuffle"

The Reagan administration touted its corporate tax reforms as the most efficient strategy for revitalizing the U.S. manufacturing sector. Unfortunately, investment in plant modernization was not a high priority of corporate America. Instead, rather than aiming for long-term international competitiveness, businesses sought to increase short-term returns on corporate investment through stock repurchases, mergers with competitors, acquisitions of highly profitable firms, and later leveraged buyouts (LBOs) of unrelated businesses (conglomerates such as RJR Nabisco). With U.S. corporations awash with cash, America witnessed one of the greatest waves of mergers, takeovers, and corporate restructurings in U.S. history: More than 25,000 deals worth over $2 trillion were transacted during the 1980s. No longer was corporate size or even market share a critical factor in evaluating merger petitions. In fact, the Federal Trade Administration and the Antitrust Division of the U.S. Justice Department routinely dismissed concerns over such undesirable consequences as less competition, fewer product choices, and unjustified price increases; federal resources devoted to antitrust enforcement were slashed more than 40 percent during the two Reagan administrations.[45]

Ironically, this "age of leverage" was instigated by cash-rich companies in mature or stagnating industries such as oil, food, and tobacco where investment in core divisions was yielding declining rates of return. This led Wall Street advisers to propose takeover strategies for companies like Chevron in order to swallow smaller competitors like Gulf Oil ($13.4 billion all-cash bid in 1984) or diversification-driven acquisitions such as Kraft's takeover of battery manufacturer Duracell, Mobil Oil's purchase of Montgomery Ward, and RJR's buyout of a wide range of companies such as Turtle Wax and Puss 'n'

Boots cat food. This drive for short-term profits led to the former Beatrice Foods being aggressively transformed into the multidivisional conglomerate Beatrice Companies in the early 1980s. According to Neil R. Gazel, in his corporate history of Beatrice, "The [management] committee recognized that if the company was to . . . maintain or increase its 16 percent return on net worth . . . it had to broaden the scope of its diversification program heretofore limited to food products." Of course, once the casino economy came into play, the hunters often became corporate prey. For example, easy credit resulted in Kraft becoming an LBO trophy of Philip Morris and Nabisco becoming a division of tobacco conglomerate RJR. Indeed, Beatrice's success led to its $8.2 billion LBO by Kohlberg Kravis Roberts & Company (KKR) in 1986.[46]

For many companies in traditional manufacturing industries, debt-financed diversification strategies were viewed as the most expedient tactic for reversing the downward slide of U.S. business profits. For instance, older industrial corporations such as Owens-Illinois first supplemented and later abandoned their core manufacturing divisions by acquiring companies in such lucrative sectors as health and financial services. In fact, the less profitable bottling division was spun off and sold as an independent company, while the more profitable service subsidiaries were preserved as a separate corporation after a $4.4 billion LBO by KKR. For many other companies, their diversification strategies were designed to penetrate the "corporate welfare" (publicly subsidized) defense-aerospace sector where profits averaged over 20 percent—regardless of product cost or quality.[47]

For example, after negotiating historic concessions from its unions, General Motors used this savings for the 1985 multibillion-dollar buyout of defense contractor Hughes Corporation rather than modernizing its plants in Flint, Michigan; Ford and Chrysler also expanded their billion-dollar defense divisions during this period. One of the most spectacular entries into the high-tech defense industry was made by corporate raider Paul Blizerian, who took control of the Singer Sewing Machine Company in 1988. Blizerian jettisoned Singer's traditional manufacturing divisions and used the proceeds to acquire several defense contractors and a furniture company. Unfortunately, the dismantling of the Berlin Wall in 1989 made this a dubious strategy, and Singer stockholders soon found themselves in bankruptcy court; Blizerian was convicted of securities fraud and declared personal bankruptcy in 1991 with pending judgments of over $100 million.[48]

On the other side of the merger frenzy, financing of corporate transactions, the Securities Exchange Commission (SEC) was not particularly vigilant in scrutinizing the evolving high-stakes gamesmanship of investment bankers—even the process of consummating mega-acquisitions. According to Benjamin J. Stein, the laissez-faire ideology of the Reagan-era SEC was determined to allow financial markets to function unfettered from government interference. That is, by promoting "greed is good" and advocating that "[federal] law was the enemy," SEC "enforcement" policies fostered an antiregulatory climate in which the unscrupulous had "a license to steal." These sentiments were underscored by F. Ross Johnson's "three rules of Wall Street." The former CEO of RJR Nabisco, who made a spectacular yet unsuccessful management buyout (MBO) bid, explained: "'Never play by the rules. Never pay in cash. And never tell the truth.'" A prominent antitrust lawyer summarized this period by declaring, "'[T]he door to corporate mergers has never been open wider than during the Reagan presidency.'"[49]

This new antiregulatory environment produced astounding business deals. For instance, minnow-sized companies were able to swallow whales as the ability to secure lines of credit (increasingly in the form of low-grade, unsecured, high-yield junk bonds) became more important than corporate equity in closing the deal.[50] Corporate managers even sought to preserve their jobs by thwarting hostile takeovers or simply ignored their fiduciary responsibility to stockholders and purchased the company themselves by taking it private with "other people's money." More disconcerting was that many complex, debt-financed mergers and acquisitions were consummated not because they created a stronger company or multidivisional synergy but because of the up-front fees they generated for the major financial players. This booming industry of corporate debt spawned ancillary networks of financial contrivance with its own legion of superstars (Michael Milken, Ivan Boesky, Martin Siegel, Dennis Levine) and insider lexicon: arbitrage, bond rigging, Chinese walls, fallen angels, friendly takeovers, hired guns, insider trading, junk, parking, tombstones, slamming, stock fixing, greenmail, golden parachutes, nuclear war, Pac-Man defenses, poison pills, raiders, target-in-play, scorched-earth policy, white knights, and of course, "leverage."[51] The greed and glamour of this ethically challenged era were glorified in Oliver Stone's *Wall Street* (1987), which yielded Michael Douglas an Academy Award for his scintillating portrayal of the malevolent corporate raider Gordon Gecko.

The now defunct Eastern Airlines Corporation is a good case study in the profound shift in the logic of corporate investment as well as the rise of debt financing. In 1978, CEO Frank Borman embarked on a six-year campaign to modernize Eastern's fleet by purchasing nearly 60 new planes and upgrading older aircraft. During this period, corporate debt increased by $1.4 billion with interest payments nearly doubling from 3.9 to 7.4 percent of total assets. At the same time, the company secured corporate "sweat equity" of over $100 million in labor concessions from 1978 to 1982. In 1984, this strategy reaped a record operating profit—$189.6 million—but it was wiped out by $227 million in debt payments. As a result, Eastern's management was able to effectively circumvent employee profit-sharing agreements by shielding company profits through the interest payments on its fleet modernization program. Hence, prior to the age of leverage, the role of corporate debt was to improve cost efficiency, enhance labor productivity, and ultimately increase market share.

In comparison, Frank Lorenzo's heavily leveraged Texas Air Corporation acquired Eastern Airlines in 1986 as part of a long-term, "horizontal" growth strategy of merging with competitors in the airline industry. Lorenzo's objective was to increase his corporate market share (Continental was acquired in 1981) and eventually to raise prices through regional airport or hub monopolies while slashing operating costs through his notorious antiunion policies. Although Texas Air (now Continental Airlines Holding) had a much higher debt-to-asset ratio (89 percent) than Eastern (63 percent) and had to pay a premium of about 25 percent above market value to acquire the company, it was able to close the deal with Michael Milken's high-yield (14 percent) junk bonds.[52]

As in most LBOs, Lorenzo's employees shouldered the greatest hardships from his junk-bond-financed acquisitions through lower wages, fewer benefits, more hazardous work conditions, and even raids on employee pension funds. Of course, troubled or even failed LBOs were not unexpected. Rather, they were simply a phase of the corporate cannibalization process that produced new streams of earnings for the debt industry. That is, new deals were consummated as parts or divisions of the acquired company were resold (often with junk bonds) or the inevitable corporate reorganization ensued (Continental Airlines is in its third Chapter 11 bankruptcy) followed by liquidation proceedings (Chapter 9 bankruptcy) and the formal corporate wake that generated millions more in fees and commissions. As for Lorenzo, he cashed out his initial $25,000 investment in Texas Air and pocketed $27 million for his Continental stock (triple its market value) from Scandinavian Airline Systems (SAS) in 1990.[53]

By the mid-1980s, corporate expansion was driven largely by business acquisitions rather than investment in more modern plant and capital equipment. For example, Chevron bought Gulf Oil instead of building new petroleum refineries. General Electric preferred to spend $6 billion for RCA than to construct more modern electronics factories. Burroughs acquired Sperry for $4 billion instead of designing new computer plants. Similarly, when General Motors paid Ross Perot and his group $730 million and then billions more in other stock repurchase programs, corporate liquidity was simply transferred to wealthy stockholders. Ironically, after the landmark antitrust settlement that led to the breakup of Bell Telephone into competing regional Baby Bells, companies engaged in a plethora of mergers and acquisitions that were largely inspired to *reduce* competition. This strategy culminated in megadeals such as Time's $13.9 billion takeover of Warner in 1989 and AT&T's $12.6 billion purchase of McCaw Cellular in 1993. Today, these deals would barely cause a ripple in the shark-infested seas of corporate LBOs.

Emboldened by this initial wave of equity-financed takeovers in the early 1980s, Wall Street salivated over the prospects of multibillion-dollar deals with greater levels of "creative" financing. According to George Anders, a *Wall Street Journal* reporter, "Banks alone in the mid-80s were pushing attitudes toward business borrowing into uncharted territory. But Milken and his Drexel acolytes helped take the pro-debt cause much further than banks alone ever would have dared." For instance, when KKR, the preeminent takeover specialist of the 1980s, needed $100 million in subordinate debt financing to consummate its modest $318 million acquisition of Cleveland retailer Cole National in 1984, it found a relatively cheap ($3 million fee plus 11 percent equity share) and convenient one-stop source in Drexel Burnham junk bonds (14.5 percent). This enabled KKR to avoid the laborious process of courting individual institutional investors (pension funds, insurance companies) and focus its energies on larger, more complex acquisitions; KKR became Milken's biggest client and borrowed about $15 billion over the next five years until Drexel's insolvency in early 1990.[54]

Ronald Perelman's debt-financed takeover of Revlon in 1985 marked the onset of the five-year LBO binge of multibillion-dollar corporations. Through the magic of junk bonds, virtually any company was susceptible to the antics of corporate raiders ("black knights") such as Paul Blizerian, Carl Icahn, and T. Boone Pickens. In fact, takeovers were a less popular strategy of corporate raiders, since simply buying stock and preparing a buyout bid often yielded a hefty "greenmail" profit. For example, T. Boone Pickens's investment group realized a $760 million profit for the resale of their stock back to Gulf Oil after securing $1.5 billion in junk-bond commitments from Milken in 1984. Ironically, the more equity and even liquidity (cash flow, reserves, pension funds) a corporation possessed—indicators of good management—the more desirable they became as LBO targets. This new trend of generating corporate growth through acquisitions led to the dramatic boom of merger and acquisition departments of commercial and investment banks.[55]

The surging demand for creative investment banking services fueled the meteoric rise of Michael Milken and his junk-bond machine at Drexel Burnham. With the deregulation of the savings and loan (S&L) industry and Milken's capture of strategic S&Ls such as Columbia (Tom Spiegel), Lincoln (Charles Keating), and CenTrust (David Paul) as well as cash-rich insurance companies including First Executive (Fred Carr) and Reliance Insurance (Saul Steinberg), corporate takeovers and their financial fees soared; by 1989, Columbia had purchased over $10 billion in bonds from Drexel, generating hundreds of millions in fees and commissions. Incredibly, knowledgeable sources estimated that Milken's junk-bond-related revenues totaled $24 billion between 1978 and 1989. With annual compensation packages that peaked at about $550 million in 1987 ($295 million in 1986), Milken ranked as one of America's wealthiest individuals even after agreeing to a record fine and criminal settlement in March 1992 that totaled about $1.1 billion (in cash and partnership assets) following his 1990 confession to six felony charges including securities fraud. Of course, Milken's financial penalty was only a drop in the bucket of losses to uninsured depositors, stockholders, bond investors, underfunded pensions, bankrupt companies, unemployed workers, and the S&L cleanup legislation that observers estimated could eventually total over $300 billion including long-term interest costs.[56]

The massive reallocation of investment capital within the U.S. economy and the profits earned by the debt industry are illustrated by the ascendance of KKR as the king of the corporate LBO. Between 1981 and 1984, KKR acquired 11 firms at an average price of $321 million with about 17 percent equity or cash down payment. KKR's equity position progressively declined from 30 percent of the $600 million Red Lion Inns buyout in early 1985 to only 8.8 percent of the $2.5 billion takeover of Storer Communications at the end of the year and then to a mere 3 percent of the $4.2 billion LBO of Safeway Stores in 1986. At the pinnacle of its power in 1989, KKR-controlled companies encompassed an industrial domain greater than Texaco, Chrysler, or AT&T and employed almost 400,000 people.

With companies in nearly every industrial sector, KKR's revenues climbed rapidly until the collapse of the junk-bond market in late 1989; the firm reaped over $6 billion in profits during the 1980s with average annual returns of 30–40 percent. Although KKR's revenues were derived from a variety of sources, most accrued from managing investors' funds, arranging corporate takeovers, monitoring acquired companies, and a 20 percent stake of the gains accruing to its investors (limited partners). KKR not only made enormous profits with little of its own money at risk but it even profited on deals that failed. In sum, the objective of takeover specialists like KKR was straightforward: to maximize short-term profits. That is, acquire a vulnerable or underpriced company, sell its assets to reduce debt payments, and then manage the remaining components for a substantial profit to be reaped at a later date. In short, they bought cheap and sold dear to someone else—fast—before getting "slammed" with an overvalued company. This explains how Henry Kravis and George Roberts could report the value of their senior partnerships at $330 million each in 1988.[57]

The escalating size and dwindling equity investments in LBOs proved to be a veritable gold mine for Wall Street; lower cash requirements meant that more deals at less risk could be pursued with potentially astounding rewards. Fueled by the tax deductibility of corporate debt interest, the soaring stock market, and subsequent corporate cost reductions (lower wages, fewer employees, sale of low-profit plants or subsidiaries, lower capital investment, less R&D), mergers and acquisitions became the mother lode of the Wall Street debt industry and an element of popular culture. For example, the complex machinations of the RJR Nabisco takeover inspired the best-selling book and controversial motion picture *Barbarians at the Gate.*[58]

For the highly paid white-collar armies of lawyers, accountants, financiers, consultants, and underwriters, KKR's ability to transact the mammoth $6.2 billion LBO of Beatrice in early 1986 represented a watershed in the history of the U.S. debt industry. Although the tightening of the corporate tax code in the late 1980s paid dividends in the form of greater investment in new plant and equipment, the biggest loophole and cost to federal tax coffers was (and still is) the deductibility of debt interest payments on LBOs. Beginning in the late 1980s, corporate deductions from debt interest exceeded $100 billion per year; also, the net operating loss (NOL) provision was estimated to have reduced corporate taxes by over $100 billion in the 1980s. For example, RJR Nabisco wrote off more than $3 billion in cash interest payments and Time-Warner deducted $2.1 billion in interest payments for 1989 and 1990 on their federal income taxes. Even with these tax advantages, many LBOs became corporate "tombstones" following the 1989 recession. For the debt industry, this was not an undesirable outcome. It simply ushered in the next phase of extracting profits from the "back end" and starting a new debt cycle through the sale of corporate assets.[59]

This disturbing trend was underscored by the growing size of the largest U.S. bankruptcies. Between 1980 and 1991, the top 30 included four non-operating bankrupt companies and 15 others that were enmeshed in Milken's network of junk bonds. The latter ranged from $2.1 billion to $15.2 billion and included Ames Department Stores, Continental Airlines, Enstar Group, First Columbia Financial, Hillsborough Holdings, and Southmark. Also, several of the other 11 bankruptcies were directly or indirectly linked to LBO debts. Their impact on the national debt was revealed by the Resolution Trust Corporation's (RTC) listings of high-yield bonds that it inherited from failed S&Ls. They included hot issues like Drexel Burnham, Eastern Airlines, and TWA.[60]

During the 1990s, the escalating number and scale of U.S. corporate mergers and acquisitions were astounding even by the standards of the go-go 1980s. For example, a total of 4,239 mergers and acquisitions in 1990 were valued at $206 billion. In 1996, the number jumped to 5,639 with a value of $1.06 trillion and then to 12,395 deals worth $1.6 trillion in 1998 and 10,698 worth $1.75 trillion in 1999. Significantly, corporate mergers also became a prominent feature of the global economy (Figure 2.3). In 1990, the value of mergers worldwide was a mere $464 billion. By 1999, it had climbed to $3.4 trillion; one-fourth of all mergers in 1998 were cross-border deals, such as Daimler-Benz's takeover of Chrysler. This was mirrored in the dramatic increase in the size of corporate mergers. Exxon's $81 billion acquisition of Mobil Corp in 1998 was considered astronomical. At the end of the decade, it barely made the top five. By then, the largest announced mergers were Great Britain's Vodafone Group PLC and AirTouch Communications ($56 billion), AT&T and MediaOne Group ($63 billion), Pfizer and Warner-Lambert ($71 billion), MCI WorldCom and Sprint ($127 billion), and Great Britain's Vodafone AirTouch and Germany's Mannesman AG ($148 billion).[61]

The bar was raised even higher in 2000 with the proposed American Online (AOL) and Time-Warner merger: $183 billion. According to Mark Clemente, a mergers and acquisition consultant, this trend will not abate in the near future because "'Companies have realized that mergers and acquisitions are the speediest and most substantive way to affect corporate growth. . . . Given the pace of today's market, companies just don't have time to grow [internally]. And deals beget deals. Companies see competitors on an acquisition spree, and they attempt to keep pace by doing their own deals.'" Not surprisingly, this ongoing trend has contributed to the staggering growth of U.S. corporate debt, almost 60 percent over the period 1994–1999. Overall, U.S. corporate debt crossed the $4.3 trillion threshold in early 2000. This represents a staggering 46 percent of GDP—a historic high.[62]

FIGURE 2.3 Worldwide Corporate Mergers: Total Value of Merger Volume,
1990–1999

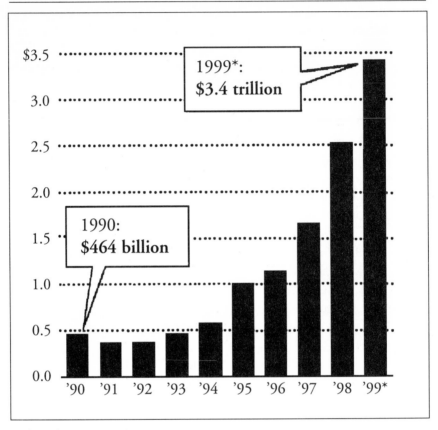

1990:
$464 billion

1999*:
$3.4 trillion

* Through Dec. 29
SOURCE: Thomson Financial Services.

Significantly, the primary beneficiaries of this corporate debt have not
been as expected. According to *The Economist*, "Study after study of past
merger waves have shown that two of every three deals have not worked; *the
only winners are the shareholders of the acquired firm who sell their company
for more than it is really worth.*" For example, AT&T acquired NCR for $7
billion in 1991 and spun it off for $3 billion in 1995; Quaker Oats' takeover
of Snapple for $1.7 billion in 1994 led to its sale three years later for only
$300 million.[63] The sharp escalation in business borrowing raises the issue
of how these macroeconomic forces impact American families—the final
leg of the triangle of debt.

Unkept Promises of Industrial Restructuring:
Stretching the Social Boundaries of U.S. Household Indebtedness

The decade of debt yielded radically different outcomes for the various actors involved in U.S. industrial restructuring. "What went wrong" was that the architects of American industrial policy were primarily concerned with short-term goals such as raising business profits, promoting economic growth, expanding politically expedient social programs, and financing U.S. military expansionism and global political hegemony. Indeed, corporate America and the U.S. government were the primary beneficiaries of supply-side economic policies. For example, corporate after-tax profits roughly doubled while stock prices quadrupled between mid-1982 and mid-1993; the Standard & Poor 500 index rose from 120.40 in January 1982 to 463.56 in August 1993. According to financial historian James Grant, the winners and losers of the 1980s are easy to identify: "'[T]he great gale of financial prosperity of the past decade . . . [means that] you've been [much] better paid to own stocks and bonds than to have been sweating down on the shop floor producing things and then selling them.'"[64]

At the beginning of the millennium, the S&P 500 had eclipsed 1,300 points and the Dow Jones reached nearly 12,000. This bull market continues to challenge the financial logic of corporate profitability while producing a nouveau riche class of Internet millionaires—many of whom have never earned a profit. CEO compensation is again an issue of stockholder concern, and the federal government is flush with a budget surplus following the successful parting of its sea of financial red ink. But who is really benefiting from this prosperity? How did corporate profits climb while the U.S. share of global trade dwindled to less than 9 percent in the 1980s? Why did the fortunate few who owned stocks gain the lion's share of the economic booms of the past two decades? And if U.S. workers endured most of the socioeconomic sacrifices, why didn't they receive a larger share of the vast wealth that was created? The latter outcome has fundamentally shaped the third (household) leg of the debt triangle.

It is emblematic of the 1990s that many of the richest and most highly rewarded people in America were investors rather than entrepreneurs or even heirs of earlier manufacturing or retailing fortunes. In 1993, superinvestor Warren Buffett, chairman of Berkshire Hathaway, temporarily supplanted William Gates (founder of Microsoft) as the richest person in America; Buffett's extraordinary financial success included favored white-knight investment deals such as protecting Salomon Brothers from a hostile corporate takeover. Also in 1993, the highest compensated person in U.S. history was

hedge-fund manager George Soros. He received at least $1.1 billion in salary
and bonuses (falling to $400 million in 1994)—more than double Milken's
astounding $550 million nearly a decade earlier. Corporate raider Ron Perel-
man nearly joined the exalted $5 billion club in 1994 (before falling on hard
times in the late 1990s), followed by fellow corporate raider Carl Icahn and
financier Robert Pritzker as multibillionaire club members.

The extraordinary redistribution of income and wealth over the past two
decades is illustrated by the growing number of billionaires at the top of the
wealth pyramid. America's first member of the billionaire club, John D.
Rockefeller, earned this distinction in 1913. As recently as 1982, *Forbes* magazine identified only 13 U.S. billionaires but by 1999 counted 267.

By the end of the decade, the super-rich possessed levels of wealth that de-
fied conventional accounting procedures. In 1999, the total net worth of the
Forbes 400—over $1 trillion—exceeded the gross domestic product of China.
Led by Gates's $85 billion, the top 25 U.S. fortunes highlighted the ascension
of the computer, information, and consumer services industries. These familiar names included Microsoft, Oracle, Dell Computer, Fidelity Investments,
Amazon.com, Metromedia, Intel, Viacom, Turner Broadcasting, and Wal-
Mart (see Table 2.3). Not incidentally, wealth had become more concentrated
than at any time since the Great Depression. In 1995, the wealthiest 1 percent of U.S. households controlled 39 percent of the nation's wealth, compared with the top 1 percent of households with the highest incomes that
received about 13 percent of U.S. after-tax income. Similarly, the wealthiest
20 percent of households owned 84 percent of national wealth, whereas the
20 percent of households with the highest incomes received a little more than
50 percent of the nation's after-tax income.[65]

Among corporate managers, executive compensation continued its rapid
ascent in the 1990s. America's middle and working classes, however, did not
fare as well in the distribution of the fruits of U.S. industrial restructuring.
A particularly revealing measure is the ratio of total compensation of corporate CEOs to average manufacturing workers. According to *Business Week*,
CEOs received 29 times the average factory worker's income in 1979, rising
to about 40 in 1985, and then climbing rapidly to almost 93 in 1989 and
then to nearly 150 in 1995. In early 2000, estimates put it at over 200.[66]

The trend of increasing U.S. income inequality not only mirrored the
enormous growth of executive compensation but also the decline in real
wages. Between 1980 and 1997, as measured in 1982 dollars, real hourly
wages in private industry dropped from an average of $7.78 to $7.55, or
3.0 percent, while weekly earnings fell from an average of $275 to $261, or
5.1 percent. Significantly, the blue-collar industries (mining, construction,

TABLE 2.3   Top 25 Richest Americans in 1999: Net Worth, Age, Residence, and Source of Fortune

Name	Worth ($ billions)	Age	Residence	Source
Gates, William H. III	85.0	43	Bellevue	Microsoft Corp.
Allen, Paul Gardner	40.0	46	Mercer Island	Microsoft Corp.
Buffett, Warren Edward	31.0	69	Omaha	Berkshire Hathaway
Ballmar, Steven Anthony	23.0	43	Bellevue	Microsoft Corp.
Dell, Michael	20.0	34	Austin	Dell Computer Corp.
Walton, Helen R.	17.0	80	Bentonville	Inheritance (Wal-Mart Stores)
Walton, John T.	17.0	53	Durango	Inheritance (Wal-Mart Stores)
Walton, Alice L.	17.0	50	Rogers	Inheritance (Wal-Mart Stores)
Walton, S. Robson	17.0	55	Bentonville	Inheritance (Wal-Mart Stores)
Walton, Jim C.	17.0	51	Bentonville	Inheritance (Wal-Mart Stores)
Moore, Gordon Earl	15.0	70	Woodside	Intel Corp.
Du Pont family (heirs of Pierre Samuel)	13.0	—	Delaware	Inheritance (Du Pont Co.)
Ellison, Lawrence Joseph	13.0	55	Atherton	Oracle Corp.
Kluge, John Werner	11.0	85	Charlottesville	Metromedia Co.
Anschutz, Philip F.	11.0	59	Denver	Oil, railroads, telecommunications
Mellon family	10.0	—	Pittsburgh origin	Inheritance
Anthony, Barbara Cox	9.7	76	Honolulu	Inheritance (Cox Enterprises)
Chambers, Anne Cox	9.7	76	Atlanta	Inheritance (Cox Enterprises)
Redstone, Summer M.	9.4	76	Newton Centre, MA	Viacom, Inc.
Rockefeller family	8.0	—	New York	Inheritance (oil)
Bezos, Jeffrey P.	7.8	35	Seattle	Amazon.com
Johnson, Abigail	7.4	37	Boston	Fidelity Investments
Kerkorian, Kirk	7.0	82	Las Vegas	Investments
Turner, Robert E. (Ted)	6.9	60	Roswell	Turner Broadcasting
Murdoch, Keith Rupert	6.8	68	New York	Media

SOURCE: Forbes Rich List Index, "Forbes Richest People in America—1999," at www.forbes.com.

manufacturing, transportation) registered a real decline in earnings, whereas some service occupations (finance, insurance, real estate) reported moderate wage gains. This trend not only belied the substantial improvement in labor efficiency (especially manufacturing), but it also contradicted supply-side economic policies that promised financial gains to more productive work- ers. In fact, Secretary of Labor Robert B. Reich declared, "Productivity im- provements are going into corporate profits not [into] workers' pockets . . . [hence] U.S. workers are enjoying none of the gain despite having endured the pain of corporate downsizing, restructuring and reengineering."[67]

Such trends defied the beguiling siren song of U.S. industrial restructur- ing that raised the expectations of America's struggling low- and moderate- income families. After all, the 1980s featured a rapidly expanding albeit fragile economic bubble that produced a sharp increase in national income. For instance, U.S. per capita earnings (1996 dollars) rose from $14,845 in 1980 to $17,785 in 1989, a net gain of almost 20 percent. In the 1990s, per capita income growth slumped to only 2.0 percent, reaching $18,136 in 1996; as a percent of median white family income, African American in- come improved only marginally, from 57.9 percent in 1980 to 59.3 percent in 1996. This pattern reflected a shocking outcome of U.S. industrial re- structuring. American society achieved the dubious distinction of having the most unequal distribution of income in the industrialized world.[68]

The dramatic increase in U.S. inequality, especially between 1977 and 1989, is revealed in figures on after-tax income. According to data and esti- mates by the U.S. Congressional Budget Office (CBO), the top 1 percent of American households registered an average gain of about 115 percent, and the top 20 percent approximately 43 percent between 1977 and 1999. In comparison, the middle fifth recorded a gain of only 8 percent; the next fifth remained stagnant; the bottom fifth registered a decline of 9 percent. Hence, the bottom 40 percent of U.S. households registered a net decline in after-tax income from 1977 to 1999. According to the CBO report, the richest 1 percent of U.S. households received a federal tax cut of 13 percent or about $40,000 per year for the 1977–1999 period—a sum nearly equal to the median U.S. household income for 2000.[69]

Clearly, middle- and working-class families effectively paid for the enor- mous upward transfer of national income through lower real wages, greater un- and underemployment, higher consumer prices, regressive tax relief, and deteriorating public services. In the process, lean-and-mean labor policies pro- foundly impacted the U.S. personal savings rate by reducing real wages and increasing un- and underemployment rates. In the aftermath of the 1981–1982 recession, personal savings dropped by one-third through the end of the decade. This was followed by another decline of about one-third after the 1989–1991 recession before plunging to virtually zero at the end of 1998. The import of this trend is significant. During the decade of debt, the national savings rate of 3.8 percent was due primarily to household savings and secondarily to business savings. This suggests that the United States will become even more dependent on future flows of foreign investment as well as the ability of the public sector to curb its previously large budgetary deficits.[70]

The Magic of Plastic:
Temporary Relief from the Middle-Class Squeeze?

The sharp decline in household saving rates mirrors fundamental economic and attitudinal shifts in American society—changes accelerated by U.S. industrial restructuring. On the one hand, American economic policy facilitated deindustrialization by rewarding disinvestment in urban manufacturing plants as well as encouraging the relocation of labor-intensive goods-production facilities to offshore sites. It also produced a "liberal" immigration policy that dramatically increased the foreign-born workforce and intensified downward pressures on labor compensation.[71] The hardest hit were high-school-educated, blue-collar union workers, who suffered an average annual loss of one million jobs in the 1980s.[72]

On the other hand, the dramatic expansion of the service sector shifted the epicenter of U.S. economic growth from corporate investment in capital goods to individual consumer decisions. By the late 1980s, consumer spending accounted for two-thirds of U.S. economic activity (GDP) and three-fourths of employment. In the process, the vast majority of newly created jobs were in low-wage, service occupations. The highly touted employment growth of the 1980s and 1990s was not led by educated professionals or skilled tradespeople but by retail cashiers and janitors followed by registered nurses, truck drivers, food servers, nurses aides, sales clerks, accountants and auditors, and kindergarten and elementary school teachers; only three of these occupations paid more than the U.S. median weekly wage. Predictions are that this job growth profile will continue at least through 2005, with the exception that the demand will decline for accountants but increase for systems analysts, business managers, and receptionists.[73]

Consequently, the transformation of the U.S. postindustrial job structure entails a fundamental contradiction: Corporate profits are increasingly dependent upon the ability to influence household consumption, but U.S. wages continue to fall as higher-wage, blue-collar union jobs in goods-production industries are replaced with lower-wage employment in services. The key factor in this counterintuitive trend (falling real wages during a period of rising labor productivity and corporate profitability) has been the concerted campaign by American corporations to redefine work relations. U.S. labor market reorganization was a central objective of most corporate LBOs,[74] especially after the company founders or longtime owners were replaced by "paper" entrepreneurs whose primary experience was in finance, accounting, or marketing. For this new class of rentier owners, company loyalty was a costly fringe benefit that could be easily squeezed to improve the bottom line. In addition, the probusiness policies of the Reagan administration emboldened U.S. corporations to deploy antiunion tactics in their quest to dismantle the post–World War II social compact with American workers.

These sentiments were succinctly expressed by the vice chairman of Safeway three years after the KKR buyout: "'We have been given a rare second chance to confront labor. . . . Only the radical surgery of the buyout and restructuring could give us the negotiating strength and resolve to rescue our core business from the insatiable appetite of the unions.'" The concessions extracted from the grocery store workers included replacing full-time workers with part-timers, instituting difficult-to-attain quota and bonus systems, increasing job responsibilities, creating new occupational classifications with lower wages, forcing older employees to quit, shrinking the workforce, limiting insurance eligibility, discouraging workers' compensation claims, and closing an entire division (Dallas) when profits failed to attain KKR-mandated targets. As Peter McGowan, the CEO of Safeway, explained, "'With the debt hovering overhead, you could get the labor concessions you deserve.'"[75]

Many corporate executives, when confronted with enormous LBO costs and intensifying competition from foreign rivals willing to modernize their production facilities, castigated unions as the primary reason for shrinking profits. Yet, the strategy of reducing overhead expenses negatively impacted labor productivity: Perelman slashed R&D expenditures after his takeover of Revlon, and KKR cut RJR Nabisco's capital equipment spending from over $1.1 billion in 1988 to under $500 million in 1990. Frank Lorenzo took this antilabor position to the extreme when Continental Airlines became the first corporation to file for bankruptcy solely for the purpose of abrogating existing union contracts. According to Lorenzo, the decision to file for Chapter 11 in 1983 "'wasn't a problem of cash. Our sole problem was labor.'" In fact, Kevin Delaney notes that Continental's cash reserves and marketable securities totaled $290 million plus other assets at the time. Therefore the purpose of this legal maneuver was to hire new, nonunion workers at 25–50 percent below the prevailing union scale as well as to relax costly rest-break work rules.[76]

The 1980s brought the sharp erosion of organized labor's collective bargaining power. Overall, union membership declined from 20.1 percent of employed U.S. workers (17.7 million) in 1983 to 13.9 percent (16.5 million) in 1999; unions lost over 95 percent of National Labor Relations Board (NLRB) elections in the 1980s, and strikes plummeted to a 50-year low. Not surprisingly, the compensation of U.S. manufacturing workers continues to lag behind that of major international competitors, including Germany, Italy, Japan, France, and Great Britain; in 1999, the United States ranked eleventh in manufacturing wages. Although U.S. wages and household income registered notable gains in the late 1990s, the latter was augmented with increased overtime and second moonlighting jobs (see Chapter 8), greater labor force participation of women, rise of entrepreneurial activities, and growth of multiple-earner households. Between 1980 and 1997, for example, the participation of women in the U.S. workforce rose steadily from 51.5 percent to 59.8 percent, whereas the rate for men declined from 77.4 to 75.0 percent. This period witnessed a net gain of 11.8 million male and 17.5 million female workers. Of course, if the gender gap in earnings had declined more rapidly (women earn about 30 percent less on average), household income would have improved considerably.[77]

To make matters worse for the American middle classes, the decline in household earnings coincided with the substantial increase in key consumption items. As companies sought to pay down their debt service obligations, they frequently succumbed to the temptation of raising their prices, as RJR Nabisco did on cigarettes and various snack foods. The largest cost increases were registered by medical care, transportation, education (especially college tuition), financial services, insurance, recreation, and tobacco products; Kevin Phillips in 1993 discussed how the official Consumer Price Index (CPI) understated this inflationary trend. Even industrial sectors facing intensifying international competition, such as car manufacturers, sought to increase their prices through government protection and even joint ventures with foreign rivals. Thus arose the inherent contradiction between the free-trade rhetoric of the Reagan and Bush administrations and their aggressive protection of U.S. consumer markets from foreign "invasions." According to Friedman, the 1980s featured "more steps away from genuine free trade than in any comparable period since World War Two."[78]

The growing divergence between the aura of American opulence and the reality of the middle-class squeeze became manifest in various forms of social anxiety. In the mass media, Susan Faludi's 1990 *Wall Street Journal* article on the social costs of the Safeway buyout became highly controversial in financial circles (eliciting a stern rebuke from KKR) yet received the Pulitzer Prize. A

U.S. News & World Report feature story in 1991 questioned whether the "vanishing dream" meant that this was the first generation in U.S. history to encounter downward mobility; other academic studies provided the intellectual foundation for this inquiry. Also, *Philadelphia Inquirer* reporters Donald Barlett and James Steele received a Pulitzer in 1991 for their series on the excesses of the LBO binge. David Broder of the *Washington Post* continued to write in-depth stories that dispelled the popular myths of the new working poor. A 1995 feature story in *Business Week* was captioned "Wages: They're Stagnant While Profits Are Soaring. Are We Headed for Trouble?" The *New York Times* followed with a seven-part front-page series that examined the social consequences of "Downsizing in America." More recently, the *Washington Post* reported on "The High-Tech Homeless: In Silicon Valley, a Dark Side to the Booming Economy." This investigation revealed that poverty in the "new" economy defied previous assumptions and financial realities. For example, a 38-year-old systems engineer explained that he was living out of his 1982 Subaru even with an annual income of $52,000 because of escalating apartment rents and "child support payments and past credit card debts."[79]

The inability of most Americans to resist the seduction or necessity of debt should not have been surprising. After all, the post–World War II period featured real wage increases through the mid-1970s that limited household installment debt to an average of about one month's income. Consumer research has shown that economic expectations are more influential than actual financial conditions in shaping the borrowing behavior of most U.S. households. As corporate marketing campaigns shifted Americans' attention from their needs to desires, banks began reinforcing this attitudinal change by offering unrestricted or "all-purpose" consumer credit cards rather than asset-specific installment loans such as for cars or furniture. This enabled Americans to satisfy their consumption goals by augmenting their declining wages with greater levels of consumer debt. According to a 1973 study of U.S. installment debt, "translating changes in attitudes into actual increases in installment debt balances . . . [will depend on] lending institutions, especially credit card agencies, to grant credit that is not associated with the acquisition of a specific asset. Any coupling of this trend with longer maturities on such debt might especially encourage the greater use of credit by families who have recently received or expect to receive substantial increases in income."[80] Consequently, the optimistic forecasts of the Reagan and Bush administrations encouraged Americans to achieve their lifestyles by increasing the role of consumer credit in their household financial strategies.

Not unexpectedly, total consumer debt as a percentage of disposable personal income climbed sharply in the 1980s, from 65.4 percent in 1980 ($1.4

trillion) to 83.5 percent in 1990 ($3.7 trillion). In 2000, it jumped to an all-time high of about $6.5 trillion, with mortgages accounting for nearly two-thirds of total consumer debt. For the vast majority of U.S. households, the new smorgasbord of consumer credit products has become the most common strategy for coping with the increasing financial pressures of the past two decades. Between 1980 and 1990, outstanding consumer installment credit such as auto loans, personal loans, gasoline charges, and retail store purchases jumped from $298 billion to $735 billion. During the 1990s, consumer installment debt escalated even more sharply—from $731 billion in 1992 to $911 billion in 1994. At the beginning of 2000, the U.S. Federal Reserve reported consumer installment debt at $1.4 trillion, with approximately $800 billion in nonrevolving consumer debt.[81]

Today, the realization that national economic growth is inextricably linked with household spending has produced increasingly sophisticated mass marketing campaigns for consumer products as well as personal credit. This glorification of consumerism has been alternately revered and reviled in the popular culture. For example, in the 1986 movie *The Check Is in the Mail*, a comic portrayal of the American middle class, Brian Dennehy makes the revolutionary declaration that "[television] commercials are all part of the [corporate] conspiracy to sell us more of what we don't want or need. . . . [As a result] we're burning all our credit cards!" Even in the fantasy world of Hollywood, however, such a draconian measure is doomed to failure; Dennehy eventually relents, and his family returns to the social mainstream of the Credit Card Nation. As a result, the fastest-growing component of consumer credit, revolving or noninstallment (bank and retail) credit, jumped from $257 billion in 1992 to $338 billion in 1994 following the employment disruptions of the 1989–1991 recession. Only five years later, consumer credit card debt nearly doubled to $600 billion.[82] And to the chagrin of consumers and the delight of the U.S. banking industry, the cost of consumer credit and related financial services rose rapidly after the onset of banking deregulation in 1980. At the forefront of this trend was industry leader Citicorp, which aggressively marketed bank credit cards to previously neglected consumer groups.

Crossroads of Debt

Citicorp and the Ascension
of the Consumer Credit Card

At the annual Travelers Group meeting on April 20, 1998, a shareholder patiently waited in line behind a microphone at the Carnegie Hall convocation. When it was his turn, he asked Chairman Sandy Weill about the proposed Citicorp–Travelers Group merger and his behind-the-scene views of the corporate courtship. The stockholder declared that Weill must have felt as if he had asked supermodel Elle MacPherson out on a date and that instead of her curtly rejecting him, she asked if he would like to spend the weekend with her. At the podium, Weill responded with a Cheshire cat grin. The nation's third-highest-paid CEO, at $167 million in 1998, Weill was elated by the outcome of his audacious overtures.[1] In fact, Weill's persistent nuptial proposals to Citicorp's CEO John Reed yielded not only the corporate bank marriage of the decade but, two years later, also the helm of the Citigroup financial services conglomerate following Reed's early retirement.

At the time, the 1998 Citicorp–Travelers Group merger was the largest business combination in U.S. history with nearly $700 billion in combined assets and a transaction value of over $78 billion.[2] The consummation of this five-week courtship catapulted Citigroup to the pinnacle of the bank-

TABLE 3.1   Top Ten U.S. Bank Holding Companies, October 1998

	Assets ($ billion)
Citigroup*	$700*
BankAmerica	$572
Chase Manhattan**	$367
J. P. Morgan**	$281
Banc One	$246
First Union	$229
Wells Fargo	$186
Bankers Trust	$173
Fleet Financial	$101
National City	$81

*   estimated

** On September 13, 2000, Chase Manhattan acquired J.P. Morgan in a $35.2 billion deal. The new company is called J.P. Morgan Chase & Co. It ranks as the sixth-largest deal in financial services history. See Noelle Knox, "Banking Titans Bury Hatchet in $35 B Deal," USA TODAY, September 14, 2000, p. B1.

SOURCE: Gary A. Dymski, *The Bank Merger Wave: The Economic Causes and Social Consequences of Financial Consolidation* (New York: M. E. Sharpe, 1999), p. 271.

ing industry by leapfrogging the enormous NationsBank-BankAmerica ($60 billion transaction) and Banc One–First Chicago ($30 billion) mergers of the same year; Citicorp had ranked behind only Chase Manhattan in corporate asset value following the latter's merger with Chemical Bank (see Table 3.1).[3] More important, unlike other transactions of the decade's merger mania that were conducted primarily among commercial banks (horizontal integration), the Citicorp-Travelers merger heralded the emergence of the first "universal" financial services conglomerate, following earlier ill-fated efforts such as Sears Roebuck–Dean Witter, Prudential Insurance–Bache securities, and American Express–Shearson securities. In fact, the two-year statutory exemption the Federal Reserve conferred upon the new Citigroup soon became irrelevant following the enactment of the 1999 Financial Services Modernization Act;[4] the joke on Wall Street was that the

U.S. Congress had no choice but to pass the bill, since the merger was "too big to litigate." Hence, this landmark legislation consecrated the illicit Citicorp-Travelers union (under the old banking regulatory guidelines) by explicitly allowing bank holding companies to affiliate with firms offering securities brokerage, investment management, mutual funds, insurance, municipal finance, and corporate investment banking.[5]

The Federal Reserve's approval of the union between the nation's second-largest bank holding company and a major insurance company (recently diversified through acquisition of brokerage Smith Barney and commodities trader Salomon) ushered in the new era of full-service banking conglomerates, albeit under protest by local community groups.[6] In the process, it marked the demise of the 70-year-old statutory framework of federal banking regulation. Indeed, it signaled the death knell of not only the 1933 Glass-Steagall Act's prohibitions against bank holding companies engaging in both wholesale and retail banking activities but also the restrictions against interstate banking in contravention of the McFadden Act of 1927.[7] As a senior Federal Reserve official explained, the regulatory challenge of the Citigroup conglomerate is that it is "'an entity unlike any other we've ever supervised.'"[8]

Today, the Citigroup bank holding company (New York Stock Exchange symbol C) features over 170,000 employees with a record $9.9 billion in net income and 22.7 percent return on equity for 1999. A truly global corporation, Citigroup provides banking, insurance, investment, and of course credit card services to more than 100 million customers in over 100 countries.[9] This full-service financial firm features brokerage services (Salomon Smith Barney), mutual funds (Primerica Financial), property/casualty insurance (82 percent ownership stake in Travelers Property Casualty), retirement products (Travelers Life and Annuity), real estate services (Citicorp Real Estate), consumer loans (Citifinancial, formerly Commercial Credit), and a state-of-the-art e-commerce unit (e-Citi), among other services.[10]

The central issue, then, is the merger's impact on the repositioning of how banks conduct their business activities. For instance, Citigroup is a diversified financial services company that can offer proprietary insurance and underwriting products as well as an insurance company that can cross-market traditional banking products. In short, it provides one-stop shopping: A home mortgage from Citibank will elicit a property insurance quote from a Travelers agent followed by a call for mutual funds from a Primerica Financial investment adviser or a retirement annuity from a Travelers Life agent.

The key to the success of financial services conglomerates is whether they will be able to derive synergistic cross-marketing efficiencies. That is, from an institutional perspective, are they getting bigger because they are effectively using economies of scale in the marketing and delivering of their financial products and services? Or are they better merely because they have become the biggest kid on the block through the absorption of their competitors?[11] In fact, analysis of bank performance in the mid-1990s indicates that smaller banks are more efficient and more profitable than the goliaths of the industry.[12]

Clearly, the neoclassical economic assumption that banking deregulation will produce corporate economies of scale that ultimately benefit consumers has not been adequately scrutinized. This fallacious and often naive view fails to examine the larger dynamics and industry trends that have emerged from banking deregulation since the early 1980s. According to Susan Kaplan, a financial planner in Wellesley, Massachusetts, "'The profits [from mergers] have been passed on to companies' shareholders [rather than lower consumer prices] because there is more demand by companies to see their stock go up than to please their consumers.'"[13] This is an instructive point. It helps to place the role of bank credit cards in a historical context as being both cause and effect in the consumer financial services revolution.

The bank credit card has played a profound role as both a statutory and technological catalyst in the transformation of the banking industry. That is, it provided the earliest and most successful legal challenges to federal regulatory restrictions (e.g., interstate banking) as well as an ideal financial product for developing automated consumer banking systems (ATMs). In the process, the circumvention of state usury laws along with the dramatic reduction in inflation led to the enormous profitability of bank credit cards in the mid-1980s. These profits were strategically allocated to augment the dangerously low capital reserves of many major money center banks in the late 1980s and early 1990s. Hence, by contributing to the stock appreciation spiral, credit cards helped to sustain the bank merger frenzy of the 1990s that further enhanced the equity position of commercial banks. These trends, along with merger-related cost-cutting and escalating bank fees, intensified the industry's diversification pressures that finally demolished the fire walls of federal banking regulation in 1997 and 1998.[14] Bank credit cards played an instrumental role in the transformation of the banking industry, with Citicorp leading the way.

The Perils of Consumer Banking: Boom and Bust of Credit and Debt

The 1980s decade of debt featured growing credit dependence among all sectors and social groups of U.S. society. For many American households, the tightening vise of the U.S. debt triangle resulted in increasing use of consumer credit for both wants and needs. That is, the common use of installment credit for the purchase of durable goods such as automobiles, washer/dryers, and furniture expanded to include auto repairs, insurance, professional services (doctor, lawyer, therapist), college tuition, and even the rent or groceries. As the go-go 1980s ushered in the austere 1990s, banks guided financially beleaguered citizens through the economic minefield of declining real wages, corporate downsizings, and skyrocketing college costs with increasingly expensive revolving consumer credit. This reflected not only the desperation of those who suffered the most from U.S. industrial restructuring but also the institutional realities of commercial banks as they assessed the realities of the newly deregulated financial services industry.

As American society adapted to the profound shift from a manufacturing- to services-based economy in the 1970s and 1980s, commercial banks like Citicorp were likewise compelled to adjust to a new set of economic realities. Indeed, the institutional pressures and larger global forces that shaped Citicorp—the industry leader in revolving bank credit cards (Visa, Master-Card)[15]—were the result of the structural changes and unique banking opportunities created by the U.S. postindustrial economy. Banks quickly realized that they had to wean themselves from the highly regulated and previously stable institutional environment in which corporate loans and low-cost deposits were the mainstays of their profitability.

As the industry faced intensifying competition and declining profits in the 1980s, banks expanded their investment portfolios to include more risky real estate and investment banking activities (e.g., junk-bond-financed acquisitions) and sought new domestic and international markets for their thriving consumer services. The success or failure of individual banks to adjust to government deregulation underlies the rapid transformation of the industry's contemporary landscape through mergers, acquisitions, and competition from nonfinancial rivals such as Sears, AT&T, and GE. These developments are illustrated by the wildly fluctuating fortunes of America's largest and most profitable bank: Citicorp. From its dominant position in the U.S. banking industry in the early 1980s to its near insolvency in the early 1990s, Citicorp has rebounded—largely due to the profitability of its credit cards and other consumer services—to become the most powerful financial institution in the world (see Appendix 2).[16]

Global Aspirations and Blind Ambitions

The architect of Citicorp's current corporate structure and institutional power was Walter Wrinston. Appointed president in 1967 and chairman in 1970, he increased the bank's size, scope, and profitability dramatically during his seventeen-year stewardship. For example, one of his most significant accomplishments was the adoption of a new organizational structure—the one-bank holding company in 1968. This strategy enabled Citicorp to enter new consumer markets through affiliated finance companies or mortgage banking subsidiaries. This decision not only facilitated the merger with Travelers Group (through a legal loophole in the Bank Holding Act of 1956) but also has yielded huge financial dividends through the expansion of the consumer services division, the creation of an overseas network of satellite branches for increasing corporate deposits while marketing an array of financial services from New York, and the development of innovative financial products such as certificates of deposits (CDs). Not incidentally, the latter has played an especially important role because low-cost capital has fueled the expansion of Citicorp's domestic and international loan portfolios.[17]

Wrinston's managerial foresight was responsible for Citicorp's current emphasis on retail banking and computerized information technologies; the former especially benefited, since it was hemorrhaging so much money in the early 1970s. For instance, Wrinston aggressively promoted the bank credit card division and increased investment in state-of-the-art automated teller machines (ATMs); both continue to pace the revolution in consumer financial services today. Indeed, by reducing the cost of soliciting new customers as well as processing small consumer transactions, Wrinston realized the bank credit card could become a formidable corporate warhorse in circumventing federal regulations against interstate banking. Furthermore, Wrinston ensured that his retail banking initiatives would be competently pursued after his retirement in 1984. His handpicked successor, John S. Reed, was head of the bank's consumer group.

Although the consumer credit division was only beginning to show signs of its profit potential upon Wrinston's retirement, the total assets of the bank had expanded at a breakneck pace: from $17.5 billion in 1967 to $150.6 billion in 1984. Also, new income climbed from $103.0 million to $890.0 million, while total loans jumped from $9.9 billion to $102.7 billion, respectively, during this period. In the process, the successful introduction of computer systems validated Wrinston's confidence in hi-tech's strategic role in improving the bank's bottom line; technology enhanced worker productivity and eventually slashed the costs of labor-intensive bank services. Overall, the Citicorp workforce increased less than threefold to 71,000, whereas new income jumped nearly ninefold during this seventeen-year period.[18]

In the early 1970s, Citicorp was well positioned for rapid growth in the U.S. and global markets. In fact, Wrinston unabashedly declared that Citicorp was poised to become the most powerful bank in the world based on his annual growth target of 15 percent. In this endeavor, the goal of revitalizing the international division received a boost from an unexpected source: the Organization of Petroleum Exporting Countries (OPEC). The successful oil embargo of the OPEC nations in 1973 increased the political clout of the cartel as well as the price of petroleum exports. Middle East oil-producing countries suddenly were awash in billions of petrodollars and sought to invest them in the safest financial institutions—particularly large U.S. banks. Citicorp recognized a potential financial bonanza if it could attract these low-interest deposits and then recycle the dollars back into the global economy through high-interest loans to cash-starved developing countries.

Citicorp masterfully courted the new oil barons as well as other Third World elites and became a major beneficiary of the revenue windfall. This is mirrored in the rapid growth of Citibank deposits—from almost $45 billion in 1975 to $70 billion in 1979. Deposits leveled off at about $80 billion during the 1981–1982 recession, climbed sharply until 1989 to nearly $140 billion, and then stabilized at about $145 billion in the mid-1990s. However, these "cheap" OPEC dollars came at an alarming price. In 1975, the U.S. Senate Foreign Relations Committee and its Multinational Subcommittee convened special hearings to investigate their potential impact on the U.S. financial system. Citicorp and other major recipients refused to divulge information about their foreign depositors. Ultimately, only aggregated data were released. Even so, they illustrate the magnitude of the petrodollar influx. At the end of 1975, a total of $11.3 billion in OPEC deposits was reported by the seven largest U.S. banks, and Citicorp ranked as the leading repository of these funds.[19]

These seemingly fortuitous events would profoundly impact both Citicorp's international and domestic lending policies a decade later. In the short term, Citicorp immediately channeled the infusion of petrodollars to developing countries such as Argentina, Brazil, Ecuador, Mexico, Peru, Uruguay, and Venezuela. These loans generated tremendous fee and interest revenues and became the single largest source of corporate earnings through the early 1980s. For example, earnings derived from international loans and related financial services constituted 54 percent of the bank's total profits in 1972 and climbed to 72 percent in 1976. At the same time, internal accusations of enhancing overseas profits by illegally "parking" financial gains from foreign exchange trades in other countries led to a Securities and Exchange Commission (SEC) inquiry, U.S. congressional hearings, and payment of over $7 million in back taxes.[20] Significantly, such accusations of questionable corporate business practices persist today.[21]

By the end of the 1970s, the performance of the foreign loan portfolio pushed Citicorp's profits above the half-billion-dollar mark for the first time in corporate history (Appendix 3). Not incidentally, these impressive profits were partially due to the federal regulations that Wrinston continually criticized. That is, Citicorp profited from the enormous spread between the low interest rates of its federally insured bank deposits (fixed at 5 1/4 percent by Regulation Q until 1982)[22] and the high interest rates (15–19 percent in the late 1970s) plus up-front fees of about 1 percent of the total loan package.[23] This easy money not only fueled Citicorp's rapid growth and inflated its profits but also helped to subsidize its money-losing retail banking operations—especially consumer credit cards—though only until the advent of the Third World debt crisis.

The overexposure of the Citicorp international loan portfolio to Third World market volatility began to manifest ominous signs by the end of the decade. For instance, Brazil began experiencing runaway inflation and spiraling levels of unemployment in 1980. The official international debt of Brazil at that time was about $60 billion, and it jumped to nearly $100 billion by the end of the decade. In 1982, the Falkland Islands war disrupted the Argentine economy and led to the suspension of payments on its foreign-held debt of $45 billion. In the same year, the collapse of world oil prices precipitated a financial crisis in another major Citicorp client: Mexico. With an international debt of about $60 billion, Mexico was forced to reschedule its loan payments as new bridge loans and unpaid interest increased its international-owed debt to $100 billion by the end of the 1980s.[24]

Altogether, developing countries owed foreign investors about $400 billion in the mid-1980s, $50 billion alone to U.S. money center banks. Surprisingly, Citicorp's profits exceeded $1 billion in 1986—its corporate high—while its stock price soared to almost $65 (Figure 3.1). This is especially impressive because Citicorp stock had been in decline, falling from about $39 in 1975 to almost $30 in 1982.[25] By the end of the year, however, the fortunes of Citicorp's $14.9 billion in Third World loans had changed drastically—from delinquent fallen angels to unperforming demonic monsters. Overall, U.S. banks wrote off as losses about $40 billion in Third World loans at the "request" of federal regulators. This decision lowered return on assets for the U.S. banking industry from a modest 0.61 percent in 1986 to an anemic 0.09 percent in 1987.[26]

With the financial hemorrhaging of unperforming Third World loans temporarily abating in 1988, Citicorp rebounded with its most profitable year—over $1.6 billion. In fact, net income on these international loans yielded $278 million in 1988. The improving performance of Citicorp's in-

FIGURE 3.1   Citicorp's Stock Price, 1975–2000

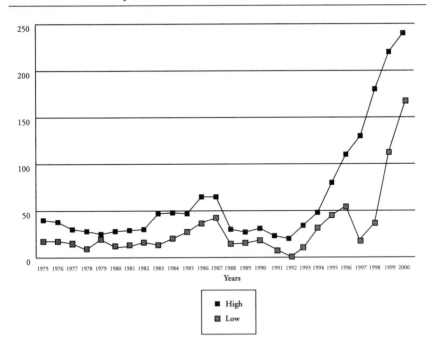

SOURCE: *Moody's Handbook of Common Stock* for years 1975–2000 (New York: Moody's Investors Service).

ternational loan portfolio proved to be short-lived. Its stock price plunged from its all-time high of $64 in 1987 to about $20 in 1988. These market concerns were justified as economic conditions in Latin America began to deteriorate rapidly. Citicorp responded by increasing its financial reserves by $1 billion and absorbing a net loss of $1.15 billion on these loans. This resulted in corporate profits plummeting from nearly $1.7 billion in 1988 to about $0.5 billion in 1989; total Third World loan exposure remained high at about $11 billion.[27]

Overexposed and Burned Again:
Corporate Arrogance and the Debt Crisis

During the early 1990s, Citicorp's financial losses from Third World loans abated; Citicorp's profits fell sharply to about $400 million in 1990. This was followed by a loss of almost $1 billion in 1991, although the major culprit was Citicorp's domestic (real estate) rather than international loans. This time, Citicorp's lending policies nearly resulted in its insolvency. Initially, Citibank's investment in domestic real estate appeared far less risky than Third World loans. With the enactment of the Economic Recovery Tax Act of 1981 (which offered generous depreciation deductions for commercial real estate) and then the Garn–St. Germain Depository Institutions Act of 1982 (which allowed interstate mergers between banks and savings and loans), a real estate boom was soon under way—largely fueled by tax shelter partnerships.

During the 1980s, over $350 billion was invested by banks in commercial real estate lending throughout the United States, accounting for one-third of all existing office space in this period.[28] The enactment of the Tax Reform Act of 1986, however, rescinded the tax advantages to commercial real estate developers. Without these tax subsidies, developers with high vacancy rates began defaulting on their loans. The trickle of corporate bankruptcies soon swelled to a torrent (including commercial bank and S&L insolvencies) as unperforming loans became unsalable real estate in glutted regional markets; in 1988, nine of the top ten banks in Texas were taken over by the Federal Deposit Insurance Corporation (FDIC). The crisis of excess capacity in commercial office space quickly spread to California, New England, and New York as the national real estate market entered a deep recession in 1989.[29]

Like other major money center banks, Citicorp eagerly expanded its real estate loan portfolio in the 1980s. In fact, it became the first major bank holding company to enter the savings and loan business in 1982 (acquiring Fidelity Savings and Loan of San Francisco) and soon became the largest home-loan mortgage originator. As early as 1985, however, potential problems were noticeable in its real estate loan portfolio as commercial loan write-offs rose to $377 million ($156 million increase), or almost twice the preceding ten-year average. Even so, Citicorp dangerously rode the crest of the real estate boom until the bottom fell out of the market in 1989. This is reflected in the growth of Citicorp's loans and deposits during this period. For example, both totaled about $71 billion in 1980 but at the end of the decade, loans had soared to nearly $158 billion while deposits increased only to about $145 billion. As Citicorp's exposure in North American commercial real estate peaked at $26.5 billion in 1989, the ramifications of this widening asset-liability gap would soon attract the attention of federal regulators.[30]

By 1991, Citicorp was in a full-blown retreat, slashing its loan portfolio by $3.5 billion to $18.6 billion. Overall, its real estate portfolio included office (35 percent), retail (21 percent), and residential (15 percent) loans with increases in nonperforming assets over the year reaching $910 million, $266 million, and $245 million, respectively. These staggering losses were primarily responsible for the almost $1 billion combined net loss recorded by Citicorp in 1991.[31] The next year was even more disastrous for Citicorp with losses of $1.3 billion in North American real estate, led by defaults on commercial office loans. Indeed, the most embarrassing and highly scrutinized losses were associated with flamboyant entrepreneur Donald Trump; in many of Trump's deals, Citicorp was either the sole lender or the lead bank of a group of lenders that were seduced with millions of dollars in up-front fees.[32]

Citicorp's failing financial health was reflected in the roller coaster price of its stock. From its high of $64 in 1987, Citicorp stock plunged to a trading range of $20 to $31 in 1989. Although it briefly rallied to nearly $38 in 1990, mounting real estate losses sent the price plummeting to $8.5 at the end of 1991. Undeniably, Citicorp was in serious trouble, and Federal Reserve regulators could no longer overlook the deteriorating condition of America's largest bank. In 1990, the president of the Federal Reserve Bank of New York met with Citicorp CEO John Reed and directed him to improve the undernourished capital base and its staggering debt-to-capital ratio. If not for the over $600 million in net profits from its consumer credit card division, Citicorp would have reported an overall loss of more than $200 million in 1989 and may have been forced to sell part of its credit card portfolio or even court a merger partner.[33]

In 1990, Citicorp embarked on an aggressive recapitalization campaign with the goal of raising between $4 billion and $5 billion. CEO Reed enticed white-knight investors with sweetheart deals such as Saudi Prince Alwaleed bin Talal's $590 million cash investment. Although federal regulators initially opposed the deal, they relented after the prince agreed to numerous restrictions as the bank's largest shareholder.[34] When finally consummated in February 1991, it generated an infusion of desperately needed capital as well as heightened enthusiasm for other Citicorp offerings. Even so, the campaign only moderately improved Citicorp's capital reserves. In fact, Citicorp's Tier I Ratio (core capital reserves) remained dangerously low at 3.73 percent, less than the 4.0 percent minimum and considerably below "well capitalized" (6.0 percent) as defined by the Federal Reserve. This led the Fed to impose restrictions on future corporate acquisitions as well as to suspend the annual stock dividend—saving about $350 million.[35]

Convinced that it could recover from its domestic real estate woes, Citicorp sought to improve its capital position without sacrificing its cash cow: consumer credit cards. This next phase of its mandated recapitalization campaign included slashing overhead expenses as well as selling noncore and low-profit operations. Between 1990 and 1991, the Citicorp workforce was reduced from 95,000 to 86,000 with a target of eliminating 8,000 more jobs by the end of 1993. As thousands of workers found themselves expendable, so did other parts of the Citicorp empire. These included the sale of a successful municipal bond insurance subsidiary (Ambac) that netted about $100 million; 25 percent of the profitable Saudi American Bank (SAMBA) that earned $203 million; the small brokerage firm Lynch, Jones & Ryan for about $15 million; Citibank Italia for $273 million; Citicorp Establishment Services for $175 million (third-largest processor of merchant credit card business in the United States); and liquidation of numerous real estate holdings. Overall, these asset sales raised almost $1.2 billion, which resolved the capitalization crisis. Citicorp also raised cash by selling securitized financial products backed by revenues from its mortgage, auto loan, and credit card receivables portfolios.[36]

Today, Citicorp has successfully overcome its liquidity crisis. After it disgorged a mountain of unperforming real estate loans, Citicorp's global retail banking division fueled the largest recorded profit in its corporate history: nearly $2 billion in 1992. Led by the Fed's decision to substantially lower the cost of money to the U.S. banking industry in 1991, the widening spread on commercial loans brought dramatically improved profitability to commercial banking. This is reflected in the rapid improvement in Citicorp's capitalization. In 1993, its Tier I Ratio climbed to 6.93 percent, and by early 1995 it had leaped above 8.0 percent based on reserves of over $5 billion and total capital of about $27 billion. By 1994, Citicorp recorded the most profitable year in U.S. banking history ($3.4 billion) and then shattered its own record in 1995. This is reflected in the impressive ascent of its stock price, which crossed the $30 plateau in 1993, the $40 threshold in 1994, and soared above $80 in 1995.[37] More important, Citicorp recovered from the costly blunders of its overzealous expansion without being forced to sell any key parts of its prized consumer credit card operations. The cash cow had been saved from the predatory wolves of the forced recapitalization campaign.

Navigating the Dangerous Economic Shoals of Banking Deregulation

The early 1980s became an especially tumultuous period for the U.S. banking industry. This was due to the initial dismantling of federal regulations and intensifying competition over consumer financial services markets. Furthermore, macroeconomic forces were wreaking havoc—particularly inflation. Beginning with the rising budget deficit and expanding money supply during the Vietnam War (unemployment fell to 3.5 percent in 1969), the U.S. economy began experiencing double-digit inflation by the end of the decade, reaching 14 percent in 1980. These pressures substantially increased commodity prices, stocks and bonds, and of course interest rates.

For small investors, who dutifully deposited their savings in federally insured bank accounts, the security of FDIC passbook investments was threatened by the erosion of their real value, the result of the relatively low interest rates mandated by the Federal Reserve under Regulation Q. Enacted in 1933, its intent was to prevent banks from ruinous competition through the overpaying of customers' deposits. However, as inflation surged in the 1970s and market interest rates jumped accordingly, the Federal Reserve only slowly raised passbook deposits from 4.5 percent in the early 1970s to 5.0 percent in 1973 and then to 5.25 percent in 1979—at a time when inflation exceeded 12 percent.[38]

Market interest rates continued to rise with the tide of inflation. The prime rate jumped from 7.9 percent in 1975 to 15.3 percent in 1980, rising to a high of 18.9 percent in 1981 and then sliding to 15.9 percent in 1982. In comparison, yields on one-year U.S. Treasury bills climbed from 6.3 percent in 1975 to 10.9 percent in 1980, peaking at 13.2 percent in 1981 and then dipping to 11.1 percent in 1982. It was not until the Depository Institutions Deregulation and Monetary Control Act (DIDMCA) of 1980 rescinded Regulation Q that federally insured passbook deposits could offer competitive interest rates, albeit over a six-year phase-in period.[39] As a result, commercial banks and thrifts could not compete, and by the mid-1980s, small depositors had fled en masse from their low-interest passport accounts to higher-yield alternatives (CDs, money market accounts, interest-bearing savings accounts). In the process, this depositor flight seriously weakened many small banks and thrifts (S&L) that relied on low-cost capital as a financial cushion. This was the first of many bumps in the road of banking deregulation that intensified downward pressures on industry profits (especially after 1979), led financial institutions to pursue increasingly riskier strategies for enhancing their bottom line, and ultimately precipitated the flurry of bank mergers and acquisitions that fundamentally shaped the current dynamics of the industry's consolidation.[40]

Federal regulations also restricted the financial operations of banks to specific regions and particular activities or financial products. Initially, the regulatory inspiration as codified by the McFadden Act of 1927 was to protect small, local community banks from the predations of regional financial goliaths that sought to enter new markets by establishing branches in other states. As restrictions on bank deposits eased in the early 1980s, the previously impervious division between commercial banks and other types of financial institutions became increasingly blurred through product innovations and bank acquisitions or special arrangements with financial subsidiaries. For example, American Express acquired the brokerage firm of Shearson Loeb Rhodes, followed by Prudential Insurance buying Bache Securities in 1981; BankAmerica Corporation merged with Charles Schwab & Company (discount brokerage firm) in 1982; Sears Roebuck added Dean Witter Reynolds and Coldwell Banker (real estate brokerage firm) to its Allstate insurance group and then created its consumer credit card company (Discover) in 1986; and Dreyfus Corporation (mutual fund management company) purchased a state bank and established a national bank within a nonbank structure (i.e., without demand deposits or commercial lending).

Even the venerable Baldwin Piano and Organ Company entered the consumer financial services "gold rush" in the early 1980s by buying an insurance company (renamed Baldwin United) that sold annuities through Merrill Lynch, albeit with disastrous consequences. Hence, by the mid-1970s, financial innovations were redefining traditional institutional distinctions. A savings and loan in Worcester, Massachusetts, offered the first NOW (negotiable order of withdrawal) account in 1970 that basically was an interest-bearing checking account. Merrill Lynch introduced its CMA (cash management account) in 1977 that later included credit card, checking account, and payment features with the traditional brokerage account. By then, commercial banks had already penetrated the once exclusive domain of finance companies by offering consumer loans.[41]

More important was the U.S. Supreme Court's challenge of federal restrictions on interstate banking. In its landmark 1978 decision *Marquette National Bank of Minneapolis v. First National Bank of Omaha*, the Court affirmed the right of banks to export higher "home state" interest rates on credit card accounts to other states. This ruling, by defining a bank's headquarters according to its bricks-and-mortar location, paved the way for credit card companies to relocate their operations to states that offered the most advantageous financial terms.[42] For Citicorp CEO Wrinston, a vociferous advocate of regulatory reform, this ruling constituted the juridical breach for surmounting federal barriers to regional and even national retail banking. As Joseph Nocera astutely notes, the "money revolution" was well under way with these seemingly isolated yet cumulatively formidable attacks on the bulwarks of the regulatory apparatus.[43]

As the regulatory ramparts began crumbling in the late 1970s, commercial banks encountered competition from unexpected sources. For example, finance companies led the growth of nonbanks in soon offering residential mortgages, consumer and commercial loans, transaction (checking) accounts, and of course credit cards. By 1990, subsidiaries of such retail giants as Sears Roebuck and manufacturing behemoths such as General Electric and Ford Motor Company were financing one-third of all consumer credit and one-quarter of all commercial loans. This trend is reflected in the substantial decline in the share of total assets of the financial services industry held by U.S. commercial and savings banks: from almost 50 percent in 1950 to 22 percent in 1991. Similarly, the increasingly important role of institutional investors is reflected in the combined assets of pension and mutual funds, which rose from 5 to 30 percent during this same period.[44]

The profound change in the institutional composition of the financial services industry was accompanied by a similar change in its loan portfolio. For commercial banks like Citibank, the most immediate impact was the decline in traditional corporate clients. Once a steady source of profits, corporate borrowing plummeted as major companies found cheaper access to short-term funds through uninsured investment banks that floated their corporate bonds. By the end of the 1970s, corporations had raised $124 billion through such debt-financing mechanisms. With extraordinary advances in telecommunications and computer technologies in the 1980s, moreover, blue-chip borrowers were able to obtain better deals from other sources, including foreign banks. As a result, the proportion of nonbank commercial paper issued by commercial firms climbed from 10 percent in 1969 to 75 percent in 1989.[45]

As with the loss of easy profits from passport savings accounts, the abrupt decline in corporate borrowing also exacerbated pressures on bank profits. Not surprisingly, banks responded to the profit crunch by engaging in new "off-balance-sheet" activities. These included issuing standby letters of credit (a bank guarantee of a loan made by a third party), "bundling" loans (auto, home mortgage, credit card receivables) and selling them as securities on secondary markets, and creating increasingly complex and risky derivative instruments. Significantly, Citicorp has been a major player in all of these activities and was the second-largest trader of derivative contracts ($2.61 trillion) after Chemical Bank ($3.19 trillion) in the mid-1990s.[46]

Citicorp's spectacular return to profitability reflects the improved performance of its international operations, recovery of the domestic real estate market, and its swift adjustment to the deregulated U.S. banking environment—especially consumer services. Corporate profits zoomed to record levels of $3.4 billion in 1994, $3.5 billion in 1995, and $3.8 billion in 1996, which resulted in Citicorp's stock price breaking the $80 barrier. Although profits slipped to $3.6 billion in 1997, the stock soared past $130 by year-end and jumped to a premerger high of $143 on April 3, 1998. Following the merger announcement with Travelers, Citicorp stock jumped 28 percent to $181; the market's euphoria quickly waned, however, as it plummeted below $85 over the summer. Citigroup posted a remarkable comeback after its tumultuous postmerger honeymoon, with $5.8 billion net income for 1998 and record net income of $9.9 billion in 1999, the latter propelled by the robust earnings of its Salomon Smith Barney commission and investment banking revenues (477 percent increase from 1998) and Global Consumer business (287 percent increase from 1998). For the first quarter of 2000, net income soared to $3.6 billion (30 percent return on equity)—a 49 percent increase from the preceding year—with a Tier I capital ratio of 9.7 percent based on total equity capital and trust securities of $55.2 billion;[47] by midyear, the adjusted Citigroup stock price had crossed the $240 threshold.[48] Consequently, in less than a decade, Citicorp has risen—like the phoenix—from the ashes of near-corporate insolvency to the largest and most profitable financial services conglomerate in the world. And it owes its extraordinary resurrection to one of its least glamorous divisions: retail banking and, especially, the almighty credit card.

Not Just a Visa, a Citibank Visa: Milking the Cash Cow

One *billion* dollars per year. This was the stratospheric figure of pretax profits that Citicorp executives giddily proposed as the objective of the consumer credit card division in the 1970s. One *billion* dollars per year. These lofty profit projections were being discussed even though Citicorp credit card operations had lost hundreds of millions of dollars annually—as recently as 1981. One *billion* dollars per year. This ambitious goal was declared even though *total* Citicorp profits had never achieved this level before the mid-1980s. By the late 1980s, however, the starry-eyed dreamers of the credit card division had climbed this mythical financial summit and even set their sights on $1 billion in *net* (after-tax) profits. For these reasons, Citicorp executives had acceded to the costly terms of the earlier corporate recapitalization campaign; the consumer credit card division had been preserved in toto. The key issue, then, is how bank credit cards became so profitable after two stultifying decades of occasionally modest earnings and more frequently substantial losses.

Birth of a (Credit Card) Nation: Sowing the Seeds of Consumer Credit Dependence

Consumer credit has played an increasingly prominent role in the rising standard of living of American households in the twentieth century.

Whether as a means to increase family purchasing power or simply for personal convenience, it has helped American families to satisfy their material aspirations. Before World War II, consumer credit was primarily used for durable goods such as the family automobile, household appliances or furniture, and, to a lesser extent, for gasoline and department store items. For most households, their consumption patterns were shaped by the indelible experiences of the Great Depression, which emphasized cash over credit as a strategy for adhering to household budgetary constraints. The exception, but only when necessary or simply for convenience, was the use of "open book" credit accounts extended by local businesses. These were based on the interwoven social networks that bound the financial trust of merchants with the commercial loyalty of their customers—the underlying social cement of American communities.

In the postwar era, increasing wages and the rapid expansion of suburbia fueled the surging materialistic impulses of the rising middle classes. New suburban bedroom communities gestated commercial shopping centers as corporate retail chains and eventually discount emporiums displaced small merchants and their informal, interpersonal networks of retail credit. As American society became increasingly mobile (socially and geographically), formal sources of installment credit became necessary as the personal bonds of main street were replaced with the impersonal relations of the antiseptic suburban mall. This is mirrored in the dramatic expansion of outstanding consumer installment credit, from $2.6 billion in 1945 to $45 billion in 1960. Sears Roebuck retail credit card accounts climbed to 25 million (nearly half of all U.S. households) in the 1950s.[49] Although these early credit cards levied 18 percent annual interest on the unpaid monthly balance, their purpose was to generate greater retail sales and to reinforce customer loyalty, not to earn a profit on finance charges. In fact, Sears was the last major retail giant to accept universal bank credit cards (Visa, MasterCard) in 1993.[50]

As economic anxieties receded from the American consciousness in the 1950s, the banking industry began to explore creative alternatives to labor-intensive, small consumer loans. The lack of efficient, computerized accounting technologies required that each installment loan application—regardless of the amount—had to be approved by bank loan officers, and subsequent loan payments required laborious and costly account documentation. At prevailing interest rates, moreover, small consumer loans were only marginally profitable to banks. The growing reluctance of first-tier banks to provide small loans contributed to the unsavory practices at the bottom of the financial food chain by loan sharks, pawnshops, and shadowy finance companies. As a result, the mid-1950s brought a flurry of bank activities that sought to tap into the growing demand for small consumer loans by developing cost-efficient delivery instruments—all-purpose revolving consumer credit cards.

Drawing on the experiences of proprietary or retail credit cards (Mobil Oil, Montgomery Ward, Sears) as well as the more recent Diners Club (a national business charge card founded in 1949), Bank of America in California developed the most prominent revolving credit card. The new bank card featured credit limits of $300–$500, a $25–$100 daily "floor" limit, and 18 percent interest on unpaid monthly balances. Initially, the commercial success of this financial innovation was not based on the growth of consumer accounts. Rather, it was contingent upon the recruitment of a vast network of merchants who would gladly accept a 6 percent transaction fee, or merchant discount, as well as a $25 monthly fee for the card processor, or "imprinter."[51] For local businesses, the advantage was that greater sales would offset the additional expense of transaction fees for several reasons: The universal bank credit card (1) offered a competitive alternative for consumers who shopped with proprietary retail credit cards, (2) lowered the merchants' costs for their own credit programs by reducing bookkeeping expenses, (3) eliminated cash-flow bottlenecks by reimbursing purchases within days, and (4) provided an entrée to a potentially large customer base that included all Bank of America clients.

By the summer of 1958, Bank of America was preparing a mass marketing campaign for the introduction of its new BankAmericard. It was inaugurated with the first "drop" (mass mailing) of over 60,000 unsolicited credit cards to Bank of America customers in Fresno, California. Over the next 12 years, until banned by legislation spearheaded by Senator William Proxmire, U.S. households were flooded with nearly 100 million unsolicited credit cards. This first volley in the money revolution soon swept across an unsuspecting American public and precipitated tremors throughout the U.S. banking industry.[52]

The launching of the BankAmericard spawned numerous imitators as well as innovators. In the travel and entertainment market for business clients, pioneered by Diners Club, the Hilton Hotel Corporation (Carte Blanche) and American Express both founded their card programs in 1958. Significantly, these accounts were marketed to business travelers as a payment convenience and offered a national network of travel and entertainment venues; cardholders continue to pay their charge balances in full each month. Other major banks such as Chase Manhattan and many small banks followed Bank of America's lead into these uncharted financial waters with financially disastrous results. Fear of intrusions by competitors led the early credit card pioneers to expand their marketing campaigns before establishing an efficient credit card operations infrastructure; Bank of America mailed 2 million credit cards throughout California over a 13-month period. This resulted in unexpectedly high rates of delinquent accounts, widespread consumer and merchant fraud, innumerable processing problems and statement errors, massive resistance to transaction fees by merchants, and, of course, enormous bank losses. Over the first 15 months, Bank of America lost an estimated $20 million and soon found the California credit card market to be its exclusive domain. Other banks critically examined their mounting losses and abandoned the credit card market. This included Chase Manhattan, which sold its credit card operations in 1962.[53]

During the 1960s, Bank of America carefully reorganized its credit card program into a statewide operation whose profitability improved with technological advances and efficiencies of scale. Between 1960 and 1968, its active cardholder base climbed from 233,585 to over 1 million, while the volume of credit card sales jumped from $59 million to $400 million. More important, profits soared from $179,000 in 1961 to $12.7 million in 1968.[54] The newfound success of the BankAmericard, however, soon demonstrated the limits of its market potential. Future consumer and merchant growth as well as investment in large-scale technologies for combating fraud and improving processing efficiency required the development of a national credit card network. As a result, Bank of America began licensing (franchising) its BankAmericard throughout the United States in 1966. Out-of-state licensees paid a $25,000 entry fee and a small additional royalty for cooperative marketing campaigns. This provoked an immediate response by rival banks in California that organized a Master Charge credit card, a group of East Coast banks that formed the Interbank Card Association, and several large Chicago banks that developed the Midwest Bank Card Association. Within a year, the number of banks issuing credit cards jumped from 70 to 627. These included such long-forgotten ventures as Town & Country, Midwest Bank, and Presto Charge cards.[55]

The establishment of regional bank consortiums facilitated the rapid expansion of merchant networks across state boundaries. Together with the resulting economies of scale, these regional systems began laying the foundation of a national infrastructure for undertaking cooperative marketing, processing transactions, and curbing fraud. By 1967, the credit card fever struck as banks began blanketing the country with unsolicited cards; over 30 million were issued during the year. Like the initially disastrous results of the BankAmericard mass mailing, these ill-conceived programs were soon drowning in their own red ink due to massive fraud (consumer, merchant, organized crime), billing and statement errors, and high payment delinquencies. To make matters worse, U.S. congressional hearings and stories in the mass media chastised banks for luring unsuspecting Americans into unnecessary debt at usurious interest rates while undermining traditional values such as thrift. The result was the first statutory regulation of bank credit cards (the mass mailing of unsolicited cards was banned in 1970) as well as a major shakeout in the industry; banks that continued to issue credit cards joined either BankAmericard or Master Charge. By 1970, BankAmericard operated in 44 states, and Master Charge had expanded into 49 states.[56]

In 1966, Citibank boldly entered the fray by purchasing 50 percent of Carte Blanche. This move provoked a strong reaction from rival banks, which feared that Citibank would gain a competitive edge in the future consolidation of the highly fragmented credit card industry. The U.S. Department of Justice concurred and, by raising antitrust concerns, forced Citibank to sell its stake in Carte Blanche. The following year, Citibank launched its own Everything Card. Like all other new entrants into the credit card industry, it suffered massive financial losses. By the end of the decade, the newly reorganized Citicorp bank holding company abandoned its Everything Card and joined the Master Charge system; other major competitors such as Chase Manhattan and First National of Chicago joined BankAmericard. Thus, as the United States braced for the impending age of inflation, the first step of mass acceptance had been accomplished; 29 million Americans had become card-carrying members of the Credit Card Nation.[57]

The Age of Inflation:
Deflated Dollars and Inflated Expectations

The post–World War II period featured remarkably low inflation and steadily rising wages through the early 1970s. These favorable trends enabled families to reliably estimate their household budgets (typically based on one wage earner) and to plan long-term purchases with accumulated savings or installment credit programs; inflation averaged only 2.3 percent per year in the 1950s and 2.4 percent in the 1960s. For most of the early bank cardholders, their initial experiences were as convenience users; they tended to pay off their monthly purchases or maintain only modest balances.[58] This was a major disappointment to the architects of the Credit Card Nation, since merchant fees and interest payments on revolving or unpaid balances were the only revenue streams flowing from their hemorrhaging credit card operations; annual membership fees were uncommon until the end of the decade. Consequently, as total outstanding consumer installment debt climbed from $45 billion in 1960 to $104 billion in 1970, credit cards accounted for only a small fraction of America's mounting consumer debt—less than 3 percent.[59]

The early pioneers of bank credit cards soon realized that a major impediment to their expansion was their limited practical use. Indeed, the growing web of enlisted merchants offered new opportunities for consumer charges, but the manual imprinter and telephone authorization technologies undermined the use "value" of credit cards. Quite simply, they were inconvenient. As the national scope of credit card operations grew and the volume of transactions increased exponentially, the credit card industry jumped into the sea of scientific progress by centralizing their processing operations through computerized switching systems. The newly formed National BankAmericard Incorporated (NBI), which was renamed Visa in 1977, blazed a technological trail after abandoning its collaboration with American Express and establishing its own national processing network in 1973. Within a year, this centralized computer system saved NBI affiliate banks $30 million in processing costs and, more important, reduced the average time for a credit card transaction from nearly five minutes to 56 seconds. Although Master Charge and American Express subsequently developed their own proprietary processing systems, NBI had already distinguished itself as the industry leader.[60]

In 1971, Citicorp surpassed Chase Manhattan and set its sights on overtaking Bank of America as the largest credit card issuer in the United States. In pursuing this objective, Citicorp executives recognized that their first problem was the technological gap in their banking operations. After observing Chemical Bank's introduction of automated teller machines (ATMs), Citicorp embarked on a modernization campaign that upgraded its ATMs and aggressively marketed them in the New York metropolitan area. Citicorp executives realized that improving the efficiency of its operations and productivity of its workers would pay big dividends in their long-term expansion plans. Led by John Reed, a research and development facility (Transaction Tech) was established at the California Institute of Technology in 1973. The willingness to invest hundreds of millions of dollars in the unprofitable credit card division showed the institutional foresight that underlies Citicorp's vanguard role in new credit card technology and product innovations today. Even so, Citicorp's current dominance of the credit card industry is the result of an opportunistic marketing ruse rather than a technological advance or product innovation.

In 1976, fearing that it would soon lose a protracted legal suit, NBI dropped its opposition to "duality" and allowed Master Charge–affiliated banks to issue BankAmericard accounts.[61] In an effort to enhance its tarnished image in the United States and abroad, NBI planned a major international marketing campaign to announce its new name: Visa. This proved to be a fortuitous opportunity for Citicorp. Although it immediately joined NBI, Citicorp did not initially offer BankAmericard accounts to any of its customers. Instead, it planned a preemptive strike of 26 million unsolicited Visa applications across the nation in late summer and early fall of 1977; this mass mailing was intentionally scheduled before Bank of America and other NBI-affiliated banks sent their credit card renewal/Visa sign-up notices.

At the time, Bank of America was the leading credit card issuer with 6.7 million cards in circulation and an annual charge volume of $3.7 billion. The number-two issuer was Citibank (5.6 million cards, $2.2 billion charges) followed by First National of Chicago (2.9 million cards), Chase Manhattan (2.9 million cards), and Continental of Chicago (2.2 million cards). Overall, industry concentration was proceeding at a rapid rate, with the top 50 banks accounting for more than one-half of all bank cards issued in the United States. Citicorp executives gambled that individual cardholders did not know which NBI-affiliated bank had issued their credit card. They speculated that many of these BankAmericard households would accept the first invitation to arrive in the mail. They were right. This unprecedented national mail drop yielded Citicorp 3 million new Visa cardholders—second only to Bank of America. Together with its existing Master Charge accounts, this marketing coup catapulted Citicorp to the apex of the credit card industry—a position it has not relinquished.[62]

By the late 1970s, the cultivation of nationwide merchant and consumer credit card networks (Visa, Master Charge) had effectively surmounted the regulatory barriers to interstate banking. With the emergence of national markets, the next goal of the major credit card issuers was to increase the cost of consumer credit. For example, the New York usury law stipulated that banks could charge a maximum of 18 percent on the first $500 loan and only 12 percent for loans above this amount. Although state usury ceilings typically ranged from 12 to 18 percent, some were as high as 24 percent (South Dakota, Ohio) and others as low as 10 percent (Arkansas). As previously mentioned, Citicorp found an unexpected ally in its efforts to evade state usury laws when the U.S. Supreme Court upheld the right of a Nebraska bank to export its higher-interest-rate credit cards to Minnesota.[63]

This 1978 judicial precedent curtailed the power of state legislatures to regulate usurious lending practices. Regional and national banks could simply relocate their operations to more lender-friendly states. As a Citibank executive explained after the landmark ruling, "'we realized that we could

[now] choose our headquarters state based on its usury laws.'" Citicorp immediately began negotiating with South Dakota politicians in an attempt to further weaken their consumer lending regulations by offering a major inducement—the 2,000 white-collar jobs of its credit card division. By January 1981, Citicorp's credit card headquarters had moved from New York to Sioux Falls, where it remains the largest employer in the city. Delaware and Maryland followed South Dakota's example of regulatory "reform" and lured the credit card divisions of many out-of-state banks in exchange for raising the costs of consumer credit for millions of their residents.[64]

After increasing the finance charges on its credit cards, Citicorp sought to expand the social frontiers of its credit card portfolio by soliciting lower-income households. This was an important marketing shift because the early focus on more affluent, middle-class households produced large numbers of unprofitable, albeit low-risk, convenience users. Bankers had hoped that a larger proportion of these cardholders would revolve a portion of their purchases or occasionally forget to pay their credit card bills. Instead, they soon realized that they were stuck with costly deadbeat clients, who zealously paid off their charges within the specified grace period. As inflation rates climbed to double digits, the architects of the Credit Card Nation encountered a crucial institutional crossroads: continue losing even more money on large numbers of low-risk, middle-class clients or increase their lending to higher-risk, lower-income households that previously had been avoided.

It did not take long before the roar of inflation created a financially insecure middle class that began assuming greater levels of consumer debt while coping with the economic distress of U.S. industrial restructuring. As real wages declined in the mid-1970s, accumulating debt rather than saving became rational behavior. That is, spiraling inflation reduced the real cost of repaying earlier loans and thus lessened the impact of falling household incomes. In the process, these trends fundamentally challenged the cultural ethos of thrift as illustrated by the popular twist of Benjamin Franklin's famous adage, "'It doesn't pay to save for a rainy day.'" Furthermore, this attitudinal shift was reinforced by demographic factors. For example, baby boomers reaching adulthood required greater borrowing for launching new households and raising young children. This trend contributed to J.C. Penney becoming the first nationwide retail chain to accept bank credit cards in 1979.[65]

Except for Bank of America, credit card operations were generating substantial losses or only marginal profits in the 1970s. Many issuers considered their credit cards to be a "loss leader." That is, they helped to cultivate customer loyalty and attract new clients. In 1976, when Citicorp imposed a monthly surcharge of 50 cents on convenience users, it claimed a loss of nearly $100 million over the preceding seven years and a small profit only when it levied this service fee. Reluctantly, Citibank discontinued the practice in spring 1978 following denunciations in the U.S. Congress and the New York Supreme Court's ruling that it was illegal. Only two years later, however, a much higher service fee was levied on cardholders following President Jimmy Carter's "emergency" restrictions on consumer credit; the latter were imposed as part of a program to combat soaring inflation. This ill-fated policy, which was quickly reversed, provided banks with a long-awaited pretext for simultaneously imposing annual membership fees ($12 to $20). To their surprise, only nine million cardholders, or about 8 percent of the national total, declined to renew their accounts.[66] As a result, total installment credit nearly doubled from $168 billion in 1975 to $298 billion in 1980, while the revolving component (primarily credit cards) jumped almost fourfold—from $15 billion to $55 billion. Overall, revolving credit climbed from 8.9 to 18.5 percent of total installment debt during this period.[67]

For the credit card industry, the late 1970s and early 1980s were a Dickensian nightmare. On the one hand, they were the best of times because the widespread use of revolving credit cards was changing cultural attitudes toward debt as evidenced by rapidly rising consumer debt levels. On the other hand, they were the worst of times because credit card operations were reporting hundreds of millions of dollars in annual losses between 1979 and 1981.[68] This was due to the inflationary squeeze on the spread between the increasing cost to banks of borrowing money and the maximum bank lending rates as mandated by state usury ceilings.

Ironically, the forces that seduced American households to increase their participation in the credit card culture were also responsible for the enormous losses that banks were incurring from their consumer loan portfolios; the prime lending rate, after adjusting for inflation, averaged only about 1 percent during the 1970s (see Appendix 4). This trend encouraged consumer borrowing, but it also meant that banks would continue to lose money on their credit card accounts so long as inflation remained intractably high. This was a contributing factor in Citicorp's decision to enter the business (travel and entertainment) charge card market. In 1978, Citicorp reacquired Carte Blanche (its upscale client base totaled about 250,000 in 1990) and then purchased Diners Club in 1981 in an attempt to compete with American Express.[69] Furthermore, overhead expenses continued to climb. These included marketing campaigns to increase merchant and consumer accounts, combating rising fraud, and offering other services such as insurance programs, retail discounts, and telephone information networks. For

Citicorp, the enormous flow of red ink in the mid-1970s became a virtual tidal wave in 1981; Citicorp lost over $500 million on its credit card operations between 1979 and 1981.[70]

From the Age of Inflation to the Decade of Debt: The Credit Card Industry Strikes Gold and Platinum[71]

Ronald Reagan's election in 1980 ushered in a dramatic shift toward banking deregulation. The decade of debt featured conservative macroeconomic policies (tight money supply) and continuing decline in worker compensation and unionization levels. Together, the architects of the Reagan Revolution sought to curb inflation and unshackle the banking industry at any cost—regardless of the social consequences. For example, the Chrysler loan bailout of 1980 was followed by a virulent antilabor campaign that began with President Reagan firing the striking air traffic controllers (PATCO) in 1981. These events heralded the unabashedly probusiness direction of U.S. government policy as the American economy plunged into the managed recession of 1981–1982. For the credit card industry, this was a fortuitous confluence of economic trends. Not only had the U.S. middle and working classes increased their reliance on consumer credit, but they also were amassing greater levels of household debt at rapidly escalating costs.

The dramatic increase in the real cost of consumer credit since 1980 is presented in Table 3.2. It lists the average credit card interest rates (column A); Federal Reserve rate, or cost of borrowing from other banks (column B); prime rate, or what banks charge their best customers (column C); and bank spread, or difference between the cost of bank borrowing and lending on credit cards (column D). At the onset of banking deregulation, the average spread on bank credit cards had shrunk from a meager 4.0 percent in 1980 to an anemic 1.4 percent in 1981. In fact, the average prime rate (16.4 percent) nearly equaled the average credit card rate (17.9 percent) from 1980 to 1982. During this brief period, when the cost of consumer borrowing was relatively inexpensive, total installment debt rose only $24 billion (8.1 percent) to $321 billion. Even so, almost one-half of this increase was attributable to revolving (credit card) debt, which rose by $10 billion to $65 billion, or one-fifth (20.0 percent) of total installment debt.[72]

With credit card membership fees an industry standard in 1981, banks waited impatiently for the harsh anti-inflation medicine to nurse corporate profitability back to health. Unexpectedly, the recovery period was short. Between 1981 and 1982, inflation plummeted from 10.3 to 6.2 percent and then stabilized at about 3.5 percent through the end of the decade. On the

TABLE 3.2   Average Annual Rates of Credit and Bank Spread, 1980–2000
(percent)

	A Credit Cards[a]	B Federal Reserve[b]	C Prime[c]	D Bank Spread[d] (A-B)
1980	17.3	13.4	15.3	4.0
1981	17.8	16.4	18.9	1.4
1982	18.5	12.2	14.9	6.3
1983	18.8	9.1	10.8	9.7
1984	18.8	10.2	12.0	8.6
1985	18.7	8.1	9.9	10.6
1986	18.3	6.8	8.3	11.5
1987	17.9	6.7	8.2	11.2
1988	17.8	7.6	9.3	10.2
1989	18.0	9.2	10.9	8.8
1990	18.2	8.1	10.0	10.1
1991	18.2	5.7	8.5	12.5
1992	17.8	3.5	6.3	14.3
1993	16.8	3.0	6.0	13.8
1994	16.2	4.2	7.2	12.0
1995	16.0	5.8	8.8	10.2
1996	15.6	5.3	8.3	10.3
1997	15.8	5.5	8.4	10.3
1998	16.3	5.4	8.3	10.9
1999	16.7	5.5	8.5	11.2
2000[e]	18.1	7.1	9.5	11.0

[a] Weighted average for the calendar year.

[b] The interest rate charged by banks with excess cash reserves to other banks needing overnight loans.

[c] The base rate that banks use in pricing commercial loans to their best customers. It is based on the Federal Reserve's prevailing interest rates for short-term borrowing.

[d] The credit card spread rates are low estimates, since they do not include the lower cost of bank borrowing through interest checking (0–2.5%), savings (3.75–4.75%), and certificates of deposit (4.75–5.75%). Also, the increasing sensitivity of credit card finance changes to prevailing interest rate changes is due to the current industry policy of shifting from fixed to variable interest rates.

[e] Estimates based on midyear CardWeb reports on average credit card interest rates and prevailing bank interest rates on July 1, 2000.

SOURCES: U.S. Federal Reserve System, *Federal Reserve Bulletins;* U.S. Federal Reserve System, *Annual Statistical Digests;* U.S. Department of Commerce, *Statistical Abstract of the United States* (Washington, D.C.: U.S. Government Printing Office, 2000); and CardWeb, "Rates Stand Still" (June 2000), at www.cardweb.com.

other hand, unemployment averaged about 10 percent during the recession and then dropped only moderately to an annual average of 6.5 percent through the 1980s.[73] Not surprisingly, the real cost of consumer credit rose sharply, especially in comparison with corporate borrowing rates.

Between 1981 and 1991, the prime rate for business loans (Table 3.2, column C) fell impressively, from 18.9 to 8.5 percent, whereas for credit cards (column A) it increased slightly, from 17.8 to 18.2 percent. A more instructive measure, however, is the interest rate spread for business loans; it is estimated by subtracting the Federal Reserve rate from the prime rate (column C minus column B). During this ten-year period, it increased modestly for corporate borrowers (2.5 percent to 2.8 percent), whereas it jumped tremendously for credit card users: from 1.4 to 12.5 percent. Over the next two years, the spread remained stable at nearly 2.9 percent for corporate loans while continuing to widen to 14.1 percent for credit cards. Even the interest rate gap between credit cards and new auto loans expanded, from 17.8 and 16.5 percent, respectively (1.3 percent), in 1981 to 18.2 and 11.1 percent in 1991, respectively (7.3 percent).[74] Together, these trends suggest that the Federal Reserve's decision to maintain a low discount rate in the early 1990s (3.6 percent average for 1992–1994) served to buttress bank profits while the industry wrote off its disastrous real estate loans and struggled with its capitalization problems.

As illustrated by the dramatic growth in the credit card spread (column D), the banks finally struck gold during the decade of debt. Not only did they increase the real cost of consumer borrowing, but their credit card write-off expenses continued to shrink as payment delinquencies and defaults fell during the economic expansion. Furthermore, economic prosperity and greater market penetration expanded the number of credit card accounts as well as the volume of card charges and accumulated balances. The targeting of lower-income households, especially those hit hard by industrial restructuring, led to escalating balances and fewer convenience users. A survey conducted by University of Maryland economist Lawrence Ausubel found that the latter declined from 31.8 percent in 1979 to 21.4 percent in 1985.[75] In addition, costly fraud-prevention programs finally began bearing fruit. Between 1983 and 1988, losses due to illicit credit card use rose only modestly, from $125 million to $159 million. This was an impressive feat in view of the massive expansion of the industry's cardholder base.[76]

By 1989, the revolving component of total consumer credit outstanding had jumped to nearly $200 billion out of a total of $724 billion. Although total installment debt grew only an additional $17 billion during the next three years to $741 billion, revolving credit increased a remarkable $55 billion—accounting for 34 percent of total installment debt in 1992. Two years later, at the end of 1994, revolving credit card debt registered an unprecedented single-year gain of $56 billion. This amount is greater than the cumulative credit card debt of 1980. Overall, revolving debt totaled $334 billion (36.6 percent) of the $912 billion in total outstanding installment credit in 1994.[77] This trend is especially revealing because the 1986 Tax Reform Act included a five-year phaseout of interest deductibility on consumer debt such as student loans, automobile financing, and credit cards. A substantial portion of this steep rise in credit card debt was attributable to the widespread use of cards by individuals and households coping with the dislocations of the 1989–1991 recession.

According to Ausubel, the leading authority on the industry's profitability, credit card issuers earned between three and five times the ordinary rate of return in banking from 1983 to 1988; the largest money center banks earned the highest profits.[78] This earlier "gold" strike yielded even more impressive "platinum" returns in the aftermath of the 1989–1991 recession. For example, between 1982 and 1985, the spread on bank credit cards averaged 8.8 percent, whereas between 1991 and 1994 it averaged 13.2 percent. Although the spread declined to about 11 percent in the late 1990s, credit card companies compensated by sharply raising fee income from late and over-limit penalties; between 1993 and 1998, fee income tripled—from $6.3 billion to $18.9 billion.[79] This explains why banks were so eager to increase their credit card loan portfolios—regardless of the creditworthiness of prospective consumers.

Not surprisingly, Citibank was a major beneficiary of the industry's newfound profitability. In 1989, after-tax profits from Citicorp's credit card operations (about $600 million) exceeded total corporate profits ($498 million) and averaged from 40 to 60 percent of Citicorp's total earnings through the early 1990s.[80] This is especially impressive in view of the modest size of the credit card portfolio. Overall, credit card receivables nearly tripled from about $8 billion in 1985 to $23 billion in 1989, while outstanding revolving credit jumped rapidly to $28.8 billion in 1989; the latter grew slowly to $33 billion in 1993 and then jumped to almost $40 billion in 1994. Even so, the proportion of outstanding revolving credit (consumer debt) to total corporate assets remained stable at between 14 and 16 percent in the 1990s. Hence, Citicorp's credit card portfolio was responsible for over one-half of total profits between 1984 and 1993 yet accounted for only one-seventh of its corporate assets; after-tax profits dipped to about $500 million in 1990 due to the recession and then climbed to an estimated $800 million in 1994.[81]

Today, Citibank's credit card revenues continue to soar. As the industry leader, Citibank's credit and charge card revenues totaled $6.9 billion in 1997; after the Travelers merger, 16 million new card accounts were added in 1998 for a worldwide total of 96 million. At the beginning of 2000, Citibank had 40.6 million domestic accounts (second only to Banc One/First USA) with over $74 billion in outstanding credit card debt (number one)—nearly double the size of its 1994 portfolio. In addition, the volume of Citibank's customer charges dwarfs that of its major competitors; for 1999, it totaled $163 billion. Overall, Citibank's credit/charge/debit card portfolio includes more than 53 million accounts and over 100 million cards in 57 countries.[82]

Significantly, Citibank's preferred strategy of expanding its U.S. cardholder base through aggressive marketing campaigns rather than corporate acquisitions has recently featured a notable shift. This is due to the rapid pace of industry consolidation. For example, Banc One's acquisition of First USA in 1997 temporarily bumped Citibank into second place. In response, Citibank acquired AT&T Universal Card Services in 1998—the eighth-largest U.S. card issuer—followed by Mellon Bank's credit card division in 1999. The AT&T acquisition added 13.6 million accounts and $15 billion in credit card receivables, and the Mellon purchase included 800,000 accounts and $1.9 billion in account balances.[83] As expected, these acquisitions—which required the payment of hefty financial premiums—restored Citibank to its familiar position at the top of the credit card industry.

As shown by Table 3.3, which lists the top ten credit card issuers in the United States, the most distinguishing feature of the credit card industry is its recent concentration. Although industry spokespeople emphasize the spirited competition among the over 6,000 credit card issuers, the rhetoric of corporate competition belies the reality of limited consumer choice. For example, at the time of the unprecedented Citibank solicitation mailing in 1977, the top 50 banks accounted for about half of all U.S. credit card accounts; Citibank had 5.6 million. Today, the top ten card issuers control nearly 77 percent of the card market and 69 percent of the $1.2 trillion in 1999 charge volume.[84] To paraphrase a popular slogan, "Where's the competition?" Indeed, industry mergers and acquisitions have reduced the number of major corporate players and thus contributed to the costly increase in consumer banking services in general (e.g., ATM fees) and credit card finance charges and fees in particular.

As the industry leader, Citibank with its recent acquisitions offers insight into future trends. For example, the transfer of highly profitable credit card portfolios, which command large financial premiums, primarily benefit the

TABLE 3.3   Top Ten U.S. Credit Card Issuers by Balance, Volume, and Accounts, December 31, 1999

Rank		Balances ($billion)	Volume[a] ($billion)	Number of Accounts[b] (millions)
1.	Citibank	74.2	162.3	40.6
2.	Bank One/First USA	69.4	129.0	43.1
3.	MBNA	65.2	101.3	28.9
4.	Discover	38.0	70.6	38.5
5.	Chase Manhattan	33.6	53.8	20.5
6.	American Express	23.4	186.4	23.5
7.	Bank of America	20.9	51.1	21.0
8.	Providian	18.7	20.0	15.2
9.	Capital One	16.4	32.6	22.0
10.	Fleet	14.3	18.0	8.5
	Total	374.1	825.1	261.8

[a]Total of charges during year (January 1–December 31, 1999).
[b]Includes multiple accounts of same households.
SOURCE: CardWeb.com, Inc. available at www.cardweb.com.

stockholders of the seller ($3.5 billion to AT&T) and secondarily the buyer; for the consumer, fewer competitors leads to higher prices as shown in Table 3.2. Also, Citibank touts its cutting-edge technology as a benefit to its cardholders. However, the acquisition of AT&T illuminates a grander scheme for Citigroup's Internet-based credit card information and transaction systems. That is, a key feature of the AT&T deal is "access to the financial profiles of all AT&T customers . . . who could be ripe for banking and investment services." In this way, credit cards are becoming the hi-tech consumer interface for tracking client transaction information that can be used in cross-marketing products and services of other subsidiaries of the Citigroup conglomerate. Just as the credit card enabled Citibank to expand its national markets in the 1980s and 1990s, its Web-based information and transaction systems offer a low-cost, fiber-optic highway for expanding its global markets; Citigroup's goal is 1 billion customers by 2012.[85]

Finally, the profitability of bank credit card portfolios inflates corporate equity for transacting future mergers and acquisitions. According to the Federal Deposit Insurance Corporation (FDIC), the number of FDIC-insured banks slipped from 14,628 in 1975 to approximately 14,500 in 1984 to 12,709 in 1989; bank assets totaled $3.3 trillion and an average of $260 million per bank in 1989. Over the 1990s, industry concentration proceeded at a breakneck pace. From 10,452 banks in 1994 to 9,940 in 1995, the merger and acquisition frenzy reduced the total to only 9,143 in 1997; industry assets totaled $5.0 trillion and averaged $548 million per bank.[86] Hence, the profitability of consumer credit cards has been both a cause and an effect of industry concentration. In the process, it has profoundly influenced the attitudes and consumption behavior of the citizens of the Credit Card Nation. This is revealed by examining America's historical views toward consumer debt and how they have shaped the moral divide that pits convenience users against revolvers.

4

Charging for Credit
(or Points or Cash)

Convenience Users and
the Ideology of the Moral Divide

As U.S. STOCK MARKETS SOARED TO DIZZYING HEIGHTS at the end of
the millennium, Americans confronted the sobering reality of the "new"
economy: the widening wealth gap. Recent reports have publicized the
trend, which has limited participation in the stock markets to about 40 percent of American households; most stock market gains have accrued to only
a small proportion of investors.[1] As a result, economist Edward Wolff of
New York University estimates that the average net worth of the richest 1
percent of American families has climbed from $7.2 million in 1983 to $9.7
million in 1997 (35.2 percent gain) while the bottom 40 percent has fallen
from $4,700 in 1983 to only $3,000 in 1997 (36.2 percent loss). This finding followed the research of sociologists Thomas Shapiro of Northeastern
University and Melvin Oliver of UCLA. They persuasively argue that the
traditional focus on U.S. income disparities understates racial and ethnic
inequality by ignoring the historically divergent patterns of "asset forma-
tion." That is, different approaches to saving and investment contribute to
the wide variation in economic well-being and financial security of different
social groups in America.[2]

FIGURE 4.1   U.S. Personal Savings Rate, 1929–1999

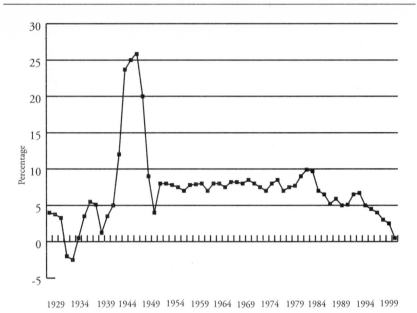

SOURCES: U.S. Bureau of Economic Analysis, *National Income of Product Accounts of the United States, 1928–94,* vol. 1; and *Survey of Current Business,* August 1997, May 1998, and May 1999.

Concerned over the precipitous decline in the U.S. personal savings rate, from a high of over 25 percent in 1943 to zero for the last quarter of 1998 followed by a modest negative rate for 1999 and an even sharper decline in 2000 (see Figure 4.1),[3] and the fact that the Social Security system may not adequately provide for future retirees, Senator Bob Kerrey of Nebraska sponsored a conference in October 1999 to promote the financial education of America's youth. At the program, Senator Kerrey proposed a personal savings account for every American: "'We hope to help people accumulate wealth because they're not doing it on their own.'" In seeking to help narrow the widening wealth gap between the rich and the rest of the U.S. population, Kerrey invited America's preeminent saver—Warren Buffett—to discuss his personal philosophy for financial success.[4]

Known as the "Oracle of Omaha," the 69-year-old Buffett bought his first stock at the age of 11. By the time he finished college, his frugality and adroit financial planning had netted him over $10,000 for future investment strategies. With this investment prowess, Buffett was on the fast track to investor lore—both for his thrifty lifestyle and penchant for picking corporate winners. As head of the investment and insurance company Berkshire Hathaway, Inc., Buffett guided the firm to financial glory. By investing in leading blue-chip companies, such as Coca-Cola and Gillette, and later insurance compa-nies such as National Indemnity and Geico as well as financial services firms such as American Express and Salomon Brothers, Buffett created a highly di-versified investment firm (including bonds) whose enormous profits have become legendary on Wall Street. In 1993, these astute investments even cat-apulted Buffett to the top of America's wealth pyramid.[5]

So, what advice did America's quintessential investor offer to his eager young listeners? A hot tip on a new dot-com? Likely corporate takeover tar-gets? How to profit from rising interest rates in the volatile bond market? None of the above. As a devoted adherent to the Puritan ethic of thrift and careful financial planning, Buffett declared at the conference that "'free-spending Americans should slice up their credit cards.'" The normally pub-lic-shy billionaire explained to the assembly of Nebraska high school students, "'My advice for you is if you can't afford it, don't buy it. . . . You can't make progress in your financial life borrowing credit at 18% to 20%.'" He later added that it was important for them to begin their professional careers with modest savings rather than debts: "'Having anything to get ahead of the game instead of behind the game is enormously important.'" The Reverend Jesse L. Jackson, who recently published a book on financial planning for the average American, amplified Buffett's message at the con-ference. While acknowledging that the next challenge of the civil rights movement was to find ways to provide low-income Americans with access to capital and technology, Jackson exhorted the students to "'Break the cycle of the debt culture. Don't be lured to use credit instead of money.'"[6]

The "Cognitive Connect":
The Cultural Origins of the Morality of Debt

The ideological pillars of the Credit Card Nation are founded upon the cul-tural precepts of individualism and free choice. The early American view of personal debt as a moral transgression and even a personal sin underlies the ideological justification for rewarding credit card "convenience users" who eschew consumer debt while punishing "revolvers" who are debt-dependent. This moral divide, which is based on historical attitudes that thrift is so-cially valued whereas debt is a personal vice, is the cultural cornerstone of the contradictory business policy of the credit card industry. That is, the re-cent growth of convenience users (see Table 4.1), who are publicly praised as the embodiment of fiscal prudence, has intensified financial pressures on

TABLE 4.1   Growth of Convenience Users of Bank Credit Cards, 1990–2000

	Percent Who Pay in Full Monthly
2000	43[a]
1999	43
1998	42
1997	40
1996	37
1995	34
1994	33
1993	32
1992	30
1991	29
1990	31

[a] Industry Estimate

SOURCE: CardWeb, "Profit Squeeze," CardTrak October 1999, p. 2.

credit card companies that reward them with free credit, gifts, and account services; these users are privately reviled by industry executives as economic "deadbeats." To address this conundrum, the focus in this section is the historical forces that fundamentally shaped the "cognitive connect," or equilibrium between household income and consumption decisions, and the moral underpinnings of American attitudes toward credit and debt.

Throughout world history, human societies have encouraged industry and thrift. From early peasant cultures, the historical record offers such homilies as "The wise man saves for the future, but the foolish man spends whatever he gets" (Proverbs 21:20).[7] This simple lifestyle, without a market economy to dispose of surplus provisions, emphasized collective subsistence over individual acquisitiveness. As societies have become more complex and market-driven, credit has played an increasingly important role by satisfying consumption needs as well as facilitating commerce. In fact, one of the earliest known written documents, the clay tablets of the Code of Hammurabi (Babylonia, about 1750 B.C.), imposed maximum interest rates (33 1/3 percent per year for grain and 20 percent for silver), and the Old Testament includes numerous references to credit, especially the evils of usury. For instance, Leviticus 25:37 states, "Thou shalt not give him thy money upon usury, nor lend him thy victuals for increase."[8]

Peasant societies embraced frugality for collective survival, whereas the rise of the market economy in seventeenth-century England rewarded industry and frugality with personal wealth. This emergent "misery of want," which flagrantly rejected New Testament directives against luxury and avarice, was accompanied by the decline of private charity; poverty was no longer a moral virtue associated with piety. According to Henry Peacham, writing in 1664, "My son better it is to dy than to be poor: for now Money is the world's god."[9] In colonial America, attitudes toward saving and debt were shaped by the secular pursuit of wealth as well as Protestantism's devotion to hard work, thrift, and self-reliance. Embodied in cultural maxims such as Ben Franklin's "A penny saved is a penny earned" and "I'd rather go to bed supperless than rise in debt," both secular and religious themes glorified individual industriousness and frugality as the cultural foundation of social and economic success in early America. In his most renowned essay on thrift, *The Way to Wealth*, Benjamin Franklin wrote in 1757: "If you would be wealthy . . . think of Saving as well as of Getting . . . remember what Poor Richard says . . . Beware of little Expenses; a small Leak will sink a great Ship . . . Buy what thou hast no Need of, and ere long thou shalt sell thy Necessaries."[10]

Significantly, Franklin's advice distinguished saving from religious restraint by offering a "morally neutral handbook" of economic life. In addition, Franklin linked personal and political freedoms with the virtues of industry and thrift: "when you run in debt; You give to another Power over your Liberty . . . The Borrower is a Slave to the Lender, and the Debtor to the Creditor, disdain the Chain, preserve your freedom; and maintain your independency: Be industrious and free; be frugal and free."[11] It is not a coincidence that the American Revolution pitted British merchants as creditors against the heavily indebted planters of the American colonies.[12]

The rise of a new Protestant ethic, influenced by John Calvin's theology of individual predestination and spiritual salvation, evoked a fanatical preoccupation with the conduct of personal affairs—especially thrift. The emphasis on personal saving entailed embracing ascetic attitudes toward consumption yet viewing them as moral virtues that Calvinism elevated to a sign of being chosen by God for spiritual salvation in the afterworld. For Max Weber, in *The Protestant Ethic and the Spirit of Capitalism* (1905), this Calvinist ethos of industry and frugality was responsible for the rise of industrial capitalism in the West and its extraordinary accumulation of wealth.[13]

English Puritans also believed that Christianity required frugality and abstinence from self-indulgence. For them, all wealth was attributed to God, and therefore any resources spent on pleasure, luxury, or sport were essentially stolen from God. Baptists and the new Methodists joined Congregationalists and Presbyterians in embracing the Weberian Protestant ethic. The common promotion of thrift included the "husbandry of time" that stressed work over leisure.[14]

The elevation of thrift to moral virtue contributed to conflicting religious and secular attitudes toward the accumulation of wealth. For instance, Methodists were instructed to give away their worldly assets because "riches were the trap that Satan had laid for industrious Christians, making them love money, pleasure, ease and luxury."[15] Therefore, industry and thrift were virtuous behaviors that could also lead to moral corruption through the pursuit of greedy individualism. The rejection of worldly materialism not only mitigated social class antagonisms in eighteenth- and early nineteenth-century America (in contrast to powerful guild and trade unions from continental Europe), but it also encouraged a high personal savings rate that the nation desperately needed in order to finance its industrial development and an independent banking system. Puritan thrift, moreover, encouraged workers to tolerate the harsh labor discipline of the new industrial order (or at least not to challenge it) by adhering to strict household budgets. That is, artisans and later factory workers were urged to avoid pauperism by establishing interest-bearing accounts in savings banks. Furthermore, the extension of consumer credit in the late nineteenth century indirectly diverted attention from the oppressive conditions of industrial employment. Households that repaid their installment loans on a regular basis were rewarded with future credit for desired consumer goods.[16]

Others whose behavior was not influenced by the "carrot" of credit-financed consumerism risked the "stick" of debtors' prisons and various forms of debt peonage. The alms- or workhouse became their worldly Hell where paupers were forced to repent for their improvident behavior by working off their debts; poverty was decried by more powerful groups as the social consequence of individual idleness and slothful spending habits. Furthermore, structural or systematic forces such as business cycles or technological advances (agricultural modernization) that produced major employment dislocations were generally ignored unless they threatened local civic authority and national political order.[17] Instead, the "sin" of impoverishment was socially defined as an individual, normative condition that required the "reform" of a person's roguish behavior. Consequently, this focus deflected attention from the vagaries of the wage labor market and the capriciousness of industrial work discipline. Those temporarily unemployed in an attempt to improve their work conditions (seeking higher wages, organizing trade unions, joining strikes) were chastised as relief-seeking frauds whose indolent behavior was the primary cause of their poverty. Not surprisingly, then, the evolution of public relief in eighteenth- and nineteenth-century America distinguished the "deserving" from "undeserving" poor. For example, widows of Civil War veterans and their children were favored over able-bodied men who were unemployed during a recession or after the harvest.[18]

As colonial America embraced the commerce and wealth of the industrial epoch, the virtue of thrift and industry was recast in the uniquely American nineteenth-century urban experience. This is exemplified by the self-made rags-to-riches lore of Horatio Alger Jr.'s *Ragged Dick* (1868), which extols the "superior" attributes of hard work, frugality, and higher education. In the novel, the protagonist (Ragged Dick) follows this blueprint for success by rising from a "poor street boy" to middle-class "office boy" in only one year. In the process, Ragged Dick's thrift and self-denial (cigars, saloons) enable him to open a savings bank account that contributes to his newfound independence, enhanced self-image, and generous benevolence. The moral of the story is that those who "favor" work over leisure (idleness as "work of the Devil") and manage to save a portion of their incomes for future needs are rewarded for not succumbing to the "worldly" temptations of self-indulgence.[19]

For most American households at the turn of the twentieth century, the emphasis on "saving for a rainy day" mirrored the economic vagaries of a rapidly industrializing, urban society.[20] Native-born and new immigrant workers increasingly persevered through recessions, strikes, work accidents, illnesses, and environmental calamities. Furthermore, the lack of public unemployment, health, and retirement systems entailed greater reliance on family and extended social networks (including mutual aid clubs, civic organizations) for emergency financial assistance. In fact, life insurance was the primary component of personal savings among working-class households; 80 percent of native white families and more than 90 percent of immigrant and black families in industrial towns were insured.[21] During this period, a nativist backlash against the "alien" menace of Irish followed by Chinese and then southern and eastern European immigrants was based on their willingness to accept low wages and a meager standard of living. Their attitude stemmed from the "sojourner" goal of saving as much money as possible before returning home or sending remittances to their families while in the United States. Interestingly, this immigrant mentality—like a cultural transfusion—reinforced the Protestant ethic of thrift and industry, a pattern that continues today.[22]

The "changing notions about economy, frugality, saving, and thrift," which fundamentally shaped the growing receptivity of American households to the use of installment credit, accelerated with the end of the ostentatious "Gilded Age" and the accompanying economic crisis of the mid-1890s.[23] This is manifest in the erosion of the traditional "cognitive connect," or fiscal equilibrium between household income and consumption decisions. This behavioral calculus defines an individual's or household's standard of living based on *present* income (total earnings) and *future* (expected/unexpected) expenses. Traditionally, it encourages the postponement of consumer purchases in order to ensure a minimal household savings rate: "make a dollar, save a dime." Yet even the U.S. government–sponsored savings movement during World War I, with its "censors of extravagance," could not repel the rising tide of new cultural attitudes toward consumption.[24] In 1916, the personal savings rate of 14.7 percent for nonfarm households would soon begin its descent.[25]

The rise of American consumerism in the late nineteenth century,[26] together with the expansion of mass advertising that "sold dreams rather than products,"[27] not only challenged the Puritan values of thrift, saving, and community but also resulted in the growing dependence of middle-class and affluent households on consumer credit. According to Milan Ayres, in a 1926 American Bankers Association report, "During the nineteenth century the things that a self-respecting, thrifty American [middle class] family would buy on the installment plan were a piano, a sewing machine, some expensive articles of furniture, and perhaps sets of books. People who made such purchases didn't talk about them. Installment buying wasn't considered quite respectable [then]."[28]

As the American Dream became increasingly shaped by mass advertising campaigns and the conspicuous consumption patterns of affluent families, middle- and working-class households began relying on itinerant merchants or "house-to-house sellers" to finance their consumer purchases on installment credit plans.[29] This practice nourished the rapid growth of the small loan industry, whose rampant abuses led to the enactment of the Uniform Small Loan Law in 1916.[30] The profound impact of these new trends on American consumerism[31] as well as the traditional attitudes of the "cognitive connect" were documented in 1929 by sociologists Robert S. Lynd and Helen Merrell Lynd in their classic community study of Muncie, Indiana:

> [I]n the early 1880s . . . when the fathers of the present generation wanted to buy a piece of land they were likely to save up the money and "pay cash" for it, and it was a matter of pride to be able to say, "I always pay cash for the things I buy.". . . Today [1920s], Middletown lives by a credit economy that is available in some form to nearly every family. The rise and spread of the dollar-down-and-so-much-per plan extends credit for virtually everything—homes, $200 over-stuffed living-room suites, electric washing machines, automobiles, fur coats, diamond rings—to persons of whom frequently little is known as to the intention or ability to pay. . . . [According to an] official of a

local company, the present-day optimistic reliance upon credit for all things great and small [is because] "People don't think anything nowadays of borrowing sums they'd never have thought of borrowing in the old days. They will assume an obligation for $2,000 today as calmly as they would have borrowed $300 or $400 in 1890."[32]

The prosperity and national optimism of the booming 1920s fueled the unprecedented growth of U.S. consumer credit.[33] The durable consumer goods industry began targeting well-to-do and middle-class Americans with sophisticated advertising and installment credit programs—especially automobile companies (led by General Motors)—while these households eagerly sought the material accoutrements of the "good life," including new electric appliances such as washing machines, refrigerators, radios, phonographs, and vacuum cleaners. This changing American attitude toward debt, especially the growing respectability of installment credit, led Frederick Lewis Allen to declare that by the 1920s "people were getting to consider it old-fashioned to limit their purchases to the amount of their cash balances."[34]

Even so, the "cognitive connect" remained the cultural cornerstone of American society's view of consumer debt in the early twentieth century. Popular and professional journals frequently issued stern warnings against these attitudinal and behavior changes even before the cataclysmic stock market crash of 1929.

> The use of credit, particularly the installment type, by consumers was characterized as "an economic sin," . . . setting "utterly false standards of living," causing judgment to become "hopelessly distorted.". . . It was attacked as "marking the breakdown of traditional habits of thrift," as tending to "weaken the moral fiber of the Nation.". . . It was accused of "breaking down character and resistance to temptations, to extravagance and to living beyond one's means, breeding dishonesty."[35]

In reality, most consumer credit continued to be provided by formal and informal noninstallment plans such as "open book" credit. Especially common in rural areas, it was based on the social relations between merchants and customers and generally was extended for less expensive items that were frequently purchased. The amount of credit was based on the strength of affective ties (trust); customers made regular payments on their accumulated balances or risked the loss of their credit account. According to the U.S. Department of Commerce, based on data collected during the first half of 1930, only 7 percent of department store sales were made on an installment contract basis; 47.4 percent were cash and 45.6 percent were open book.[36] Moreover, credit cards were initially offered by large retailers (beginning in 1914) only to their most affluent customers as a strategy for selling expensive items and fostering consumer loyalty. In the process, retail credit cards conferred social prestige and convenience to the cardholder. It was only with the extension of credit to lower-income, middle-class households in the 1920s that retail credit cards were used to increase sales through revolving debt. By emulating the behavior of elite and affluent households, moderate-income, middle-class families were able to mask their consumer debt from public scrutiny. Only the company's accountant knew for sure.

The mounting challenge of consumerism to the "cognitive connect" was thwarted by the economic and psychological devastation of the Great Depression. Only the most devoted adherents of the principle were able to avoid financial ruin. Even those who followed the old rules, by entrusting their life savings to financial institutions, often were severely punished as bank failures led to the loss of homes, farms, and automobiles. For many who experienced the social and moral confusion of the 1930s, their collective frustrations produced cultural responses and even political movements that contested dominant attitudes toward poverty and indebtedness. For instance, the distinction between "God's poor" and the "Devil's poor" was temporarily ignored. In fact, these forces profoundly challenged and eventually transformed the social and economic landscape of the nation. Widespread unemployment (especially among the middle classes) begat the "liberal" public relief programs of FDR's New Deal—including reform of the insolvent banking system (Glass-Steagall Act of 1933).

For survivors of the Great Depression—the parents and grandparents of today's baby boomers—debt became an anathema while the "cognitive connect" became the cultural blueprint for pursuing their postwar American Dream. This is revealed in the Lynds' 1937 sequel, *Middletown in Transition*. According to a local carpenter, "We were all damned fools in the 1920s! We thought we had the world by the tail and forgot the old truths that 'a nickel saved is a nickel made!' I'm never again going to get caught the way I was in this crash. From now on I'm going to live within my income and you bet I'll save."[37]

From Monopoly to Mall Madness: Replacing the Calvinist Ethos of Saving with the Spirit of Consumption

During the depths of the Great Depression, Charles B. Darrow of Germantown, Pennsylvania, developed a board game "to amuse himself and pass the time" while coping with unemployment. Ironically, the objective of the game "is to become the wealthiest player through buying, renting, and selling property." With the help of a friend, who was a printer, Darrow sold 5,000 sets to a Philadelphia department store. As demand for his game soared, Darrow could not satisfy the volume of orders, and in 1934 he offered the licensing rights to the Parker Brothers company. Sixty-five years later, Monopoly is still sold by Parker Brothers in 80 countries and in 23 languages; it is the leading proprietary game in United States and throughout the Western world.

The rules of the game, which reward shrewd investment skills, do not allow players to obtain unsecured loans or consumer credit from the bank. Hence, it inculcates the "cognitive connect" by penalizing players for falling into debt; money cannot be spent on discretionary purchases, personal consumption, or business entertainment. Even collateralized business loans, offered by the bank at 10 percent, are significantly above the prevailing market rate. And, not incidentally, defeated players must declare bankruptcy before liquidating or transferring ownership of their assets.[38] This public pronouncement of the personal shame of their financial condition affirms the underlying tenets of Puritan thrift. As a reflection of the individualistic ethos of the American Dream and the social confusion produced by the extension of consumer credit in the early twentieth century, the game of Monopoly has offered "moral" guidance in the conduct of personal financial affairs over the last several generations. Today, Monopoly is the most popular marketing promotion of the world's most popular fast-food restaurant: McDonald's.

With fresh memories of the deprivations of the Great Depression followed by the rationing programs of World War II, Americans again saved; the U.S. personal savings rate jumped to nearly 14 percent during the 1940s, peaking at nearly 24 percent during the war (1942–1945).[39] Unlike in World War I, the U.S. government did not mobilize a national savings campaign. Savings bonds were sold as a patriotic duty, without moralistic references to the virtues of thrift: "They give their lives; you lend your money."[40] More important, the rise of secular reasoning over religious dogma as well as the influence of socialist ideologies inspired macroeconomic doctrines that promoted government spending as a sound social and economic policy. The most prominent intellectual voice was British economist John Maynard Keynes. By arguing that the Great Depression arose from excessive saving rather than high wages and prices, Keynes advocated an activist government spending agenda that appealed to a wide political spectrum: from New Deal liberals of the 1930s to supply-side conservatives of the 1980s.[41]

The return to a peacetime economy raised concerns that Americans might "save" themselves into another depression. Keynesian economic planners and corporate business leaders jointly reviled the "curse of thrift" and extolled the new "age of affluence" with its rising wages, labor productivity, and standard of living. Together, they ushered in a new phase of American consumerism. Led by the rapid expansion of the mass manufacturing industries and the preeminent position of the United States in the global economy, the surge in national optimism and economic prosperity led to the profound transformation of U.S. society: from urban neighborhoods to suburban housing developments (Levittowns). The rapid suburbanization of metropolitan America, fueled by federally guaranteed (VA, FHA) mortgages and publicly financed highways, featured the replacement of public trolleys with private cars and community parks with private lawns while labor-saving appliances aided women in the discharge of their domestic responsibilities.[42]

In the process, downtown business districts with local mom-and-pop stores were being supplanted with suburban shopping malls dominated by corporate retailers. The increasing mobility of Americans, together with the decline in affective social ties (trust) and stable residential communities, rendered obsolete such common forms of consumer credit as open book that were increasingly susceptible to fraudulent abuse. Furthermore, as merchants no longer grew up in the same communities as their customers and corporate retailers sought to expand their client base, a standardized method for noncash transactions was necessary for stimulating sales and encouraging customer loyalty. Beginning with the major petroleum companies (Mobil, Gulf, Standard Oil), the mass solicitation of gasoline credit cards occurred immediately after the war; some even permitted installment payment plans. In 1952, Standard Oil introduced the metal embossed Chevromatic charge cards that were the precursors to the now familiar plastic credit cards.[43]

At the same time, groups of large retailers began developing cooperative "charga-plate" operations that included revolving credit plans for "soft" purchases such as clothes and that supplemented installment credit programs for "hard" purchases such as washing machines. In 1948, a consortium of major New York department stores was formed that included Bloomingdale's, Arnold Constable, Franklin Simon, Gimbel's, and Saks; typically, a 1 percent finance charge was levied on outstanding monthly balances. Similarly, nonproprietary (universal) charge cards were being introduced for travel and entertainment expenses, beginning with Diners Club in 1949, followed by Carte Blanche and American Express cards in 1958.[44] These programs did not offer revolving payment plans, and thus their appeal was primarily to business travelers or to affluent consumers who could pay their balances in full at the end of the month. These charge cards were designed for convenience, with fees derived from merchant discounts and memberships. Hence, they did not permit consumption levels that exceeded the discretionary income of the cardholders.

For the rapidly growing mass production workforce, financing the American Dream with installment credit served to reinforce the bread-and-butter unionism of the politically conservative policies of the AFL-CIO.[45] The expanding ranks of the American middle class benefited from the escalating wages and productivity of the U.S. manufacturing sector as well as the active role of the public sector in subsidizing the cost of higher education, medical care, and home mortgages. Although household income was normally based on only one wage-earner, the rising standard of living of the middle class during the postwar *Pax Americana* was financed primarily through higher wages and the modest cost of installment credit from retailers; the personal saving rate remained stable at about 7.6 percent in the 1950s and 1960s. Even so, banks began to realize the business potential of universal credit cards as the combination of merchant discount fees, finance charges, and annual membership fees offered a profitable mix of revenues. In 1947, John C. Biggins introduced the first universal (third-party) credit card called Charg-It for use in a two-square-block neighborhood near the Flatbush National Bank of Brooklyn.[46]

By the 1950s, the race was on as hundreds of groups of regional banks formed cooperative associations—as retailers did—for recruiting merchants, financing advertising campaigns, and underwriting the infrastructural costs of processing credit card transactions. The largest credit card operation was launched by Bank of America in 1958. The successful adoption of the BankAmericard throughout California led Bank of America to pursue a regional expansion strategy that offered licensing agreements to banks across the United States in 1966. Other rivals responded by creating their own consortium, the Interbank Credit Association, which became Master Charge in 1969. The following year, Bank of America spun off its credit card division and formed a membership association called NBI; the name was changed to Visa in 1976. Although intense competition between these two credit card giants fundamentally shaped the consolidation of the industry, this market dynamic was dramatically altered in 1972 following a U.S. District Court decision that ruled in favor of "duality." That is, any bank could now issue both Master Charge (MasterCard) and BankAmericard (Visa) to its customers.[47]

The initial wave of unsolicited credit card solicitations in the late 1960s became a virtual tidal wave in the 1970s and 1980s as households received applications for both Visas and MasterCards. Indeed, banks began to realize that the market for noninstallment consumer credit had tremendous growth potential. This is because American attitudes toward debt were changing with the increasing availability of retail credit and the psychological optimism of the age of affluence. However, the primary goal of proprietary credit cards (which were financially unprofitable) was to increase sales and customer loyalty only within their retailing operations, which limited the future expansion and use of consumer credit. In comparison, universal cards offered consumers nearly unlimited shopping possibilities (even before the Internet) and a largely untapped source of income to issuing banks.

In 1970, the first national examination of consumer use and attitudes toward credit cards was conducted by Lewis Mandell (currently dean of the State University of New York at Buffalo School of Management) under the auspices of the University of Michigan's Survey of Consumer Finances. He found that only 16 percent of U.S. households possessed bank credit cards, and 9 percent had travel and entertainment charge cards. This compares with more than twice as many U.S. households (35 percent) with at least one retail credit card and 34 percent with gas cards. More instructive, Mandell found a clear pattern in the unequal access to consumer credit that was an extension of earlier marketing strategies; 81 percent of families with an income of at least $25,000 used credit cards versus less than 20 percent of families earning under $3,000.

The most intriguing finding of the study is the ambivalent attitudes of Americans toward bank credit cards. According to Mandell, "75 percent of all respondents said that credit cards made it too easy to buy things that they may not really want or can't really afford . . . [yet] when asked about the advantages of credit cards, the most frequent response related to the credit feature—a family could buy without having the money and pay the bank back over time." Among wealthier families, he was shocked to find that 15 percent reported a balance, which suggested cognitive confusion if not outright financial irrationality. Mandell concluded that Americans, regardless of their household incomes or education levels, "are far more likely to use credit cards than to approve of them." In fact, he noted that "[F]ully three-quarters of all American families said that such a card tempts one to buy more than is necessary."[48]

As real wages began stagnating in the mid-1970s and inflation soared to double digits at the end of the decade, universal credit cards became the angel of mercy to struggling middle-class households. With the onset of federal deregulation of banking in 1980, the rising cost of real interest rates led banks to expand into increasingly profitable consumer financial services. Not since the unprecedented expansion of consumer credit in the 1920s had the cognitive connect confronted such a serious challenge, as baby boomers faced the dismal reality of declining real wages and rising material expectations. Over the next two decades, the economic dislocations produced by U.S. industrial restructuring contributed to the successful marketing of consumer credit to traditionally neglected groups: low-income workers, blue-collar households, and college students. This is mirrored in the sharp decline in the U.S. personal saving rate. During the 1970s and early 1980s, it remained stable at about 8.4 percent and then steadily declined following the 1981–1982 recession—from 5.6 percent in the late 1980s to 3.7 percent in the mid-1990s—plummeting to zero at the end of 1998.[49]

The most striking feature of the decade of debt is the role of consumerism in eroding the Puritan ethos of frugality and saving. Pepsi's narcissist "me generation" promotions of the 1980s, a sharp contrast to Coca-Cola's earlier "We are the world" advertisements, have been reinforced by Nike's "Just do it" consumption-oriented campaigns of the 1990s. The central theme of these marketing promotions is that self-denial is "old school" and instant gratification is "new school." Hence, their objective is to exalt the commodification of fun for immediate, personal enjoyment. This is exemplified by a 1998 Sony-Citibank cross-marketing campaign directed at twenty-something professionals: "Workaholics take note: make some time for play . . . Don't deny yourself. Indulge with the Sony [Visa] Card from Citibank . . . The official currency of playtime."

The profound shift in America's cultural attitudes toward credit and debt are epitomized by a popular board game of the late 1980s, Mall Madness: The Talking Shopping-Spree Game. Introduced by Milton Bradley in 1989,[50] for players "9 years and up," it promotes instant gratification and unrepentant consumption, the antithesis of the cultural values inculcated in preceding generations of Monopoly aficionados. The game instructions declare, "Now you can shop till you drop as you rush from store to store! [The] Object of the Game [is to] be the first to buy 6 items on your shopping list and get back to the parking lot." But, how do you get enough money for making these purchases? Ask for an increase in your weekly allowance? Withdraw money from your saving account? Get a job at Pizza Hut? Like, no way! After exhausting the initial $200 allotment, players "have to go to the bank to get more money . . . [by] insert[ing their] credit card into the bank slot. The voice will tell you to take $50, $75, or $100."

Clearly, in this game, the social relations of consumption are not linked to work, saving, or earned rewards. Instead, the amount of money a player has to spend is due to good fortune (mom or dad is in a generous mood) or simply the work-pleasure disconnect that is miraculously provided by the easy money of bank credit cards. The only incentive to "save money [is] to head for a store that's having a sale or clearance. But hurry! You may arrive too late to get the bargain!" Not incidentally, in order to ensure that players learn how to buy rather than save, there is a specific set of instructions and a visual portrayal of buying an item: "put your credit card into the buy slot . . . You [will] hear 'Ching Ching!' This is the sound of the cash register ringing up your purchase. You've made a successful buy."[51] Is it really surprising that the magic-of-plastic fantasy of this board game continues in the real world of postadolescence?

"Save for Your Future": Cognitive Befuddlement and the Social Construction of the Moral Divide

The increasingly successful assault of the Credit Card Nation on traditional attitudes toward saving and consumption is exemplified by a popular 1999 holiday radio advertisement:

Motorcycle jacket for kid brother on the Internet—$300.
Monogrammed golf balls for dad on the Internet—$50.
Vintage smoking robe for husband on the Internet—$80.
Not having to hear "attention shoppers"—not even once—priceless.
The way to pay on the Internet and everywhere else you see the MasterCard logo.

This brilliantly conceived commercial features the triumvirate of key credit card marketing themes: (1) modern technology that is associated with professional success (successor to the "future of money" campaign); (2) emotional spending on close family members (extension of the "priceless" series); and (3) long-standing emphasis on personal convenience ("It's everywhere you want to be," "Don't leave home without it"). This focus on technology-driven consumerism, which satisfies important social responsibilities, is designed to deflect attention from the Puritan tenets of frugality and saving. And these campaigns have been impressively effective. If whipping out plastic money at the checkout counter has aided impulsive consumption, by fracturing the attitudinal link between earnings and spending, imagine the future impact of Web-based point-and-click shopping carts in the virtual-mall environment, where even the spatial connection of "going shopping at the mall" is no longer operative.

The cognitive confusion created by technology-driven consumerism is illustrated by a recent U.S. Department of the Treasury promotion. Using the

Internet, consumers can log on and "buy" U.S. savings bonds—with credit cards. The logic of this campaign is dubious from the perspective of the traditional earnings-spending connection. The federal government is encouraging the purchase of "savings" bonds with money borrowed from a bank through the transactional mechanism of a credit card. Since most Americans are revolvers, the purchase of a savings bond could be an immediate money-losing transaction: a 19.9 APR finance charge versus a 5.25 percent annual bond yield. Who benefits from this exercise of the magic of plastic? Other common examples that exacerbate our cultural befuddlement include monetary awards for paying off credit card debts. For example, a popular Washington, D.C., radio station recently sponsored a call-in contest in which the winner didn't receive cash but instead had his credit card balance paid off. Fortunately, he was a revolver, but that was the point of the promotion. Most of the station's listeners are saddled with large credit card debts.

The blurring of the financial boundaries of money (American Express uses "cash money" in a 1998 advertisement) and the mechanisms of commercial transactions (MasterCard's "future of money" campaign) further contribute to the confusion that underlies the magic of plastic. For example, debit cards are the technological embodiment of Puritan thrift, since each purchase (plus a small transaction fee) is immediately debited at the point of sale (POS), and thus purchases are limited to the amount of money in the cardholder's bank account. The rationale of the system is that a person cannot spend more money than is in the account. However, the banking industry has circumvented this fiscal constraint by providing automatic lines of credit that are typically charged at the prevailing interest rate of the bank's credit card. Similarly, most checking accounts offer overdraft protection that includes a line of credit at the standard credit card interest rate. Hence, by offering features that give financial flexibility—as a "customer courtesy"—banks are encouraging the erosion of the traditional "cognitive connect."

Even more perplexing is the tiered system of credit card finance charges. An account may have several low introductory teaser rates (0–7.9 percent), higher fixed rates for balance transfers (7.9–12.9 percent), standard rates for purchases (15.9–22.9 percent), and the highest rates for cash advances (19.9–26.9 percent plus transaction fees). The cost of credit is especially confusing since each tier may have a different "life" (expiration period), and the outstanding balances at the lowest interest rates are paid off before the balances at the highest rates. Is it any wonder that the banking industry's obfuscation of the terms of credit card accounts leads so many people to give up on their personal finances and internalize the social and emotional shame of abandoning the Puritan ethic?

Ironically, the most striking attack on the traditional savings ethic emanates from the very bastion of American culture: the Smithsonian Institution. In 1997, during its 150th anniversary celebration, the Smithsonian contracted with Discover to offer an affinity credit card. The primary marketing theme of the Smithsonian Discover card is the promotion of "emotional spending": "It's Ben Franklin's credit card. And Harriet Tubman's. In fact, it's the credit card of just about any historic American you can name. It's the Smithsonian Card. Every time you make a purchase you'll help the Institution preserve America's past." Of course, the use of traditional values in this way subverts their initial intent. Even more astounding is the secondary marketing theme of financial self-interest: "Ben Franklin [said] 'A penny saved is a penny earned.' But now a penny spent can earn you free U.S. Savings Bonds . . . Save for your future, and support the Smithsonian . . . because you'll earn points toward free U.S. Savings Bonds." The venerable Smithsonian is encouraging the use of credit cards—even invoking the historical legacies of our founding fathers and mothers—in order for you to "earn" a savings bond. Would Ben Franklin really think this is a deal—at 19.8 percent?[52]

In the illusory world of the Credit Card Nation, it is noteworthy that more people have not succumbed to the alluring work-pleasure disconnect offered by bank credit cards. Like the sirens' songs of Homer's *Odyssey*, the most serious challenge to the traditional savings ethic is the mass marketing of fun and the desire for immediate gratification that underlies impulsive consumption.[53] Unlike the consumerist bravado of the 1980s bumper sticker "He who dies with the most toys, wins," the motto of convenience users and other adherents of traditional financial virtue is "It's not how much money you make. It's how much money you save."

Significantly, the average American's ability to accumulate wealth by practicing Puritan thriftiness has been recently discovered through media reports of generous philanthropic gifts. These include middle-class people like Anne Scheiber, whose annual salary at the IRS never exceeded $4,000 until her retirement in 1944. Yet, upon her death at 101 in 1995, she had left $22 million to Yeshiva University. Another case is Raymond Fay, whose annual salary of $11,400 at his retirement in 1969 still enabled him to donate $1.5 million to Philadelphia's public library. Even more impressive is Oseola McCarty, a Mississippi "washerwoman." In 1995, she donated $150,000 to the University of Southern Mississippi to aid African American students.[54]

Such examples of America's unpretentious rich and how they accumulated their wealth received national attention in 1996 with the publication of Thomas J. Stanley and William D. Danko's *The Millionaire Next Door:*

The Surprising Secrets of America's Wealthy. Eager to learn the wealth-building lessons of the nation's affluent families, many Americans were shocked by the key findings. For example, the authors found islands of fiscal restraint in a sea of indolent consumption but could not identify any secret formula to explain the economic success of America's rich. Instead, Stanley and Danko discovered that "many people who live in expensive homes and drive luxury cars do not have much wealth . . . [while] many people who have a great deal of wealth do not live in upscale neighborhoods." In fact, as a group, American millionaires are much less likely to be swayed by consumerist pressures and more likely to buy U.S.-made rather than imported goods such as automobiles. Like Juliet Schor's "downshifting" consumers, they often drive the same car for many years and then trade up to a newer, preowned model.[55]

Stanley and Danko's other key discovery was that "it is seldom luck or inheritance or advanced degrees or even intelligence that enables people to amass fortunes . . . [rather] wealth is more often the result of hard work, perseverance, planning, and most of all self-discipline." Hence, a common trait shared by America's wealthy is their attitudinal devotion to the Puritan ethic. Typically, America's millionaires invest 15–20 percent of their household income while resisting the social pressure to maintain a standard of living that matches their level of earnings.[56] As adherents of the cognitive connect (traditional view of savings), they abhor the temptations offered by credit cards and the financial irresponsibility promoted by the culture of consumption. For them, "fun" is not their central goal, nor is it a commodity that can be simply bought and sold. In fact, shopping is perceived as a means to the end of satisfying needs rather than as a path to emotional catharsis through commodity fetishism.

The conflict between the modern mentality of consumerism and the traditional Puritan ethic has become an increasingly salient theme in American popular culture. This is illustrated by a 1987 episode of the popular *Newhart* television show; the sitcom was set in rural Vermont and featured Dick (Bob Newhart) as the proprietor of a bed-and-breakfast inn. During this period of rampant consumerism, George (Tom Postman), the local handyman, receives a large inheritance from his uncle; George is portrayed as an unsophisticated, rural hayseed. Dick, a New York city slicker, explains to George that he needs to loosen up and learn how to enjoy his money by spending some of it. For Dick, it is important to have the newest gadgets (electronic memo minder) and ride the wave of technological progress such as a home laser light show. George, on the other hand, is happy with his simple life and makes purchases based on personal need and functional utility; he prefers his old black and white television over a state-of-the-art entertainment system.

In an early scene, Dick takes George on a shopping trip. The ostensible goal is to show George that money can be used to provide pleasure by buying anything he wants. Unfortunately for George, he discovers that shopping is not fun. He already has all of the things he needs and sees no reason to buy something new simply because he can. After a few hours, George pleads with Dick, "Can we go home yet? We've been to eight stores and I'm shopping spree-ed out." For George, shopping without the purpose of satisfying a need is a wasteful use of time. Dejected, Dick retorts, "Technically, it's not a shopping spree until you buy something."

Later, George apologizes. "I'm sorry, Dick. I tried to enjoy spending money. But it doesn't make me happy the way it does for you. It sort of makes me crazy. I guess I'm just screwed up. . . . Everyone told me I should spend my money if I wanted to be happy." Dick attempts to soothe George's guilt: "It's all right to not spend money if there's absolutely nothing you really *want*." Indeed, the primary issue for George is not saving money but the avowed purpose of spending it. Like other disciples of Puritan thrift, he needed a reason to make a purchase—the satisfaction of a need rather than an indulgent want. This leads George to confide, "What I [really] want is a jungle gym . . . for the playground in the park. All the equipment is rusted and falling apart. It'd be nice for the kids to have it shiny and new." Dick, realizing that George's desire is motivated by utilitarian and philanthropic reasons, declares, "I think it's a great use for your money. This leads George to exclaim, "Great! You mean I finally got what I really want . . . and this [boxes of electronic components] can go? Approvingly, Dick responds, "It's only fair that I take this state-of-the-art baby off your hands" and writes a check to George for the cost of the expensive home entertainment system.

Ultimately, both men satisfied their consumptive desires but for very different reasons. George, the consummate saver, affirmed the Puritan ethic by purchasing a functional item that served an important social need. Dick, the unrepentant consumer, satisfied his personal desire to acquire the newest electronic gadgets—regardless of whether he actually needed them or not. Interestingly, this clash of competing cultural values—which fundamentally shapes the ideological moral divide between savers and debtors—reveals an important shift in American attitudes toward debt.

Historically, personal debt in America has been portrayed with religious overtones—a moral battle between "good" and "evil."[57] Today, however, it features more secular representations such as a struggle of "new" versus "old" lifestyles. In fact, at the end of the *Newhart* show, a rumor circulates that Dick

is "broke" and "[he] and the missus are close to living out of a shopping cart
. . . [due to his shopping] disease." Rather than being ostracized for his "sick-
ness" and publicly punished for his behavior, the townspeople offer their moral
support. They even present Dick with a charity basket of money and implore
him to "get [professional] help."[58] Hence, the program reflects the larger social tensions of the decade of debt by raising questions about whether the new
way of debt-financed consumerism is really superior to the old way with its
simple, debt-free lifestyle. The show analogizes to other addictions by imply-
ing that even responsible, God-fearing people may not be able to withstand
the consumerist pressures of the Credit Card Nation. Significantly, the growing influence of secular attitudes has sharply reduced the social stigma of personal debt and contributed to more lenient penalties through twentieth-
century amendments to the U.S. Bankruptcy Code.[59]

The Growing Social Inequality of the Moral Divide

With changing attitudes toward debt and the relentless marketing of consumer credit, the role of bank credit cards has increased dramatically
throughout American society. Today, they can be used to enhance one's
household standard of living as well as to provide temporary financial relief
from employment disruptions or family crises, and even to provide start-up
capital for aspiring entrepreneurs. In fact, with the ascendance of the service-based society, national economic growth has become more sensitive to
family debt levels and consumer interest rates than to fluctuations in real
wages or even household income. It is surprising, then, that one of the most
neglected topics in the study of U.S. consumerism is the growing inequality
in the cost and availability of credit to different social groups. Even the Economic Policy Institute, in its biannual *State of Working America* series, does
not report the consumer debt levels of American households or estimate the
annual costs of financing their loan obligations.[60] With nearly 46 million
revolver households, carrying an average of over $11,000 in outstanding
credit card debt, this translates into a substantial annual expenditure: over
$2,000 per household in finance charges plus penalty fees.[61] This figure,
moreover, does not include other forms of installment debt, such as home
equity, debt consolidation, finance company, student, and auto loans.

On the Puritan side of the moral divide, convenience users of bank credit
cards essentially receive free loans, as long as they pay off their monthly
charges. This continues the earlier policy of retail credit cards whose initial
purpose was to reward consumer loyalty and, indirectly, adherence to the
Puritan ethos of thrift. Ironically, one of the biggest benefactors of bank

credit cards—the most affluent convenience users—was initially hostile to them. Many resisted the widespread acceptance of revolving credit cards for the very reasons the struggling middle and working classes so eagerly embraced them: They obscured the widening gulf between rich and poor.

This cultural anxiety toward the massive expansion of credit—but not more exclusive charge cards—was expressed in numerous interviews that were conducted for this book. For example, a middle-aged, upper-middle-class woman declared, "Working [class] people have to buy on credit because they don't have enough money. . . . I'm not poor so why should I use credit cards like them when I can pay with cash?" This sentiment is especially evident among immigrants and their children. According to a 27-year-old Iranian immigrant, "paying with credit is shameful" and "is not acceptable for someone belonging to my wealthy social class." Similarly, a 28-year-old Italian exemplified traditional attitudes toward the earning-consumption connection. She explained that having a debt on her credit card is considered an embarrassment to her prominent family, indicating that they cannot afford to pay for her expenses. As a result, she initially paid her credit card charges the following day at her bank in an attempt to "wipe away the shame of owing money."

Today, the robust economy and recent appreciation of the residential housing market have substantially reduced the number of highly profitable revolvers; home equity and debt consolidation loans have enabled many property owners to reduce or even pay off their high-interest credit card debts. For instance, at the end of the recession in 1991, 71 percent of credit card accounts paid monthly finance charges. By 2000, this proportion was only 57 percent (see Table 4.1).[62] This is one of the reasons that credit card penalty fees have escalated so fast since the mid-1990s[63] and why some banks have canceled the accounts of convenience users. The latter led U.S. Congressman John J. LaFalce (D-N.Y.) to propose federal legislation in 1998 that would forbid this practice.[64] Nevertheless, banks publicly laud the fiscal prudence of their "deadbeat" clients and declare that they "earn" the financial carrot of free credit. For the credit card industry, this is a small price to pay for legitimating the ideological divide that pits the disciplined restraint of savers ("God's children") against the purportedly undisciplined behavior of debtors ("Devil's poor"). This traditional perspective—with its attitudinal focus on the flawed moral character of debtors—underlies the contemporary bank practice of offering economic incentives to its deadbeat credit card clients.

On the debtor side of the moral divide, the real cost of consumer credit has soared since the early 1980s—especially bank credit cards. This trend is particularly noteworthy because corporate loan rates have only slightly increased during this period. Furthermore, the effective cost of consumer credit has remained relatively low for affluent groups and segments of the middle classes (e.g., tax-deductible home equity loans), whereas it has climbed rapidly for the struggling middle classes and especially the working poor. Not unexpectedly, the banking industry defends its punitive lending rates as reflecting the cost of conducting business with high-risk groups; it also contends that expensive finance charges encourage fiscal responsibility and frugality. A closer examination, however, reveals that this view obfuscates and further punishes those social groups that have suffered the most and benefited the least from the past two decades of U.S. industrial restructuring. Indeed, the unequal access to and cost of consumer credit constitute emergent features of U.S. postindustrial inequality. For example, both "God's poor" as well as the "Devil's apostles" pay as much as 35 percent APR (plus membership fees) on low-end bank cards.

The widening financial chasm obscures the increasingly ambiguous distinction between "worthy" and "unworthy" debtors. For example, affluent convenience users who pay off their monthly charges receive free or low-cost credit, while some even make money on rebates, gifts, plane tickets, retail discounts, and even cash-back offers. This business practice contrasts sharply with the high cost of credit for financially dependent revolvers who may carry a credit card balance due to personal or household crises that are beyond their control, such as unemployment, illness, or divorce.

The most expensive consumer credit—the "fringe banks" of last resort—are found in the nefarious world of second-tier financial services. Here, low-end credit cards are a bargain compared with the rates of "poverty banks," such as cash-checking outlets, finance companies, pawnshops, rent-to-own stores, and even loan sharks. These sources of credit typically feature interest rates that range from 5 to over 30 percent per month; popular payday loans cost 10 to 15 percent *per 15 days*. An even more costly variant of the latter is "cash leasing," which charges 30 percent for a 15-day loan. Not incidentally, these subprime loans are often directly or indirectly linked to some of America's largest financial institutions.[65] Table 4.2 summarizes the varying costs of consumer credit by social background of borrower and type of loan.

American attitudes toward credit are much more complex than implied by the ubiquitous marketing campaigns of the credit card industry. Cards can be useful for those able to adhere to the Puritan financial ethos, but they can become a merciless burden when convenience use revolves into financial dependence. This attitudinal ambivalence is reflected in the anxiety of the middle and working classes over the moral laxity of embracing debt as a temporary fi-

TABLE 4.2 Cost and Sources of Consumer Credit by Social Class

Type of Consumer	Source	Cost
Convenience (Affluent or frugal user)	Preferred bank credit card (Gold, Platinum), special professional accounts (U.S. Medical)	Free with zero to moderate ($20 to $60) annual fee for "frequent flier" programs with credit lines up to $100,000

Benefits: Extended warranties on purchases, buy big-ticket items on sale, annual itemized summaries for tax records or business reimbursements, retail discounts, cash rebates, free air travel and gifts for volume purchases.

Money makers (Entrepreneurs, hustlers)	Bank cards with high limits ($5,000–$35,000)	1% to 1¼ % per month without annual card fee
	Unsecured revolving credit ($10,000–$35,000)	Variable rate (12–16%), effective cost includes business expense deduction

Benefits: Line of credit with "pooled" cash advances from $5,000 to over $100,000. Instant short-term loans that avoid bank loan delays and create wealth such as for stock market, real estate, autos, "quick" deals as well as small-business cash-flow loans. If not quickly "flipped" (sold), can be converted to less costly conventional bank loans.

Middle class (Homeowners)	Bank home equity loans $10,000 to $150,000	Fixed and variable rate loans at 6% to 12.5% APR plus zero to 2% loan origination and insurance fees

Benefits: Debt consolidation, purchase of big-ticket items on sale such as cars and appliances, home improvement, and college expenses. Due to tax deductibility of home mortgage interest, effective cost of credit ranges from about 5.0% to 9.0%.

Working and middle class	Basic or prestige bank credit card	12% to 22.9% with zero to modest ($15 to $30) annual card fee
	Retail credit card	19.8% to 24.8% annual card fee (Sears, CompUSA)

Benefits: Extended warranties on purchases, purchase big-ticket items on sale, receipts for tax records or business reimbursements, retail discounts, free gifts for volume purchases, and instant loans for emergencies (car repairs, medical expenses, clothing, rent, parking tickets, personal income taxes, legal bills, unemployment expenses, and groceries).

(continues)

College students	Basic or prestige bank credit card	17.8% to 26.7% with zero to moderate ($10 to $25) annual card fee

Benefits: Loans for educational and recreational expenses, computer equipment, life-enrichment experiences. Offers retail discounts, free gifts for volume purchases, and opportunity to establish a personal credit history.

High risk (recently bankrupt, underemployed, new immigrants)	"Special offer"	24.9% to 34% APR with processing (0 to $89) and annual fees ($25 to $100)
	Secured bank or Collateralized credit cards	19.9% to 26.9% APR plus processing ($0 to $89) and annual fees ($25 to $99) plus required savings deposit

Benefits: Offers those without (divorced women, young adults, immigrants) or with a poor credit history (bankrupt) to establish responsible repayment history. Features low credit limits ($300 to $1,500) but offers a starter credit card by matching the cardholder's bank deposit from zero to 300%. For example, a $300 deposit would yield a credit limit of from $300 to $600 and as high as $900. After 6 to 18 months of regular payments, many secured clients are mainstreamed into regular credit accounts.

Working poor	Payday loans (postdated checks) Finance companies	10% to 25% (up to 2 weeks) or 260% to 540% APR and higher for daily loans 16% to 25% and up to 40+% with application and origination fees
	Check-cashing outlets	1–2% to 9% for 1- to 5-day loan or 350% to over 700% APR

Benefits: Avoid foreclosure of home or eviction for nonpayment. Immediate puchase of furniture, stereo, or other household items on difficult-to-obtain credit and provides way to establish personal credit history. Instant loans for satisfying other creditors or emergencies such as home or auto repairs and medical bills.

Financially desperate	Rent-to-own stores Pawnshops	180% to over 450% per year 2.5%–25% per month to over 260% per year (plus fees)
	Car title loans	2.5%–25% per month with loss of auto for nonpayment
	cash leasing	30% for two weeks, over 730% per year

Benefits: Short-term loans for surviving personal or family crises, unexpected income interruptions, credit card bills, back taxes, child support payments, and other household resource shortages.

nancial crutch. In contrast, affluent groups perceive bank credit cards simultaneously as a useful convenience but also a threat to the less visible economic bulwarks of their privileged social status. With the democratization of credit, elite tastes such as designer clothes, foreign cars, and European vacations are no longer reliable markers of social class background. And, ironically, the ideological legitimacy of the Credit Card Nation that features free credit—a perceived entitlement of the U.S. upper and middle classes—is effectively subsidized by both "deserving" and "undeserving" debtors.

In terms of the ideological ramparts of the moral divide, credit cards are no longer merely a transactional mechanism for deserving convenience users. Nor can their role be lauded as simply a means of democratizing credit by providing financial resources to groups that have been previously denied small consumer loans. Rather, they are the corporate warhorse of the banking industry for cheaply and efficiently penetrating into new consumer markets and extending the complex web of new financial services. In the process, as American society adjusts to the new patterns of postindustrial inequality, credit cards have both obscured the gap between middle-class respectability and an elite lifestyle as well as confounded the moral distinction between deserving (e.g., involuntarily unemployed) and undeserving (e.g., spending-binge) debtors. Consequently, under the guise of democratic access and the moral legitimacy of appropriate use, credit cards are obscuring the widening gap between the haves and have-nots. This view is amplified by Clara, a 30-something upper-class Italian:

> America invented credit cards so that people can enjoy a taste of the upper-class lifestyle and then quietly return to their original social [class] positions. Credit cards give Americans a taste but not a share of the pie. In this way America can preserve a social system based on a very unequal distribution of income. Only in America can you go to the shopping mall, buy an Armani suit with credit cards, and then go back to your trailer, which by the way belongs to the bank.

Hence, the easy availability of consumer credit cards is the driving force of a striking conundrum of contemporary U.S. society. It both obscures and accentuates the complex social, cultural, and economic inequality of postindustrial America.

5

Life on the Financial Edge

Maxed Out, Surfing, and Playing the Credit Card Shuffle

FOR THE REVEREND ROBERT G. TRACHE, March 4, 2000, was to be a highly anticipated and joyous occasion. A widely respected rector of St. James Episcopal Church in Richmond, Virginia, the 52-year-old priest had been elected the previous October to head the tenth-largest Episcopal diocese in the United States. As the bishop of Atlanta, he would have had a diocese that included over 53,000 parishioners and the Cathedral of St. Philip in the heart of the affluent Buckhead section of the city. The long-awaited consecration was the culmination of a meticulously conducted search that required a 15-year background check into all candidates' employment, education, credit, and legal history—even investigation of past traffic violations. It also included rigorous physical and psychiatric exams. Yet, only eight days before the lavish ($20,000) ceremony, the diocese's standing committee announced its controversial decision to rescind Trache's nomination because it was "no longer confident in Trache's ability to function as bishop of Atlanta." Although candidates had withdrawn earlier in the nomination process in the past, usually following revelations of sexual or financial improprieties, it was an unprecedented action to cancel a bishop's consecration at such a late date.[1]

So, what egregious act did Reverend Trache commit that necessitated such an embarrassing institutional spectacle? Why did Reverend Frank Griswold, presiding bishop of the Episcopal Church, and retiring Atlanta Bishop Frank Allan approve of this abrupt cancellation? After all, church officials have insisted that there was no evidence of illegal or immoral acts by Trache and thus no need for further disciplinary action. According to a statement released by the Atlanta diocese on February 25, the committee's action was "'a result of very recent discoveries of lack of disclosure in personal financial and family matters.'" Trache was deemed guilty of a "'violation of trust'" and "'lapses in good decision-making'" that led to the termination of his $110,065 annual salary, which also included a comfortable housing allowance.[2]

At the heart of the controversy and the future of Trache's career is his secretive filing for Chapter 7 personal bankruptcy on January 20, 2000. Court records at the U.S. Bankruptcy Court in Richmond list Trache's assets at less than $18,000 and his outstanding debts at over $122,000—primarily owed to credit card companies. Reverend Richard Callaway, the committee's chairman, explained that "'the issues are not so much what has gone on, but how they handled the decisions they made and how they were disclosed to the body of the faithful.'" This statement was made, of course, after a thorough review of the candidate's background that included testimonials by former colleagues praising his character, devotion, and theological training at Harvard Divinity School. According to retired bishop Joseph T. Heistand, who temporarily filled in as rector of the Richmond parish following Trache's resignation to become bishop in Atlanta, "'I know Bob Trache. I think he's an outstanding person. He's very prominent in the religious life of this city. He's an outstanding preacher, an outstanding teacher.'" Bette Wanamaker, who served as a lay minister on Trache's staff in Virginia, declared that he "'is one of the most talented clergy I have known. He's a man with a lot of heart, a lot of energy, a lot of insight . . . [whose] strong preaching didn't leave you in the same place when you left . . . [whose leadership skills] attracted new members and moved the parish to a new place, to new ministries and opportunities.'"[3]

Even so, like the 1.3 million Americans that filed for bankruptcy in 1999, Reverend Trache became overwhelmed with the worldly affairs of personal finance. According to Wanamaker, "'What line he went over I don't know. I'm just so very, very sorry that he could not face up to the difficulties . . . in his life and gotten help from the church. I don't know whether he thought that would have destroyed him or that he was too embarrassed [to ask for help].'"[4] What is striking about this case is that Reverend Trache belies the popular stereotype of the financially irresponsible by instead being highly educated with a good salary and spiritually guided. Indeed, the cultural bases of economic savings as a moral virtue and debt as a sign of improvident behavior are deeply rooted in America's religious heritage. For a clergyman of his stature not to withstand the temptations of personal indulgence underscores the difficulty of resisting the intensifying social and economic pressures of the Credit Card Nation.

Rising Tides and Sinking Ships: Are U.S. Households Treading Water in a Sea of Red Ink?

As illustrated by the Trache case, the transformation of the Puritan ethos of thrift and savings is one of the most important cultural revolutions of the U.S. postwar era. This profound attitudinal and behavioral shift began with the erosion of real U.S. wages in the mid-1970s. Americans were encouraged to respond to declining household resources by assuming higher levels of installment (auto, furniture, appliances) and revolving (bank, retail credit card) debt. This trend mirrors the more aggressive lending practices of U.S. retailing and banking sectors as well as sophisticated corporate marketing campaigns that are informed by the burgeoning research literature on consumer behavior.[5] That is, Americans' consumption patterns tend to be influenced by their perception of future economic conditions (based on past financial experiences or optimistic forecasts such as President Ronald Reagan's "Morning in America" mantra) rather than by current trends—even during periods of declining real wages or economic difficulty.[6] The growing importance of consumer credit in influencing domestic economic policies contributed to President Jimmy Carter's ill-fated decision to propose temporary restrictions on bank credit cards in an effort to rein in the double-digit inflation rates of the late 1970s.[7] Overall, studies by the U.S. Federal Reserve report that American household debt exploded from about 50 percent of disposable income in 1970 to over 80 percent in 1995.[8]

The most striking features of the trend in U.S. household indebtedness are the rise of personal bankruptcy and the corresponding decline in its social stigma.[9] For example, the Great Depression produced a rate of 4.65 bankruptcy filings per 1,000 households during the 1930s. This rate fell sharply in the 1940s and remained below 4.0 in the 1950s. Although the rate nearly doubled in the 1960s and exceeded 9.0 per 1,000 households in the 1970s, the most dramatic increase in personal bankruptcy occurred in the 1980s (see Figure 5.1). Between 1980 and 1984, personal bankruptcy filings remained stable at almost 300,000 per year, then soared to 718,107 in 1990 and to 874,642 in 1995; between 1990 and 1995, this constitutes

FIGURE 5.1   U.S. Personal Bankruptcy Filings and U.S. Unemployment Rate,
1980–1999

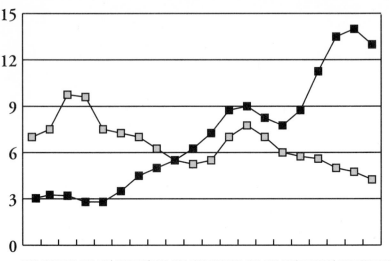

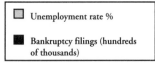

Unemployment rate %

Bankruptcy filings (hundreds
of thousands)

SOURCES: American Bankruptcy Institute, "Annual Filings," www.abiworld.org; and U.S.
Bureau of Labor Statistics, *Employment and Monthly Earnings,* vol. 47, no. 1 (January 2000),
p. 219, available at www.stats.bls.gov.

about 35 filings per 1,000. Over the next five years, filings averaged over
1.25 million per year, or more than 52 filings per 1,000 households. This
number peaked at 1.4 million in 1998 and dropped by 112,000 to 1.3 million in 1999.[10]

Unlike what occurred during the Great Depression era, the extraordinary
rise in personal bankruptcies coincides with the nation's current economic
prosperity and low unemployment. In fact, personal bankruptcy filings fell
immediately after the 1989–1991 recession (from 900,874 in 1992 to
780,455 in 1994) before they surged to unprecedented levels at the end of
the decade. In comparison, the 1990s featured the longest economic expansion in U.S. history; unemployment peaked in 1991 and steadily declined to
its current rate of about 4 percent. This counterintuitive relationship—falling
unemployment and escalating bankruptcy rates—is at least partially attrib-

TABLE 5.1   U.S. Personal Bankruptcy Rates by Household and State, 1998

	Households	Rank		Households	Rank
National average	68		Missouri	73	24
			Montana	92	36
Alabama	50	5	Nebraska	103	42
Arizona	144	51	Nevada	39	1
Arkansas	56	22	New Hampshire	88	33
California	52	9	New Jersey	63	14
Colorado	82	6	New Mexico	78	27
Connecticut	88	29	New York	86	32
Delaware	96	38	North Carolina	104	43
District of Columbia	80	28	North Dakota	113	46
Florida	70	22	Ohio	75	26
Georgia	45	3	Oklahoma	58	12
Hawaii	67	17	Oregon	69	19
Idaho	56	9	Pennsylvania	98	40
Illinois	65	16	Rhode Island	69	19
Indiana	56	9	South Carolina	118	49
Iowa	116	47	South Dakota	119	50
Kansas	74	25	Tennessee	40	2
Kentucky	67	17	Texas	96	38
Louisiana	69	19	Utah	46	4
Maine	107	45	Vermont	116	47
Maryland	53	8	Virginia	58	12
Massachusetts	104	43	Washington	64	15
Michigan	88	33	West Virginia	82	29
Minnesota	93	37	Wisconsin	100	41
Mississippi	52	6	Wyoming	82	29

SOURCE: American Bankruptcy Institute, "Personal Bankruptcy Filings by Quarter" (1999), available at www.abiworld.org, based on data from the Administrative Office of the U.S. Courts (1998 bankruptcies) and the U.S. Bureau of the Census (1996 household data).

uted to the lax lending policies of the banking industry that offered easy consumer credit to increasingly higher-risk, lower-income workers. Table 5.1 presents U.S. bankruptcy filings by household rates and national ranking of each state: The national average is one bankruptcy per 68 households in 1998.

After the 1989–1991 recession, U.S. financial institutions substantially increased lines of revolving and installment credit to recently employed as well as existing clients. According to George M. Salem, a Wall Street securities analyst with Gerard Klauer Mattison & Company, "'The banks and other credit lending institutions brought this problem [of soaring personal bankruptcy rates] upon themselves. They shot themselves in the foot by using some of the weakest and most pitiful loan underwriting techniques that I have ever witnessed.'"[11] And in light of the economic anxiety of high unemployment and declining real wages, Americans were eager—even flattered—to be considered worthy of such potentially large consumer loans. Revolving credit became the new social safety net of the American middle class as well as the source of start-up capital for aspiring entrepreneurs. Hence, U.S. households willingly accepted increasing amounts of consumer credit as a hedge against an abrupt decline in their economic circumstances.

According to Dr. Stephen Brobeck, executive director of Consumer Federation of America (CFA), "'the credit card companies bear the lion's share of responsibility for the bankruptcy crisis'" because of their overzealous competition for highly profitable accounts—regardless of the ability of consumers to repay their loans. Between 1993 and 1998, according to CFA reports, unused lines of cardholders' credit more than tripled—from $580 million to over $2 trillion. This has led Brobeck to assert that "'banks are hypocritical to seek bankruptcy restrictions when their irresponsible marketing and extension of credit card debt [have] been an important cause of rising bankruptcies.'"[12] Significantly, banks began implementing more stringent lending policies in the late 1990s, and there was a corresponding absolute decline in personal bankruptcies in 1999. This trend is consistent with the research of David Moss and Gibbs Johnson, who found that bankruptcy rates jumped in the 1990s following the extension of credit to economically marginal households.[13]

During the 1990s, the convenience of bank credit cards changed dramatically, from providing people with a way to avoid carrying cash to providing "bridge loans" during periods of financial distress or social crises. This logic of household budgeting shifted from the influence of the Great Depression generation, which subscribed to the importance of savings, to the attitude of baby boomers, who sought simply to balance their budget without incurring substantial debt. As the social pressures of competitive consumption influenced households to adopt budgets based on a revenue mix of earnings and credit rather than earnings and savings, as described by Juliet Schor in *The Overspent American,* the U.S. personal savings rate plummeted to zero by the end of 1998.[14] This is reflected in the massive growth of high-interest credit card debt following the 1981–1982 recession; revolving consumer debt increased from nearly $60 billion in 1982 to about $515 billion in 1999.[15] These concurrent trends are particularly intriguing, since wages have been rising since 1998 and convenience users have increased sharply over the last decade—from 29 percent in 1991 to 43 percent in 2000.[16] Clearly, they reflect the dramatic increase in U.S. income inequality over the past two decades—the worst among the Western industrialized countries—along with the changing role of revolving consumer credit.

As astutely noted by Lendol Calder, installment credit historically has enforced the Puritan values of frugality and hard work by requiring strict adherence to household budgets and prompt loan repayment in order to receive future consumer credit.[17] The recent marketing of revolving credit, however, serves to undermine work discipline and personal thrift by providing unrestricted consumer loans that may be used during periods of employment disruption, family emergencies, and personal crises. That is, instead of promoting the Puritan ethos of saving for a rainy day, consumer credit cards have become the "savings account" of the heavily indebted middle class and, more recently, the working poor. For example, one study of the national Survey of Consumer Finances (1983–1995) found that the proportion of "poor" households with bank credit cards more than doubled during this period, while those with credit card debts more than twice their monthly incomes nearly quadrupled. The finding leads the authors to speculate that "the poor used the 1980s to build down their debt, leaving them in decent financial condition when the 1990–1991 recession hit. Then perhaps the recession induced the poor to use credit card debt to maintain consumption . . . the most interesting development [is] that the poor have not reduced their debt in the growth period of the 1990s as they did in the 1980s."[18] This is consistent with the pattern of credit card use by middle-income households. During the labor force layoffs of industrial restructuring in the 1980s and ongoing labor market reorganization in the 1990s, bank credit cards rather than household savings became the economic safety net for financially embattled Americans. A key issue, then, is the cost of this "democratically" allocated consumer credit.

As discussed in Chapter 3, the dramatic increase in the profitability of consumer credit cards in the mid-1980s precipitated corporate marketing campaigns that systematically penetrated more marginal consumer niche markets (lower-income workers, students, elderly) while simultaneously shaping societal attitudes toward frugality and debt.[19] By offering credit cards to high-risk social groups ("democratization" of credit), the banking industry asserts that it is helping financially overburdened households as well as encouraging the responsible use of consumer credit through the individual choice of the carrot-or-stick incentives of its flexible finance charge system. As the moral divide between debtors and savers has narrowed, however, the industry confronts mounting opposition to its unequal loan "pricing" policies. That is, cardholders who can pay off their monthly charges receive free credit, whereas hardworking households that are debt-dependent due to circumstances beyond their control must pay dearly for their credit. Furthermore, in its quest for more stringent consumer bankruptcy laws, the banking industry's credibility has been questioned due to its simplistic contention that the main problem is the lack of individual responsibility for financial debts. By focusing on the "poor" decisions of individuals, this view neglects the larger social and economic context of consumer indebtedness and, in the process, tends to confound the causes of personal bankruptcy with the consequences.

Financial Armageddon: Contemporary Patterns of Personal Bankruptcy

The public debate over the growth of personal bankruptcies tends to obscure the different causes of this financial strategy of last resort. On the one hand, the credit card industry has contended that Americans are not overburdened with consumer debt. Dr. Lawrence Chimerine, chief economist at the Washington, D.C.–based Economic Strategy Institute and MasterCard consultant explains, "'We've been hearing that the sky is falling under the weight of consumer debt for years. All economic trends continue to support the ability of American consumers to manage their credit card spending and debt appropriately.'"[20]

From this perspective, the recent surge in personal bankruptcy rates reflects the growing irresponsibility of consumers in seeking to evade their financial obligations under the guidance of aggressive bankruptcy attorneys. This view, shaped by the Puritan ethos that underlies the moral divide, asserts that consumer debt is an individual choice that can be controlled through self-discipline and frugality. According to the American Bankers Association, "'Current bankruptcy law encourages "bankruptcy of convenience" by people who could afford to pay back some of their debts.'" The argument is buttressed by a 1997 industry-financed report, albeit widely criticized for its methodological flaws, that estimated about 30 percent of its sample of Chapter 7 bankruptcy petitioners could have repaid a sizable amount of their personal debts.[21] Hence, from the banking industry's point of view, if you play then you must pay, regardless of whether you should have been offered a loan.

On the other hand, consumer advocates and researchers have emphasized the increasingly important role of credit card companies in encouraging dangerously high levels of personal debt. According to Elizabeth Warren, Leo Gottlieb Professor at Harvard Law School:

Virtually all independent academic studies and all government studies of the rate of bankruptcy filings demonstrate that a rise in bankruptcy filings follows a sharp rise in the amount of consumer debt per household. . . . As families carry more short-term, high-interest credit card and similar debt, they are more at risk for financial failure. . . . For a family loaded with debt, any setback—such as a job loss, an uninsured medical loss, or a divorce—will put the family over the edge of financial stability.[22]

Even U.S. Federal Reserve Chairman Alan Greenspan, in his February 23, 2000, testimony before the U.S. Senate Banking Committee, mentioned the indiscriminate solicitation of credit card customers with concern: "'Children, dogs, cats, and moose are getting credit cards.'"[23] Furthermore, unwary consumers have wrongly assumed that bank lending policies are based on the ability to repay their loans. As CFA's Brobeck explains, "'Issuers should be more discriminating and responsible in their allocation of credit . . . issuers [should] deny credit to anyone whose credit card debt is already 20 percent of his income. . . . At the same time, we need for society to view substantial high-cost, short-term debt as foolish.'"[24] Significantly, this rejection of credit-based consumerism, the proverbial "shopping on steroids," has inspired a personal empowerment movement with "debt freedom" as its new status symbol.[25]

Unfortunately, media reports of personal bankruptcy tend to further distort these conflicting perspectives. America's fascination with the cult of celebrity, which celebrates the meteoric rise of the rich and famous and their spectacular fall into the pit of public ridicule, distorts popular portrayals of personal bankruptcy. For example, the "Going Broke on $33 Million a Year" cover story in the February 1997 issue of *People Magazine* highlights the financial dirty linen of many fallen pop icons. Singer M. C. Hammer's 1995 bankruptcy filing cited $9.6 million in assets and $13.7 million in debts; only five years earlier, *Forbes* estimated his 1990 earnings at more than $33 million. The financial intrigue, however, concerned the cost of his 40-person entourage, the elaborate home sound system with 22 miles of electrical wiring, and the elaborate design of the six-bedroom "Hammer Time" estate with its $68,000 worth of mirrors and an initial budget of $600,000–$900,000 for Italian marble. After her Chapter 11 bankruptcy in 1993, actress Kim Basinger of *Batwoman* fame and wife of Alec Baldwin was forced to sell her financial stake in Braselton, Georgia (population 418), for $4.3 million; she had bought the town through a partnership in 1989 for $20 million. Her court filing listed monthly expenses of $575 for dry cleaning, $7,000 for pet care, and $9,000 in alimony for her ex-husband.[26]

The media's glamorizing of celebrities' profligate spending and conspicuous consumption sprees (remember Imelda Marcos's collection of shoes?) masks the more mundane causes of even their high-profile bankruptcies. Burt Reynolds attributes his 1996 bankruptcy to bad investments in two restaurant chains and the abrupt decline in his box-office appeal; he listed $6.6 million in assets and $11.2 million in debts. His ex-wife, Loni Anderson, claims that her financial insolvency (including $105,000 in back taxes to the IRS for 1995) is due to the failure of Reynolds to pay her home mortgage. Lorraine Bracco, star of the popular television program *The Sopranos,* blamed her 1999 bankruptcy on the costly custody battle over her daughter with actor and former husband Harvey Keitel. The financial woes of country singer and social activist Willie Nelson began when the IRS rejected his tax shelter losses and seized his property in 1990 for $16.9 million in back taxes and penalties. Nelson negotiated a repayment plan that included the recording of a collection of songs, subsequently entitled *The IRS Tapes,* whose proceeds were garnished by the federal government while fans rescued his possessions from public auctions. In explaining the settlement, Nelson laconically explained, "'25 percent of what I make ain't bad.'"[27] In sum, the media's fascination with conspicuous consumption and celebrity misfortune has served in the past to deflect attention from the most common causes and consequences of personal indebtedness.

So, who are America's highly indebted and recently bankrupt? Are they compulsive shoppers who are seeking an easy way to escape their financial obligations? Are they poor households that are unable to control their use of previously unavailable sources of credit? Are they families exploiting the financial relief provision of the U.S. Bankruptcy Code by discharging debts that could have been paid if bankruptcy courts were not so sympathetic to debtors?[28] According to a recent and thorough examination of national bankruptcy trends, conducted by Teresa Sullivan and Robert Warren at the University of Texas–Austin and Elizabeth Warren at Harvard, the results fail to support the common portrayal of debtors as unable or unwilling to control their discretionary spending. The authors' previous pathbreaking study of 1,547 bankruptcy cases filed in 1981 was reported in *As We Forgive Our Debtors: Bankruptcy and Consumer Credit in America* (1989); their later analysis of 2,650 bankruptcy cases filed in 1991 indicates that more recent debtors represent a typical cross-section of middle-class America. Their sequel, *The Fragile Middle Class: Americans in Debt* (2000), presents a compelling and surprising snapshot of American debtors.[29] They are more likely to have lower incomes and much greater consumer debts than their counterparts of the preceding decade.

The authors contend that "by every social measure, bankruptcy is a middle-class phenomenon." In the early 1990s, people who filed for bankruptcy had comparable educations and worked in the same occupations and in the same industries as other middle-class Americans. They were employed and owned homes at about the same proportion as all other Americans.[30] Based on inflation-adjusted figures, however, the annual income of bankruptcy filers has fallen over the past two decades—from $23,254 in 1981 to $17,652 in 1997. More striking is the debt burden of the recently bankrupt. In 1997, the average consumer debt of bankruptcy filers had jumped to 1.64 times their annual income—nearly double the debt burden of 0.87 in 1981.[31] These data suggest that the banks' aggressive marketing of consumer credit had effectively penetrated the lower-income groups by the late 1980s. It is not surprising, then, that the credit card industry expanded its marketing campaign to the untapped populations of teenage college students and senior citizens and then to millions of new bankruptcy survivors.

Significantly, contrary to the banking industry's attack on "convenience bankruptcy" abuse, many heavily indebted families are reluctantly declaring bankruptcy—as a last resort—because their escalating consumer debts offer no other recourse. In fact, many American families are finding fewer alternatives to personal bankruptcy due to changing policies of the banking industry. For instance, in a 1998 survey, the Consumer Federation of America (CFA) found that "in violation of a long-standing industry practice, the largest credit card issuers are becoming increasingly unwilling to reduce interest rates for consumers who enter debt management programs [and] major banks have instituted across-the-board funding cuts of at least a third for the nation's credit counseling agencies." Credit card issuer MBNA, for example, recently increased its interest rate to consumers in debt management programs from 10.0 to 15.9 percent. The highest rates are Sears (21.9 percent), American Express Optima (21.7 percent), Capital One (19.8 percent), and First Card (17.65 percent); Bank of America, First North American National Bank (FNANB), Mellon Bank, and U.S. Bancorp do not levy a finance charge on credit counseling clients. Additionally, the CFA survey found that virtually all credit card issuers have sharply reduced their fair-share contributions to credit counseling agencies below the traditional industry standard of 15 percent. Two of the top ten issuers, MBNA and Household Credit Services, contributed only 6 percent. This belies the dramatic increase in the household demand for credit counseling services. Between 1988 and 1998, the number of consumers that entered nonprofit, debt management programs nearly doubled.[32]

According to Sullivan, Warren, and Westbrook (2000), the U.S. Bankruptcy Code provides an effective strategy for the most vulnerable members
of the American middle class to avert their fall into the lower class, especially those hardest hit by economic reversals.[33] Their research indicates that
the most common causes are unemployment (over one-half report a significant period of unemployment before filing), particularly in single-parent
households; marital dissolution (divorced filers are 300 percent more likely
to file than the general U.S. population), especially for women with children; and medical expenses (40 percent of older filers [50–65]), particularly
for households without health and automobile insurance. In addition,
African American and Latino families are more likely to declare bankruptcy,
largely due to their lack of assets (retirement plans, stock portfolios, real estate) in comparison with white households. For many of these families,
bankruptcy is filed to prevent the loss of their homes.[34] Last, a small but
growing factor is the rising popularity of casino gambling. Recent studies of
bankruptcy petitions in states with legalized gambling have found that some
large consumer debts are due to gambling-related cash advances from bank
credit cards. As Eric Rajala, a Missouri bankruptcy attorney explains, "'The
credit card companies want to push this credit on anybody that has a pulse
. . . when they put ATMs in a casino, it's like giving a bottle to an alcoholic
and saying, don't get drunk.'"[35]

"It's the Economy, Stupid!" Shuffling and Surfing in the Turbulent Seas of Economic Uncertainty

As American society continues to enjoy the ninth consecutive year of uninterrupted economic growth in 2000, a period of sustained prosperity unri-
valed in U.S. history, the "new" economy features unusual schizophrenic
tendencies. Corporate profits have soared while workers' wages have fallen.
America's billionaires have multiplied while personal bankruptcies have
climbed to record levels. U.S. income inequality has become the worst in
the industrialized West while the stock markets have reached the strato-
sphere. Most disconcerting are the frequent layoffs at some of America's
largest corporations. For instance, during the last week of January 2000,
Amazon.com, Lockheed, Coca-Cola, Venator (Woolworth), and Marriott
all announced major personnel "reduction in force" policies.[36] This increasingly common trend of employment disruption, which has been regularized
through the enormous growth of temporary or contingent workers, has fundamentally changed the nature of employee loyalty and, in the process, created often unmanageable personal debt burdens. For members of a

generation who have never witnessed an economic downturn, the perceived lack of an imperative to accumulate financial reserves (savings, lines of credit) suggests a potential social crisis when they must endure longer periods of un- and underemployment. This is illustrated by the experience of "Daniel," whose graduation from college in the early 1990s resulted in unfulfilled expectations, disappointing job prospects, and insurmountable consumer debt obligations.

The case of Daniel, who was at the beginning of the employment life cycle, reveals how the impact of credit card debt amassed in college can be obscured by the middle-class squeeze after graduation. That is, recent graduates tend to assume greater levels of consumer debt during their job search. This includes employment-related expenses (résumés, business attire, transportation) as well as personal living expenses (rent, food, car, entertainment). Significantly, recent graduates who are financing their lifestyle with credit cards are classified as neither students nor new workers. During this transitional period, personal credit card debt often grows at a rapid rate—especially during a tight labor market.

Daniel's unexpected odyssey into the financial depths of credit card debt began innocuously when he was offered a Citibank Visa application by a corporate representative while he was walking through the student center. A sophomore at a private university, he was struggling to pay for his college expenses and enjoy a modest social life in Washington, D.C. Daniel's middle-class, professional family is from Kenya, and his goal was to become an accountant. With limited personal funds, Daniel was eager to receive "free money" but was skeptical that a major bank would give him a credit card, since he was several years away from earning a middle-class salary. From Daniel's perspective, an undergraduate college student was a major loan risk.

In 1988, however, Citibank was aggressively marketing credit cards to college students like Daniel whom it viewed as potentially lucrative customers for high-interest consumer loans. Citibank was so desperate to expand its credit card portfolio that it abandoned the industry policy of requiring parental cosignatures for unemployed students. Banks realized that the threat of lawsuits could persuade parents to pay for their children's credit card debts, as could informing parents that nonpayment would damage their children's credit history. Citibank required only a copy of his university ID, and Daniel quickly completed the application and received a $600 line of credit. He immediately used it all for schoolbooks, food, and an occasional cash advance. At the time, Daniel thought that his plastic cash had been exhausted and he would have to survive on his previous "starving student" budget. Instead, to Daniel's surprise, he began receiving new credit cards in the mail—a peculiar reward for maxing out his Citibank Visa. Over the next seven months, Daniel received Citibank MasterCard and Visa Gold cards with rapidly rising credit limits as well as several retail credit cards. Daniel found it amazing that all of these cards were preapproved before he had even applied for his first job. Apparently, he thought, this reflected the banks' confidence in his future earning ability.

By the time Daniel finished his B.A. degree in 1990, he had over $5,000 in credit card debt. Although he does not remember most of these purchases, Daniel is grateful that his credit cards enabled him to enjoy a middle-class lifestyle before he had a well-paying job. In fact, this consumer debt did not seriously concern him because he was convinced he would earn a good salary soon after completing his studies. This is why Daniel justified the frequent payment of his consumer debts through cash advances and balance transfers from bank cards—the credit card "shuffle." Over the next two years, Daniel used students loans and credit cards to finance his master's degree in accounting. Upon graduating in fall 1991, Daniel had amassed over $15,000 in credit card debt. As a certified public accountant (CPA), he expected to be able to pay off his debts quickly, but to his shock, the 1989 recession severely affected his employment prospects. Daniel spent the summer interviewing for jobs as an accountant and paid his living expenses with his credit cards. His debts were approaching $20,000 when he took a temporary position as a security guard. Daniel was stunned that his first annual salary of approximately $15,000 was less than his total credit card debt.

Even when an accounting job did not materialize, Daniel did not perceive his credit card debt as a serious problem. He was certain that it was simply a matter of time before he became financially solvent. Undeterred by his escalating debt, Daniel found that his full-time job and extensive credit history enabled him to obtain even more credit and buy whatever he wanted. "In stores, I would apply for instant credit cards and be set to buy in a few minutes." Unfortunately for Daniel, his temporary position lasted nearly two years. As he explains, "During this time, I was basically surviving off credit cards. They paid my rents, entertainment, gas, and shopping." In 1993, Daniel finally joined a Washington, D.C., firm as an accountant. His initial salary was over $50,000, and he believed he could begin reducing his $25,000-plus in credit card debt. However, Daniel's newfound professional success persuaded him to ignore his original goal of escaping credit dependence, and he quickly accepted preapproved offers for Chevy Chase Gold Visa, American Express, and Diners Club cards. Emboldened by his new buying power, Daniel bought a condominium and furnished it with his credit cards. He rationalized the condominium as a good investment, and after all, interest on the mortgage, unlike on his credit card debts, would be tax deductible. After a couple of salary increases, Daniel's rising standard of living soon included a new car and of course auto loan payments in 1994. Now Daniel felt his hard work was being rewarded as he became a taxpaying member of the American middle class.

By 1996, even with an annual salary of nearly $60,000, Daniel's credit card debts exceeded $30,000—and were rising: "My paycheck could only pay my condo, car, and credit cards. Then I had to depend on the credit cards for gas, groceries or anything else I wanted to buy. No savings. [Over] a few months, I would make thousands of dollars in credit card payments, and the debts were not going anywhere." Efforts to replace his high-interest credit card debts with lower-interest debt consolidation loans were time-consuming and ultimately fruitless. Banks were disinclined to approve new consumer loans for anyone with such a high debt-to-income ratio. Reluctantly, Daniel believed he had no option but to file for personal bankruptcy. In early 1997, his Chapter 7 filing was approved by the D.C. bankruptcy court, and all of his credit card debts were discharged.

Today, Daniel is recovering from the personal pain of bankruptcy and thankful for the opportunity to rebuild his financial future. "Without it [bankruptcy], I would still be increasing my credit card debt, and they [banks] would still be increasing my credit limits . . . instead of relying on cash [advances] from my credit cards I can now get cash from my savings account." Daniel still uses plastic money but only for convenience and prestige. To minimize suspicions about his past financial problems, he has a debit card and a secured Visa credit card.[37] The credit line on his collateralized card has been raised twice, and Daniel hopes he will be approved soon for a retail credit card after being rejected twice. Although the days of easy credit are temporarily over, Daniel knows that in time he will rejoin the ranks of the middle class with the full privileges of a Gold credit card.

For Daniel, life without credit cards requires more careful planning and fewer discretionary purchases. His salary enables him to pay all of his bills and even begin planning financial investments. Fortunately, Daniel has been able to keep his personal bankruptcy a secret and thus avoid public ridicule from his colleagues. "I don't want anyone in the office to know in case it could be used against me later on. . . . I don't want anyone to say that I can't be trusted or that money problems may affect my work . . . someone might try to use it against me later on to hurt my career. You know office politics." In sum, a review of Daniel's bankruptcy petition portrays a well-paid professional who appears to have been unable to control his consumption desires. In reality, however, about two-thirds of his credit card debt was accumulated during college and his initial job search. Hence, the roots of Daniel's financial insolvency were sown by his credit dependency as a university student and the unforeseen difficulty in obtaining a job in the aftermath of the 1989 recession.

Breaking Up Is So Easy to Do:
Picking Up the Pieces After a Leveraged Buyout

In 1990, Susan Faludi incurred the ire of the business community with her investigative article on the leveraged buyout (LBO) of the Safeway grocery store chain. Faludi's story, which was published on the front page of the *Wall Street Journal*, examined the social costs of this highly profitable LBO.[38] Although the owners of the company were handsomely rewarded and the merger and acquisition specialists of the debt industry pocketed millions of dollars in fees,[39] Faludi and the newspaper were widely criticized in financial circles (including a virulent attack from KKR) for reporting the social consequences: professional careers ruined, long-term unemployment, sharp decline in wages, forced early retirements, spouse abuse, divorce, alcoholism, bankruptcy, and even suicide. The near collapse of KKR's spectacular LBO of RJR Nabisco, Wall Street's retreating bull market, and the surprising commercial success of Michael Moore's critique of corporate America's labor policies in his movie *Roger and Me* underscored the fragility of the go-go 1980s. For the captains of industry and corporate raiders, the fear was that the party could end before they enjoyed "last call." Therefore, the attack against Faludi, who was awarded a Pulitzer Prize, was simply an attempt to kill the messenger of bad news that middle America had been enduring for over a decade.

When 33-year-old Ron Taylor heard the news about the LBO of his new employer, Revlon, he expressed concern but did not foresee the life-altering experiences that he would soon encounter. Corporate raider Ron Perelman, whose net worth was once reported at almost $5 billion, promised to transform the company and dramatically increase its market share through his aggressive management strategies.[40] At the time, Taylor did not realize that this meant sacrificing long-term research and development for short-term profits and stock appreciation gains. But as the research lab's seats emptied and fewer new projects arrived, it became clear that the high-interest junk bonds that enabled Perelman to acquire Revlon were being partially serviced with the financial savings from the R&D department. Ron was appalled at the indiscriminate dismantling of the research teams and agonized over the years of research that were being lost. "Most people don't realize the time and human resources that are necessary for assembling a lab team . . . and the time required through trial and error to complete a project. Perelman claimed to be pruning the department through careful surgical procedures, but it was really a series of crude battlefield amputations . . . he didn't care. It was only about how to save money. I quickly realized that my time was up. . . . It was a question of what to do next."

A talented African American chemist, Ron is one of the least likely people to have a promising career derailed by such corporate machinations. An up-from-the-bootstraps achiever, he was raised in a modest working-class family from Chicago's South Side and is the first in his family to graduate from college. Inspired by his mother, a Mississippi native who emphasized the virtues of higher education, Ron earned a doctorate in organic chemistry. He rarely mentions the enormous odds he overcame in joining the exclusive club of black Ph.D. chemists, though he once remarked that "when I graduated [in 1985], you could count the number of black chemistry doctorates awarded in the entire U.S. that year on your hands and still have fingers left over." After working four years as a postdoctoral researcher at a major public university, at an annual salary of less than $20,000, Ron finally abandoned his quest to become a college professor. Numerous research publications and journal articles had failed to yield admission to the ivory tower. So Ron followed the lead of his mentor, who had resigned from a tenured academic position three years earlier for the excitement and financial rewards of the private sector. Unfortunately for Taylor, the timing of the Revlon offer in 1989 could not have been worse.

Revlon's compensation package was generous by academic standards— nearly double his university salary. Along with savings from his graduate and postgraduate stipends, Ron invested his money (nearly $10,000) in a two-bedroom condominium and believed that the American Dream was within his grasp. Less than a year after relocating to sunny San Diego, Ron found himself out of a job; he received one month of severance pay and accumulated sick and retirement benefits in May 1990. Undaunted, Ron actively sought a similar research position in the San Diego area. However, as local defense companies began downsizing after the end of the Cold War and the collapse of the real estate market deepened the recession, Ron began exploring other sources of income while coping with the frustrations of unanswered job inquiries. "After Perelman took over, we all became expendable . . . even with my doctorate in organic chemistry, the market was saturated [with well-trained chemists], and then of course the recession hit southern California. . . . As weeks [of unemployment] turned into months . . . my best friend became my credit cards . . . and I learned how to play the credit card shuffle with the best of them. . . . Without playing the shuffle, I would have had to declare bankruptcy. . . . The banks love me because I need them as much as they need me with all the losses they're taking in real estate."

Significantly, the credit card companies encouraged this financial strategy by extending new offers and higher credit limits during the recession. For example, one year after being laid off by Revlon, Ron received a letter from First Chicago Bank: "Congratulations! We are very pleased to inform you that we have increased your First Card credit limit to $9,000. We appreciate your responsible use of your First Card and commend you for the excellent record you have established. We look forward to continuing to serve your needs."

As weeks of unemployment turned into months of accumulated bills, Ron realized that his job prospects and those of his past colleagues were not going to improve in the near future. Ignoring public embarrassment, he soon reversed roles in his favorite men's clothing store; Ron became a part-time salesman at an hourly wage of less than $7. He also encouraged a friend, Kevin, to move into his condo and share living expenses. Unfortunately, Kevin was a union construction worker and had an even more difficult time finding work. Three months later, after a courtesy call from his investment counselor, Ron enrolled in a seven-week program that "licensed" him as a stockbroker. Ron immediately joined a major brokerage firm. However, he was essentially an independent contractor whose income was derived solely from commissions minus various office expenses such as rent, supplies, and insurance. Although enthusiastic about his earnings potential, Ron was unable to meet his basic living expenses and left the following year over his concerns about possibly unethical corporate sales practices.

By 1992, after affiliating with another firm in a similar sales capacity, Ron had exhausted his savings and was financing his stockbroker career through the credit card shuffle. In fact, he charged his personal computer and professional supplies on his Visa, which he paid with cash advances from his MasterCard. By the end of the year, Ron "could no longer see any light in my financial tunnel of darkness." This is mirrored by an October 8, 1992, letter from First Chicago:

> We have previously notified you that your account is past due and have told you that we would like to help you work out a plan for meeting your obligations. We may be able to accept a smaller payment than the amount shown above ($407.80 amount due, $9,225.06 balance). . . . Unless we hear from you right away, it may become necessary for us to revoke your account and recall your First Card credit cards. These actions will seriously affect your credit standing.

Ron's credit card arrears were the least of his problems. In 1993, while underemployed in temporary research positions and as a part-time salesman, Ron fell three payments behind on his condo; his modest 1985 Toyota had been paid off several years earlier. In an effort to free up his life's savings, he put the condo up for sale but without success. After nearly two years, "the vultures began to circle." A December 14, 1992, letter from HomeFedBank explained: "We sent to you our letter of 'Intent To Foreclose.' That letter expires soon and we intend to begin formal foreclosure proceedings without further notice to you. Funds in the amount of $2375.07 are needed to cure the default. . . . A trustee's sale (foreclosure) proceeding will result in additional expense to you and the possible loss of your property." Subsequent efforts to sell the condo without further financial expense proved fruitless, and an attempt by some friends to buy it for Ron to rent also fell through. Ron realized it was time to minimize his losses as he sought every possible strategy to avert personal bankruptcy. His financial crisis was a struggle for professional survival, and Ron saw his only option to be "strategic amputation" by jettisoning his depreciating asset—"Ron's Resort."

Agents of the debt industry—lawyers, mortgage relief specialists, distressed-property buyers, real estate agents—wasted no time in descending on their prey. On May 19, 1993, Ron heard from a bankruptcy attorney: "I am writing this letter to introduce myself and the services that my firm offers. I am an experienced bankruptcy attorney who provides aggressive and personalized legal representation specifically for individuals facing foreclosure." A mortgage company wrote the same day, "Mortgage relief, 'money . . . when you really need it!' . . . Don't wait for the bank to take your home away from you! I know that the pressure you are under is tremendous, and I am truly sorry that you are experiencing these heartaches." The next day, a letter from a realty company arrived: "I can help you! Never give up hope! I've done it for others, I can do it for you! It has come to my attention via county records that your loan is in default. By selling your home quickly, you can possibly save your credit and in many cases, you receive money at the close of escrow." On May 22, 1993, another attorney offered his legal services: "When creditors foreclose on your property or harass or sue, they can drive you up the wall! They are masters at power tactics. How do you stop them? . . . You need an expert on your side."

The deluge of letters from bankruptcy lawyers continued through the summer. One stated, "I acquired your name from a Notice of Default published in the San Diego County Records." Another noted, "The records at the county recorder's office show that your property was recently placed in foreclosure. . . . I have counseled many clients in the same position as you."

These letters were followed by solicitations by home mortgage lenders and realty brokers: "Don't allow the lender to acquire your property. I can help you. You have a limited amount of time left." Ron didn't need further reminders. The most painful letters were from real estate agents with hopeful news: "Don't lose your home equity and credit to foreclosure. . . . Your home . . . is scheduled for Public Auction. . . . We would like to purchase your property prior to foreclosure sale. We pay all fees and costs . . . absolutely no expense to you. You receive cash value immediately." Unfortunately, when his condo was sold in September 1993 for $79,900, Ron did not receive a cent and lost all of his equity—nearly $10,000. The mortgage company was paid in full, a $4,794 seller's commission was deducted from the sale price, and the rest went for various transactional expenses. In fact, the condo sale cost Ron an additional $2,000 in miscellaneous closing fees, but he at least achieved his goal of avoiding an official foreclosure on his credit report.

After moving to a one-bedroom apartment, Ron negotiated a repayment plan with his family of bank credit cards. With these debts approaching his annual salary, the financial future was challenging but not impossible; he continued making reduced payments on his five-figure credit card debt and avoided bankruptcy. This was possible because the regional economy was regaining its health. Ron's luck improved with a full-time temporary research assignment at the end of 1993. The next year, with a steadily growing portfolio of clients, he was offered a permanent, senior-level research position in a large corporation with a $15,000 raise over his Revlon compensation. After four years of underemployment, he finally rejoined the ranks of the middle class with a well-paying research position in a large corporation. Chemistry was his chosen profession, and he felt comfortable to be in the lab again. Even so, Ron's slow and tedious recovery was not complete. With a total compensation of over $55,000 per year, he still was being rejected for bank credit cards. His secured credit card was a constant reminder of his financial marginality, and he finally resigned himself in 1996 to the outrageous terms of a low-end MasterCard: $100 first-year membership fee for a $700 line of credit at 19.9 APR. Ron rationalized his decision as a form of "financial triage . . . I've stopped the bleeding and it's time to get out of the hospital and save the patient—me!"

Ron soon became frustrated with the continual corporate maneuvering of the chemical industry as the resurgence of mergers and acquisitions intensified his employment anxiety. Indeed, he realized that his long-term economic future was as a stockbroker. Ron continued to monitor his clients' accounts each day before work and executed trades during lunch or on personal breaks. Each passing week in the corporate jungle brought him closer to another company layoff. In 1996, while faced with an impending corporate merger, Ron "saw the handwriting on the wall, and I wasn't going to let them decide my future with a pink slip . . . rather than agonize over who and when . . . I made the decision for them. I bailed."

Although Ron is heavily dependent on "every source of available credit," his decision to return to his secondary job on a full-time basis has been professionally satisfying albeit fraught with new forms of economic insecurity. Highly volatile stock markets yield unstable broker commissions. Immediately after the sharp stock market corrections of late summer 1999, he was seriously concerned that his carefully cultivated client base might leave him after suffering substantial financial losses. Furthermore, rapid changes in the new economy make his old 9-to-5 routine seem like part-time employment. For him, the incessant demands of "market research" have replaced his primary "leisure activity"—sleep. Still, he laughs about the popular bumper sticker "I pay MasterCard with my Visa" and says that "if this [bull stock] market goes in the drink, then I'm back to Z & Z selling men's clothes." Nevertheless, he sees his future in trading stocks rather than monitoring reactive agents or organic syntheses. For this opportunity, he is grateful to his credit cards, since millions of other displaced workers are only one corporate downsizing away from playing the credit card shuffle—again.

Rising Educational Achievement and Faltering Economic Realities: Coping with the Changing U.S. Labor Market

Today, the lingering effects of student loan obligations and personal bankruptcy as strategies for coping with credit card debt can persist for several decades. The impact is especially burdensome to single women, who were the fastest-growing subgroup of bankruptcy petitioners in the 1990s.[41] As illustrated by Catherine, a 50-something social policy specialist in the New York City Mayor's Office, neither of these options has provided an easy escape from her credit card debts. As a recent survivor of Chapter 7 bankruptcy, Catherine offers a warning to students who routinely shift their credit card debts into federally insured loan programs: "Federal student loans cannot be washed away with consumer bankruptcy." In the early 1970s, Catherine started transferring her credit card debt into student loans. She is still paying for purchases that she charged over 20 years ago—even after filing for bankruptcy. This is because personal bankruptcy and unemployment can defer but not erase student loan obligations.

When Catherine completed her undergraduate degree in 1971, she graduated without any financial debts. Of course, tuition was free at City University of New York (CUNY), and she lived at home with her parents while employed part-time; Catherine worked in a gift shop during high school and in a Lord & Taylor retail store while in college. For Catherine, whose parents constantly reminded her of their financial difficulties during the Great Depression, personal debt was anathema. Her father refused to buy household items like a TV or stereo through installment credit programs at nearby department stores. Although earning only a moderate salary as a municipal civil servant, he adhered to the cognitive connect by limiting household purchases to available savings. Like most members of this generation, he viewed personal debt with fear and moral disdain. According to Catherine, her family regarded debt as a social stigma, "a kind of Jewish Calvinist guilt thing." The prevailing cultural emphasis on saving even pervaded familial attitudes toward her impending work career: "Make sure you take a job with a good pension plan . . . save now and you will not have to worry later . . . for retirement."

After a stint as an editorial assistant with a major publishing house in New York City, Catherine enrolled in a master's degree program at Washington University—debt-free (including her bank credit cards). She saw graduate school as a means for professional advancement that would enable her to avoid personal debt. Initially, Catherine's scholarship paid for tuition and a modest monthly stipend. Over the next two years, however, tuition increased and her scholarship was reduced. At this time, Catherine became more dependent on her credit cards and began "carrying an increasing balance." Initially, she took out student loans in order to defray living and educational expenses. A good "investment" that even her family would approve, the interest rate of the National Direct Student Loan program was only 3 percent and the Guaranteed Student Loan Program was 7 percent. Although Catherine justified her student loans as a "necessary evil," due to escalating college costs, her view toward them quickly changed. One day, while Catherine was "venting" about the financial and emotional costs of her escalating credit card debts, a fellow graduate student offered the astoundingly simple solution: "Why pay 18 percent on your credit cards when you can get a student loan and defer the interest at 3 percent?" Indeed, thought Catherine, why not? When Catherine finished her master's degree in 1974, she had accumulated $5,000 in student loans, which included at least $2,000 of credit card bills. At the time, Catherine thought she had made a smart decision. After all, she saved on the higher interest rates and now had a job to pay off her student loans.

When Catherine became the educational director of a St. Louis theater company, she looked forward to enjoying a social life in the real world. After seven years of college, she felt entitled to "enjoy the finer things in life" such as assembling a professional wardrobe from Saks Fifth Avenue and Neiman Marcus. The problem was that the low salaries of the nonprofit sector contrasted sharply with those in its social networks of economically successful and culturally sophisticated professionals. For Catherine, this meant that her job required "champagne taste with a draft-beer pocketbook." As she explained, "Why should the bourgeoisie have all the nice things?" In 1974, her first bank credit card had a $400 limit that was quickly exhausted. Catherine received another bank card with a higher credit limit to go with her growing collection of retail, travel, and gasoline cards. During the mid-1970s, moreover, inflation began its rapid ascent. Catherine realized that credit cards could be used to beat the system and believed that "the more you spent, the more you saved." These macroeconomic circumstances profoundly influenced her decision to abandon the cognitive connect between earnings and consumption. In fact, she felt justified in "no longer differentiating between needs and wants." Unfortunately, Catherine was laid off at the end of 1977 and survived on unemployment compensation and her credit cards. After several months of fruitlessly searching for a job, Catherine returned to New York and moved in with her parents.

In 1979, Catherine joined a market research firm and married a Middle Eastern graduate student. After a year, irreconcilable cultural differences led to divorce and her enrollment at Rutgers University for a second master's degree. Over the next two years, she received $10,000 in student loans and used $5,000 to pay off her various credit cards. At this point in her life, Catherine decided to make another career shift and enrolled in a graduate program in an elite East Coast university. She accepted an administrative position that paid her tuition and most of her living expenses with a $19,000 annual salary. Over the next five years, Catherine managed her budget without assuming additional student loans. In 1987, she received an $8,000 fellowship to conduct her research overseas and quit her administrative position. To pay for her living and travel expenses, Catherine borrowed $8,000 in federal student loans. During this period, moreover, the credit limits on her bank cards began to rise sharply. For instance, she charged a $3,000 personal computer on her MasterCard and supplemented her modest fellowship stipend with charges on her other credit cards. Overall, Catherine received $16,000 in student loans while completing her graduate degree in the early 1990s; about half was used to pay off her bank credit cards.

Catherine returned from her field research in the fall of 1988 and began working as a program specialist in a nonprofit organization. Her salary was "in the low twenties," which she viewed "as a temporary sacrifice while in the homestretch of [writing] my thesis." After completing her degree in 1991, Catherine felt justified in indulging a higher standard of living, which included new clothes, theater tickets, a more powerful computer, costly cosmetics, and dining with friends. Unfortunately, her job search was stymied by the recession, and her material "wants" became increasingly satisfied by the rising credit limits on her bank cards. In the early 1990s, Catherine's salary did not keep up with inflation. However, this financial crunch was alleviated by her available plastic money as the credit limits on her bank cards climbed sharply. By 1993, Catherine had become dependent upon the credit card shuffle simply to pay her monthly bills. Over the following year, with nearly $20,000 in total credit card debt, Catherine began to explore personal bankruptcy as an option for regaining control over her personal finances. After all, she declared, "Why should I feel so bad after all the S&Ls that went broke and the corporations that filed for bankruptcy?"

In the summer of 1996, after more than five years of actively searching for a higher-paying job, Catherine was laid off. The nonprofit sector was implementing serious budget cuts, and many senior-level staff were accepting positions at lower salaries. To make matters worse, she already had almost maxed out her credit cards, so these once helpful friends could offer little assistance during this stressful period of professional rejection and financial crisis. Catherine painfully recalls how quickly her "credit cards turned on me when I became delinquent." Although Catherine was able to defer her student loans while unemployed, she could not negotiate a similar arrangement with the credit card companies. The situation angers her. "If I could have paid them, dammit, I would have. I was unemployed. They gave me no choice but to file [for bankruptcy]."

Without any serious job prospects, Catherine tearfully accepted her predicament and filed for Chapter 7 bankruptcy in the fall of 1996. This was such a "gut-wrenching" decision for Catherine—due to the personal and professional stigma it entailed—that she has still not informed her family or closest friends. "It's been hell. I don't need to hear my brother moralize about my behavior . . . or scrutinize my spending . . . my friends know I've been through a tough time . . . but no one wants to be with a loser and it's best that they think that I've survived my difficulties . . . Besides, Americans respect winners, especially those that overcome the odds."[42] With the guidance of an attorney, Catherine had nearly $23,000 in credit card debts discharged by the bankruptcy court. However, the court would not absolve her from the financial responsibility of her remaining federal student loans. Catherine estimates that of a total of approximately $21,000 (she had paid off her undergraduate loans and some other graduate loans), over one-half—

at least $12,000—is attributable to transferring her earlier credit card debts into student loans.

After a two-year job search, Catherine found a position paying an annual salary of $37,000, but finds it still a stretch to pay her modest living expenses and nondischargeable student loans. An impending raise, which will inch her closer to $40,000, is crucial for Catherine because "I'm not a spring chicken anymore . . . I need to repay loans from my pension and start catching up with all of the years I missed [contributing to a retirement account] while in school and unemployed. This raise will not appreciably improve my standard of living." Furthermore, if not for her rent-controlled apartment of nearly twenty years, "I would be leading the workers' revolution. . . . There is no way a single woman can survive on my salary and pay a market-rate rent in New York City."

As illustrated by Catherine's experience, personal bankruptcy is not the financial panacea that is commonly portrayed in the media. Indeed, the flood of preapproved credit card applications is unrelenting—the junk mail of the 1990s—but the reality is "It's still extremely difficult for me to get any credit. It took me almost three years [after bankruptcy] to be mainstreamed from my secured [credit] card to a regular credit card. . . . The credit limit is only $1,100. College students who've never had jobs get more [credit] than that. . . . It's a stark reminder of how fragile my finances are." Without the second income of a spouse or live-in friend, Catherine knows her future household finances will remain shaky. "I can't afford my [impending] hospital bills [for minor surgery], but I can't afford to lose my health and not be able to support myself. . . . After all, who knows what will be left of the welfare state when I retire? . . . I just hope that I can eat *and* pay my credit card bills [in retirement]."

It Takes Two to Tango . . . and Pay the Bills: Struggling with Divorce and the Suitors of the Financial Services Industry

Geoff Matheny remembers vividly the first time he heard the Nation's Bank advertisement for a home equity loan. It was the spring of 1998. He was driving to work in Washington, D.C., and singing along with a golden oldie. Suddenly the radio program shifted from the upbeat Elton John standard "Bennie and the Jets" to the depressing topic of his generation's debt problems: "The 'D' word . . . it's what you get into when you buy on credit. . . . It's not necessarily bad . . . with debt consolidation. . . . Why not make *it* work for you instead of you working for *it?* My monthly payments are less after consolidating high-interest loans, and they are tax deductible!"

Talk about "turning a vice into virtue," thought the 40-year-old Geoff as he reflected on his personal odyssey from convenience user in the mid-1980s to over $70,000 in credit card debt and nearly $40,000 in home equity loans in 1999. In 2000, Geoff's consumer debt was more than double his income, with interest rates ranging from 8.9 to 27.7 percent. More instructive, however, are the unexpected twists and turns in Geoff's life that have profoundly shaped his ambivalent attitudes toward consumer credit and the enormous growth of his personal debts. Indeed, Geoff's conservative views toward debt challenge the conventional stereotypes of maxed-out consumers as profligate spenders. This is because the most important factor in his precarious financial condition is Geoff's divorce.

When Geoff married in 1986, his attitudes toward credit were primarily influenced by his mother's fear of debt as a sign of personal shame. Money was tight during Geoff's childhood as his father's business ventures produced a succession of financial disappointments. A Protestant in his religious upbringing, Geoff perceived economic debt as a moral choice in the conduct of one's personal affairs. For him, debt was not simply an impersonal statistic in an accounting ledger. It was a social indicator of personal problems and potential failure, the moral equivalent of the Puritans' scarlet letter in the realm of personal finance. By the time he entered college in 1975, he had been saving for over a decade to pay for his education, and he continued working part-time jobs during the school year and semester breaks. Although education was highly valued by his parents, their modest income did not permit them to contribute to Geoff's university expenses.

Geoff's former wife, in comparison, was less "virtuous" in managing her financial affairs. Although Mary was influenced by Calvinist views toward debt through her religious upbringing, her behavior alternated between Puritan thriftiness and impulsive consumption that was primarily fueled by her credit cards. This Jekyll-and-Hyde approach to debt was subconsciously reinforced by her father's binge spending; his affluent parents frequently bailed him out of financial crises and six marriages until their deaths in the early 1990s. Fortunately, Mary's college education was largely paid by her grandparents, whose travails during the Great Depression greatly influenced their frugality and long-term economic planning. Even so, their financial wisdom had little effect on Mary, as she brought considerable debt into the marriage, including credit cards, while Geoff's debts were limited to college student loans.

Geoff tried to maintain a household budget that was shaped by the Calvinist-inspired ethos of maintaining equilibrium between earnings and consumption. The objective is to define one's standard of living based on *present* income (total earnings) and *future* (expected/unexpected) expenses. This attitudinal approach, which eschews debt in favor of "saving for a rainy day," was bolstered by his grandparents' experiences during the depression that reinforced the values of thrift and economic sacrifice; his paternal grandfather lost his prosperous business and opulent home in the mid-1930s. Not surprisingly, when Geoff received his first credit card in 1984, he used it primarily for convenience and rarely carried a balance.

By the early 1990s, Geoff was losing the behavioral battle of adhering to the cognitive connect. Although Mary worked part-time while in graduate school, the birth of the couple's child followed by the purchase of a house increased their financial pressures. The unrelenting solicitations of easy credit—jumping from 2 billion per year in the early 1990s to over 3 billion in the late 1990s—proved too enticing to ignore. Plastic money became the carefree currency for their postponed purchases and delinquent bills: business suits, car repairs, day care expenses, home products, and even college fees. Furthermore, escalating marital discord over household finances could be temporarily ameliorated with bank credit cards. Disputes about long-overdue vacations, well-earned evenings out, or bridal-shower gifts could now be avoided through the magic of plastic.

The short-lived domestic peace was an emotional relief from the incessant heated arguments with Mary, who insisted that their financial difficulties were a temporary phase of their marriage. After all, she insisted, they would be enjoying the economic prosperity of a dual-income household soon after she finished her degree. In the meantime, they "deserved to relax from the financial strains" and not have to worry about the additional stress of asking for loans from family members. As Geoff recalls, Mary explained that "some people borrow money from their families but have to explain why [they need the money] . . . and then are reminded [of the financial help] for the rest of their lives. . . . This way we're just borrowing for a short time [from MasterCard] . . . no one has to know. I'll have no problem finding a job and paying them off."

The unbridled optimism of people like Mary fundamentally shaped consumer expectations and spending attitudes during the 1980s. More important, it provided an opportunity for the credit card industry to intensify its attack on the traditional economic ethos by encouraging impulsive consumption through sophisticated mass marketing campaigns. Such narcissist advertising promotions as Pepsi's "me generation" and Nike's "Just do it" touted the material entitlements of middle-class life and transformed "fun" into a commodity to be purchased.[43] And, by promoting instant gratification, they began recasting the moral stigma of debt into a common feature of modern society. As a result, the newfound ability to satisfy individual "wants" meant that the cognitive distinction between "needs" and "desires" would become increasingly blurred.

This cognitive breakdown is illustrated by the dramatic change in the consumption patterns of Jennifer Jones following her graduation from high school in 1994. "'The [banks] would send me an application, I would fill it out, and lo and behold, there would be a credit card in the mail. If I saw something I wanted, I would just take out a credit card and buy it. I wouldn't plan ahead for it. I wouldn't think how am I going to pay for this bill when it comes. I was out of control.'" Three years and eight credit cards later, the 23-year-old Virginia administrative assistant could no longer afford the minimum payments on her nearly $10,000 in credit card debt and was on the verge of filing for personal bankruptcy.[44]

When Geoff divorced, four years after completing graduate school, Mary had finally finished school and was beginning her professional career. To Geoff's chagrin, he never enjoyed the promised financial benefits of a second household income that could have quickly paid off the couple's mounting consumer debts. Instead, the marriage ended, and Geoff assumed half of Mary's credit card debts, substantial legal bills, a 10-year-old car, and out-of-state rental property. Furthermore, the divorce settlement included $550 in monthly child support even though Mary's salary was greater than Geoff's and she received the couple's house, which included an income-generating boarder. In addition, Mary's boyfriend moved into the house the same day the divorce became final and a few months later became Mary's third husband. Today, Mary has the financial stability of two incomes, tax advantages of homeownership, and Geoff's monthly child support payments.

For Geoff, who was struggling on his modest $43,000 annual salary in a federal agency in Washington, D.C., and with over $300 monthly in student loan payments, divorce entailed a sharp decline in his standard of living. His experience is not atypical. There have been over 1.1 million divorces annually over the past two decades (see Table 5.2),[45] but these statistics fail to convey the enormous human and economic costs of family disruptions. For those who do not remarry, postdivorce reality is a higher cost of living and much less income.[46] Besides child support payments, Geoff faces the divorce hangover of credit card debts, legal bills, higher insurance costs, and the expenses of establishing a new household. He laughs about wanting to "throw a divorce party" with a banner proclaiming the civil rights slogan "Free at last, free at last. Oh thank God, I'm free at last," but was too embarrassed to invite friends to his modest rented house with its spartan furnishings.

TABLE 5.2   U.S. Marriages and Divorces 1980-1998

	Marriage		Divorce	
Year	Number	Rate	Number	Rate
1980	2,406,708	10.6	1,182,000	5.2
1981	2,438,000	10.6	1,219,000	5.3
1982	2,495,000	10.8	1,180,000	5.1
1983	2,444,000	10.5	1,179,000	5.0
1984	2,487,000	10.5	1,155,000	4.9
1985	2,425,000	10.2	1,187,000	5.0
1986	2,400,000	10.0	1,159,000	4.8
1987	2,421,000	9.9	1,157,000	4.8
1988	2,389,000	9.7	1,183,000	4.8
1989	2,404,000	9.7	1,163,000	4.7
1990	2,448,000	9.8	1,175,000	4.7
1991	2,371,000	9.4	1,187,000	4.7
1992	2,362,000	9.2	1,215,000	4.8
1993	2,334,000	9.0	1,187,000	4.6
1994	2,362,000	9.1	1,191,000	4.6
1995	2,336,000	8.9	1,169,000	4.4
1996	2,334,000	8.8	1,150,000	4.3
1997	2,384,000	8.9	1,163,000	4.3
1998	2,256,000	8.4	955,000	3.5

SOURCE: U.S. Department of Health and Human Services, National Center for Health Statistics. www.dhhs.gov.

During this period, new "suitors" began calling through the mail on a regular basis. First, they invited Geoff to join their exclusive memberships. Among these were the MBNA "Platinum Plus [MasterCard], the new standard of excellence, offered by invitation only, no annual fee. Credit line up to $50,000 . . . 2.9% introductory APR preapproved invitation"; and FirstUSA with its "3.9% fixed introductory APR." Others, like Citibank Visa, announced "special offers" of "5.9% APR on all balance transfers," while Chase MasterCard trumped its competitors with a 9.9% fixed APR. At the time of his divorce, Geoff was appreciative of the banks' solicitations. He thought these low-interest credit cards would enable him to regain control over his finances by buying him time to obtain a conventional debt consolidation loan. After all, with a part-time consulting job, he could soon begin tackling his growing credit card bills while perfecting the art of the credit card shuffle. Indeed, he learned to "surf" his high-interest credit balances to the lowest introductory rates. When the introductory interest rates had expired at the end of 1994, Geoff transferred the card balances with the highest interest rates to a

$10,000 tax-deductible debt consolidation loan. This enabled him to negoti-
ate lower interest rates and higher credit lines on the zero-balance credit cards,
which resulted in the secondary transfer of high-interest credit card debt to
the reduced-rate cards. Indeed, Geoff otherwise could not have paid for the
increasingly frequent repairs on his aging Toyota.

The following year proved to be even more financially disastrous. His
elderly father's illness and subsequent divorce forced Geoff to support two
households on a single income. As an only child, Geoff felt obligated to pay
his father's mortgage and car payments while he recovered. With over
$35,000 in high-interest credit card debt, Geoff surfed $30,000 to a second
mortgage on his father's home the following year. Due to federal tax laws
that favor mortgage debt, this became an increasingly popular trend in the
1990s. According to a 1998 study sponsored by the Federal Reserve, 48 percent of second mortgages and 38 percent of home equity loans are used to
pay high-interest credit card debts.[47] For Geoff, all he had to show for this
bank loan was a "new" 7-year-old Mazda and a used computer and printer.
More disturbingly, the additional $410 monthly payment as well as his rent
were frequently being paid by "courtesy checks" from his bank credit cards.
During the summer of 1996, costly auto repairs convinced Geoff to buy a
more reliable, new car. This led to a charge of $3,500 on his MasterCard
for the down payment. Geoff justified this decision by insisting that the additional $300 monthly payment would be partly offset by lower gasoline
and maintenance expenses.

Geoff thought he had "hit financial rock bottom" in 1997. Little did he
know that he could and would sink much deeper. At the time, Geoff described himself as an "accident victim in the ER [emergency room]" with "a
tourniquet to stop the [financial] bleeding." Geoff slashed his living expenses by nearly $400 per month by moving into a modest two-bedroom
apartment in an area "where my colleagues would be afraid to park their
cars." He "finally saw light at the end of a very dark tunnel" with the final
year of his student loans approaching and the recent refinance of his rental
property that paid off nearly $15,000 in credit card debt. Furthermore,
Geoff was recommended for a job promotion, and because his retirement
account had benefited handsomely from the surging stock market, he expected to borrow from his pension to pay off the remaining credit card debt.
To Geoff's shock, his promotion was rejected, and he became embroiled in
costly litigation over his unfair treatment. This led Geoff to seek more lucrative work in the private sector. Unfortunately, after seven months of part-
time employment, he had to accept a full-time job at a lower salary.

In 1998, Geoff "finally hit the financial brick wall." As he maxed out on all but four of his sixteen credit cards, the banking industry began implementing more stringent lending standards. For the first time, solicitations for debt consolidation loans exceeded those for preapproved credit cards, and secured credit cards "with as little as a $49 deposit" outnumbered regular credit card applications. More sobering was the response of the credit card companies as Geoff's financial distress worsened. On the one hand, Geoff was grateful that his credit cards had enabled him "not to panic" during his employment search and take the most desirable job. They also enabled him to hire an attorney and litigate his lawsuit. On the other hand, they were creating enormous emotional strain.

Although Geoff had never been delinquent on any of his credit cards, the banks began a "vicious assault on my personal character" beginning in 1998. Over twenty applications for additional credit cards were rejected over the next two years. Bank of America abruptly slashed his credit line from $7,000 to $900, and a retail credit card was reduced from $1,500 to $200. Two other retail credit cards were suddenly canceled, and the only bank credit card that did not have a balance—Geoff's emergency "cash"—was also terminated. When Geoff inquired about these actions, company representatives responded that they were concerned about customers maxing out their credit cards with cash advances and purchases (often for resale, such as computers) before filing for personal bankruptcy. In response, Geoff asked family members to cosign a $15,000 loan and obtain credit cards in their names in order for him to continue credit card surfing while he regained his financial equilibrium. The latter was especially important, since many banks began raising interest rates on his credit cards. MBNA jumped from 15.9 percent to 22.9 percent, and FirstUSA climbed from the introductory rate of 2.9 percent to 17.9 percent and suddenly rose to 21.9 percent and then to 27.7 percent. To add insult to injury, the minimum monthly payment of the FirstUSA card was less than the monthly finance charge.

Geoff describes his current economic condition as "I'm out of intensive care and slowly on the road to recovery." Although he occasionally suffers the embarrassment of having his credit card declined, a cinematic flashback of Will Smith in *Enemy of the State,* he is now able to begin paying down his debts. He landed a new job that increased his annual income to over $54,000, and his car note and student loans were recently retired. Furthermore, unlike assetless debtors, Geoff has benefited from the robust economy: His retirement account has more than doubled over the past five years; his rental property has appreciated nearly 30 percent over the past three years. Geoff intends to use these financial gains as collateral to pay down his credit cards. Furthermore, he invested his last Gold card in the stock market in 1998, and it has provided impressive returns: "My investment nearly tripled. Last year I paid my rent for several months as well as numerous car payments [with stock sales]. . . . I probably would have filed for bankruptcy if the market had tanked before I cashed out. . . . Fortunately, I thought that the dot-coms were going to crash, and I pulled out [my money] just in time."

Interestingly, Geoff's improving financial condition is not reflected in his current mail or credit rating. He still is rejected for new credit cards, and most of his credit card interest rates are between 19.9 and 27.7 percent. "Imagine," sighs Geoff, "I was even rejected for a $1,000 K-mart credit card. I applied just to break my string of [credit card] rejections." His most common solicitations are from Capital One Bank. These letters are designed to appeal to those desperate for consumer credit. Some convey the excitement of winning the lottery: "This is not a bill. You have just been *guaranteed approval* for a new Visa account. (See inside for the amount of your guaranteed credit line.)" Another explains, "We've reserved a Visa Gold card in your name . . . no security deposit [required] . . . use your card to buy groceries, fill your gas tank or even buy plane tickets . . . buy much, much more than if you had to pay cash. . . . You can use your card in thousands of money machines (probably including the one down the street). So you never really have to worry about running short of cash."

In a consoling and nonjudgmental tone, other Capital One mailings offer advice: "Forget about your credit history. Let's talk about your future. . . . Everyone deserves a second chance. Financial freedom could be just around the corner! Simply send in a security deposit of as little as $49 and receive a Visa or MasterCard with a credit line up to $400! You don't have to send any money right now. Just call the toll-free number below . . ." Geoff is sarcastic: "Can you see me calling a [Capital One] rep and asking for a $49 increase in my credit limit?" He contends, moreover, that the most recent credit card solicitations feature the highest finance charges.

> Look at this mailing for the Aspire Diamond Visa. You might think that it is a good deal because it states "For immediate acceptance processing, respond on-line at www.AspireYes.com!" Well, look at the microscopic fine print . . . "your APR may vary, but will in no event be less than 29.00%. . . . Your delinquency APR may vary, but will in no event be less than 35.00%." What happened to the usury laws?

Today, Geoff's suitors reflect the polarity of the credit card moral divide. The American Express solicitations for its new Blue card trumpet "Zero interest for six months" as a middle-class entitlement, while Capital One and other high-interest cards underscore the reality of Geoff's maxed-out predicament. The most noticeable trend, however, is the arrival of "pre-approved home equity loans for up to $70,000 or more" that promise "Here's the easy way to cut your bills up to 50% and save hundreds of extra dollars each month!" According to Geoff, "Upland Mortgage and Citifinancial are the most aggressive. . . . If you look at their letters, they don't even tell you what the interest rate is, and you have to look carefully at the fine print to understand that there are lots of closing costs involved. . . . No wonder Citibank wants me to pay off their Visa with a home equity loan."

Although Geoff's attorney and many close friends have recommended personal bankruptcy, he has adamantly rejected this advice: "Bankruptcy is not an option for me. If it means working a couple of extra years instead of retiring, so be it. I will honor my financial obligations rather than impugn my hard-earned reputation." In fact, he is grateful that his credit cards offered the choice of "short-term [economic] sacrifices rather than long-term [emotional] misery of a dysfunctional marriage." As Geoff explains, "How can you place a monetary value on escaping a disastrous marriage and the possibility of finding a fulfilling relationship in the future?" Ironically, he acknowledges that a solution to his financial woes "is to marry a professional woman with a comparable income. . . . Next time, however, I will marry for the right reason. I will marry only for love."

Nevertheless, Geoff admits that he occasionally regrets the choices that the availability of easy consumer credit provided, such as pursuing costly litigation: "I definitely could not have continued my case and would have avoided at least $30,000 of [consumer] debt." And he worries about the consequences of offering large lines of credit to inexperienced and naive consumers—especially the working poor and teenagers. Not surprisingly, the latter groups are the most desirable and rapidly growing market segments of the Credit Card Nation. Indeed, the enormous expansion of consumer credit cards on American college campuses is contributing to major social shifts, with potentially profound future consequences.

Credit Cards on Campus

The Social Consequences
of Student Credit Dependency

Introduction

On June 8, 1999, the Consumer Federation of America (CFA) convened a major press conference on student credit card debt at the National Press Club in Washington, D.C. The program featured leading consumer advocates, mothers of two college students whose credit card debts contributed to their recent suicides, and the release of the first major academic study of student credit card debt that was based on both in-depth interviews and cross-sectional survey data.[1] The highly publicized event drew national attention to the previously neglected social consequences of credit card debt. The topic was discussed in front-page newspaper stories, magazine articles, newspaper editorials, morning and evening television news programs, cable TV interviews, and radio call-in shows.[2]

Although Americans have become inured to the tremendous growth of the national debt and economic consequences of corporate mergers, the newly reported social impacts of student debt struck a chord in the national consciousness. Most Americans had assumed that college administrators were responsible for providing a safe, nurturing environment where parents could expect that their children would acquire the personal skills and professional experiences necessary for a rewarding future. Instead, it was a national revelation that young lives were being ruined by credit card debt that led to dropping out of college (misclassified as academic casualties), health problems (physical and emotional),[3] family conflicts, bankruptcy, job rejections (due to poor credit histories), loan denials, inability to rent apartments, professional school rejection, and even suicide. Many people were aware of anecdotal stories of family members or friends whose collegiate careers were disrupted or abruptly ended by credit card debts. However, most had been persuaded by the assurances of the credit card industry that the problem affected only a small number of students (3–4 percent)[4] and most of them would suffer only a minor financial inconvenience after beginning their work careers.[5]

The personal testimonies of parents whose children committed suicide challenged the benign image of student credit card debt as a new adolescent rite of passage of the "Just do it" and "Shop 'til you drop" generation.[6] Their anguish resonated with the concerns of all Americans who realized that their own sons and daughters were at risk of the predatory marketing policies of the credit card industry. Janne O'Donnell described the despair of her 22-year-old son, Sean, a National Merit finalist and a liberal arts "letters" major, who succumbed to the temptations of easy money:

> A week before Sean killed himself [we] had a long talk about his debts and about his future. He told me he had no idea how to get out of his financial mess and didn't see much of a future for himself. He had wanted to go to law school but didn't think he could get a loan to pay tuition because he owed so much on his cards. . . . Sean tried to pay off his debts. He went through credit counseling but fell further behind . . . and moved [from the University of Dallas] back home with us to attend the University of Oklahoma. He was working 2 jobs while attending OU. Still he couldn't make ends meet. . . . By the time he died he had 12 cards including 1 MasterCard, 2 Visas, Neiman-Marcus, Saks 5th Avenue, Macy's, Marshall Fields, Conoco, and Discover. How those companies can justify giving credit to a person making $5.15 an hour is beyond me. . . . Credit must be based on the applicant's present income—not on potential to earn. . . . There simply has to be some limits set on credit card companies before more students end up in bankruptcy or dead.[7]

O'Donnell later described the emotional pain of making the difficult decision not to help Sean with his mounting credit card bills. In previous years, Janne and her husband had paid some of his debts. In retrospect, however, they believed that their assistance had actually been a "disservice" by not "holding him responsible for his debts." At the time, Sean expressed his desire to attend graduate school and become a lawyer. With his younger brother preparing to start college in the fall, Janne explained that "we thought our money should be spent paying for Tim's bachelor's degree rather than graduate school for Sean. It was a [difficult] choice of allocating our [limited] resources." As Janne pondered this agonizing dilemma, she related that "I don't know if it was the right decision, and I do not know if Sean would be here today if we had paid his bills. It haunts us still."

Sadly, Janne and her family are regularly reminded of their personal tragedy due to ongoing debt collection activities. The aggressive tactics of one particular bill collector continue to haunt her: "He called about Sean's credit card debt [a year later]. I left two messages explaining his death and where to get a copy of his death certificate. I just couldn't believe it when I received the third phone call. . . . [This time] he insisted that I pay [Sean's] debt. I'll never forget [that conversation] . . . he said to me 'Wouldn't you want to honor his memory by paying off his debts?' I was so angry. If I had the money, I would have paid them [earlier] and Sean might be with us today." The O'Donnells need no further reminders of their ordeal, but Chase and other credit card companies still mail preapproved credit card applications in Sean's name to their home. Worse, "the creditors still call but not as often."

To the displeasure of the credit card industry, the national debate continues to intensify over the seriousness of the student debt problem and who is ultimately responsible. Criticism of the industry's methodologically flawed research (which has been previously used to soften and systematically underestimate student credit card debt)[8] elicited a flurry of journalistic and academic investigations that confirmed many key findings of Manning's 1999 CFA study. Significantly, the most striking feature of the ongoing furor over predatory marketing to college and high school students has been the adamant refusal of the credit card industry to acknowledge publicly any culpability. In fact, industry representatives have rejected all requests to participate in live national television or radio programs that specifically address the issue of student credit card debt. As CNN reporter Brooks Jackson concluded the "Headline News" story on the CFA press conference, he explained that "credit card companies say most students use credit responsibly, but the representatives [of] Visa, MasterCard, [and] American Express would not go on camera to discuss this story." The following week, Visa withdrew its spokesperson from an interview on *Good Morning America* that included O'Donnell and Manning. A miffed Diane Sawyer curtly commented that "the credit card companies, by the way, would not come on our program to talk with us [about the CFA study]."[9]

For the credit card companies, their initial public relations strategy was to dismiss the scholarly criticism and its relevance to the public as unrepresentative of national trends and the student suicides as anecdotal anomalies. By ignoring the negative publicity, they gambled on the expectation that the public's attention would shift during the summer to baseball pennant races and family vacations—financed by friendly credit cards of course. Instead, the groundswell of opposition to credit card marketing and lending policies led to mounting public pressures for corrective action in the form of federal bills and legislative amendments as well as the introduction of restrictive marketing bills in at least twelve state legislatures. The most prominent federal response is HR-3142, the College Student Credit Card Protection Act, which was introduced by U.S. Congresswoman Louise Slaughter (D-N.Y.) in October 1999.[10]

Additionally, student groups, parents, and alumni have intensified pressure on college administrators to ban or restrict credit card marketing on their campuses. During the academic year 2000–2001, over 800 colleges and universities formulated official policies that restricted on-campus credit card marketing, and over 300 other schools were considering similar restrictions. Significantly, the most effective policies have been instituted by small liberal-arts colleges where the loss of even a few students has social and economic repercussions. Conversely, the 250 largest public schools with their highly profitable student populations are where credit card companies most aggressively direct their marketing energies. This includes the threat of potential lawsuits against uncooperative universities, persuasive tactics of corporate lobbyists, major donations, and, of course, lucrative marketing contracts. The most prominent example is the seven-year, $16.5 million deal with the University of Tennessee. The latter has provoked greater public scrutiny of "exclusive licensing" agreements with colleges that generate millions of dollars in annual fees.[11]

In addition to the public scrutiny of college administrators in providing a safe environment for students, there has been greater attention to the role of colleges and universities in promoting complacent attitudes toward personal debt and to the need for effective credit card education and financial literacy programs. The latter focus is reminiscent of the beer industry's "drink responsibly" campaign, which publicly lauds cautious attitudes toward alcohol consumption but loathes the impact on its financial bottom line. Unfortunately, the current business climate of higher education rewards revenue-enhancement programs over instructional excellence. This explains why many college administrators are willing to sacrifice the long-term interests of their students and their institutions for the short-term financial inducements of the credit card industry.[12]

From Part-Time Jobs to Full-Time Debt:
The Political Economy of Middle-Class Indenturement

The post–World War II American Dream is based upon the twin pillars of higher education (vocational, junior college, university) and homeownership. Both entail personal sacrifice, long-term planning, and increasingly higher levels of debt. In fact, these are the only "investments" that Americans consider worthy of long-term indebtedness.[13] Over the past generation, however, these exalted accoutrements of middle-class status have become increasingly difficult to achieve. Today, baby boomers have found that homeownership requires two incomes rather than one and typically a 30-year rather than a 10- or 15-year mortgage.[14] Furthermore, the modest cost of the boomers' college education stands in sharp contrast to the pricey reality of their children's. Beginning with the G.I. Bill, which offered financial assistance to World War II veterans, the federal government has provided most college financial aid through free grants. This was expanded with the enactment of the 1965 Higher Education Act—the cornerstone of the boomers' financial aid entitlement—which produced the need-based Pell Grant Program in 1972 as well as the present student loan system.

Since the 1970s, the cost of attending college has risen dramatically. In 1975, Bruce Springsteen was the "boss" of American campuses as manual typewriters clattered to the beat of "Born to Run" on stereophonic LP records and 8-track cassette players. Floor-level concert tickets to a Springsteen concert cost $6 to $7, and Volkswagen Beetles and Ford Pintos retailed for under $2,000. The student staple—a six-pack of Old Milwaukee beer—could be purchased for less than a dollar. Summer employment, federal work-study, and part-time jobs during the academic year financed a substantial portion of college expenses even at the federal minimum wage of $2.10 per hour. This was especially true for students living with their parents and commuting to public colleges; in-state tuition for full-time students enrolled in state universities averaged less than $800 for the academic year. Overall, a four-year undergraduate degree at a public university (including tuition, room, board, and fees) averaged about $11,300 in 1975.[15]

Even private universities were affordable to students without much financial assistance from their families. At American University in Washington, D.C., for example, the cost of tuition ($2,880), housing ($954), and board ($588) totaled $4,422 during the 1975–1976 academic year; an undergraduate degree at a private university (including tuition, room, board, and fees) beginning in 1975 averaged about $26,400 for all four years (see Appendix 5).[16] In 1979, students at a moderately priced private school like American

University who were primarily responsible for financing their education typically graduated with less than $5,000 in student loans; most left school with less than $2,000 in debts due to the availability of federal grants. For those attending public colleges, the respective debt levels were less than half that of their private school counterparts. Furthermore, the financial burden of student loans was eased considerably with the deductibility of interest on federal income taxes through the late 1980s and the double-digit inflation of the late 1970s and early 1980s. Therefore, a virtually debt-free undergraduate degree was the norm for the baby-boomer generation as college expenses were paid with personal savings, college jobs, family contributions, federal grants, federally subsidized student loans, and high inflation. Significantly, as these students left their college campuses, a Visa was more likely to be needed for studying abroad than for paying university fees.

Today, the boomers' children confront immensely different social, cultural, and financial pressures. Lauryn Hill, Celine Dion, and Sheryl Crow rule on campus CD and DVD players, and students are more likely to spellcheck their course assignments on $1,000 laptop computers than peruse a dictionary or thesaurus. A floor-level concert ticket to a major rock or hip-hop concert costs $50 to $60.[17] A Volkswagen Beetle is difficult to find for under $15,000.[18] Although Old Milwaukee beer is available for less than $9.00 per case, students are more likely to enjoy a pricier Corona, Sam Adams, or Wicked Pete's Ale. More striking, however, is the sharp escalation in the price of a college education. At American University, for example, tuition has jumped more than sevenfold. Incredibly, 1979 AU graduates will pay nearly as much for their children's freshman year of tuition ($21,144 in 2000–2001) than they paid for their entire four years of college (1975–1979).[19] Overall, tuition at private colleges and universities exceeded $14,000 per year, and the total cost of a four-year degree (including tuition, room, board, and fees) averaged over $80,000 in 1999–2000. Not surprisingly, nearly four out of five U.S. students attended public colleges and universities where in-state tuition averaged about $3,100 per year and the cost of a four-year degree was almost $32,000 in 1999–2000.[20]

From Work-Study to College Debt: The Student Loan Generation

As the cost of a college degree has skyrocketed, the strain of paying for higher education has been exacerbated by falling real wages. For instance, median U.S. household income has risen only 6.9 percent over the past 20 years, from $36,259 in 1979 to $38,885 in 1998 (measured in 1998 dollars).[21] As a result, the financial ability of middle- and lower-income families to pay for their children's college education through household savings has diminished sharply. A 1991 national survey reported that only 26 percent of all U.S. families paid for at least one-fifth of their children's college expenses. Today, university financial aid officials estimate this proportion at about 10 percent.[22] This is confirmed by a 1998 study by the Institute for Higher Education Policy. Between the 1986–1987 and 1997–1998 periods, according to the study, which was adjusted for inflation, parental financial assistance dropped by 8 percent, while college costs at four-year institutions rose 38 percent. Overall, it found that parents had saved an average of only $9,956 for their children's college education. This represents about one-fourth of the total cost of attending public universities and only about one-eighth of the cost of private colleges.[23]

The intensifying financial strain on middle-class families is shifting the economic burden to their children. However, students rarely are able to compensate for the middle-class squeeze on their parents, as college inflation has greatly outpaced their earnings since the mid-1970s.[24] For instance, tuition at American University has jumped from $2,880 in 1975–1976 to $21,144 in 2000–2001; the federal minimum wage for students has increased less than threefold during this 25-year period—from $2.10 to $5.25. In order to maintain the same earning power for tuition as their parents in 1975 (assuming the same number of work hours), American University students must earn at least $15.42 per hour in 2000. Instead, they receive only one-third of this rate.[25] With university scholarships and financial aid grants dwindling, especially at underfunded private schools with meager endowments like American University, it is not surprising that students and their families have increasingly opted to finance their college educations through various subsidized and unsubsidized loan programs. The result has been an unprecedented increase of college-related debt that parallels the tremendous growth of public-sector and corporate indebtedness in the 1980s and 1990s.

In 1998–99, the majority (52 percent) of U.S. college students paid less than $4,000 per year for tuition, and 79 percent paid less than $8,000.[26] Even so, the dependence of students on various grant and loan programs is staggering: one-half of all students matriculating at public institutions and nearly three-fourths (72 percent) at private colleges and universities.[27] More than 7 million students relied on federally guaranteed education loans for the year 1997–1998, borrowing over $38 billion—an 11 percent increase over 1996–1997;[28] the 1997 National Student Loan Survey reported that 60 percent of college students borrowed for college-related expenses during the 1997–1998 academic year.[29] This represents a substantial jump from 5.3 million students and $17.6 billion in loans for 1992–1993.

Overall, college students borrowed more than $140 billion during the 1990s, which exceeds the cumulative total of the past three decades. Moreover, about 80 percent of total federal aid to higher education is allocated in the form of personal loans—a dramatic reversal from the 25 percent levels of the 1970s when grants were the primary form of governmental assistance.[30] In the process, the tremendous demand for student loans has fueled the rapid expansion of the highly lucrative student loan, processing, and service industry; the federal government paid nearly $4 billion in service fees while absorbing $2.8 billion in defaulted loans in 1996.[31]

The relative decline in federal student aid has continued. Between 1991 and 1997, the proportion of college financial aid paid by federal programs fell from 7.7 to 4.5 percent.[32] Not surprisingly, median student debt jumped dramatically—from $2,000 in 1977 to about $7,000 in 1990 and then more than doubled to $15,000 in 1996.[33] Although private tuition has fueled this trend, the public-private student debt gap is narrowing substantially. For instance, the College Board reported that the average public university student graduated with $11,950 of loans in 1996 (an increase of 70 percent from 1993), and graduates of private colleges averaged $14,290 (an increase of 43 percent from 1993); this represents a debt gap of only 16.4 percent.[34] A comparison of debt levels of 1997 graduates from 11 selected public and 17 private colleges and universities is consistent with this trend.[35]

Several Republican House members proposed legislation in 1996 that would have reduced the availability of subsidized student loans, arguing that the program was an impending "budget buster." Instead, the U.S. Congress passed several tax relief bills in 1997 that benefit parents of students as well as recent college graduates.[36] Furthermore, the Clinton administration championed the expansion of the Pell Grant program (from a maximum of $2,700 to $4,000 per year) as well as student work-study funds.[37] Nevertheless, the affordability gap for college continued to widen in the late 1990s. As a result, credit cards became an increasingly popular source of easy money for financing basic educational costs as well as the inflated lifestyles prevalent on many college campuses.

"Plastic Money for Real People":[38]
Penetration and Expansion of the Student Market

In the mid-1970s, the proposed mass marketing of unsecured consumer loans to financially inexperienced and unemployed students in the form of credit cards was ridiculed and routinely dismissed by credit card executives.[39] The discretionary income of college students was limited primarily to summer earnings, part-time jobs, monthly allowances, and gifts from family members. Indeed, because of concern that young and impressionable consumers would act irresponsibly with "gifts" of unearned money, the starving-student financial services market was largely ignored through the early 1980s. The advent of banking deregulation in 1980, however, precipitated profound changes in the financial services industry that were accelerated by major advances in computer technologies permitting easy segmentation of the market. Furthermore, financial losses in other loan portfolios[40] and the dramatic decline in inflation made consumer credit cards an increasingly profitable venture for the banking industry.

From the precipice of financial insolvency, the banking industry embarked on two daring offensives that epitomize the decade of debt: (1) financing corporate mergers and acquisitions[41] and (2) expanding into consumer financial services.[42] The second strategy, in the aftermath of the 1981–1982 recession, resulted in the mass marketing of bank credit cards to struggling middle- and working-class families. By the end of the decade, consumer credit cards had emerged as the profit center of the struggling banking industry. But the enormous success of these marketing campaigns foreshadowed an impending profitability crisis: the saturation of the high-yield consumer services market. Banks could either accept lower growth and profit rates or aggressively pursue new markets. Not surprisingly, many opted to shift their attention to highly impressionable and trend-conscious college students as well as new groups of the financially desperate.[43]

Today, college students are becoming an even more profitable and strategically important market than their baby-boomer parents. This is because it is cheaper to conduct mass marketing campaigns on college campuses (about half the cost of marketing to their parents), students forge long-term corporate loyalties (an average of at least 15 years for credit cards), they offer profitable cross-marketing opportunities with other corporations (GM, American Airlines, Time, Wal-Mart, MCI), and their present and future needs include a wide range of financial services (private student loans, debt consolidation loans, checking accounts, savings accounts, auto loans, home mortgages). Finally, unlike other nearly saturated credit card niche markets, at least one-third of the population of four-year colleges and universities is replenished each year with new students (freshmen and transfers).

Penetration of the student credit card market began in the late 1980s. The banking industry was confronting serious financial difficulties, and college campuses became its next target. In 1990, when Citibank (largest and most aggressive marketer of student credit cards) was close to financial insolvency, about one-half of U.S. students enrolled in four-year colleges and universities used bank credit cards—either their own or their parents'. A 1990 market research study conducted by Claritas, Inc., found 54 percent of this student population had bank credit cards.[44] At the time, a major obstacle to sustained expansion of the student market was the industrywide practice of requiring parents to cosign credit card contracts for minors under 21 years old.

In the face of continuing economic losses during the 1989–1991 recession, banks informed their credit card divisions that they could ignore this policy and sign up students without parental consent. This aggressive marketing strategy, which focuses on the social and cultural pulse of campus life, led U.S. Congressman John Kennedy to direct the U.S. House of Representatives Subcommittee on Consumer Credit to investigate the credit card industry's often unsavory solicitation and debt collection techniques in 1994. In particular, it found two particularly questionable practices. First, introductory "kiddie cards" (with a $300 or less line of credit) were being routinely increased without the request or consent of account holders in order to increase the debt capacity of the student market. Second, and more disconcerting, were the harassment and even lawsuits against parents of students in default on their credit cards—even if they had not cosigned the loan agreement.[45] Significantly, both of these practices persist and are major complaints of students and their parents.[46]

Today, the successful solicitation campaigns on college campuses are yielding a steadily growing harvest that is approaching nearly three-fourths of the undergraduate student population of four-year colleges and universities. A 1996 national study by Claritas, Inc., reported that two-thirds (67 percent) of undergraduate students at four-year colleges and universities possessed credit cards.[47] This proportion is consistent with a 1998 survey by the Institute for Higher Education Policy and the Education Resources Institute that found 64 percent of its respondents had at least one credit card.[48] These studies closely mirror the results of the 1997 Nellie Mae "National Student Loan Survey" that found 65 percent of undergraduates had credit cards (the sampling universe was federally guaranteed student loan recipients).[49] Similarly, the 1998 national survey by the Student Monitor market research firm reported that 56 percent of undergraduate students had credit cards in their own name and an estimated 15 percent were secondary users of their parents' credit cards.[50] Hence, the available data indicate that about 70 percent of all undergraduates at four-year colleges and universities have at least one major bank credit card. In addition, Manning's 1998–1999 survey of more affluent undergraduate students at the University of Maryland and Georgetown University found that 85 percent had bank credit cards.[51] The results of the survey are presented in Appendix 6.

The most controversial and hotly debated issue concerns college students' level of credit card indebtedness. According to industry-sponsored studies, over one-half (56 percent) of all undergraduate students are convenience users who pay their credit charges in full each month. On the surface, this is much better than the general population's rate of 43 percent. Indeed, industry representative Charlotte Newton, vice president of consumer and government affairs of MasterCard International, declares, "College students can pay, do pay and are using their plastic cards responsibly."[52] However, the frequent use of this statistic—without further explanation—is misleading. This is because it obscures rather than illuminates the complexity of student credit card debt—both in terms of what students charge and how they pay.

In general, this commonly reported proportion of student credit card debtors—only 44 percent—is unreliable because it ignores several important factors: (1) At least 15 percent of undergraduate student credit card bills are paid directly by their families (students often do not know if their parents pay the bills in full and in surveys simply respond that they do not have a monthly credit card balance to pay);[53] (2) student indebtedness is measured only at the time of the survey rather than during the entire school year; (3) there are many more convenience users at private than at public schools; (4) new freshmen users have much lower debt levels than do upperclassmen; and (5) students are increasingly using federal student loans, private debt consolidation loans, and informal family loans or gifts to pay credit card bills.

As the following interviews demonstrate, student credit card debts are especially difficult to measure due to the dynamic nature of college survival strategies. Even so, the most credible studies verify the rapid increase of student card debt—especially among upperclassmen and graduate students. For instance, national surveys of undergraduates at four-year colleges by the market research firm Claritas, Inc., found that average student credit card debt climbed 134 percent between 1990 and 1995—from $900 to $2,100.[54] More compelling are the results of the National Student Loan Surveys sponsored by Nellie Mae. Between 1996 and 1997, the average credit card debt among its undergraduate respondents rose from $1,879 to $2,226. Moreover, those with credit card debts between $3,000 and $7,000 doubled from 7 to 14 percent; those with debts over $7,000 also doubled from 5 to 10 percent. The trend among graduate students is even more disturbing. The average number of credit cards in 1997 was seven with an average credit card balance of $5,800; 21 percent of students owed between $6,000 and $15,000, and 9 percent owed over $15,000.[55] In sum, the banking industry's mass marketing of credit cards to college students has been very successful. More than 70 percent of undergraduate students in four-year colleges and universities have at least one bank credit card. And they are obtaining them at a much earlier age. About 80 percent of students with credit cards receive their first card by the end of their freshman year of college.[56]

Paying Pizza Hut by MasterCard with University Loans: College Students' Survival Strategies

One of the most important and underexamined features of student credit card debt is its dynamic nature. In some cases, it reflects seasonal variation, such as school-related expenses at the beginning of the academic year or holiday gift-giving such as for Christmas and Hanukkah. In other cases, it may mirror the exhaustion of summer savings or the family's college nest egg; among a smaller number of students, it may be due to irregular parental support payments. Additionally, students may confront family-related economic demands that are satisfied through charges to their credit cards. Furthermore, the general assumption that credit card debt increases incrementally during college or is unrelated to the changing lifestyle activities on college campuses belies the contemporary reality of students' survival strategies. In short, credit cards are used to bridge financial gaps in student budgets. However, the availability of credit cards has profoundly changed a typical student's consumption patterns. As a result, credit cards have so altered the perception of personal "emergencies" that students must distinguish between an on-campus financial crisis from an urgent need at home. Finally, the experiences described in the following interviews illuminate the increasingly important role of college life in shaping the attitudes of future generations toward credit and debt. These issues are highlighted by "Jeff," a 1999 graduate.

During his middle-class upbringing in Indiana, Jeff's father inculcated the midwestern values of frugality and debt avoidance, and Jeff enrolled at Georgetown University in 1995 with a commitment to conduct his financial affairs on a cash-only basis. Initially, he socialized with students like himself—from moderate-income midwestern families—who shared similar social backgrounds and cultural experiences. But Jeff soon realized that he wanted to transcend his family background and enjoy the more exciting lifestyle of his more affluent and urbane friends such as his roommate. At first, his adherence to the cognitive connect (income and other resources dictate level of consumption) made him stand out among his peers. For instance, Jeff's father always paid restaurant bills in cash. His motto was "If

you don't have the cash, then you shouldn't buy it." Jeff's new friends, however, associated this behavior with the quaint and backward cultural practices of depression-era farmers. Only rarely did their parents use cash for
common financial transactions.

This clash of cultures led Jeff to apply for a credit card. He received two
credit cards his first semester, including a Gold MasterCard. Although Jeff
initially obtained the cards for convenience, he was impressed by the favorable response of others to his Gold card: "It made me feel like I had made it
. . . people treated me differently when they saw [the Gold card]." Jeff acknowledges that this new respect was premature, since he did not yet have a
real job, but he perceived it as an early recognition of his future social status
as a graduate of a prestigious university. Significantly, Jeff first began using
his credit cards like cash, paying off the balances at the end of the month:
"Why pay cash? [After all] what's the point of having a credit card?" His
other reason for obtaining credit cards was for emergencies. Hence, as long
as Jeff's savings and loans could finance a carefree lifestyle, his credit cards
served as a modern convenience that befitted his status as a student at an
elite, private university. Of course, this situation quickly changed when his
financial resources were exhausted in the fall of his sophomore year.

As a freshman, Jeff saw his credit cards as his best friend, a guardian angel
during crisis situations: "At first, I decided that my credit cards would only
accumulate debt in case of emergencies, such as being stranded in an airport and needing a [plane] ticket. After a while, I decided that it was okay
to charge necessary things like books and other school-related expenses . . .
Then, after charging for needs, it was just so easy . . . I decided that it was
okay to charge anything I damn well wanted." As his debt increased, with 8
new credit cards during his sophomore year, Jeff became disheartened. Although they enabled him to rebel against the strict social control of his father, Jeff was now encumbered with several thousand dollars of debt. Over
time, Jeff confounded his pursuit of personal independence with the rejection of the cultural ethos of the cognitive connect. After all, he argued, consumer debt was a common—even modern—trend of professionally
successful people: "Everyone else I knew was in debt . . . and so were many
of their parents." His peers rationalized their indolent spending behavior by
emphasizing "the great jobs that we will get [after graduation] that will enable us to pay off our credit card [debts]."

At the onset of his college career, Jeff's conservative midwest background
made him an unlikely candidate for accumulating a large credit card debt.
However, with tuition over $23,000 per year at Georgetown University, Jeff
quickly exhausted the $40,000 "loan" that his parents saved for his college

education. And because the combined income of Jeff's parents was over $100,000, his financial aid was primarily limited to student loans. Unlike students at less costly public colleges, moreover, Jeff was unable to transfer any of his personal debts into student loans. This is because Jeff's student loans covered only a fraction of Georgetown's tuition while his duties as an on-campus resident hall adviser (RA) provided his room and board. For Jeff's family, credit card use was acceptable only if one had sufficient savings or earnings that "could back up your purchases." Initially, Jeff succumbed to the temptations of credit cards for noneconomic reasons. They offered emotional security in case of personal emergencies and alleviated social-status anxiety because "people treat me so much better when they see my Gold [American Express, MasterCard] cards." Jeff's first credit card was an impulsive response to a Citibank advertisement "that was hanging on the wall in the dorm." The Visa card offered a credit limit of $700 with an introductory rate of 4.9 percent. By the end of his freshman year, Jeff had received three credit cards, which he used primarily for entertainment-related activities.

The shift from using credit cards for convenience to financing an inflated standard of living was a normal extension of Jeff's college experience. "Everyone has to take on debt to go to college . . . everyone is expected to have student loans. . . . Even in my Midwestern [culture,] which emphasizes that debt is bad, college loans are viewed as good debt. . . . Low interest rates . . . [on student loans combined with the] high price of college equals high value . . . [which produces] a greater return on your investment." By the middle of Jeff's sophomore year, he had exhausted his parents' college "loan." At this point, he confronted a profound crossroads in his college career: either fundamentally alter his consumer-oriented lifestyle, or abandon his familial attitudes toward debt. Faced with the choice of losing his new friends, who viewed debt as a necessary means to a justifiable end, Jeff succumbed to the temptation of easy money and accumulated eight more credit cards in 1997.

The most striking feature of Jeff's credit card use is how quickly he discarded the virtue of frugality as a necessary means for establishing his own social identity outside of his father's strict control. After all, the culture of consumption that permeates college life views saving as a practice of "hicks," whereas debt is the "breakfast of champions." By the end of his sophomore year, Jeff had accumulated a couple of thousand dollars in credit card debt. Instead of beginning his junior year with savings from his summer job, most of Jeff's earnings were used to pay off his credit cards. Significantly, as his credit card balances rose, Jeff received complimentary letters from credit card companies congratulating him on his good credit history and raising his credit limits as a "courtesy to our best customers" so that he could avoid over-limit fees. Although he had never earned $10,000 in annual income, the deluge of credit card offers obscured the fragility of Jeff's financial circumstances: "With the constant arrival of new preapproved credit card applications *and* the raising of my credit limits, the credit card companies made it seem like [my level of debt] was okay. . . . When I started to fall behind, I even received letters that allowed me to 'skip a payment' because the company 'understood' that sometimes debts can back up, such as during the holidays." During this period, Jeff eagerly embraced the marketing ploys of the credit card industry so that he could accumulate miles or points for frequent-flier and consumer gift programs. More important, this practice led to surfing—transferring debt from high- to low-interest "introductory rate" credit cards to maximize the financial benefits.

As Jeff learned to tread water by surfing in this period, he learned the next lesson of the credit-dependent: the credit card shuffle. When he was short on cash, Jeff paid his credit card bills with other credit cards through monthly balance transfers and courtesy checks. This acceptance of his new debtor status was "disheartening . . . but I rationalized it by telling myself that everyone else is in debt. . . . After all, I'm going to get a great job and pay it off." The "good" (responsible) credit card debt, such as school-related expenses, a personal computer, and work suits, was soon overtaken by entertainment on weekends, restaurant dinners, spring break in Florida and then London and Canada. One ten-day vacation cost over $5,000—"I even charged the passport application fee"—and Jeff found himself on the verge of exhausting his available cash and credit. Fortunately, the university credit union was willing to assist students like Jeff who found themselves "drowning in credit card debt . . . most of the people I know that go to the credit union are getting loans to pay their credit cards." Without the option of federally guaranteed student loans to service his credit card debts, Jeff received a $10,000 credit union loan at a moderate 11.9 percent. This loan essentially bought Jeff some time before he entered the job market—an option not available to most college students. Not incidentally, a condition of the loan disbursement was that $3,000 had to be used to pay off one of his credit cards. The balance of the loan was spent on school expenses as well as catching up on his other monthly credit card payments.

During his junior year, Jeff began to engage in riskier and more creative credit card schemes. For instance, he began receiving new preapproved credit card solicitations and congratulatory letters announcing that he had "earned" an increase in his credit limits. He even began receiving letters that encouraged him to miss a payment, such as during holiday gift-giving sea-

sons, while lauding his good credit history. These mixed messages are easy
for college students to misinterpret. Indeed, Jeff rationalized that his accumulating debt was not very serious, since the credit card companies "made
it seem that everything was okay by sending new applications and raising
existing credit limits." During this period, moreover, Jeff became so dependent on ATMs (his parents *never* used them) that he did not even think
about the transaction costs ($1.50–$3.00). As cash advances became more
frequent, he did not want to know that the fees and higher interest rates
made their cost comparable to short-term pawnshop loans. Eventually, he
realized his meager stipend as an RA was making it difficult to send even
minimum credit card payments. The $10,000 debt consolidation loan from
the university credit union averted an economic crisis but proved to be only
a temporary band-aid. Jeff's finances had spiraled out of control.

Ironically, a contributing factor to his financial crisis was two failed business ventures with his roommate that were intended to eliminate their debts.
The first was a service to translate résumés of Mexican and other Latin
American students who were seeking internships or applying to colleges in
the United States. Encouraged by friends seeking their assistance, Jeff and
his roommate purchased all the necessary office items of a high-tech company—computer, fax machine, cell phones, executive chairs, high-quality
business cards and fliers—and incurred other fees for a website, P.O. box,
and legal assistance for formal incorporation in Delaware. After several
months without clients and rapidly depreciating business technology, Jeff
and his roommate opted to cut their losses and terminate the business. Each
lost over $2,500. Further financial pain came when they had to pay addi-
tional legal fees to dissolve their corporation, and they only recently paid off
the two-year contract for their listing with an Internet search engine.

After this entrepreneurial debacle, they sought to recoup their losses
through the stock market. Instead of becoming more cautious about debt,
"our credit cards allowed us to get too big for our britches." According to
Jeff, "My roommate found out that his company [where he was employed
part-time] was going to be bought out. So, he was convinced that we would
make a quick profit if we bought some stock before [the acquisition] . . . a
sure winner! We each bought $5,000 worth of stock with cash advances
from our credit cards . . . with e-trade we even saved on brokers' commissions. . . . The company was bought out all right, but then it was cannibal-
ized and the stock fell. . . . We each lost over $3,000." When asked why
they pursued such risky ventures while still in school, Jeff responded, "Because we could! The courtesy checks gave us the opportunity to act on our
impulses."

By the end of Jeff's junior year, the social empowerment provided by his 11 bank and 5 retail credit cards had changed dramatically: They had evolved from friends to foes. The social doors they had previously opened were now increasingly closed. Jeff recalled that he was "so concerned about meeting the right people and fitting in with them . . . that I didn't think twice about $50 bar tabs and spending spring break in London . . . To think otherwise would have meant certain social death." Fortunately, Jeff was forced to confront his situation after realizing that "I no longer had control over my credit cards. Now, they controlled me." The earlier freedom to "act like an adult" had been replaced with the financial responsibility of paying for his earlier excesses. Indeed, rather than enjoying his final year at college, Jeff endured a form of "social hell" by working full-time while taking a normal course load and applying and interviewing for jobs. He worked at least 30 hours per week at two part-time jobs (in addition to his RA position) simply to make the minimum payments on his $20,000 credit card debt and $10,000 debt consolidation loan. Most of his friends stopped calling to make plans for the weekend because he was "shackled to my credit cards. . . . I can't go out with them like I used to because I have to work . . . ultimately, to pay for the fun that I charged on my credit cards a couple of years ago."

Today, Jeff views his credit cards with disdain: "I hate them." He is delinquent on many of his accounts and has threatened to declare bankruptcy unless the banks offer him more favorable interest rates. Ironically, Jeff's social and financial odyssey has brought him full-circle to affirming his father's mantra toward debt: "If you can't afford it, don't buy it." He is most angered about how the credit card companies' marketing literature on campus praises the benefits of "responsible use" but neglects to inform impressionable and inexperienced students about the downside, such as the impact of poor credit reports on future loans and even potential employment. This is crucial, as Jeff explains, because "the credit card industry knows exactly what it is doing [in encouraging debt] while taking advantage of students who are trying to learn how to adjust to living away from home, often for the first time. . . . Let's face it, how can these banks justify giving me 11 credit cards on an annual income of only $9,000? These include a Gold American Express and several Platinum Visa cards."

Although Jeff does not dismiss his financial responsibility, he states that "I almost feel victimized. . . . Giving credit cards to kids in college is like giving steroids to an athlete. Are you *not* going to use them after you get them?" Furthermore, as an RA, Jeff emphasizes that the university offers a wide range of student informational programs and services but with one notable exception: "There is nowhere to go for debt counseling . . . everything is discussed in freshman orientation or incorporated in resident advisor training and residence hall programs . . . AIDS, suicide, eating disorders, alcohol, depression, peer pressure, sex ed, academic pressures, learning handicaps . . . all but financial crisis management."

As Jeff has "gone full circle" in his attitudes toward credit cards, he is now coping with the unexpected pain of his past credit card excesses. With over $20,000 in credit card debt (plus his $10,000 debt consolidation loan and over $30,000 in student loans), Jeff has washed ashore from his surfing escapades. Although working two part-time jobs during his senior year, Jeff is delinquent on several of his 16 credit cards. A business major, he is anxiously awaiting the outcome of his job search. He is optimistic, as some of his peers have already received starting salaries ranging from $40,000 to $55,000 per year. In addition, several have received signing bonuses of between $3,000 and $10,000. For Jeff, the latter is especially important because he plans to use this money to reduce his credit card debt.

Unfortunately, Jeff's promising career is encountering obstacles from an unexpected source—his credit cards. During a recent interview with a major Wall Street banking firm, Jeff was asked, "How can we feel comfortable about your managing large sums of our money when you have had such difficulty in handling your own [credit card] debts?" Jeff was stunned. It was obvious that the interviewer had reviewed his credit report—without prior notification—in evaluating Jeff's desirability to the firm. "Can you believe it?" Jeff declares. "They want an explanation about my personal finances in college, and yet they lost over $120 million last year!"

The firm did not offer him employment, and Jeff wonders how much the decision was based on his GPA and how much on the "score" calculated by the consumer credit reporting agency. This is certainly not a potential consequence that the credit card industry explains in its marketing pitch to "Build your credit history . . . you'll need [it] later for car, home or other loans." As Jeff passes by the MBNA Career Center on campus, which is named after the credit card company that he owes several thousand dollars, the irony of his catch-22 situation is not lost on him. "How can I pay them back when their credit reports are hurting my chances of getting a good job?" It is not surprising that growing numbers of students like Jeff are using sexual analogies in describing their unforeseen circumstances, denouncing the predatory policies of the credit card industry as a form of "financial rape."

As Jeff's experience shows, student financial strategies are becoming increasingly complex as credit card companies offer "the [financial] freedom to hang ourselves." Even students at expensive private schools are finding ways to transfer their credit card debt into supplementary loans without the knowledge of their parents. This increasingly popular practice helps to explain the wide vacillation in student credit card balances due to infusions of cash from other sources of loans. In addition, Jeff demonstrates how access to credit cards can lead to costly and unnecessary purchases that would not have been considered under the financial constraints of a fixed student budget. The latter is especially disconcerting. It reflects the strong influences of escalating peer consumption pressures as well as sophisticated marketing campaigns that target the youth culture. One of the most seductive is the Sony advertisement, "Don't deny yourself. Indulge with the Sony [Visa] Card from Citibank . . . The official currency of playtime," or, more succinctly, the ubiquitous Nike slogan, "Just do it."

After the Magic of Plastic Wears Off: The Social Costs of Student Debt

Credit card debt negatively impacts the personal and professional futures of college students in a variety of ways. For some, the need to work extra jobs may lead to deficient grades and loss of scholarships and other financial aid. This may compel students from moderate-income families to drop out of private colleges and attend less prestigious public universities, while those in state colleges may drop out and enroll in junior colleges. Other students may find that their debts are overwhelming and, in the absence of family assistance, are forced to file for bankruptcy while still enrolled in school. For still others, the impact may be delayed until after graduation. The combined burden of student loans and credit card debt may lead to bankruptcy after their employment fails to offer an adequate income for servicing their financial obligations. Last, the newest and most disturbing trend concerns the use of credit reports by employers. Student credit card debts are increasingly scrutinized during the recruitment process and may be an important factor in evaluating prospective employees. As a result, many recent graduates may be unaware that their employment prospects are limited due to their college legacy of credit card debt.

George and his parents were elated with his acceptance into the class of 1999 at American University. Although neither of his parents had attended college, they had always encouraged him to pursue a professional career—as an accountant, lawyer, maybe even a doctor. George was born and raised in a small town outside of Columbus, Ohio, and these were ambitious career goals, as George's mother is a secretary at an insurance company and his father is a shoe salesman in a department store. Their combined annual income of about $35,000 places them in the economic vice of the middle-class squeeze. Finances have always been tight for the family of five, and George understood at an early age that he would be financially responsible for his college education. Indeed, his enrollment in an eastern private college would have been an "impossible dream" without a substantial financial aid package.

George was prepared for the demanding college course work, especially because of the academically competitive atmosphere. Some of his classmates had attended exclusive prep schools, and many came from families with professional parents—even university professors. But George was not prepared for the social pressures of university life: CD players, designer clothes, dining at expensive restaurants, and the late-night D.C. bar scene. One student he met even drove her own BMW—George's dream car. Clearly, this was a different world, with its own rules, a virtual fantasyland compared with small-town life in northern Ohio. Indeed, whereas he spent 15 hours per week at his work-study job and carefully managed his modest personal budget, most of his peers enjoyed an active and expensive social life. In fact, few students had part-time jobs, and yet nearly all of his acquaintances had credit cards—what they called plastic money.

George had been warned by his parents about the evils of credit cards, and he was shocked that his classmates had such a cavalier attitude about them. As he tried to adjust to this new social milieu, he became frustrated and uncertain about the values imparted by his family. Away from home for the first time and without a strong social support system at the university, George began to crave the sophisticated lifestyle of his more popular classmates—a classic case of Durkheim's social "anomie." In order to be accepted by his peers, George believed that he needed more discretionary resources so that he could participate more frequently in their activities. George's only option, as he recalls, was to reject his parents' advice and get a magical piece of plastic. This proved to be a far more important decision than he could have ever imagined at the time. The financial freedom and social independence promised by the credit card advertisements on campus obscure their lesser-known dark side. For naive students from modest-income households like George, the social consequences of credit card dependency may deeply influence their college experiences and even their future professional careers.

George remembers vividly the day his plastic "gift" arrived in the mail. "I really didn't think that Citibank would give me a Visa. I saw the advertisements in the [student] newspaper, sign-up tables [in the student center], and applications [inserted] with my textbooks [from the bookstore]. . . . I sent in an application but did not expect to be approved." When George received his credit card nearly six weeks later, he was ecstatic: "I felt like a kid in a candy store. I had my own credit card. I was somebody, and I couldn't wait to show *them* that I could go out and enjoy myself like everyone else." For George, the Citibank Visa truly possessed magical powers. It unleashed the freedom to partake in a social life that respected few financial boundaries. For the first time since he had arrived on campus, he felt empowered and the "rush" was "intoxicating." One night he even paid the beer tab for all of his friends. George was eager to impress them, as he desperately wanted to join a fraternity in the spring.

George's emotional high abruptly ended with the arrival of his first credit card statement—over $600. He was stunned. George assiduously recorded purchases he made by cash or check, but he had not kept track of his credit card charges. And few of these purchases were really necessary: bar tabs, restaurant dinners, schoolbooks, concert tickets, clothes, and flowers for his girlfriend's birthday. He bought a dozen long-stemmed roses for $49, and a single bar tab was $165—just so he could pretend to be a "big shot." If his parents ever found out, he confided, "they would kill me." Even so, George was reluctant to give up his newfound freedom. He decided to work a few extra hours at his campus job and then use the money from his Christmas job and holiday gifts to pay down his bill. This seemed like a reasonable strategy at the time. Besides, he could not worry over a few hundred dollars while coping with the stress of final projects and exams. Midterms had not gone very well, and he "felt entitled to all the help I could get to concentrate on my studies."

George returned for the spring semester with low grades and a high debt. His GPA was less than a C, and his credit card balance was approaching its limit of $1,000. Instead of saving his money from the holidays, he spent much more than usual on Christmas gifts. Since he could not turn to his parents for financial assistance, his only option was to take a second job at an off-campus copy center. It paid $6.00 per hour, which was good by standards back home but did not provide much relief from his credit card obligations. Despondent over the inauspicious start of his college career, George began "burning the candle at both ends" with late nights of working, studying, and partying. In fact, the more he worked at his part-time jobs, the more he felt he deserved to eat out, enjoy a concert, and go to bars with friends. George did not realize then that his credit card had opened a Pandora's Box of rising expectations that could be satisfied only with greater levels of debt and more hours of paid employment. In the meantime, his financial situation was temporarily alleviated when the credit limit on his Visa was raised and he received a second credit card.

By midterm exams of the spring semester, George was very nervous—in fact, near panic. The additional hours he worked at his part-time jobs meant fewer hours for studying and sleeping. Yet what he once perceived as luxuries were now necessities for coping with the stresses of college. Indeed, his lifestyle was not extravagant. He was not out of control with his spending, as were other students he had met and heard about. Why was this happening to him? By spring break, George realized that "the sky was falling down on me." His grades continued to plummet, which led to a prophetic warning from his academic adviser: Financial aid was contingent upon satisfactory academic performance. George hoped he could catch up with his studies while many of his friends partied in Miami, Cancun, and the Caribbean. Unfortunately, it was too little, too late.

George was emotionally "fried" when he took his final exams. His "miserable" performance resulted in his being placed on academic probation, a far cry from the dean's list to which he had once aspired. To make matters worse, American University subsequently cut its institutional aid and scholarship award. George would have to replace several thousand dollars of university grants with additional student loans and summer savings while drastically reducing his moderate standard of living; the university's estimated budget for personal expenses was unrealistically low. "Almost a couple of thousand dollars in the red" with his credit cards, George accepted the reality that he could not afford to return to the university in the fall. Instead, he decided to go back to Ohio and commute from home to a local junior college while working full-time at a retail store.

George hopes to return to Washington, D.C., eventually. However, he reluctantly admits that he may have lost his opportunity to graduate from a prestigious private university. Although listed as an academic casualty, George explains his fate as a product of youthful naïveté and the inability to resist campus social pressures. George regrets that he was unprepared for the social temptations offered by his credit cards. Most of his classmates could appeal to their parents for financial help and remain at the university; he had no choice but to accept the full consequences of his actions. Even so, "it was much easier to tell my parents that college [course work] was harder than expected than to explain that I was running around at night with my buddies [at the bar] . . . and working extra hours during the day to pay my credit card bills."

Unlike George, Cris chose a local state university in order to retain her social network of friends and minimize the costs of her college education. She is a resident of suburban Maryland; her mother is a registered nurse and her stepfather is a doctor. When Cris graduated from high school, their combined household income was well in excess of $100,000, and they enjoyed a comfortable albeit frugal lifestyle. In fact, it was much too frugal for Cris's tastes—simply turning on the air conditioner or taking a hot shower could incite a heated exchange with her "stingy" stepfather, Karl. The conflict over personal consumption was so contentious that Cris and her mother were forced to hide their purchases—clothes, shoes, cosmetics—"even when we used our own money." In fact, Cris worked full-time at an auto-parts store during her senior year of high school. This enabled Cris to pay her car loan and most personal expenses. For Cris, attending the University of Maryland in College Park offered a refuge from the social control that Karl exercised over her life. Although she lived at home during her freshman year, she spent most of her time at the university or socializing with friends. The only problem was money, as she was responsible for most of her educational expenses.

At the university, Cris embarked on a rebellious "wild roller coaster ride" of partying, day trips to the mall, and academic irresponsibility. This unfettered freedom of college life contrasted sharply with the harsh discipline of living at home. At the time, Cris's parents were oblivious to her new college lifestyle, since she was limited to her meager savings from high school. Unbeknown to them, however, the credit card industry was aggressively expanding into the previously ignored student market in the late 1980s. For Karl, it would have been ludicrous to think that major banks would give essentially unsecured loans to unemployed teenagers who lacked experience in managing their economic affairs or discipline in controlling their consumption. In the end, it was Karl who was naive when it came to student finances and bank loan policies. The junk-bond-financed frenzy of corporate mergers and acquisitions, which defined the 1980s, had spilled over into the rampant consumerism of American campus life. Indeed, banks were eager to make high-interest loans to students, and credit cards became their financial vehicle of choice. Ultimately, credit cards became the personal junk bonds of Generation X.

Cris's initial encounter with plastic money began early in the fall of 1989—her first semester of college. Citibank Visa advertisements "were plastered all over the university," and she thought she had nothing to lose in submitting an application. Besides, Cris was curious about the power of plastic, since her parents would not permit her to use a credit card in high school and she did not want to provoke an argument by asking now. Furthermore, all of her friends were receiving financial assistance for college from their parents and thus had considerably more discretionary resources for "play." Emboldened by the prospect of financial independence, Cris eagerly filled out the form, which did not require the consent of her parents—only a copy of her student ID. At the time, Cris was 18 years old and working part-time at a telephone answering service for about $5.00 per hour. To her surprise, Citibank granted a $500 line of credit, which she immediately used to pay a large library fine and "buy a bunch of clothes at the mall that I couldn't otherwise afford." More important, Citibank's decision had a greater impact on Cris than the monetary value of its loan: "It made me feel emotionally and financially mature. . . . [The credit card] helped me become independent [in my relations] with my family and my friends. . . . It made me realize that I deserved to be responsible—that I should not have to beg my stepfather for money or call my grandfather for [financial] help."

Cris's new social and economic empowerment transformed her attitudes toward consumption and debt. No longer forced to earn the ability to consume through work-related savings (cognitive connect), she was also liberated from the social control of her parents. At first, Cris limited her charges to school expenses and personal items. By the end of the academic year, Cris was routinely using her credit card for mall excursions, restaurant meals, bar tabs, concert and professional sports tickets, and weekend trips to the beach. These activities underscored her newfound freedom and were reflected in her rising credit card debts. Indeed, the power of Cris's first credit card convinced her to get a second by the end of the fall semester and two or three more in the spring. During this period, Cris learned the flip side of the power of plastic: the need to refuel its financial engine with monthly infusions of cash. By the second semester, Cris's top priority was maintaining her lifestyle, and she began working full-time at the answering service company.

Not surprisingly, Cris's grades plummeted. For the first time in her life, she received a D and an F, which resulted in academic probation from the university. As conflicts with Karl intensified over her social activities, Cris moved into an apartment with some of her college girlfriends. These additional financial pressures reinforced her dependence on credit cards. They were her most dependable asset. When she needed economic help, they were always there for her. And they did not ask questions about why she needed the money or moralize about her spending patterns. The only problem was that they were high-maintenance. But it was a small financial price to pay for their invaluable assistance. At least that was what Cris thought at the time.

Cris enjoyed a largely carefree summer, and to reduce her expenses, she enrolled in a local community college for the fall semester. Already over $3,000 in debt and earning only $5.00 per hour, Cris was deluged with preapproved credit card offers. She believes the credit card industry found her desirable because of her prompt remittance of minimum monthly payments. During this period, Cris began to view her credit cards differently. "After spending my paycheck, I used my credit cards like savings. . . . I used them for everything . . . books, tuition, gas, food, hotel rooms at the beach . . . whether for school, emergencies, or simply to enjoy an evening with friends." This intermingling of credit and earnings, which is common, was reinforced by unexpected situations such as car repairs and medical emergencies. After all, she had to get her car fixed in order to drive to work, and her health deserved immediate attention or she could not perform her job.

Cris then began to engage in more creative and costly credit card practices that would foreshadow her eventual debt crisis. First, she started using her credit cards regularly to generate additional cash flow. This strategy usually entailed charging all of her friends' meals at a restaurant and then collecting their money afterward. Second, she began to take cash advances routinely from her credit cards "when I realized that I could." Initially, Cris would use cash advance checks to pay bills like rent, utilities, or car loan. As she got further into debt, however, Cris learned a sophisticated version of the credit card shuffle: She took cash advances at the end of the month and then deposited the money into her checking account so that she could send the minimum payments to the credit card companies. "It got to the point where I had written down all of the PIN numbers of my credit cards and, at the same ATM, I would take cash advances and then deposit the money directly into my [checking] account." Significantly, this financial management tactic was encouraged by her credit card companies, which profit from high interest rates, cash advance fees, and over-limit penalties. "Every time I began to bump against my limits, the banks would raise them. [Because of this practice,] it did not become a crisis early when I could have realized the seriousness of my situation." At the same time, marketing inducements such as 10 percent off and free merchandise were "too easy" to pass up.

Over the next two years, Cris's credit card debt jumped from about $5,000 to over $15,000. Cris marveled at the sum and how she was completely unaware of the debt that had accumulated on her 8 or 9 credit cards: "After being relatively stable for a couple of years, it just [tripled] overnight." She moved back with her parents to reduce expenses that now included payments on a stereo, VCR, and TV. However, the recurrent conflicts with her stepfather ensured that this was only a short-term move. The following year, she moved in with her boyfriend. Although Cris had received a moderate raise to $6.50 per hour and earned as much overtime as possible, the economic burden of rent and utilities plus her car payment led to a sobering realization: Her basic expenses exceeded her income. Cris had been content to send minimum payments on her credit cards because she had convinced herself that she would soon get "a good job and pay them all off." Instead, at 21 years old, Cris was forced to accept the reality that she would have to work full-time and remain a part-time student while attempting to reduce her credit card debts. A $5,000 debt consolidation loan offered only temporary relief.

As Cris slipped closer to her financial abyss, she was stunned by a debt counseling announcement she saw on television. It explained that merely sending minimum payments would require over 30 years to pay off existing credit card balances. "With no end in sight," Cris's attitude toward her credit cards changed dramatically. From generous companions, they quickly became her worst enemy—"I hated them." Dependent on the credit card shuffle "simply to get by," Cris sought help at a local debt counseling agency. To her surprise, she received a "shock . . . I thought that they could help anyone . . . instead, they told me that they could not help me at all . . . that I should declare bankruptcy. I was mad. They implied that I was beyond help. . . . I had nowhere else to go. . . . I could not believe that this was happening to me." Cris did not want to abandon her debts, but she could not find anyone interested in helping her "put my life back together" unless she "started over again."[57] In fact, the first lawyer she consulted recommended that she max out all of her credit cards before filing for bankruptcy. Cris was appalled by his suggestion: "I am not irresponsible. I was not looking for an easy way out. . . . He made me feel bad about myself and the whole [bankruptcy] process . . . I was doing it because there was no other option." Cris declined his offer to represent her during the bankruptcy proceedings.

In December 1994, at the age of 23, Cris had her bankruptcy petition approved with the aid of her attorney, at a cost of $695. The court discharged a total debt of $22,522 on 13 credit cards and a $5,000 consumer loan; she reaffirmed two credit cards and continued payments on her car loan. "I felt awful about abandoning my debt. After all, I tried to renegotiate through debt counselors, but no one was interested in helping me." Indeed, the striking feature of Cris's story is her emphasis on individual responsibility while at the same time criticizing credit card companies for aggressively marketing excessive lines of credit to naive and emotionally vulnerable students. "I admit that I charged way too much . . . my debts were all my fault. . . . [However] they should never have given me all those credit cards at my age [under 22]. . . . There was just too little effort to get them. The banks make it too easy to get into debt."[58]

Fortunately for Cris, bankruptcy was a prudent decision because it enabled her "to put the pieces of my life back together." In fact, she was able to complete her junior college studies as a full-time student and is now enrolled at a four-year university. For those who contend that the bankruptcy system is too lenient, Cris's experience is instructive. She agrees that the social stigma is diminishing but has strong feelings about taking this presumably painless path:

> You don't know how bad [bankruptcy] is. They said [my bad credit] would last only seven years, but it will take ten years before the bankruptcy is erased from my credit report. . . . I can't get a real credit card, AT&T just rejected me for their card, and forget about a house mortgage. . . . I've talked to people who are thinking about declaring bankruptcy for only $4,000–$5,000 of debts. As little as they knew about credit cards, they know even less about bankruptcy. . . . Kids need to understand the future repercussions of accumulating multiple credit cards. Many young people see only the immediate benefits, the gratification. They are so [financially] ignorant. It is so sad.

After Cris filed for bankruptcy in December 1994, the last thing on her mind was providing financial assistance to her mother. Cris was only 23 years old and had just started working full-time as an account technician at a suburban government agency. Her only major expenses were the $327 monthly payment for the new car she purchased in October (the 12.75 percent auto loan would have been much higher after her bankruptcy filing) and the modest tuition at the local junior college. Also, she chose to reaffirm her Montgomery Ward and Circuit City credit cards. This decision averted the repossession of her bed and stereo as well as initiated the agonizing process of rebuilding her credit history. Although Cris felt insecure without her financial backup of cash advances, she did not need them after the bankruptcy court discharged over $600 in monthly credit card payments. For the first time since high school, Cris was making more money than she was spending.

Cris's newfound financial stability was a sharp contrast to the precarious situation of her mother. In 1993, Bette filed for a separation from her husband and bought a small house near the college where Cris was continuing her studies. Burdened by the down payment on the house and her mounting credit card debt, Bette immediately experienced financial problems. Although she earned over $50,000 as a registered nurse, Bette's mortgage payments were almost half her monthly take-home salary. Her financial situation was exacerbated by her husband's refusal to grant an uncontested divorce. There would be no imminent division of community property and thus no economic relief in the near future. As a result, Cris moved into the house to help with her mother's living expenses.

At first, Cris used her mother's credit cards for her own personal expenses such as schoolbooks and gas. She would later reimburse her mother in cash, which Bette used for the minimum monthly payments. Other times, Cris gave her mother cash for living expenses, and Bette used these funds for the minimum payments on her credit cards. This led to a strategy of paying down one credit card and then sending the minimum payments for the other cards via balance transfers. The arrangement ended when all of Bette's credit cards reached their limits. However, Cris and Bette continued to barter through another creative use of credit. Cris had obtained two secured credit cards—which required deposits of $400—enabling Bette to charge some of her expenses in exchange for rent. These included her pager, utilities, and car loan. Even so, Bette was accumulating too much debt and was still having difficulty making her mortgage payments. With Cris's encouragement, Bette entered a consumer debt counseling program and negotiated a repayment plan for her other personal debts. Significantly, Bette was required not to use any of her credit cards until all of her debts were paid off. By the end of 1996, Bette could no longer postpone the inevitable and reluctantly accepted the foreclosure of her house. She rented a nearby apartment, and Cris moved in with an aunt.

In 2000, Cris continued to help her mother financially with her secured credit cards. Cris has "loaned" Bette one of her secured credit cards for emergencies and allows her to charge small items on another credit card that has less than $1,000 of remaining credit. This arrangement has been facilitated by Cris's eligibility for the maximum federal guaranteed student loan (beginning in 1997) and the "loan" of an unsecured Visa from her aunt; she was offered the credit card after her auto repairs exceeded the $1,000 limit on her credit card. "The first thing I do with my student loans is pay down my credit cards. I receive half of my Stafford loan ($2,750) at the beginning of the fall semester and the other half at the beginning of the spring semester. . . . At least a half goes [as payment] to my credit cards." Hence, the student loans serve essentially as cash advances for paying down her credit cards.

For Cris, the magic of plastic has been an alternating source of personal freedom and financial anguish. Halfway through the ten-year "scarlet B" on her credit report, she reflects on her roller coaster ride of credit cards: "At 17, I was too young to handle so much credit . . . It was just too easy [to get credit cards] . . . but I don't deny my responsibility. . . . I just wish that I didn't have to go through bankruptcy. It is so hard. People think that it is easy, but it is not." Indeed, ten years after receiving her first credit card, Cris will finally graduate with an accounting degree in spring 2001. Even so, credit cards are providing a valuable service for both mother and daughter today. Cris is proud to be able to help her mother through this personal and financial ordeal. The creative sharing of her credit cards has helped to strengthen the relationship with her mother and heal the lingering wounds of past familial conflicts. In fact, for her fall 2000 wedding, Cris and her fiancé decided to purchase Bette's engagement ring, rather than a new ring, through a combination of paying cash and assuming existing bills—including credit card debts. In this case, the accumulating balance on Cris's credit cards is a small price to pay for strengthening the cherished relationship with her mother.

Mom, Did You Borrow My (Master)Car(d)?
Confronting the Realities of the Middle-Class Squeeze

The most neglected trend among college students is the use of credit cards for providing financial assistance to family members and close friends. This phenomenon has been ignored by researchers and industry analysts who limit the scope of their investigations to the personal expenditures of individual students. Indeed, this source of indebtedness defies the common portrayal of "irresponsible" student consumption and the last-ditch efforts of parents who are traditionally viewed as bailing out their children from massive credit card debt. However, the roles are often reversed as parents plead for—and even demand—economic help from their children who are enrolled in college. Furthermore, the social pressures that lead to these requests for assistance are not unusual. The major difference is that these "loans" are provided by credit cards (charges or cash advances) rather than from personal savings and by full-time students rather than employed family members. For these students, the economic burden that results from their strong familial bonds becomes an enduring financial obligation for many years after graduation. And for those whose parents' economic circumstances do not markedly improve, the prospects of personal bankruptcy are an unrelenting reality.

The past two decades of U.S. industrial restructuring have intensified the economic squeeze on American middle-class families. Some high-salaried workers have lost their jobs through corporate mergers or management streamlining. Others have been downsized through layoffs or outsourced through subcontracting agreements. Most middle-class families have borne the economic pressures through stagnant real wages and rising costs such as college tuition and medical care. These circumstances are exacerbated, moreover, by social crises such as divorce or health problems. Also, tensions between parents over personal financial expenditures have led to increased use of children's credit cards for shielding potentially contentious purchases from volatile spouses. The following examples illustrate the wide range of family dependence on children's credit cards.

When Kristin applied for a credit card in fall 1995, she never dreamed that her father's health problems would have such a dramatic impact on her credit history or her relationship with her mother. The oldest of three children, Kristin enjoyed an upper-middle-class lifestyle in an affluent white community of suburban New Jersey. Five-bedroom homes, stay-at-home moms, memberships in exclusive country clubs, private prep schools, vacations in Europe, and expensive foreign cars were the norm of her adolescence. Money was not a constraint on the family's activities, as John, her father, was a vice president of a large insurance company. Unfortunately, during her senior year of high school, Kristin's father suffered a severe heart attack. The timing of his health problems could not have been worse, as his company soon embarked on a policy of downsizing its workforce. During his convalescence, John was unable to protect his job, and he was forced into early retirement at only 49 years old. Kristin did not know at the time that the family had been living beyond its financial means. Not only were there little savings, but her parents had accumulated substantial debts from their inflated standard of living.

Kristin's mother, Mary, did not accept the inevitable consequences of her husband's medical and career misfortunes. Although Mary reluctantly began to work part-time while John slowly recovered from bypass surgery, she refused to adjust the family's upper-middle-class lifestyle to reflect their new economic reality. For Kristin, her mother's behavior was a source of mounting tension. Kristin had accepted the responsibility of financing her private college education with student loans and part-time jobs while lowering her standard of living. Furthermore, she was angry that her matriculation at a private university in Washington, D.C., would require many years of personal sacrifices after graduation, whereas her mother simply portrayed it as a testament to the family's affluent social status—the equivalent of vacationing at a three-star hotel. The reality of the middle-class squeeze was more quickly understood by Kristin than her mother. Indeed, Kristin cautiously budgeted her limited student resources, whereas Mary pretended that the family's financial woes would soon pass. Mary's refusal to accept her downward mobility contributed to her denial of the mounting "past due" notices from multiple credit card and debt collection companies.

Early in her first semester, Kristin quickly realized that the costs of books, personal items, and weekend activities were far more than she could afford on her meager savings and university financial aid. In order to stretch her limited resources, Kristin decided to get her own credit card, since she no longer had access to her parents' plastic. The slogan "It pays to Discover" was appealing because the "no annual fee," "build your own credit history," and "cash back bonus" features satisfied her need for financial control. When she mailed the application, she unconsciously wrote down her parents' address.

As Kristin prepared for her first set of midterm exams, she forgot about the Discover application. Her finances were tight, but she had enough money for the semester, and she would get a job over the Christmas holidays. Not until she received a phone call in early December from a Discover representative did she learn that her credit card application had been approved two months earlier. More startling, she was informed that it was maxed out and in a delinquent status. Kristin owed over $1,500, and her credit history was already tainted with late and over-limit penalties. Convinced that she was a victim of credit card fraud, Kristin demanded that Discover investigate the charges to her account. To her shock, the credit card had been used (and abused) by her own mother. When Kristin returned home for the semester break, she confronted Mary about the unauthorized use of the Discover card. What angered Kristin was her mother's explanation: "With your father out of work . . . all of the credit cards were at their limit . . . I needed [yours] for family expenses." In fact, Mary scolded her daughter for being so "selfish," reminding her, "we provided well for you, and we still have to take care of your [two] younger sisters."

For Kristin, it was her mother's unrepentant attitude that was most disturbing. Unwilling to accept her husband's situation, Mary embraced the end-justifies-the-means mentality for prolonging her lifestyle. As Kristin exclaimed, "Can you believe it . . . she says that I'm selfish, but she refuses to give up her Jag[uar], country-club [membership], and shopping sprees." Unfortunately for Kristin, her well-intentioned strategy of establishing a record of financial responsibility through the cautious use of credit cards backfired through no fault of her own. The "payback" from Discover was not the promised 1 percent cash-back bonus or a carefully constructed credit history.[59] Instead, Kristin discovered that she was contributing financially to her parents' struggling household and unexpectedly suffering the consequences of their irresponsible credit card use. As a result, Kristin embarked on a nearly one-year crusade to restore her financial reputation. In the process, she confided that the relationship with her mother had deteriorated beyond repair. Mary continues to deny the irresponsibility of her actions or the long-term consequences her daughter may suffer. In the end, this example illustrates that the social cost of credit can far exceed its economic value.

Unlike Kristin, Sheila fully expected that she would financially contribute to her family's household expenses after graduating from high school in West Point, Mississippi. The oldest of four children, all of whom are enrolled in college, Sheila is a 22-year-old junior at Georgetown University. Although her father is a steelworker and her mother is a schoolteacher, their combined household income of $62,000 is inadequate for maintaining their middle-class lifestyle. For Sheila and her family, who are considered successful by the standards of the local African American community, their goal is to provide themselves with new clothes, proper educations, a socially acceptable home with new furnishings and appliances, personal grooming items, medical care, and exposure to high-class culture. Hence, they play the all-American game of "keeping up with the Joneses," which included "new Sunday dresses, piano lessons, and braces." Without adequate resources, however, the family must rely on high-cost loans from finance companies, credit cards, and pawnshops. In fact, all of her family members have learned to accept their dependence on debt, and their creative financial strategies have evolved into a precariously fragile standard of living.

Sheila and her siblings are proud of their academic accomplishments. Her brother attends Alcorn State University, and her sister is at the University of North Carolina. They all agree that college is essential for continuing their membership in the middle-class, and, of course, each has at least two credit cards. As the oldest, Sheila was the first to receive a credit card—Discover—during her senior year of high school. Significantly, she received the credit card application, with the unnecessary inducement of a free T-shirt, while visiting a prospective college; a part-time job paid for her monthly payments. This marketing encounter proved particularly effective, as all three siblings currently have a Discover credit card. Although Sheila's mother, Karen, was heavily in debt, she supported her daughter's decision because she believes credit is a middle-class entitlement. That is, credit cards are a financial supplement—a form of extra income—for purchasing necessary items after exhausting one's earnings. To Karen, the more, the better. Not surprisingly, all of Sheila's and her siblings' credit cards are maxed out. In fact, Sheila is currently unable to send even the minimum payments on her Discover and Citibank Visa cards. She owes a total of $3,500 plus interest and penalties. In addition, she is negotiating with debt collection agencies over other unpaid bills, including medical expenses resulting from a recent illness.

The key to how Sheila and her siblings amassed credit card debt is that it resulted from their collective efforts to maintain the family's social status. In high school, all of the children had part-time jobs and contributed to household expenses. By the time Sheila's siblings had enrolled in college, the family's consumer debt had swelled to over $30,000. In 1997, with interest rates falling sharply, Karen and her husband refinanced the family house and paid off nearly all of their high-interest debts—over $27,000. This debt consolidation loan, however, only temporarily stabilized their tenuous financial situation. Today, Sheila estimates that her parents' household expenses exceed their income by nearly $900 per month. And as she and her siblings did in their teenage years, they still help with household finances. As full-time students, however, their financial contributions are more likely to be through loans from their credit cards than cash from part-time jobs. They charge or take cash advances for family expenses such as food, utilities, and medical bills. Thus both parents and children are constantly applying for credit cards. "You do it for the family," declared Sheila. "[You] charge to satisfy needs . . . it is a constant cycle . . . After all, if [the banks] give you a credit card . . . they expect you to use it. They don't care if it is for a night at the opera or for groceries."

The goal of presenting the appearance of middle-class respectability is so important to Sheila and her family that they have accepted the "by any *legal* means necessary" strategy for survival. In fact, Sheila matter-of-factly explains that most of her credit card debts are "caused by helping my family." Sheila's indifference to debt, however, should not be interpreted as an expression of financial irresponsibility. Just the opposite. Her emphasis on "legal" is very important, because her strong Christian upbringing has left her with no sympathy for those who ignore their financial obligations. According to Sheila, avoiding economic responsibilities through personal bankruptcy is the "ultimate form of cheating." For her, moral debts are more binding than legal debts. Thus Sheila is not concerned about falling behind on her credit card debts because she will eventually pay back the borrowed money. She is fully aware of all aspects of her debts (including interest rates and penalties) as well as those of her siblings and parents. To Sheila, this attention to financial detail is natural, since "debt is a way of life." In the end, she describes her family's reliance on credit cards as a "present-day form of sharecropping." She is well aware of the downside: "Credit cards give you a false consciousness. . . . You think that they [offer] a higher status—at least by your appearance—but they really keep you down with their high interest charges . . . especially with wages not even keeping up with inflation."

Paper or Plastic?

Since the mid-1970s, rapidly escalating college costs and declining financial aid and real wages have forced students increasingly to rely on credit cards to help pay for their college educations. This has led to a new trend in which credit card debts are being revolved—paid off with federal student loans or even with private debt consolidation loans. For growing numbers of students, credit cards are becoming a savior for financing their educations—especially in public schools. For others, consumer credit initially offers freedom but may become a financial shackle by the end of their college career. The most unfortunate may find that their only option for regaining personal control in the just-do-it culture of credit dependency is to withdraw from school and work full-time in order to pay off their debts. Indeed, official dropout rates (attributed to low grades) include growing numbers of students who are unable to cope with the stress of both their debts and the part-time jobs they must take to service those debts. For others, the reality of their credit card indebtedness may not be realized until after graduation when prospective employers question their past financial recklessness or when they must accept a sharp decline in their standard of living.

A key factor in college marketing campaigns is that adolescence and early adulthood are the formative periods for shaping consumer attitudes (immediate gratification versus the cognitive connect) as well as consumer tastes for specific products and corporate brand loyalty. This has produced new cross-marketing campaigns in which banks join with corporate retailers in reaching students through credit card advertisements (American Airlines, *Time* magazine, Wal-Mart, L.L. Bean, Sony). Not surprisingly, the social pressures of college—especially for students from modest-income families—constitute an ideal setting for manipulating parental authority conflicts and status anxiety among young, impressionable students. The ability to acquire credit cards, without parental consent, is exacerbating family tensions over unapproved behavior (drinking, sex, drugs, body piercings, tattoos, holiday trips, expensive clothes). In fact, many students with credit cards provided by their parents are acquiring their own in order to conceal their social, sexual, and consumption activities. Hence, student credit cards are contributing to heightened family tensions as well as shielding potential financial responsibility from the purview of parents or guardians.

A final issue concerns the seduction of college and university administrators by the credit card industry. This Faustian pact includes sponsoring school programs, funding student activities, renting on-campus solicitation tables, and paying "kickbacks" for exclusive marketing agreements such as college or alumni affinity credit cards. As a result, rather than protecting the economic and educational interests of their students, college administrators are playing an active and often disingenuous role in promoting the societal acceptance of consumer debt as well as the prominence of credit cards in college life. For instance, bank-sponsored "smart" (computer chip) cards are being used as student IDs (automated dorm entry "key") as well as bank credit cards (Visa, MasterCard). Their multifunction "stored value" features facilitate the collection and transmission of personal data throughout the fiber-optic network of the global information economy with only limited privacy protections. In the absence of direct parental guidance, together with a social environment that promotes immediate gratification (attitudinal disconnect between cash and credit) and the deferment of economic responsibility (e.g., student loans), the financial education of American college students is increasingly being auctioned by universities to the highest corporate bidders. This suggests that one of the most enduring lessons of college—often beginning with the first tuition loans—is the uncritical acceptance of credit dependency. Most likely, it will help to shape the sharp disjuncture between current discretionary lifestyle activities and the inability to satisfy future consumption desires due to the burdens of college indebtedness and modest household incomes.

7

Where Ace Is Not a Hardware Store

Fringe Banking and the Expansion of Second-Tier Financial Services

IN A DECEMBER 1999 SPEECH, Comptroller of the Currency John D. Hawke Jr. lauded the recent passage of the landmark Financial Services Modernization Act (FSMA).[1] He explained that U.S. consumers are the major beneficiaries of the increased availability of lower-priced financial services that will be offered:

> The market works, the profit motive will lead [banks to offer] more services at competitive prices . . . this legislation will enable banks to respond [more efficiently] to customer demands. . . . Banks will be able to provide their customers with all of their financial needs—insurance, investments, credit cards, consumer loans, checking [accounts]—basically one-stop shopping for all their [financial service] needs.[2]

Hawke predicted that the cost of consumer financial services will decline at least 5 percent over the next two decades. For American households, this amounts to a hefty savings—nearly $18 billion per year. But where will these gains come from? According to Hawke, they will be realized from new corporate efficiencies resulting from the dismantling of the 1933 Glass-Steagall Act[3] whose regulatory firewalls prevented financial institutions from engaging in both wholesale and retail banking. Indeed, the explicit mandate of these depression-era regulations was to prevent the formation of financial services conglomerates (insurance, brokerage, underwriting, credit cards, banking services) like Citigroup and Morgan Stanley Dean Witter Discover.[4]

Today, the political climate regarding supervision of the banking industry has changed dramatically, even after the S&L fiasco of the 1980s and the Microsoft antitrust trial of the late 1990s. The U.S. government's objective has shifted from restricting bank activities (protecting consumer deposits from risky investment schemes) to actively promoting deregulatory policies that facilitate the creation of financial services conglomerates. By encouraging potential corporate synergies, public officials have tended to overlook the steadily rising costs of consumer financial services, with the notable exception of ATM fees. At the same time, bank mergers and acquisitions have reduced competition and precipitated major employee layoffs while yielding unprecedented industry profits. Admittedly, not all Washington insiders have supported this profound policy shift. Many are voicing concerns over the political influence of financial services conglomerates with their penchant for oligopolistic pricing practices and disregard for consumer confidentiality in their cross-marketing campaigns.[5]

The most controversial issue concerning the deregulation of financial services pertains to the "self-banked" population—households without banking accounts in state-chartered financial institutions. When Hawke was queried about the FSMA's impact on low-income groups—at least 20 million people do not have checking or savings bank accounts—Hawke acknowledged that there may be some short-term problems but asserted that market forces would ultimately resolve any difficulties in providing them with necessary financial services. In fact, Hawke emphasized that additional federal oversight was unnecessary due to the relief mechanisms of the 1977 Community Reinvestment Act (CRA); the Clinton administration staunchly defended the CRA against the concerted efforts of the bank lobby to have it abolished.[6]

The industry maintains that the CRA's bank regulations are burdensome. Banks are required to provide loans in the same low-income or minority areas where they accept deposits. Ironically, the CRA is difficult to enforce because of the complexity of monitoring the consumer loans of thousands of banks that have been absorbed by regional or national behemoths. Its most threatening regulatory power is the authority to deny a proposed merger or acquisition based on the deficient compliance record of a pro-

posed bank partner—albeit a very rare occurrence.[7] Even so, Hawke expressed concern over the increasing number of "unbanked" households after
the defeat of an amendment to the FSMA that would have offered low-cost
checking accounts to the poor.[8]

In summary, Hawke contended that the FSMA will lead to greater competition, more innovative products, and lower prices—the optimal outcome of
unfettered market forces. The key is whether *all* consumers will benefit from
the market-driven reform of the financial services industry. That is, will the
primary beneficiaries be high-income households that conduct their business
in first-tier banks where personal advisers cater to their individual financial
needs?[9] Or, will the gap in consumer financial services between the working
poor and more affluent clients begin to narrow over the next decade through
the invisible hand of the market? This issue is especially important, since the
banking industry's massive investment in high-tech information systems tends
to neglect low-income groups and others that lack technological training, In-
ternet-wired personal computers, and access to local bank branches.

The latter trend is suggestive because it raises questions about the neoclassical economic assumption of unified markets. In fact, based on consolidation
trends in the financial services industry—especially the recent flurry of bank
mergers and acquisitions (See Table 3.1)—there is little evidence to suggest
that the increasing bifurcation of the consumer financial services industry will
abate in the near future.[10] Significantly, this is largely due to corporate policies of first-tier banks rather than the personal preferences of the working poor
and highly indebted middle class. That is, rapidly rising bank fees (particularly for returned checks) and minimum account balances together with the
closing of full-service bank branches—especially in the central city—are
sharply reducing the availability and desirability of basic financial services of
first-tier banks for low-income families and new immigrants.[11]

The departure of traditional banks from poor neighborhoods does not
necessarily reflect a declining demand for financial services or the lack of a
profitable consumer market. Instead, the emergent void of first-tier financial services is swiftly being filled by a second-tier system of high-interest
"fringe banks"—many with direct ties to first-tier banks. According to
Jonathan I. Lange, lead organizer of Baltimoreans United for Leadership
Development, "'We see banks closing up in the inner city and being replaced by these parasitical financial [fringe banking] institutions. It's one
more example of the poor paying more for services.'"[12]

Aptly called "merchants of misery" by Michael Hudson,[13] corporate loan
sharks are enjoying a feeding frenzy in the murky and largely unregulated
waters of fringe banking. Their operations include check-cashing outlets,

pawnshops, car-title pawns, sale-leaseback loans, rent-to-own stores, sub-prime auto lenders, and even cash leasing. The once forlorn landscape of the second tier is rapidly changing as the corporate loan sharks also target locally owned mom-and-pop shops. With finance rates that commonly range from 180 percent to 520 percent (APR) and even higher, it is no wonder that second-tier financial services are proliferating at a dizzying pace. And they are not low-profile, with their bright neon signs flashing corporate logos such as Aaron's, Ace Cash Express, Almost A Banc, Cash-2-U, Cash Cow, EZLoan, Famous Pawn, Kwikash, Mr. Payroll, Rent-A-Center, and Last Chance Finance. But at what social cost is this expansion coming?

Deregulation of Consumer Financial Services: Where Did the Banks Go?

The Citicorp-Travelers merger—which will produce the world's first trillion-dollar financial services conglomerate—is accelerating the bifurcation of the consumer financial services market. Industry consolidation in the 1980s and early 1990s resulted in the withdrawal of first-tier banks from low-income and minority (especially urban) communities. A continuation of earlier geographic redlining policies, this trend has been accompanied by only minimal satisfaction of the CRA's requirements; banks want the deposits of poor people but do not want to provide them with moderate-cost loans. For example, the Parkchester branch in New York City was one of Citibank's most profitable with deposits of $65 million. Yet in 1996, it was closed, and customer accounts were transferred to a branch one mile away. This led a South Bronx community organization to examine the nationwide pattern of Citibank's branch closings. It concluded that "'Citibank is opening new branches in affluent, non-minority communities while closing and downgrading branches in low-income and predominantly minority communities.'"[14]

Today, Wall Street–financed banking consolidations are spawning new consumer services conglomerates that are tailoring their marketing and investment policies toward higher-income households that use a wider range of financial products and services. According to Richard Hartnack, vice chairman of Union Bank of California, "'[Most] banks seem to be focusing on the upscale market, such as investment products.'"[15] Hence, the sharp increase in economic inequality over the past two decades has fundamentally shaped the two-tiered banking industry. That is, banks have increased their highly profitable consumer financial services in the affluent suburbs while they have reduced their low-profit retail banking services in low-income, especially urban, communities.

For example, Citigroup's expanding array of financial services currently includes brokerage services (Salomon Smith Barney), mutual funds (Primerica Financial), property and casualty insurance (Travelers Property Casualty), real estate services (Citicorp Real Estate), and retirement products (Travelers Life and Annuity). Typically, the demand for nonbanking products is relatively modest in lower-income middle- and working-class neighborhoods. This is why first-tier banks spent the 1990s developing new technologies (ATMs, automatic paycheck deposit, bank-by-phone, Internet banking services) that reduced the demand for routine and relatively costly banking services. In the next expected stage, the new full-service banks will embark on a secondary exodus from these communities in order to focus their resources on more affluent areas that use the full range of their more profitable consumer financial services. This explains the banking industry's tenacious lobbying against consumer privacy laws; intercorporate sharing of consumer information (Citigroup and AT&T) is the cornerstone of their cross-marketing strategies. An auto loan application at a Citibank branch could generate solicitations from Travelers Life for insurance or Primerica Financial for mutual funds.

As first-tier banks close their full-service branch locations, they are replacing them with inferior substitutes such as ATMs or limited-service supermarket offices. Together with sharply rising fees and bank policies that discourage the participation of low-income customers, it is not surprising that the number of households without first-tier bank accounts rose sharply during the first decade of banking deregulation: from 6.5 million (9 percent) in 1977 to 11.5 million (14.9 percent) in 1989. In 2000, the most credible estimates are that 13–15 percent of U.S. households are "unbanked" or without checking or savings accounts,[16] nearly double the proportion in England.[17] However, it is the poorest of the poor who are the most disadvantaged by the new era of deregulation. For instance, in the poverty-stricken South Bronx of New York City, Citicorp has only one consumer bank branch for approximately 500,000 residents.[18] Overall, only about 60 percent of households with less than $10,000 annual income are estimated to have banking accounts, versus 99 percent with over $50,000 income, according to the Federal Reserve's 1995 Survey of Consumer Finances; the Federal Reserve estimates that as many as 41 percent of working-class households do not have a checking account. This translates into over 20 million Americans who do not have access to basic banking services.[19]

Not surprisingly, the highest consumer debt burdens are borne by the lowest wage-earning households. This pattern is documented by a study of family wealth patterns based on analysis of the 1995 Survey of Income and Program Participation, which found that the median U.S. family had net financial assets of only $1,000. For families with an annual income of less than $12,940 (lowest family income quintile), their mean consumer debt of $4,104 is an enormous 52.8 percent of their mean family income of $7,779. This compares with 27.9 percent for the second quintile of family income ($12,940–$23,138), 22.6 percent for the third quintile ($35,919–$54,946), 20.3 percent for the fourth quintile ($35,919–$54,946), and 16.2 percent for the fifth quintile (over $54,946).[20] Clearly, the working poor are the most debt-dependent households in America. The key issues are where they get their consumer credit, and how much it costs.

Corporate Loan Sharks:
"Relationship Banking" for the Working Poor

The success of first-tier banks in influencing cultural attitudes toward debt, even promoting the use of credit cards as the "currency of fun," has inspired second-tier banks to embark on similarly beguiling marketing campaigns. The goal is to enhance their image as "lenders of last resort" while simultaneously justifying the enormous profits they extract from primarily lower-income clients. In attempting to change the public perception that they are "ghetto bankers" and "poverty pimps," these corporations are pursuing some of the same tried-and-true strategies used by their first-tier counterparts: associate with popular activities (NASCAR auto racing) and celebrities of the cultural mainstream. For example, NFL broadcasting icon John Madden is in great demand as a corporate spokesman. For years, his endearing television advertisements have exhorted middle-class Americans to shop at "Ace, the place of the helpful hardware folks." Emblematic of the Protestant work ethic, Madden has marketed his public persona as a hardworking Six-Pack Joe and a straight shooter—someone you can trust—albeit one with an eight-figure bank account.

At the same time that Madden promotes Ace, he is also paid handsomely by Rent-A-Center to cross over into the business realm of "no credit needed" and "first week free when second week is paid," pitching customers through the storefront windows of the industry's largest rent-to-own company. In fact, many stores feature a nearly life-size likeness of the former Oakland Raiders football coach. On large cardboard cutouts and magazine-quality fliers, Madden talks the talk: "Get the good stuff. Get the best brands today with no long-term obligation . . . Sony, Philips, JVC, Toshiba, Sealy, Whirlpool, Dell."

Madden, whose imposing physical presence is hard to ignore, is especially conspicuous because celebrities are rarely recruited as pitchmen in this business sector. Why pay the extra marketing expense if customers shop in rent-to-own stores only when they have no other retailing options? In this case, as corporate consolidation intensifies competition among the dwindling number of chain outlets, Madden offers a subliminal connection to the corporate mainstream. In the process, he offers a marketing credibility edge against Rent-A-Center's rivals in attracting highly indebted, middle-income households. Ironically, another corporate chain with its distinctive green corporate logo—Ace Cash Express—is a common fixture near many rent-to-own stores. Although both companies serve many of the same customers, these people rarely associate John Madden with being the corporate spokesman of the Ace hardware stores. Nevertheless, he bridges the social chasm of corporate respectability for Rent-A-Center and its customers. With his reassuring smile radiating throughout the store, its clients know where at least a small portion of their hard-earned money goes.

As banking deregulation has accelerated the bifurcation into first- and second-tier financial services, many myths concerning the undesirability of the working poor as consumer markets have been dispelled. These stereotypes of low-income households include (1) they receive little corporate attention because of their modest disposable income; (2) they are served primarily by small mom-and-pop stores due to their marginal profitability; and (3) their irresponsible financial behavior underlies the punitive "stick" of high-cost credit. The latter view—a variant of the blame-the-victim syndrome—is a cultural legacy of the Puritan-influenced morality of debt; usurious interest rates are socially justified as negative incentives for encouraging more diligent work and frugal spending habits. Indeed, most customers of second-tier services are erroneously characterized as erratically employed, unmotivated, or welfare-dependent.

These enduring misconceptions have been revealed following the withdrawal of first-tier banks from poor and low-income communities. That is, the emergent vacuum of financial services has exacerbated the desperation of these residents and their willingness to pay usurious interest rates. As explained by a West Baltimore man, who owed about $4,000 to several check cashers, "'Right now, people who are being gouged feel there is no choice. . . . If you're victimized, it doesn't mean that you are ignorant and aren't aware you are being victimized. It just means you're desperate.'"[21] Furthermore, the employment dislocations of U.S. industrial restructuring and labor market reorganization (rise of temps), normal social crises (divorce, accidents, family emergencies), recurrent personal difficulties (auto repairs, medical expenses, life-cycle needs), rapid growth of new immigrant communities (lack of ties with first-tier banks), dramatic rise in personal bankruptcies (6 million over the past 5 years), enormous expansion of modern fringe-banking outlets, and aggressive corporate marketing campaigns have attracted millions of temporarily and persistently "broke" customers. As the social composition of fringe-banking clients has become more diverse, so too has the array of new products and services—especially with the arrival of heavily indebted middle-income households. With U.S. unemployment rates hovering at 4 percent in 2000, future economic conditions cannot be expected to improve appreciably for most clients of the second tier.

Like the marketing of relationship banking in the first tier, the rapid expansion of the fringe-banking sector has been fueled by the "merchandising of respect" to traditionally neglected customers and their neighborhoods: "'The customer should feel like this is home, a place [to] feel comfortable and [where the staff] cares about you.'" In fact, the industry's market research has shown that potential customers are more pride- than price-sensitive, "craving good treatment even more than low prices." This has led to the refurbishing of the image and business practices of the second tier by upscaling showrooms, offering state-of-the-art models, emphasizing products with premium features, personalizing greetings to customers, introducing high-technology services, fostering long-term relationships with clients, and even sending inexpensive flower arrangements to funerals of local residents.[22]

The emphasis on personal respect is illustrated by two television commercials for Rent-A-Center. In a night-shift ad (3–5 a.m.), a middle-aged working-class woman explains, "If somebody goes to work every day and they have bad credit or no credit, there's really no reason why [they] shouldn't be able to have nice things. With Rent-A-Center you can." In another ad that targets Latinos, a young woman declares, "For what it cost me at the laundromat, I got a washer/dryer at Rent-A-Center . . . And you don't need credit to get it!" The ads conclude with "*free* delivery, *free* setup, *free* service, *no* commitment!" After luring potential clients with these advertisements, the sharks of the rent-to-own industry go for the kill as soon as their quarry walk through the door. As explained by Carol, a waitress at a resort hotel in Bolton Landing, New York, "'The prices could be cheaper but they treat me like I'm somebody.'" Her home is almost completely furnished by Rent-A-Center.[23]

"Buddy, Can You Spare a Loan?" Corporate Loan Sharks and the Growth of Second-Tier Financial Services

The dramatic growth of second-tier financial services has been propelled by the successful evasion of state usury laws—a distinguishing feature of bank deregulation. For example, Ohio's Small Lending Act limits consumer loans to a maximum of 28 percent state (APR) on balances up to $1,000; in New York the state usury law ceiling is 25 percent, in Missouri 26.6 percent (APR) plus 5 percent of the loan, in New Jersey 30 percent (APR), in Florida 31 percent (APR), and in Maryland 33 percent (APR); Illinois abolished its state usury laws in the early 1980s during the initial phase of bank deregulation.[24] So, how does the industry legally command 20 to 70 percent APR *per month*? This victory of corporate avarice was won by aggressively soliciting state legislators throughout the country and hiring powerful lobbyists to promote special safe-harbor provisions for fringe-banking activities.[25] Essentially, these laws exempt fringe-banking transactions from state usury laws by redefining them as check-cashing "fees" and product "leasing" services rather than consumer loans. The most outrageous example is the "sale-lease-back loan." A customer ostensibly "sells" an appliance such as a refrigerator to a lender and then "leases" it back; the item never leaves the client's home.

The most recent strategy for circumventing state usury laws is the "exportation" of high interest rates. That is, by partnering with banks or thrifts (S&Ls) that are chartered in unregulated states, check cashers are able to import interest rates that exceed local usury rate caps. For example, a national class action suit filed in California accuses Eagle National Bank of "renting" its bank charter to Dollar Financial Group. The purpose is to evade otherwise applicable consumer loan regulations in order to raise the fees charged by its Cash Til Payday loans; one-third of Eagle's profits were derived from these payday loans in 1998. Significantly, this exportation strategy is based on a 1978 Supreme Court decision that permits out-of-state banks to charge higher interest rates on their credit cards than allowed by the usury laws of the receiving state. Consequently, the enactment of these safe-harbor laws in the 1990s (23 states and D.C.) precipitated the rush into fringe banking.[26] This is demonstrated by the enormous growth of its three main pillars.

Gus's Pawnshop: "See Why They Call Us the People's Bank"

The first fringe-banking pillar, pawnshops, has nearly tripled in size during the first two decades of banking deregulation. From about 4,849 in 1985 to 7,760 in 1991 (across the United States but especially in the South), the number of pawnshops jumped to 8,787 by the end of the recession in early 1992. Today, distressed urban neighborhoods and even new suburban strip malls are littered with almost 14,000 pawnshops with names like Best Pawn, Cash America, Castle Pawn, EZPawn, Famous Pawn, The Jewelry Exchange, Metro Pawn, First Cash, and Mr. Cash.[27] Although about 30 percent of customers default on their "pawns," this financial loss (loans are typically 25–30 percent of appraised value of pawned items) is praised as a desirable feature. That is, failure to "renew" (pay monthly interest) or "redeem" (pay loan and interest) a pawned item is not reported to a credit bureau; delinquent payments or defaulted loans are confidential information. Amazingly, many customers confide that this is a preferred business practice. They have internalized the ideology of the oppressed—"you play, you pay"—even if the cards are stacked against them.

The largest chain of pawnshops, a subsidiary of Cash America Investments, illustrates the meteoric rise of the industry as well as the flow of second-tier profits to first-tier corporate balance sheets. Beginning with 4 Texas pawnshops in 1984, founder Jack Daugherty had an ambitious vision for an aggressive acquisition strategy that required a large infusion of investment capital. This was realized through a public stock offering in 1987 that made Cash America the first pawnshop company to be traded publicly on the New York Stock Exchange (PWN). At the time, its initial public offering (IPO) was one of the most profitable of the pre-dot-com era, and Cash America immediately became the industry leader. In 1991, it had grown to 178 pawnshops in seven states. Only four years later, it had amassed 365 stores, including operations in Europe; the first English pawnshops were acquired in 1992. Aided by its financial ties with Bank of America, Cash America has continued its expansion through acquisition strategy. In 1999, it totaled 414 domestic shops in 16 states and 50 foreign (United Kingdom and Sweden) operations. Overall, Cash America's 1.25 million outstanding loans average $102 (totaling $129 million in early 1999) at monthly interest rates from 12 to 25 percent; corporate financing costs 6–8 percent APR, and gross profit margins on the sale of pawned merchandise were 37 percent in the late 1990s.[28]

Cash America is constantly exploring expansion opportunities in other fringe-banking activities. This began at its inception with negotiations to acquire the nation's largest check casher (ACE) in 1987 and the largest rent-to-own company (ColorTyme) in 1988. In 1997, Cash America established a separate subsidiary, Rent-A-Tire, that offers only new tires and wheels; it grew from 4 stores to 27 by the end of 1999. More strategic, Cash America Investments, Inc., forged a joint venture with Wells Fargo Bank in 1999: InnoVentry Corp. Both companies are equal equity partners (45 percent) in Mr. Payroll (founded in 1997), the first fully automated check-cashing and financial services company. Wells Fargo's investment includes $21 million in equity capital and assets of an existing network of 200 ATMs valued at $6 million. This business venture constitutes a technological leap into the second (albeit related) pillar of fringe-banking services, including check cashing, payday loans, money orders, and bill paying. Most important, it provides access to highly indebted segments of the U.S. middle class by placing Mr. Payroll kiosks in convenience (Circle K) as well as oil company stores (Texaco, Conoco, BP) and Ralph's supermarkets in 20 states; the goal is 1,700 check-cashing ATMs by the end of 2000.[29]

Check-Cashing Outlets:
The High Cost of Convenience and Financial Desperation

The proliferation of check-cashing outlets (CCOs) reflects both the growth of the self-banked population and the magnitude of its financial transactions. The primary service provided by CCOs is cashing checks (government, payroll, bank) for a fee (typically 1.0–3.25 percent) and more recently payday and small consumer loans. Most CCOs also offer ancillary services such as money orders, money wire transfers, bill payment services, bus and subway cards, prepaid phone cards, lottery tickets, fax transmissions, notary services, copying machines, mailboxes, and postal services. Between 1985 and 1987, the number of CCOs increased moderately—from about 2,000 in 1985 to 2,151 in 1987. Over the next five years, however, they more than doubled to almost 5,000 and then stabilized at about 5,500 in 1999; CCO revenues are expected to approach $2 billion in 2000.[30]

Significantly, the modest growth of CCOs in the late 1990s is not an indication that the market is nearing its saturation point. Rather, it reflects the mass entry of pawnshops and predatory lenders into the most profitable segment of fringe-banking services: payday loans. These are essentially postdated checks ($100–$300) that are cashed at a specified "service" premium. Typically, a customer writes a check for $240 and receives $200 in cash for a maximum two-week loan (520 percent APR). However, if the customer does not have enough money in his or her checking account and wants to avoid returned-check fees, the debt is simply "rolled over" like a pawnshop loan by paying the interest for another two weeks. In this case, the fee would be $40, or 20 percent of the check's face value. Overall, the U.S. Federal Reserve estimates that payday loan fee revenues are soaring, from $810 million in 1998 to $1.44 billion in 1999 and to an estimated $2 billion in 2000. Analysts predict that payday revenues could climb to over $6 billion by 2003.[31]

The newfound profitability of poverty has produced a rush to satisfy the demand for desperation loans. This is illustrated in the sharp increase in payday loan outlets—from only 300 in 1992 to over 10,000 today. In fact, a hybrid of payday "deferred deposits" and pawnshop loans has become very popular in the South: car-title pawns. Legal in about 25 states and flourishing in at least 12 and carrying names like Fast Title Loans and Last Chance Finance, they offer larger loans than pawnshops (typically $300–$1,200) and are quickly obtained by pledging one's car title at monthly interest rates of from 2.5 to 25 percent. Some of the most commonly cited reasons for obtaining these loans are to avoid eviction, utility shutoffs, and even arrest for back child support payments or income taxes. Unlike payday loans, however, these loans are secured with the title of the car, which can be confiscated after the borrower has failed to make two consecutive payments. This has been a major point of contention of consumer groups and social service agencies, since the forfeiture of one's car often results in job loss and the inability to pay any financial obligations. Not incidentally, first-tier banks are integral to the expansion of this new industry. The national leader, Georgia-based Title Loans of America (TLA) with over 300 stores nationwide (established in 1993), has secured lines of credit from major financial institutions such as Fleet Capital and a subsidiary of Union Planters Corporation; Union is one of the 50 largest bank holding companies in the United States. Featured in a 1999 *60 Minutes* investigative report, TLA's largest shareholder (Alvin I. Malnik) reputedly has long-standing ties with organized crime and is notorious for hiring high-priced lobbyists to push for enactment of special exemptions for car-title loans in Florida and other state legislatures.[32]

The largest check-cashing company is Ace Cash Express (NASDAQ: AACE), established in 1968. Its corporate literature describes it as "the nation's largest owner, operator and franchiser of retail financial service stores." In spring 2000, ACE celebrated its 1,000th location: 854 company-owned stores and 146 franchises in 30 states. Initially, ACE's impressive expansion pace was propelled by its financial ties with American Express. More recently, however, it has partnered with other corporations in an effort to modernize its processing systems and to offer new financial services. For example, in collaboration with Travelers Express Company (subsidiary of Viad Corp.), ACE now provides bill payment services for walk-in customers in all of its stores. This state-of-the-art system enables ACE to process any retail bill that a customer needs to pay; it is the same as "home banking" with a PC on the Internet.

ACE is also entering the new market of automated check-cashing services that was pioneered by Cash America. In late 1999, ACE introduced 21 advanced-function ATMs (developed by Diebold, Inc.) in the Dallas–Ft. Worth area. The machines are user-friendly, with touch-screen menus that can verify personal information and disburse cash within a few seconds. This foray into automatic financial services will enable ACE to remain competitive in the burgeoning payday loan industry; between 1996 and 1998, its loan revenues doubled to $100 million, fueled by its Cash 'n' Go stores. Not incidentally, ACE has negotiated an exclusive agreement with e-Power International to provide prepaid Internet service through its retail network.[33] Hence, those who cannot enter the high-tech financial corridors of first-tier banks can enter through the back door of the second tier. But the financial toll is very expensive.

While modernizing its processing systems and offering high-tech services are important goals (its secondary objective is to upgrade its corporate image), ACE has continued to diversify into traditional fringe-banking services. For example, ACE is allied with Instant Auto Insurance, an underwriter of "specialty" (high-risk) insurance. Customers can discuss policies over the phone with licensed insurance agents and then activate their new policies at an affiliated ACE store; this service is currently offered at 385 locations in 10 major markets. However, diversification into other financial services has been constrained by ACE's limited access to corporate credit. With over 2 million monthly customers, the volume of cash transactions at ACE locations has reached staggering proportions. For instance, ACE cashed $2.9 billion worth of checks and issued 14.5 million money orders totaling $1.9 billion in 1999. These enormous daily cash demands necessitate large lines of credit from first-tier banks at favorable rates. Indeed, without reliable access to a cash spigot, second-tier fringe banks would wither away from credit starvation. As a result, ACE has recently partnered with Goleta National Bank and now provides small consumer loans ($100–$500) and money orders (maximum of $500)—the most profitable services of CCOs.[34]

The most recent trend in the booming check-cashing industry is the joint ventures among first-tier banks and major CCOs. This symbiotic relationship promises potentially huge profits for modest effort. For instance, first-tier banks have plenty of money to lend, but they do not want to invest in new branch locations or provide basic banking services in inner-city or low-income communities. Check cashers, on the other hand, have the office facilities and the trained staff but lack the capital for financing the tremendous increase of uncollateralized consumer loans. On the national level, this is illustrated by the expansion of American Express into automated check-cashing services through ATMs in 7-eleven convenience stores. At the local level, Union Bank of California (state's third largest) recently purchased 40 percent of Nix Check Cashing. With 47 storefronts that serve 600,000 customers, Union is profiting from the lucrative check-cashing markets of impoverished South Central Los Angeles and Santa Ana.[35]

With returns on payday loans in the incredible range of 30–48 percent, even Citibank has reassessed the poverty market. In 1999, it partnered with a national check-cashing trade group for distributing debit cards to welfare recipients who receive their government benefits electronically. Significantly, the monthly fees charged by Citibank are about the same and potentially even higher than the cost of cashing paper checks. Needless to say, these corporate partnerships are not what community groups had envisioned in their efforts to coax banks to return to the inner city. In fact, not even Comptroller Hawke would laud the efficiency of market forces in providing these banking services to the poor. According to Elizabeth Renuart, staff attorney of the National Consumer Law Center in Washington, D.C.: "'It is ironic that banks, after closing their branches in low-income neighborhoods [and] thus relegating the poor to using check-cashing outlets, are now trying to profit from the same high-fee business they helped to create. This could perpetuate a two-tiered system of delivering financial products that discriminate against the poor.'"[36]

Rent-to-Own: *"And You Don't Need Credit to Get It"*

A third major pillar of the fringe-banking sector is the burgeoning "lease ownership," or "rent-to-own," industry. Its most popular merchandise includes TV/VCRs, stereos, sofas, dining sets, kitchen appliances, bedroom furniture, washer/dryers, computers, and even jewelry. Usually located in low-rent storefronts or strip malls, these outlets feature obscure corporate logos such as Aaron's, Buddy's, ColorTyme, HomeChoice, Rainbow Rentals, Rent-A-Center, and Rent-Way. But their folksy names and brief corporate histories mask a major trend: These companies are growing so large and so quickly that major manufacturers are eagerly courting them to forge strategic alliances. In spring 2000, for example, Gateway negotiated an exclusive rental-supply agreement with Rent-Way and its 1,100 stores for low-cost Internet-equipped computers.[37]

Like pawnshops, sardonically referred to by clients as the "poor man's bank," rent-to-own stores are often viewed by their customers as the last-chance consumer romance for the poor. This is because "everyone is preapproved . . . no credit [is] needed" and thus "no dream is denied." Direct-mail advertisements regularly flood the mailboxes of poor communities much the way preapproved credit card applications flow into middle-class neighborhoods. Rent-to-own pronouncements to "Buy it! Charge it! Lease it!" have a hollow ring, since few people would shop there if they had cash or even credit cards. Indeed, the cost of realizing their consumer dreams exceeds state usury laws by enormous margins. This is why the financial terms are not clearly explained to customers and why industry spokesmen argue that "lease ownership" is not subject to installment loan regulations.[38]

The most alluring aspects of rent-to-own programs are that clients are not subject to an embarrassing credit check, they make only a small down payment, and they have instant purchasing power through seemingly low weekly payments. This is illustrated by Rent-A-Center's typical consumer-baiting strategy: "one week–one dollar [special] when one week is paid. Una semana por un dolar"—literally "a dollar down and payments for life." The industry has experienced tremendous growth over the past two decades—from 2,000 stores in 1982 to nearly 7,000 in 1996. According to its leading trade group, the Association of Progressive Rental Organizations, there are about 8,000 rent-to-own stores currently serving over 3.3 million customers. In 1999, it estimated total industry revenues at $4.7 billion, a rapid climb from $3.6 billion in 1991; the average store generates about $500,000 in annual revenues.[39] Although corporate representatives attribute the growing popularity of their services to client referrals and an expanding customer base, this trend reflects the tremendous increase in U.S. social inequality as well as a sharp decline in the credit options of the working poor in the aftermath of banking deregulation.

For the most economically and educationally disadvantaged, it is hard not to succumb to the industry's aggressive marketing campaigns. According to a former Rent-A-Center store manager in describing the company's "blanket brochuring" in South Carolina, this practice bears a striking resemblance to the old debt peonage system: "'You would brochure [hang fliers on apartment doors] the projects one week before the [welfare] checks came out. . . . Then the day the checks came out, you'd go back and knock on doors and fill out the work forms. Corporate was in on it, the stores were in on it. These people didn't stand a chance.'"[40] It is not surprising that few of these clients can afford their purchases and thus have accumulated little if any equity after many years of lease-ownership payments.

Even so, these "retail rejects" understand that high-pressure rent-to-own stores constitute their only opportunity to enjoy the consumer fruits of the longest economic expansion in American history. This helps to explains why a 1999 survey by the U.S. Federal Trade Commission (FTC) found that 75 percent of rent-to-own patrons reported being generally satisfied with their lease-ownership experiences; overall, 2.3 percent of all U.S. households patronized rent-to-own stores during the previous year. In addition, the FTC survey of 12,000 randomly selected households (including 532 rent-to-own customers) provides important sociodemographic characteristics of the industry's clients: 73 percent have a high school education or less, 59 percent have household incomes under $25,000, 53 percent live in the South, and 31 percent are black. It is important to note that this profile of disproportionately low-income, low-educated, minority customers contrasts sharply with the industry's description of an older, more educated, higher-income, and predominantly white clientele.[41]

The undisputed leader in the lease-ownership industry is Rent-A-Center (NASDAQ: RCII) with 26 percent ownership of all rent-to-own stores. Although founded in 1986, Rent-A-Center (RAC) acquired its market position through recent corporate acquisitions. It controlled only 27 stores in 1993 before initiating its extraordinary expansion. In May 1998, RAC purchased Central Rents and its 176 stores for $100 million in cash. This transaction, however, was a mere prelude to its massive acquisition three months later: Thorn Americas. For $900 million in cash plus assumption of Thorn's outstanding debts, RAC received the industry's prize network of 1,409 company-owned outlets (including the subsidiary ColorTyme) and 65 franchise stores in 49 states and the District of Columbia; it issued $260 million in preferred stock to help finance the Thorn purchase (most through an affiliate of Bear Stearns & Co.) and another $175 million in senior subordinated notes in late 1998.[42]

Today, RAC owns and operates over 2,300 stores in 50 states, Washington, D.C., and Puerto Rico. In just the first quarter of 1999, RAC reported spending $109.3 million on new rental merchandise. RAC is an archetype of buying cheap and selling dear, and its financial success is primarily due to its relations with first-tier banks, which explains the enormous spread between the corporate cost of borrowing and the high returns on lending to the poor. RAC reported that its average rate for corporate borrowing was a mere 7.9 percent APR in 1999—on a total debt of nearly $1 billion—while the rent-to-own rate to its customers typically ranges from 180 to 360 percent APR.[43] These usurious rates do not include multiple resale of individual items due to repossession; a customer does not build up any equity in a leased item until the contract is fulfilled. It is no wonder Wall Street is so bullish on the purveyors of the "good life" to the working poor.

The Golden Age of Predatory Lending: When a Loan Is Not a Loan

The most striking feature of second-tier financial services is their extraordinarily high cost. Indeed, the *financial* definition of "loan sharking" fails to reflect adequately the realities of the new economy; federal law considers 36 percent APR the threshold for "'extortionate extension of credit.'"[44] The fact that interest rates in the second tier are commonly in the 360 to 720

percent APR range suggests that the term "loan shark" is no longer sufficient for describing extremely usurious rates. As Gary L. Calhoun, who provides legal services for a national union explains, "'I know of loan sharks in
New York who wouldn't charge this kind of interest.'"[45] Apparently, based
on the honor code of their predecessors, the new corporate loan sharks are
considered morally bankrupt.

For these new lenders of last resort, the "fleecing of the needy by the
greedy" no longer entails the second criterion of loan sharking—violent collection techniques. Instead, whenever possible, this cost of conducting business is simply shifted to the public through the court system.[46] This is because
banking deregulation has produced a plethora of new consumer financial
services that are so innovative that second-tier banks do not even consider
them loans. For example, cashing a check is now termed a "service," payday
loans are "deferred deposits" or "payment instrument sales," car-title pawns
are "advances," and rent-to-own purchases are "leases." An enterprising payday lender, Checkstop, even offers payday loans on the Internet through an
FDIC-insured institution, Web Bank.[47] Unlike comparison shopping in the
first tier, which enables consumers to find the lowest loan rates on the Internet, "banking without boundaries" in the second tier means that state usury
laws become "lost in [virtual] space." Furthermore, under the new rules of
retail banking, people can even "lease" money at rates that would make real
loan sharks blush. So, how much do these innovative services really cost?

The answer to that question is based largely on the author's field research
(summarized in Table 7.1). The APR of *unregulated* financial services typically ranges from 180 to 391 percent; the primary exceptions are cash leasing at 730 percent APR and especially exploitative payday loans that range
from 442 to 988 percent APR. Check-cashing services include obtaining
cash for payroll or government checks at 1.0–3.0 percent of the face value
(essentially a 2- to 3-day loan at an APR of 122–365 percent) and payday
loans of $100 to $300 (maximum of $500–$600) from check-cashing stores
and pawnshops at 15–20 percent for two weeks (391–520 percent APR),
which are transacted as postdated checks.[48] Pawnshop loans range from
monthly rates of 5 percent in regulated states to 25 percent (300 percent
APR) in essentially unregulated states. Car-title loans range from 2.5 percent per month (30 percent APR) in regulated states to over 25 percent (300
percent APR) in deregulated states such as Wisconsin and Georgia.[49] Rent-
to-own financing typically ranges between 180 and 360 percent APR; rates
are often higher for items in greater demand. Cash leasing is a legal ruse to
circumvent state usury loan ceilings; it is basically a high-rate payday loan
(30 percent per 15 days).

TABLE 7.1   Cost of Second-Tier Financial Services

Check Cashing	Pawnshop Loan	Car Title Loan[a]	Rent-to-Own	Cash Leasing
1.0–3.0%	5–25%[b] month	2.5–25% month	15–30% month	30% per 15 days
2–3 days	15–25% month (unregulated)			
APR 122–365%	60% (regulated) 180–240% (unregulated)	30–300%	180–360%	730%

Payday loans (2 weeks)
   11–21%   12–21%
APR
286–546% 312–546%

CFA-PIRG National Survey[c]
APR
260–988%

[a]Established by state and local usury laws. For instance, Wisconsin and six other states do not have an interest rate ceiling for consumer loans. In comparison, New Jersey limits most consumer loans to a maximum of 30% APR.

[b]Both Virginia and the District of Columbia restrict pawnshop loans to a maximum of 5% per month, although related fees can increase the total cost of loans. In comparison, the maximum monthly rate in Florida is 25%.

[c]In a 1999 survey of 230 payday lenders in 20 states, conducted by Consumer Federation of America and Public Interest Research Group (2000), the average APR was 474%. Nationally, only 19 states currently prohibit payday lending through statutory interest rate ceilings or usury laws.

SOURCE: Author's fieldwork in metropolitan Washington, D.C., and Orlando, Florida.

The annual cost of fringe-banking services (check cashing, money orders, utility payments) in the early 1990s has been estimated at $199 for take-home pay of $10,000, rising to $313 for $16,500, and jumping to $444 for household take-home pay of $24,000 in the early 1990s.[50] Today, this cost has escalated sharply due to the increasing use of high-interest services (pawnshops, payday loans, and the like)—especially by middle-income households ($25,000 to $50,000). By comparison, the annual cost of a traditional checking account with less than a $300 minimum balance has nearly doubled from about $60 per year in 1991 to over $100 today plus $2.50–$3.50 per ATM transaction and $29 returned-check fees.

The increasing participation of middle-income households in second-tier banking services has recently received attention through the enormous popularity of "refund anticipation loans" (RALs). RALs are secured by electronically filed tax returns and are essentially 1- to 2-week high-interest loans (146–452 percent APR). In fact, H & R Block—the nation's largest tax return preparation service—has partnered with Household Bank in providing this high-cost service to 2.4 million clients in 1998. The growing demand for RALs by the highly indebted working and middle classes has led AmScot Tax Service in Tampa to offer RALs on a portion of the Earned Income Credit—a federal subsidy for low-income workers. To process a $1,500 RAL requires a $69 bank fee plus tax return and document preparation expenses.[51] Not surprisingly, this back door to fringe-banking services has channeled increasing numbers of middle-income households to other forms of high-interest loans—even to pawnshops.

As previously discussed, pawnshops are the most popular source of collateralized credit due to their confidentiality and fast access. In Virginia, a regulated state, the interest rates of pawned items are limited to 5 percent per month (60 percent APR); in unregulated Florida, they range as high as 25 percent per month (300 percent APR). Particularly noteworthy is that fieldwork in Virginia, the District of Columbia, and Maryland revealed a striking pattern of different interest rates according to the social class of a store's clientele. That is, not all pawnshops are created equal. High-end or upper-middle-class pawnshops offer monthly rates of 4 to 5 percent that are negotiated on an individual basis. Loans can be made up to $50,000, and pawned items are typically designer jewelry, Rolex watches, silver sets, artwork (a real Picasso), cars (BMWs, Mercedes, Infinitis), and even a chandelier (appraised at $250,000). Middle-income patrons are able to negotiate monthly rates of 10 to 15 percent in unregulated areas. These pawnshops feature new laptops, expensive stereos, wide-screen Sony televisions, costly athletic equipment, valuable coins, baseball card collections, and lots of jewelry; loans commonly range from $70 to $150.[52]

In contrast, the poorest of the poor have no choice but to accept 25 percent per month to pawn gold necklaces, Timex watches, Fender guitars, Magnavox televisions, power tools, bicycles, fishing equipment, and winter coats. Pawns are small and typically range from $20 to $75. Not incidentally, as pawnshops have become active in the payday loan business, there is evidence of similar patterns of stratification in lending rates. For instance, fieldwork in metropolitan Washington, D.C., revealed significant rate variation by the social class of the store's clientele. Even the same corporate pawnshop chain was found to charge different rates in the same state. For example, low-income working-class clients paid the highest rates of 15 percent and even more for two-week loans (391 percent APR), whereas middle-class customers paid only 12 percent (284 percent APR), even though the pawnshops were only a few miles apart.[53]

The growing popularity of lease-ownership companies, which has precipitated a flurry of recent class action suits,[54] merits further examination of the true cost of the "dollar-down" industry. Indeed, the promotion of "convenient" weekly payments obscures usurious finance charges, and high-pressure sales staff are trained to prey on low-income consumption desires. In fact, stores specifically hire salespeople who reflect the sociodemographic characteristics of their clientele: bilingual Latinos (especially U.S.-educated immigrants), young African Americans, and working-class white men. The strategy is to pair a salesperson (shark) immediately with a client (raw meat) of the same socioeconomic background. The feeding frenzy commences immediately as salespeople befriend potential customers, assess their initial needs and desires, trump them with "special offers" for higher-quality products or models with "premium features," and then swiftly seal the deal with instant credit approval and same-day delivery and installation. Unsuspecting customers, especially those who have been frequently rejected for retail credit, are overwhelmed by the slick sales pitches, personal flattery, and instant fulfillment of their consumer romance. But, again, at what cost?

The interest rates of lease-ownership programs are presented in Table 7.2. The three popular consumer electronics products used for the research—19-inch Magnavox television, Fisher VCR, and JVC CD stereo—were selected due to their availability at both electronics retail (Circuit City) and rent-to own (Rent-A-Center) stores located in the same metropolitan Washington, D.C., suburb. The credit price of the electronics chain store includes the cost of financing with a retail credit card (22.8 percent APR) for the same period as the rent-to-own contract. The rent-to-own credit price is the total of all weekly payments required to fulfill the lease-ownership contract. Hence, the two columns showing credit price offer a direct comparison of the cost of financing in the first and second banking tiers. Note, rent-to-own contracts include a onetime processing fee (typically $7.50), late fees (usually $5 per week), and costly "customer protection" plans.[55]

Clearly, the price data show that rent-to-own economics do not reflect prevailing retail market conditions. On average, RAC prices are between two and one-half and three times the retail price of the same item in nearby electronics stores. This is illustrated by comparing retail prices for the Fisher VCR: $199.99 at Circuit City, $599.00 at Rent-A-Center. Furthermore, RAC credit prices do not directly correspond with retail prices. The CD

TABLE 7.2   Cost Comparison of Retail Electronics Chain Versus Rent-to-Own

Consumer Product	Chain Cash Price	Retailer[a] Credit Price	Rent-to-Own[b]	
			Cash Price	Credit Price
New 19" TV				
(Magnavox)	$195.99	$231.46	$549.00	$779.22
78 weekly payments		$2.97		$9.99
Cost of credit		$35.47		$583.23
Annual percentage rate (APR)		22.8%		238.4%
New 4-head VCR				
(Fisher)	$199.99	$236.22	$599.00	$935.33
78 weekly payments		$3.03		$11.99
Cost of credit		$36.21		$735.23
Annual percentage rate (APR)		22.8%		283.6%
New CD stereo				
(JVC)	$189.99	$212.32	$469.55	$659.56
44 weekly payments		$4.83		$14.99
Cost of credit		$22.33		$469.57
Annual percentage rate (APR)		22.8%		357.1%

[a] Depending on the size of the product, Circuit City will deliver to the customer's residence for a fee of from $19.97 to $29.97. The cost of credit (22.8%) is the interest rate of the company's own retail credit card, which is financed by an affiliated bank. If a customer uses a personal bank credit card, the interest rate would be lower.

[b] The contractual terms of agreement clearly specify "no ownership until paid in full." The rental price includes delivery within 24 hours and, if necessary, any repair service during the life of the contract. The cost of credit for the rent-to-own items is based on the completion of the lease-ownership contract. As illustrated by the 19" TV, it is calculated by (1) subtracting the retail price at Circuit City ($195.99) from the total payment price at Rent-A-Center (78 weeks × $9.99 = $779.22), which yields the total finance charge of $583.23, and then (2) calculating the annual percentage interest rate (APR), which is 238.4 percent. See "Debt Zapper" calculator at www.creditcardnation.com.

NOTE: Data are from Circuit City and Rent-A-Center stores that are located in the same suburban Maryland area and are accessible by public transportation. The retail price of the item at Circuit City is the base price used to calculate the cost of credit.

SOURCE: Author's fieldwork in metropolitan Washington, D.C.

stereo has the shortest contract life (44 weeks) but the highest APR, while the retail price of the VCR—only $4 more than the television—costs an additional $156 ($2 more per week) over the 78-week lease. Cash prices, moreover, are deceptive at rent-to-own stores. Only previously leased items, which usually do not include a service warranty, are sold at these prices.[56] The key question, then, is why the disparity? Is this industry practice merely an example of corporate price gouging, or are other factors involved?

Fieldwork observations and interviews with customers and salespeople suggest the answer is much more complex and offer instructive insights into the marketing dynamics of second-tier fringe banks. Inflated "cash" prices are a carefully designed industry policy for discouraging potential consumers who have alternative sources of financing. These prohibitively high cash prices essentially serve to filter out the more creditworthy customers while simultaneously ensuring a large inventory of products for multiple lease-ownership contracts. This is why a cash sale is such a rare occurrence in rent-to-own stores. Simply stated, the creditworthy are undesirable customers because they are not desperate enough to accept the costly terms of a lease-ownership contract. Instead, the rent-to-own industry seeks the most financially distressed, whom they benevolently call "our people." By "treating them like royalty," rent-to-own companies foster long-term relationships that keep their customers dependent on their costly "no credit needed" services.[57]

A comparison of the credit prices in Table 7.2 reveals the subterfuge of the weekly payment schedule. Although rent-to-own payments are only three to four times greater than respective credit card payments, the APR is 10 to 16 times greater. For example, the cost of credit for the 19-inch Magnavox TV is $35.47 with a Circuit City retail credit card (22.8 percent APR) versus $583.23 through the RAC 78-week lease-ownership plan (238.4 percent APR). Significantly, the shorter finance period for the CD stereo (44 weeks) has the highest interest rate: $22.33 by retail credit card (22.8 percent APR) versus $469.57 at RAC (357.1 percent APR).

Not surprisingly, the response of rent-to-own representatives to public criticism is to deflect attention from usurious APRs. Their contention is that the industry serves a growing population that has been abandoned by traditional retailers. Industry spokespeople assert, moreover, that comparisons of APR costs are fallacious because they fail to recognize the valuable services offered by lease-ownership programs. Representatives cite automatic preapproval, short-term contracts, little money down, a way to build credit, fast delivery, free repairs, no transfer fee at end of lease, and, like pawnshop loans, confidentiality of delinquent payments or repossessions.[58] Last, they argue that three-fourths of all contracts are not renewed by the end of four months (17 weeks), and therefore it is unfair to calculate the cost of credit on an APR basis. The latter point, however, offers an important insight into rent-to-own economics. After 4 months of payments, a customer has paid 85 percent of the retail cost of the television, 102 percent of the VCR, and 134 percent of the CD stereo. Hence, most of the merchandise expenses of rent-to-own companies are repaid by the first or second customer. Similarly, customers could pay for the items in cash if they could save their weekly payments for only four months.

Clearly, the cost of rent-to-own leases defies a rational explanation *if* the marketplace includes sufficiently educated consumers with access to alternative sources of financing. The reality is that for many highly indebted low-income families, the only retail stores that welcome their business are rent-to-own companies like Buddy's and Rent-Way. Yet, as with getting a good job or hitting the lottery, their goal of ownership is usually unfulfilled. Of course, it is not the fault of the rent-to-own industry that its customers earn minimum wages, lack medical insurance, have costly auto repairs, or are behind in child support payments. Rent-to-own companies simply exploit these unfavorable circumstances to their maximum financial advantage. It is not surprising, then, that each item in a rent-to-own store conceivably can generate thousands of dollars in revenues through a continuous lease-repossession-lease cycle. Alix M. Freedman reports that a single $119 Philco VCR earned $5,000 in revenues over a five-year period in the early 1990s for a Victorville, California, Rent-A-Center.[59]

Consequently, desperation underlies the tacit acceptance of and even thankfulness for usurious rent-to-own financing by the working poor. Those who beat the odds rarely accumulate much equity for future emergency loans—even when they pay off the ownership lease. For this reason, community groups have followed up their class action lawsuits with educational programs through popular culture and local mass media. In fact, the Consumers League of New Jersey has orchestrated an anti-rent-to-own campaign that includes pamphlets, posters, and a 60-second public service announcement. The latter includes the "Rent-to-Own" rap lyrics "With rent-to-own your paycheck's blown, you keep on paying 'til you turn to stone."[60]

The Market Works but for Whom? New Innovations in Second-Tier Consumer Financial Services

The dearth of available credit and the rising cost of consumer financial services have recently produced two particularly egregious forms of high-cost lending to the working poor and highly indebted middle-class households. The most expensive credit offered by corporate loan sharks is the "cash lease" scam of companies like Cash-2-U Leasing. To evade state usury laws, these companies technically "lease" (rather than loan) money at a cost of 30 percent per 15 days. A maximum of $300 can be leased at any time. Clients must have an active checking account and verify ownership of at least three electronic items that can be pledged as collateral, such as a stereo, computer, or television. Advertising to low-income and economically distressed groups is aggressive, with particular attention to the maxed-out, lower-income, working-class minorities and, more recently, to college students. Radio and print advertising targets racial and ethnic minority communities, with the emphasis on "helping you out" during those "cash crunch periods"—especially holiday gift-giving seasons. Information will not be sent through the mail. Applications must be submitted in person at their offices, and interviews are conducted in order to document personal information and filter out less desperate potential clients. The APR is an outrageous 730 percent.

The second trend is the direct marketing of highly exploitative credit cards. For those with bad credit histories, a collateralized (secured) credit card may be worth the price for beginning the torturous process of rebuilding a worthy credit history. This "credit you deserve," exclaims a Providian Bank television advertisement, can require processing and membership fees of over $100 for the privilege of borrowing your own money at 21.9 APR through a savings account held in escrow by the credit card company. Others desperately seek a credit card as a "bank account of last resort." But an investigation of recent marketing to the poor reveals a new and very costly type of credit card that imposes the purchase of unwanted educational materials and high membership fees but grants little available credit. This is illustrated by the terms of the United Credit National Bank Visa. Its direct-mail solicitation declares, "ACE Visa Guaranteed Issue or we'll send you $100.00! (See inside for details.)" For those who bother to read the fine print (and a magnifying glass would be useful in this case), the terms of the contract are astounding:

> Initial credit line will be at least $400.00. By accepting this offer, you agree to subscribe to the American Credit Educator Financial and Credit Education Program. The ACE program costs $289.00 plus $11.95 for shipping and handling plus $19.00 Processing Fee—a small price to pay compared to the high cost of bad credit! The Annual Card Fee [is] $49.00. . . . For your convenience, we will charge these costs to your new ACE Affinity Visa card. [*They*] *are considered Finance charges for Truth-in-Lending Act purposes.*[61]

An unsuspecting applicant could pay $369 for a net credit line of only $31 at a moderate 19.8 APR. Significantly, this practice is not limited to small credit card issuers. Providian National Bank, the sixth-largest U.S. credit card company, agreed to an out-of-court settlement for a record $300 million in June 2000. John D. Hawke Jr., U.S. comptroller of the currency, explained: "'We found that Providian engaged in a variety of unfair and deceptive practices that enriched the bank while harming literally hundreds of thousands of its customers.'" For example, one of its "no annual fee" programs failed to disclose that the card required the purchase of a $156-a-year credit-protection plan. Customers who complained were informed that the plan was mandatory unless an annual fee was paid.[62]

Living on the Margins of the American Dream: *"Brother, It Ain't Cheap to Be Poor"*

As Josephina Gutierrez Zaccaro emerged from Castle Pawn, on the barrio side of the rapidly gentrifying neighborhood of Mount Pleasant in the District of Columbia, her smile radiated a sense of accomplishment. Josie had reclaimed her favorite gold necklace. Born in Washington, D.C., in 1976, she is the only member of her extended family to graduate from high school. This is because in the rural countryside (*campo*) of El Salvador, where Josie's family is from, only a few years of formal schooling is the norm. As is typical of Salvadoran immigrant households in Washington, D.C., Josie's parents are unskilled blue-collar workers: Rafael is a construction laborer, and Anna is a maid for a domestic service agency. Although Josie's family has not found the streets paved with gold, life has been much better than in El Salvador—especially during the civil war.[63] There is, however, one recurrent problem: money.

Money is a daily concern for Josie and her family. It is especially scarce because Rafael is seldom employed; he is suffering from the long-term, debilitating effects of manual labor and chronic drinking. In addition, Josie is the primary provider for her baby boy, one-year-old Carlito. Her boyfriend, 24-year-old Hector, has worked a variety of minimum-wage dead-end positions such as busboy and fast-food worker but has difficulty keeping a job. Josie attributes Hector's employment problems to his short temper, personal pride, and lack of education—a volatile combination both at work and at home. And without additional job skills, Hector is limited to erratic employment in the low-wage service economy.

Not surprisingly, the lack of earnings by the men has produced considerable turmoil within the household. On the one hand, the men resent the financial independence of the women, but on the other, they realize that these incomes are necessary for paying basic living expenses. Currently, Josie works at night as a waitress in a nearby Latino restaurant. This enables her to watch Carlito during the day while supplementing her income as a babysitter. Although Josie has applied for other jobs, she is concerned that the additional cost of child care may be prohibitively expensive. At the moment, she is waiting to hear from District Cablevision about a bilingual customer service position.

Josie's life is shaped primarily by the demands of her family and social ties to the local Latino community. As happens in so many households in the barrio, Josie fights daily to juggle mounting financial obligations. For her, there is no need for a checking or savings account because there is rarely any money left over at the end of the week. Instead, as with so many of her neighbors, Josie's use of financial services is relegated to second-tier institutions like Crown Pawn, ACE Check Cashing Express, and Rent-A-Center. Although Josie's jobs pay her in cash and thus she does not need check-cashing services, ACE essentially functions as Josie's checking account, since she routinely buys money orders to pay for household bills. Also, there are occasionally unavoidable familial pressures that require sending money orders to El Salvador. However, the financial demands faced by Josie and other members of her household have increased the social and psychological distance of family members who remain in El Salvador. It is easier to sever these social ties than to endure the shame of not being able to send baptismal gifts or medicine to ailing relatives.

As for a savings account, Castle Pawn serves this purpose. Both Josie and her mother regularly have at least two or three items in the pawnshop. Today, these include a radio, her boyfriend's PlayStation (video game system), and some jewelry. When she has some extra money, Josie goes to Castle Pawn and redeems an item. Conversely, when she needs extra money, which is more frequent with the extra expenses of Carlito, she pawns one or more items. Hence, Josie carries her savings with her (gold necklace, bracelet, earrings) or "stores" them at Castle Pawn when in urgent need of money. Typically, Josie's pawns net her $25 to $55.

The integration of the different pillars of second-tier financial services is illustrated by Josie's patronage of Rent-A-Center. Two years ago, when Hector moved in with Josie's family, they all moved to a larger apartment. Since Hector and Josie did not have enough money to purchase furniture, they got a bedroom set from RAC. About three months later, however, they fell behind on their payments due to the unexpected medical expenses of Josie's pregnancy; without medical insurance, they had to pay for her visits to the doctor. Only two weeks of missed payments resulted in the repossession of the furniture. According to Josie's calculations, they lost about $400 in payments, a typical rent-to-own experience. Fortunately, a month later, one of their neighbors moved to Texas and gave them some bedroom furniture.

The most revealing aspect of Josie's experience is that the social networks of the working poor discourage savings in the traditional middle-class sense.[64] Josie, her family, and friends are intertwined in a complex web of reciprocal borrowing and lending relationships. Their ambivalence toward government agencies and nonprofit organizations reflects a general mistrust of public institutions as well as the importance of relying on one another to cope with emergencies. As Josie explains, this is because "life is so unpredictable . . . when problems happen, you must handle them immediately . . . if your baby is sick, you can't go sit and wait to talk with a social worker. . . . If you need help in the middle of the night [from friends], you also have to give it [to them]." Thus, the working poor develop strong ties and honor the unrelenting demands for financial assistance.

According to Josie, it seems impossible to save money: "I'm either repaying a loan [friend or pawnshop] or giving a loan . . . there's always someone who needs money [more urgently] or someone you owe." Indeed, it may seem strange from a middle-class perspective that Josie is lending money at the same time that she is borrowing from Castle Pawn or from other friends. For the poor, however, the strength of their social ties is a matter of utmost importance that cannot be measured in mere dollars and cents. Consequently, at least in the short term, Josie will continue to bank at Castle Pawn even though community activists finally pressured Citibank to open a branch bank only a few blocks down the street—the first bank in the neighborhood since the riots of 1991.[65]

The experience of Josie and her family provides insight into the use of second-tier financial services among the working poor in urban America. Joe and Jeannie Anderson, in comparison, offer a vista into the experience of the white working poor of suburban America. The Andersons, who are in their late 30s, live in a modest residential neighborhood outside of Orlando, Florida. They face a perpetual and often losing struggle "to make ends meet" for themselves and their three children. When he can, Joe sends child support for his daughter from a previous marriage, but Jeannie rarely receives any financial contributions from her oldest son's father.

Both parents are hard workers when their health permits. Joe injured his back in an automobile accident a few years ago, and Jeannie has recurrent bouts of a thyroid condition. A high school graduate, Jeannie works about 30 hours per week at a Martin Marietta assembly plant where she makes $6.35 per hour; she also earns extra money cleaning houses on the weekends and sometimes in the evenings. Joe is a construction worker who makes a decent wage by nonunion standards of around $8.50 per hour; he earned an equivalency degree (GED) after dropping out of school in his junior year. His problem is that the Florida weather makes construction work unreliable, and his bad back often prevents him from working on a good day. Joe still owes about $3,500 in medical bills from his car accident (only Jeannie has limited health insurance from her job) and needs $1,100–$1,500 worth of repair work on his car. Joe was laid up for about eight months after the accident, and he and Jeannie are facing "an uphill battle against our bills." Loans from Joe's mother and Jeannie's sister helped them get by when Joe was hurt. But now they have to "make our basics [expenses]" and start paying back some of the money they borrowed. When both Joe and Jeannie are working, it is daunting but doable. The problem is when circumstances beyond their control—health or weather—limit their earnings. That is why the Andersons have become well acquainted with their "friends" in the second tier of financial services.

Unlike middle-class couples who go shopping in electronics stores, department stores, or discount warehouse clubs, Jeannie and Joe go window-shopping at Buddy's—a regional rent-to-own chain. Their credit history, to be polite, is classified by the major reporting agencies as unsatisfactory. They used to have a Sears card and a $1,200 MasterCard, but they maxed out those years ago; their credit card accounts have all been canceled. They would love to shop at the mall and get a better deal, but they are realistic. "Who's gonna give us credit while we're tryin' to get back on our feet?" And, of course, they can't imagine saving up to buy a couch or a computer with cash. "By the time we save enough to buy a computer, it won't do the kids no good . . . they'll be out of school." Instead, they are consigned to their consumer fate of rent-to-own stores; they have been regular customers at Buddy's for several years.

For them, Buddy's is their friend, a secure island in a sea of financial shoals and predatory loan sharks. They are grateful to have a washer/dryer and living room furniture—even if "it costs a bit more"—because their life is hard and "Buddy's makes it a little bit easier." In fact, they are proud they have not missed a payment in over five months thanks to their "understanding" friends at Buddy's. Interestingly, they refer to their "good credit history" with Buddy's as an indicator of their financial integrity and newfound creditworthiness. When asked if they thought that it was a contradiction to have good credit at a rent-to-own store, they seemed to be genuinely puzzled by the question. The Andersons are doing the best they can under their trying circumstances. And they are quick to distinguish themselves from others who are less financially responsible.

The numerous rent-to-own showrooms that are visible along the highways compete for attention with even more car-title loan stores and pawnshops. Like the summertime growth of weeds, fringe banks proliferate in Florida, which offers the key ingredients for this growth: low wages and high state usury caps. Indeed, the Andersons are too familiar with easy-money offers that end up costing "400 and 500 percent." Their survival strategy has been to develop a good relationship with a pawnshop manager; they are afraid of car-title loans because of the possibility of losing their only means of transportation. Indeed, not only does Joe get a better deal ("around 20 percent per month without fees"), but he also does some shopping; "I got the kids' fishing poles, a necklace for Jeannie, and some mechanic's tools for me." Even so, their most expensive electronic goods were "purchased" at Buddy's, which requires proof of ownership before they can get a pawnshop loan—an embarrassment for many people but not for Joe and Jeannie. In fact, it is a source of pride because proof of ownership shows that they "beat the odds" and paid off their debt—at least this time. After several years of financial failure, they want people to notice their small economic achievements.

The Andersons struggle to make their basic bills each month. Their biggest problem is that their financial legacy of bad credit continues to haunt them with inflated costs. For example, their auto insurance has jumped sharply, and they will probably have to let it lapse after renewing the car registration. They hope that "lightning don't strike us twice" with another accident. Similarly, they cannot afford the deposit for telephone service required of those deemed at high risk for nonpayment ($400), so their only option is a prepaid plan for the disconnected. They currently use Reconex, which costs $55 per month—more than twice the cost of regular service. As for banking services, several $25 returned-check fees have forced them to use money orders and pay their bills in cash. According to Jeannie, "It's not so bad. It takes more time and it's sure not convenient . . . but it does give me an opportunity to visit with people I don't usually get to see."

The last comment is especially poignant because, unlike Josie, the Andersons are unable to participate in social networks of reciprocal lending. It is not that they are unfriendly or not interested in helping others. Rather, it is shame, because borrowing without the ability to lend would lead to their eventual social isolation. They would prefer not to have friends avoid them for fear that they could not honor their financial obligations. Unfortunately, by exhausting their social capital for obtaining informal loans, the Andersons have become even more dependent than their peers on fringe banks. When this point was raised, Joe laughed and exclaimed, "Well, at least I know that I'll always have a friend at Buddy's."

The Two-Tiered Banking System: Reflecting or Reinforcing U.S. Social Inequality?

The social and economic integration of second-tier financial services underscores the spiraling cost of credit for the most economically disadvantaged.

That is, as first-tier banks abandon lower-income and minority neighbor-hoods—especially in the inner city—their residents often have little choice but to accept the usurious terms of the new financial innovations of bank deregulation: deferred deposits, cash advances, car-title pawns, lease-owner-ship, and even cash leasing. As a result, the credit strategies of the working poor are becoming more complex than can be assessed by examining only discrete segments of the system such as pawnshops or rent-to-own stores. Imagine trying to estimate the cost of consumer credit where $200 televi-sions cost over $700 and then are pawned for $45 at a 20 percent monthly interest rate. In the process, the circumvention of state usury laws has essen-tially redefined "loan sharking" and thus renewed the interest of first-tier banks in the profitability of poverty. Through joint ventures such as Mr. Payroll (Wells Fargo Bank and Cash America Pawn) or indirectly such as Fleet Capital extending credit lines to Title Loans of America, first-tier banks are reaping windfall profits from their earlier withdrawal from low-income communities.

A new and disturbing trend of banking deregulation is the emergence of financial services conglomerates such as Citigroup (Citibank and Travelers Group merger) that are focusing their resources on the more affluent seg-ments of the U.S. population. As these full-service companies embark on their secondary exodus from working-class and modest-income communi-ties, many of the highly indebted households are finding themselves en-snared by fringe banks. The Association of Progressive Rental Organizations contends that most of its rent-to-own clients have household incomes be-tween $24,000 and $50,000. This is consistent with an industry study of payday lenders, which indicates that the average customer earns from $25,000 to $40,000, and a report commissioned by the car-title loan indus-try found that 30 percent of its borrowers had household incomes over $50,000 and nearly half were above $39,000.[66] Not surprisingly, now that legal loan sharking has become a middle-class rather than merely a poverty-level issue, the public's "discovery" of abusive lending policies has provoked a regulatory backlash; in summer 2000, Florida rescinded its 1995 car-title loan law and reduced the monthly interest cap from 22 to 2.5 percent. In response, the fringe-banking industry is attempting to reshape its corporate image with national celebrities like John Madden or popular local figures; for example, NBA team mascot "Benny the Bull" has been used for Chicago-area promotions of Check Into Cash.[67]

Of course, first-tier banks and their beneficiaries feign ignorance and decry the high cost of conducting business with the poor. They even trum-pet their business practices as providing a valuable service to disadvantaged communities by "democratizing" access to consumer credit that otherwise would be denied to needy residents. The reality, of course, is that Citigroup is making large profits reselling subprime loans through its Salomon Smith Barney subsidiary. Other banks such as Wells Fargo, Union Polanters, Fleet Capital, Eagle National, and Goleta National are making huge profits on payday loans and providing the lines of credit for check-cashing and car-title pawn operations. In addition, brokerage companies are making millions of dollars in commissions selling the stocks and bonds of second-tier banks, and mutual fund managers are eager to benefit from their appreciating stock portfolio of fringe banks. Significantly, the profitability of corporate fringe banks is due to their emulation of the successful strategies of first-tier banks: (1) industry concentration by acquiring or merging with competitors (Rent-A-Center); (2) technological modernization and expansion of new services (ACE's universal electronic bill payment system); and (3) evolving conglomerate corporate structures (Cash America establishing separate cash-checking and rent-to-own subsidiaries).

In sum, as long as the proliferation of corporate loan sharks is not effectively regulated, the most economically disadvantaged will find themselves ensnared in new forms of debt peonage relationships. Ultimately, the growing chasm between rich and poor suggests that lower-income households will continue to depend on pagers rather than telephones, money orders rather than personal checks, and pawnshops rather than bank savings accounts. These profound changes in the allocation of credit and the cost of debt are fundamentally shaping another important sector of the Credit Card Nation: small businesses. The new banking policies are having long-term and potentially deleterious impacts on the entrepreneurial backbone of the U.S. economy.

8

The Credit Card Hustle

The Commercial Credit Crunch and the Crisis of Small Business

WHAT DO SPIKE *"40 Acres and a Mule"* LEE, Robert *"The Clerk"* Smith, and Eduardo *"Blair Witch"* Sanchez have in common? Like many small business start-ups, these talented young filmmakers were initially spurned by banks for financing of their projects. After exhausting their social networks of friends and family members for economic assistance—"angel" financing—they eventually completed their breakthrough movies with credit cards. According to 30-year-old Sanchez and 35-year-old cowriter/director Daniel Myrick, "'We were at the end of our rope. We had nothing to our name—we didn't even have cars. We were wondering how many more independent films we could put on our credit cards. [This movie] was like the last roll of the dice [for us].'" Myrick was so desperate after maxing out all of their credit cards that he "'was resigned to going back to shooting wedding videos if nobody bought [our] film.'"[1]

Today, the University of Central Florida film school graduates no longer have to worry about how to make the rent or how to buy 16 mm black-and-white film stock. In fact, they have been able to pay off all of their credit cards (Myrick even bought a house) following the stupendous success of their 1999 horror mockumentary *The Blair Witch Project*. According to

Sanchez and Myrick, the eight-day film shoot was financed with $25,000 in credit card cash advances, or about "the cost of a new Ford Taurus." The total cost of making the film, which received rave reviews at Sundance, was approximately $60,000. After its distribution rights were acquired by Artisan, for the astounding price of $1.5 million, *Blair Witch Project* grossed an estimated $140 million in box-office revenues. At least another $60 million was subsequently generated from comic book, novel, and video sales. Altogether, the commercial success of *Blair Witch Project* makes it the Holy Grail of independent films and the most profitable movie ever released.[2]

Small Business and the Credit Card Hustle:
"Democratizing" Credit or Price Gouging?

Recent U.S. business history is replete with examples of billion-dollar companies whose entrepreneurial seeds were nurtured with bank credit cards during their formative start-up years. For example, Computer Associates International (CAI) Inc., the third-largest independent software company in the world, was founded by Charles Wang in 1976. A Chinese immigrant, Wang started with three employees and boasts that his initial financing consisted of "'maxing out credit cards as fast as [I] could order them. [I] took no [bank] loans or venture capital.'" In 1999, with software sales of over $5.6 billion, CAI ranked behind only Microsoft and IBM. Its national and international expansion was fueled by over 200 corporate acquisitions, including the five largest in the history of the software industry.[3]

Some banks have begun reconsidering their commercial lending policies toward the rapidly expanding small business sector. Between 1995 and 1998, small business loans increased 22 percent to a record $186 billion.[4] Even so, this amount is dwarfed by the escalating credit demands of small businesses; nearly 2.5 million new enterprises were founded between 1995 and 1997.[5] As Todd McCracken, president of National Small Business United, explains, "'Relying on credit cards is a "quick fix" for many small business owners—demonstrating their ingenuity in finding ways to help their business move ahead.'"[6]

If ingenuity is the mother of invention, then it should not be surprising that credit cards have become the number one source of financing for small businesses—supplanting bank loans in the late 1990s. Indeed, the breakneck pace of the Internet industry is incompatible with the dilatory loan process of commercial bank lenders. Imagine if Jerry Yang had to spend several months collecting financial documents for a bank loan before launching the Internet search engine Yahoo in 1994. Or, if Jeff Bezos had to spend afternoons on the phone tracking the status of his loan applications rather than embarking on his revolutionary concept of selling books directly to consumers via the Web. Significantly, as Amazon.com begins a second decade with spectacular sales growth, its financial balance sheet would make most bankers leery of offering Bezos a loan—especially during Amazon's infancy.[7] This underscores a crucial issue confronting the small business sector. The business media lavish praise on successful companies that were launched with credit cards. These reports present a Horatio Alger image of hardworking entrepreneurs that ignore the more common experience that high-interest credit is a serious obstacle to small business prosperity.

Today, most business start-ups owe their early survival to plastic money. According to a 1998 Arthur Andersen/National Small Business United report, based on a survey of 504 enterprises, 47 percent of small and midsized business owners use credit cards—nearly double the proportion of only two years earlier. This source of financing exceeds commercial bank loans (45 percent), leasing (which nearly doubled to 36 percent), vendor credit (17 percent), private loans (14 percent), inventory used as collateral (13 percent), and personal/home equity loans (12 percent); Small Business Administration (SBA) loans account for only 2 percent followed by venture capital at 1 percent. The majority of credit card users (62 percent) do not pay off their balances. This trend shows little evidence of subsiding, as 43 percent of the respondents indicated that they intended to use credit cards to boost their businesses over the next year.[8] It is supported, moreover, by the research of PSI Global. This study found that the use of credit cards by small businesses climbed 10 percent between 1997 and 1998.[9]

Data from the 1994 National Survey of Small Business, cosponsored by the SBA and Federal Reserve Board, confirm these patterns. For example, personal credit cards were most common for small firms (fewer than 10 employees) at 40 percent compared with 22–24 percent for larger firms (50 or more employees). Significantly, 16 percent of small businesses reported that bank mergers had negatively impacted their ability to secure commercial loans.[10] This trend is consistent with the recent experience of Eric Rosenfeld, who founded Adoptive Creative Partners (research/consulting firm) in 1997: "'I haven't found many banks that are interested in small-business loans.'" His experience with corporate vendors has been equally frustrating. Dell rejected his application to lease $5,000 of computer equipment, which contributed to the $25,000 in start-up costs that are being financed on his three credit cards.[11]

For new entrepreneurs, credit cards are their most reliable source of start-up funds. As Rosenfeld explains, "'Everyone respects Visa.'"[12] And, unlike bank loan officers, private angel investors, or SBA bureaucrats, credit cards do not require extensive documentation or entail second-guessing of business decisions. Furthermore, borrowing from friends, family members, or professional associates often leads to unexpected social costs such as stressful personal conflicts and intrusive inquiries. For those committed to blazing their own entrepreneurial paths, the limited financing options invariably lead to bank credit cards. In fact, their use is touted in the business press as evidence of entrepreneurial daring: "If you have confidence in your business, using your credit cards should not be an issue. Go ahead and open as many [credit] card [account]s as you can, and charge whatever you need to make your business run."[13]

After founding a company with credit cards and demonstrating their business acumen, most inexperienced entrepreneurs are shocked to learn that business growth and longevity do not necessarily attract greater interest from commercial lenders. This is due to the banking industry's discrimination, or "redlining," policy against small businesses—especially entrepreneurs in the information- and service-based economy. For instance, Jo-Anne Dressendorfer uses her six credit cards with combined credit lines of $100,000 to finance computers, software, and office supplies for her 10-year-old technology marketing business in Morristown, New Jersey. Even with $10 million in annual revenues, "banks still spurn requests for loans [because] All I have is bodies. They cannot collateralize anything. [I] shop for teaser credit-card rates of around 4.5% and switch when the rates go up. It is a brilliant strategy."[14] It is also becoming more risky with fewer banks competing for consumer accounts due to the ongoing consolidation of the credit card industry.

Even small business owners with substantial equity for collateral are finding that their local banks are reluctant to refinance their credit card debts with conventional loans. For instance, Robert Allen and his wife Mae invested their life savings of $30,000 as well as an additional $15,000 from a military credit union loan in a Cleveland restaurant in 1998. Although they have a stable outside income (Mae's full-time job, Robert's part-time job, military pension), the Allens had no choice but to go plastic after five banks rejected their loan applications. According to Robert, a certified chef and former Arthur Treacher's franchisee, "'You don't have to explain to anybody what you're going to do with it. You can make a cash advance and just work with it.'" After only five months in business, they are now encumbered with $30,000 in credit card debt at 14 to 18 percent APR. They now realize that there is little chance of refinancing with a bank loan in the near future.[15]

For those who have exhausted their credit card limits, the need for financing has even spawned television and on-line small business "beauty pageants."

For example, the *Money Hunt* TV show features aspiring entrepreneurs who, as contestants, compete on-air for potential financial angels and venture capital. By summer 1999, this contemporary version of Ed McMahon's *Star Search* had expanded to nearly 100 metropolitan markets.[16] The escalating demand for commercial financing has led the SBA to develop a website—ACE-Net—for matching entrepreneurs with angel investors. Both groups must submit registration and certification documents before they can be listed in the on-line database for funding from $250,000 to $5 million.[17]

One issue is whether the credit card industry merits commendation for the expansion of the U.S. small business sector in the 1990s. Industry representatives often point to these entrepreneurial success stories as evidence of the increasing importance of bank credit cards in leveling the playing field for aspiring entrepreneurs. They even refer to the proliferation of bank credit cards as a way of "democratizing" access to credit for those most in need or excluded from traditional sources of credit.[18] The industry fails to explain, however, that the low approval rate of small business loans does not correspond with their risk assessment profiles. The banking industry's rule of thumb that four out of five business start-ups will fail is not empirically substantiated. For instance, Bruce Kirchhoff's 1989 analysis of the SBA's small business database found that only 18 percent of all new businesses end in involuntary failure after eight years, and other subsequent studies have confirmed the higher-than-expected longevity rates of small business start-ups.[19] In 1996, for instance, there were about 5.4 million companies with fewer than 500 employees but only 71,811 business failures and 53,549 official bankruptcies; the latter fell to 44,367 in 1998. Furthermore, SBA research indicates that only one out of seven enterprises that go out of business has unpaid loan obligations.[20]

Not surprisingly, as the credit card industry faced a profitability crisis due to the saturation of its traditional consumer markets, American Express and Visa began aggressively marketing corporate credit cards to fledgling small enterprises and the self-employed in the late 1990s. In two 1999 television ads, for example, two novice male entrepreneurs "go for it" and lease business furniture for their new office on their Corporate Visa card. Similarly, American Express touts the benefits of its Corporate Card, which includes a wide range of financial and consulting services (tax and business services [TBS]), to the young founders of a fast-growing landscaping company. Today, TBS generates one-quarter (26 percent in 1999) of AMEX's corporate revenues—up from 10 percent in 1994. The growing demand and profitability of small business credit have fueled the expansion of American Express's initial foray into the consumer credit market (Optima card) with its new hi-tech Blue card.[21] Significantly, the emphasis on personal freedom and empowerment is strikingly similar to the marketing themes on college campuses. Aspiring entrepreneurs are encouraged to take advantage of a good investment opportunity or the once-in-a-lifetime chance to escape an unsatisfying job and become their own boss.

In contrast to the generous offer of easy money to unemployed students, the growing use of credit cards by small businesses is often the result of increasingly restrictive lending policies by commercial banks. In the same way the withdrawal of first-tier banks from low-income communities has sharply increased the demand for costly second-tier loans, banks are profiting handsomely from the commercial credit crunch by issuing credit cards rather than approving small business loans. The problem is that credit card applications do not ask questions about long-term business plans and how the loans will be repaid. As a result, rather than paying 6–8 percent interest on profit-enhancing small business loans, eager entrepreneurs soon find themselves burdened with 14–24 APR consumer loans that they often cannot repay.

According to Maria Coyne, director of the Small Business Development Center in Cleveland, "'In many cases, these [entrepreneurs] are desperate. This is the only recourse they have to get money. . . . Without it, their business might go under or they might not be able to pay critical vendors.'" As a result, the flip side of this "democratization" of credit is the growing number of families in financial difficulty due to the increasing use of consumer credit cards for business expenses. Jay Seaton, president of Consumer Credit Counseling Services (CCCS) of northeast Ohio, has found this problem "so staggering" that CCCS began offering seminars in 1999 to inform business owners about the signs of credit trouble and the potential hardships that it could impose on family members.[22]

In sum, the decision to go plastic reflects (1) a lack of access to alternative sources of start-up capital (including community-based "incubators" and other nonprofit programs);[23] (2) a calculated preference not to exhaust the "last lines of defense" of other informal sources of credit; (3) the expectation that high-interest debt will be paid off with future business revenues; and (4) the assumption that banks will refinance with lower-interest loans after the business demonstrates a viable track record. For most aspiring entrepreneurs, higher-cost credit card loans are well worth the nonpecuniary costs of SBA and personal loans in the short term. And the immediate use of bank cards could be the difference between whether a lucrative business opportunity is pursued or lost. Consequently, this trend has important implications for future success rates of individual entrepreneurs as well as U.S. employment and macroeconomic growth patterns.

The Changing U.S. Economic Landscape:
Are Small Firms Bountiful, or Are Big Corporations Lean and Mean?

Over the past two decades, the rapid restructuring of the U.S. economy has featured contraction of the goods-production sector (especially manufacturing) and dramatic expansion of information and consumer services. Today, the broadly defined service sector accounts for approximately two-thirds of U.S. domestic economic activities. This structural shift has brought the spectacular rise of new corporate giants such as Microsoft, Yahoo, Amazon.com, Viacom, and Wal-Mart as well as the decline of traditional industrial behemoths such as Kodak, Xerox, Burlington Northern–Santa Fe railroad, and U.S. Steel and even the demise of previous industry leaders such as Commodore Computers, Eastern Airlines, and Singer Sewing Machines.

The ongoing transformation of the U.S. economy, which mirrors the ascendance of these new postindustrial goliaths, has been accompanied by leaner-and-meaner labor policies. That is, many corporations have fundamentally reorganized their most desirable and highly compensated primary labor markets as a strategy for preserving their internationally high rate of profit.[24] The latter is being challenged by the new patterns of global production, national subsidies and tax policies, and strategic corporate alliances.[25] This process typically includes replacing high-wage, blue- and white-collar (often unionized) jobs with lower-wage, semiskilled, nonunionized employment or even subcontracted work.[26]

Furthermore, white-collar professionals and middle managers began facing the employment ax by the mid-1980s as corporate mergers and acquisitions led to massive layoffs in previously secure workforces such as AT&T, Citicorp, Digital Equipment, General Electric, General Motors, IBM, and Kodak. As a result, while U.S. corporations were enjoying the age of leverage, they became fixated with reducing labor costs in order to service their spiraling debt obligations and to maintain high profits and extravagant executive compensation packages. In the process, millions of workers were downsized and outsourced throughout their respective occupational and seniority pyramids with the specious explanation that they were necessary casualties of global competition.

According to the U.S. Census, an annual average of 1.2 million 20-plus-year-old workers with three or more years of tenure in a job were displaced between 1987 and 1992. In the 1980s, most were blue-collar workers, but in the mid-1990s nearly half were white-collar managers and professionals. The annual number of displaced workers increased in the mid-1990s (4.2 million between January 1993 and December 1995) with about one-fifth becoming self-employed, at least temporarily (especially white-collar workers).[27] Significantly, as humorously highlighted by Michael Moore in his best-selling 1996 book *Downsize This!*, the comical 1998 movie *The Big One*, and the popular 1999 cable television program *The Awful Truth*, corporate layoffs in the late 1980s and 1990s were accompanied by record company profits.[28]

Ironically, as U.S. industrial restructuring produced ever larger multidivisional conglomerates, their share of U.S. economic growth has dwindled. In 1979, for example, the Fortune 500 companies accounted for $1.4 trillion in sales (58 percent of GNP) and employed 16.2 million workers. Ten years later, 1989, their combined sales rose sluggishly to almost $2.2 trillion (falling to only 42 percent of GNP), whereas their total workforce declined sharply to 12.5 million. Overall, between 1979 and 1989, the entire American economy added nearly 19 million jobs while the Fortune 500 lost 3.7 million. This job creation gap, however, is not simply the product of the decline of major manufacturing giants and their replacement with big service-oriented corporations. For instance, the largest service-sector companies (Fortune's Service 500) account for only a modest share of this employment growth—about 2 million new workers from 1982 to 1989.[29]

Some observers have argued that simply examining the absolute numbers of jobs generated by large companies neglects the quality of jobs offered in the corporate sector. Factors pertaining to quality include comprehensive health insurance, retirement programs, and stock options. However, as attested by Microsoft's efforts to limit benefits to full-time permanent workers,[30] this fallacious assumption ignores the recent rise of contingent workers who have lower total compensation (wages and benefits) and fewer career mobility opportunities than comparable permanent employees. These include part-time, temporary, and contract employees whose labor is leased from temporary employment agencies and then discharged without fear of fracturing company loyalty or undercutting employee morale.[31] In the case of Microsoft, the total number of contingent workers has risen from 440 in 1989 to about 6,000 in 2000—about one-fifth of its total U.S. workforce— even while the company was unsuccessfully litigating a class action suit by past and present temporary workers.[32] In general, major corporations have been much more likely to eliminate high-paying positions, whereas smaller firms are more likely to generate average- and high-wage occupations.[33]

At the end of the 1980s, contingent workers accounted for about one-fifth of the U.S. labor force; 18.1 percent of the U.S. nonagricultural workforce was employed part-time in 1989.[34] The plight of overqualified and undercompensated workers, with little prospect for promotion, permanently entered the workplace lexicon and was even glorified by Hollywood in the 1993 movie *The Temp*. In this film, a temporary office worker's only successful strategy for moving up the corporate ladder is to murder her competition. Although the U.S. economy has rebounded impressively from the 1989 recession (the movie's inspiration), with robust expansion continuing through the 1990s, temps still constitute the fastest-growing category of employment. For instance, the number of workers in the U.S. temporary-help industry more than doubled from 417,000 in 1982 (0.5 percent of total employment) to 1.22 million in 1989 (1.1 percent) and then more than doubled again to 2.65 million in 1997 (2.2 percent of total employment). Overall, the proportion of part-time (nonagricultural) workers remained basically unchanged at 17.8 percent in 1997.[35]

The fundamental question is where the new jobs are coming from. Some researchers emphasize the role of computer-aided technologies in revolutionizing the ability of decentralized yet highly integrated producer networks to adjust rapidly to changing market demands. By promoting "flexibly specialized" production processes and "just in time" delivery schedules, large corporations are able to coordinate networks of smaller and more efficient producers that can outcompete older and more highly centralized, standardized mass production systems.[36] This "second industrial divide," some argue, entails the development of highly efficient industrial districts that are nurtured by local and regional planning policies.[37] This perspective is amplified by economist Bennett Harrison of the Massachusetts Institute of Technology (MIT). He contends that large corporations are no longer the lumbering dinosaurs epitomized by IBM's previously rigid organizational structure and conservative management culture. Instead, Harrison asserts that multinational corporations have successfully adapted to the "age of flexibility" and thus remain the most important source of desirable employment in the United States. This is due to their more flexible and efficient management and production forms as well as the continuing dominance of their respective markets.[38] In sum, this view asserts that big corporations—industry-leading titans—will continue to be the organizational backbone of the dynamic and rapidly expanding U.S. economy in the twenty-first century.

Other investigators offer less sanguine views of highly concentrated industries and their corporate behemoths. They challenge the perspective that "big is better" by emphasizing that "small is bountiful." That is, new start-up and small companies (fewer than 500 workers and, especially, fewer than 100) have generated the bulk of recent job growth by swiftly and creatively responding to the new opportunities of the postindustrial economy—particularly in the service sector. According to the SBA's Office of Advocacy,

businesses with four or fewer employees accounted for about 95 percent of
U.S. job growth between 1989 and 1991. The Department of Commerce
substantiates this assertion by reporting that the vast majority of the 3.5
million jobs created in 1994 were generated by enterprises with fewer than
five employees.[39] Overall, David Birch contends, the astoundingly successful small companies ("gazelles") that account for less than 3 percent of U.S.
businesses created 5 million jobs between 1990 and 1994, while all others
produced a loss of 800,000 jobs.[40]

The largest corporations were still trimming or only modestly expanding
their workforces in the mid-1990s, so it is not surprising that small business
growth has continued to climb. Between June 1996 and June 1997, according to SBA data, a record 885,000 new companies were created (excluding
sole proprietorships)—up from 758,000 in 1993. Significantly, this 16.8
percent increase in new companies compares with a nearly constant level of
700,000 business failures per year during this same period (1993–1997).
Overall, as measured by business tax returns, there were 23.3 million nonfarm businesses (corporations, partnerships, sole proprietorships) in 1996,
and 99 percent had fewer than 500 workers; only 5.3 million in 1994 reported fewer than 500 employees; the vast majority (nearly 16 million) were
classified as either full- or part-time entrepreneurial ventures.[41]

A Gendered Path to Business Success:
The Dramatic Rise and Triumph of Female Entrepreneurship

One of the most neglected and dynamic components of the U.S. small business sector is the proliferation of female entrepreneurs. Whether self-
employed as personal service providers or white-collar professionals, or
establishing and managing small businesses, women have become an increasingly potent force in the ongoing transformation of the U.S. economy—especially the service sector. According to the National Association
of Women Business Owners and Dun & Bradstreet Information Services,
women owned over 9.1 million enterprises (38 percent of all firms), employed over 27.5 million people, and contributed over $3.6 trillion in rev-
enues to the U.S. economy in 1999.[42] These figures represent an impressive
increase over the previous four years. In 1995, women-owned businesses
numbered over 7.7 million (about one-third of all firms) with about 15.5
million employees and nearly $1.4 trillion in revenues. The overwhelming
majority (90 percent) were individual proprietorships and over one-half (55
percent) were concentrated in service industries, followed by retail trade (20
percent).[43] Overall, the most popular metropolitan areas for female entre-

preneurs are New York followed by Los Angeles, Chicago, Philadelphia, Seattle, Houston, Washington, D.C., and Dallas.[44]

Between 1987 and 1999, the number of women-owned firms increased by 103 percent nationwide, employment by them tripled (320 percent), and sales quadrupled (436 percent). Not incidentally, women entrepreneurs are more likely to remain in business than the national average. Women-owned enterprises are retaining their traditional base in retail trade and services, but they are growing faster than the national average in construction, manufacturing, transportation/communications, wholesale trade, and finance/insurance/real estate. In fact, the establishment of women-owned enterprises outpaced those founded by men more than threefold between 1983 and 1993; the number of women-owned businesses increased a spectacular 43 percent from 1991 to 1994 and a more moderate 18.2 percent from 1994 to 1999.[45] The somewhat slower growth rate for women entrepreneurs in the late 1990s reflects the improved promotional opportunities for younger professional women and the substantial number of older women who previously opted out of the corporate workforce due to downsizings, frustrations over the gendered "glass ceiling," and age discrimination.[46] Significantly, women have been making progress in guiding larger enterprises; between 1991 and 1994, women-owned businesses with at least 100 employees grew by 18.3 percent compared with 9.1 percent for all commercially active women-owned businesses.[47]

Although they tend to mirror the general performance of all U.S. firms, with nearly three-fourths (72 percent) of women-owned enterprises in 1991 still in business in 1995, female entrepreneurs cite a common obstacle to success: difficulty in obtaining commercial credit.[48] A 1995 survey of women business owners found that two-thirds reported problems in securing loans from their financial institutions, including one-third who "perceived some degree of gender-based discrimination."[49] This pattern, though not uncommon among small firms (especially in services), greatly influences the prosperity and potential growth of women-owned enterprises. In fact, the National Association of Women Business Owners concludes that "despite the solid [business] record, other research has shown that difficulty in obtaining financing is one of the biggest obstacles faced by women business owners." This is an especially difficult problem for minority women entrepreneurs, who now account for one-eighth (13 percent) of all women-owned businesses, especially African Americans who report the least success in obtaining bank loans.[50]

In sum, higher educational levels and labor force participation rates of women are contributing to the entrepreneurial boom in the United States—

especially in the service sector. Although more women are pursuing self-employment and establishing small businesses, they are less successful in expanding the size of their enterprises and thus less likely to become powerful actors in their respective markets. Not surprisingly, the lack of access to commercial loans and limited (albeit growing) "old girl" business networks have consigned most female entrepreneurs to industries with low capital requirements and reliance on low-wage labor. This explains the relatively small size of female-owned enterprises (including self-employed) and modest volume of business revenues.[51] Overall, the SBA estimates that about 70 percent of female entrepreneurs initially finance their businesses with credit cards and other personal resources and are three times more likely than others to use high-interest credit cards for their short-term commercial credit needs.[52] Consequently, although women entrepreneurs report greater personal satisfaction and social esteem than their male counterparts, they face higher hurdles for business success, greater financial risk, lower economic rewards, and increased likelihood of failure due to the lack of access to bank loans. Against these improbable odds, the performance of women-owned businesses has been remarkable. It suggests that the popular bumper sticker "I'd rather go shopping" may soon be replaced with "Visa—A (business)woman's best friend."

The Age of the Gazelle:
Small Job Engines or Big Industry Innovators

As corporate downsizing and labor market reorganization reduced company payrolls and eroded employee loyalty in the late 1980s, subsequent job growth in the largest U.S. corporations has been deliberately limited by "flexible" employment policies. That is, major corporations have curbed the expansion of their more costly permanent workforces by using temporary employment agencies and creative subcontracting arrangements with small firms and independent consultants. More important, many laid-off and disgruntled employees of the 1980s (especially professional women) possess the work experience, technological and management skills, business contacts, and access to start-up capital that often constitute formidable synergies for penetrating specialized niche markets. When successful, these new private start-ups or corporate spin-offs excel and may even dominate their markets. Often referred to as "gazelles," these include such high-flying companies as America Online, Boston Market restaurants, Dell computers, OfficeMax, Starbucks Coffee, and Yahoo.[53] The key to their success is maximizing labor productivity and managerial creativity through state-of-the-art production technologies and streamlined corporate bureaucracies.

A classic example of a corporate gazelle is Continental Promotion Group, Inc., of Tempe, Arizona. Founded by Sam Garvin in 1989, Continental processes rebates, coupons, and mail-in promotions for the Fortune 500 and other large organizations. His experience is strikingly similar to that of Mitch Michaelson (see next section). Garvin enthusiastically started his own business even though he had been promoted to merchandising manager after less than five years at Heinz USA. Ironically, his former supervisor asked him to resign, and Garvin saw his dismissal as a fortuitous business opportunity rather than a career setback. Instead of pleading for his job, Garvin immediately acted on his small business instincts. At 25 years old, he followed his entrepreneurial vision and established his own consumer promotion company, which initially operated out of the "roomy trunk" of a leased Ford Taurus.

Ten years later, the 35-year-old entrepreneur could reflect on the dozens of competitors throughout the country that went out of business during the 1990s. According to Garvin, who has a master's degree in business management and a bachelor's degree in political science and German studies, "'They were living in the past. They didn't see the [power] of the personal computer, its lower cost and longer life. They couldn't compete with people like us that were fast and agile.'" In addition, Sam's global focus (he reads 7 U.S. and European newspapers and 10 business magazines) has enabled Continental to expand internationally, with offices in Canada and Ireland.

For corporate marketing offices, rebates and coupon redemptions are important sales and advertising tools because they offer consumer profiles of who is buying their products and at what price. In 1997, Continental was responsible for processing 20 million pieces of mail as well as sending out tens of thousands of promotional items (from Snickers soccer balls to Snow White figurines) and conducting sweepstakes for new cars and cash; it uses over 100 postal boxes.

One of Garvin's first clients, Dial, required relentless persistence before he landed the contract—over 100 phone calls just to schedule his sales pitch. This tenacity, innovativeness, and attention to customer service have produced a client portfolio of over 300 major companies in less than a decade. They include CompUSA, Disney, Fuji Photo Film, Memorex, Microsoft, Quaker State Auto, Sony, Sutter Home Winery, Warner Home Video, and Western Digital. The company is so successful that it opened a new $4.2 million headquarters at the Scottsdale Airpark in 1998 in an effort to expand its share of the $4 billion consumer promotion market. With 150 employees in Tempe and another 150 independent contractors, Continental's revenues soared from $56 million in 1996 to over $200 million in 1998. The hiring of a new sales staff and the continuing expansion of international operations led Garvin to forecast that corporate revenues would exceed $300 million in 1999.

This high-flying gazelle got off the ground with modest savings and the creative use of consumer credit—a half-dozen credit cards and huge cellular phone bills. Indeed, Continental began as a "virtual" company; the office was the physical space of Garvin's leased car. Without small business loans, Garvin realized that he had to be "'willing to risk everything to start my business.'" And he did. A decade later, even with Continental's success, the initial scarcity of commercial credit continues to shape his corporate business plan. Instead of financing Continental's expansion with costly bank loans, he waited until the company could pay for a new corporate headquarters with cash—no outside loans or costly mortgage fees. According to Garvin, "'We're very careful about debt. We don't owe on anything except the head to the postage meter, because they won't sell it to us.'" This corporate frugality, however, has not affected the quality of services or employee compensation, as Continental offers a 401(k) plan, profit sharing, and quarterly bonuses. Garvin is like most successful entrepreneurs in the service sector in realizing that "'people are where it's at. You could have the best computer system in the world, but if you don't have [quality] people to interact with the Dials and Disneys, you're never going to make it.'"[54]

The tremendous success of small businesses like Continental reflects the structural transformation of the postindustrial economy as well as the profound impact of innovative technologies. According to John Case, the unexpected surge of entrepreneurship in the United States is due to three basic factors. First, increasing global competition has intensified pressures for corporate efficiency; unproductive units or divisions are being sold off in order to focus on core business activities. Second, the technological revolution of the computer age has created not only new industries but also new methods of producing goods and delivering services. The relatively low cost of this technology, moreover, makes it accessible to small firms and even the self-employed. Third, the rapid expansion of the small business sector has produced an entrepreneurial snowball effect. That is, the growth of new companies is increasing the demand for business products and services that, in turn, stimulates the secondary demand for independent suppliers.[55] As Case explains:

> Facing an uncertain environment and stiff new competition, the giant corporations flailed about in the 1970s and 1980s. They slashed payrolls, shutting down or selling off whole divisions, and contracted out what they had once done for themselves. They scrambled to get into newer, more profitable industries. . . . Meanwhile . . . thousands upon thousands of new businesses

came into existence. Some of these new companies grew very big very quickly. Most remained relatively small. Unlike . . . [in] the past, the new companies were oriented toward growth. They were technologically and managerially sophisticated, typically leading their larger competitors into new markets rather than following them. Newer, smaller businesses created many of the 18 million private-sector jobs that were added during the 1980s.[56]

Although research on small business has recently produced a vast literature, from the psychology of entrepreneurial risk-takers to the managerial/organizational limits of success,[57] it is important to note a crucial flaw in the analysis of the rise of small business during the age of leverage. The return-on-investment rates demanded by large U.S. corporations are typically much higher than accepted by small businesses.[58] This is due to huge debt interest payments, high executive compensation, and shareholder pressures; an annual return on investment of less than 12 percent will tend to result in depressed stock values and management shake-ups. Hence, large corporations are abandoning lower-profit ventures and are reluctant to pursue risky business strategies that require high start-up costs.

In comparison, SBA data show that only 49 percent of small businesses reported a profit in 1994; entrepreneurs typically have multiple sources of income and, more important, are willing to make economic sacrifices to be self-employed.[59] As a result, it is often more cost-effective for major corporations to acquire innovative companies than to invest in expensive research and development programs. Indeed, Microsoft's use of this strategy has been frequently lampooned by Gary Trudeau in his acerbic comic strip *Doonesbury*, but the tactic has proved to be a very effective corporate policy for developing new product lines and minimizing future competition. Consequently, the widening gap between the "acceptable" rate of profit for large U.S. corporations and small businesses ensures that entrepreneurial activities will continue to flourish within the market space that is fundamentally shaped and defined by low returns on investment. For most aspiring entrepreneurs, this means that credit cards and home equity lines of credit will continue to be their most reliable source of start-up capital.

Last, both the large-is-powerful and small-is-bountiful perspectives share a major conceptual flaw. They focus on the macroeconomic processes of *labor demand* as measured by job growth rather than examining *how workers cope* with a tumultuous labor market.[60] These top-down approaches result in several important omissions. For example, they overlook various contingent job statuses that generate high worker turnover and multiple job holders (e.g., performing two part-time jobs); ignore informal-sector enterprises that creatively use social networks and human capital that compensate for their smaller firm size and older production technologies; and neglect the growing importance of self-employment during this era of "flexible accumulation."

By focusing on jobs rather than job seekers, both approaches fail to recognize the growing significance of supplementary earnings by full-time workers who must generate additional income in order to augment their declining real levels of compensation and their rising cost of living. As a result, these researchers tend to overstate the extent of job creation in the formal labor market, since workers are increasingly assuming more than one job (two or three part-time jobs or one full- and one part-time) during a given employment period. Significantly, some moonlighting activities may develop into full-time self-employment and even blossom into small business enterprises and even a potential gazelle. These financial "hustles" include real estate speculation, stock market investment, rental housing, ornamental plant maintenance services, and cinematic productions. Of course, bank credit cards play a role in these ventures as well.

Potential Gazelle Versus Goliath: Credit-Starved, Undercapitalized, and the Darwinian Struggle to Survive

Mitch Michaelson has a penchant for competitive sports and an intense determination to succeed. A lifelong St. Louis resident and an avid Cardinals baseball fan, he usually finds himself rooting for the underdog. Although Mitch's free afternoons are now nearly as rare as a St. Louis championship, he is always accessible via e-mail on his personal computer. This is because he is consumed with rooting for a new underdog, Caravell Computer Supplies, his fledgling computer supply company. Only five years old, Caravell is a rookie upstart compared with the major-league veterans of the industry. Even so, Mitch is not averse to challenging the goliaths of the marketplace. A savvy and accomplished player, with nearly nine years of sales experience in the computer supply market, he is a small-business man with an attitude. He is a potential gazelle in the making.

For Mitch and Caravell, the main concern is to play on a level ballfield. Not surprisingly, the primary obstacle to company expansion and profitability is the lack of inexpensive commercial credit. Without access to conventional small business financing, Caravell is forever at bat with two strikes against it: high-interest debt, low-volume sales, and few wholesaler rebates. Hence, the crisis of undercapitalization means that small businesses like Caravell continually face a major disadvantage in their Darwinian struggle to survive the cutthroat competition from the goliaths of their respective industries. For American society, this also entails important social and economic costs, such as higher consumer prices, creation of fewer new jobs, greater likelihood of small business failure, more limited range of available products and services, and lower long-term aggregate growth for the U.S. economy.

Farewell to 9-to-5: A Small Business Is Born

Unlike Ron Taylor (Chapter 5), whose employment anxiety led him to the path of self-employment, Mitch Michaelson had no trouble finding and keeping a well-paying job. Born into a white middle-class family in suburban St. Louis, Mitch had the generational advantage of entering the job market toward the end of the economic expansion. In fact, after graduating from a large midwestern university in 1988, Mitch found that his business degree yielded job offers from several blue-chip corporations including Coca-Cola and IBM. When asked why he turned down such promising career opportunities, he replies with the foresight of a savvy entrepreneur: "The entry-level salaries were low, $16–$18 to $18–$20 thousand plus benefits . . . but the real issue was the job . . . only learning one part of sales. . . At Coca-Cola I'd have managed 2,000 accounts—imagine troubleshooting for 2,000 clients. . . . At IBM I'd have been in sales but would not have learned about marketing. . . . I wanted to learn it all . . . sales, project [development], cultivating clients."

Instead, Mitch accepted a less glamorous job offer from an independent regional computer supply company based in St. Louis. Although the salary was somewhat higher than was offered by the big corporations ($22,000 plus benefits), the crucial difference was the opportunity to learn all facets of the business: sales, marketing, finance, customer relations, and management. Here, Mitch not only could acquire the varied business experiences that he craved, but also was assured that he could apply his creative talents to future marketing initiatives. The president of the firm, moreover, promised a special enticement. Mitch's career ladder would lead directly to sales manager and possibly even to company president. For an ambitious 22-year-old fresh out of college, these were impressive prospects, even by the lofty standards of the late 1980s.

A natural in his chosen profession (he spent one summer selling books door-to-door in Texas), Mitch quickly established himself as the "big kahuna"—the number one salesman in the company. Over the next two years, his salary more than doubled, and he received numerous bonuses and material awards in recognition of his outstanding sales achievements. The latter included a microwave, stereo, golf clubs, and furniture. Nevertheless, Mitch became increasingly dissatisfied with his job. The personal secretary was promised but not hired, the promotion was discussed but never materialized, and most important, his creative influence in developing new marketing strategies was only occasionally solicited and rarely implemented. For Mitch, it soon became evident that management was interested in his talents only on its terms. As a go-getter, he was valuable only so long as he furthered the aims of the company within its organizational structure and prevailing business practices. Change was anathema to the business culture of the firm—a familiar refrain previously echoed by Sam Garvin.

From management's perspective, the company was thrilled with the "kid's" production and content with its market position. This complacent attitude, however, further rankled Mitch as he chafed under company policies that he perceived as stifling, poorly designed, and ultimately self-destructive. Although his financial expectations were satisfied, with a base salary and bonuses approaching $60,000 in 1992, Mitch's professional creativity and ambitions were so stymied that he resigned at the end of the year. To the disappointment of his sales manager, Mitch voluntarily relinquished the "golden handcuffs" of a steady income for the personal freedom and economic insecurity of self-employment. As he explains it, he gave up "the [company's] box seats at the baseball park" for the challenge of "working for myself."

Mitch's family background helped to prepare him for the challenges of the business world. His father works in sales, and his mother is a real estate agent. Indeed, it was clear relatively early on that a business career would be Mitch's chosen vocation, and his college studies provided a solid foundation for attaining this goal. Although Mitch earned a decent salary while employed, he was a "boomerang baby" who lived with his divorced mother in order to maximize his savings. In retrospect, this frugality proved foresightful. This was due to his difficulties in obtaining commercial credit for nurturing the growth of Caravell and the necessary economic discipline for becoming a successful small business owner.

In January 1993, after the expiration of the one-year "no compete" clause (within 90 miles of St. Louis) in his employment contract, Mitch formally embarked on his new entrepreneurial venture from the basement of his mother's house. Without the financial overhead of a home mortgage or office rent, he was able to offer competitive prices that attracted both old and new clients; about 85 percent of his computer supplies are "drop-shipped" (mailed directly from wholesalers). In addition, unshackled from the marketing constraints of his previous employer, he began an aggressive direct-mail campaign. This included advertisements in major trade publications, promotional blitzes by fax, and even contracting an outside telemarketing service. For Mitch, his previous routine as a salesman seemed like a part-time job, as his workday now included other responsibilities such as marketing, shipping, billing, payroll, office management, and, of course, small business loan applications. Thus, the 9-to-5 work regimen was replaced with longer hours, lower salary, and greater anxiety. Still, Mitch relished the opportunity.

As Caravell sales grew steadily, Mitch moved out of the basement and rented an office suite in downtown St. Louis. This business expansion, however, did not signify a substantial improvement in the profitability of the company. Rather, it was a necessary but not sufficient condition for sustaining economic competitiveness. That is, Caravell's sales volume is sensitive to both the price and credit/financing terms offered to its retail customers. Inevitably, then, outstanding billings or company credit continued to increase in absolute terms as the volume of Caravell's sales continued to swell; Mitch faced payment delays and cash-flow bottlenecks, which are common problems encountered by all small businesses. As a result, "My credit card debt grew from day one until my suppliers finally decided to grant me credit in the winter of 1995."

The Chicken or Egg Conundrum:
Small Business Success and the Commercial Credit Divide

The computer supply business, like most retail enterprises of the postindustrial economy, is highly competitive, since it essentially serves as a middleman between the manufacturer and the consumer. This makes customer loyalty more difficult to cultivate because the primary feature that distinguishes competing supply companies is price followed by secondary factors such as speed and efficiency of delivery and credit or financing terms. For Caravell and other small companies, the key to business success is to increase sales volume and minimize costs, as epitomized by the retail gazelle—now goliath—Wal-Mart. The lack of commercial credit, however, is Mitch's major obstacle to business expansion, since it limits the ability of Caravell to qualify for manufacturer and wholesaler rebates. This is due to three factors. First, manufacturers' rebates are based on amount of purchases; the greater the sales volume, the greater the percentage discount. Second, wholesalers offer discounts for prompt payment, 5 percent for payments within 10 days and 2 percent within 30 days. Third, in order to qualify for volume discounts and manufacturer rebates, Mitch is forced to specialize in only one brand of computer supplies. Although this enables Caravell to sell this particular manufacturer's products at a lower price, it also excludes any potential customers who prefer other name-brand products.

Within a year, Mitch had exhausted his savings and was relying on his "string of 5 or 6 credit cards" to maintain an adequate inventory and to compensate for periods of negative cash flow. Indeed, without this costly form of credit, Caravell would not have been able to survive during this crucial phase of company expansion. For example, whenever Mitch received a large order of computer supplies ($3,000 to $15,000), he would pay by maxing out his personal credit cards. Only after Caravell received payments from its customers could Mitch pay those debts. Of course, his credit card balances would then climb back to their limit when another large order was accepted. Hence, this source of commercial credit is very expensive, ranging from about 15 to 18 percent APR. This includes the merchant discount fee of 2.5 to 3.0 percent of the credit card charge, which is passed on by his wholesalers, plus the 12 to 15 percent interest rates levied by his bank credit cards (Visa, MasterCard). At this time, Mitch began to apply for small business loans from local and regional banks. This was precipitated by the refusal of wholesalers to extend him credit and the rapid growth of his credit card debt, which peaked at almost $30,000.

The reluctance of Caravell's suppliers to offer short-term credit is not unusual to new companies in the industry. This is due to a common business scam whereby a company receives supplies or equipment on credit, sells them quickly at a substantial discount, and then declares bankruptcy or simply disappears with the sales revenues. In order to minimize such losses, Mitch uses the Dun & Bradstreet computerized credit report service. This enables him to determine quickly the amount and terms of credit he is willing to extend to a prospective customer. So far, this risk assessment method has proved very effective, since he has written off only $158.28 in unpaid computer supplies. Even so, unforeseen events can lead to disastrous consequences. For instance, a customer's impending bankruptcy will force Caravell to absorb an $8,000 unpaid balance ($7,200 net loss) from an $18,000 equipment purchase.

By the end of the second year, Caravell's sales had grown to nearly $40,000 per month. Like the goliaths of the marketplace, however, Mitch more than doubled his sales volume through an acquisition rather than a costly marketing campaign. The purchase of a small computer equipment company (Zanadu), which had been a Caravell supplier, was financed by assuming its existing bank loan obligations plus a short-term monthly payment. Although Zanadu's profit margin of 10 percent was substantially lower than Caravell's 20 percent, its larger revenue stream warranted its purchase; Caravell was grossing about $500,000 annually compared to about $750,000 for Zanadu. With over $1.25 million in combined annual sales, Mitch thought he would easily qualify for a small business loan of from $25,000 to $75,000. After all, he believed the marketing campaigns of local banks that promised to "bend over backwards to meet your financial needs."

Mitch's greatest frustration as a small business owner is not the plethora of advantages held by his largest competitors but the "runaround" he gets from his "friendly community banks," which have become fewer and less ingratiating since the recent flurry of mergers. He describes the humiliating process of dealing with loan officers who tell him how to run his business, make promises that they never intend to keep, and fail to respond to his telephone inquiries. Worse, Mitch fears that only a handful of banks will survive the consolidation pressures of deregulation (which he supports) and that this will result in less competition and higher-cost loans. Mitch's voice rises in anger as he bitterly recites a litany of excuses proffered by bank loan officers in explaining why his loan applications have been rejected—a total of six and counting: "I am so tired of talking to banks, even the 'sure things' fall through. . . . It's always the same thing . . . lack of collateral . . . lack of managerial experience. . . . I even applied to a local bank in my area that was deficient in small business loans with the same result . . . turned down. . . . What a hassle!"

As Mitch explains it, the banks present a catch-22 scenario for justifying their lending practices. They want collateral in the form of home or office building ownership so that "in case you go bankrupt, it's nice to know there's something [of value] to fall back on." One local bank assured him that he would receive a small business loan of between $25,000 and $50,000. Inexplicably, however, they stopped returning his phone calls and did not even bother to inform him of the decision to reject his application. This was particularly ironic because the same loan officer finally called Mitch to ask why he was making the monthly payments on the two Zanadu loans that he had assumed after acquiring the company. Exasperated, Mitch sarcastically told him, "I need to buy you some new shoes since you've been dragging your feet on my loan [application] for so long."

Even more irksome to Mitch is the fact that some banks based their high-risk evaluation on his credit card debt. He declared in disgust, "I wanted a business loan, but all I got was a[nother] credit card instead." Uncertain about whether this is a conscious policy directed toward struggling entrepreneurs like himself, he emphatically expressed his hostility toward the U.S. banking system. Mitch is especially angry about the banks' rhetorical support of small businesses—the backbone of American capitalism—then the banks "turn around and starve me out [of credit]." This negative experience has reinforced his underlying resentment toward perceived preferential treatment of minorities: "Some bagel company can get a bank loan to open a store in Harlem, but I can't get a loan without substantial collateral." Although Mitch does not have supporting evidence for this claim, he views government programs that promote minority businesses as an affront to white male entrepreneurs like himself; he asserts that there are "high odds against me."

Significantly, Mitch believes his inability to secure a small business loan is not because of the discretionary lending policies of the banking industry but "because the government overregulates the banks, which discourages them from giving loans to me." Although cognizant of governmental policies that provide legal mechanisms for contesting discriminatory lending practices, such as the 1977 Community Reinvestment Act, he perceives such laws as counterproductive, since "overregulation of banks is the reason they choose to loan me money on credit cards rather than less-profitable business loans." Mitch's misguided laissez-faire perspective ignores the numerous deregulatory policies of the 1980s and 1990s that made credit card loans enormously profitable to member banks. At the same time, these policies accelerated the concentration of the banking industry, which further eroded the social commitment of financial institutions to providing low-interest business and residential mortgage loans to their local communities.

Mitch employs three people in sales and marketing as well as a secretary-receptionist. The celebration of his third year in business was rewarded by an extension of credit by his wholesalers, who now perceive him as a much better credit risk. Each successive year he has received more vendor credit but has watched nervously as his profit margins shrink due to intensifying competition from new upstart wholesalers. Surprisingly, Mitch seems more concerned about his ability to extend his customers credit than to secure more commercial credit for himself. In fact, Caravell accepts Visa and MasterCard for customer payment but adds the merchant discount fee of 2.78 percent to the sales price, since its slim profit margin cannot absorb any additional costs. Unlike lower-volume enterprises, Mitch is receiving a reduced merchant fee (Discover recently called to sign up Caravell), and his PC software precludes the need for a costly credit card processing system. He simply inputs the credit card account number, and the software routes his authorization requests through his regional bank's computer system; he pays a modest fee of $5 per month for the service. Mitch's credit risks are low due to the use of computerized credit information services, especially in comparison with the low-tech systems used by small business owners on the economic fringes.[61] (Remember the manual credit card imprinter and its accompanying deadbeat list for checking delinquent or frozen accounts?)

Mitch remains frustrated and angry about not receiving a bank loan. He views it as the primary reason for the modest growth of his company's sales and, indirectly, as a factor in the moderate expansion of the U.S. economy, which he sees as dominated by lazy corporate goliaths rather than aggressive "street fighters" like himself. Indeed, if he could retire his high-interest (15 rising to 18 percent in 1998) credit card debt, which has finally dipped below $25,000, Caravell could more easily qualify for early-payment discounts from suppliers, integrate and modernize the separate company data systems, expand the selection of different product brands, and increase its sales and marketing staff. Together, these factors would enable Caravell to compete for a larger share of the computer equipment and supplies market.

In retrospect, even though Mitch's salary is less than half of his previous compensation as a salesman, he remains committed to building his own company. If Caravell's lines of credit continue to increase, Mitch is confident that the company will sustain its growth and soon record a profit. After all, Amazon.com has yet to escape its red ink. Although Mitch's accumulated credit card debt is a drag on company profits, he realizes that Caravell has outgrown its initial dependence on them, and in time his company will receive a small business loan from a bank. At this juncture of the business life-cycle, Mitch has survived the most daunting challenges that few new companies are able to overcome. In fact, his goal is that his future credit card use will be only for company-related travel and entertainment rather than for short-term financing of a new shipment of computer supplies. Who knows, maybe his cards will eventually pay for a corporate box at Bush Stadium where he can watch his beloved Cardinals and enjoy the games as a business expense. After such a momentary flight of fantasy, however, Mitch remembers that his corporate finances evoke a more ominous reality. Without improved capitalization and access to lower-cost credit, his narrow margin of error in making business decisions leaves him only a step away from having his entrepreneurial ambitions crushed by an insolvent customer, a recalcitrant supplier, or the aggressive marketing of a competing goliath.

Hustling on Plastic Money:
Trump Wanna-Bes, Flippers, and Spread Beaters

The restructuring of the American economy and the reorganization of U.S. labor markets over the past two decades have intensified financial pressures on American households. This has led to the greater participation of secondary workers in the wage labor market such as spouses, partners, relatives, or children. For others, new sources of income have entailed renting rooms, taking in laundry, or babysitting. Some wage earners have increased their workweek by moonlighting on a second job or during the weekends; others have pursued alternative sources of income through entrepreneurial activities. Although most of these commercial ventures are designed simply to supplement existing household resources, others constitute initial forays into potential full-time self-employment. The following examples highlight a variety of typical and atypical revenue-generating activities, or "hustles," that are being financed with bank credit cards.

Gary Phillips is a 36-year-old real estate broker in Orlando, Florida. Raised in a white middle-class family in suburban Ohio, he attended an expensive private university in Miami. Gary's education was funded primarily by an athletic scholarship, and he remains an avid booster of the school's nationally renowned athletic program. In fact, he uses these university networks whenever possible in expanding his portfolio of potential investors. Even so, Gary confides that his social and economic ambitions would have been hindered by plying his trade in the intensely competitive market of south Florida. Instead, he joined a real estate company in booming central Florida, near Walt Disney World. As a full-time salesman, with a steady income of real estate commissions, he quickly recognized the growth of new investment opportunities—especially bankrupt and foreclosed properties. For Gary Phillips, who aspires to be a real estate magnate like his hero, billionaire tycoon Donald Trump, the lack of investment capital was his biggest obstacle to acquiring wealth. And, like The Donald, he relies on high-interest borrowed money to "make the deal," which often featured cash advances of tens of thousands of dollars on his portfolio of several Gold Visas and MasterCards.

Exposed to the affluent lifestyles of his college classmates and wealth of local alumni, Gary is obsessed with making it in U.S. society. Emphasizing that the winners of the American Dream are distinguished by their individual motivation and talent, he epitomizes the narcissist attitudes of the yuppie wanna-bes of the go-go 1980s. In fact, Gary often hosts evenings with friends and family members who play spirited rounds of Trump: The Game, which mirrors his view of the cutthroat competition that characterizes the path to business success. For Gary and his late-thirty-something friends, Monopoly is too passé without the quick-strike opportunities and duplicitous dealmaking that define the age of leverage. Not surprisingly, his personal goals are unencumbered with moral concerns or personal empathy toward those whose often dire situations result in fire-sale prices. Rather, his business philosophy is simply to make as much money as possible with the least amount of invested capital: "Why should I let someone else make a killing? . . . It's a free market . . . anyone can play . . . to the victor goes the spoils." A few examples illustrate the crucial role of the credit card hustle in launching his real estate empire.

Just as the financial companies that are perpetually "trolling" for potential debtors, Gary constantly scours the local tax rolls for out-of-state property owners who may be experiencing economic distress. He sends out hundreds of letters per year with unsolicited "low-ball" offers in the hope of "hooking" a highly motivated seller who desperately needs money—immediately if not yesterday. Gary estimates that the response rate to his mailings is less than 1 percent; from this small group, he negotiates with the few willing to accept a cash price on his terms. After negotiating a favorable deal, such as the purchase of a $75,000 duplex for $49,000, Gary pays with cash advances from his credit cards in increments of $5,000 or $10,000; in this example, the interest charges of nearly $1,000 per month are tax deductible as a business expense. After the property title is transferred, Gary seeks conventional bank financing (70 percent to 85 percent of market value) from his carefully cultivated network of friendly financial loan officers (usually low, variable-rate mortgages) and is often able to cash out a few thousand dollars in the process. He then attempts to sell, or "flip," the property at a 10 to 15 percent discount to someone on his list of investors and quickly earns a substantial profit. If his target price is not tendered, Gary fixes up the property and generates a new stream of rental income.

Another of Gary's favorite strategies is to make low bids (at least 20 percent below market value) on bankrupt or foreclosed properties whose mortgages are insured by federal government agencies (FHA, VA, HUD). On a $60,000 house or condominium, the down payment and closing costs often total less than $3,500—a modest cash advance from his credit cards. In these cases, since Gary represents both the buyer and seller, his broker's commission occasionally exceeds the cash requirements of the transaction. Gary then resells the property for an immediate profit—with no cash outlay—or simply rents the house and creates another source of income. In 2000, he owned over 50 residential rentals and offers a rental management service (tenant screening, collections, repairs and renovations) for past and present clients. In addition, his financial success enabled him to quit his sales position and open his own real estate office. With the flourishing central Florida housing market, Gary has parlayed his professional contacts and investment knowledge into a thriving company with over 20 sales agents. In fact, he has cultivated a national client base and established his own investment fund that requires a minimum "participation" of $5,000. Rarely dependent on his $100,000-plus in combined bank card credit, Gary relishes the fact that his economic success has resulted in banks soliciting him for financing his various business ventures. Even so, he realizes that bank lending policies can quickly change with the health of the real estate market. For this reason, Gary confides that he will continue to increase his bank credit card limits in case of a future economic recession.

Like Gary, Eugene Bergman works for himself; he is 49 years old and is his own financial consultant. His ambitious personal goals were shaped largely by the social expectations of his upper-income New England family, which includes his father, a doctor, and several uncles who are successful professionals and businessmen. A graduate of a local private university, Eugene joined a large brokerage house on Wall Street in 1973. After a moderately successful career as a stock trader, he was unexpectedly fired in 1985 following a dispute with his supervisor. At first, Eugene's family supported his decision to leave Wall Street until they realized that his short-term goals violated their central tenets of success: hard work and personal sacrifice. Instead, Bergman chose an alternative route that avoided the high pressure and questionable business practices of Wall Street yet potentially offered the six-figure rewards of a stock trader's salary. He decided to play the stock market.

Eugene collected a lump-sum severance package and, with his savings, reaped the rewards of investing in the stock market during the bull market of the 1980s. With his prior experience and contacts on the Street, the timing was fortuitous for playing the market, as nearly everyone was making impressive profits from its rising financial tide. Of course, the key was to invest as little of his own money as possible and leverage his equity with higher levels of credit (other people's money, or OPM) in order to generate the largest possible trading profits. With his financial acumen, Eugene shrewdly multiplied his investment clout through complicated stock "calls" and "options." Without a source of income, he turned to credit cards for paying his living expenses. However, he did not have a credit card when he lost his job—only an American Express charge card. Although he faithfully "never left home without it," AMEX could not offer relief for his cash-flow woes. So, with his stellar credit rating and based on his previous income, Eugene immediately obtained three bank credit cards—all while unemployed. Initially, Eugene used his unemployment checks to make his minimum credit card payments and then later diverted a small portion of his trading profits to meet his credit card obligations.

At the end of the decade, Eugene was a wealthy man. In fact, he had shifted his assets into low-risk mutual funds before Black Monday when the sharp decline in the stock market signaled the end of the bull run. Today, 15 years after his involuntary career shift, Eugene's investment income affords him a very comfortable standard of living in an affluent New York suburb. In fact, he profited handsomely—again—by the "running of the bulls" in the late 1990s. Although he acknowledges the role of timing and general "good luck," Eugene justifies his leisurely lifestyle as a reward for shrewd financial planning. Otherwise, how could he explain his favorable circumstances to the hardworking professionals in his family? Even so, Eugene remarks that without credit cards, "who knows what my life would be like now?"

The economic forces that created profitable opportunities for Gary Phillips and Eugene Bergman are also responsible for Doug Mathews's hustle. He remembers the shock of house hunting after completing graduate school at the age of 31 in late 1988. The housing-price spiral had peaked with a median price of over $170,000 in the metropolitan Washington, D.C., area. Although he landed a good job in the federal government, the $37,000 annual salary was insufficient for buying a home, especially with nearly $25,000 in maturing student loans. Furthermore, earlier federal tax reforms of 1982 and 1986 had eliminated important tax savings for recent graduates, such as income tax averaging and interest deductibility of student loans, car loans, and credit cards. For Doug, entering the full-time job market seemed like a new form of generational debt peonage. Without the traditional tax deductions and tax saving allowances, he could not buy a house. But without the tax advantages of mortgage interest deductibility, it did not seem possible to save for a down payment on a house.

The inflated housing prices led Doug to spurn buying a home in the D.C. area, an assessment soon validated by the decline of the real estate market the following spring. In order to accumulate savings, however, he was convinced that the tax advantages of homeownership were too substantial to ignore, and he began exploring the purchase of a rental property in various parts of the country. With the onset of the recession, a wave of federally insured foreclosures began flooding the real estate market by the end of the summer. In November 1989, Doug purchased a HUD-insured condominium for $44,000 in central Florida and paid the down payment and settlement costs of nearly $7,000 with cash advances from his MasterCards; the $5,000 in renovations were also financed by credit cards. He rented the condo, which is managed by his retired father, and then refinanced it at an appraised value of $58,500 in order to pay off the accumulated credit card debts.

Over the next three years, Doug purchased three more houses with cash advances from his credit cards and then paid off the balances with his higher income tax returns; the first condominium was financed with a ten-year mortgage, which he views as an emergency savings account to be tapped at any time via a second mortgage. Significantly, Doug realizes that the economic success of this strategy is due to the financial difficulties of people like Ron Taylor who lost their jobs and homes in the late 1980s and thus increased the demand for rental housing in the 1990s. As a result, Doug often "carries" his tenants for several months during periods of economic distress (unemployment, illness, divorce, or separation) by paying the mort-

gages with credit card checks. In fact, he notes with pride that he could easily raise the rents but instead has helped several families from becoming
homeless. By summer 1992, the decline in local housing prices and accumulated tax savings enabled Doug to buy a house in suburban Maryland.
Again, he financed the down payment and closing costs on the $125,000
home—about $12,000—with his growing retinue of six credit cards. At the
end of the 1990s, with residential housing prices soaring, Doug's home had
appreciated to over $170,000. A contented homeowner, Doug acknowl-
edges the crucial aid provided by his credit cards. In fact, Doug laughs that
without them, he might still be living in a student apartment.

Connie Crenshaw is a 29-year-old bartender at a popular restaurant in a
medium-sized town in northern Florida. A vivacious woman, she has only a
high school diploma but will not permit that to limit her career ambitions.
Raised in a local working-class family, Connie enjoys a comfortable lifestyle
with her blue-collar boyfriend, largely due to her earnings at the restaurant
and a secondary income from her plant maintenance service. She would like
to start a family. However, she is concerned about her companion's commitment to marriage as well as the long-term prospects of her job. As a ten-year
veteran of the restaurant industry, she is well aware that today's "in" place is
tomorrow's forgotten hangout.

Connie sees her impending thirtieth birthday as a major event for planning her future. Weary of the frantic pace of the bar trade, she yearns for
more social respect as she explores the transition to a more conventional
work regimen. Although both marriage and a family are high priorities,
Connie remarks that a higher-status occupation might command greater respect from her boyfriend or even attract a more desirable companion. Regardless, she is consumed with the prospect of becoming self-employed and
expanding her small ornamental plant business; she delivers plants and provides maintenance services to local offices. In fact, her keen business instincts have already cultivated an impressive network of clients from the bar
and restaurant—primarily hotels, professional offices, and small businesses.

Connie eagerly coordinates her dual work schedules by operating the
plant service out of a Toyota hatchback on her off days and after the evening
shift. As the business has expanded, Connie's investment has grown accordingly with more plants, fertilizer, and planters. The very success of this venture, however, has brought her to an important professional and financial
crossroads. In order to expand, she must buy a larger delivery vehicle and
expand her greenhouse; she has accumulated over $4,000 of credit card debt
in order to finance her current inventory of plants, supplies, and a storage

facility. Furthermore, as her business has grown, so too have her cash-flow difficulties, as she must spend more time on billings and collections.

Connie's optimistic business plan has received disappointing responses from bank loan officers. Her application for a $15,000 small business loan was rejected, and a loan for a used van was contingent on a hefty down payment; local lenders confirmed their lack of interest in making small business loans under $25,000—regardless of collateral pledges. This irony is not lost on Connie. She recognizes that the same banks that consider her an unacceptable risk for an 8 percent small business loan routinely offer her a credit card for the same purpose at 18 percent APR. Even so, Connie is not disheartened by the skepticism she has encountered. Instead, she is saving money for a van (possibly supplemented with a credit card cash advance) and expanding her plant selection via MasterCard. Thus, Connie is well aware that when she shifts into her Plants-R-Us business full-time, she will become even more dependent on bank credit cards for business expenses. In a business environment with "two strikes against me," Connie knows her social class and gender leave her with little margin for error due to the limited access to business loans. She hopes her goal of swapping her miniskirt for a professional suit will be delayed only temporarily and not permanently.

Finally, while most credit card hustles entail active strategies for financing moneymaking activities, a more recent trend features passive "spread beating" investment strategies. This reflects the frustrations of the credentialed but struggling-to-survive twenty- and thirty-something middle-class professionals who witnessed the prosperity of the 1990s but did not benefit financially from it. This is especially true of the most highly educated, who not only missed the enormously profitable bull market while in school but also are now burdened with large education-related debts. For many of these households, their lack of savings increasingly entails the use of borrowed money in their initial investment forays. For example, in the "passive" investment clubs emerging in cities across the country, members learn how to take cash advances from their credit cards and then buy "shares" in a particular business venture or become partners in a new company by pooling the necessary start-up capital. Others join "syndicates" through which their cash advances are used to purchase products cheaply (such as government surplus equipment or auctions) and then resold at a profit. In fact, there are now professional credit entrepreneurs who assist clients in upgrading their credit ratings in order to obtain new bank credit card accounts for investment purposes. As a recent notice on the Internet proclaims:

I'll show you how to use OPM (other people's money) to create income $$$ get amazing credit secrets. . . . [I am] the only credit specialist attorney in California . . . I'll show you exactly how . . . to get a drawer full of credit cards even if you have little or no income. Then you'll be able to start using your new credit status to make money with my proven methods. I'll show you exactly how you can use credit (OPM) to create a dependable and regular income . . . by using some secret, little-known and new information and laws along with your computer to do things that until recently were impossible! . . . Use new credit cards to create passive income of $2,100 to $6,300 a month![62]

The ongoing proliferation of low-interest introductory credit card rates (teaser rates) has recently spawned a surge in spread-beater investment strategies. For example, a spread beater borrows money at a low interest rate (from 0 to 8.9 percent) through cash advances on credit cards and then invests it in higher-yield stocks, bonds, futures, or other valuable commodities. The low-interest credit card debt (loan), which is a tax-deductible business expense, can be replaced with (surfed to) a new introductory-rate credit card in an attempt to maximize the spread (profit) between the cost of borrowing and the yield on the investment. Although a potentially risky strategy, as illustrated by the college students in Chapter 6 who lost most of their credit card–financed investments, it has enabled many individuals and households to begin building an investment portfolio during the bull market of the 1990s.

Today, the middle-class entitlement of low-cost credit is enabling many earnest hustlers to earn supplementary earnings for their lifestyle needs or wealth for their future retirement with other people's money (OPM). Sadly, this option is not available to the working poor and struggling middle class who must wait to accumulate investment capital through personal savings. In fact, their financial plight contributes to the success of this wealth-generating strategy because they subsidize low-cost introductory teaser rates with high-interest (18–24 percent) credit card accounts and costly transaction fees and penalties. In addition, by paying extremely high finance charges, they contribute to the lucrative investment opportunities in the highly profitable deregulated financial services industry. Significantly, this risky and potentially profitable use of bank credit cards contrasts sharply with the experiences of older Americans. Their conservative and disciplined use of bank credit cards reflects the cultural legacy of personal debt as a social stigma as well as their fear of unforeseen economic calamities.

9

Aging into Debt

Crisis or Convenience
in the Golden Years?

For millions of older Americans, the tumultuous transformation of the U.S. banking system is cause for concern and even anxiety. A generation that endured the financial calamities of the Great Depression and the sacrifices of World War II, most of the nation's elderly are skeptical about the advantages that the new information technologies offer to their lifestyle needs and are reluctant to embrace computer-based banking services during their golden years. As Pat, an 85-year-old senior from Buffalo, New York, scoffed, "Computers are for the younger generation. No way am I touching them, I don't care how easy they are to learn. . . . I'm happy enough [reconciling monthly bank statements] with my calculator. . . . This dog is too old to learn new tricks—even in retirement."

Although the passage of the 1999 Financial Services Modernization Act offers all consumers a smorgasbord of new financial products and services, the vast majority of seniors will not have a hearty appetite for the confusing array of insurance, investment, and other unfamiliar banking offerings. The allure of high-yield mutual funds or more complex stock options will not entice many elderly customers who are fearful of unknown financial risks as they manage their limited financial resources. Instead, the rise of aggressive marketing campaigns based on the corporate sharing of detailed customer information will exacerbate the fear of the elderly toward the new financial services giants.[1] Indeed, most disconcerting to America's seniors is the decline of institutional stability and corporate trust. For a generation whose shopping and banking were based on long-standing friendships and mutual trust, the replacement of familiar community banks with impersonal corporate logos and Madison Avenue slogans is not a change that is easily embraced.

A key issue confronting today's seniors is the erosion of individual relations in conducting their banking affairs. The personal trust that is based on many years and even generations of transactions with the same bank employees is being supplanted by impersonal electronic communication, computer technology, and a rapidly changing workforce. The replacement of community bank presidents with out-of-state transfers and the development of bank policies dictated by corporate officials in New York rather than the local board of directors have led to greater confusion and mistrust of the new banking relationships. This increasingly common situation is described by Harold, a 95-year-old senior from central Florida. He explained the frustration of dealing with his local bank after several decades of direct, personal relationships with the previous bank presidents:

> I never had a problem getting a loan [until now]. No way would I fill out a loan application! Hell, I knew Jack [the bank president] when he was a kid. His father and his grandfather are [members of the] Elks [Club]. I've been drinking with his grandfather for nearly 50 years . . . before Jack was even born. I still see him at the [Elks] Club. Sometimes I'll have a drink with him and his son [Jack's father] . . . [In the past] whenever I needed to borrow some money . . . to buy a [used] car or a house to resell, I'd walk right into Jack's office and tell him how much money I needed and the interest rate that I was going to pay. Hell, I'd even tell him that I wasn't paying any points [on the loan]. . . . After all these years, do you think he would doubt [my creditworthiness]? If he even flinched [at my loan request], I'd have the whole board [bank directors] calling him. That includes his father and grandfather (with a laugh).

For older Americans, whose long history of financial affairs was conducted under the shadow of their personal and family reputations, banking deregulation has fundamentally changed the rules of the game. Impersonal risk-assessment models and credit agency reports fail to adequately respect their past financial achievements. America's seniors are disturbed that creditworthiness is more likely to be defined by current income and amount of money in the bank rather than a spotless credit history and a paid-off mortgage. Hence, in the world of financial conglomerates, only the most economically secure seniors are finding that their banking services have improved.

One year after the interview with Harold, Barnett Bank merged with Nation's Bank, which is now Bank of America. For older Americans of modest financial means, the consequences of this corporate transaction are far greater than simply exchanging inflated shares of stock. After more than 60 years of successful entrepreneurial hustles, Harold confided later that these big banks would not give him a loan due to his limited financial assets. According to the American Association of Retired Persons (AARP), the largest membership organization of senior citizens in the United States, Harold's experience is not unusual. In fact, credit discrimination by banks against older adults (especially widows and those who pay in cash) is "very serious," even though seniors rarely declare bankruptcy and have a default rate on consumer loans of only 1 percent compared with 5 percent for younger borrowers.[2] Incredibly, college students who have never had a job can obtain a consumer loan in the form of bank credit cards more easily than can their grandparents who have retired from 40- or even 50-year work careers.

Although Harold and most members of his generation believe that the interest rates of bank credit cards are usurious (Harold even exclaimed that "this [form of] easy money is how the big banks getcha"), America's seniors are increasingly finding that the erosion of personal relations and the plummeting value of their past credit histories leave them with few credit options. After all, Citibank does not ask what they need a Visa for (as inquisitive children do) or demand extensive application forms. Even for a debt-abhorrent generation, among whom "saving for a rainy day" still resonates with depression-era experiences, it is not surprising that bank credit cards are becoming the loan of last resort for increasing numbers of older adults. Indeed, the use of bank credit cards by U.S. seniors—the group that most adamantly upholds the Puritan ethos that debt is a manifestation of social shame—is rapidly changing to include credit-dependent revolvers. As will be illustrated, older Americans tend to be either devoted convenience users or desperate revolvers.

America's Demographic Bulge:
Aging into the Golden Years of Retirement

While the United States experiences its longest period of uninterrupted prosperity—economic conditions that belie the social and economic hardships of the previous period of U.S. industrial restructuring—it faces an unrelated yet imposing demographic challenge: the grandparent boom. The increasing life

FIGURE 9.1   Growth of U.S. Older Adult Population: 1900–2050

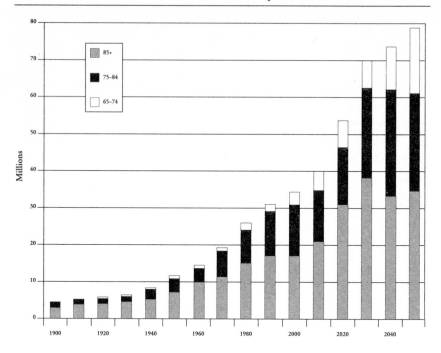

SOURCE: U.S. Bureau of the Census.

expectancy of Americans, together with the aging of the 76 million post–World War II baby boomers (born between 1946 and 1964), translates into an impending gerontological explosion. Demographic estimates by the U.S. Census Bureau indicate the number of Americans at least 65 years old has increased modestly from 33.2 million in 1994 (12.7 percent of the U.S. population) to 35.3 million in 2000 (12.8 percent). Based on medium growth assumptions, however, demographic projections indicate that the 65-plus population will climb from 40.1 million (13.3 percent) in 2010 to 53.3 million (16.4 percent) in 2020 and then jump sharply to 70.1 million (20.1 percent) in 2030 as the baby-boomer "bulge" enters retirement.[3] By 2040, between 20 and 25 percent of all Americans will be at least 65 years old, which will nearly double the number of Social Security beneficiaries. This compares with only 4 percent at the turn of the twentieth century. Similarly, the number of children under 5 years old outnumbered seniors over 84 years old by 12 to 1 in 1970; by 2040, it is estimated that these groups will nearly achieve numerical parity.[4] Overall, U.S. seniors will exceed 80 million by 2050. Figure 9.1 shows the growth of the U.S. older adult population during the twentieth century and demographic projections through 2050.[5]

Significantly, the "graying of America" is not a static gerontological phenomenon or simply the inexorable progression of a relatively homogeneous proportion of the U.S. population aging into retirement. Rather, this demographic bulge comprises a heterogeneous population that includes more highly educated citizens, dual-income households, geographically dispersed extended families, single and divorced elderly, immigrants and minorities, as well as seniors with fewer (if any) children. Furthermore, the increasing longevity of Americans means that the lifestyles of the elderly will vary radically among the active "young-old" (65–74), more sedentary "old" (75–84), and the "oldest old" (85+) who are most dependent and medically frail. Last, as the senior population rises from one in eight in 2000 to one in six in 2020 and then to one in five in 2030, its political and economic clout may radically change retirement, consumption patterns, and even entitlement programs provided by the federal government. And, in contrast to the 1996 "liberal" welfare reform, based on compulsory employment of healthy public-aid recipients,[6] public support is very low for programs that would force grandpa to work for food (see McDonald's recruitment materials for "non-traditional" workers) or grandma to hold bake sales for the rent.

Unlike their parents and grandparents, many future U.S. seniors will experience more severe hardships in their older years due to greater household debt, more limited and fragmented family support networks, higher medical costs, increased longevity, and shrinking public assistance programs. The escalating economic demands on America's older adult population are colliding increasingly with the diminished ability of both private and public programs to address these mounting social needs adequately.[7] As a result, many older adults are finding that they have little choice but to abandon their conservative attitudes toward debt and embrace a credit-dependent lifestyle. Inevitably, the replacement of fiscally cautious depression babies with younger credit-reliant boomers ensures that this attitudinal transformation will be completed over the next two decades as the use of bank credit cards among older adults mirrors their use in the general U.S. population.

The Moral Divide: Intractable Attitudes or Changing Behaviors?

Older adults are the most sensitive, as a group, to the social implications of the moral divide between revolvers and convenience users (Chapter 4).[8] Even after they complete their work careers, the generational influences of the Great Depression continue to shape their abhorrence of personal debt of any kind. For most U.S. seniors, debt is a sign of personal failure—either professionally or behaviorally. Members of this generation, which endured

the sacrifices of economic catastrophe and wartime rationing, recognize that
they cannot control the impact of larger trends on their lives (e.g., unemployment, war), but they can discipline their personal consumption urges.
As a result, debt is the generational yardstick of personal success or failure—
a standardized measure for all social classes. The difference between social
condemnation ("she never could manage a budget" or "he still has to work
because they refused to live within their financial means") and approval ("the
poor dear always managed at least to put food on the table" or "he was able
to provide for a comfortable retirement") is based on a moral code that includes rejection or deferral of immediate gratification and self-indulgence.

For these reasons, many older adults adamantly refuse to accumulate any
debt if at all possible on bank credit cards. This is illustrated by 71-year-old
Janice, a lifelong convenience user of consumer credit from Yonkers, New
York. For Janice, the prospect of accumulating debt on her credit cards is
morally repugnant and must be avoided at all costs. She emotionally re-
counted a heated argument with her son over the use of her Visa credit card:
"I know he had a good reason to borrow the money [$4,000], it was an
emergency. . . . All of my money was tied up in CDs (bank certificate of deposits), and he promised to pay the entire amount [of the loan] at the end
of the month. Still, it bothered me so much that I couldn't sleep until he
sent me a check and I paid off the bill. It would have upset me terribly if I
had to pay a finance charge. . . . You have to understand, it's not [paying]
the interest that bothers me. It's the thought that people would think that I
needed the money and couldn't pay it back."

The preoccupation of American seniors with the social stigma of accumulated debt is reflected in the limited available data. Older adults are the
least likely to have bank or universal credit cards and the most likely to pay
off their monthly charges. For example, 66.4 percent of all U.S. households
reported using a bank credit card in 1995. As expected, the proportion of
credit card users steadily increases by age of household head until the oldest
age groups: under 35 years (59.0 percent), 35 to 44 years (68.5 percent), 45
to 54 years (75.4 percent), 55 to 64 years (71.9 percent), 65 to 74 years
(68.3 percent), and 75 years and older (54.6 percent). More striking is the
different rates of convenience use by age cohorts. In 1995, approximately
one-third (34 percent) of all U.S. credit card holders paid off their balances
in full at the end of the month. As reported in the 1995 Survey of Consumer Finance, however, the percentage of credit card holders who "almost
always pays off" monthly charges ranged from 40.2 percent among the
under-35 age group to 85.8 percent among those 75 years old and over (see
Table 9.1); the next highest is 72.0 percent among the 65-and-over age

TABLE 9.1 Credit Card Payment Patterns by Age Group, 1995 (self-reported, in percentages)

Age of Family Head	Almost Always Pay off Balance	Sometimes Pay off Balance	Hardly Ever Pay off Balance
Under 35	40.2	23.5	36.3
35–44	40.7	26.9	32.4
45–54	47.1	22.5	30.4
55–64	59.3	18.4	22.3
65–74	72.0	12.9	15.1
75 and older	85.8	2.5	11.7

NOTE: General-purpose credit cards include MasterCard, Visa, Optima, and Discover.

SOURCE: Federal Reserve Board, unpublished data from the 1995 Survey of Consumer Finance, reported in table 823, *1998 Statistical Abstract of the United States* (Washington, D.C.: U.S. Government Printing Office, 1999), p. 524.

group.[9] Today, even with convenience users rising to 43 percent, older Americans are still about twice as likely to pay off their charges than the average U.S. account holder under 65 years old.[10] And the concern over paying their accounts off each month is not a simple issue of frugality but is a moral imperative. In fact, most seniors boast that their status as credit card "deadbeats" is a social affirmation of their generation's moral code of conduct.

In marketing credit cards, the banking industry's advertisements reflect the extreme experiences of older adults, with the underlying themes of moral rectitude (self-discipline) and misfortune (bad luck). Seniors are portrayed as either financially and socially vigorous or economically dependent with serious health infirmities. This polarized view of the contemporary experiences of older Americans is illustrated in the recent marketing campaigns of Visa. On the one hand, a 1998 American Airlines–Visa promotion portrays an active and well-groomed grandmother smiling with, presumably, her young grandson. The advertisement implies that Visa can help "earn" free airline tickets so that seniors can enjoy more precious time with family members during their golden years. The objective is to encourage seniors to use their credit cards more frequently with the reward of free airline tickets.[11] Hence, this emphasis on convenience and frugality—charging as the means to a financially responsible end—is an extension of this generation's moral code of conduct. From the industry's perspective, the more charges made by older adults, the greater the potential that some will eventually become profitable revolvers.

The image of healthy and vigorous seniors contrasts sharply with Visa's 1999 "homebound elderly" program. These advertisements, often displayed at the cash registers of retail checkout counters, feature an infirm elderly woman in a wheelchair in what appears to be a nursing home. The scene conveys loneliness, despair, and impoverishment. In this case, Visa appeals to consumers' empathy by declaring that 1 percent of all proceeds from the program will be dispersed to help the most needy of America's seniors. Only the most insensitive can ignore the silent plea—as carefully orchestrated by the photographer—of someone's grandmother in an understaffed nursing home despondently pondering her final years.

In this case, Visa is publicizing the plight of the nation's most unfortunate and undeserving poor as a "public service to the community." The campaign implores us to help—even in a small way—those whose disadvantaged circumstances are outside of their control: the bad luck of financial, familial, or health-related misfortune. Of course, a more effective response would be to contribute directly to nonprofit groups that aid older adults, but that is not the point. The goal of this campaign is to encourage greater credit card use by praising the social good that these charges will provide for the neediest of senior citizens. In sum, the public images of older Americans that are presented by the credit card industry reflect a wide range of changing economic and lifestyle demands. Together with declining public services, the mass marketing of consumer credit is both a cause and an effect of the profound behavioral changes experienced by some older adults. These trends are illuminated through the personal experiences of the senior citizens portrayed in the following sections.

The Magic of Plastic:
Patching the Social Safety-Net of Elderly Survival

Jeannie May Lawson has worked hard, all of her life, to raise three children and generally "just to get by." Divorced for over 40 years, she survives on a Social Security check of $648 per month and part-time work in the "old folks home" in the small town where she lives in upstate Illinois; the rent for her subsidized one-bedroom apartment is $196 per month. Unlike many of her generational peers, Jeannie May lacks an accumulated nest egg for retirement. Her low-income, blue-collar jobs did not offer a private pension, and divorce deprived her of the opportunity for greater household savings. More important, the modest home that she and her ex-husband purchased with a VA loan after the war was sold years ago. This seemingly uneventful decision has had a major, unforeseen impact on her later years because home equity is the most important source of personal wealth for retirement, especially among working-class families. Today, nearly four out of five seniors (79.1 percent) over 64 years old are homeowners, only 8 percent are still paying on their first mortgages, and 28 percent have various home equity and second mortgages.[12] Not surprisingly, home equity accounts for most assets of older adults.[13]

Jeannie May symbolizes the plight of America's working-class elderly. The United States was still a largely rural society—especially in the Midwest—when she was born in 1915 in northern Illinois, the youngest of five children. Her parents worked the small family farm that produced mostly corn and some vegetables for the market as well as pigs, cows, and chickens primarily for household consumption. Money was scarce as the family, second-generation immigrants from England, struggled to make ends meet in a local farm economy where credit was informally negotiated and debts were satisfied through bartered exchanges. For example, the local dentist was frequently paid for his services "in-kind" with eggs, butter, and freshly dressed chickens, and the schoolteacher received food and housing that were supplemented with a small monetary salary. This practice of nonmonetary exchange was especially common during the 1930s when Jeannie May's most vivid memories about credit and debt were molded. "Money was hard to come by in those days. . . . Many people were losing their farms and even their homes . . . it was tough times."

Jeannie May's rural life experiences, Calvinist religious upbringing, and recollections of the Great Depression strongly influenced her attitudes toward personal debt. On the one hand, the economic rhythms of the seasonal farm economy required rural families to rely on credit for agricultural and household supplies during the planting and fallow seasons, which would then be repaid after harvesting the corn or selling some livestock in the cash economy. Hence, even among yeoman farmers, credit and debt were natural features of their modest lifestyle. On the other hand, the local Protestant churches emphasized the Calvinist values of hard work and frugality as evidence of a virtuous life. This emphasis on savings as a sign of potential spiritual salvation contrasts sharply with the negative views of leisure activities and personal consumption. Jeannie May remembers sermons in the little white church that chastised "idle hands" and indolent "material desires" as moral sins that would lead to disastrous personal debt. The painful experiences of the depression, when friends and family members "lost everything to the banks," stayed with Jeannie May as she entered her later years with very conservative attitudes about credit and debt.

At 78 years old, Jeannie May still enjoys an active lifestyle that belies her age. Unlike her affluent brother, John, she was unable to translate the generational advantages of rising wages, inexpensive housing, and low educational costs into economic security in retirement. This is partially due to Jeannie May's divorce and inability to remarry, which forced her to assume the economic responsibility of raising her three children on a single income. Although national poverty rates among older adults at least 65 years old have been falling, from 15.7 percent in 1980 to 10.8 percent in 1997, older women are nearly twice as likely as older men to live in poverty. Also, African American and Latino seniors are more than twice as likely as whites to live in poverty; Asian and Pacific Islander rates are nearly the same as for whites.[14]

For Jeannie May, her fragile financial circumstances mean that she cannot enjoy a leisurely life in her final years; she would prefer to catch up on her "patchin' [a quilt] or knittin' [an afghan]" for a newborn nephew or niece. Instead, when her health permits (she has diabetes and high blood pressure), Jeannie May works 15 to 30 hours per week in the "[retirement] home's" kitchen and does housework and errands for neighbors who are usually several years younger. Her experience, of course, is not unusual. The U.S. Census Bureau reports that 8.6 percent of women and 17.1 percent of men over 64 years old were still officially employed in 1997, with projected increases in 2006 to 8.7 percent for senior women and 17.8 percent for senior men. Significantly, this rate for men has declined from 19.0 percent in 1980, whereas it has risen from 8.1 percent for women.[15] Although Jeannie May occasionally receives small financial gifts from a son in Seattle, the only source of economic assistance she could depend on in case of an emergency was her brother John—that is, until the day she received that miraculous piece of plastic in the mail.

Jeannie May does not recall the first Visa solicitation that arrived in late 1987, but she does remember her excitement over the financial "freedom" it offered. As a struggling single mother, she was grateful for the higher standard of living that installment credit had provided for her and the children in the 1940s and 1950s: the VA home mortgage loan, used-car loans from finance companies, corporate loans for appliances and furniture, store credit from local merchants for clothing, and a charge card for gasoline. Jeannie May confides that she rarely paid off the balance of her credit accounts at the end of the month and was often late with her payments. Although she accepts most of the responsibility as a poor "budget keeper," she laments that her ex-husband's irregular child support increased her dependence on consumer credit by "stretching" her meager earnings.

Unlike the proprietary credit cards (Sears, Montgomery Ward) she had previously used, the new universal Visa card offered her the magic of purchasing items nearly anywhere she wanted and whenever she wanted them: local merchants, mail order, and even over the telephone. More important, it enabled Jeannie May to avoid the scrutiny of her financially secure brother (a successful dentist) and his condescending wife, who frequently criticized Jeannie's lifestyle when "helping" with her financial crises. Hence, by avoiding such embarrassing financial assistance, Jeannie May did not have to confront the Calvinist guilt that would eventually erupt from her escalating mountain of consumer debt. This attitudinal denial was reinforced by the marketing strategies of the credit card industry. As long as she "paid her minimums [monthly credit card payments]," Jeannie May convinced herself that she was satisfying her financial obligations and thus adhering to her generation's moral code of conduct.

Unaware of the technological advances in mass marketing, Jeannie May was flattered by the personalized invitations for bank cards that arrived in her mailbox. Jeannie's limited education (she did not complete high school), low self-esteem (modest family background), meager income as a divorced blue-collar worker ("scarred" credit history), and respect of authority figures (bankers) made her especially susceptible to the marketing ploys that affirmed her self-worth as a valued client. Even after violating her ingrained values by consuming more than she could afford, Jeannie willingly accepted the bank's explanation that she *was* creditworthy and that she "deserved" to be "rewarded" with a higher line of credit. After all, she did what she was told, at least for the first few years: promptly remit the minimum payment at the end of each month. "I never really looked at the credit card bills much. What was important [to me] was what I had to pay at the end of the month. . . . I didn't really keep track of how much I owed. I paid 'em what they wanted [minimum payment]. They were happy and I was happy."

The especially disturbing feature in Jeannie May's experience is the ease with which the industry manipulated her into assuming debt levels that she was incapable of financing much less ever paying off. Indeed, the predatory marketing strategies of the credit card companies are very effective in exploiting the low self-esteem and falling standard of living of America's senior citizens. As a divorcée who never remarried, for example, Jeannie May found her material lifestyle had plunged below that of her brother and even of her children—especially after her retirement. Although she embraced her generation's values of hard work and frugality, she yearned for some of the indulgences that members of the middle class take for granted: vacation trips, new cars, household furniture, restaurant outings, gift-giving, and even chocolate candies. With few friends (most deceased or in nursing homes) and a disconnected extended family (children in Seattle, Milwaukee, New York), she began coping with her loneliness by embracing material rewards during her leisure time. In the process, she sought to emulate the consumption privileges of many middle-class wives (such as her sister-in-law), who balanced their husbands' economic success as "producers" by being the primary household "consumers."[16] Through the magic of Jeannie May's piece(s) of plastic, she was finally able to enjoy a comfortable life that previously had been denied her.

For Jeannie May and millions of elderly citizens, credit cards are serving important purposes during the current era of fragmented families and an increasingly fractured social-welfare system. Indeed, Jeannie May did not use her credit cards frivolously by middle-class standards, at least at the beginning. The car needed repairs and new tires; her automobile insurance premiums were raised; her diabetes and high blood pressure medications were more costly; she replaced her reading glasses and finally bought a new winter coat. Jeannie May's newfound purchasing power also unleashed the ability to satisfy other wants that she felt had been unfairly denied. This led to such purchases as a sofa and dining room table for her apartment, a set of pots and pans for the kitchen, new clothes, knitting and sewing materials and supplies, restaurant dinners, and small gifts for family members during the holiday season.

Although supermarkets did not initially accept credit cards, she charged groceries and household supplies at drugstores and even mail-order steaks (delivered by dry ice) from Nebraska. Later, she began making purchases over the telephone via the Home Shopping Network. Jeannie May described with irrepressible glee her anticipation of the UPS truck as it made its appointed deliveries of her eagerly awaited "surprises." For her, the magic of plastic offered the opportunity to enjoy the consumer lifestyle promoted by mass advertising yet denied by Social Security.

By the time Jeannie May had maxed out her first credit card in late 1988, about $3,000 in less than a year, she truly believed the banks' form letters that praised her responsible credit history. In fact, she began to accept the preapproved credit card solicitations that arrived in her mailbox with the now familiar logos of Visa and MasterCard, as these were not just any banks that were "callin' on her." Esteemed financial institutions such as Citibank, First Chicago, Continental Bank, and Chase Manhattan were actually vying for her business. "I figured if the banks keep on sending 'em to me, then I figured I'd keep on usin' 'em. . . . [The banks are] in the business of lending money. I trusted 'em. I thought they knew what they were doing." And they did. Instead of a financial warning after reaching her credit card limit, Jeannie's "mature" account status triggered a second and then a third card in 1989 followed by a fourth credit card in early 1990. By 1991, Jeannie May had amassed a huge credit card debt and was having difficulty making her minimum payments.

Jeannie May really did not know how much debt she had accumulated (over $12,000) or even how bad her financial situation was at the time. She did admit that the infirmities of old age were finally catching up to her. "I never thought of myself as one of the old folks [in the retirement home]. . . . I could get around on my own and even helped them with their own chores. With my car and job, my life really hadn't changed much [in retirement]. . . . I just didn't have to work as hard [at a full-time job]." The reality, however, was that she could not live adequately on her Social Security income—even with participation in public programs for the elderly such as subsidized housing and medical care. As a result, it became increasingly difficult to budget her modest monthly income due to rising health-related expenses and an uncertain level of supplementary earnings. On the one hand, her high blood pressure and diabetes required more costly medicines—even with Medicaid assistance—which increased her need to work. On the other, her poor health meant that she could not work regularly at the retirement home and thus could not rely on extra earnings to supplement her meager Social Security check. Although Jeannie May's children remain in contact with her, they provide little financial help; occasionally they send money, but it amounts to only a "couple a hundred dollars a year." Hence, with a limited family support system and America's shrinking social safety-net, Jeannie May turned to credit cards as her most reliable form of assistance against the unforeseen and debilitating exigencies of the aging process.

It was primarily for economic reasons that Jeannie May ignored her doctor's advice to "slow down" and stubbornly continued to work part-time. For her, employment was crucial to continuing her newfound independence. Work enabled her to shield the escalating credit card debt from outside scrutiny while maintaining the illusion that her industriousness provided for a relatively comfortable lifestyle. Unfortunately, the combination of financial duress, failing health, and a long life of manual labor finally culminated in a mild stroke at the end of 1991. She was already stretched to her financial limit, and the temporary end of her part-time job forced Jeannie May to confront the reality that she could no longer make the minimum payments on her credit cards. While she was convalescing at home, the tone of her credit card statements shifted radically—from friendly to concerned and then to threatening. At this time, Jeannie May desperately sought help from the source of last resort, her brother, even though she knew that this decision would require a humiliating explanation as well as the end of her credit-reliant lifestyle.

Jeannie May's brother, John, remembers the phone call that led to his dismay over the predicament of his sibling. John lived in a posh, northside suburb of Chicago and immediately made the three-hour drive to Jeannie May's apartment. He had always been protective of his youngest sister and was surprised by her agitation over what he assumed was a relatively minor problem. After all, she was a frugal person, and there were no obvious warning signals to indicate a sudden change in her lifestyle. In fact, John was unaware that Jeannie May had any bank cards. Upon reviewing her credit card charges, he found not one but four separate accounts. Furthermore, John was able to reconstruct her consumption patterns. What were normal and modest purchases for him were often unnecessary or too costly for Jeannie May. Even so, John was impressed by the general pattern of essential charges: car repairs, gasoline, medicine, groceries, clothes, insurance, and other necessary household items.

After compiling all of Jeannie May's outstanding credit card bills, John was shocked by what they revealed. In less than five years, Jeannie May had amassed over $12,000 in consumer debt. Fear and shame had led her to ignore the cumulative outstanding balance, yet the marketing campaigns of the credit card industry continued to persuade her that she was a good customer and thus worthy of more credit. For Jeannie May, elevation to a middle-class standard of living proved to be a temporary respite. After she paid rent, medicine, and food, her Social Security check barely covered the "minimums" on her credit card accounts. Clearly, if she ever was to regain economic self-sufficiency, Jeannie May had to escape from this financial albatross and return to her more modest lifestyle. With the help of John's lawyer, Jeannie May filed for personal bankruptcy and is no longer responsible for her past credit card debts. In addition, John purchased a small annuity that supplements Jeannie May's retirement income (about $200 a month) for the rest of her life. Although this was a compassionate and foresightful act, John's recent death of a heart attack at age 87 means that Jeannie May has lost her only dependable source of economic assistance. For her and increasing numbers of impoverished elderly, the ability to secure a bank credit card is the most realistic strategy for obtaining a modicum of financial security in their later years. And this is not an unlikely prospect in view of the intensifying competition by credit card companies for new accounts of revolvers.

Coping with Credit:
Conflicting Attitudes and Divergent Lifestyles

Jeannie May Lawson's experience is emblematic of the social crisis confronting America's poorest senior citizens. Her story reveals the aggressive efforts of the credit card industry in its quest to expand into the few remaining unsaturated market segments. This unique intersection of escalating consumer demand and institutional growth of the financial services industry—a trend accentuated by the dislocations of U.S. industrial restructuring—explains the successful recruitment of new credit card holders from the most economically marginal social groups: unemployed college students and retired seniors. For instance, the only age groups with a market penetration of less than 50 percent in the early 1990s were those 18 to 24 years old and over 64 years old.[17] Not surprisingly, these percentages increased rapidly throughout the decade.

Older Americans were not specifically targeted by the credit card industry until the mid- to late 1980s. Although respected by banks, due to their accumulated assets and favorable credit histories, seniors typically generated few profits for credit card divisions. This is because seniors initially obtained credit cards in the 1960s and early 1970s and tended to use them sparingly or promptly paid off their balances at the end of the month. Furthermore, these convenience users have been much less likely than other groups to purchase big-ticket items (furniture, appliances, stereos) and have been erroneously stereotyped as socially inactive and frugal retirees.[18] The latter is particularly important, since young executives have been preoccupied with marketing to more youthful households while assuming that older adults eschew discretionary consumption expenditures. Of course, this perception changed quickly as more economically marginal seniors such as Jeannie May Lawson received credit cards in the late 1980s and swiftly began accumulating high-interest consumer debt.

In a report summarized in 1995 by AARP, which presented sophisticated predictions of credit card expansion by age cohort in 2000, the most striking feature of these trends is that even the fast-growth projections have substantially underestimated the pace of this market expansion. In 1992 (see Table 9.2, panel 1), as expected, the proportion of credit card holders steadily increases over the life-cycle until the oldest age cohorts: for 18 to 24 years old, 37.8 percent; 25 to 34 years old, 52.4 percent; 35 to 44 years old, 62.2 percent; peaking at 45 to 54 years old, 65.0 percent; declining at 55 to 64 years old, 58.1 percent; and at 64-plus years old, 44.6 percent. The next two panels of the table present the growth projections of cardholders

TABLE 9.2   Credit Card Holders by Age Group, 1992, and by Growth Projections to 2000

Age Groups	Number (thousands)	Possess Credit Cards (percent)	Market Share (percent)	Percent Change (1992–2000)
		1992		
Total, 18 and older	98,614	53.5	100.0	—
18 to 24	9,623	37.8	9.8	—
25 to 34	23,158	52.4	23.5	—
35 to 44	23,345	62.2	23.7	—
45 to 54	16,407	65.0	16.6	—
55 to 64	12,003	58.1	12.8	—
65 and older	13,420	44.6	13.6	—
		2000 (slow-growth projections)		
Total, 18 and older	122,911	60.2	100.0	24.6
18 to 24	11,860	45.4	9.6	23.3
25 to 34	21,579	57.7	17.6	-6.8
35 to 44	30,536	68.4	24.8	30.8
45 to 54	26,478	71.5	21.5	61.4
55 to 64	15,325	63.9	12.5	21.0
65 and older	17,133	49.1	13.9	27.7
		2000 (fast-growth projections)		
Total, 18 and older	145,152	71.1	100.0	47.2
18 to 24	19,034	72.9	13.1	97.8
25 to 34	24,513	65.5	16.9	0.6
35 to 44	34,035	76.2	23.4	45.8
45 to 54	32,371	87.4	22.3	97.3
55 to 64	15,992	66.7	11.0	26.3
65 and older	21,214	60.8	14.6	58.1

NOTE: Data from Mediamark Research, Inc., combined with U.S. Census population-growth projections.

SOURCE: American Association of Retired Persons (AARP), "Credit Marches On," *Horizons,* February 1995, p. 6.

in 2000 based on slow-growth rates and fast-growth rates. The total net increase over this eight-year period is estimated from 24.3 million (24.6 percent) to 46.5 million (47.2 percent) cardholders with the largest increase attributed to the youngest (from 37.8 percent to 72.9 percent) and oldest (from 44.6 percent to 60.8 percent) age groups. By 1995, however, the slow-growth estimates had already been exceeded, and most of the fast-growth estimates were nearly achieved: under 35 years old, 59.0 percent; 35 to 44 years old, 68.5 percent; 45 to 54 years old, 75.4 percent; 55 to 64 years old, 71.9 percent; 65 to 74 years old, 68.3 percent; and over 75 years old, 54.6 percent.[19] In 1999, approximately 70 percent of all students enrolled in four-year colleges and over 62 percent of older adults 65–74 years old used bank credit cards.[20]

The use of bank credit cards by the elderly will continue to increase over the next two decades. This is primarily due to two factors. First, deteriorating economic circumstances will force many financially desperate seniors to change their attitudes toward consumer credit and amass increasing levels of personal debt. For the impoverished elderly, like Jeannie May Lawson, credit cards are becoming their social safety-net of last resort. In fact, there is a noticeable rise in telemarketing scams that prey on economically distressed seniors. With promises of low-interest credit cards, these representatives of fictitious credit card companies demand application fees as high as $300. The success of these fraudulent boiler-room operations underscores the financial ignorance and appalling economic plight of America's most disadvantaged elderly. Fortunately, highly publicized complaints have led to greater scrutiny of these high-pressure sales pitches (even though most seniors fail to report these crimes) and even some successful criminal prosecutions.[21]

Second, the oldest and most debt-abhorrent age cohorts are being steadily replaced with younger boomers who already rely on the convenience of bank cards or have become credit-dependent for their lifestyle needs. This means that the age structure of the U.S. population will soon bulge with credit-dependent cohorts of the "new old" while the oldest age cohorts will eventually disappear through natural attrition. Consequently, the progressive market saturation of America's senior citizens by the credit card industry is ensured due to economic and demographic forces as well as the effectiveness of mass marketing campaigns. These trends are illustrated by the conflicting attitudes and divergent lifestyle patterns of the different age cohorts of U.S. seniors.

The most striking difference in consumer credit card use among older Americans is associated with their social class background as it interacts with lifestyle patterns that vary by age and gender. Indeed, U.S. seniors are not a homogeneous population, as reflected in their social activities and consumption patterns. Instead, the lifestyles of Americans aged 55 to 70 are clearly distinct from senior retirees 70 to 85 years old. First, the younger group is more physically active, and through advances in geriatric medicine, its middle-class members are more likely to take advantage of their leisure time and discretionary income by engaging in sports, physical fitness activities, travel, hobbies, entertainment, education, and cultural events. AARP first offered a fixed-rate Visa in 1990. Only four years later, membership demand and lucrative sponsorship fees led AARP to offer four AARP Visa affinity cards and a fifth AARP Gold card. Not surprisingly, over two-thirds of AARP Visa cardholders are between 50 and 65 years old, and most of their purchases are classified as discretionary, such as hotel accommodations, plane tickets, restaurant meals, and consumer catalog products.[22] Of course, these primarily middle-class seniors are more familiar with consumer credit, are more likely to have continued their credit card use after completing their employment careers, and are more likely to have adequate retirement incomes.

Often, the intersection of age and social class is difficult to distinguish in shaping the attitudes of senior citizens toward consumer debt. For instance, 64-year-old Katherine Papademetrios, a white professional woman who lives in suburban Maryland, expressed her concern over the rising levels of household debt among middle-class families. During our interview, she pointed to the house across the street and confided in an exasperated tone, "I can't believe that my neighbor has three or four thousand dollars [of debt] on her Sears credit card and has no intention to pay it off. Imagine, she's still paying for things—at over 20 percent interest—that wore out years ago." For Katherine, whose parents immigrated from Greece at the turn of the century, the use of credit in the financial world is like courteous manners in the social world: Its undisciplined use will produce shameful outcomes. This leads her to view consumer debt as a sign of imprudent personal behavior that should elicit social reproval rather than become more socially acceptable. Of course, the reality may be that intransigent consumer debt is masking household crises (employment disruptions, health problems, separation and divorce, family obligations, investment fiascoes) that otherwise might be publicly visible and socially embarrassing. Even so, the common assumption still prevails that credit card debt is a personal problem that must be addressed at the level of flawed individual values and inflated consumption patterns.[23]

Although the past two decades have brought an enormous increase in household debt, its origins and meanings differ markedly, especially among younger senior citizens. For some, debt in retirement implies professional failure or a life of personal indulgence; for others it suggests dysfunctional family support networks or simply poor financial planning. More recently, employment disruptions arising from corporate bankruptcies and workforce downsizings have challenged traditional views toward credit and debt.[24] Unlike economically active workers, seniors regard consumer debt as a more damning stigma, since it implies long-lasting and potentially insurmountable hardships in their later years. These different attitudes are mirrored in the experiences of the following "young old" seniors.

Janice Goldsmith is a 71-year-old white divorcée from Yonkers, New York. A high school graduate from a middle-class family, she had a glamorous modeling career, then performed more mundane jobs as a retail clerk and a small-town librarian. Today, Janice's generally good health and substantial inheritance have enabled her to enjoy an active retirement in central Florida at a relatively youthful age; she retired at 62 with partial Social Security benefits rather than endure the mounting stress of disciplining teenage "rowdies" in the public library. A grandmother and avid traveler, Janice has eagerly embraced consumer credit cards as a transactional godsend:

> Credit cards have made my life so much easier. I don't have to worry about carrying cash [in case of being robbed] or waste time writing a check. . . . If I want to make a hotel reservation, send my grandson an airline ticket, or go out and have lunch with my girlfriends, I can simply use my cards. . . . Also, I can earn frequent flier miles for a free [airline] ticket. . . . It's not like I can't afford to pay [for my purchases].

Hence, Janice is the quintessential convenience credit card user—the type of clients banks love to promote as "responsible" consumers and detest as financial "deadbeats." A relatively high-volume charger, she invariably pays her balance in full at the end of the month, and thus the banks rarely make money on her account. Indeed, Janice is proud to report that she has almost never paid a bank finance charge, or what she considers a "tax on poor money managers." The only times that Janice remembers carrying a balance was when she was out of the country, or waiting for her quarterly investment dividends to pay for an expensive trip or a costly medical procedure.

Janice's conservative attitudes toward credit and debt—especially common among retirees—reflect her social Darwinist views toward material success. That is, she measures personal achievement and social worth by one's level of economic affluence. "If you have money, then you deserve the better things in life. If you can't pay for things, then you don't deserve them and shouldn't enjoy them." This view is mirrored in her attitudes toward retirement. According to Janice, people should prepare for retirement through financial planning (long-term investments) or frugal living. Otherwise, she believes that economic difficulties constitute a "final grade" of professional failure, a previously inflated standard of living, or some nefarious family problem. For Janice, economic success during one's work career should translate into a comfortable lifestyle in retirement.

Even so, Janice realizes that financial security in retirement may attract "smooth operators" who prey on the loneliness and physical infirmities of older adults—especially widows and divorcées. She describes with compassion the personal experiences of friends or highly publicized stories of modest-income seniors who have fallen victim to fraudulent schemes that were paid with credit cards: over $10,000 for dancing (lessons, gowns, competitions), $5,000 for a modeling portfolio, and even $15,000 for church-sponsored youth-outreach programs that was squandered by a philandering pastor.[25] Indeed, Janice expresses concern that credit cards do not always provide the convenience and peace of mind that are portrayed in mass marketing campaigns. Fear of theft and even physical abuse are growing risks among the elderly but not because of stashes of cash hidden under their mattresses. Rather, the generally low balance that most older adults carry on their credit cards means that even fixed-income seniors can be victimized for hundreds and even several thousand dollars of unauthorized charges or cash advances. Assaults, home burglaries, purse snatchings, and even theft of credit cards by medical staff in hospitals and nursing homes are being reported with greater frequency by the media—even in Canada and Great Britain. One of the most disturbing cases involves the murder of a 73-year-old Phoenix woman by her 49-year-old son over his use of her credit cards. Robert Davis, who used cash advances from his mother's credit cards for "gambling and drinking at a topless bar," was convicted of first-degree murder in 1998.[26]

Janice expresses intolerance and general disdain toward those who accumulate long-term personal debt: "I have little sympathy for people with large credit card debts. If they can't afford it, they shouldn't buy it." As for retirees, "Debt at that age is disgraceful. What did they do with their lives? . . . It is shameful if they have to depend [financially] on their children." When asked if she knew people who had lost their pensions and health insurance after their companies went bankrupt or were laid off immediately before qualifying for full retirement benefits, she replied, "Poor devils. Today, companies do treat you much differently than before. I guess there are more people who really don't deserve the situation they're in now . . . like my cousin who was laid off at 53 years old." Even so, Janice responds that "they shouldn't use their credit cards unless it's an emergency. Using credit cards [for loans] only makes it more difficult to survive later on. They have to pay back what they borrowed with high interest rates. They [retirees] should be relying on savings or help from their family. . . . In a capitalist society, you have to take care of yourself."

Janice's leisurely retirement lifestyle and harsh attitudes toward personal debt contrast sharply with the experiences of Beatrice Williams. A 63-year-old African American woman and lifelong resident of the District of Columbia, she suffers from high blood pressure and the emotional stress of possibly losing her job—again. Beatrice finds her situation especially disconcerting since she had planned to join her husband in retirement soon and finally relieve her weary body of the daily rigors of "being on my feet." Unfortunately, she is still paying a high economic and physical price for the mistakes of others. That is, she suffered the consequences of the [mis]management and subsequent 1990 bankruptcy of Washington's most prestigious department store: Garfinckle's. This once haughty and seemingly invincible retailer, a century-old downtown fashion institution, became a highly coveted trophy in the merger and acquisition frenzy of the 1980s. Like a small boat in an ocean storm, it was tossed from one corporation to another during the tumultuous financial gale of the age of leverage. In fact, Garfinckle's once stable ownership suddenly shifted from retailing giants Federated and then Allied to flamboyant retailing entrepreneur Neil Fox—all during the 1980s. For longtime employees like Beatrice, who became unwitting pawns in the gamesmanship of high-stakes finance, the results were often devastating: careers abruptly ended, health insurance terminated, savings depleted, new debts incurred, and well-earned retirements postponed.

Beatrice was laid off from Garfinckle's in June 1990 following 23 years of continuous service. After climbing the company job ladder, from merchandising assistant to office administrator, she suddenly found herself without work, medical insurance, and retirement benefits. Nearly 58 years old, Beatrice received only unemployment compensation and three months of medical insurance (COBRA); she never received her final salary, severance pay, accumulated sick leave, or vacation time. Hence, Beatrice was thrown into the perilous sea of corporate downsizings without even a temporary financial life preserver. This was an especially difficult period, moreover, because her husband had recently retired. And, as was true for many other older workers, Beatrice's reentry into the labor market proved to be a frustrating experience; she failed to attract a serious job offer for almost two years.

Beatrice was not particularly selective about her job search even though most of the available positions featured substantially lower hourly wages and few benefits. She was nearing retirement and she had only a high school diploma. At first, she believed that the recession was responsible for her employment difficulties. Only later did she realize that age discrimination was a major factor. "Companies today want younger people who work harder ... for less pay ... also, their health insurance costs are much lower ... [whereas] we older workers are more risky ... we cost more." Indeed, the emotional stress of unemployment aggravated her high blood pressure and menopausal conditions. It was during this "rough time" that she became dependent on bank credit cards, especially for medicine and other personal expenses. "Oh, yes, I had to use my credit cards to get by. I had no choice. ... Sometimes I had to choose between [charging] my blood pressure or hormone pills. ... After a while, I decided I could learn to live with the hot flashes ... but not without the high blood pressure pills."

Beatrice's economic woes were exacerbated with the end of her unemployment benefits and the continuation of the job search into a second year. As her personal debts soared, Beatrice was forced to make an agonizing financial decision. She began to withdraw savings from her 401(k) retirement account, a move compounded by a "substantial financial penalty." Not until January 1992 was she finally offered a clerical position at a nonprofit organization in downtown Washington, D.C.; the hourly wage was much lower than her previous job at Garfinckle's and did not include health insurance or a private pension program. Although Beatrice is thankful to be employed, she remains bewildered by the unexpectedly high costs of her employment disruption. Her health is worse (she has no medical insurance), credit card debts remain high, and retirement savings are only now returning to prelayoff levels nearly six years later. As a result, "early" retirement—that is, retiring before qualifying for full Social Security benefits—is no longer an option for her.

Beatrice's expectations for retirement have plummeted sharply as she adjusts to the economic realities of the prosperous "new" economy. Not only will she have to continue working for at least two more years, but her economic goal also has shifted dramatically: from saving a substantial nest egg by age 62 to paying off as much debt as possible by 65. This experience is not unusual among older female workers. Between 1965 and 1991, the proportion of employed women aged 55–64 increased from 41 to 45 percent and dipped only slightly (from 10 to 9 percent) among women over 64 years old. During this same period, the employment of men aged 55–64 dropped from 85 to 67 percent and fell more sharply among men aged 62–64 (73 to 46 percent) and over 64 (28 to 16 percent). By 1997, the proportion of employed women aged 55–64 had risen to 50.9 percent and is projected to climb to 55.8 percent in 2006 (women workers over 64 years old will remain stable at 8.7 percent), whereas male workers aged 55–64 remained virtually unchanged at 67.6 percent with a projected increase to 70.2 percent in 2006; male workers over 64 years old are projected to rise modestly to 17.8 percent in 2006.[27]

These divergent employment trends are not surprising, since older women tend to have less job seniority, lower incomes, smaller pensions, higher poverty rates (especially in retirement), and greater longevity than their male counterparts. Consequently, as illustrated by Jeannie May Lawson and Beatrice Williams, older women have little choice but to remain in the labor force in order to increase household savings (or decrease debt) for retirement or to supplement their meager retirement income after the death or divorce of their spouse. Indeed, Beatrice Williams hopes to pay down her financial obligations and eventually become a convenience user rather than an involuntary credit card "abuser" in her retirement years. Of course, only her credit card representative will know for sure.

Among America's oldest seniors, a similarly wide range of attitudes characterizes their credit card usage patterns: abhorrence, delight, and of course desperation. First, those over 70 are more likely to be personally averse to using consumer credit due to harsh memories or family experiences during the depression; about one-third of AARP credit card holders are over 64, which is consistent with the data in Table 9.1. These people tend to pay for their purchases directly with cash or checks. This is illustrated by 95-year-old Harold Whitaker. Born in "the hills of Tennessee," Harold was attracted to the "fast life of city livin'" and eventually sought his "fame and fortune" in Knoxville, where he had a successful sales career "sellin' Chevies" at a major car dealership. A self-described "wheeler-dealer" in retirement, he earned money in retirement by "flipping" (short-term buying and selling) various items such as used cars, houses, and real estate with bank financing. Even with his profitable use of credit, Harold vehemently objects to the growing popularity of bank credit cards because of his personal experiences during the 1930s: "Credit is the root of financial ruin. I saw people lose everything during the depression. . . . Credit cards are how they [banks] getcha today. . . . Shell [petroleum company] sent me a gas card a few years back. I cut it up and mailed it right back to 'em. They ain't gettin' me."

Credit card use of the oldest seniors not only is more complex than for other groups but also is profoundly influenced by gender-based relations. First, this group is far less active than younger retirees and tends to be limited by physical infirmities, the emotional strain of changing professional and familial roles, and the loss of a spouse. In particular, it is more likely to be composed of single women (especially widows) who tend to have had limited experience with family financial responsibilities and even less employment experience outside of the household; among seniors over 65, nearly one-half of all women versus only 14 percent of all men are widowed.[28] As a result, women over age 65 are more likely to be primarily dependent on the retirement and Social Security benefits of their husbands. This explains why two-fifths (41 percent) of all women over 65 are classified by the federal government as "poor" and why they account for nearly three-fifths (73 percent) of the total elderly poor; the average income of women over 64 is $7,200.[29] Not incidentally, these elderly women are least likely to have a credit card due to the lack of their own established credit history; many lose their credit cards following the loss (divorce, death, institutionalization) of their authorizing spouse.

These generational experiences condition the cautious and often misinformed views of many elderly Americans toward consumer credit. As Eleanor Cockwell, a 79-year-old, white, middle-class widow explains: "My husband and I used to buy with credit every once in a while, but we paid it back right away. . . . Now that I'm a widow, I'm really scared that the balance might get away from me. . . . I've even heard that there are many outrageous fees and high interest [charges] that would make something you bought for only $10 really end up costing more like $300." This lack of familiarity with consumer credit underlies the befuddlement of many of the oldest seniors who either are skeptical of such "amazing" credit card offers or fearful that the banks will charge exorbitant interest rates. According to an AARP spokeswoman, some older members actually believe in "the magic of plastic" and inquire if their purchases are "a gift." She explained that such phone calls are not unusual and added: "It seems shocking, but we really get people who honestly ask, 'Do you have to pay it back?'"

On the other hand, AARP analysts have detected a distinctly different pattern of credit use among seniors over age 65 who often endure a bored and lonely existence. Many seek excitement, entertainment, and even brief interludes of companionship by discussing their orders over the telephone with catalog salespeople. In fact, AARP Visa charge records indicate a consistent purchase-return cycle among their most elderly cardholders, especially orders from the Home Shopping Network and other telephone retail enterprises. For example, AARP frequently receives desperate phone calls from "a hysterical little Aunt Esther who just purchased $300 worth of merchandise *by accident* . . . who pleads 'Can I please send it back before someone finds out?' After they realize that, in fact, everything [purchased by credit card] is returnable, this process becomes a 'real entertainer' for them."[30] Such behavior is consistent with scholarly research that suggests "television allows for the illusion of being in a populated world . . . [it brings] the sound of life into an otherwise empty and silent room."[31] For many of the oldest seniors, participation in the mass consumption society provides new social and cultural connections that promote growing receptiveness to the less restrained use of credit in their final years. As a popular bumper sticker of older adults proclaims, "I'm spending my children's inheritance."

From Boomers to Bust: Aging into a Retirement of Debt

Frank Cain announced his 50th birthday with the mirthful remark that he was celebrating "a half-century of wisdom and folly." A white native of the District of Columbia—he jokingly refers to himself as part of an "an endangered urban species"—Frank has witnessed the dramatic social and demographic transformation of the Washington, D.C., metropolitan area from a biracial city to a multicultural metropolis. As a teenager, he was part of the first urban exodus of white working-class families who abandoned the city in the late 1950s and 1960s for the metropolitan suburbs of northern Virginia and Maryland. During this period, the District of Columbia experienced its demographic shift from a white to a black majority, as its economic base shifted from the urban core of the federal city to the postindustrial growth "poles" or satellite "edge" cities of suburbia.[32]

As a young adult, Frank participated in the second mass migration of white families who moved from the inner to the outer D.C. suburbs in an effort to escape the rising costs and social problems of the city. Today, he lives in a rapidly suburbanizing area of rural northern Virginia from where he and his wife commute each day to their jobs in D.C. Although they would prefer to avoid the grueling 90-minute drive (each way), Frank explains that they have little choice but to accept their lifestyle, since "there are not many jobs out here that offer a decent income for [working-class] people like us." In reality, Frank is trapped by mounting household debts and unyielding family obligations that are disrupting his plans for a middle-class lifestyle in retirement. His predicament reflects the anguish and confusion of both his social class and his generation as middle-aged Americans ponder the unexpected prospect of financial insecurity in their later years.

If you call Frank Cain a baby boomer, he will give you a wry look of "Who, me? I'm just a good ol' country boy." His birth in 1946, after his father returned home from the "Big War," marks the inception of the demographic explosion that has fundamentally shaped and recast employment, consumption, residential, leisure, and now retirement patterns. For instance, Frank's parents, with only one blue-collar job and military benefits, enjoyed a comfortable middle-class lifestyle in the post–World War II period, including homeownership, an automobile, summer vacations, and an adequate retirement income. The rapid ascent of the U.S. standard of living, which was accompanied by rising socioeconomic aspirations, is especially impressive because it occurred only one generation after the Great Depression. This rising tide of prosperity was propelled by the impressive growth in real wages and household income, expansion of federal education grants (G.I. Bill, student loans) that facilitated occupational and interclass mobility, new mortgage insurance (FHA, VA) programs that greatly increased homeownership among the working and middle classes, improved private and public pension programs, greater public benefits for retirees and their spouses (Social Security), and relatively inexpensive health care and insurance costs. Together, these factors contributed to high personal savings rates (Chapter 2) as well as the substantial appreciation of residential dwellings.

Frank, like millions of early boomers, followed in his father's footsteps after graduating from high school: "Patriotism called" but, unlike for his father, the male rite of passage of his generation was involuntary induction into the U.S. Army—"getting one's number called by the draft board." Whereas their parents were revered in the postwar period, young military veterans like Frank were reviled upon their return from Vietnam. The dramatically different civilian experience awaiting the first boomer vets began with their initial reception in the United States followed by the difficulties they encountered in the job market. According to Frank,

> We were America's forgotten heroes . . . Hell, it didn't rain on our parade, we weren't given one. . . . In fact, coming back home was a nightmare with anti-war protests and the liberal [mass] media. What did we do [wrong]? We did what we were told just like our fathers [in World War Two]. . . . But nobody wanted us. Telling [potential employers] that you were a Vietnam vet was a kiss of death. It hurt you much more than it helped you. Those were really tough times.

Frank did not think much about a work career while serving in Vietnam. His thoughts focused on coming home "with my boots on rather than in a wooden box." A voracious reader, Frank considered the possibility of using his G.I. benefits for attending a local junior college. These plans were quickly dismissed, however, when he married his high school sweetheart and she swiftly "became in a family way." Already at the end of his four-year enlistment tour, the Cains returned to Washington, D.C., and prepared to start their own family. Unfortunately, Frank had a hard time finding a full-time job, and Marlene was having problems with her pregnancy. They did not have any health insurance, and the baby was delivered stillborn. Thus, instead of leaving the hospital with the hopes and joyous anticipation of parenthood, they were encumbered with a large collection of medical bills. Only 24 years old, Frank found himself heavily in debt to family members and the hospital, and Marlene's health complications left her weak and unable to work for quite some time.

Like his father before him, a maintenance technician for the U.S. government, Frank finally secured a job in the public sector where his military experience was valued: federal security operations. As a Vietnam vet, he qualified for preferred recruitment and joined the staff of the U.S. Department of Transportation as an entry-level guard, or "security officer." Since then, he has been assigned to several federal agencies; his responsibilities include monitoring basic internal security procedures such as opening and closing the buildings, checking visitor authorizations, combating office theft, and responding to general breaches of security. Marlene eventually recovered from her difficult pregnancy and was hired as an entry-level clerk-typist in another federal agency.

By the end of the Vietnam War, the Cains had successfully surmounted their earlier problems and joined the middle class as a dual-income household; the family now included a healthy baby boy and infant girl. As the age of inflation eroded their personal debts, Frank used his veteran status to qualify for a VA home mortgage and buy a more spacious house for his growing family in the less costly outer suburbs of Howard County, Virginia. Although it meant a long commute even by D.C. standards, the Cains felt that the trade-off in their standard of living was worth this daily sacrifice. They failed to realize, however, that the previous increases in their family income would soon come to an end, and the unexpected expenses of their commute, together with the rising costs of rearing teenagers, would contribute substantially to their financial difficulties during the decade of debt. And, unlike previous generations who managed on one income, the Cains' deteriorating situation was based on two incomes.

From the mid-1970s to the early 1980s, the Cains enjoyed a comfortable lifestyle as their household income rose slowly but steadily. Although real earnings were falling in this period, as double-digit inflation exceeded single-digit wage increases, these unfavorable conditions were obscured by job promotions and the abundant overtime available to Frank. However, because the Cains were low-level and relatively unskilled workers without college degrees, their promotional potential peaked early in their work careers. Frank reached his ceiling almost 15 years ago at a government service rank of GS-5 (step 7) and Marlene nearly a decade ago at a GS-5 (step 3). In 1998, he earned nearly $30,000 with overtime, and she earned almost $22,000. With an annual family income of approximately $51,000, the Cains were only slightly below the national median of dual-income households—$54,770 in 1998.[33] With the recent marriage of their daughter, they have only their adult son living at home. So, why are they falling deeper into a financial abyss, and what are the economic prospects for their impending retirements?

Ask Frank about credit cards or his consumer debt and his friendly smile quickly fades into a scowl. The combination of declining real wages and rising consumer credit costs has put families like the Cains in the classic middle-class squeeze. Enter the credit card industry and, of course, the financial vise tightens. The oldest boomers are most likely to have credit cards, and they are much less likely to be convenience users (Table 9.1). Instead, they are using consumer credit to soften the financial blows of life-cycle crises, family obligations, and employment disruptions. As Frank explains, "My credit cards aren't run up from dining out or taking fancy vacations like the three-piece-suit guys here. . . . They've grown from things that we needed . . . car repairs, new tires, gasoline, the wife's medicines, and insurance. These aren't discretionary . . . We have to have 'em to survive. What else can I do?"

The increasingly important role of consumer credit is illuminated by its role in solving basic household problems as well as coping with unexpected crises such as a car accident or sudden medical ailment. For instance, the Cains' biggest expense after their mortgage (which is modest by D.C. standards) is their daily commute. Only three years old, their car is already having serious mechanical and maintenance problems after nearly 100,000 miles of wear and tear: new tires, brakes, and transmission repairs. But with a five-year auto loan, they cannot consider buying a new car in the immediate future. In addition, escalating pump prices have inflated their gasoline bills, and their automobile insurance premium jumped recently due to an accident by their last dependent child.

Clearly, without their credit cards, the Cains would have much greater difficulty in satisfying basic household demands such as car repairs, health-related medicines, or even climbing gasoline prices. In fact, Frank claims that his Sears card is "run up" simply by charging the annual insurance premiums on the car (Allstate) and the service contracts on various household appliances. Significantly, even with finance charges that exceed 22 percent, Frank is resigned to sending only minimum payments for his Sears account. This is a deliberate decision that reflects the fragility of the Cains' household finances. By using proprietary credit cards for fixed expenses, the Cains free up their universal bank cards (Visa, MasterCard, Discover) for unexpected household emergencies. And these have been occurring with increasing frequency due to problems involving their son, Frank Junior.

For Frank, as for most suburban commuters, his work in the city has become increasingly detached from his life in rural Virginia. Employment in

D.C. is the economic means for realizing his personal goals in the suburbs. Today, however, he readily admits that many of the urban problems that he sought to shield from his family are occurring with greater regularity in Howard County. Violence, crime, teenage pregnancy, alcoholism, drugs, and unemployment mar the social landscape of his suburban paradise. These trends have contributed to his biggest problem and unpredictable financial expense: Frank Jr. At 25 years old, Frank Jr. exemplifies the social crisis of Generation X—especially high-school-educated, blue-collar, white males. Rebellious and unfocused in his adult goals, Frank Jr. refused to "straighten out" and enlist in the military after finishing high school. After he rejected this traditional avenue for social advancement, his father encouraged him to take classes at the nearby junior college, but he quit after one frustrating semester. Instead, he prefers to hang out with friends, drive fast cars, and pursue romance in local bars.

For Frank Jr., the future appears bleak with a monotonous succession of low-wage, dead-end jobs and continued financial dependence on his family. This grim scenario is exacerbated by the prospect that even the moderate standard of living of his parents is probably beyond his grasp. Furthermore, several classmates have already died from irresponsible behavior such as drunken driving, drug overdoses, and barroom brawls. Fearful of such a possibility awaiting his son, Frank hopes that his guidance and supervision will eventually help Frank Jr. get over "this dark period" of low self-esteem and lack of discipline. Frank therefore has grudgingly accepted the reality that his son is a "boomerang baby" and will live at home for the foreseeable future. The problem is bad timing: Frank Jr. is increasing the economic pressures on the Cain household when it is already financially overburdened. This situation is exacerbated by federal budget cuts that have substantially reduced Frank's opportunities for overtime pay, and by Marlene's physical maladies that will require more costly medications as she grows older.

Frank's concern over his son's behavior is well justified. Last year, Frank Jr. had a major automobile accident and was insured only because his father included him as a dependent driver on his policy; Frank Jr. argued that he could not afford auto insurance *and* make his car payments. At the time, he was delivering pizzas for Domino's, which of course required a car for employment. Not surprisingly, Frank "loaned" his son the $500 insurance deductible that was necessary for repairing the car and absorbed the higher household insurance premiums; both expenses were eventually added to the Cains' credit card debts. A couple of months later, Frank Jr. broke his hand in a fit of rage over the reported death of a friend. The hospital bills totaled over $800, and Frank felt he had no choice but to "loan" his uninsured son the money for these necessary medical services. Again, this unexpected emergency expense was ultimately financed by Visa and, again, Frank laments, "What choice do I have as a [concerned] father?"

As Frank struggles with escalating household debt and ponders his future, he reflects on the experience of his parents and how the economic advantages of their generation have continued in retirement. Not only do they own their own home "free and clear [from the bank]," but its value has climbed sharply—more than sixfold over 30 years. In comparison, the value of Frank's house has only doubled over the past 18 years (increasing moderately over the past three years) and is encumbered with a modest home equity loan. Additionally, the ability of Frank's parents to accumulate savings and participate in private pension programs enabled them to accumulate income-generating wealth in their retirement years. For Frank, this is not a feasible goal in the near future, especially with the rising medical expenses of his wife and the continued economic dependence of his son. As a result, Frank is coping with the reality that he must postpone his long-awaited retirement for at least a couple of years, assuming that he can endure the mounting physical rigors of the daily commute.

The generational differences in national wealth accumulation patterns are revealed by comparisons of age cohorts. In 1989, for example, housing assets accounted for only 56 percent of total wealth among homeowning households aged 65–74. For those aged 55–64, the proportion was 70 percent, leading the Congressional Budget Office to conclude, "Households that own their homes have enjoyed sizable capital gains [in the late 1970s and 1980s], but nonhousing wealth has not increased as a percentage of income since the early 1960s for most households."[34] Hence, homeownership (tax deductibility of mortgage interest) and the related capital gains allowance for sellers 55 and older (up to $300,000 tax-free for single homeowners or a total of $600,000 for joint ownership) have become the most important determinants of net household wealth among older Americans.[35] This is an especially ominous trend for late boomers whose homeownership rates fell in the 1980s and were deferred for several years in the 1990s. Their future ability to accumulate wealth for retirement through their homes will be hindered by rising borrowing costs (especially adjustable rate mortgages), greater home equity loans, and much lower price appreciation.[36] This explains why home equity accounted for only about 47 percent of the net worth of all U.S. families in 1995—ranging from 45 to 53 percent by age group.[37]

Some analysts attribute the sluggish growth of household wealth accumulation among the early boomers to delayed savings at peak income levels due to higher education costs, later child rearing, and other household mainte-

TABLE 9.3   1995 Mean and Median Family Net Worth, with and without Home Equity, by Age Group (dollars)

Family Age of Head	Net Worth		Home Equity		Net Worth Less Home Equity	
	Mean	Median	Mean	Median	Mean	Median
25–34	23,505	5,579	11,052	0	12,454	3,275
35–44	62,167	25,588	32,381	9,070	29,787	8,000
45–54	108,343	53,975	50,595	28,449	57,747	14,675
55–64	146,604	86,478	65,440	49,927	81,165	19,873
65–74	155,586	97,474	71,486	55,000	84,100	26,004
75 or older	127,379	80,000	61,141	40,000	66,238	18,104
All[a]	89,634	35,459	42,341	14,641	47,293	10,005

[a] Families with head at least 25 years and older.

SOURCE: Capital Research Associates analysis of the national Survey of Income and Program Participation (SIPP), reported in Joseph Anderson, "American Family Wealth: Analysis of Recent Census Data" (Washington, D.C.: Consumer Federation of America, 1999), pp. 22–23.

nance expenses. On the other hand, more pessimistic explanations point to the greater employment disruptions of mid- and late-career workers who are more likely to experience voluntary "early outs" and mandated retirements. Indeed, corporate downsizing policies have featured the contraction of the most highly paid segments of the U.S. workforce, including middle managers and well-paid senior workers. In addition, lower wage growth, greater household maintenance costs (especially medical care and college education), and increasing financial support of adult family members have mired the boomer generation in greater depths of household debt. For example, between 1977 and 1986, the debt/income ratio rose only modestly for the age groups 35–44 (81.4 percent to 81.5 percent) and 45–54 (58.4 percent to 62.0 percent) but jumped enormously for the older age groups 55–64 (35.7 percent to 51.8 percent) and 65–74 (19.4 percent to 41.2 percent).[38] Instead of accumulating income-earning assets for retirement, aging boomers and more recent retirees have been adding greater levels of household debt that have obscured their financial insecurity through dubious estimates of appreciated home equity and recent stock market gains. This trend is demonstrated through the examination of the net financial assets of U.S. households.

As shown in Table 9.3, the net economic worth of U.S. families is highly skewed, especially in the 25–34 and 35–44 age groups. For example, the mean net worth of the youngest group ($23,505) is more than four times greater than the median level ($5,579), whereas this wealth inequality diminishes to only 1.6 in the 75-plus age group. This means that wealth has become much more unevenly distributed in the younger age groups than in the oldest age cohorts. Although net worth consistently increases with age of household head, it is striking that most is attributable to home equity. In fact, median home equity is more than double nonhome equity wealth in the groups over 44 years old. Overall, the analysis of the U.S. Census Bureau's 1995 Survey of Income and Program Participation (SIPP) reveals a shockingly low level of family net worth when home equity is excluded. This median family net worth (excluding home equity) ranges from only $8,000 among the youngest boomers (35–44 years old) and $14,675 among the oldest boomers (45–54 years old) to $19,873 among the preretirees (55–64 years old) and $26,004 among the young seniors (65–74) and then drops to $18,104 among the oldest seniors (75 and older).[39]

Today, the relatively favorable economic condition of older Americans is masked by the prominent role of public programs such as Social Security (indexed to inflation in 1972) and Medicare/Medicaid health insurance programs; elderly poverty rates have been declining over the past three decades. In fact, if not for government cash transfer payments, one-fourth (23.4 percent) of the total U.S. population and one-half (50.8 percent) of the elderly would have been living at the official poverty level in 1993.[40] This is mirrored in the growing share of Social Security benefits to total income, from 22 percent in 1958 to 36 percent in 1990, whereas the contribution of pensions (14 percent to 18 percent) and personal assets (23 percent to 25 percent) grew only modestly in this same period.

Of greater concern is the spiraling cost of health care for the elderly. In 1987, 94 percent of all people at least 65 years old incurred medical expenses at an average annual total expense of about $4,600—excluding long-term care costs. Medicare (48 percent) and Medicaid and other public programs (14 percent) paid for nearly two-thirds of these expenses, whereas individuals paid about only one-fifth (21 percent); private insurance covered the remaining 16 percent. A 1993 study by the Congressional Budget Office underscores the extent of this intergenerational transfer program. For people who became 65 years old in 1992, Medicare will pay at least 60 percent more per person over their lifetimes than the value of the combined contributions of these workers and their employees, or an annual subsidy of about $2,000 per enrollee. The subsidy is even more generous for enrollees in the Supplementary Medical Insurance program.[41]

For present and future generations of retirees, it is doubtful that federal entitlement programs will continue to offer such generous benefits, especially with the impending geriatric explosion of the next three decades. For boomers like Frank Cain, the "tough times ain't gonna end any time soon" as the generational advantages of their parents intensify economic pressures on the boomers' long-anticipated retirements. In the short term, these shifts will prolong the work careers (part- and full-time) of aging boomers as they will try to increase their retirement wealth or at least pay down their household debts. In the long term, many of those who missed the great real estate appreciation "gift" of the 1980s and again in the late 1990s will become increasingly dependent upon more costly forms of consumer credit. This is particularly important to highly leveraged baby boomers who will soon be confronting their golden years with a much smaller nest egg and much greater personal indebtedness than their parents did. Thus, while today's older Americans have been relatively successful in resisting credit card debt, tomorrow's senior citizens may find it an unwelcome but increasingly necessary burden. This is because personal credit cards are becoming the social safety-net of the struggling middle class and working poor as they cope with the increasing difficulties of saving for retirement coupled with the dwindling social programs of the U.S. welfare state.

Didn't Leave Home Without It

Future Trends of the Credit Card Nation

IN A 1995 "GEM OF THE DAY," advice columnist Ann Landers recommended that Americans' wallets and, presumably purses, would be better off if they left home without their plastic money.[1] Landers intimated that for most people, the temptation to spend money they do not have is too difficult to resist and thus is the root of the growing social problem of consumer debt. By simplistically presenting the issue as a choice between good and evil, where bank credit cards represent the allegorical temptations encountered by Adam and Eve in the Garden of Eden, Landers expresses the traditional Puritan-inspired view that consumer debt is a personal vice that many Americans cannot control without external moral guidance.

With this popular emphasis on individual behavioral flaws, it is not surprising that the mass media frequently associate high credit card debts with compulsive personality traits. For example, journalists are as punctual as holly wreaths with postholiday reports of shopping "hangovers" among those unable to restrain their gift-giving impulses. Or the media offer periodic state-of-the-nation investigations of middle-class indebtedness that routinely portray chronic credit card–induced shopping binges as cathartic releases driven by the narcotic influences of "free" money. Like the Hobbesian notion that society must protect itself from the innately selfish acquisitive motives of man (and woman), the postindustrial twist on human nature is that people must guard against the socially conditioned desire to consume against their best interests. Indeed, the issue is far more complex than simply the struggle between good and evil. As illustrated by the increasing popularity of gambling on the Internet—a growing social problem on college campuses—many students could not have amassed such large financial debts without credit cards. However, their compulsive behavior probably would have been expressed in some other ways. Hence, from an individualistic perspective, it is often difficult to ascertain accurately the role of credit cards as the cause or the effect of personal indebtedness in the absence of important contextual information.

As previously discussed, it is clear that bank credit cards have fractured the culturally conditioned "cognitive connect" between earnings and consumption. In the process, they have profoundly changed the determinative role of work in defining one's consumption or even employment decisions. This is the key to understanding the social outcomes of the easy access to plastic money. For Landers and others who embrace the "old school" Puritan ethic, credit cards are anathema, representing for those unable to resist the Devil's proverbial temptation the unshackling of the moral restraints of socially responsible behavior. Without the financial guideposts that historically enforced the cognitive connect, together with the declining social stigma of public indebtedness, the unsuspecting innocents of the Credit Card Nation may become the victims of the socially inspired yearning to consume, especially in the citadels of mass consumption—shopping malls.

Consumption in contemporary American society has become the secular raison d'être of postindustrialism as well as the primary means of forging personal identities in the mass culture. In the temporary absence of fiscal constraints, the rational response is to enhance one's identity and social status through the cloak of credit card–financed consumption. After all, our identity in the impersonal culture of American materialism is largely defined by what we do and do not consume. For example, it may be rational for affluent individuals to accumulate debt privately in order to finance an inflated standard of living that includes designer clothes, private schools, imported cars, and homes in exclusive neighborhoods if the goal is to enhance their social capital for career mobility or the future success of their children.

Even so, whereas consumption decisions are generally shaped by larger social forces, their consequences are typically portrayed as individual responsibilities. As University of Maryland sociologist George Ritzer asserts in *Expressing America: A Critique of the Global Credit Card Society*, "People are not helpless victims. . . . Before they can take steps to deal with credit card abuse, people must accept the fact that their credit card debt is a personal trouble. They must overcome the common tendency to deny the existence of any difficulty; they must admit to themselves and to others that they are too deeply into debt to the credit card companies for their own good."[2]

Thus, a key issue from this normative, individualistic perspective is the role of social agency in the explanation of soaring consumer debt. Are Americans innocent victims of their lack of moral discipline when tempted with free money? Are inflated lifestyles rational investments for realizing future opportunities for upward mobility? Or, is the lack of personal restraint a conscious decision reflecting a general societal decline in individual responsibility that necessitates the restoration of the previous moral order?

On the other hand, the institutionalist perspective emphasizes the role of the banking industry and its sophisticated mass marketing machinery (along with its strategic alliances with consumer-oriented companies such as Citibank–Sony Visa) in transforming traditional attitudes toward debt in order to promote greater levels of consumption—the fundamental dynamic of postindustrial capitalism. From this point of view, debt is not an individual "problem." Instead, it is a creative "new school" strategy for coping with the changing realities of postindustrial inequality and the "Just do it" ethos of immediate personal gratification. Indeed, the age of leverage featured all sectors of U.S. society embracing unprecedented levels of debt. If the U.S. government is not troubled with trillion-dollar debts and corporations routinely assume billion-dollar junk-bond obligations, what is the problem with individual households taking on a few thousand dollars in consumer debt?

During the decade of debt, the banking industry shrewdly expanded its consumer financial services divisions and actively sought to recast its "evil" reputation and transform its image to become the financial savior or knight in shining armor of the middle and working classes. By associating the industry with the heartfelt emotional bonds of social life and the core institutions of American society, these mass marketing campaigns have been very successful. In the Credit Card Nation, for example, bank cards are portrayed as being responsible for heartwarming family reunions, father-son bonding sessions at baseball games, romantic husband-wife evenings at the opera, long-overdue anniversary vacations, money for travel emergencies, and even solutions to currency exchange problems during overseas excursions in unfamiliar locales. Indeed, through ubiquitous advertising that woos us— "There are some things that money can't buy. For everything else there's MasterCard," "Visa, it's everywhere you want to be," or "American Express, don't leave home without it"—the credit card industry has transformed the traditional view of consumer bank loans from a time-consuming option of last resort to the first choice of financial convenience.

Furthermore, by affiliating with college alumni associations, favored political or professional groups, benevolent social (e.g., children's literacy) programs, and even major cultural institutions like the Smithsonian, the credit
card industry has attempted to portray itself as a socially responsible corporate citizen and even a community benefactor. The underlying reasons, however, are not necessarily altruistic. As an internal Citibank marketing memo
explains, "While brand loyalty is strong, it is getting harder and harder to
attract and keep cardmembers due to better or lower-priced offers that come
along. That's why a differentiating feature, such as the donation to a municipal program or project, offers an additional competitive advantage."[3] Not
incidentally, affinity (e.g., university alumni or environmental organizations) and cobranded credit cards tend to offer higher interest rates.

A notable feature in the marketing of the Credit Card Nation is the lack
of reference to any financial or social costs arising from serious financial difficulties. The American Express campaigns, which feature popular celebrity
spokespersons such as Jerry Seinfeld, extol their charge/credit cards as contemporary angels of mercy. In this idyllic world of unlimited credit lines
and extended grace periods, credit cards are presented as the means to satisfying one's needs and desires as well as solving unexpected emergencies. And
if one adheres to old-school values that buttress the moral divide, such as
Puritan thrift, then the use of bank credit cards is virtually free with "di-
vine" connotations such as payment within the "grace" period. Hence, this
institutionalist framework presents credit cards as the servant of account
holders. Individual members of the Credit Card Nation have the choice of
selectively using their cards for maximum personal utility or even opting
not to use them at all—only for "emergencies." A great deal.

The most neglected feature of the Credit Card Nation in these sanitized
images is the dark side of indebtedness. The credit card companies' profitability is based largely upon the amount of finance charges and penalty fees paid
by their account holders; consumer "deadbeats" who pay in full each month
are the bane of the industry. Although the grace period has served to legiti-
mate the rising cost of consumer credit, as a punitive "stick" ostensibly to encourage "responsible" consumption patterns among "deserving" debtors, the
escalating *social* costs of these high-maintenance friends have typically been
ignored. Indeed, a perceived short-term personal solution often becomes a
long-term pact with the devil. This is illustrated by 28-year-old Florence,
whose attitude toward her $25,000-plus in accumulated bank card debt is
changing: "My credit cards are like an abusive companion. . . . At first, they
made me very happy, bringing me flowers and later [the euphoria of] a diamond ring . . . then, when I couldn't pay them, it became a nightmare of emo-

tional beatings . . . that would not go away." Florence has a part-time income of less than $15,000, and her most effective method for paying her monthly bills is to negotiate lower interest rates with the credit card companies (under the threat of filing for personal bankruptcy), which reduces her monthly minimum payments. For others, the personal ramifications of credit card debt far exceed the financial costs due to the resulting physiological and emotional distress—including the extreme resorting to suicide.[4]

A third view of consumer debt examines the profound changes in the historically unique patterns of U.S. postindustrial capitalism. These macrostructural trends include declining real wages, shrinking welfare programs, and rising material expectations. During the contemporary epoch, the fundamental shift from highly unionized goods-production industries to hi-tech information and unskilled services has dramatically increased U.S. economic inequality with often devastating impacts on specific communities and individual households. For example, Michael Moore's 1989 *Roger and Me* film documented the enormous social consequences of General Motors' decision to close its domestic auto plants in Flint, Michigan, and open state-of-the-art production facilities in Saltillo, Coahuila (the "Detroit of Mexico"); similarly, Dale Maharidge captured the social costs of the mid-1980s demise of U.S. Steel in Homestead, Pennsylvania.[5] For these households suffering from unexpected job displacement and lingering un- and underemployment, the decade of debt ushered in an era of unfulfilled expectations, intergenerational downward mobility, and the reluctant acceptance of mounting levels of consumer debt. And, with inflation under control, the credit card industry swiftly responded to the financial distress of lower-income households struggling to survive the economic dislocations of U.S. industrial restructuring with high-interest consumer credit cards.

Cultural Contradictions:
Will the Puritan Morality of Debt Be Sustained?

The enormous success of the consumer credit card harvest in the 1980s and 1990s reflects the changing patterns of U.S. inequality as well as the increasing profitability of consumer financial services. This has produced two important trends. First, contrary to the provocative analysis by Harvard sociologist Daniel Bell of the "cultural contradictions of capitalism," which posited the emergence of conflicting social roles of disciplined workers in public and voracious consumers in private,[6] the rapid expansion of consumer debt has not been used necessarily for hedonistic purposes. The rise of bank credit cards has actually provided opportunities to resist intolerable labor conditions by financially supporting workers while they look for better jobs, participate in labor strikes, seek higher education or vocational job training, pursue alternative forms of self-employment or small business activities, and even escape oppressive marriages or other abusive household relationships.

The bottom line is that banks do not care if mounting charge balances are for a ski vacation, book-writing expenses, college tuition, a small business line of credit, a family reunion, the rent, or a divorce lawyer. Each of these loans is equally profitable to the card-issuing banks as revolving consumer debt. However, as a source of "bridge loans" during the contraction of the welfare state and reorganization of the U.S. labor market (part-time, temporary full-time, temps), bank credit cards provide opportunities or political "space" for Americans to challenge the profit-driven forces of structural change that have profoundly traumatized their lives and the future well-being of their children. This may be less apparent today, in the shadow of the longest economic expansion in U.S. history. However, with the impending conclusion of this "up" business cycle, Americans will increasingly resort to their credit cards for "political" purposes such as resisting undesirable employment or intolerable household living arrangements.

Hence, the rapid expansion of bank credit cards has not necessarily reinforced the schizophrenic division between public (disciplined work) and private (hedonistic consumption) spheres of capitalism. Rather, bank credit cards—which offer a potentially subversive form of political empowerment for their users—may actually mediate the cultural contradictions of American capitalism by providing unrestricted loans for enhanced negotiating power in the labor market, financing self-employment activities, and establishing stable household arrangements. Conversely, bank cards could play a politically conservative role by obviating the short-term need for widespread social movements to expand the programs of the welfare state and demand more socially responsible corporate investment and employment policies. Regardless of this future outcome, the systemic contradictions of postindustrial society will be attenuated by the growing cultural acceptance of higher levels of household debt.

A second trend concerns the ideological legitimacy of the moral divide. Based on the Puritan ethos that underlies the cognitive connect, punitively high finance charges are morally justified as the conscious choice of informed consumers who "voluntarily" accept the consequences of their accumulated debts. These high card interest rates constitute a form of secular punishment that the banks are happy to accept in cash. However, this equilibrium between "good" debtors who are rewarded with free interest as convenience users and "bad" debtors who are punished with high interest rates as revolvers is increasingly being publicly challenged as morally bankrupt. That is, as revolvers increasingly include people whose debts are due to circumstances beyond their control (job loss, illness, divorce) and the contraction of the welfare state leads to the use of consumer credit for nonhedonistic purposes, the imposition of escalating consumer finance charges is becoming more difficult to justify based on traditional Puritan morality. As a result, the corporate avarice of the banking industry is eroding its moral legitimacy as well as its benevolent image. The key question concerns the limits to Americans' tolerance of the excesses of the banking industry.

As described earlier, the most striking and underexamined feature of the Credit Card Nation is the role of consumer debt in the new patterns of postindustrial inequality. On the one hand, bank cards simplify the stratification system by distinguishing those who qualify for consumer credit cards and then ranking them by their credit "worthiness" according to the prestige of their plastic identities. In this hierarchical order, status is conferred by one's "complexion" (Providian Bank's Visa [Blue] Classic, Visa Gold, and Visa Platinum ranking system), charge versus credit program (American Express, Diners Club), and marginal status such as debit or even secured cards. As bank cards have become essential to middle- or upper-middle-class lifestyles, membership in the Credit Card Nation is presumed and even validated by the prestige ranking of one's computer-chip-enhanced piece of plastic. But, at what cost?

As suggested by ongoing trends, the cost of consumer credit will continue to increase in the short term. Unlike during the early 1990s, when the banking industry faced enormous domestic and international losses on defaulted loans, the rising cost of consumer credit coincides with record-breaking profits for the banking industry; credit card portfolios are no longer needed to subsidize unperforming loans in Brazil or Dallas. In 1996, the banking industry recorded a record profit of $52.4 billion, which was followed by a 13.1 percent increase in 1997; two-thirds of all commercial banks reported higher earnings in 1997 compared with 1996. Overall, net bank interest income rose 7.2 percent, and return on equity grew from 14.46 to 14.70 percent. This was followed by another record profit in 1998, albeit somewhat less than the previous increase in 1997.[7]

What does the increasing profitability of financial services mean to consumers? Enhanced banking services? More highly compensated and enthusiastic employees? Larger number of bank branches? Greater choice of financially sound financial institutions? Lower consumer prices due to greater competition? Actually, none of the above. Instead of sharing the prosperity of the late 1990s with employees and customers through more cost-efficient services, banks have used rising corporate profitability to fuel the frenzy in mergers and acquisitions. Banking deregulation has rapidly accelerated industry consolidation—there were over 14,600 FDIC-insured banks in 1975 and fewer than 9,000 in 2000—as well as the conglomerate structure of the Citigroup behemoth. The result has been rapid stock appreciation, higher CEO compensation packages, and much more costly consumer services. In fact, as recently as 1995, the average bank was acquired for 1.7 to 1.9 times its book value, whereas it was not uncommon in the late 1990s for banks to be acquired for as much as 3.0 times their book value.[8]

Not surprisingly, corporate growth has been a defining characteristic of the banking industry during the past decade. Between 1989 and 1997, the number of FDIC-insured banks declined by 28 percent, but average assets per bank more than doubled from about $260 million to $548 million; aggregate industry assets climbed from $3.3 trillion to $5.0 trillion (51.5 percent). As reported in Table 3.1, the top nine banks in 1998 had assets of more than $100 billion, and the top five ranged from an estimated $700 billion (Citigroup) to $246 billion (Banc One). This top group included such megamergers as Bank of America and NationsBank, which cross geographic boundaries, and Citicorp and Travelers Group, which cross industry boundaries. For 1997, the top five banks accounted for 29.3 percent of total industry assets.[9]

As industry consolidation has accelerated the pace and scope of bank mergers and acquisitions, it is not surprising that competition within the credit card industry has focused on the acquisition of prized credit card portfolios. Incredibly, the highly fragmented credit card industry of only 20 years ago is one of the most concentrated industries today. For instance, in 1980, the top 50 card issuers accounted for less than 60 percent of the U.S. market, whereas in 2000, the top five credit card issuers control nearly 57 percent of the market, and the top ten control almost 77 percent; overall, there are more than 6,000 credit card issuers in the United States.[10] This trend is exemplified by Banc One's acquisition of major credit card issuer First USA in 1997 and explains why the rhetoric of intense competition belies the stark reality of oligopolistic pricing practices and steeply rising fees and interest rates. For example, Laurence Popofsky, lead attorney for Visa in its ongoing antitrust litigation, describes the credit card industry as "'one of the most extraordinarily competitive markets imaginable.'"[11] Yet a quick review of most consumers' credit card statements would question the veracity of this assertion.

With rising finance charges (variable rates tied to inflation rather than fixed rates), higher average daily balances, and sharply increasing penalty fees, the consolidated structure of the industry ensures that its pricing policies will continue to gouge its "best" customers. For example, when the proportion of convenience users jumped from 34 percent in 1995 to 43 percent in 2000, credit card issuers responded with sharp increases in penalty fees—from $8.3 billion in 1995 to $18.9 billion in 1998; note, escalating penalty fees are derived from a smaller pool of revolvers (Fleet raised its late fee to $35 in 2000). Of course, this greed-inspired policy does not reflect stagnant growth in credit card interest income; the latter rose from $34.8 billion in 1994 to $58.1 billion in 1998.[12] Nor does it mirror an increase in default accounts; Citibank's bank card credit losses have improved substantially, to only 4.43 percent in 1999.[13] Hence, "market competition" has one meaning for card issuers (greater concentration and higher profits) but a quite different one for consumers (fewer choices and more costly services). In fact, the estimated consumer rip-off for the current decade (2000–2009)—based on conservative projections of average household debt and credit cost (interest and penalty fees) increases—suggests that American consumers will pay at least $300 billion more this decade than during the profitable late 1980s; 1989 is selected for the price-gouging baseline.[14]

The tremendous concentration of corporate power in the credit card industry underlies the arrogance of Visa's and MasterCard's dismissive response to the antitrust suit filed by the U.S. Department of Justice in response to complaints from American Express and Discover. The credit card industry is the cash cow of consumer financial services, and the small club of leading issuers is not going to relinquish its market share to upstarts like Discover and American Express without a fight. Ironically, when NBI dropped its opposition to duality in 1976, which allowed banks to issue both Visa and Master-Card to their customers, the move was viewed as an important event in increasing competition in the credit card industry. Today, the consolidation of the industry has proceeded at such a rapid pace that it has obviated this competitive feature. However, in the process, it also has created the market space for new competitors that want to join the credit card gold rush. This competitive pressure is the focus of the U.S. Department of Justice's antitrust suit, which points to the negative consequences suffered by American consumers such as advances in "smart card" technology that have proceeded much faster in European markets. Regardless of the outcome of the litigation, leading issuers like Citibank are forging their own corporate identity and could conceivably launch their own separate credit card systems in the future.

The Global Village Goes Plastic:
Technological Advance or Societal Distress?

At the end of the millennium, Citibank achieved the goal that defied the wildest dreams of even the most enthusiastic executives of consumer banking. In 1999, the net income of nearly $1.2 billion in its bank card division slightly exceeded the combined profits of the other three components of its global consumer business division: Citibanking North America, Mortgage Banking, and Citifinancial.[15] The profit engine of consumer financial services continues to deliver impressive profits for fueling the global expansion of the Citigroup empire. Although the refinement of new transactional mechanisms (such as cash checking and debit cards with overdraft protection) contributes to new bank card revenues, it is clear that the limits of sustained growth through U.S. market consolidation and rising household debt levels will soon be reached. As Citibank shifts its attention to international markets, the central question is whether similar consumer revenue gains can be achieved abroad.

At first glance, the ongoing growth of universal bank credit cards overseas is staggering. In 1998, according to Visa International, over 800 million Visa, Interlink Plus, and Visa Cashcards purchased $1.4 trillion in products and services. This sum accounts for 55 percent of the electronic point of sale (POS) market. According to Visa, its 21,000 member financial institutions throughout the world enable members to charge at over 16 million locations, in 300 countries and territories, in 160 different denominated currencies, "making Visa the closest thing to a universal currency"; its VisaNet system can process as many as 2,700 transactions per second. In 1998, MasterCard International's nearly 700 million MasterCard, Maestro, Cirrus, and Mondex cards charged over $650 billion in products and services. MasterCard, the second-largest credit card association (one-quarter of global volume of sales), reports that its 23,000 member financial institutions offer cardholders over 16.2 million commercial locations, in 220 countries and territories.[16]

According to Ritzer, this trend reflects the inevitable expansion of technologically efficient transaction systems that he describes as the coming "global credit card society." From this perspective, the major U.S. credit card issuers will also dominate their international markets and, through a process that Ritzer calls global "Americanization," will accelerate the replacement of cash and checks with technologically superior credit cards.[17] Ritzer refers to this inexorable process of Americanized patterns of modernization as the "McDonaldization" of society; expansion into the middle classes of Europe, Japan, and Latin America is presented as an inevitable product of "the culture that conquered the world."[18] In light of the rapid growth of overseas infrastructural development and credit card accounts, it would seem that this cultural supremacist view of globalization is at least somewhat accurate. However, closer inspection of international credit card trends reveals a strong cultural resistance to the expansion of American-style consumer credit card systems.

As illustrated by Citigroup's aggressive international growth, the Credit Card Nation is being franchised throughout the world; China is the second-largest MasterCard market outside of the United States. Citigroup has established a state-of-the-art regional credit card processing headquarters in Taiwan and is establishing European centers in low-wage countries such as Ireland. Furthermore, Citigroup has embarked on a global acquisition campaign to expand its retail banking operations in both developed and developing countries. Its recent purchases include banks in Italy, Hungary, Ukraine, Vietnam, Argentina, and Mexico.[19] On the one hand, its growth in developing countries has been limited by market volatility; the Latin American financial crisis of 1995 was followed by the Asian contagion of 1997 and the Russian currency collapse of 1998. The relatively small, upper middle class has been easy to recruit in these countries, but the mass market of rising middle-class households has produced uncertain revenues, based on the macroeconomic fortunes of the countries' respective economies. For example, the profitable growth of credit cards in Mexico during the prosperous late 1980s led to an abrupt curtailment of retail banking activities after the recession of the early 1990s and especially after the currency crisis of 1995.

The striking feature of the international expansion of bank credit cards is that it is being fiercely resisted as both a nationalist rejection of American corporate intrusion in the country's financial system and a cultural rejection of the accompanying American attitudes toward credit, savings, and debt. In Germany, for example, protesters marched in the street in opposition to Citibank's proposal to bundle discount rail and Visa cards in 1995; the program was interpreted as an arrogant attempt to impose credit cards on people who did not want them. In Japan, where the vast majority of consumer spending is with cash (less than 10 percent is transacted with credit cards), many people consider credit cards inconvenient and, most important, are fearful of "American-style debt."[20] In Mexico, a long-deprived middle class actively embraced credit cards until interest rates, driven by escalating inflation, exceeded culturally acceptable levels—commonly over 150 percent APR. This factor, together with restricted access to credit for rural farmers and small businesses, led to the emergence in 1993 of a national debtors movement—El Barzón—whose adherents refused to pay socially defined, usurious finance charges.[21] Citibank responded by temporarily suspending the extension of additional consumer credit.

Increasingly, the successful growth of bank credit cards abroad does not necessarily reflect the desire for technologically superior transaction systems.

Rather, this growth mirrors the emergence of new patterns of socioeconomic inequality in countries where consumer credit offers an economic transition for buffeting the decline in national living standards. For example, whether it is the intensifying assault on the European welfare state or IMF-imposed structural adjustment programs in developing countries, the middle classes of these societies are encountering rising medical care costs, increasing higher education expenses, and sharp reductions in retirement pensions.

As in the United States, many households abroad are using consumer credit cards to augment financial shortfalls rather than adopting American-style attitudes toward debt or the efficacy of rational transaction systems. Their receptivity more often reflects household desperation rather than the eager embrace of the credit card society. In fact, the rapid expansion of consumer credit since the late 1990s is already the focus of national media reports. Concern over the rise of credit card debt as an impending social problem has been voiced in culturally diverse countries such as England, Scotland, Ireland, Australia, Japan, Hong Kong, and Mexico.[22] Finally, the acceptance of bank cards in foreign markets tends to be limited to large, corporate chain merchants. This is producing an unexpected problem: Credit card users are abandoning the less expensive, small shopkeeper sector. The result is the purchase of more expensive products (financed at high interest rates) as well as the potential demise of large segments of community-based businesses that have traditionally offered credit during periods of economic distress.

What's Credit Got to Do with It?

Over the past two decades, universal or bank credit cards have played a prominent role in the profound transformation of American attitudes toward savings and debt. One of the most important cultural revolutions of the postwar epoch, the dramatic expansion of consumer bank credit cards has fundamentally influenced household subsistence strategies as well as macroeconomic policies. In the process, the drive for higher bank profits to satisfy Wall Street's profit and growth expectations has led to the abandonment of lower-income communities and even aspiring entrepreneurs. Hence, it is important to recognize the indirect role of national banks in contributing to urban decay and the proliferation of low-wage service occupations through their increasingly restrictive lending policies. In fact, the recent flurry of bank mergers and acquisitions has made it even more difficult to monitor compliance with Community Reinvestment Act (CRA) obligations.

Economists frequently discuss "opportunity costs" that result from various investment decisions. As national money center banks increasingly shift their portfolios from productive (corporate expansion, public works, home mortgage, auto, small business) to unproductive loans (credit cards, currency exchange, derivatives, LBOs, stock repurchases), the public (social) costs of their private gain are mounting through potentially lower aggregate economic growth (GDP), fewer good jobs due to the credit starvation of promising start-up "gazelles" (e.g., Starbucks Coffee), rapid growth of low-wage service jobs (due to proliferation of suburban malls and office complexes), and the incalculable expense attributable to the decline of urban, minority, and low-income communities.

The public costs of record bank profits even exclude many of the highly productive workers of the banking industry. While profits have soared, employment has plummeted as mergers and acquisitions have resulted in fewer workers performing more tasks at lower levels of compensation. Not surprisingly, net employment in the U.S. banking industry declined sharply over the 1990s. For example, following the announced merger between Citicorp and Travelers Group, a total of 10,400 jobs were cut. Wall Street immediately responded with a 5 percent jump in the stock price.[23] Furthermore, banks are outsourcing consumer services by building fiber-optic networks of bank processing centers in low-wage countries like Ireland and Taiwan, and labor-intensive tasks in the United States are being shifted to bank customers via ATMs and PC banking technologies.

For those workers fortunate enough to retain their jobs during this tumultuous transition, the reward is increasingly part-time employment, decreased medical and pension benefits, and fewer high-salary advancement opportunities. Sadly, the employees of retail banking are generating the highest profit revenues of the financial services industry, yet their low salaries consign them to dependence on the high-interest credit cards that fuel their jobs as purveyors of debt. Consequently, the credit card industry is ensuring its own future demand by creating armies of low-wage, low-skill service occupations that constitute the backbone of the U.S. postindustrial economy.

So, who enjoys the profits of the current bank bonanza? The cost savings and record profits have been used to finance stock repurchase programs ($2 billion by Citigroup in 1998), increase stock dividends, enhance executive compensation packages ($167 million for Citigroup CEO Sandy Weill in 1998), finance corporate acquisitions (AT&T Universal Card by Citibank in 1998), and inflate stock prices (Citigroup jumped from $85 in summer 1998 to over $260 in 2000). As the banking industry lobbies for more stringent personal bankruptcy reform laws (to reduce losses from overzealous lending practices) and further erosion of personal privacy protections (for cross-marketing campaigns), it is clear that the financial revolution inaugurated by the national marketing of bank credit cards has reached a new and more perilous crossroads.

Today, debt reigns supreme as the marketing and refinancing of paper obligations take precedence over the previous industry standard of investing in tangible commodities with potentially useful social purposes, such as homes, small businesses, and automobiles. These profound social and economic transformations have even achieved frequent expression in the popular culture. For instance, vanity license plates, presumably purchased with borrowed money, have been observed that proclaim to friends and strangers alike of the car owner's current financial woes: INDEBT, BROKE 2, and BANKRUP. In an earlier era, such public pronouncements of privately shameful behavior would have been anathema. Today, however, they are apparently not only a sign of the times but also an expression of personal identity. How quickly the cultural norms have changed in the Credit Card Nation.

A frequent advertisement in the "Personals" section of the *Washington City Paper* in the late 1990s. The point of the ad is that credit cards are the most common means for "singles seeking singles" to initiate potentially amorous liaisons through impersonal telephone introductions. Like the commodification of fun, "love" begins with a charge to Visa or MasterCard.

Appendix 1: Note on Sources

The credit card advertising trends reported in Chapter 1 are based on a systematic sample of eleven magazines; the sampling time frame was magazine issues published between 1974 and 1997. A content analysis was then conducted on the manifest and latent meanings of the selected credit card advertisements (defined as retail, bank, and charge). The sampling strata were defined by the presumed social class background, race, and gender of the readers: *New Yorker* (gender-neutral affluent), *Gentlemen's Quarterly* (affluent men), *Vogue* and *Elle* (affluent women), *Newsweek* and *Time* (gender-neutral middle class), *Ebony* (African American middle class), *Better Homes and Gardens* and *Self* (middle-class women), and *Sports Illustrated* (middle- and working-class men). A "rolling" sample selection interval was chosen due to the small number of advertisements in the 1970s and large number in the 1990s; in the 1970s, all advertisements were selected and the selection interval was increased to every third advertisement in the 1990s. The data collection began with February 1974 (or the first year that the magazine was published). Every third issue of each magazine was examined, and photocopies were made for the study's archive. The content analysis of *Time, Newsweek,* and the *New Yorker* was subsequently extended through 1999. The combined sample totals 984 credit and charge card advertisements. This includes multiple copies of the same advertisement that appeared in different issues of the same magazine or in different magazines.

The data for examining the three components of the "U.S. triangle of debt" in Chapter 2 were derived primarily from official federal government statistics and reports. For information on the national debt and the federal budget, the primary sources were the U.S. Bureau of the Public Debt of the U.S. Department of Treasury and the U.S. Congressional Budget Office's historical data and reported estimates of the federal budget. Statistics on foreign direct investment and other capital flows were obtained from various reports of the U.S. Department of Commerce and the International Monetary Fund. For trends on corporate debt obligations and mergers and acquisitions, most data were obtained from reports by the U.S. Bureau of Economic Analysis (especially Survey of Current Business), U.S. General Accounting Office reports, the "Merger and Corporate Transactions Database" compiled by Securities Data Company, and the junk-bond listings of the U.S. Office of Resolution Trust. Employment, earnings, and occupational trends were obtained from reports by the U.S. Bureau of Labor Statistics, and savings rate information was derived from information provided by the U.S. Bureau of Economic Analysis. Last, post–World War II data on consumer installment and revolving credit were provided by monthly reports of the U.S. Federal Reserve, and credit card industry trends and consumer use patterns were based on reports by CardWeb, Inc.

The primary sources used in the examination of the deregulation of U.S. banking in Chapter 3 were the corporate archives of Hoover's Inc., *Standard & Poor's, Moody's Handbook of Common Stock, Federal Reserve Bulletins,* and reports by the U.S. Congressional Budget Office and U.S. General Accounting Office. Corporate information on Citicorp and, after 1998, on Citigroup was obtained from their respective annual reports and corporate press releases. Trends in U.S. banking were gleaned from the financial business press, including *Bloomberg News* and *Dow Jones/News Retrieval* as well as various print media such as *Business Week, The Economist, Fortune, Money,* and *Financial World.*

The interviews reported in Chapters 4, 5, 7, 8, and 9 were selected via a nonrandom selection protocol that was initially based on the author's Postindustrial Economic Inequality Project. This study was begun in 1993 with the examination of seven corporate mergers and acquisitions that included interviews with corporate human resources staffs, AFL-CIO lists of recently laid-off workers, and referrals from meetings of job seekers who were involuntarily unemployed (Five O'clock Clubs). These initial contacts were used to select a purposive sample of approximately 50 workers who had lost their jobs in the 1990s due to corporate reorganization or bankruptcy. From this initial group of displaced workers who resided in San Diego, New York, and Washington, D.C., a snowball sample was collected based on respondents' referrals and the author's contacts with various nonprofit and government organizations. A matrix of possible credit card use patterns was subsequently developed (convenience, dependence, self-employment), and respondents were selected in a purposive manner to represent differences by educational background, income, occupation, gender, race and ethnicity, age, and geographic origin. All interviews with respondents were conducted in person or by telephone. In-depth interviews were conducted with a total of 128 people. Pseudonyms have been used for all respondents discussed in the text.

The next study focused exclusively on college students. Between fall 1994 and spring 1999, in-depth interviews were conducted with 332 college students from American University (N=112), Georgetown University (N=168), University of Maryland (N=23), and other miscellaneous colleges and universities (N=29); 284 were undergraduate students (85 percent) and 48 were graduate students (15 percent). Respondents were subsequently classified according to a matrix of possible use patterns (none, convenience, dependence, extravagant use, support family members) and cross-classified by sociodemographic characteristics such as family economic background, parents' occupation, family educational attainment, race and ethnicity, gender, geographic origin, parents' credit card use, and age at which respondents received their first credit card. Respondents reported in Chapter 6 were selected based on their representativeness of specific profile groups (credit card use patterns). The frequency distribution of these respondents is reported in Appendix C of Robert D. Manning, *Credit Cards on Campus: Current Trends and Informational Deficiencies* (Washington, D.C.: Consumer Federation of America, 1999), available at www.creditcardnation.com. Again, pseudonyms have been used for all of these respondents.

A parallel survey was conducted during the 1998–1999 academic year at Georgetown University (N=303) and during the late spring 1999 semester at University of Maryland (N=103). The Georgetown University survey was conducted in introductory-level liberal arts classes (response rate of 87.3 percent), which resulted in a sample bias of first-year students; the University of Maryland survey was composed of a random sample of students who walked into the university student center during randomly selected hours of the day (response rate of 76.3 percent). The frequency distribution of these two subsamples is presented in Appendix 6. The survey and sample selection protocols are explained in Robert D. Manning, *Credit Cards on Campus: Current Trends and Informational Deficiencies* (Washington, D.C.: Consumer Federation of America, 1999), available at www.creditcardnation.com.

The results of the final study on second-tier financial services are reported in Chapter 7. Fieldwork was conducted by the author in pawnshops, rent-to-own stores, and cash-checking outlets in the District of Columbia, the metropolitan Washington, D.C., inner suburbs of Maryland and Virginia, and central Florida between 1995 and 2000. The areas were selected based on the level of state regulation, ranging from weak (Florida) to strong (District of Columbia). Also, a sample of 15 pawnshops was studied during summer 1999 with the assistance of Liana Prieto; it was stratified by the socioeconomic background of clientele, urban-suburban location, private versus corporate ownership status, and race and ethnic composition of the nearby residential community. This fieldwork was supplemented by the review of the annual reports (SEC form 10-K) of Cash America International, First Cash Financial Services, Ace Cash Express, RentWay, and Rent-A-Center.

The data presented in Chapter 8 on small business trends were derived primarily from reports of the Small Business Administration and, for women entrepreneurs, from reports authored by the National Association of Women Business Owners. Finally, the data in Chapter 9 describing the demographic and employment trends among senior citizens were obtained from reports by the U.S. Census, U.S. Bureau of Labor Statistics, U.S. Congressional Budget Office, and the American Association of Retired Persons. The credit card use and wealth patterns of American senior citizens were largely obtained from unpublished data from the 1995 Survey of Consumer Finance and the 1995 Survey of Income and Program Participation.

Appendix 2

APPENDIX 2   The Citicorp Roller Coaster Ride: Emergence of the Global
Financial Services Conglomerate, 1975–2000

1975   Citicorp is largest beneficiary of OPEC deposits. U.S. Senate convenes
        hearings on the impact of huge foreign deposits on the American
        banking system.
        Citicorp uses OPEC and other Third World deposits to make high-
        interest loans to developing countries such as Brazil, Mexico, and
        Argentina.

1976   Citicorp's international operations account for 72 percent of income.
        Name changed from First National City Bank to Citibank, N.A.
        Statewide branch banking law permits Citicorp to expand through the
        state of New York.
        National BankAmericard (NB) accedes to pressure from U.S. Justice
        Department and drops opposition to credit card duality. National
        BankAmericard (NBI) changes name to Visa.

1977   Citicorp's enormous mass mailing of Visa applications yields 3 million
        new accounts, and Citicorp becomes bank credit card leader.
        Citicorp currency trader reports illegal foreign-exchange "parking" in
        European office; SEC inquiry and congressional hearing result in
        payment of over $7 million in back taxes.

1978   U.S. Supreme Court's landmark decision in *Marquette v. First National*
        upholds the right of "national" banks to charge interest rates on credit
        cards at prevailing levels in the "home" states. Citicorp acquires Carte
        Blanche.
        Citicorp drops 50-cent surcharge on convenience accounts.

1979   Citicorp becomes the world's leading foreign-exchange dealer. J.C.
        Penney becomes the first nationwide retail chain to accept Visa credit
        card.

Chase drops its Master Charge operation due to unprofitability. Citicorp's losses on consumer bank credit cards exceeded $600 million between 1979 and 1981.

1980   President Carter imposes controls on consumer credit, including bank cards, in his campaign against inflation.

Banks respond with annual credit card membership fees. Federal deregulation of U.S. banking industry begins; enactment of Depository Institutions Deregulation and Monetary Control Act of 1980 phases out Regulation Q.

Citicorp inaugurates the new Choice credit card.

Interbank Card Association changes name from Master Charge to MasterCard.

1981   Citicorp opens banks in Delaware and South Dakota to facilitate expansion of credit card operations.

Citicorp relocates its New York credit card processing division to Sioux Falls after South Dakota eases state usury laws.

Citicorp acquires Diners Club charge card company.

MasterCard launches its Gold card.

1982   Latin American markets in chaos as Brazil is unable to make interest payments on loans, Mexican economy enters deep depression, and Argentina begins war on Great Britain.

Citicorp is the first beneficiary of the Garn–St. Germain Depository Institutions Act of 1982, by acquiring Fidelity Savings and Loan. Key Federal Savings and Loan (Maryland) inaugurates first secured credit card. Visa launches Premier card, which is changed to Visa Gold. Citicorp posts modest profits on credit card operations.

1983   Federal government approves the reinterpretation of the McFadden Act (1927) that allows out-of-state banks to offer limited banking services.

Citicorp's Choice credit card subsidiary relocates to Denver.

Citicorp targets college students for new credit card accounts.

1984   John S. Reed, architect of Citicorp's global consumer business and hi-tech visionary (ATMs), elected chairman.

U.S. devalues dollar against other leading currencies.

Citicorp initiates a direct-mail blitz to solicit business accounts for its Diners Club charge card.

1985   The Citicorp bill permits entry into lucrative suburban D.C. market as a limited-service bank; agreement moves its enormous credit card processing center to Hagerstown, Maryland.

Citicorp enters District of Columbia via special legislation that includes a community development plan and then buys National Permanent Bank.

Citicorp's default rate on its commercial loan portfolio (especially real estate) begins to increase.

Visa and MasterCard launch first cobranded affinity cards.

1986   Collapse of petroleum market sends oil below $15 per barrel.

Sears launches Discover credit card.

Bank One offers first securities backed by credit card receivables with issue of $50 million (CARDS).

Tax Reform Act of 1986 rescinds the deductibility of interest paid on consumer credit cards over five-year phase-out period.

1987   Brazil suspends payments on foreign loans.

Competitive Equality in Banking Act (CEBA) limits growth of so-called nonbank banks.

American Express inaugurates its Optima card.

Citicorp announces sale of South African subsidiary.

Citicorp's stock price peaks at historic high of $64.

1988   Michael Milken's junk-bond markets network implodes with the bankruptcy of Drexel Burnham.

Citicorp earns $4 million fee for arranging $425 million loan to Donald Trump for buying Plaza Hotel.

Citicorp begins aggressive penetration of non-U.S. bank card market such as Diners Club.

Fair Credit and Charge Card Disclosure Act is passed.

1989   Brazil and Argentina suspend payment on loans.

U.S. real estate and junk-bond markets collapse.

Citicorp participates in largest LBO: RJR Nabisco.

Japan's JCB credit card enters U.S. market.

Visa introduces VisaPhone telephone charge service.

Citicorp begins marketing bank credit cards in Europe.

Citicorp's consumer credit card division earns over $600 million in after-tax profits.

1990   Citicorp is instructed by the U.S. Federal Reserve Bank of New York to substantially improve its total capital position of $16 billion; asset sales are explored to raise new capital.

Donald Trump suspends interest payments to banks and junk-bond holders including Citicorp.

AT&T launches no-fee, low-rate Universal card.

Citicorp begins targeting those with low incomes, poor credit histories, and recent bankruptcies for its new secured credit card and becomes the industry leader.

Citicorp eliminates 3,600 positions and announces 4,400 more job cuts over the next two years.

Citicorp's consumer credit card division earns over $500 million in after-tax profits, which is impressive due to rising delinquency rates attributed to the recession.

1991   Citicorp's Tier I (core capital) ratio falls to 3.73 percent, far below the 6.0 percent level that is defined as "well capitalized." Reserves are only $3.3 billion and total capital is $17.1 billion.
Citicorp records a near $1 billion loss for the year.
Citicorp embarks on a recapitalization campaign by selling $660 million in Series 13 shares, $1.13 billion of "Percs," and $590 million in shares to Saudi investor.
Citicorp sells 25 percent of its shares in Saudi American Bank (SAMBA), first part of AMBAC (bond insurance company), Lynch, Jones & Ryan, and CAMPAC.
Citicorp finally links its ATM system to the nationwide Cirrus network.
Citicorp introduces a floating (adjustable) rate card.
Citicorp's consumer credit card division earns over $630 million in after-tax profits.

1992   Citicorp becomes largest bank in the United States.
Citicorp sells its Indian operations to an Italian firm after the crash of the Indian stock market.
Citicorp sells the second part of AMBAC.
Citicorp sells its Establishment Services to Welsh, Carson, Anderson, and Stowe.
Citicorp receives equity stake in Alexander's retail chain, Plaza Hotel, and other Trump properties in return for restructuring his loan obligations.
Citicorp's consumer bank credit cards division earns profits of $635 million.

1993   Citicorp becomes the largest credit and charge card issuer and servicer in the world.
Sears becomes the last major national retail chain to accept bank credit cards.
Citicorp announces elimination of 8,000 more jobs.
Citicorp's net income almost triples to nearly $2 billion.
Citicorp's profits on credit cards estimated at over $800 million.

1994   U.S. revolving consumer debt jumps a record $53 billion to a total of $334 billion.
Citicorp's net income of $3.4 billion (54 percent increase) is the highest ever by a domestic banking company.
Citicorp ranks second (after Chemical) in derivative contracts with $2.61 trillion at the end of the year.
Payment of common stock dividend resumed following 1991 suspension.

1995   Citicorp's risk-adjusted Tier I capital ratio rises above 8 percent.

Citicorp sells its 27.1 percent of Alexander's shares (from Trump bailout) to Vornado for $54.8 million.

Citicorp's assets climb to $250 billion.

Citicorp sells $1.06 billion of securitized credit card receivables on the New York bond market followed by the sale of $625 million in London market (tied to U.S. Treasury note yields), which significantly lowers the cost of raising new capital.

Citicorp announces its intention to repurchase $3 billion in publicly held Citicorp stock.

Citicorp reports a record first quarter of $4.7 billion in total adjusted revenues (13 percent increase) with 56 percent of its net income of $436 million attributed to worldwide consumer revenues.

Citicorp's global network includes over 3,300 offices, branches, affiliates, and subsidiaries in 92 countries.

1996   Citicorp becomes largest credit card issuer in Asia. Taiwan first country outside United States with over 1 million credit cards.

1997   Citicorp announces acquisition of AT&T's credit card division (18.1 million accounts and $15 billion balances) for $3.5 billion and 10-year strategic cobranding and cross-marketing alliance.

1998   Citicorp and Travelers Group merge to form the world's largest financial services conglomerate.

Citigroup authorizes $2 billion stock repurchase program.

Citibank opens bank in Ukraine, its 100th country.

Citibank's agreement with Blockbuster expands its network of proprietary banking machines from 9 to 39 states and D.C.

Citigroup's strategic alliance with WorldGate Communications enables cable operators to offer e-Citi financial services to 69 million U.S. cable-TV households.

1999   Citibank introduces "e-Citi commerce solutions," for consumer Internet transactions, based on technological advances of Transpoint, joint venter of Microsoft and First Data.

Citigroup reports a net profit of $1.2 billion on its credit cards.

Citicorp reports record profit of $9.9 billion.

Citicorp acquires Mellon Bank's credit card division of 800,000 accounts and $1.9 billion outstanding receivables.

2000   Citigroup chairman John R. Reed retires and is succeeded by Sandy Weill, chairman of Travelers.

Citigroup and Commerce One announce plan to build Internet marketplace.

Citigroup reports record core income for first quarter.

Citigroup stock price rises above $250.

APPENDIX 3   Citicorp's Annual Reported Profits: 1975–1999 (millions of dollars

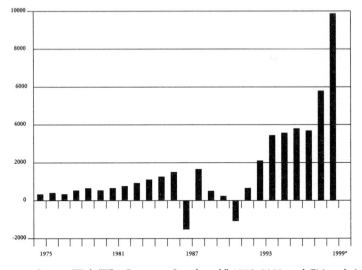

SOURCES: *Business Week*, "The Corporate Scoreboard," 1975–2000, and Citicorp's Annual Reports.

* 1998 and 1999 report the combined profits of Citicorp and Travelers Group for the new company Citigroup.

APPENDIX 4   The Real Cost of Borrowing: Inflation Rate, Real Discount Rate, and Real Prime Rate, 1970–1999 (percent)

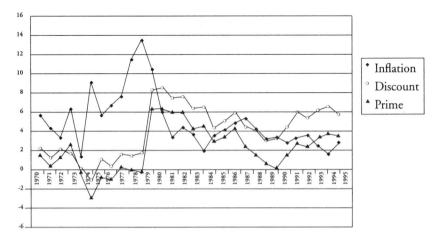

SOURCE: The Board of Governors of the Federal Reserve system, "Selected Interest Rates," www.federalreserve.gov.

APPENDIX 5   Spiraling Cost of Higher Education: Undergraduate Room, Board, and Tuition at American University (nominal dollars)

	1975–1976	*1985–1986*	*1995–1996*	*2000–2001*
Tuition	2,880	8,200	16,890	21,114
Housing	954	2,400	4,040	5,350
Board	588	1,528	2,800	3,022
Total	4,422	12,128	23,730	29,516

SOURCE: American University, Office of Financial Aid, Washington, D.C.

APPENDIX 6   Undergraduate Student Surveys: Frequency Distributions of Gender, Race/Ethnicity, Household Income, Student Loans, Credit Card Accounts, and Credit Card Use (percent)

	University of Maryland *(N=103)*	*Georgetown University* *(N=303)*
Gender		
Male	53.4	49.9
Female	46.6	50.1
Total	100.0	100.0
Race/ethnicity/national origin		
White	63.0	67.7
African American	15.2	13.2
Latino	10.9	8.9
Asian	6.5	5.9
Other	4.4	4.3
Total	100.0	100.0
International Students	10.9	7.6
Household income		
Under $25,000	8.7	3.6
Under $35,000	6.8	3.3
Under $45,000	1.9	6.9
Under $55,000	10.7	5.0
Under $65,000	8.7	4.6
Under $75,000	15.6	3.3
Under $85,000	12.6	5.3
Under $95,000	6.8	5.6
Under $105,000	10.7	9.9

(continues)

316

APPENDIX 6   *(continued)*

	University of Maryland (N=103)	Georgetown University (N=303)
Under $155,000	10.7	18.8
Under $205,000	6.8	8.9
Over $205,000	0.0	24.8
Total	100.0	100.0
Student loans		
Yes	51.5	38.9
No	48.5	61.1
Total	100.0	100.0
Joint credit card account with parents		
Yes	19.5	44.2
No	80.5	55.8
Total	100.0	100.0
Receive free gift with credit card application		
Yes	71.7	29.7
No	28.3	70.3
Total	100.0	100.0
Ever take cash advance [a]		
Yes	26.1	20.5
No	73.9	79.5
Total	100.0	100.0
Currently have account balance [a]		
Yes (revolvers)	68.9 (58.8 of total)	43.0 (36.3 of total)
No (convenience)	31.1 (41.2)	57.0 (63.7)
Total	100.0	100.0
Number of credit cards [b]		
None	14.6	15.5
One	43.7	47.9
Two	21.3	23.1
Three	8.7	8.9
Four	4.9	2.6
Five	1.9	1.0
Six or more	4.9	1.0
Total	100.0	100.0

[a] These percentages are based on students with an active universal credit card account: Visa, MasterCard, Discover, American Express (Optima). Hence, students with only retail and gasoline credit cards or Visa debit and/or cash checking cards are classified as "none."
[b] These percentages are based on students with an active universal credit card account: Visa, MasterCard, Discover, American Express (Optima). They exclude retail and gasoline credit accounts as well as debit and cash checking cards.

Notes

Chapter 1

1. "Clinton's Credit Card Not Accepted: Expired American Express Forces President to Ask Aide for Help," *Houston Chronicle*, 2 March 1999, p. A3.

2. Such bizarre situations are described by sociologist Max Weber as the "iron cage" of rationality. For the irrationality of rationally inspired bureaucratic organizations and procedures, see Max Weber, *The Protestant Ethic and the Spirit of Capitalism* (London: Unwin Hyman, 1930), p. 181.

3. Daniel Bell, *The Cultural Contradictions of Capitalism* (New York: Basic Books, 1996).

4. Benjamin R. Barber, *Jihad vs. McWorld: How Globalism and Tribalism Are Reshaping the World* (New York: Ballantine Books, 1995).

5. Lendol Calder, *Financing the American Dream: A Cultural History of Consumer Credit* (Princeton: Princeton University Press, 1999).

6. David M. Tucker, *The Decline of Thrift in America* (New York: Praeger, 1991), p. 114.

7. Calder, op. cit., p. 24.

8. This is consistent with Lenin's view of the hegemonic power of banking. Indeed, the emerging international division of labor features relatively low profits for industrial production in developing countries (depending on the role of the state in suppressing labor rights) and among the highest profits in financing corporate and consumer loans in the developed countries. See V. I. Lenin, *Imperialism: The Highest Stage of Capitalism* (New York: International Publishers, 1939).

9. The Financial Services Modernization Act of 1999 (HR-10), or the Gramm-Leach-Bliley Act, is the statutory cornerstone of the deregulation of financial services. This legislation effectively eliminated depression-era restrictions against firms conducting both wholesale and retail banking (Glass-Steagall Act of 1933) and paved the way for the eventual elimination of restrictions against interstate banking (McFadden Act of 1927). The result is the emergence of trillion-dollar financial service conglomerates such as Citigroup. See Chapters 3 and 7.

10. Estimates from HSN Consultants Inc., *The Nilson Report*, "Credit Cards—Holders, Numbers, Spending, and Debt," reported in table 822, *1998 Statistical Abstract of the United States* (Washington, D.C.: U.S. Government Printing Office, 1999), p. 523.

11. Approximately 78 million out of 102 million households in 2000 have a bank credit card. See CardWeb, "Rates Stand Still," CardTrak, June 2000, at www.cardweb.com. On credit card solicitations, see Lawrence M. Ausubel, "Personal Bankruptcies Begin Sharp Decline: Mil-

lennium Data Update," Department of Economics, University of Maryland (18 January 2000); Marcy Gordon, "More Consumers Show Credit Restraint," *Boston Globe* (January 19, 2000), p. C2; and Richard Snathmary, "Credit Card Offers Hit Record Volume," *DM News,* 31 July 1995, p. 5.

12. Gary Hendricks and Kenwood C. Youmans with Janet Keller, *Consumer Durables and Installment Debt: A Study of American Households* (Ann Arbor, Mich.: Institute for Social Research, 1973), p. 134.

13. Margaret Webb Pressler, "At Giant, a New Meaning for 'Paper, or Plastic?'" *The Washington Post,* 14 March 1996, p. D11; Vivien Kellerman, "A Credit Card with a Little Bonus for Retirement," *The New York Times,* 11 June 1994, p. A36; Ruth Susswein, Executive Director, Bankcard Holders of America, testimony before the U.S. House Subcommittee on Consumer Credit and Insurance, 10 March 1994. For a selected review of credit card marketing campaigns and specific programs, CardTrak offers a comprehensive compilation of industrial information at www.cardweb.com.

14. On how to evaluate different credit card reward programs, see "So Many Credit Card Choices, So Little Time: How to Choose the Best Deal for You," Module 2, in the "Financial Education" section at www.creditcardnation.com.

15. Quoted from Susswein, op. cit.

16. Robert D. Manning, *Credit Cards on Campus: The Social Consequences of Student Debt* (Washington, D.C.: Consumer Federation of America, 1999), examines the marketing to college students in greater depth. See Appendix F. The report is available in the "Research Reports" section at www.creditcardnation.com.

17. As identified by Competitive Media Reporting during the period May 1993 through April 1994. *National Directory of Advertisers* (New Providence, N.J.: National Register Publishing, 1995), pp. xvii–xxi.

18. The probability of winning Visa's 1999 Magic of Plastic campaign, assuming one credit card charge each day of the promotion, was 1 out of 86,400. Similarly, the largesse of the credit card industry tends to satisfy only the minimum criteria for charitable donations. "Visa has guaranteed a $2.5 million contribution to the United States Olympic Committee related to the number of Visa card sales transactions from 1/31/97 through 9/30/00." This is a minimum contribution of less than $700,000 per year.

19. Quoted in Kevin Sullivan and Mary Jordan, "In Japan, Cash Registers, Many Merchants Start Accepting Credit Cards at Urging of Olympic Officials," *The Washington Post,* 4 February 1998, p. C3. On the emergence of credit cards as rational expression of modern commerce, see George Ritzer, *Expressing America: A Critique of the Global Credit Card Society* (Thousand Oaks, Calif.: Pine Forge Press, 1995).

20. *The Economist,* 2 November 1991, p. 69; Bankcard Holders of America, *Bankcard Consumer News,* vol. 15, no. 6 (November/December 1995), pp. 1–2; and Lawrence M. Ausubel, "The Failure of Competition in the Credit Card Market," *American Economic Review,* vol. 81, no. 1 (March 1991), pp. 50–81.

21. U.S. Department of Commerce, *1994 Statistical Abstract of the United States* (Washington, D.C.: U.S. Government Printing Office, 1995), tables 810 and 812, pp. 525–526; and Snathmary, op. cit., p. 5.

22. As identified by Competitive Media Reporting during the period May 1997 through April 1998. *National Directory of Advertisers* (New Providence, N.J.: National Register Publishing, 1998), pp. xxiii–xxvii.

23. CardWeb.com, "Credit Card U.S. Brand Market Share," February 2000, available at www.Cardfacts.com.

24. Estimates from HSN Consultants Inc., *The Nilson Report,* op. cit., p. 523. On bank credit card revenues and profits, see CardWeb, "Profit Squeeze," CardTrak, October 1999, at www.cardweb.com.

25. Admittedly, these debt statistics are reported in nominal dollars. After adjustment for inflation, the $78 billion increase in credit card debt would be less than $55 billion in 1980 dollars. U.S. Department of Commerce, *1994 Statistical Abstract of the United States*, op. cit., tables 810 and 812, pp. 525–526; Bankcard Holders of America, op. cit., p. 1; and Federal Reserve System, *Federal Reserve Statistical Release*, "Consumer Credit," reported monthly at www.bog.frb.fed.us.

26. The U.S. Federal Reserve estimates that its statistics on revolving consumer debt are overstated by about 14 percent; approximately 9 percent of credit card debt is paid off before interest charges are incurred and another 5 percent is not credit card debt. As a result, for the purposes of this analysis, the official Federal Reserve statistics on revolving consumer credit outstanding (credit card debt) are deflated by 14 percent. The monthly *Federal Reserve Bulletin*, which reports revolving and nonrevolving consumer debt levels, is available at www.bog.frb.fed.us.

For a more detailed discussion of this methodological issue, see Stephen Brobeck, "Expanding Credit Card Debt: The Role of Creditors and the Impact on Consumers" (Washington, D.C.: Consumer Federation of America, 16 December 1997), available at www.consumerfed.org. The 2000 figures are based on 78 million households with at least one credit card that have accumulated an unadjusted total of $603.5 billion in revolving debt; 43 percent of these households with credit cards are convenience users. The first quarter 2000 estimates are based on 81 million households with credit cards and 43.5 percent convenience users. The proportion of convenience users in the 1990s is reported in Card-Web, op. cit. For 2000, see Marcy Gordon, "Credit Cards at 50: The Problems of Ubiquity," *The New York Times*, 12 March 2000, p. A11.

27. National and personal U.S. savings rates are examined in Chapter 2. U.S. Bureau of Economic Analysis, National Income and Product Accounts of the United States, 1929–1995, cited in table 775, "Gross Saving and Investment: 1990 to 1997," in the *1998 Statistical Abstract of the United States* (Washington, D.C.: U.S. Government Printing Office, 1999), p. 458.

28. Eric Schurenberg, "Getting on Top of Your Debt," *Money*, April 1987, pp. 95–99.

29. Marcia Vickers, "A Hard Lesson on Credit Cards," *Business Week*, 15 March 1999, p. 107. Jeff sent a formal letter of complaint to the *Business Week* ombudsman complaining about his inaccurate portrayal in the article.

30. See Calder, op. cit.; Bell, op. cit.; Tucker, op. cit.; Martha L. Olney, *Buy Now, Pay Later: Advertising, Credit, and Consumer Durables in the 1920s* (Chapel Hill: University of North Carolina Press, 1991); and Daniel Horowitz, *The Morality of Spending: Attitudes Toward the Consumer Society in America, 1875–1940* (Baltimore: Johns Hopkins University Press, 1985).

31. This cultural emphasis underlies Max Weber's classic explanation of the rise of Western economic dominance in the nineteenth century. See Weber, op. cit.

32. Frank Levy, *The New Dollars and Dreams: American Incomes and Economic Change* (New York: Russell Sage Press, 1998); David M. Gordon, *Lean and Mean: The Corporate Squeeze of Working Americans and the Myth of Managerial "Downsizing"* (New York: Free Press, 1996); and David Halberstam, *The Fifties* (New York: Ballantine Books, 1994).

33. Joseph Nocera, *A Piece of the Action: How the Middle Class Joined the Money Class* (New York: Simon & Schuster, 1994); and Lewis Mandell, *The Credit Card Industry: A History* (Boston: Twayne Publishers, 1990).

34. The study of consumer credit cards has generally been limited to financial and institutional histories. The most important books on these topics are Nocera, op. cit., and Mandell, op. cit. Although Ritzer, op. cit., offers a sociological overview of contemporary trends in the industry, he ignores the fundamental political, economic, and institutional forces responsible for the tremendous growth of revolving credit cards since the mid-1980s. Without adequately contextualizing this phenomenon, Ritzer simply "explains" the global expansion of consumer

credit cards from a dubious, culturally deterministic perspective. Significantly, this modernization paradigm, or "McDonaldization" of society, fails to explain its central theoretical contradiction—that is, the emergence of social and cultural resistance to the expansion of consumer
credit because of its homogenizing influences. In sum, the academic studies fail to address two
fundamental issues: (1) the increasing cost of consumer credit by social class and (2) the different uses of consumer credit in the daily lives of individuals in these various groups. Not incidentally, none of these authors collected primary data on consumer credit patterns, and they all
tend to interpret their findings from a distinctly white, male, middle-class perspective.

35. See U.S. Federal Reserve System, *Federal Reserve Bulletins*; U.S. Federal Reserve System, *Annual Statistical Digests*; and U.S. Department of Commerce, *Statistical Abstract of the
United States*, op. cit., tables 798, 819, and 820.

36. Table 4.2, Chapter 4, summarizes this pattern of the different costs of credit by social
group. Also see Robert D. Manning, "Poverty, Race, and the Two-Tiered Financial Services
System," in Chester Hartman (ed.), *Challenges to Equality: Poverty and Race in America* (New
York: M. E. Sharpe, 2000 forthcoming).

37. For example, 50 bank branches closed in the New York City boroughs of the Bronx
and Brooklyn between 1978 and 1992. Several closings are attributed to the merger of Chemical and Manufacturer's Hanover. See Matthew Purdy and Joe Sexton, "Short of Banking
Services, the Poor Are Improvising," *The New York Times,* 11 September 1995, p. A1. According to Gary A. Dymski, in *The Bank Merger Wave* (New York: M. E. Sharpe, 1999, chap.
2), the impact has been much greater on lower-income communities because they had so
few bank branches before the mergers were consummated.

38. Gregory D. Squires and Sally O'Connor, "Fringe Banking in Milwaukee: The Rise of
Check Cashing Businesses and the Emergence of a Two-Tiered Banking System," *Urban Affairs Review,* vol. 34, no. 1 (1998), pp. 126–163; John P. Caskey, *Fringe Banking: Check Cashing Outlets, Pawnshops, and the Poor* (New York: Russell Sage, 1994); and Michael Hudson
(ed.), *Merchants of Misery: How Corporate America Profits from Poverty* (Monroe, Maine:
Common Courage Press, 1996).

39. Corporate programs, stock price data, and annual reports (SEC form 10-K) of Cash
America (PWN) available through EDGAR Online at http://biz.yahoo.com.

40. The current amount of the national debt is available at www.publicdebt.
treas.gov/opd/opdpenny. In September 2000, it was $5.68 trillion.

41. This is illustrated by the experience of "Chris" in Chapter 6. Also see Teresa A. Sulli-
van, Elizabeth Warren, and Jay Lawrence Westbrook, *The Fragile Middle Class: Americans in
Debt* (New Haven: Yale University Press, 2000); Teresa A. Sullivan, Elizabeth Warren, and
Jay Westbrook, *As We Forgive Our Debtors: Bankruptcy and Consumer Credit in America* (New
York: Oxford University Press, 1989); and Katherine Newman, *Falling from Grace: The Expe-
rience of Downward Mobility in the American Middle Class* (New York: Free Press, 1988).

42. The Administrative Office of the U.S. Courts reports 1,286,000 bankruptcies in
1999. This represents a decline of 8 percent from 1,397,000 in 1998. See Lawrence M.
Ausubel, "Personal Bankruptcies Begin Sharp Decline: Millennium Data Update," Department of Economics, University of Maryland. The report is available at www.bsos.
umd.edu/econ/bankruptcy.

43. John Meehan, "All That Plastic Is Still Fantastic for Citibank," *Business Week*, 28 May
1990, p. 90; and Linda Punch, "Citicorp: Where Does the Giant Go from Here?" *Credit
Card Management* (October 1991), p. 42.

44. *Time,* 8 April 1974, p. 14; and *Family Circle,* 19 May 1978, p. 221.

45. *Time,* 18 May 1981, p. 2; *Gentlemen's Quarterly,* August 1985, p. 37; and *Gentlemen's
Quarterly,* August 1987, p. 21.

46. *Time,* 24 November 1980, p. 17; 18 May 1981, p. 2; 24 November 1986, p. 75; 23
June 1986, p. 79; 28 November 1988, p. 76; and 21 August 1989, p. 27.

47. Robert L. Black, Don L. Boroughs, Sara Collins, and Kenneth Sheets, "Heavy Lifting: How America's Debt Burden Threatens the Economic Recovery," *U.S. News and World Report*, 6 May 1991, pp. 51–54; and Peter Passell, "A Mystery Bankers Love: How Do Credit Cards Stay So Profitable?" *The New York Times*, 17 August 1995, p. D2.

48. Max Weber, "Class, Status, Power," in Richard Swedberg (ed.), *Essays in Economic Sociology* (Princeton: Princeton University Press, 1999), p. 92; and Thorstein Veblen, *The Theory of the Leisure Class* (New York: Macmillan, 1899). On Veblen, see John Patrick Diggins, *Thorstein Veblen, Theorist of the Leisure Class* (Princeton: Princeton University Press, 1999).

49. For Weber's influence on the study of credit cards as the "rational" expression of the technological efficiency of modern society, see Ritzer, op. cit. Surprisingly, Ritzer ignores Weber's insightful analysis of the social impact of economic pressures on national stratification systems and the potential backlash against these new consumption patterns.

50. *Time*, 1 June 1981, p. 9; 6 June 1983, p. 44; and 5 December 1983, p. 61.

51. Michael Lewis, *The Money Culture* (New York: Penguin Books, 1992), pp. 15–20. In 2000, Providian Bank marketed a color-coded hierarchy of credit cards ranging from blue Visa Classic ($1,000 credit limit) to Visa Gold ($5,000 limit) to Visa Platinum ($10,000 limit).

52. *Time*, 5 December 1983, p. 61; 13 June 1988, p. 29; and 20 November 1989, p. 90.

53. *Time*, 4 December 1989, p. 16; 20 May 1991, p. 38; 2 December 1991, p. 77; *Elle*, March 1992, p. 58; and *The Washington Post*, 8 March 1995, p. F11.

54. Quoted in Vanessa O'Connell, "New Risk in Credit Cards: Punitive Rates," *Dow Jones News*, 13 July 1995; and Bankcard Holders of America, *Bankcard Consumer News*, op. cit., p. 2.

55. The August 31, 1999, program featured Catherine West, executive vice president of First USA; Carter Warren, executive vice president of marketing for First USA; and Ed Mierzwinski, director of consumer affairs, Public Interest Research Group (PIRG). The transcript is available at the *Nightline* page of www.abcnews.com.

56. "Ames CIA Mole," *The Washington Post*, 8 March 1993, p. A1; and Bankcard Holders of America, *Bankcard Consumer News*, op. cit., p. 6.

57. Elizabeth Judge, "Briton Comes Home to Face Music over $10,000 Tip," *The Times*, 10 June 2000, p. 5; Becky Beaupre, "$10,000 Tip Rejected by Credit Firm," *Chicago Sun-Times*, 8 June 2000, p. 1; Donald Liebenson, "Will 'Blair Witch Project's' Marketing Spell Continue?" *Los Angeles Times*, 18 October 1999, p. F2; *Boston Globe*, 10 August 1999; Marla Harper, "Not a Doctor, Either," *The Washington Post*, 25 July 1995, p. B3, and "A Grand Tip in Oregon Ignites a Grand Dispute," *The Washington Post*, 14 March 1996, p. A5. For other recent anecdotes, see "Stories" at www.creditcardnation.com.

Chapter 2

1. U.S. Department of Commerce, Bureau of Economic Analysis, *Survey of Current Business*, summarized in "U.S. Personal Savings Rate 1929–1999," at www.asec.org. Note, this estimate of personal savings was revised in 1999 to include appreciation of investment assets as well as value of durable goods. Only the new definition of savings is now reported by the Bureau of Economic Analysis at www.bea.doc.gov/briefrm/saving. See note 3 of Chapter 4 for a discussion of the new set of assumptions that distinguish the old versus new U.S. personal savings rates.

2. ABC *Nightline*, "Americans in the Red," 29 December 1998, at www.abc.com.

3. Vince Passaro, "Who'll Stop the Drain? Reflections on the Art of Going Broke," *Harper's*, August 1998, pp. 38–39.

4. Juliet B. Schor, *The Overspent American: Upscaling, Downshifting, and the New Consumer* (New York: Basic Books, 1998).

5. Passaro, op. cit., p. 39.

6. ABC *Nightline*, op. cit.

7. Passaro, op. cit., p. 39.

8. This book was originally entitled "The Debtor Society" in 1995. The following year, economists James Medoff and Andrew Harless published an instructive but more narrowly focused book, *The Indebted Society: Anatomy of an Ongoing Disaster* (Boston: Little, Brown, 1996).

9. The phrase "fat and mean" refers to a distinctive feature of U.S. labor relations in the 1990s: The growth of corporate management is directly related to downsizing the frontline workforce. According to David M. Gordon, the former is the "stick" for extracting concessions from the latter with bureaucratic expansion becoming a key organizational trend. See *Fat and Mean: The Corporate Squeeze of Working Americans and the Myth of Managerial "Downsizing"* (New York: Free Press, 1996).

10. Consumer debt combines all sources including installment (revolving and nonrevolving), consumer loans, and mortgages. See U.S. Bureau of the Public Debt, U.S. Department of Treasury, *The Public Debt to the Penny*, at www.house.gov; U.S. Federal Reserve System, *Flow of Funds Accounts*, March 1998, reported in table 795, "Flow of Funds Accounts—1980 to 1997," and table 799, "Flow of Funds Accounts—Liabilities of Households," *1998 Statistical Abstract of the United States* (Washington, D.C.: U.S. Government Printing Office, 1999), pp. 512 and 515; and Gregory Zuckerman, "U.S. Boom: Living on Borrowed Dime?" *The Wall Street Journal*, 31 December 1999, p. 1.

11. The early sociological discussion of this phenomenon is the focus of Thorstein Veblen's classic, *The Theory of the Leisure Class* (New York: Macmillan, 1899).

12. Fred L. Block, *The Origins of International Economic Disorder* (Berkeley: University of California Press, 1977); Michael J. Piore and Charles F. Sabel, *The Second Industrial Divide: Possibilities for Prosperity* (New York: Basic Books, 1984); David P. Calleo, *The Bankrupting of America: How the Federal Budget Is Impoverishing the Nation* (New York: Basic Books, 1992); and David P. Calleo, *Beyond American Hegemony: The Future of the Western Alliance* (New York: Basic Books, 1987).

13. David Halberstam, *The Fifties* (New York: Ballantine Books, 1994); Lester Thurow, *Head to Head: The Coming Economic Battle Among Japan, Europe, and America* (New York: William Morrow, 1992); Paul Kennedy, *Preparing for the Twenty-First Century* (New York: Vintage Books, 1993); and David P. Calleo, *The Bankrupting of America: How the Federal Budget Is Impoverishing the Nation* (New York: Basic Books, 1992).

14. U.S. Bureau of Labor Statistics, *Employment and Earnings*, reported in table 677, "Unemployed Workers: 1980 to 1997," *1998 Statistical Abstract of the United States* (Washington, D.C.: U.S. Government Printing Office, 1999), p. 423; and U.S. Department of Labor, *Handbook of Labor Statistics—1975* (Washington, D.C.: U.S. Government Printing Office, 1976), p. 26.

15. U.S. Bureau of Labor Statistics, *Handbook of Labor Statistics* (Washington, D.C.: U.S. Government Printing Office, 1993); John Allen, "Fordism and Modern Industry," in Stuart Hall, David Held, Don Hubert, and Kenneth Thompson (eds.), *Modernity: An Introduction to Modern Societies* (Cambridge: Basil Blackwell, 1996), pp. 280–306; and David Harvey, *The Condition of Postmodernity* (Cambridge: Basil Blackwell, 1989), pp. 121–197.

16. See U.S. Census Bureau, "Historical Income Tables," at www.census.gov/hhes/income/histinc; Samuel Bowles, David M. Gordon, and Thomas E. Weisskopf, "Power and Profits: The Social Structure of Accumulation and the Profitability of the Postwar U.S. Economy," *Review of Radical Political Economics*, vol. 18 (1986), pp. 132–167; G. Dumenil, M. Glick, and J. Rangel, "The Rate of Profit in the United States," *Cambridge Journal of Economics*, vol. 11 (1987), pp. 331–359; David Harvey, *The Condition of Postmodernity* (Cambridge: Basil Blackwell, 1989); David M. Gordon, "The Global Economy: New Edifice or Crumbling Foundations?" *New Left Review*, March-April 1988, pp. 24–64; Bennett Harri-

son and Barry Bluestone, *The Great U-Turn: Corporate Restructuring and the Polarizing of America* (New York: Basic Books, 1988); Charles B. Craver, *Can Unions Survive?* (New York: New York University Press, 1995); and Arthur Shostak, *Robust Unionism* (Ithaca: Industrial Relations Press, 1991).

17. Frank Levy, *The New Dollars and Dreams: American Incomes and Economic Change* (New York; Russell Sage, 1998); Denny Braun, *The Rich Get Richer: The Rise of Income Inequality in the United States and the World* (Chicago: Nelson-Hall, 1997); Lawrence Mishel, Jared Bernstein, and John Schmitt, *The State of Working America* (Ithaca: Cornell University Press, 1999); David M. Gordon, *Fat and Mean: The Corporate Squeeze of Working Americans and the Myth of Managerial "Downsizing"* (New York: Free Press, 1996).

18. Kenneth T. Jackson, *Crabgrass Frontier: The Suburbanization of the United States* (New York: Oxford University Press, 1985); Halberstam, op. cit., chap. 9; U.S. Bureau of the Census, Current Housing Reports, Series H121-90-2, *Homeownership Trends in the 1980s* (Washington, D.C.: U.S. Government Printing Office, 1991); Frank Levy, *Dollars and Dreams: The Changing American Income Distribution* (New York: W. W. Norton, 1988); Katy Butler, "The Great Boomer Bust," *Mother Jones,* June 1989, pp. 33–38; Eva Jacobs and Stephanie Shipp, "How Family Spending Has Changed in the U.S.," *Monthly Labor Review,* March 1990, pp. 20–27; Glenn B. Canner and Charles A. Luckett, "Payment of Household Debts," *Federal Reserve Bulletin,* April 1991, pp. 218–229; and Arthur Kennickell and Janice Shack-Marquez, "Changes in Family Finances from 1983 to 1989: Evidence from the Survey of Consumer Finances," *Federal Reserve Bulletin,* January 1992, pp. 1–18.

19. Jackson, op. cit.; Mark Baldassare, "Suburban Communities," *Annual Review of Sociology,* vol. 18 (1992), pp. 475–495; Halberstam, op. cit., chap. 9; John Palen, *The Suburbs* (New York: McGraw-Hill, 1995); Thomas Stanback, *The New Suburbanization: Challenge to the Central City* (Boulder, Colo.: Westview Press, 1991); Peter Saunders, *A Nation of Home Owners* (London: Unwin Hyman, 1990); and Martha L. Olney, *Buy Now, Pay Later: Advertising, Credit, and Consumer Durables in the 1920s* (Chapel Hill: University of North Carolina Press, 1991).

20. The post–World War II consumer behavior of Americans has been influenced more by *perceptions* of short-term economic trends than the reality of their personal economic circumstances. This pattern was empirically verified in the late 1960s by the Institute for Social Research's four-year panel study of 2,604 family units that concluded: "[F]or individual families it is perception of financial progress rather than income change itself that is likely to be most important in influencing whether major discretionary expenditures, particularly major consumer durables, occur." See Gary Hendricks and Kenwood C. Youmans with Janet Keller, *Consumer Durables and Installment Debt: A Study of American Households* (Ann Arbor, Mich.: Institute for Social Research, 1973), p. 152.

21. The monthly *Federal Reserve Bulletin* reports revolving and nonrevolving consumer debt levels. See Federal Reserve Statistical Release "Consumer Credit," which is available at www.bogfrb.fed.us.

22. For instance, between 1948 and 1973, the U.S. share of worldwide production fell from 44.4 to 29.5 percent. This geopolitical shift in industrial manufacturing, or "global recomposition," was most pronounced in Japan (1.6 percent to 7.8 percent), Germany (4.6 percent to 7.4 percent), Soviet Union (6.3 percent to 12.4 percent), and other centrally planned economies (2.2 percent to 7.1 percent), respectively. See David M. Gordon, "The Global Economy: New Edifice or Crumbling Foundations?" *New Left Review,* March-April 1988, pp. 24–64; Calleo, *The Bankrupting of America;* Thurow, op. cit.; Kennedy, op. cit.

23. Benjamin M. Friedman, *Day of Reckoning: The Consequences of American Economic Policy* (New York: Vintage Press, 1989), chap. 3; U.S. Congress, Congressional Budget Office, *Displaced Workers: Trends in the 1980s and Implications for the Future* (Washington, D.C.:

U.S. Government Printing Office, 1993); Barry Bluestone and Bennett Harrison, *The Deindustrialization of America: Plant Closings, Community Abandonment, and the Dismantling of Basic Industry* (New York: Basic Books, 1982); George Bouvier, *Free Trade Fraud* (New York: St. Martin's Press, 1991); Levy, op. cit.; Bennett Harrison and Barry Bluestone, *The Great U-Turn: Corporate Restructuring and the Polarizing of America* (New York: Basic Books, 1988); Lawrence Mishel and David M. Frankel, *The State of Working America* (New York: M. E. Sharpe, 1993); Robert D. Manning, "U.S. Industrial Restructuring, Immigrant Workers, and the American State: The Political Economy of Mexican Migration," Ph.D. dissertation, Department of Sociology, Johns Hopkins University (Baltimore, 1989), chap. 5; Donald L. Barlett and James B. Steele, *America: What Went Wrong?* (Kansas City: Andrews and McMeel, 1992).

24. Bowles, Gordon, and Weisskopf, op. cit., pp. 132–167; Dumenil, Glick, and Rangel, op. cit., pp. 331–359; Frank Levy, op. cit.; Harrison and Bluestone, op. cit.; Braun, op. cit.; David P. Calleo, *The Bankrupting of America: How the Federal Budget Is Impoverishing the Nation* (New York: Basic Books, 1992); David P. Calleo, *Beyond American Hegemony: The Future of the Western Alliance* (New York: Basic Books, 1987); Frances Fox Piven and Richard A. Cloward, *Regulating the Poor: The Functions of Public Welfare* (New York: Vintage Press, 1997); and Terry Boswell and Albert Bergesen (eds.), *America's Changing Role in the World System* (New York: Praeger Press, 1987).

25. Friedman, op. cit.

26. U.S. Bureau of the Public Debt, U.S. Department of Treasury, "The National Debt," at www.publicdebt.treas.gov/opd/opdpenny. Reported annual deficits are actually higher due to the "paper shuffle" of raiding the Social Security surplus ($56.8 billion in 1994) and hiding other "off-budget" expenses such as the S&L bailout and U.S. Post Office subsidies after 1988. See U.S. Congress, Congressional Budget Office, *The Economic and Budget Outlook: Fiscal Years 1996–2000* (Washington, D.C.: U.S. Government Printing Office, 1995).

27. Quoted in Friedman, op. cit., p. 216; and National Republican Committee, "A Strategy for Growth: The American Economy in the 1980s" (mimeo, 1980), p. 8.

28. U.S. Congress, Congressional Budget Office, *Assessing the Decline in the National Saving Rate* (Washington, D.C.: U.S. Government Printing Office, 1993), pp. 3–4.

29. For example, only 37.4 percent of federal R&D dollars went to U.S. civilian projects versus 86.3 percent for Germany and 94.6 percent for Japan. Similarly, Germany invested 15 percent of total government R&D in industrial development (U.S. less than 1 percent), while Japan invested 23 percent in energy research (U.S. 4 percent). More striking is the nearly equal contributions of federal (46 percent) and private (49 percent) sector resources to total U.S. R&D. In Japan and Germany, R&D investment is led by the private sector, reaching a high of nearly 80 percent in Japan. See National Science Foundation, *Research and Development Expenditures in the U.S.* (Washington, D.C.: U.S. Government Printing Office, 1991); and Sam Natapoff, *Defenseless? Or Less Defense? A Comparison of U.S., German, and Japanese Public Expenditures* (Washington, D.C.: Campaign for New Priorities, 1992).

30. Arms exports account for only 2 percent of international trade. Hence, U.S. arms exports—which are heavily subsidized by U.S. taxpayers—represent less than one-tenth of 1 percent of global trade. See Natapoff, op. cit.

31. Interest payments on the national debt stabilized in the early 1990s: $184.2 billion in 1991, $194.5 billion in 1992, $198.8 billion in 1993, $202.9 billion in 1994. This was due to a "hedging" strategy by the Clinton administration whereby higher-interest, long-term debt was replaced with lower-interest, short-term debt. The potential economic consequences could be higher interest payments in the future if interest rates increase, even with a balanced budget. Note, net interest payments rose modestly at the end of the decade: $234 billion in 1995, $241 billion in 1996, $244 billion in 1997, and $243 billion in 1998. U.S.

Office of Management and Budget, *Historical Tables,* "Federal Budget Outlays," reported in table 538, *1998 Statistical Abstract of the United States* (Washington, D.C.: U.S. Government Printing Office, 1999), p. 339.

32. Eric Pianin and John M. Berry, "The Clinton Budget: A Sobering Surplus Scenario," *The Washington Post,* 8 February 2000, pp. A1, A15. For Congressional Budget Office estimates, see *The Budget and Economic Outlook: Fiscal Years 2001–2010* (Washington, D.C.: U.S. Government Printing Office, 2000), table 2, available at www.cbo.gov.

33. U.S. Federal Reserve, 1991. The latter two factors raised the effective rate of return to foreign investors without increasing the yield to domestic lenders. At the end of 2000, about two-thirds of the $5.7 trillion national debt was held by domestic borrowers. See Bureau of the Public Debt, "Public Debt: To the Penny," at www.publicdebt.treas.gov; and U.S. Congress, Congressional Budget Office, *The Economic and Budget Outlook: Fiscal Years 1996–2000* (Washington, D.C.: U.S. Government Printing Office, 1995), table 517.

34. International Monetary Fund (IMF), *Direction of Trade Statistical Yearbook* (Washington, D.C.: International Monetary Fund, 1999); "U.S. International Transactions: 1980 to 1992," and "International Investment Positions: 1980 to 1992," reported in tables 1306 and 1309, *1994 Statistical Abstract of the United States* (Washington, D.C.: U.S. Government Printing Office, 1995), pp. 804, 807. This is an ominous trend since it portends greater political as well as economic costs of sustaining current patterns of foreign investment. See Norman J. Glickman and Douglas P. Woodward, *The New Competitors: How Foreign Investors Are Changing the U.S. Economy* (New York: Basic Books, 1989); Sara L. Gordon and Francis A. Lees, *Foreign Multinational Investment in the United States: Struggle for Industrial Supremacy* (New York: Quorum Books, 1986); Martin Tolchin and Susan Tolchin, *Buying into America: How Foreign Money Is Changing the Face of Our Nation* (New York: Times Books, 1988).

35. U.S. Department of Commerce, "U.S. Total Trade Balances with Individual Countries, 1991–98," available at www.ita.doc.gov/industry; U.S. Department of Commerce, "U.S. Balances on International Transactions" and "Foreign Direct Investment in the United States," reported in tables 1303 and 1309, *1998 Statistical Abstract of the United States* (Washington, D.C.: U.S. Government Printing Office, 1999), pp. 788, 791.

36. See U.S. House of Representatives, Subcommittee on Oversight, Committee on Ways and Means, transcript of "Federal Tax Payments by U.S. Subsidiaries of Foreign-Controlled Companies," 9 April 1992.

37. The much lower social responsibility of American corporations, as reflected in declining corporate taxes and rise of contingent workers in the 1990s, underlies the much higher "cultural rate-of-profit" that distinguishes the management policies of American-based corporations. For example, a comparison of the largest U.S. and Japanese corporations in 1987 revealed that American corporations reported about double the returns on equity of their Japanese counterparts in the same industries. Overall, major U.S. corporations demand at least 12–15 percent return on investment. See Manning, op. cit., chap. 5.

38. U.S. Bureau of Economic Analysis, *Survey of Current Business,* "International Investment Position," reported in table 1305, *1998 Statistical Abstract of the United States* (Washington, D.C.: U.S. Government Printing Office, 1999), p. 789.

39. At the end of 1997, the market value of foreign assets in the United States was $6.330 trillion. U.S. Bureau of Economic Analysis, op. cit., p. 789; and John Burgess, "1999 Trade Gap Hits Record $271 Billion," *The Washington Post,* 19 February 2000, p. E1.

40. U.S. corporate tax policy is the most important factor in explaining fluctuations in the reported rates of profit in the post–World War II period. See Dumenil, Glick, and Rangel, op. cit., pp. 331–359. Also see Friedman, op. cit., chap. X; Richard C. Zeimer, "Impact of Recent Tax Law Changes," *Survey of Current Business,* vol. 65 (April 1985), pp. 28–31; and

U.S. Congress, Congressional Budget Office, *The Economic and Budget Outlook: Fiscal Years 1996–2000* (Washington, D.C.: U.S. Government Printing Office, 1995).

41. A neglected component of U.S. indebtedness concerns the rapid growth of earnings, interest charges, and royalties and fees that are remitted back to foreign investors from their U.S. investments (private and corporate). The data show a substantial increase since 1987 that requires greater national savings to compensate for increased pressure on the U.S. capital account. For example, between 1990 and 1997, net U.S. investment income fell from $24.2 billion to –$5.3 billion. See "U.S. International Transactions by Type of Transaction," reported in table 1302, *1998 Statistical Abstract of the United States* (Washington, D.C.: U.S. Government Printing Office, 1999), p. 786. Overall, tax evasion by foreign corporations was estimated at $25 billion to $35 billion per year in the late 1980s. See U.S. House of Representatives, Subcommittee on Oversight, op. cit., p. 75.

42. Citizens for Tax Justice, *It's Working, but . . . The Resurgence of Business Investment and Corporate Income Taxes* (Washington, D.C.: Citizens for Tax Justice, 1989); U.S. House of Representatives, Subcommittee on Oversight, op. cit., p. 23; and U.S. Congress, Congressional Budget Office, op. cit.

43. Barlett and Steele, op. cit.; and Friedman, op. cit., author's emphasis, p. 264.

44. Gary Shilling, *The World Has Definitely Changed* (New York: Lakeview Press, 1986); John M. Berry, "Takeovers Eroding Corporate Equity, Increasing Debt," *The Washington Post*, 28 October 1988, p. H1; and Merrill Lynch, cited in *U.S. News & World Report*, "Heavy Lifting: How America's Debt Burden Threatens the Economic Recovery," 6 May 1991, pp. 52–61.

45. Peter Behr, "Wave of Merges, Takeovers Is a Part of Reagan Legacy," *The Washington Post*, 30 October 1988, p. H1.

46. Neil R. Gazel, *Beatrice: From Buildup Through Breakup* (Chicago: University of Illinois Press, 1990), p. 78.

47. Manning, op. cit., chap. 5.

48. Blizerian currently lives in a palatial estate, protected by Florida bankruptcy laws, near Tampa, Florida. George Anders, *Merchants of Debt: KKR and the Mortgaging of American Business* (New York: Basic Books, 1992); Sarah Bartlett, *The Money Machine: How KKR Manufactured Power and Profits* (New York: Warner Books, 1991); and CBS News, transcript of *60 Minutes* TV news program "Bankrupt in Florida," 28 November 1993.

49. Benjamin J. Stein, *A License to Steal: The Untold Story of Michael Milken and the Conspiracy to Bilk the Nation* (New York: Simon and Schuster, 1992); the "three rules" quote in Bryan Burrough and John Helyar, *Barbarians at the Gate* (New York: HarperCollins, 1990), p. 34; James B. Stewart, *Den of Thieves* (New York: Simon and Schuster, 1992); and "[T]he door" quote in Behr, op. cit., p. H1.

50. Junk bonds became increasingly important in the mid-1980s as the "subordinate" debt that was necessary to close the LBO. According to George Anders (1992, chap. 5), commercial banks would lend up to a maximum of 60 percent in "senior" loans, and the "limited partners" of the acquiring company (e.g., KKR) would provide between 5 and 20 percent. In order to complete the takeover financing, the remaining unsecured loans (20–40 percent) were the riskiest and thus required the highest yields of the loan package. Michael Milken's junk bonds, which originated from Drexel Burnham, typically paid interest twice per year and matured in from 3 to 20 years. Sold in $1 million units, they yielded 11–15 percent versus 8–10 percent for high-grade bonds. Also see U.S. General Accounting Office, *High Yield Bonds: Nature of the Market and Effect on Federally Insured Institutions* (Washington, D.C.: U.S. Government Printing Office, May 1988).

51. The 1991 movie *Other People's Money* starred Danny DeVito as the ruthless corporate raider "Larry the Liquidator" Garfield. See Michael Lewis, *Liar's Poker* (New York: W. W. Norton, 1989); Michael Lewis, *The Money Culture* (New York: W. W. Norton, 1991); Stein,

op. cit.; Stewart, op. cit.; and Mary Zey, *Banking on Fraud: Drexel, Junk Bonds, and Buyouts* (New York: Aldine de Gruyter, 1993).

52. John E. Parsons, "Bankers and Bargaining: The Eastern Airlines Case," *Economic Notes,* April-May 1986, pp. 6–8; Aaron Bernstein, *Grounded: Frank Lorenzo and the Destruction of Eastern Airlines* (New York: Simon and Schuster, 1990); Kevin J. Delaney, *Strategic Bankruptcy: How Corporations and Creditors Use Chapter 11 to Their Advantage* (Berkeley: University of California Press, 1992), chap. 3; Kevin Kelly, "The Airline Industry's Haves and Have-Nots," *In These Times*, 1–7 May 1991, p. 2; and Office of Resolution Trust, listing of junk-bond holdings, mimeo (1992).

53. Barlett and Steele, op. cit., chap. 4; Kevin J. Delaney, op. cit., chap. 3; and Allan Sloan, "Airlines That Are Loaded Down with Debt Will Have Struggle to Stay Aloft," *The Washington Post*, 30 October 1990, p. D3.

54. Anders, op. cit., p. 82.

55. Lewis, op. cit.; Barlett and Steele, op. cit.; and Zey, op. cit.

56. Even after Milken became subject to prosecution by the SEC and to numerous other civil suits, the Milken family fortune was estimated at over $1.2 billion in mid-1992. See Stewart, op. cit., p. 523. Savings and loan institutions were permitted to purchase junk bonds from 1982 to 1989. See Barlett and Steele, op. cit.; Zey, op. cit.; Stein, op. cit., chap. 8; Michael Waldman and Public Citizens Congress Watch Staff, *Who Robbed America? A Citizen's Guide to the Savings and Loan Scandal* (New York: Random House, 1990); Stephen Pizzo, Mary Fricker, and Paul Muolo, *Inside Job: The Looting of America's Savings and Loans* (New York: HarperCollins, 1991); and Kirstin Downey Grimsley, "After Closing Many Doors, RTC Shuts Its Own," *The Washington Post,* 29 December 1995, p. D1.

57. Bartlett, op. cit.; and Anders, op. cit.

58. Burrough and Helyar, op. cit.; and the 1993 HBO movie with the same title starring James Garner.

59. Barlett and Steele, op. cit.; Burrough and Helyar, op. cit.; Paul Farhi, "Getting a Grip on Debt, Time Warner Owes $18.5 Billion," *The Washington Post*, 25 June 1995, p. H1; American Bankruptcy Institute, "1994 Personal and Business Bankruptcies," mimeo, 1995; and Anders, op. cit.

60. For instance, Manville declared bankruptcy in order to shield its corporate assets from impending settlements from asbestos class action suits. See Delaney, op. cit., chap. 3; and Stein, op. cit., chap. 8.

61. Securities Data Company, "Merger and Corporate Transactions Database," cited in "Mergers and Acquisitions—Summary," reported in table 884, *1998 Statistical Abstract of the United States* (Washington, D.C.: U.S. Government Printing Office, 1999), p. 556; *The Economist*, "After the Deal," 9 January 1999, p. 21; and Sandra Sugawara, "Merger Wave Accelerated in 1999," *The Washington Post*, 31 December 1999, p. E1.

62. Quoted in Sugawara, op. cit., p. E1. The enormous corporate debt service obligations are currently not a significant problem due to robust earnings, relatively modest interest rates, substantial stock appreciation, and continuous macroeconomic growth. In fact, profits of U.S. companies are currently reported at four times their net interest expenses, which are up from two times in the early 1990s. Even so, concern over bloated debt interest payments is mounting. Defaults on corporate bonds jumped from 0.7 percent in 1997 to 2.9 percent in 1999. See Richard Siklos and Catherine Yang, "Welcome to the 21st Century," *Business Week*, 24 January 2000, pp. 36–44; Securities Data Company, op. cit., p. 556; and Zuckerman, op. cit., p. 1.

63. Author's emphasis as quoted in *The Economist*, op. cit., p. 21.

64. Quoted in Brett D. Fromson, "Warren Buffett, Taking Stock: Berkshire Hathaway's Chairman Rides a Bull Market to the Top of the Billionaires' Club," *The Washington Post*, 4 September 1993, p. B1.

65. Forbes Rich List Index, "Forbes Richest People in America—1999," at www. forbes.com. Also see Isaac Shapiro and Robert Greenstein, *The Widening Income Gulf* (Washington, D.C.: Center on Budget and Policy Priorities, 1999), pp. 10–11, available at www.cbpp.org; Edward B. Wolff, "Top Heavy: A Study of the Increasing Inequality of Wealth in America" (New York, a Twentieth Century Fund Report, 1999); Dinesh D'souza, "The Billionaire Next Door," *Forbes*, 11 October 1999, pp. 50–61.

66. Fromson, op. cit., p. B1; *Forbes*, "The Billionaires," 17 July 1995, pp. 110–223; *Forbes*, "America's Highest-Paid Bosses," 22 May 1995, pp. 180–182; Stephen Taub and David Carey, "The Wall Street 100," *Financial World*, 5 July 1994, p. 33; and Lee Nathans Spiro and Ronald Grover, "The Operator: An Inside Look at Ron Perelman's $5 Billion Empire," *Business Week*, 21 August 1995, pp. 54–59. Also see Anthony Bianco, "Charles Wang, Software's Tough Guy," *Business Week*, 6 March 2000, pp. 132–144; and AFL-CIO, "Worker Fact Sheet," 2000.

67. Kevin Phillips, *The Politics of Rich and Poor: Wealth and the American Electorate in the Reagan Aftermath* (New York: HarperCollins, 1991), pp. 179–180; U.S. Bureau of Labor Statistics, *Employment and Earnings* (June issues), reported in table 692, "Average Hourly and Weekly Earnings," *1998 Statistical Abstract of the United States* (Washington, D.C.: U.S. Government Printing Office, 1999), p. 434, at www.stats.bls.gov; quoted in Steven Pearlstein, "U.S. Finds Productivity, but Not Pay, Is Rising," *The Washington Post*, 11 January 1995, p. A1; Steven Pearlstein, "Wages Lag Worker Productivity," *The Washington Post*, 25 June 1995, p. 23; and AFL-CIO, "Worker Fact Sheet," 2000.

68. U.S. Bureau of the Census, "Per Capita Money Income" and "Money Income of Families," reported in tables 755 and 746, *1998 Statistical Abstract of the United States* (Washington, D.C.: U.S. Government Printing Office, 1999), pp. 476, 472, at www.census. gov/hhes/income; Braun, op. cit.; Kevin Phillips, *Boiling Point: Democrats, Republicans, and the Decline of Middle-Class Prosperity* (New York: Random House, 1993); Kevin Phillips, *The Politics of Rich and Poor: Wealth and the American Electorate in the Reagan Aftermath* (New York: HarperCollins, 1991); Shapiro and Greenstein, op. cit.; Gary Burtless and Timothy Smeeding, "America's Tide: Lifting the Yachts, Swamping the Rowboats," *The Washington Post*, 25 June 1995, p. C3; and Harrison and Bluestone, op. cit.

69. U.S. Congressional Budget Office Memorandum, "Estimates of Federal Tax Liabilities for Individuals and Families by Income Category and Family Type for 1995 and 1999," Washington, D.C. (May 1998). For a discussion of methodological issues and impact of various personal income tax laws during this period, see Shapiro and Greenstein, op. cit.

70. The importance of personal savings nearly doubled in this period. For each dollar of national savings, personal savings contributed $0.59 in the 1960s and $0.77 in the 1970s before jumping to $1.24 in the 1980s due to the large budget deficits of the public sector. See U.S. Congress, Congressional Budget Office, *Assessing the Decline in the National Saving Rate* (Washington, D.C.: U.S. Government Printing Office, 1993), pp. 4–5; and U.S. Department of Commerce, Bureau of Economic Analysis, *Survey of Current Business*, summarized in "U.S. Personal Savings Rate 1929–1998," at www.asec.org, and "U.S. Personal Saving Rate," at www.bea.doc.gov/briefrm/saving.

71. On "liberal" U.S. immigration policy and its relationship to U.S. industrial restructuring, see Robert D. Manning and Anita Butera, "Global Restructuring and U.S.-Mexican Economic Integration: Rhetoric and Reality of Mexican Immigration Five Years After NAFTA," special issue "Globalization, Transnationalism, and the End of the American Century," *American Studies*, vol. 41, nos. 2–3 (Summer/Fall 2000), pp. 183–209. For an empirical analysis, see Robert D. Manning, "U.S. Industrial Restructuring, Immigrant Workers, and the American State: The Political Economy of Mexican Migration," Ph.D. dissertation, Department of Sociology, Johns Hopkins University (Baltimore, 1989), chaps. 6–8. Also see

George J. Borjas, *Heaven's Door: Immigration Policy and the American Economy* (Princeton: Princeton University Press, 1999).

72. U.S. industrial restructuring had a particularly deleterious impact on low-educated, semiskilled, blue-collar workers—regardless of race or ethnicity. For example, the proportion of white men in the prime of their work careers (25–54) with 12 years of education who earned less than $12,000 (1987 dollars) rose from 6.5 percent in 1973 to 8.9 percent in 1979 and then jumped to 15.0 percent in 1987. Similarly, among comparable black workers, the proportion climbed from 15.8 percent in 1973 to 21.8 percent in 1979 and then 36.5 percent in 1987. Latino men exhibited the same trend, from 13.1 percent in 1973 to 16.8 percent in 1979 and then leaping to 27.0 percent in 1987. See Sheldon Danzinger and Gregory Acs, *Educational Attainment, Industrial Structure, and Male Earnings, 1973–1987* (Madison, Wis.: Institute for Research on Poverty, 1990); U.S. Congress, Congressional Budget Office, *Displaced Workers: Trends in the 1980s and Implications for the Future* (Washington, D.C.: U.S. Government Printing Office, 1993); Frank Levy, *The New Dollars and Dreams: American Incomes and Economic Change* (New York: Russell Sage, 1998); Braun, op. cit.; Lawrence Mishel, Jared Bernstein, and John Schmitt, *The State of Working America* (Ithaca: Cornell University Press, 1999); and Gordon, op. cit.

73. U.S. Bureau of Labor Statistics, *Monthly Labor Review,* November 1997, cited in "Employment Projections, by Occupation: 1996 and 2006," reported in table 673, *1998 Statistical Abstract of the United States* (Washington, D.C.: U.S. Government Printing Office, 1999), p. 420; and George Silvestri and John Lukasiewicz, "Outlook: 1990–2005, Occupational Employment Projections," *Monthly Labor Review*, November 1991, pp. 64–94.

74. The successful drive of U.S. corporations to raise the returns on investment while servicing their spiraling debt obligations has featured various combinations of the following: increase production efficiency through modernization of plant and equipment (Owens-Illinois), raise prices through joint ventures or acquisition of competitors (RJR Nabisco), diversify into highly profitable, unrelated industries (Beatrice), lobby for direct public subsidies and lower tax rates (1981–1982 tax reform acts), and "reorganize" the labor market for reducing per-unit labor costs (Safeway Stores). The last strategy, both facilitated and necessitated by the LBO wave of the 1980s, has most profoundly affected U.S. labor relations in general and household indebtedness in particular.

75. Quoted in Anders, op. cit., p. 184; and McGowan quoted in Susan C. Faludi, "The Safeway LBO Yields Vast Profits but Exacts a Heavy Human Toll," *The Wall Street Journal*, 16 May 1990, p. 1.

76. Steven N. Kaplan, "Taking Stock of the RJR Nabisco Buyout," *The Wall Street Journal*, 30 March 1995, p. 1; and quoted in Delaney, op. cit., p. 96.

77. By creating an international labor compensation index, with 1999 U.S. rates set at 100 (adjusted for exchange rate fluctuations), the U.S. Department of Labor estimated that the following countries featured higher labor costs in goods-production occupations: unified Germany (136), Norway (125), Switzerland (123), Denmark (120), Belgium (119), Austria (114), Sweden (112), Finland (110), Netherlands (109), and Japan (109). See U.S. Bureau of Labor Statistics, "International Comparisons of Hourly Compensation Costs for Production Workers in Manufacturing" (Washington, D.C.: U.S. Government Printing Office, September 2000), available at www.stats.bls.gov.flshome. Also see U.S. Bureau of Labor Statistics, *Employment and Monthly Earnings,* vol. 47, no. 1, January 2000, p. 219. Also see U.S. Bureau of Labor Statistics, "Civilian Labor Force and Participation Rates, with Projections: 1980 to 2006," reported in table 645, *1998 Statistical Abstract of the United States* (Washington, D.C.: U.S. Government Printing Office, 1999), p. 714 and p. 403.

78. Bryan Burrough, "Barbarians in Retreat," *Vanity Fair,* March 1993, pp. 190–230; Eva Jacobs and Stephanie Shipp, "How Family Spending Has Changed in the U.S.," *Monthly*

Labor Review, March 1990, pp. 20–27; Kevin Phillips, *Boiling Point: Democrats, Republicans, and the Decline of Middle-Class Prosperity* (New York: Random House, 1993); and Friedman, op. cit., p. 57.

79. Faludi, op. cit., p. 1; "The Vanishing Dream: Upward Mobility Is No Longer Possible for Millions of American Workers," *U.S. News & World Report*, 22 April 1991, pp. 39–43; Barlett and Steele, op. cit.; Joseph Berger, "The Pain of Layoffs for Ex-Senior I.B.M. Workers," *The New York Times*, 22 December 1993, p. B1; quoted in Mark Leibovich, "The High-Tech Homeless: In Silicon Valley, a Dark Side to the Booming Economy," *The Washington Post*, 12 February 2000, p. A13; and Abby Goodnough, "The Day the Jobs Got Up and Moved Away," *The New York Times*, 23 July 1995, p. A13.

80. See Gary Hendricks and Kenwood C. Youmans with Janet Keller, *Consumer Durables and Installment Debt: A Study of American Households* (Ann Arbor, Mich.: Institute for Social Research, 1973), p. 156.

81. Glenn B. Canner and Charles A. Luckett, "Payment of Household Debts," *Federal Reserve Bulletin*, April 1991, pp. 218–229. The largest increase was due to mortgage debt—from 47.3 to 63.1 percent. See also Zuckerman, op. cit., p. 1; U.S. Federal Reserve System, *Flow of Funds Accounts*, March 1998, reported in table 799, "Flow of Funds Accounts—Liabilities of Households," *1998 Statistical Abstract of the United States* (Washington, D.C.: U.S. Government Printing Office, 1999), p. 515; and Federal Reserve, "Consumer Credit," at www.bog.frb.fed.us.

82. The monthly *Federal Reserve Bulletin* reports revolving and nonrevolving consumer debt levels. See Federal Reserve's Statistical Release "Consumer Credit," which is available at www.bog.frb.fed.us. For an explanation of the Federal Reserve Board's reported revolving consumer debt levels and more precise estimates (downward adjustment of 14 percent), see note 26 of Chapter 1.

Chapter 3

1. Gary Silverman and Leah Nathans Spiro, "Citicorp and Travelers: Is This Marriage Working?" *Business Week*, 7 June 1999, pp. 127–134.

2. At the time of the merger, Citicorp reported 93,700 employees with $310.9 billion of corporate assets; in 1997, revenues were $21.6 billion and profits were $4.1 billion. Its corporate partner, Travelers Group, reported 68,000 employees with $386.6 billion of corporate assets; in 1997, revenues were $27.1 billion and profits were $3.4 billion. See Amy Feldman, "Shareholders Embrace Citi/Travelers Pairing," *Daily News*, 23 July 1998, p. 39; and Hoover's Inc., *Hoover's Online*, 11 December 1999, at www.hoovers.com.

3. "Merger: Who's Next," *Dow Jones News Service*, 13 April 1998; Feldman, op. cit., p. 39; and Gary A. Dymski, *The Bank Merger Wave: The Economic Causes and Social Consequences of Financial Consolidation* (Armonk, N.Y.: M. E. Sharpe, 1999), chap. 9. On September 13, 2000, Chase Manhattan acquired J.P. Morgan in a $35.2 billion deal. The new company is called J.P. Morgan Chase & Co. and ranks behind only Citigroup with combined assets of nearly $700 billion. A week earlier, Citigroup announced its acquisition of consumer finance giant Associated First Capital in a mammoth $31.0 billion deal. See Noelle Knox, "Banking Titans Bury Hatchet in $35 B Deal," *USA Today*, 14 September 2000, p. B1.

4. The historical impetus for these statutory barriers was the 1929 depression when financial institutions did not separate their commercial and investment-banking activities. This financial Armageddon was exacerbated when banks sought to control their losses in the stock market by using their depositors' savings as a backup reserve. However, the bank depositors also wanted to use their own money to control personal losses in the stock market. It was this confluence of cash demands that devastated U.S. financial markets and led to the collapse of the private banking system.

5. A key statutory loophole was provided by the Bank Holding Company Act of 1956, which excludes nonbanks from its regulatory purview. At its inception, it was enacted to rescind an exception to laws against interstate banking granted in the 1930s to Transamerica, a holding company that an insurer formed in 1928. In essence, it prohibited bank alliances with insurance companies. However, since Travelers Group was not a commercial bank, its application to become a bank holding company did not conflict with restrictions imposed on traditional banks engaging in other nonbank activities. Thus, it offered a legal justification for circumventing interstate banking restrictions. It is for this reason that Travelers was granted a two-year exception in its acquisition of Citicorp. For a discussion of these legal issues, see Jonathan R. Macey and Geoffrey P. Miller, *Banking Law and Regulation* (New York: Aspen Publishers, 1997), chap. 4; and Stephen Biggar, "Industry Surveys: Banking," *Standard & Poor's*, vol. 166, no. 24, sec. 1 (11 June 1998), pp. 11–12.

6. For a summary of grassroots political opposition to the merger, see Matthew Lee, "The First Comment ICP Filed with the Federal Reserve Board Opposing the Citicorp-Travelers Merger," *Inner City Press*, available at www.innercitypress.org/.

7. The 1933 act established the Federal Deposit Insurance Corporation (FDIC) and denied banks the legal ability to engage in investment banking, especially the sale of security-based investment products. By preventing banks from purchasing large blocks of stock and then reselling them in smaller blocks at a profit, this regulation sought to protect individual investors as well as the FDIC from bank failure due to speculative investments. See Macey and Miller, op. cit., chaps. 3, 6; Davita Silfen Glasberg and Dan Skidmore, *Corporate Welfare Policy and the Welfare State: Bank Deregulation and the Savings and Loan Bailout* (New York: Aldine de Gruyter, 1997), chap. 2; and Dymski, op. cit., chap. 3.

8. Quoted in Silverman and Spiro, op. cit., p. 134.

9. Citigroup, "Citigroup Reports Record Core Income for the Fourth Quarter and for 1999," Citigroup news release, 18 January 2000; "Citigroup Reports Record Core Income for the First Quarter," Citigroup news release, 17 April 2000; Citigroup, "Citicorp and Travelers Group to Merge," Citigroup news release, 6 April 1998, available at www.citibank.com; and Bob Violino, "Banking on E-Business," *Information Week*, 3 May 1999, pp. 1–6.

10. Associated Press, "$70 Billion Deal: Citicorp, Travelers to Merge," *Seattle Times*, 6 April 1998, p. D1; and Hoover's Inc., *Hoover's Online*, 11 December 1999, at www. hoovers.com.

11. James Surowiecki, "Mindless Merging," *The Motley Fool Slate Archives*, 23 April 1998, available at www.slate.msn.com/motleyfool/.

12. For empirical examination of the "big is better" assumption, see Dymski, op. cit., chaps. 4 and 6; and "Merger Mania, Sobering Statistics," *The Economist*, 20 June 1998, p. 89.

13. Quoted in Jon Friedman, "Travelers Group–Citicorp Merger May Mean Higher Prices," *Bloomberg News*, 7 April 1998, p. 1.

14. The relaxation of the 1933 Glass-Steagall Act's regulatory restrictions began in 1987 when banks were allowed to earn up to 5 percent of their revenues from securities underwriting; the limit was raised to 10 percent in 1989 and to 25 percent in late 1996. These statutory changes precipitated the new wave of bank takeovers. In 1997, commercial banks that acquired investment banks included Bankers Trust New York Corp. (Alex. Brown Inc.), NationsBank Corp. (Montgomery Securities), First Union Corp. (Wheat First Butcher Singer), and BankAmerica Corp. (Robertson Stephens). Similarly, Banc One acquired credit card issuer First USA in 1997, and First Union acquired the Money Store (home equity lender) in 1998. See Biggar, op. cit., pp. 9, 11; and Dymski, op. cit., p. 54.

15. Linda Punch, "Citicorp: Where Does the Giant Go from Here?" *Credit Card Management*, October 1991, p. 42; John Meehan, "All That Plastic Is Still Fantastic for Citibank," *Business Week*, 28 May 1990, p. 90; and Joseph Nocera, *A Piece of the Action: How the Middle Class Joined the Money Class* (New York: Simon & Schuster, 1994), p. 303.

16. A brief corporate history of Citicorp is available at www.citibank.com. Also, earlier periods are competently discussed in Richard B. Miller, *Citicorp: The Story of a Bank in Crisis* (New York: McGraw-Hill, 1993).

17. Nocera, op. cit., pp. 140–143; Miller, op. cit., pp. 87–93.

18. Miller, op. cit., p. 96.

19. The subcommittee chairman, Senator Frank Church, requested that the subpoenaed banks reveal the specific amount of their OPEC deposits; Citicorp, Chase Manhattan, Bank of America, J.P. Morgan, and other major banks refused to comply. They argued that the deposits would be withdrawn if their confidentiality was compromised. See Miller, op. cit., pp. 96–106.

20. Miller, op. cit., chap. 7; Robert A. Hutchinson, *Off the Books* (New York: William Morrow, 1986); and Roy Rowan, "The Maverick Who Yelled Foul at Citibank," *Fortune*, 10 January 1983, pp. 46–56.

21. For example, the U.S. Justice Department has been investigating whether Citibank allegedly devised money-laundering schemes on behalf of Raul Salinas de Gortari, brother of the former president of Mexico. *The New York Times, The Washington Post,* and other major newspapers have reported that over $100 million was reputedly channeled through his private Citibank accounts from Mexico to Switzerland and the Cayman Islands. See Lee, op. cit., pp. 14–15.

22. The Depository Institutions Deregulation Committee (DIDC), headed by U.S. Secretary of the Treasury Donald Regan, failed in its attempts to double the passport savings rate to 10 1/4 percent in 1981. Pressures from the thrift industry to maintain low, fixed passport rates prevailed until the passage of the Garn–St. Germain Depository Institutions Act of 1982. The law deregulated the savings and loan industry and allowed thrifts to engage in most of the same activities as commercial banks. This resulted in enormous fraud, mismanagement, hundreds of insolvent thrifts, and the huge federal bailout—estimated as high as $500 billion over 40 years. See Nocera, op. cit., pp. 207–228. Also, Glasberg and Skidmore, op. cit., p. 1.

23. A special tax loophole (since abolished by the 1986 Tax Reform Act) virtually eliminated U.S. corporate tax liabilities on interest revenue derived from foreign loans. This provision enabled Citicorp to pay a tax rate of only 1.8 percent in 1985. Hence, loans made by U.S. banks to developing nations were basically subsidized by American taxpayers—twice. First, the corporate tax rate was low while these loans were generating high corporate profits. Second, these delinquent loans effectively shielded other highly profitable revenues from federal taxation by reducing net corporate income. See Karin Lissakers, *Banks, Borrowers, and the Establishment: A Revisionist Account of the International Debt Crisis* (New York: Basic Books, 1991).

24. U.S. Congressional Budget Office, *The Changing Business of Banking: A Study of Failed Banks from 1987 to 1992* (Washington, D.C.: U.S. Government Printing Office, 1994), p. 12; and Miller, op. cit., pp. 108–114.

25. *Business Week,* "Corporate Scoreboard," 16 March 1987, pp. 125–146; *Moody's Handbook of Common Stock* (New York: Moody's Investors Service), 1976–1983; and *Citicorp Annual Report 1989* (New York: Citicorp, 1990).

26. Brazil led the push by suspending interest payments on all of its foreign debt obligations in February 1987; the subsequent demands of other countries to restructure their international-held debts resulted in Citicorp's placing $3.8 billion of its intermediate and long-term outstandings on a cash basis. This action reduced Citicorp's after-tax earnings by $200 million in 1987 and forced the bank to increase its financial reserves by $3 billion in May 1987. For the year, Citicorp reported a record loss of almost $1.2 billion. Although Citicorp reduced its Third World exposure by $1.3 billion, it still held $11.7 billion in cross-border and foreign-currency outstandings in its refinancing portfolio at the beginning of 1987. See *Citicorp Annual Report 1989* (New York: Citicorp, 1990); U.S. Congress, Congressional Budget Office, op. cit., p. 12; and Miller, op. cit., pp. 109–111.

27. *Business Week,* "Corporate Scoreboard," 20 March 1989, pp. 62–116; *Moody's Handbook of Common Stock* (New York: Moody's Investors Service), 1987–1990; Miller, op. cit., pp. 35–36; *Citicorp Annual Report 1992* (New York: Citicorp, 1993), p. 41; *Business Week,* "Corporate Scoreboard," 18 March 1991, pp. 52–93; and *Business Week,* "Corporate Scoreboard," 16 March 1992, pp. 64–92.

28. The high prevailing interest rates of the early 1980s generated large losses on real estate partnerships. These "passive" losses were then syndicated by investors through shell corporations and then profitably "sold" to people with tax liabilities. Also, the Garn–St. Germain Depository Institutions Act of 1982 eliminated margin limits on real estate lending. This resulted in such intense competition for financing construction projects that little or no equity from borrowers was required, and even closing costs were often paid by the lender. See U.S. Congress, Congressional Budget Office, op. cit., pp. 16–17.

29. Robert S. McIntyre, Douglas P. Kelly, Bruce L. Fisher, David Wilhelm, and Helene Luce, *It's Working, but . . . The Resurgence of Business Investment and Corporate Income Taxes* (Washington, D.C.: Citizens for Tax Justice, 1989); Patrick Hendershott and Edward Kane, "Office Market Values During the Past Decade: How Distributed Have Appraisals Been?" Working Paper no. 4128, National Bureau of Economic Research, Cambridge, Mass., July 1992; and U.S. Congressional Budget Office, op. cit., pp. 17–18.

30. *Citicorp Annual Report 1993* (New York: Citicorp, 1994), pp. 35–40; and Miller, op. cit., pp. 36–37.

31. The global financial group that includes the geographic areas of Japan, Europe, and North America (JENA) reported a precipitous drop in net income—from $614 million in 1989 to a loss of $299 million in 1990. While this division registered flat revenue growth, its credit costs jumped from $318 million in 1989 to $1.45 billion in 1990. This was largely due to a half-billion-dollar increase in the commercial loan loss allowance, a jump in net write-offs, cost of carrying nonperforming assets, and expenses from "other real estate owned" (OREO). Furthermore, cash basis and renegotiated loans doubled to $4.9 billion while OREO expenses climbed $1 billion to a total of $1.3 billion at the end of 1990. U.S. real estate problems continued to mount as JENA's losses rose to $1.02 billion in 1991. From 1990 to 1991, total net credit losses on the U.S. portfolio more than doubled from $431 million to $941 million, and on U.S. commercial real estate lending jumped from $228 million to $511 million. See Miller, op. cit., pp. 36–37; *Citicorp Annual Report 1992* (New York: Citicorp, 1993), p. 29; and *Business Week,* "Corporate Scoreboard," 18 March 1991, pp. 52–93.

32. Robert J. McCartney and Kathleen Day, "Huge Fees May Have Blinded Trump's Lenders," *The Washington Post,* 26 June 1990, p. C1; Neil Barsky, "Trump to Ask Bondholders for Debt Relief," *The Wall Street Journal,* 26 July 1990, p. A3; Richard Karp, "The Donald's CFO," *Financial World,* 14 May 1991, pp. 27–29; "New Jersey Board Gives Trump Slight Nod," *The Washington Post,* 18 June 1991, p. C5; and Mitchell Pacelle, "Trump to Give Up Plaza Stake to Saudi Prince, Hotel Firm," 12 April 1995, *Dow Jones/News Retrieval.*

33. *Citicorp Annual Report 1993* (New York: Citicorp, 1994), p. 31.

34. In 1998, the market value of Prince Alwaleed's 41.1 million shares (4.8 percent of Citicorp stock) was nearly $10 billion. See Timothy L. O'Brien and Joseph B. Treaster, "Shaping a Colossus: Citicorp Plans Merger with Travelers Group," *The New York Times,* 7 April 1998, p. A1. For foreign policy objections to Prince Alwaleed and other sales to institutional investors, see Miller, op. cit., chap. 1.

35. After the 1981–1982 recession, Citicorp's debt as a percentage of its capitalization rose to perilously high levels: From 23 percent in 1983, it climbed to almost 29 percent in 1984 and then peaked at 31 percent in 1986 before stabilizing at about 29 percent through the end of the decade. By 1991, the situation was exacerbated with nearly one-fifth of its U.S. real estate loan portfolio in nonperforming statuses. See Dean Orser, "Citicorp Buyback Seen Paving

Way for Dividend Increase," 20 June 1995, *Dow Jones/News Retrieval;* "Citicorp Buyback, Analyst Sees Other Bank Buyback This Year," 20 June 1995, *Dow Jones/News Retrieval;* John Meehan and Leah Nathans Spiro, "Wanted: $5 Billion, Contact Citicorp," *Business Week,* 11 February 1991, pp. 64–65; Meehan, op. cit., pp. 90–92; and Punch, op. cit., pp. 42–51.

36. By the end of 1991, Citcorp's reserves were $3.3 billion and total capital was $17.1 billion. Only one year later, Citicorp's Tier I (5.88 percent) had nearly attained the well-capitalized threshold. See Punch, op. cit., pp. 42–43; *Citicorp Annual Report 1993* (New York: Citicorp, 1994), p. 48; Meehan and Spiro, op. cit., pp. 64–65; and Miller, op. cit., pp. 6–7 and 25–27.

37. *Moody's Handbook of Common Stock* (New York: Moody's Investors Service), 1994–1996.

38. Nocera, op. cit., pp. 197–198; and *Federal Reserve Bulletin, Annual Statistical Digest,* and time series of trends reported in "Money Market Interest Rates," U.S. Department of Commerce, *1993 Statistical Abstract of the United States* (Washington, D.C.: U.S. Government Printing Office, 1994), p. 525.

39. Nocera, op. cit., pp. 77–78; Kenneth Scott, "The Future of Bank Regulation," in John H. Moore (ed.), *To Promote Prosperity: U.S. Domestic Policy in the Mid-1980s* (Stanford, Calif.: Hoover Institution Press, 1984), pp. 260–262; and U.S. Congress, Congressional Budget Office, *The Changing Business of Banking: A Study of Failed Banks from 1987 to 1992* (Washington, D.C.: U.S. Government Printing Office, 1994), pp. 7–11.

40. Dymski, op. cit.; James Barth, R. Dan Brumbaugh, Jr., and Robert E. Litan, *The Future of American Banking* (New York: M. E. Sharpe, 1992), pp. 63–65; and U.S. Congress, Congressional Budget Office, op. cit., pp. 7–11.

41. Nocera, op. cit., pp. 126–127 and 257–259; Lewis Mandell, *The Credit Card Industry: A History* (Boston: Twayne Publishers, 1990), pp. 49–51; and Scott, op. cit., p. 264.

42. The U.S. Supreme Court recognized the broader implications of its ruling, 439 U.S. 299 (1978), when it declared: "'Close examination of the National Bank Act of 1864 . . . makes clear that, contrary to the suggestion of petitioners, Congress intended to facilitate . . . a "national banking system. . . ." Petitioners' final argument is that the "exportation" of interest rates . . . will significantly impair the ability of States to enact effective usury laws. This impairment, however, has always been implicit in the structure of the National Bank Act . . . [and] may be accentuated by the ease with which interstate credit is available by mail through the use of modern credit cards. . . . [T]he protection of state usury laws is an issue of legislative policy and . . . is better addressed to the wisdom of Congress than to the judgment of this Court.'" Quoted in Macey and Miller, op. cit., p. 196. Also see Nocera, op. cit., pp. 194–197; and Mandell, op. cit., pp. 75–76.

43. Nocera, op. cit., pp. 126–127.

44. The remaining financial assets were held by other depositories such as life insurance firms and nondepository institutions such as finance companies, automobile companies, retail department stores, and telephone companies. See Roger Vaughan and Edward Hill, *Banking on the Brink* (Washington, D.C.: Washington Post Company, 1992), p. 19; Herbert L. Baer and Larry R. Mote, *The U.S. Financial System* (Chicago: Federal Reserve Bank, 1990); and U.S. Congressional Budget Office, op. cit., p. 8.

45. U.S. Congress, Congressional Budget Office, op. cit., p. 11; Frederick T. Furlong and Michael C. Keeley, "Capital Regulation and Bank Risk-Taking: A Note," *Journal of Banking and Finance,* November 1989, pp. 883–891; *Citicorp Annual Report 1993* (New York: Citicorp, 1994), pp. 13–20 and 44–77; and "U.S. Banks Fourth Quarter Derivatives Activity Remains at $15 Trillion," 31 March 1995, *Dow Jones/News Retrieval.*

46. Overall, the volume of off-balance-sheet items was four times greater than the volume of balance-sheet items in 1989, and fee income (percentage of total income before operating costs) from these activities rose from 20 percent in 1979 to 33 percent in 1991. This proportion was even higher for Citicorp in the 1990s. Also, the category of "fees, commis-

sions, and other revenues" exceeded "net interest revenues" for the first time during the 1990s. See Eileen Maloney and George Gregorash, "Banking 1989: Not Quite a Twice-Told Tale," *Economic Perspectives*, Federal Reserve Bank of Chicago (July-August 1990); John H. Boyd and Mark Gertler, "U.S. Commercial Banking: Trends, Cycles, and Policy," Working Paper no. 4404, National Bureau of Economic Research, Cambridge, Mass. (July 1993); and *Citicorp Annual Report 1993* (New York: Citicorp, 1994).

47. "Citigroup Reports Record Core Income for the Fourth Quarter and for 1999," Citigroup news release, 18 January 2000; "Citigroup Reports Record Core Income for the First Quarter," Citigroup news release, 17 April 2000, available at www.citibank.com; and Silverman and Spiro, op. cit., pp. 129–130.

48. The stock market conversion price of Citigroup includes two important adjustments. First, the merger entailed a 5-for-2 stock swap of Citicorp (NYSE: CCI) for the new Citigroup (NYSE: C). Second, Citigroup declared a 3-for-2 stock split on April 20, 1999. Hence, the Citigroup price must be multiplied by 3.75 (2.5 x 1.5) to yield an equivalent premerger Citicorp stock price. For example, at the end of June 2000, Citigroup stock was trading at $64. This is equivalent to an old Citicorp stock price of $64 x 3.75, or $240. On August 25, 2000, Citigroup offered a 4-for-3 stock split to shareholders and announced the repurchase of $5 billion in common stock. See "Citigroup Declares 4-3 Stock Split," July 19, 2000, at www.citibank.com/corporate affairs.

49. David Halberstam, *The Fifties* (New York: Ballantine Books, 1994); Mandell, op. cit., p. xvii; Nocera, op. cit., p. 137; and the monthly *Federal Reserve Bulletin*, which reports revolving and nonrevolving consumer debt levels. See *Federal Reserve Statistical Release*, "Consumer Credit," available at www.bog.frb.fed.us.

50. Nocera, op. cit., p. 306; Mandell, op. cit., pp. 48–49.

51. Nocera, op. cit., pp. 24–33.

52. Joseph Nocera, "The Day the Credit Card Was Born," *Washington Post Magazine*, 4 December 1994, pp. 15–17 and 39–43; Nocera, *A Piece of the Action*, pp. 23–33; and Mandell, op. cit., pp. 23–33.

53. Nocera, "The Day the Credit Card Was Born," p. 42; and Nocera, *A Piece of the Action*, pp. 38–31.

54. Nocera, *A Piece of the Action*, p. 33; and Mandell, op. cit., pp. 33–40.

55. Nocera, *A Piece of the Action*, pp. 56–57; and Mandell, op. cit., pp. 30–32.

56. Mandell, op. cit., pp. 33–35.

57. Nocera, *A Piece of the Action*, p. 62; and Mandell, op. cit., p. 35.

58. U.S. Bureau of Labor Statistics, *Handbook of Labor Statistics*, cited in "Consumer Price Indexes (CPI-U), by Major Groups: 1939–1997," table 772, *1998 Statistical Abstract of the United States* (Washington, D.C.: U.S. Government Printing Office, 1999). For credit card balances in the early 1970s, see Lewis Mandell, *Credit Card Use in the United States* (Ann Arbor, Mich.: Institute for Social Research, 1972).

59. See *Federal Reserve Statistical Release*, "Consumer Credit," available at www. bog.frb.fed.us.

60. Nocera, *A Piece of the Action*, pp. 100–105; and Mandell, *The Credit Card Industry*, pp. 62–64.

61. In 1971, NBI passed an amendment to its bylaws (Bylaw 216) to prevent any of its members from offering both BankAmericard and Master Charge cards. Worthen Bank Trust Company of Little Rock, Arkansas, filed suit in U.S. District Court under sections 4 and 16 of the Clayton Act arguing that NBI was in violation of the Sherman Antitrust Act. After five years of costly litigation and strong pressure from the U.S. Department of Justice, NBI finally discontinued its opposition to duality in 1976. As a result, banks currently offer their customers both Visa and MasterCard accounts. See Nocera, *A Piece of the Action*, p. 144; and Mandell, *The Credit Card Industry*, pp. 40–42.

62. Nocera, *A Piece of the Action,* pp. 142–148; and Mandell, *The Credit Card Industry,* pp. 37–40.

63. See note 42.

64. Quoted in Nocera, *A Piece of the Action,* p. 194.

65. Ibid., p. 192. Also, Mandell, *The Credit Card Industry,* pp. 48–49.

66. Nocera, *A Piece of the Action,* pp. 195–196; and Mandell, *The Credit Card Industry,* pp. 75–78.

67. The *Federal Reserve Bulletin* reports revolving and nonrevolving consumer debt levels by month since January 1943. See *Federal Reserve Statistical Release,* "Consumer Credit," available at www.bog.frb.fed.us.

68. According to Lewis Mandell, the Federal Reserve's functional cost analysis data indicate that "net pretax margins on bank credit card debt were positive from 1972 to 1979 [but] the return was significantly below that on other types of bank debt. Many banks actually lost money on their credit card operations during this period, as did the industry as a whole in the inflationary period from 1979 to 1981." See Mandell, *The Credit Card Industry,* pp. 74–75.

69. The problem was the huge advantage that American Express had in its client base: about 15 million cardholders versus only about 2 million members of Diners Club in 1985. The gap was smaller in international markets; American Express had almost 5 million cardholders compared with nearly 3 million for Diners Club. Between 1983 and 1985, Citibank spent over $70 million in its campaign to promote the Diners Club charge card. In 1984, Citibank embarked on a direct marketing campaign for Diners in order to expand its preferred customer base: business travelers. The mass mailing began, "Frankly, Citicorp Diners Club wants your business, and we are willing to work for it!" Citicorp also offered popular inducements to join Diners, such as free Citicorp traveler's checks and round-trip airline travel to any destination in the United States (including Hawaii and the U.S. Virgin Islands) for $175. See Monci Jo Williams, "The Great Plastic Card Fight Begins," *Fortune,* 4 February 1985, pp. 18–23.

70. Nocera, *A Piece of the Action,* pp. 143–148; and Meehan, op. cit., pp. 90–92.

71. The prestige hierarchy of Citibank Visa cards ranges from no-frills Choice for price-sensitive customers to Citibank Classic and then the preferred or elite Gold and Platinum cards. Today, the least prestigious account is the "fall from grace" (secured) credit card. This is for cardholders whose credit history is so poor that they are considered too high of a risk for an unsecured consumer loan. With an annual average of over 1.2 million bankruptcies between 1995 and 1999, this is a growing market niche. See Chapter 5.

72. U.S. Federal Reserve System, *Federal Reserve Bulletins*; U.S. Federal Reserve System, *Annual Statistical Digests*; and U.S. Department of Commerce, *1999 Statistical Abstract of the United States* (Washington, D.C.: U.S. Government Printing Office, 2000); and CardWeb, "Rates Stand Still," June 2000, at www.cardweb.com.

73. U.S. Bureau of Labor Statistics, *Handbook of Labor Statistics,* reported in table 772, "Consumer Price Indexes (CPI-U), by Major Groups: 1939–1997," p. 489; and U.S. Bureau of the Census, *Current Population Reports,* P60–197, reported in table 754, "Per Capita Money Income," *1998 Statistical Abstract of the United States* (Washington, D.C.: U.S. Government Printing Office, 1999), p. 476, at www.census.gov/hhes/income.

74. U.S. Federal Reserve System, *Federal Reserve Bulletins*; reported in table 798, "Consumer Credit—Installment Credit Finance Rates," p. 521, and table 807, "Money Market Interest Rates," *1998 Statistical Abstract of the United States* (Washington, D.C.: U.S. Government Printing Office, 1999), p. 525.

75. Lawrence M. Ausubel, "The Failure of Competition in the Credit Card Market," *American Economic Review,* vol. 81, no. 1 (March 1991), p. 70.

76. The percentage of credit card fraud to outstanding revolving credit fell from 0.16 percent in 1983 to 0.09 percent in 1988. The dramatic expansion of credit card accounts in

the 1990s, however, contributed to escalating fraud as it jumped from $209 million (0.11 percent) in 1989 to $720 million (0.26 percent) in 1992. See George Ritzer, *Expressing America: A Critique of the Global Credit Card Society* (Thousand Oaks, Calif.: Pine Forge Press, 1995), pp. 98–106; and "Fraud Costs," *The Washington Post*, 31 March 1994, p. D12.

77. Federal Reserve Board, *Federal Reserve Statistical Release*, "Consumer Credit," available at www.bog.frb.fed.us.

78. Ausubel, op. cit., pp. 60–68.

79. CardWeb, "Profit Squeeze," CardTrak, October 1999, p. 3, available at www.cardweb.com.

80. Meehan, op. cit., p. 90; and Punch, op. cit., p. 42.

81. Punch, op. cit., p. 46; Meehan and Spiro, op. cit., pp. 64–65; and *Citicorp Annual Report 1994* (New York: Citicorp, 1995), pp. 50–53.

82. *Citigroup Annual Report 1998* (New York: Citicorp, 1999), p. 9; and O'Brien and Treaster, op. cit., p. A1.

83. Citigroup, "Citibank to Acquire Mellon Bank's Credit Card Business," *Citibank News*, 23 March 1999, pp. 1–2, available at www.citibank.com; AT&T, "Citibank Acquires AT&T Universal Card Services," AT&T news release, 18 December 1997, pp. 1–2, available at www.citibank.com; and Associated Press, "Citicorp Gets Gold Mine of Choice Sales Targets," *Ottawa Citizen*, 19 December 1997, p. D9.

84. CardWeb, "Market Power," CardTrak, February 2000, available at www.cardweb.com; and Mandell, *The Credit Card Industry*, p. 37.

85. Quoted in Associated Press, op. cit., p. D9; and Silverman and Spiro, op. cit., pp. 127–134.

86. Biggar, op. cit., p. 8.

Chapter 4

1. Isaac Shapiro and Robert Greenstein, *The Widening Income Gulf* (Washington, D.C.: Center on Budget and Policy Priorities, 1999), available at www.cbpp.org; and Lawrence Mishel, Jared Bernstein, and John Schmitt, *The State of Working America* (Ithaca: Cornell University Press, 1999).

2. Edward B. Wolff, *Top Heavy: A Study of the Increasing Inequality of Wealth in America* (New York: Twentieth Century Fund Report, 1999); Melvin L. Oliver and Thomas M. Shapiro, *Black Wealth, White Wealth: A New Perspective on Racial Inequality* (New York: Routledge, 1997). See also Dalton Conley, *Being Black, Living in the Red: Race, Wealth, and Social Policy in America* (Berkeley: University of California Press, 1999); and Michael Sherraden and Neil Gilbert, *Assets and the Poor: A New American Welfare Policy* (New York: M. E. Sharpe, 1991).

3. U.S. Department of Commerce, Bureau of Economic Analysis (BEA), *Survey of Current Business*, summarized in "U.S. Personal Savings Rate 1929–1998," at www.asec.org. Based on the BEA's traditional assumptions, the U.S. savings rate as a percentage of disposable personal income was about –1.2 percent for 1999 and about –3.0 percent for the first quarter of 2000. In 1999, this time series was revised due to criticism that the BEA measure did not reflect personal savings attributed to stock market assets, personal IRAs, and value of consumer durable goods such as household appliances and automobiles. The revised time series shows the same sharp downward trend based on this broader definition of personal savings—from 10.9 percent in 1982 to 3.7 percent in 1998 and about 0.5 percent in the first quarter of 2000; available at www.bea.doc.gov/brieffrm/saving. See Employee Benefit Research Institute (EBRI), "The Savings Paradox?" June 1999, at www.ebri.org/facts. Significantly, this more complex measure does not include the rising cost of financing outstanding consumer debt, which would lower the personal savings rate.

4. Quoted in Owen Ullmann, "Billionaire and Activist Give the Same Advice: Avoid Credit Cards," *USA Today,* 12 October 1999, p. A5.

5. *Forbes* estimates that Buffett with a $31 billion personal fortune ranks third behind MicroSoft founders Bill Gates and Paul Allen. See Dinesh D'Souza, "The Billionaire Next Door," *Forbes,* 11 October 1999, pp. 50–61; "The Forbes 400: A Century of Wealth," *Forbes,* 11 October 1999, p. 169; Bloomberg News, "Bond Sales Boost Berkshire," *Montreal Gazette,* 4 August 1998, p. C3; Roger Lowenstein, *Buffett: The Making of an American Capitalist* (New York: Random House, 1995); Brett D. Fromson, "Warren Buffett, Taking Stock: Berkshire Hathaway's Chairman Rides a Bull Market to the Top of the Billionaires' Club," *The Washington Post,* 4 September 1993, p. B1. Also see Table 2.3 for the 25 richest people in the United States.

6. Quoted in Owen Ullmann, "Billionaire and Activist Give the Same Advice: Avoid Credit Cards," *USA Today,* 12 October 1999, p. A5. See Jesse L. Jackson Sr., Jesse L. Jackson Jr., with Mary Gotschall, *It's About the Money: The Fourth Movement of the Freedom Symphony* (New York: Time Books, 2000).

7. Quoted in David M. Tucker, *The Decline of Thrift in America: Our Cultural Shift from Saving to Spending* (New York: Praeger, 1991), p. 2.

8. Quoted in Lewis Mandell, *The Credit Card Industry: A History* (Boston: Twayne Publishers, 1990), p. 12; also see chap. 2 for a review of early forms of credit and the distinction between types for consumption and for commerce. Also see Sidney Homer and Richard Sylla, *A History of Interest Rates* (New York: Rutgers University Press, 1996); Tucker, op. cit., chap. 1; Paul Einzig, *Primitive Money* (London: Erie and Spottiswoode, 1949); and Rolf Nugent, *Consumer Credit and Economic Stability* (New York: Russell Sage Foundation, 1939).

9. Henry Peacham, *The Worth of a Peny or a Caution to Keep Money* (London: S. Griffen, 1664), pp. 15 and 17, quoted in Tucker, op. cit., p. 8.

10. Leonard W. Labaree (ed.), *The Papers of Benjamin Franklin,* vol. 7 (New Haven: Yale University Press, 1963), pp. 342–347.

11. Ibid., pp. 342–347. Also see *The Autobiography of Benjamin Franklin,* edited by Leonard W. Labaree et al. (New Haven: Yale University Press, 1964), pp. 148–150; and J. E. Crowley, *This Sheba, Self: Conceptualization of Economic Life in Eighteenth-Century America* (Baltimore: Johns Hopkins University Press, 1979).

12. Tucker, op. cit., pp. 11–14; T. H. Breen, *Tobacco Culture: The Mentality of the Great Tidewater Planters on the Eve of Revolution* (Princeton: Princeton University Press, 1985); and Edmund S. Morgan, "The Puritan Ethic and the American Revolution," *William and Mary Quarterly,* vol. 24 (January 1967), pp. 3–15.

13. Max Weber, *The Protestant Ethic and the Spirit of Capitalism* (London: Unwin Hyman, 1930); Giafranco Poggi, *Calvinism and the Capitalist Spirit: Max Weber's Protestant Ethic* (Amherst: University of Massachusetts Press, 1983); and Gordon Marshall, *In Search of the Spirit of Capitalism* (London: Hutchinson, 1982).

14. See Tucker, op. cit., chap. 2. Also Stephen Foster, *Their Solitary Way: The Puritan Social Ethic in the First Century of Settlement in New England* (New Haven: Yale University Press, 1971), pp. 104–126; Philip Greven, *The Protestant Temperament* (New York: Alfred A. Knopf, 1977), pp. 13–50; and E. P. Thompson, "Time, Work-Discipline, and Industrial Capitalism," *Past and Present,* vol. 38 (December 1967), pp. 88–91.

15. Tucker, op. cit., p. 20.

16. Lendol Calder, *Financing the American Dream: A Cultural History of Consumer Credit* (Princeton: Princeton University Press, 1999); Tucker, op. cit., chap. 3; Alan Teck, *Mutual Saving Banks and Savings and Loan Associations* (New York: Columbia University Press, 1968); and Paul Johnson, *Saving and Spending: The Working-Class Economy in Britain 1870–1939* (Oxford: Clarendon Press, 1985).

17. Frances Fox Piven and Richard A. Cloward, *Regulating the Poor: The Functions of Public Welfare* (New York: Vintage Books, 1996), chap. 1.

18. Michael B. Katz, *Improving Poor People: The Welfare State, the "Underclass," and Urban Schools as History* (Princeton: Princeton University Press, 1997); Theda Skocpol, *Protecting Soldiers and Mothers: The Political Origins of Social Policy in the United States* (Cambridge: Harvard University Press, 1995); John Myles and and Jill Quadagno, *States, Labor Markets, and the Future of Old-Age Policy* (Philadelphia: Temple University Press, 1991); and Jill Quadagno, *The Transformation of Old-Age Security: Class and Politics in the American Welfare State* (Chicago: University of Chicago Press, 1988).

19. Horatio Alger Jr., as edited by Carl Bode, *Ragged Dick* (New York: Penguin Books, 1985).

20. The role of credit and savings in household subsistence and life-cycle strategies is examined in nineteenth-century Newburyport, Massachusetts, in Stephan Thernstrom, *Poverty and Progress: Social Mobility in a Nineteenth-Century City* (Cambridge: Harvard University Press, 1964). See also Tucker, op. cit., for an excellent review of this topic. For an insightful view of the symbiotic role of credit between small shopkeepers and working-class households, see Johnson, op. cit., chap. 6.

21. According to Tucker, op. cit., p. 51: "[L]aboring classes were apparently more concerned with respectability than large bank accounts. Typical families desired security and respect within their class more than upward mobility into the capitalist class."

22. Ivan H. Light and J. Steven Gold, *Ethnic Economies* (New York: Academic Press, 2000); Daniel Soyer, *Jewish Immigrant Associations and American Identity in New York, 1880–1939* (Cambridge: Harvard University Press, 1997); Tucker, op. cit., chap. 8; Alejandro Portes and Robert D. Manning, "The Immigrant Enclave: Theory and Empirical Examples," in Joan Nagel and Susan Olzak (eds.), *Ethnicity: Structure and Progress* (New York: Academic Press, 1986), pp. 47–68; and Michael J. Piore, *Birds of Passage: Migrant Labor and Industrial Societies* (New York: Cambridge University Press, 1979).

23. Charles O. Hardy (ed.), *Consumer Credit and Its Uses* (New York: Prentice-Hall, 1938), p. 127. See also Margaret G. Reid, *Consumers and the Market* (New York: F. S. Crofts, 1938); Calder, op. cit., chap. 1; Martha L. Olney, *Buy Now, Pay Later: Advertising, Credit, and Consumer Durables in the 1920s* (Chapel Hill: University of North Carolina Press, 1991), chap. 4.

24. For an excellent review of these programs as well as the mobilization of public schools and civic/fraternal organizations in this "patriotic" campaign, see Tucker, op. cit., chap. 7. For example, Tucker cites an elementary school play, *Save Your Pennies*, containing the stanza "'Save your pennies for a rainy day; It's not what you earn but what you put away,'" from Nan Oppenlander-Eberle, *Good Fairy Thrift* (Swarthmore: Chatauqua Association of Pennsylvania, 1917).

25. Raymond W. Goldsmith, *A Study of Savings in the United States*, vol. 1 (Princeton: Princeton University Press, 1955), p. 241.

26. See Calder, op. cit.; chaps. 3, 4; Pamela Walker Laird, *Advertising Progress: American Business and the Rise of Consumer Marketing* (Baltimore: Johns Hopkins University Press, 1998); Susan Strasser, Charles McGovern, and Matthias Judt (eds.), *Getting and Spending: European and American Consumer Societies in the Twentieth Century* (Cambridge: Cambridge University Press, 1998); William Leach, *Land of Desire: Merchants, Power, and the Rise of a New American Culture* (New York: Pantheon Books, 1993); Andrew R. Heinze, *Adapting to Abundance: Jewish Immigrants, Mass Consumption, and the Search for American Identity* (New York: Columbia University Press, 1990); Daniel Horowitz, *The Morality of Spending: Attitudes Toward the Consumer Society in America, 1875–1940* (Baltimore: Johns Hopkins University Press, 1985); and Richard W. Fox and Jackson Lears, *The Culture of Consumptionism: Critical Essays in American History* (New York: Pantheon Books, 1983).

27. Jackson Lears, *Fables of Abundance: A Cultural History of Advertising in America* (New York: Basic Books, 1994); Olney, op. cit., chap. 5; Susan Strasser, *Satisfaction Guaranteed: The Making of the American Mass Market* (Washington, D.C.: Smithsonian Institution Press, 1994); Carole Shammas, "Explaining Past Changes in Consumption and Consumer Behavior," *Historical Methods*, vol. 22 (Spring 1989), pp. 61–67; and Ronald Marchand, *Advertising the American Dream: Making Way for Modernity, 1920–1940* (Berkeley: University of California Press, 1985), chap. 5.

28. Milan V. Ayres, "Installment Selling and Its Financing: A Report by the Economic Policy Commission to the Executive Council and a Report to the Economic Policy Commission," American Bankers Association, 1926, quoted in Olney, op. cit., pp. 130–131.

29. According to Reid, op. cit., p. 247: "During the closing decade of the nineteenth century the practice of installment selling spread more rapidly and came to be widely used by house-to-house sellers. . . . [T]here was much fraud and deception in charges and in repossessions."

30. David J. Gallert, Walter S. Hilborn, and Geoffrey May, *Small Loan Legislation: A History of the Regulation of the Business of Lending Small Sums* (New York: Russell Sage Foundation, 1932); Louis N. Robinson and Rolf Nugent, *Regulation of the Small Loan Business* (New York: Russell Sage Foundation, 1935); and Irving S. Michelman, *Consumer Finance: A Case History in American Business* (New York: Frederick Fell, 1966). The 1916 law was a response to the ineffectiveness of state usury laws. It was developed by a national group of small lenders under the auspices of the Russell Sage Foundation. Lenders generally agreed to a maximum monthly interest rate (typically 3 percent), and by 1931 twenty-two state legislatures had passed small loan acts. For an excellent summary, see Olney, op. cit., pp. 132–133; Calder, op. cit., chap. 3; and Mandell, op. cit., chap. 2.

31. A key theoretical issue concerns the relative influence of institutional forces in shaping the material standard of living of middle-class America. That is, are corporate manufacturers and advertising agencies responsible for stimulating greater consumer demand for durable goods, or did it emerge from social pressures to redefine middle-class identity and the material foundation of the American Dream? For a perceptive view on this debate, see Martha L. Olney, "Demand for Consumer Durable Goods in 20th-Century America," *Explorations in Economic History*, vol. 27 (July 1990), pp. 322–349; and Shammas, op. cit., pp. 61–67.

32. Robert S. Lynd and Helen Merrell Lynd, *Middletown: A Study in Contemporary American Culture* (New York: Harcourt, Brace & Co., 1929), pp. 45–47.

33. Calder, op. cit., chap. 4; Olney, *Buy Now, Pay Later*; Nugent, *Consumer Credit and Economic Stability*; Hardy (ed.), op. cit.; and Reid, op. cit.

34. Frederick Lewis Allen, *Only Yesterday: An Informal History of the 1920s* (New York: Harper & Row, 1931), pp. 139–140.

35. These quotes were excerpted from articles published between 1926 and 1928 by William Clyde Phelps, *The Role of Sales Finance Companies in the American Economy* (Baltimore, Md.: Commercial Credit Company, 1952), pp. 39–40. Also see Calder, op. cit., chap. 5.

36. Mandell, op. cit., p. 17.

37. Robert S. Lynd and Helen Merrell Lynd, *Middletown in Transition* (New York: Harcourt, Brace & Co., 1937), pp. 479–481.

38. Parker Brothers, "Official Monopoly Game Rules," Beverly, Mass., Parker Brothers Company, 1995.

39. It is important to note that the 1940s saving rate includes personal contributions to the national retirement fund as mandated by the Social Security Act of 1935. Hence, comparisons to pre–Social Security Act years must recognize the forced matching payments of both workers and their employees after the enactment of this legislation.

40. Tucker, op. cit., p. 133.

41. John Maynard Keynes, *A Treatise on Money* (London: Macmillan, 1930); *The General Theory of Employment, Interest, and Money* (London: Macmillan, 1936); and *How to Pay for the War* (London: Macmillan, 1940).

42. David Halberstam, *The Fifties* (New York: Ballantine Books, 1994); David Harvey, *The Condition of Postmodernity* (Cambridge: Basil Blackwell, 1989); and Kenneth T. Jackson, *Crabgrass Frontier: The Suburbanization of the United States* (New York: Oxford University Press, 1985).

43. Joseph Nocera, *A Piece of the Action: How the Middle Class Joined the Money Class* (New York: Simon & Schuster, 1994), chaps. 3–5; and Mandell, op. cit., chap. 3.

44. See Chapter 3; also Marcy Gordon, "Credit Cards at 50: The Problems of Ubiquity," *The New York Times*, 12 March 2000, p. A11; Nocera, op. cit., chaps. 3–5; and Mandell, op. cit., chap. 3.

45. Melvyn Dubofsky, *The State and Labor in Modern America* (Chapel Hill: University of North Carolina Press, 1994); Bruce E. Kaufman, *The Origins and Evolution of the Field of Industrial Relations in the United States* (Ithaca, N.Y.: Industrial & Labor Relations Press, 1993); and Patricia Cayo Sexton, *The War on Labor and the Left* (Boulder, Colo.: Westview Press, 1991).

46. U.S. Department of Commerce, Bureau of Economic Analysis, *Survey of Current Business*, summarized in "U.S. Personal Savings Rate 1929–1998," at www.asec.org; and Mandell, op. cit., chap. 3.

47. Mandell, op. cit., chap. 3.

48. Gary Hendricks and Kenwood C. Youmans with Janet Keller, *Consumer Durables and Installment Debt: A Study of American Households* (Ann Arbor, Mich.: Institute for Social Research, 1973), chap. 7; and Lewis Mandell, *Credit Card Use in the United States* (Ann Arbor, Mich.: Institute for Social Research, 1972), pp. 7, 35, 50.

49. U.S. Department of Commerce, Bureau of Economic Analysis, *Survey of Current Business*, summarized in "U.S. Personal Savings Rate 1929–1998," at www.asec.org.

50. The game has been primarily marketed to young girls. For example, the cover photographs of the game feature four young, middle-class teenage girls cavorting in a mall with shopping bags; the backdrop photos include a rack of clothes, a music boom box, CDs, an easy-money credit card (Cash 'n' Carry Bank), and a printed announcement, "Attention Mall Shoppers! Sale in the record store!" Significantly, the game socializes young girls that shopping is a gendered social role, even as economic pressures are requiring more women to become full-time workers and more women are completing college and pursuing professional careers.

51. Milton Bradley Company, "Mall Madness: Store Directory and Instructions," 1990.

52. Smithsonian Institution–Discovery credit card contract, 1997. A $50 Series EE Savings Bond is awarded for charging $5,000. This might look like a deal. But if you charge $5,000 in a year and average a $1,000 account balance (debt), the $25 present value of the bond will have cost you over $200 in finance charges.

53. For a brief review of recent credit card advertisements, see "Cultural Literacy Quiz," at www.creditcardnation.com.

54. Evelyn Tan Powers, "Just How Did They Get Rich?" *USA Today*, 22 February 2000, p. 4B.

55. Thomas J. Stanley and William D. Danko, *The Millionaire Next Door: The Surprising Secrets of America's Wealthy* (Atlanta: Longstreet Press, 1996), p. 9; and Juliet B. Schor, *The Overspent American: Upscaling, Downshifting, and the New Consumer* (New York: Basic Books, 1998), chap. 5.

56. Stanley and Danko, op. cit., p. 5.

57. Calder, op. cit.; and Tucker, op. cit.

58. *Newhart* television show, produced by MTM Enterprises, Inc., 1987. The series continues to be aired on Nickelodeon's "Nick-at-Night" cable show.

59. For information on federal and state bankruptcy law, see Teresa Sullivan, Robert Warren, and Elizabeth Warren, *The Fragile Middle Class: Americans in Debt* (New Haven: Yale University Press, 2000); and the American Bankruptcy Institute at www.abiworld.org.

60. Mishel, Bernstein, and Schmitt, op. cit., and research updates at www.epinet.org. The authors are developing a new section for the next edition that will address some of these consumer debt burden issues.

61. See Chapter 1 (note 26) for an explanation of these figures. It is important to note that they are somewhat inflated due to the increasing use of credit cards in financing start-up businesses and other commercial ventures such as stock market investments. However, when these businesses fail, their credit card debts must be repaid, since they are consumer rather than small-business loans. On the other hand, the popularity of home equity, debt consolidation, and student loans over the past decade deflates the credit card debt figures by shifting some revolving debt into the consumer installment debt category.

62. CardWeb, "Profit Squeeze," CardTrak, October 1999, at www.cardweb.com/cardtrak. For 2000, see Marcy Gordon, "Credit Cards at 50: The Problems of Ubiquity," *The New York Times*, 12 March 2000, p. A11.

63. See CardWeb, op. cit.

64. LaFalce, the ranking Democrat on the U.S. House of Representatives Banking and Financial Services Committee, is the most influential politician in the fight against the misleading and financially exploitative practices of the credit card industry. His legislative effort to make illegal the imposition of additional fees and/or cancellation of credit card accounts that pay in full their monthly charges was defeated in the 1998 session. See Jerry Zremski, "End Wrongful Penalties for Paying on Time," *Buffalo News*, 19 August 1998, p. 2B.

65. Robert D. Manning, "Poverty, Race, and the Two-Tiered Financial Services System," in Chester Hartman (ed.), *Challenges to Equality: Poverty and Race in America* (New York: M. E. Sharpe, 2000 forthcoming); Jean Ann Fox, "The Growth of Legal Loan Sharking: A Report on the Payday Loan Industry" (Washington, D.C.: Consumer Federation of America, 1998); Gregory D. Squires and Sally O'Connor, "Fringe Banking in Milwaukee: The Rise of Check-Cashing Businesses and the Emergence of a Two-Tiered Banking System," *Urban Affairs Review*, vol. 34, no. 1 (Winter 1998), pp. 126–163; Michael Hudson (ed.), *Merchants of Misery: How Corporate America Profits from Poverty* (Monroe, Maine: Common Courage Press, 1996); and John P. Caskey, *Fringe Banking: Check-Cashing Outlets, Pawnshops, and the Poor* (New York: Russell Sage, 1994).

Chapter 5

1. Bill Broadway, "The Bishop Who Wasn't: Atlanta Diocese Loses Faith in Episcopal Priest," *The Washington Post*, 4 March 2000, p. B9.

2. Quoted in Gayle White, "Diocese Cancels Bishop's Appointment," *Atlanta Journal-Constitution*, 26 February 2000, p. B1.

3. Quoted in Broadway, op. cit., p. B9; White, op. cit., p. B1; and bankruptcy petition of Robert G. Trache (00-30328-DOT), Eastern Virginia District, Richmond, Virginia, 20 January 2000. Trache's bankruptcy was approved on 27 April 2000, and his debts were discharged with "no assets available to creditors."

4. Quoted in Broadway, op. cit., p. B9.

5. See Pamela Walker Laird, *Advertising Progress: American Business and the Rise of Consumer Marketing* (Baltimore: Johns Hopkins University Press, 1998); Greg Myers, *Ad Worlds: Brands, Media, Audiences* (New York: Edward Arnold, 1998); and Benjamin R. Barber, *Jihad*

vs. McWorld: How Globalism and Tribalism Are Reshaping the World (New York: Ballantine Books, 1996), chap. 4.

6. Gary Hendricks and Kenwood C. Youmans with Janet Keller, *Consumer Durables and Installment Debt: A Study of American Households* (Ann Arbor, Mich.: Institute for Social Research, 1973), p. 134.

7. Joseph Nocera, *A Piece of the Action: How the Middle Class Joined the Money Class* (New York: Simon & Schuster, 1994).

8. Arthur B. Kennickell and Janice Shack-Marquez, "Changes in Family Finances from 1983 to 1989: Evidence from the Survey of Consumer Finances," *Federal Reserve Bulletin,* January 1992, pp. 1–18; Arthur B. Kennickell and Martha Starr-McCluer, "Changes in Family Finances from 1989 to 1992: Evidence from the Survey of Consumer Finances," *Federal Reserve Bulletin,* October 1994, pp. 861–882; and Glenn B. Canner, Arthur B. Kennickell, and Charles A. Luckett, "Household Sector Borrowing and the Burden of Debt," *Federal Reserve Bulletin,* April 1995, pp. 323–328.

9. Rising personal bankruptcy reflects the diminished influence of the Calvinist ethos of thrift and savings in maintaining social control, that is, constraining individual consumption behavior.

10. The growth of personal bankruptcy filings peaked between the fourth quarter 1995 and the third quarter 1996; the bankruptcy rate increased at an annual rate of 30 percent for the 12-month period. In the second quarter of 1997, the personal bankruptcy filings increased at a much slower annual rate—less than 4 percent. Filings increased about 1.5 percent in 1998 and then slowed to less than 1 percent in fourth quarter 1998. Bankruptcy filing data are available at www.uscourts.gov.

11. Quoted in "The Bankruptcy Express Slows Down," *Business and Industry,* August 1998, p. 2; David Hosansky, "Potent Forces Brace for Battle on Bankruptcy Law Overhaul," *Congressional Quarterly,* 18 October 1997, p. 2536; and "The Latest Round of Finger Pointing," *Credit Card Management,* June 1999, p. 5.

12. Quoted in Hosansky, op. cit., p. 2536. See also Consumer Federation of America, "Banks Expand Card Marketing and Credit Extension While Seeking to Restrict Consumer Access to Bankruptcy," 28 July 1998, available at www.consumerfed.org.

13. David Moss and Gibbs Johnson, "The Rise in Consumer Bankruptcy: Evolution, Revolution, or Both," *American Bankruptcy Law Journal,* Spring 1999, report a strong relationship between lending to less creditworthy consumers and the sharp rise in bankruptcy filings in the 1990s. See also Lawrence M. Ausubel, "A Self-Correcting 'Crisis': The Status of Personal Bankruptcy in 1999," unpublished manuscript, Department of Economics, University of Maryland, College Park.

14. Juliet B. Schor, *The Overspent American: Upscaling, Downshifting, and the New Consumer* (New York: Basic Books, 1998). The national savings rate is discussed in Chapter 2 and the personal savings rate is discussed in Chapter 4. See Figure 4.1.

15. U.S. Federal Reserve, "Consumer Credit," at www.bog.frb.fed.us. For a discussion of the statistical adjustment for estimating outstanding revolving consumer debt, see note 26 of Chapter 1.

16. The increase of consumers who pay off their credit card charges at the end of the month is discussed in Chapter 4. See also CardWeb, "Profit Squeeze," CardTrak, October 1999, at www.cardweb.com.

17. Lendol Calder, *Financing the American Dream: A Cultural History of Consumer Credit* (Princeton: Princeton University Press, 1999), p. 24.

18. Edward J. Bird, Paul A. Hagstrom, and Robert Wild, "Credit Card Debts of the Poor: High and Rising," unpublished paper, Department of Public Policy, University of Rochester, Rochester, N.Y., 1998, p. 5. Between 1983 and 1995, the authors found, the proportion of

cardholders increased across all household income levels: below poverty line (17.0 percent to 36.2 percent); 100–150 percent of poverty line (35.0 to 56.9 percent); 150–200 percent of poverty line (47.2 to 65.7 percent); and above 200 percent of poverty line (78.5 to 87.6 percent). In terms of debt levels, 3.6 percent of all households had credit card debts greater than their monthly incomes, and 1.0 percent had more than twice their monthly incomes in 1983. In 1995, these proportions had risen to 16 and 8 percent, respectively. Among poor households, 3.4 percent had credit card balances more than twice their monthly income in 1983; this proportion jumped to 11.9 percent in 1995.

19. See Laird, op. cit.; Myers, op. cit.; and Barber, op. cit., chap. 4.

20. Quoted in "Consumer Debt Rises at Weak Pace," *Los Angeles Times*, 9 July 1998, p. D3.

21. Quoted in Jonathan P. Decker, "Bankruptcies Drop, but Not by Much," *Christian Science Monitor*, 20 March 2000, p. 16. See John M. Barron and Michael E. Staten, *Personal Bankruptcy: A Report on Petitioners' Ability to Pay* (Washington, D.C.: Credit Research Center, Georgetown University, October 1997); and Michael E. Staten, "A Profile of Debt, Income and Expenses of Consumers in Bankruptcy," testimony before the national Bankruptcy Review Commission, Washington, D.C., 17 December 1996. For critiques of methodology and legal analysis, see General Accounting Office, "Personal Bankruptcy: Analysis of Four Reports on Chapter 7 Debtors' Ability to Pay," GAO/GGD-99-103, June 1999; and Teresa Sullivan, Robert Warren, and Elizabeth Warren, *The Fragile Middle Class: Americans in Debt* (New Haven: Yale University Press, 2000), pp. 289–290.

22. Elizabeth Warren, "Consumer Bankruptcy: Issues Summary," unpublished paper, Harvard Law School, Cambridge, Mass., April 1999, p. 1.

23. Quoted in Decker, op. cit., p. 16. For example, 3-year-old Alessandra Scalise's parents listed her occupation as "preschooler" and stated that she was applying for a credit card to buy toys. The preapproved application from Charter One Bank—which was sent in Alessandra's name to the family residence—was approved—even without a Social Security number, no listed income, and no other relevant financial information. Furthermore, Ali's card came with a credit limit of $5,000—more than her parents' card. For more, see "Stories," at www.creditcardnation.com.

24. Quoted in Margaret Mannix, "Goodbye to Debt," *U.S. News & World Report*, 27 April 1998, p. 65.

25. This is a key theme of Schor, op. cit. Also, practical advice guides include Nancy Lloyd, *Simple Money Solutions: Ten Ways You Can Stop Being Overwhelmed by Money and Making It Work for You* (New York: Times Books, 2000); Suze Orman, *The 9 Steps to Financial Freedom* (New York: Crown, 1998); Dave Ramsey, *Financial Peace: Restoring Financial Hope to You and Your Family* (New York: Viking Press, 1998); David Heitmiller, *Getting a Life* (New York: Viking Press, 1997); Olivia Mellan, *Overcoming Overspending* (New York: Walker Press, 1995); Mark S. Waldman, *The Way of Real Wealth* (New York: HarperCollins, 1993); Arlene Modica Matthews, *Your Money, Your Self* (New York: Simon & Schuster, 1991); and Jerrold Mundis, *How to Get out of Debt, Stay out of Debt, and Live Prosperously* (New York: Bantam Books, 1990). For further information on debt liberation as a lifestyle choice, see Center for a New American Dream at www.newdream.org/. Also, for a Christian fundamentalist perspective, see the extensive financial educational materials authored by Larry Burkett, founder of Christian Financial Concepts, Inc., at www.cfcministry.org.

26. George Kalogerakis, "Going Broke," *People Magazine*, 24 February 1997, p. 7.

27. Ibid., p. 11.

28. The most popular personal filing is under Chapter 7 of the U.S. Bankruptcy Code. A common misconception is that it erases all personal debts; only short-term, high-interest debt (primarily credit cards and finance company loans) and some medical debts can be discharged. After bankruptcy, all payments on the family home must be made, including inter-

est, late charges, and penalties, or it will be lost through foreclosure. Furthermore, debt secured by a home mortgage or home equity line of credit cannot be reduced through bankruptcy. Auto loans must be paid as well as outstanding tax bills and educational loans. Additionally, all child support and alimony obligations must be satisfied, and any reaffirmation agreements on debts that otherwise would be discharged in bankruptcy must also be paid. Consequently, the fresh start offered by Chapter 7 is not total debt relief. Under Chapter 13 of the U.S. Bankruptcy Code, a repayment plan is negotiated whereby the debtor's future earnings are budgeted to pay creditors all or part of outstanding debts—usually over 3 to 5 years. Since the mid-1980s, however, about 2 out of 3 debtors who filed for Chapter 13 have not survived the duration of the repayment period due to unexpected expenses, unemployment, or both. For others, their plans were unrealistic based on their inadequate sources of income. When these Chapter 13 repayment plans fail, most debtors leave the bankruptcy system without having discharged any debt. Hence, Chapter 13 offers little relief for many who try to repay their debts. For more information, see the American Bankruptcy Institute at www.abiworld.org.

29. The 1981 study, "Consumer Bankruptcy Project Phase I," examined bankruptcy filings in Illinois, Pennsylvania, and Texas based on different state exemptions and laws; these selected districts vary greatly in the ratio of Chapter 7 filings to Chapter 13 filings. See Teresa Sullivan, Robert Warren, and Elizabeth Warren, *As We Forgive Our Debtors: Bankruptcy and Consumer Credit in America* (New York: Oxford University Press, 1989), app. 1, pp. 342–354. The 1991 study, "Consumer Bankruptcy Project Phase II," examined the same states of phase one plus the two states with the highest bankruptcy rates: California and Texas. See Teresa Sullivan, Robert Warren, and Elizabeth Warren, *The Fragile Middle Class: Americans in Debt* (New Haven: Yale University Press, 2000), app. 1, pp. 263–287.

30. For a brief summary, see Teresa Sullivan, Robert Warren, and Elizabeth Warren, "Consumer Debtors Ten Years Later: A Financial Comparison of Consumer Bankrupts, 1981–91," *American Bankruptcy Law Journal*, vol. 68 (1994).

31. The analysis is based on the 1981 and 1991 studies by Sullivan, Warren, and Westbrook (cited in note 29) as well as 1997 data provided by Judge Barbara Sellers and a research project by Professors Marianne Culhane and Michaela White of Creighton Law School. See Elizabeth Warren, "The Bankruptcy Crisis," *Indiana Law Journal*, vol. 73, no. 4 (1998), at www.law.indiana.edu.

32. Consumer Federation of America, "Large Banks Increase Charges to Americans in Credit Counseling: New Practices Will Hurt Consumers on the Brink of Bankruptcy," 28 July 1999, available at www.consumerfed.org. The CFA report states that the largest network of nonprofit credit counseling agencies, the National Foundation for Consumer Credit (NFCC), handles a little over one-half of all consumer debt that is being repaid through such agencies. In 1998, NFCC member agencies assisted over 1.4 million Americans; 504,000 entered debt management programs with consumer debt obligations of $2.3 billion—a sharp rise from 254,000 program participants in 1988.

33. For examination of contemporary patterns of downward mobility, see Barbara Ehrenreich, *Fear of Falling* (New York: HarperCollins, 1987); Katherine S. Newman, *Falling from Grace: The Experience of Downward Mobility in the American Middle Class* (New York: Free Press, 1988); *U.S. News & World Report*, "The Vanishing Dream: Upward Mobility Is No Longer Possible for Millions of American Workers," *U.S. News & World Report*, 22 April 1991, pp. 39–43; Katherine S. Newman, *Declining Fortunes: The Withering of the American Dream* (New York: Basic Books, 1993); David Bensman and Roberta Lynch, *Rusted Dreams, Hard Times in a Steel Community* (Berkeley: University of California Press, 1988); and Frederick R. Strobel, *Upward Dreams, Downward Mobility: The Economic Decline of the Middle Class* (Lanham, Md.: Rowman & Littlefield, 1993).

34. Sullivan, Warren, and Warren, *The Fragile Middle Class*, especially chap. 2; and Teresa Sullivan, Robert Warren, and Elizabeth Warren, "Bankruptcy and the Family," *Marriage and Family Review,* vol. 21, nos. 3–4 (1995), pp. 194–215.

35. Quoted in Joyce Smith, "When Luck Runs Out," *Kansas City Star*, 9 January 2000, p. A1; and SMR Research Corporation, *The Personal Bankruptcy Crisis, 1997: Demographics, Causes, Implications, and Solutions* (Hackettstown, N.J.: SMR Research Corporation, 1997). For a review of recently published bankruptcy studies, see Sullivan, Warren, and Warren, *The Fragile Middle Class*, app. 2, pp. 288–296.

36. Denise Lavoie, "Xerox to Cut Payroll by 5,200," *The Washington Post*, 1 April 2000, p. E8; Dana Hedgpeth and Ariana Eunjung Cha, "Amazon Announces Layoffs," *The Washington Post*, 29 January 2000, p. E1; Greg Schneider, "Lockheed to Reorganize, Cut 2,800 Jobs," *The Washington Post*, 28 January 2000, p. E3; Martha M. Hamilton, "Coke to Cut 6,000 Jobs in Major Reshuffling," *The Washington Post*, 27 January 2000, p. E1; and Rachel Beck, "Venator to Trim Jobs, Shut 358 Stores," *The Washington Post*, 26 January 2000, p. E3.

37. Secured credit cards are the Visas and MasterCards of last resort and serve to hide the cardholder's inability to obtain a regular bank credit card—especially after bankruptcy. They feature high interest rates (19.0 to 25.9 APR), generally require an annual membership fee (from $30 to $125), and are secured or collateralized with a financial deposit—usually in increments of $100. The bank will limit the riskiest clients to a line of credit equal to the deposit. As a reliable payment history is established, the bank will extend credit in multiples of the cardholder's deposit. For example, a $500 deposit may be doubled or tripled to produce a credit limit of $1,000 or $1,500. Eventually, responsible cardholders can request a regular credit card, usually after a minimum of one year of punctual payments.

38. Susan C. Faludi, "The Safeway LBO Yields Vast Profits but Exacts a Heavy Human Toll," *The Wall Street Journal*, 16 May 1990, p. 1.

39. Sarah Bartlett, *The Money Machine: How KKR Manufactured Power and Profits* (New York: Warner Books, 1991); and George Anders, *Merchants of Debt: KKR and the Mortgaging of American Business* (New York: Basic Books, 1992).

40. Lee Nathans Spiro and Ronald Grover, "The Operator: An Inside Look at Ron Perelman's $5 Billion Empire," *Business Week*, 21 August 1995, pp. 54–59; and Allan Sloan, "How You Can Invest with Revlon's Ronald Perelman," *Money*, July 1994, pp. 19–20.

41. According to Teresa Sullivan and Elizabeth Warren, between 1981 and 1999, bankruptcies for couples rose about 150 percent, men filing alone grew nearly 375 percent, and women filing soared over 900 percent. See Teresa Sullivan and Elizabeth Warren, "The Changing Demographics of Bankruptcy," *Norton Bankruptcy Law Advisor,* no. 10 (October 1999), pp. 1–7; Oliver B. Pollak, "Gender and Bankruptcy: An Empirical Analysis of Evolving Trends in Chapter 7 and Chapter 13 Bankruptcy Filings, 1967–1997," *Commercial Law Journal*, vol. 102 (Fall 1997), pp. 333–338.

42. For a superb discussion of the socioeconomic forces that shape America's winner-take-all ethos, see Robert H. Frank and Philip J. Cook, *The Winner-Take-All Society* (New York: Free Press, 1995).

43. Barber, op. cit.

44. Quoted in Christine Dugas, "Going from Debt-Ridden to Debt-Free: Credit Cards Are Hard to Control," *USA Today*, 18 September 1998, p. B3.

45. The marriage and divorce rates in the United States have fallen substantially over the past two decades. The decline in official civil marriages has necessarily led to fewer divorces. Of course, the dissolution of unrecorded informal unions (cohabiting couples) causes similar emotional and financial hardships. See Andrew Cherlin, *Marriage, Divorce, Remarriage: Social Trends in the United States* (Cambridge: Harvard University Press, 1992).

46. The sociological research on divorce has tended to neglect the economic consequences to men. In fact, the most prominent research on the financial impact of divorce on women,

Lenore J. Weitzman's *The Divorce Revolution: The Unexpected Social and Economic Consequences for Women and Children in America* (New York: Free Press, 1985), played an influential role in the political movement to reform no-fault divorce laws in the late 1980s and early 1990s. Since its publication, however, it has been severely criticized for its lack of methodological rigor as well as its exaggerated claims of financial hardship for former wives and minimal hardship for their ex-husbands. See Saul Hoffman and Greg Duncan, "What Are the Economic Consequences of Divorce," *Demography*, vol. 25 (1988), pp. 641–645; Jed H. Abraham, "'The Divorce Revolution' Revisited: A Counter-Revolutionary Critique," *Northern Illinois Law Review*, vol. 9 (1989), pp. 251–298; Martin David and Thomas Flory, "Changes in Marital Status and Short-Term Income Dynamics," in H. V. Beaton, D. A. Ganni, and D. T. Frankel (eds.), *Individuals and Families in Transition* (Washington, D.C.: U.S. Bureau of the Census, 1989), pp. 15–22; Richard R. Peterson, *Women, Work, and Divorce* (Albany: State University of New York Press, 1989); Leslie A. Morgan, *After Marriage Ends* (Newbury Park, Calif.: Sage, 1991); and Richard R. Peterson, "A Re-Evaluation of the Economic Consequences of Divorce," *American Sociological Review*, vol. 61 (1996), pp. 528–536.

47. The 1998 national survey of home equity indebtedness was conducted by the University of Michigan's Survey Research Center. Between 1988 and 1998, the proportion of first mortgages (60 percent) and second mortgages (5 percent) remained stable while home equity lines of credit increased from 6 to 8 percent. See Kenneth R. Harney, "The Portrait of a Homeowner Who Is Debt-Free," *The Washington Post*, 31 October 1998, p. E1.

Chapter 6

1. Robert D. Manning, *Credit Cards on Campus: The Social Consequences of Student Debt* (Washington, D.C.: Consumer Federation of America, 1999), is based on over 350 in-depth interviews and over 400 survey questionnaires of students at two private universities (American, Georgetown) and one public university (University of Maryland–College Park). The study is available in the "Research Reports" section at www.creditcardnation.com.

2. A sampling of national and regional media reports is available in the "Media" section at www.creditcardnation.com.

3. Personal communication with Dr. Edward Ehlinger, director of the Boynton Health Service at the University of Minnesota, 19 September 1999. Dr. Ehlinger first conducted a 1995 survey at the University of Minnesota that "showed a correlation between heavy credit-card use and health and academic problems." In 1998, the survey was expanded to four postsecondary schools (University of Minnesota, Augsburg College, Hamline University, and Bethel College) and included more credit card–related questions. Overall, the survey found that nearly 80 percent of the students had at least one bank credit card and "students with unpaid credit card balances of $1,000 or more a month smoke more, drink more and use more medications for depression. They also work more hours at their jobs than students owing less. And their grade point averages are lower." See Kay Miller, "Charging into Debt," *Minneapolis Star Tribune*, 12 September 1999, p. 1A; also Patricia Drentea and Paul J. Lavrakas, "Over the Limit: The Association Among Health, Race and Debt," *Social Sciences and Medicine*, vol. 50 (2000), pp. 517–529.

4. The credit card industry's opposition to marketing restrictions on college campuses was articulated by Dr. Michael Staten, director of the Credit Research Center, Georgetown University, in his 16 December 1999 testimony before the Joint Senate Subcommittee on the Status of the African American Male, General Assembly of Virginia, Richmond, Virginia. These arguments were emphatically disputed in the 16 December 1999 testimony of Dr. Robert D. Manning, Department of Sociology, Georgetown University, during the same subcommittee hearing.

5. These arguments tend to ignore the ease of accumulating credit card debt and the difficulty in paying it off with finance charges typically 19.9 percent and higher. For example, if a student graduates with $5,000 of credit card debt and can only afford to pay for new charges due to a low starting salary, then the initial debt at a finance charge of 19.9 percent will grow to $13,348 in only five years. At a finance rate of 22.9 percent, the amount will rise to $15,544 in five years. See credit card "Debt Zapper" at www.creditcardnation.com. Not incidentally, credit card interest is no longer a deductible expense on federal income taxes. This tax change was phased in over five years beginning with tax year 1986.

6. The view that student credit card debt is simply a personal choice that has become a common feature of the college experience is presented by Marcia Vickers, "A Hard Lesson on Credit Cards," *Business Week*, p. 107, 15 March 1999. The banking industry argues that excessive credit card debt is the product of impulsive consumer decisions and inadequate financial education rather than its predatory marketing policies. Significantly, the student featured in the *Business Week* story, "Jeff," is profiled in this chapter, and he vigorously disputes Vickers's portrayal of his financial predicament. See his 8 June 1999 interview on CNN Headline News available in the "Media" section at www.creditcardnation.com.

7. The summary of the CFA report and the testimonies of Janne O'Donnell and Trisha Johnson are included in "Credit Card Debt Imposes Huge Costs on Many College Students," 9 June 1999, available in the "Press Releases" section at www.consumerfed.org.

8. For an explanation of the methodological flaws of the credit card industry's research reports, see Manning, *Credit Cards on Campus: Current Trends and Informational Deficiencies* (Washington, D.C.: Consumer Federation of America, 1999), in the "Research Reports" section at www.creditcardnation.com.

9. Transcripts of the 8 June 1999 CNN Headline News and 14 June 1999 *Good Morning America* programs are available in the "Media" section at www.creditcardnation.com.

10. See U.S. Congresswoman Louise Slaughter, "Why We Need HR-3142," *Rochester Democrat*, 31 August 1999, p. 9, available in the "Legislation" section at www.creditcard nation.com. The bill's restrictions on campus marketing and student credit card limits were proposed by Dr. Robert D. Manning at the June CFA press conference and were incorporated in the 1999 version of HR-3142.

11. See Tina D. Tapas, "Issuers Graduate to the Risky, but Lucrative, College Market," *Card Marketing*, July/August 2000, pp. 12–15. For an investigative report on the University of Tennessee's exclusive credit card marketing contract with First USA, see CBS's "Eye on America" program, 3 May 2000, available in the "Media" section at www.creditcardnation.com. This "Confidential Affinity Group Bankcard Agreement," signed 28 June 1998, guarantees the university a minimum of $16.5 million over seven years. However, the annual payment will increase significantly over the life of the contract based on the following royalty fees: $1.00 per each new account, $3.00 on the one-year anniversary of each "existing" account, and between 0.40 percent and 0.50 percent of net retail sales charged to each account. The 1999 royalty payment was $2,357,142.86. Also see Marcia Vickers, "Big Cards on Campus," *Business Week*, 20 September 1999, p. 136. Also, MBNA donated $25 million for financing the new MBNA student center at Columbia University in 1996 and $7 million for the new MBNA Performing Arts Center at Georgetown in 1999. See Karen W. Arensen, "Columbia's Colossal Student Center, Designed by Dean of Architecture, Is to Open in September," *The New York Times*, 28 July 1999, p. B8; and Jean Weinberg, "GU to Submit Plans for New MBNA Performing Arts Center," *The Hoya*, 17 September 1999, p. 1.

12. Robert D. Manning, "Credit Cards on Campus: Are Colleges Responsible for the Social Consequences?" unpublished manuscript, Department of Sociology, Georgetown University, Washington, D.C., 2000, available at "Research Reports" section at www. creditcardnation.com.

13. The "Credit Cards on Campus" study indicates that there is growing dissatisfaction within the college student population over the relatively low social and economic returns deriving from investment in a college education—especially for those from moderate-income families. Many recent college graduates (single and married) report that their long-term student loan debts and disappointingly low economic returns from their college degrees have forced them to defer homeownership in the short term and possibly even preclude it in the long term. Additionally, several respondents (including graduate students) expressed frustration that their student debt obligations are forcing them to choose between homeownership and parenthood. This is a new dilemma that was not commonly encountered by their parents—particularly among two-income households.

14. Katie Butler, "The Great Boomer Bust," *Mother Jones,* June 1989, pp. 35–42; David Halberstam, *The Fifties* (New York: Ballantine Books, 1994); and Peter Saunders, *A Nation of Home Owners* (London: Unwin Hyman, 1990).

15. Joshua Wolf Shenk, "In Debt All the Way up to Their Nose Rings," *U.S. News and World Report,* 9 June 1997, p. 38.

16. Ibid.

17. In 1975, a ticket to a premier rock concert cost the equivalent of three hours of work at the federal minimum wage. Today, a comparable concert ticket costs about 8–10 hours of minimum-wage work.

18. The cheapest cars in the U.S. market, such as the Saturn GEO series, retail for less than $10,000.

19. At American University, the cost of tuition ($21,144), housing ($5,350) and board ($3,000) totaled $29,494 for the 2000–2001 academic year. It is important to note that this figure does not include the cost of university activity fees, books, travel, and living expenses. A realistic student budget in Washington, D.C., is at least $35,000 for the 2000–2001 academic year.

20. Shenk, op. cit.; Fred Vogelstein, "How High Can It Go?" *U.S. News and World Report,* March 1998, at www.usnews.com/usnews/edu.

21. Isaac Shapiro and Robert Greenstein, *The Widening Income Gulf* (Washington, D.C.: Center on Budget and Policy Priorities, 1999), at www.cbpp.org; U.S. Bureau of the Census, *Current Population Reports,* P60–197, cited in table 739 in the *1998 Statistical Abstract of the United States* (Washington, D.C.: U.S. Government Printing Office, 1999), p. 468, at www.census.gov/hhes/income; and Denny Braun, *The Rich Get Richer: The Rise of Income Inequality in the United States and the World* (Chicago: Nelson-Hall, 1997).

22. Shenk, op. cit., 1997; Joanne P. Cavanaugh, Sue De Pasquale, Melissa Hendricks, and Dale Keiger, "Scrambling for Dollars: Why Is a Hopkins Education So Expensive?" *Johns Hopkins Magazine,* September 1998, pp. 12–27.

23. Albert B. Crenshaw, "Options for Parents As College Costs Climb," *The Washington Post,* 18 October 1998, p. H1.

24. The term "college inflation" refers to the consistently greater increase in the cost of college education–related expenses than in the general "basket" of goods and services that are the basis for estimating the national rate of inflation. For instance, a 1996 GAO report found that tuition increases at four-year public colleges tripled the rate of inflation between 1980 and 1995; the Consumer Price Index tuition rose 85 percent, whereas tuition at four-year colleges jumped 254 percent. See Robert J. Samuelson, "The Hypocrisy Scholarship," *The Washington Post,* 12 February 1997, p. A23; and Rene Sanchez, "5% College Tuition Increase Still Outpacing 2% Inflation," *The Washington Post,* 25 September 1997, p. 3. This trend continues today. For example, American University raised the price for tuition, room, and board by 4.0 percent for academic year 2000–2001 while the inflation rate was about 2 percent.

25. The federal minimum wage was $5.75 and the student minimum wage was $5.25 per hour in 2000. See U.S. Employment Standards Administration, cited in table 699 in the *1998 Statistical Abstract of the United States* (Washington, D.C.: U.S. Government Printing Office, 1999), p. 438, at www.dol.gov.

26. According to the College Board at www.collegeboard.org, the breakdown by cost of tuition and fees for all full-time students in 1998–1999 was as follows: under $4,000 (52.2 percent of students), $4,000–$7,999 (20.2 percent), $8,000–$11,999 (6.7 percent), $12,000–$15,999 (9.0 percent), $16,000–$19,999 (5.5 percent), and $20,000 or higher (6.4 percent).

27. Vogelstein, op. cit. Under the federal Guaranteed Student Loan Program, the maximum loan undergraduates could receive in 1999 was $46,000 and for graduate students it was $138,500. At present, the federal government offers four types of loans to families: (1) subsidized Stafford, (2) unsubsidized Stafford, (3) Perkins, and (4) Parent Loans for Undergraduate Students (PLUS). The subsidized Stafford (capped at 8.25 percent) and Perkins (5.0 percent) loans are based on financial need; the federal government pays the interest until the end of the student's grace period following graduation or withdrawal from school. The unsubsidized Stafford (capped at 8.25 percent) and PLUS (9.0 percent) loans accrue interest immediately. During matriculation in college, however, loan payments may be suspended and then capitalized for repayment after graduation. In general, the repayment schedule is ten years, although the current trend is to consolidate personal loans over longer periods (15–20 years).

28. Public Interest Research Group (PIRG), *The Campus Credit Card Trap* (Washington, D.C.: PIRG, 1998).

29. Allison Schlesinger, "College Students Urged to Avoid Credit-Card Debt," *St. Louis Post-Dispatch*, 31 August 1998, p. 5.

30. Jamie P. Merisotis and Ernest T. Freeman, "A Look at the Rising Cost of College," *The Washington Post*, 3 November 1996, p. A23.

31. It is estimated that the loan industry has collected over $50 billion in student loan fees. See Charles R. Babcock, "Rising Tuitions Fill Loan Firm Coffers," *The Washington Post*, 27 October 1997, p. A1.

32. Cavanaugh et al., op. cit.

33. Shenk, op. cit.

34. Troy Flint, "Students Graduate to Huge Debts," *The Times-Picayune*, 22 November 1998, p. 1. The 1997 Nellie Mae "National Student Loan Survey" found a larger gap of 25.7 percent with the average debt of public (four-year) students at about $13,000 compared to $17,500 for private college graduates. This somewhat inflated figure is partially explained by the different composition of the NSLA sample. That is, the sampling universe is loan recipients that began repayment between 1993 and 1996. Hence, graduates from the early 1990s would be expected to have a larger debt gap than graduates from the mid-1990s. See Sandy Baum and Diane Saunders, "Life After Debt: Results of the National Student Loan Survey," in *Student Loan Debt: Problems and Prospects* (Washington, D.C.: Institute for Higher Education Policy, 1998), pp. 77–96.

35. Robert D. Manning, *Credit Cards on Campus: Costs and Consequences of Student Debt* (Washington, D.C.: Consumer Federation of America, 1999), apps. A and B, available in the "Reports" section at www.creditcardnation.com.

36. Beginning with the 1998 tax year, parents may claim a $1,500 Hope Scholarship and $1,000 Lifetime Learning credit based on their children's college expenses. Also, recent graduates can claim up to $2,500 in interest on their student loans for tax year 2001. See Cavanaugh et al., op. cit.; Jane Bryant Quinn, "New Tax Credits May Bring Cuts in Student Aid," *The Washington Post*, 31 August 1997, p. H2; and Richard W. Riley, "Give the Middle

Class a Break on Education," *The Washington Post*, 24 April 1997, p. A25. For information on how to qualify and calculate these federal tax deductions, see "[Financial] Reality Bytes: New Tax Relief for Recent Graduates and Parents of College Students," module 5, in the "Financial Education" section at www.creditcardnation.com.

37. Cavanaugh et al., op. cit.; Quinn, op. cit.; and Riley, op. cit.

38. This is the title of a 1999 mass marketing Visa campaign by Associates National Bank.

39. George Ritzer, *Expressing America: A Critiquing of the Global Credit Card Society* (Thousand Oaks, Calif.: Pine Forge Press, 1995); Joseph Nocera, *A Piece of the Action: How the Middle Class Joined the Money Class* (New York: Simon & Schuster, 1994); and Lewis Mandell, *The Credit Card Industry: A History* (Boston: Twayne Publishers, 1990).

40. Many large banks incurred enormous losses during the decade due to the Third World debt crisis, collapse of the U.S housing market, glut of commercial office buildings and shopping malls, decline of traditional corporate lending, and two national recessions.

41. George Anders, *Merchants of Debt: KKR and the Mortgaging of American Business* (New York: Basic Books, 1992); Benjamin M. Friedman, *Day of Reckoning: The Consequences of American Economic Policy* (New York: Vintage Press, 1989); Bennett Harrison and Barry Bluestone, *The Great U-Turn: Corporate Restructuring and the Polarizing of America* (New York: Basic Books, 1988).

42. Gary A. Dymski, *The Bank Merger Wave: The Economic Causes and Social Consequences of Financial Consolidation* (New York: M. E. Sharpe, 1999); Nocera, op. cit.; Mandell, op. cit.

43. The other untapped social frontiers of the credit card industry are the elderly and newly bankrupt. See Chapters 5 and 9.

44. Cited in Michael Moore, "Campus Curbs on Card Eyed in Two States," *American Banker*, 20 May 1997, p. 7.

45. U.S. Congress, hearing before the Subcommittee on Consumer Credit and Insurance, Committee on Banking, Finance, and Urban Affairs, U.S. House of Representatives, "Kiddie Credit Cards," 10 March 1994.

46. Kenneth Reich, "Son's Debt Plagues Dad for 7 Years," *Los Angeles Times*, 17 January 1999, p. A4.

47. Cited in Moore, op. cit.

48. Education Resources Institute (ERI) and Institute for Higher Education Policy, *Credit Risk or Credit Worthy? College Students and Credit Cards, a National Survey* (Boston: ERI, 1998).

49. Baum and Saunders, op. cit.

50. See College Monitor, "Chapter 2: Credit Cards," which summarizes its 1998 survey results at www.collegemonitor.com.

51. For industry estimates based on a national survey of 100 colleges (approximately 12 students per college), see College Monitor, "Chapter 2: Credit Cards," at www.college monitor.com. The 1998–1999 surveys at Georgetown University and University of Maryland are based on a total of 406 students. See Manning, *Credit Cards on Campus: Social Consequences of Student Debt*, app. B. For a review of survey studies on student credit card use and a critique of this methodology, see Robert D. Manning, *Credit Cards on Campus: Current Trends and Informational Deficiencies* (Washington, D.C.: Consumer Federation of America, 1999), in the "Research Reports" section of www.creditcardnation.com.

52. Charlotte Newton, "Students' Credit Good," *USA Today*, 8 June 1998, p. A11.

53. This is illustrated by a University of Maryland senior who responded, "I know the balances of my 2 [Visa and Discover] credit cards [but] I don't know about the other one [because] my parents pay it"; quoted in Manning, *Credit Cards on Campus*, p. 18.

54. Cited in Moore, op. cit.

55. Baum and Saunders, op. cit. The lowest estimates, based on questionable methodological assumptions, are reported by the Institute for Higher Education Policy and the Education

Resources Institute. This study found that 59 percent of its survey respondents reported paying their monthly charges in full, and only 18 percent reported a balance of over $1,000; see Education Resources Institute, op. cit. Similarly, the 1998 Student Monitor survey reports that 54 percent of undergraduate students do not revolve their debt and that their average credit card debt is $503. At least one-seventh of student credit card accounts are paid directly by their parents. Nevertheless, the Student Monitor confirms the trend that credit card balances climb sharply during the last two years of college: freshmen ($316), sophomores ($378), juniors ($536), and seniors ($636). See College Monitor, "Chapter 2: Credit Cards," which summarizes its 1998 survey results at www.collegemonitor.com.

56. Manning, op. cit., table 2.

57. The most common question asked by students (in interviews, surveys, workshops) is how long it takes to pay off their credit cards. The difficulty in answering this question is twofold. First, from an industry standard of approximately 2.0 percent in the mid-1990s, the minimum payment has been commonly reduced to 1.0 percent of outstanding principal balance. Incredibly, some companies such as First USA require minimum payments that are less than the monthly interest charge. Second, the industry's emerging "springboard" finance rate system now includes low introductory (teaser) interest rates, variable or adjustable rates, large interest rate penalties (even if the account has only one late payment), and additional price increases through contract amendments.

The confusion over the precise finance charge of a credit card account means that calculating the payoff of a specific outstanding balance is a problematic exercise. As a University of Maryland student exclaimed, "Every card issuer should give specific scenarios of cash advances, missing payments, etc., in their booklets to illustrate how their card works. People mostly don't know what percentage will apply to them if they skip a payment." For calculating the specific cost of credit card finance charges or the number of months required to pay off a credit card debt at a specific interest rate, see the "Debt Zapper Calculator" at www.creditcardnation.com.

58. This is a common criticism of college students who question the credit card industry's policy of extending high lines of credit to unemployed students. As a University of Maryland senior declared, "Why do credit card companies offer credit cards with high credit limits [to] young people who can't afford them? . . . Of course many of them end up with debts that they can't pay for."

59. The application states, "Through responsible use of your Discover Card, you will be building the credit history you'll need later for car, home or other loans."

Chapter 7

1. The Financial Services Modernization Act of 1999 (HR-10) is also referred to as the Gramm-Leach-Bliley Act. The final agreement was brokered between the Clinton administration and U.S. congressional leaders on 22 October 1999. It was then easily ratified by the U.S. Senate (90 to 8) and the U.S. House of Representatives (362 to 57).

2. Keynote address at the conference "The Consumer in the Financial Services Revolution: Challenges and Opportunities," Consumer Federation of America, Washington, D.C., 2 December 1999.

3. The 1933 act established the Federal Deposit Insurance Corporation (FDIC) and denied banks the legal ability to engage in investment banking, especially the sale of security-based investment products. By preventing banks from purchasing large blocks of stock and then reselling them in smaller blocks at a profit, this regulation sought to protect individual investors as well as the FDIC from bank failure due to speculative investments. See Davita Silfen Glasberg and Dan Skidmore, *Corporate Welfare Policy and the Welfare State: Bank Deregulation and the Savings and Loan Bailout* (New York: Aldine de Gruyter, 1997), chap. 2; and

Gary A. Dymski, *The Bank Merger Wave: The Economic Causes and Social Consequences of Financial Consolidation* (Armonk, N.Y.: M. E. Sharpe, 1999), chap. 3.

4. CitiGroup was formed from the merger of Citicorp and Travelers Group in 1998. It has retained the Travelers red umbrella logo and offers credit card, banking, insurance, and investment services in over 100 countries. It also offers brokerage services (Salomon Smith Barney), mutual funds (Primerica Financial), property and casualty insurance (82 percent ownership of Travelers Property Casualty), retirement products (Travelers Life and Annuity), and real estate services (Citicorp Real Estate), among other services. Hoover's Inc., Hoover's Online, 11 December 1999, www.hoovers.com.

Similarly, MWD emerged after the Sears financial services division spun off its Dean Witter and Discover subsidiaries and then merged with Morgan Stanley. According to Hoover's Online, "The merger of blue-blood Morgan Stanley and blue-collar Dean Witter took the financial world by storm, creating an investment banking and retail brokerage powerhouse. The number two retail broker in the U.S. behind Merrill Lynch, the company has more than 430 branches in the U.S. and some 30 more abroad. Its Discover unit is a leading credit card issuer, and Discover Brokerage Direct is a top online broker. The company offers assets and investment management services to individuals and institutions. Other services include securities underwriting, corporate finance, and research and advisory services. The firm is an investor in Bernard L. Madoff Securities' Primex Trading Company, in electronic communications network (ECN)."

5. The fear of rising consumer prices (contrary to the assertions of Comptroller of the Currency John D. Hawke Jr.) and withdrawal of basic banking services from low-income communities are central themes of consumer advocates. See Ralph Nader, "Banking Jackpot," *The Washington Post*, 5 November 1999, p. A33. Also, intra- and intercorporate information sharing was a major issue during the debate on the 1999 FSMA. For instance, there are not sufficient consumer safeguards against insurance subsidiaries sharing personal medical information with other corporate divisions that then could be used by employers (e.g., life insurance rejection) and result in serious consequences for employees (dismissal, career disruption, discrimination). This consumer privacy issue is examined by Robert O'Harrow Jr., "Consumer Advocates Fear Pitches by Companies Will Breach Personal Privacy," *The Washington Post*, 31 October 1999, p. H1. See Stephen Katsanos, "FDIC Board Proposed Rule on Privacy of Consumer Information," Federal Deposit Insurance Corporation, Washington, D.C., spring 2000, available at www.fdic.gov/news/press/2000.

6. Senator Phil Gramm (R-Texas), chairman of the Senate Banking Committee, is one of the most powerful and vocal critics of the CRA. He finally relented to the Clinton administration's insistence on its preservation (but with "sunshine" provisions that substantially weaken its enforcement), since it was the final obstacle to enactment of the FSMA. For a comprehensive review of Senator Gramm's opposition to the Community Reinvestment Act and the compromise provisions of the CRA that led to the passage of the FSMA, see "Inner City Press Community Reinvestment Reporter," www.innercitypress.org. For current CRA statutes, the Consumer Compliance Task Force of the Federal Financial Institutions Examination Council (FFIEC) provides a legislative history at www.ffiec.gov/crac.

7. Bankers complain about onerous CRA paperwork and occasional lawsuits. However, enforcement penalties are rare; less than 2 percent fail to satisfy CRA compliance provisions in a given year. The most effective use of the CRA in challenging unfair bank lending policies was a 1994 suit filed by the U.S. Department of Justice against Chevy Chase Bank of Maryland. The government persuasively argued that the bank had engaged in discriminatory lending or "redlining" practices; Chevy Chase Bank opened branches primarily in the suburbs. White, suburban residents of metropolitan Washington, D.C., were far more likely to receive home mortgage loans than the primarily African American residents of the District

of Columbia. Significantly, Chevy Chase contended that its high-interest credit card accounts should be considered as part of its consumer loan portfolio in the central-city neighborhoods. This argument was ultimately rejected, and the bank agreed to an out-of-court settlement. See Chevy Chase Bank, *Community Lending Performance*, 14 May 1994; and Kim I. Eisler, "Say Uncle: Chevy Chase Bank Decided Not to Fight Back," *Washingtonian Magazine*, July 1995, pp. 47–53. For a list of CRA organizations and Internet research sources, see www.innercitypress.org/links.

8. The fallaciousness of Hawke's argument was acknowledged by President Clinton only six months later. In May 2000, he announced legislation that would provide the Treasury Department with $30 million to fund programs to subsidize banks that offer checking accounts and ATM service to underserved households. This initiative was announced after the president visited some inner-city neighborhoods in New York City where concerns were voiced over the lack of affordable banking services and the rise of unregulated predatory lenders. Significantly, banks complain that they often lose money on low-income customers. See "Low-Income Banking Programs," *Milwaukee Journal Sentinel,* 8 May 2000, p. D1; and White House Office of the Press Secretary, "President Clinton Unveils 'First Accounts': Bringing the 'Unbanked' into the Financial Mainstream," May 2000, available at www.whitehouse.gov/WH/.

9. In California, a major bank has a visual screening system that alerts employees to affluent clients by means of a flashing green light that signals "preferred" treatment and a yellow light for patrons with only modest financial resources.

10. Robert D. Manning, "Poverty, Race, and the Two-Tiered Financial Services System," in Chester Hartman (ed.), *Challenges to Equality: Poverty and Race in America* (New York: M. E. Sharpe, 2000 forthcoming); Dymski, op. cit., chap. 6; Gregory D. Squires and Sally O'Connor, "Fringe Banking in Milwaukee: The Rise of Check Cashing Businesses and the Emergence of a Two-Tiered Banking System," *Urban Affairs Review*, vol. 34, no. 1 (Fall 1998), pp. 126–163; Gary A. Dymski, "The Theory of Credit-Market Redlining and Discrimination: An Exploration," *Review of Black Political Economy*, vol. 23, no. 3 (Winter 1995), pp. 37–74; and John P. Caskey, *Fringe Banking: Check Cashing Outlets, Pawnshops, and the Poor* (New York: Russell Sage, 1994).

11. See Jarrett Murphy, "Don't Bank on It," *City Limits,* December 1999, at www.city limits.org/lores/archives. These issues are some of the reasons that community organizations opposed the Citicorp-Travelers merger. See Matthew Lee, "The First Comment ICP Filed with the Federal Reserve Board Opposing the Citicorp-Travelers Merger," *Inner City Press,* available at www.innercitypress.org; and Woodstock Institute, "Community-Bank Partnerships Creating Opportunities for the Unbanked," *Reinvestment Alert,* no. 15, June 2000, available at www.woodstockinst.org.

12. Quoted in Greg Garland, "Payday Loans Exact High 'Fees' from the Desperate," *Baltimore Sun,* 19 September 1999, p. A8.

13. Michael Hudson (ed.), *Merchants of Misery: How Corporate America Profits from Poverty* (Monroe, Maine: Common Courage Press, 1996).

14. Quoted in Matthew Lee, "The First Comment ICP Filed with the Federal Reserve Board Opposing the Citicorp-Travelers Merger," *Inner City Press,* available at www.inner citypress.org/, pp. 3–4. the study found one bank branch for every 25,000 residents in the Bronx compared with one for every 2,000 Manhattan residents. Also see Dymski, *The Bank Merger Wave,* chap. 6; Gary A. Dymski and John M. Veitch, "Financial Transformation and the Metropolis: Booms, Busts, and Banking in Los Angeles," *Environment and Planning,* vol. 28, no. 7 (July 1996), pp. 1233–1260; John P. Caskey, *Lower-Income Americans, Higher-Cost Financial Services* (Madison, Wis.: Filene Research Institute, Center for Credit Union Research, 1997); Angela Chang, Shubham Chaudhuri, and Jith Jayaratne, "Rational Herding and the Spatial Clustering of Bank Branches: An Empirical Analysis," Federal Reserve Bank of New

York, Research paper no. 9724 (August 1997); and John P. Caskey, *Fringe Banking: Check-Cashing Outlets, Pawnshops, and the Poor* (New York: Russell Sage Foundation, 1994), chap. 5.

15. Quoted in Edmund Sanders, "Banking Takes Interest in Check-Cashing Industry," *Los Angeles Times*, 16 March 2000, p. A1.

16. Recent studies, based on different data sources, estimate that between 13 and 20 percent of American households do not have checking or savings accounts in first-tier banks. For the perspective of low-income communities, see Ray Boshara, *Federal and State Individual Development Accounts (IDA) Overview* (Washington, D.C.: Corporation for Enterprise Development, October 1999). The most recent government estimate, based on the 1998 Survey of Consumer Finances, reports that the proportion of families without a checking account has fallen from 18.7 percent in 1989 to 13.2 percent in 1998; 82.6 percent of families without checking accounts had incomes less than $25,000. See Arthur B. Kennickell, Martha Starr-McCluer, and Brian J. Surette, "Recent Changes in U.S. Family Finances: Results from the 1998 Survey of Consumer Finances," *Federal Reserve Bulletin*, January 2000, pp. 8–9, at www.bogfrb.fed.us. For trends in the 1980s and 1990s, see Dymski, *The Bank Merger Wave*, chap. 6.

17. In comparison, a recent study of "financial exclusion" in England found that 7 percent of all households (1.5 million) do not have a bank checking, savings, or credit card account. The result is a thriving "alternative banking" system among the poorest segments of British society. See Elaine Kempson and Claire Whyte, *Understanding and Combating Financial Exclusion* (London: Policy Press, 1999); and Alexandra Frean and Karen Wolfson, "Poor Using Alternative Bank System," *The Times*, 22 March 1999, p. A1.

18. Murphy, op. cit.; and Dymski, *The Bank Merger Wave*, chap. 6. In Chicago, a 1999 survey found that 37 percent of lower-income city residents did not have a checking account and over 40 percent lacked a savings account. See Metro Chicago Information Center, *1999 Metro Survey* (Chicago: MCIC, 1999). For grassroots community opposition to the Citicorp-Travelers merger, partially due to Citibank's withdrawal from underserved inner-city communities, see Matthew Lee, "The First Comment ICP Filed with the Federal Reserve Board Opposing the Citicorp-Travelers Merger," *Inner City Press*, available at www.innercity press.org.

19. An examination of the 1996 Panel Survey of Income Dynamics (PSID) found 78 percent of all U.S. households had a bank account. However, only 47 percent of minority households and 54 percent of lower-income households reported a checking or savings account. See Paul Huck and Lewis Sepal, "New Data on Mortgage Lending," Federal Reserve Bank of Chicago, *Chicago Fed Letter*, no. 119 (July 1997), pp. 1 and 4; and Arthur B. Kennickell and Myron L. Kwast, "Who Uses Electronic Banking? Results from the 1995 Survey of Consumer Finances," *Finance and Economics Discussion Series*, 1997, no. 35 (Washington, D.C.: Board of Governors of the Federal Reserve System, 1997). Also see Sanders, op. cit., p. A1; Jamal E. Watson, "Banking on a Costly Alternative, Low Earners Turn to Check-Cashing Stores," *Boston Globe*, 28 February 2000, p. A1; and Peter T. Kilborn, "New Lenders with Huge Fees Thrive on Workers with Debts," *The New York Times*, 18 June 1999, p. A1.

20. Joseph M. Anderson, *American Family Wealth: Analysis of Recent Census Data* (Washington, D.C.: Consumer Federation of America, 1999), table 11, at www.consumerfed.org.

21. Quoted in Garland, op. cit., p. A8.

22. Quoted in Alix M. Freedman, "Peddling Dreams," in Michael Hudson (ed.), *Merchants of Misery: How Corporate America Profits from Poverty* (Monroe, Maine: Common Courage Press, 1996), pp. 157–158.

23. Ibid., p. 161.

24. John Roska, "How High Can the Finance Companies Go? With Interest Rates, the Sky Is the Limit," *St. Louis Post-Dispatch*, 16 July 1998, p. 4.

25. Public Interest Research Group (PIRG) and Consumer Federation of America (CFA), *Show Me the Money! A Survey of Payday Lenders and Review of Payday Lender Lobbying in State Legislatures* (Washington, D.C.: PIRG, 2000), available at www.pirg.org/reports. For Florida, see Editorial Staff, "A Payoff to Loan Sharks," *St. Petersburg Times*, 8 March 1999, p. A8.

26. PIRG and CFA, op. cit.; and Jean Ann Fox, "States Grant Payday Lenders a Safe Harbor from Usury Laws" (Washington, D.C.: Consumer Federation of America, September 1999), at www.consumerfed.org. Also see Chapter 3 (note 42) for the 1978 Supreme Court decision, *Marquette National Bank of Minneapolis v. First National Bank of Omaha,* on the initial exportation of high interest rates to circumvent state usury laws.

27. Marketdata Enterprises, *The U.S. Pawn Shops Industry* (New York: Marketdata Enterprises, Inc, 1999), p. 1; Robert Minutaglio, "Prince of Pawns," in Hudson (ed.), *Merchants of Misery,* chap. 6; and see Caskey, *Fringe Banking*, chap. 3.

28. Cash America International, Inc., *1999 Annual Report*, SEC Form 10-K, pp. 1–3.

29. Ibid., pp. 1–5; and Sanders, op. cit., p. A1.

30. PIRG and CFA, op. cit.; Edmund Sanders, "Banking Takes Interest in Check-Cashing Industry," *Los Angeles Times,* 16 March 2000, p. A1; and Marketdata Enterprises, *Check-Cashing and Money Transfer Services* (New York: Marketdata Enterprises, 1999), p. 1.

31. PIRG and CFA, op. cit.; and Christopher Bowe, "The Americas: Fed Rules over APR Rates for Payday Loans," *The Financial Times*, 27 March 2000, p. 3.

32. Rick Romell, "Title Loans Provide a Fast Lane to Cash, Debt," *Milwaukee Journal Sentinel,* 30 November 1999, p. 1; Pat Kossan, "Quick Cash, Easy Credit," *Arizona Republic,* 14 February 1999, p. A1; and Adam C. Smith, "Price of Fast Car Cash Can Put Unwary on Foot," *St. Petersburg Times,* January 1999, p. A1.

33. Ace Cash Express, Inc., "General Information" and "Ace Store Services," 2000, at www.acecashexpress.com; Ace Cash Express, Inc., *1999 Annual Report*, SEC Form 10-K, pp. 1–2; Steve Jordon, "Quick Cash, High Fees: More Are Using Loans to Make It to New Payday," *Omaha World-Herald,* 9 April 2000, p. M1; and Minutaglio, op. cit., chap. 5.

34. Ace Cash Express, Inc., op. cit., pp. 3–7; and Kilborn, op. cit., p. A1.

35. Jordon, op. cit., p. M1; Sanders, op. cit., p. A1; and Marketdata Enterprises, *Check-Cashing and Money Transfer Services* (New York: Marketdata Enterprises, 1999).

36. Quoted in Edmund, op. cit., p. A1. For a discussion of this issue from the perspective of the federal banking system, see Jeanne M. Hogarth and Kevin H. O'Donnell, "Banking Relationships of Lower-Income Families and the Governmental Trend Toward Electronic Payment," *Federal Reserve Bulletin,* vol. 85 (July 1999), pp. 459–473. Also see Jordon, op. cit., p. M1; and Jane Bryant Quinn, "Little Loans Come at Staggering Cost," *The Washington Post*, 13 June 1999, p. H2.

37. Bloomberg News, "Rent-Way Will Offer Gateway's Computers," *Los Angeles Times,* 22 April 2000, p. C2; and Hudson (ed.), op. cit., chaps. 16 and 17.

38. Teresa Dixon Murray, "The Choice Is Yours," *The Plain Dealer,* 3 April 2000, p. C1; Dennis Chapman, "Bill Would Alter Regulation of Rent-to-Own Firms," *Milwaukee Journal Sentinel*, 29 March 2000, p. 3B; and Michael Quinlan, "Committee Kills Rules for Rental Stores," *The Courier-Journal,* 4 February 2000, p. B1.

39. Sharon Linstedt, "No Credit, No Problem," *Buffalo News,* 25 April 2000, p. E1; Murray, op. cit., p. C1; and Salt Lake Tribune, "Rent-to-Own," reprinted in *The Plain Dealer,* 3 January 2000, p. C3.

40. Quoted in Freedman, op. cit., p. 159.

41. Bloomberg News, "Rent-to-Own Customers Satisfied, Survey Shows," *Arizona Republic,* 10 April 2000, p. D1; Murray, op. cit., p. C1; and Hudson (ed.), op. cit., chap. 16.

42. Rent-A-Center, Inc., *1999 Quarterly Report*, SEC Form 10-Q, 12 May 1999, pp. 2–3.

43. Ibid., p. 5.

44. Quoted in Roska, op. cit., p. 4.

45. Quoted in Kilborn, op. cit., p. A1.

46. Jordon, op. cit., p. M1; "Borrowing Loophole: Some Loans Better to Be Outlawed in Texas," *Houston Chronicle,* 16 March 1999, p. A18; Kilborn, op. cit., p. A1; and Jean Ann Fox, *Payday Lenders Charge Exorbitant Interest Rates to Cash-Strapped Consumers* (Washington, D.C.: Consumer Federation of America, 1998). Some state prosecutors have argued that the payday industry is attempting to make local sheriffs departments their low-cost collection agencies and hence essentially their new corporate "muscle." Increasingly, local courts (through the aid of class action suits) are taking the position that since payday loan checks were never written as "good" checks, the borrowers cannot be prosecuted for writing "bad" checks.

47. PIRG and CFA, op. cit., p. 8; Editorial Staff, "Crack Down on Those 'Payday Loans,'" *Tampa Tribune,* 5 February 2000, p. 10; Editorial Staff, "Controlling Loan Sharks," *St. Petersburg Times,* 29 February 2000, p. A16; Ted Jackovics, "Cash Crunch: People Are Flocking to Payday Advance Shops," *Tampa Tribune,* 21 November 1999, p. 1.

48. According to a 1999 survey of 20 states, conducted by Consumer Federation of America (CFA) and Public Interest Research Group (PIRG), payday loans ranged from 260 percent (Helena, Montana) to 988 percent (Atlanta); the average APR was 474 percent. At present, only 19 states currently prohibit payday lending through statutory interest rate ceilings and usury laws. See PIRG and CFA, *Show Me the Money!*

49. In Florida, which is renowned as the capital of the car-title pawn industry, industry representatives primarily led by Title Loans of America funneled over $112,000 in political donations to state legislators and their lobbyists (including former House speakers Don Tucker and Ralph Haben) between 1996 and 1999 to thwart the enactment of lower rate ceilings; Kentucky passed a bill in 1998 that reduced the maximum interest rate to 36 percent, which led to an exodus of car-title pawn operations. In spring 2000, a broad coalition of religious and community groups led to the Florida House unanimously passing legislation that reduced the maximum monthly interest rate from 22.0 to 2.5 percent. The loss of these financial services probably will be filled by other fringe-banking activities such as payday loans. Romell, op. cit., p. 1; Will Rodgers, "Car Title Lenders Say Rates Cheap," *Tampa Tribune,* 25 August 1999, p. 1; Michael Quinlan, "Title-Loan Firms Extinct in State," *The Courier-Journal,* 28 April 1999, p. B1; Kossan, op. cit., p. A1; Smith, op. cit., p. A1; and "Special Report: Poverty Inc.," *Consumer Reports,* vol. 63, no. 7 (July 1998), pp. 28–35.

50. Caskey, *Fringe Banking,* p. 60.

51. RALs are based on the calculated income tax return minus a "loan fee" and tax preparation fee or a separate electronic filing fee (typically $20) if the tax return was prepared by the filer; the IRS electronically deposits the refund within 10 business days. For example, H & R Block charges 19.95 for an RAL of $200 to $500 plus $20.00 for electronic filing; the finance charge for a two-week RAL of $500 (minus $39.95 fees) is 226 percent APR. The APR for a two-week RAL of an average refund of $1,500 (minus $59.95 and $20.00) is 146 percent. If the refunds are deposited by the IRS to H & R Block in one week, then the APRs are twice as high (452 and 292 percent respectively). Similarly, Jackson-Hewitt charges a $60 bank fee, a $24 application fee, and a $35 processing fee for a $1,500 RAL (minus $119 fees), or 224 percent APR for a two-week loan; Santa Barbara Bank and Trust provides the loans. See Pamela Yip, "RALs Can Be Quick Money, but There's a Price to Be Paid for Getting Tax Refund in a Hurry," *San Diego Union-Tribune,* 5 March 2000, p. 12; and Rex Henderson, "1040 Blues: For the Impatient Taxpayer, Refund Anticipation Loans—at a Stiff Price," *Tampa Tribune,* 14 February 1999, p. 1.

52. Manning, op. cit.; and Robert D. Manning and Liana Prieto, "I Have to Pawn to Pay My Credit Cards: The Social Stratification of American Pawnshops," unpublished manuscript, Department of Sociology, Georgetown University (2000).

53. Manning, op. cit.; Manning and Prieto, op. cit.

54. Dennis, op. cit., p. 3B; Donna Halvorsen, "Rent-A-Center Customers Are Getting Refund Checks," *Star Tribune,* 8 March 2000, p. B1; and Michael Quinlan, "Committee Kills Rules for Rental Stores," *The Courier-Journal,* 4 February 2000, p. B1. The most successful efforts to restrict the effective interest rates of lease-ownership purchases through state legislation have been in New Jersey, Minnesota, and Wisconsin. In fact, Rent-A-Center lost a class action lawsuit in New Jersey, and the state assessed RAC $163 million. These class action suits were settled for $60 million. See Consumers League of New Jersey at www.clnj.org.

55. Lease contracts, Rent-A-Center and Aaron's; Hudson (ed.), op. cit., chaps. 16 and 17.

56. Murray, op. cit., p. C1; and Hudson (ed.), op. cit., chaps. 16 and 17.

57. For instance, Mike Kilbane, regional director for Rent-A-Center in northern Ohio, engaged in a heated exchange with Cleveland *Plain Dealer* reporter Teresa Murray over her story on the rent-to-own industry. In response to her question regarding the services that RAC provides that justify its inflated prices, he exclaimed, "'It really doesn't matter what [your readers] think. They can't do anything for me or against me. My customers aren't reading your paper.'" Quoted in John J. Kroll, "Getting the Goods on Rent-to-Own," *The Plain Dealer,* 3 April 2000, p. C1. Also see Freedman, op. cit., pp. 157–161.

58. Linstedt, op. cit., p. E1; Murray, op. cit., p. C1; and Hudson (ed.), op. cit., chaps. 16 and 17.

59. Freedman, op. cit., pp. 155–156.

60. For an example of grassroots organizing campaigns against the rent-to-own industry, see the informative website of the Consumers League of New Jersey at www.clnj.org.

61. United Credit National Bank, "Disclosure of Terms," Visa Credit Card Contract, 1999 (author's emphasis).

62. Quoted in Terence Chea, "Providian Agrees to Restitution and Fine," *The Washington Post,* 29 June 2000, p. E1.

63. Robert D. Manning, "Multicultural Washington, D.C.: The Changing Social and Economic Landscape of a Post-Industrial Metropolis," *Ethnic and Racial Studies,* March 1998, pp. 328–355.

64. This pattern of the social embeddedness of reciprocal debt obligations is reported in a recent ethnographic study of minority communities in California and Mississippi. See John P. Caskey, *Beyond Cash-and-Carry: Financial Savings, Financial Services, and Low-Income Households in Two Communities* (Washington, D.C.: Consumer Federation of America, 1997).

65. Manning, "Multicultural Washington," pp. 373–389.

66. Murray, op. cit., p. C1; Quinn, op. cit., p. H2; and Romell, op. cit., p. 1.

67. Raymond R. Coffey, "Even Benny Is on Payday Loan Act," *Chicago Sun-Times,* 23 March 1999, p. E1.

Chapter 8

1. Quotes from Ruthe Stein, "A Haunting Tale of Success," *San Francisco Chronicle,* 11 July 1999, p. 29.

2. Donald Liebenson, "Will 'Blair Witch Project's' Marketing Spell Continue?" *Los Angeles Times,* 18 October 1999, p. F2; Richard Natale, "The Summer's Other Hitting Streak," *Los Angeles Times,* 31 August 1999, p. F1; and Lewis Beale, "Now It's 'Blair's' Bewitching Hour, Low-Budget Flick Set to Scare Up Big Box-Office Bucks," *New York Daily News,* 29 July 1999, p. 46. The movie's website address is www.blairwitch.com.

3. Quoted in Mark Leibovich, "Computer Associates Backs Off on Bid," *The Washington Post,* 6 March 1998, p. G1. Also see Anthony Bianco, "Charles Wang, Software's Tough Guy, *Business Week,* 6 March 2000, pp. 132–144.

4. Dennis Bergman and Jeremy Quittner, "Credit Cards: Entrepreneurs Are Tapping Them More Than Ever," *Business Week*, 14 December 1998, p. 42.

5. The majority of new business start-ups are initially part-time entrepreneurs; three-fourths of new business owners are also employed in a wage-and-salary job. Frances D. Stanley, *Accessing Capital: Start to Finish* (Richmond, Va.: Federal Reserve Bank of Richmond, September 1998), at www.rich.frb.org/comaffairs; and Small Business Administration, *The Facts About Small Business* (Washington, D.C.: U.S. Government Printing Office, 1997), at www.sbaonline.sba.gov.

6. Quoted in *CNN Financial Network News*, "Charging Your Business: More Owners Than Ever Are Relying on Credit Cards to Finance Their Businesses," 19 November 1998, p. 11.

7. Mark Leibovich, "Amazon.com, Service Workers Without a Smile," *The Washington Post*, 22 November 1999, p. G1; and Mark Leibovich, "AOL Deal Could Weaken Market's Love for Online Stocks," *The Washington Post*, 15 January 2000, p. E1.

8. *CNN Financial Network News*, "Charging Your Business: More Owners Than Ever Are Relying on Credit Cards to Finance Their Businesses," 19 November 1998, p. 11.

9. Bergman and Quittner, op. cit., p. 42.

10. *CNN Financial Network News*, op. cit., p. 11.

11. Quoted in Bergman and Quittner, op. cit., p. 42.

12. Ibid.

13. Steven Jo, "Financing Your Business: The Uphill Battle," *New Vision in Business,* vol. 1, no. 3 (September 1999), p. 19.

14. Quoted in Bergman and Quittner, op. cit., p. 42.

15. Quoted in Teresa Dixon Murray, "Maxing Out Credit Cards Is Way to Get Started in Small Business," *The Plain Dealer,* 31 January 1999, p. H1. See also E. Holly Buttner and Rosen Benson, "Entrepreneurs' Reactions to Loan Rejections," *Journal of Small Business Management,* vol. 1 (1992), pp. 59–66.

16. Shannon Henry, "Venturing onto TV for Capital," *The Washington Post*, 3 June 1999, p. E1.

17. Jo, op. cit., p. 19. The ACE-Net Internet address is http://ace-net.sr.unh.edu.

18. According to Dr. Lawrence Chimerine, managing director and chief economist, Economic Strategy Institute, and MasterCard consultant, during an interview with financial news correspondent Paul Solomon on PBS's *The News Hour* with Jim Lehrer, 21 December 1996: "Credit cards have essentially democratized the availability of credit in [the United States]. . . . Ten or 15 years ago low-income and high-risk families could not get any credit. Now at least they do get credit cards, some get home mortgages . . . in the process it has improved the quality of a lot of families' lives." The "Consumer Credit Debate" program included Dr. Robert D. Manning, Department of Sociology, Georgetown University.

19. Bruce A. Kirchhoff, *Entrepreneurship and Dynamic Capitalism* (Westport, Conn.: Praeger Press, 1994). See also John Case, "The Wonderland Economy," in John Case (ed.), *The State of Small Business* (Boston, Mass.: Goldhirsh Group, 1995), pp. 13–16.

20. Stanley, op. cit.; and Small Business Administration, op. cit.

21. Since the end of 1993, the stock price of American Express has increased 465 percent. See Stephen Gandel, "Is American Express Headed for a Fall?" *Individual Investor,* November 1999, pp. 76–79. Also, the successful marketing of its small business Corporate charge card enables American Express to promote its very profitable tax and business services (TBS) program. According to its 2000 advertising campaign, "Where else but American Express can you find comprehensive help for your business?" The small business services offered include commercial loan development, tax planning and preparation, strategic business planning, accounting and bookkeeping, financial planning, and accounting software. The advertisement concludes by exclaiming "Learn how American Express Tax and Business Services can help your business succeed!" Available at www.americanexpress.com.

22. Quoted in Murray, op. cit., p. H1.

23. Jan Norman, "Business Incubators," in Robert W. Price (ed.), *Entrepreneurship 1999–2000* (Guilford, Conn.: Dushkin/McGraw-Hill, 1999), pp. 117–119; and Vikki Ramsey Conwell, "Church 'Business,'" *New Vision in Business,* vol. 1, no. 3 (September 1999), p. 19.

24. The "cultural rate of profit," whereby U.S.-based corporations demand higher rates in the 1980s than comparable companies in other countries, is examined in Robert D. Manning, "Industrial Restructuring, Immigrant Workers, and the American State," unpublished Ph.D. dissertation, Department of Sociology, Johns Hopkins University (1989), chap. 5.

25. See Bennett Harrison and Barry Bluestone, *The Great U-Turn: Corporate Restructuring and the Polarizing of America* (New York: Basic Books, 1989); David Harvey, *The Condition of Post-Modernity* (London: Basil Blackwell, 1989); M. Patricia Marchak, *The Integrated Circus: The New Right and the Restructuring of Global Markets* (Montreal: McGill University Press, 1993); David M. Gordon, *Fat and Mean: The Corporate Squeeze of Working Americans and the Myth of Managerial Downsizing* (New York: Free Press, 1996); and Dean Baker, Gerald Epstein, and Robert Pollin (eds), *Globalization and Progressive Economic Policy* (Cambridge: Cambridge University Press, 1998).

26. On labor market "degradation" and other "flexible accumulation" policies, see Manning, op. cit., chaps. 7–8; Leann Tigges, "On Dueling Sectors: The Role of Service Industries in the Earning Process of the Dual Economy," in George Farkas and Paula England (eds.), *Industries, Firms, and Jobs* (New York: Aldine de Gruyter, 1994), pp. 281–302; and Ash Amin (ed.), *Post-Fordism: A Reader* (London: Basil Blackwell, 1996).

27. On worker displacement, see Carolyn C. Perrucci, Robert Perrucci, Dena B. Targ, and Harry R. Targ, *Plant Closings: International Context and Social Costs* (New York: Aldine de Gruyter, 1988); Harrison and Bluestone, op. cit.; and U.S. Bureau of Labor Statistics, *News,* USDL 96-446, cited in table 669 in the *1998 Statistical Abstract of the United States* (Washington, D.C.: U.S. Government Printing Office, 1999), p. 416. On the self-employment of displaced workers, see Anne Murphy, "Do-It-Yourself Job Creation," *Inc.* (January 1994), pp. 36–48; Betsy D. Gelb, "Selling Your Service Business," *Business Horizons* (November-December 1995), pp. 71–76; and Kathi S. Allen and Gloria Flynn Moorman, "Leaving Home: The Emigration of Home-Office Workers," *American Demographics,* October 1997, pp. 57–61.

28. *The Big One* is based largely on Moore's national book tour for *Downsize This!* (New York: HarperCollins, 1996). The movie had a very short and limited distribution in theaters. As with most of Moore's movies, its popularity is more accurately measured by video-rental revenues. A weekly series, *The Awful Truth,* was one of the most watched programs on the Bravo cable channel during 2000.

29. John Case, *From the Ground Up: The Resurgence of American Entrepreneurship* (New York: Simon & Schuster, 1992), pp. 32–33.

30. Kirstin Downey Grimsley, "Revenge of the Temps: Independent Contractors' Victory in Microsoft Case May Have Wide Impact," *The Washington Post,* 16 January 2000, pp. H1, H7.

31. Chris Tilly, *Half a Job* (Philadelphia: Temple University Press, 1996); Robert E. Parker, *Flesh Peddlers and Warm Bodies: The Temporary Help Industry and Its Workers* (New Brunswick, N.J.: Rutgers University Press, 1994); and Virginia L. duRivage (ed.), *New Policies for the Part-Time and Contingent Workforce* (New York: M. E. Sharpe, 1992).

32. On 10 January 2000, the U.S. Supreme Court refused to hear an appeal from Microsoft Corp. regarding the ruling against it by the 9th Circuit Court of Appeals. This decision upholds the lower court's ruling that thousands of temporary workers at Microsoft were essentially "common-law" employees and thus qualified for some of the same benefits as permanent workers employed in the same occupation. In this case, the court specified that pension rules apply to all employees who worked at least 20 hours per week with at least five months of con-

tinuous employment. The key issue is the right to purchase discounted Microsoft stock (85 percent of market value without commission fees) as part of the company's pension plan. A worker who bought 20 shares of stock in January 1987 would have paid only $818. By January 1998, after stock splits, the number of shares would have grown to 720 and would be worth over $107,000. See Kirstin Downey Grimsley, "Temporary Workers Win in Lawsuit," *The Washington Post*, 11 January 2000, p. E3.

33. David Birch, cited in Steven Pearlstein, "Fleet-Footed Firms Reshape Economy: 'Gazelles' Represent a Business Revolution," *The Washington Post*, 4 July 1994, pp. A1, A11. Birch reports the following distribution of job gains and losses by firm size between 1989 and 1993. For large firms, −352,000 low-wage, −481,000 average-wage, and −2,520,000 high-wage; for small firms, +906,000 low-wage, +1,479,000 average-wage, and +1,433,000 high-wage. The overall totals are +554,000 low-wage, +1,479,000 average-wage, and −1,093,000 high-wage.

34. Lawrence Mishel, Jared Bernstein, and John Schmitt, *The State of Working America, 1998–1999* (Ithaca: Cornell University Press, 1999), pp. 247–248. See research reports and updates by the Economic Policy Institute at www.epinet.org.

35. The 1997 statistic is not strictly comparable with earlier years due to changes in the Bureau of Labor Statistics survey methodology. See Mishel, Bernstein, and Schmitt, op. cit., pp. 248–249.

36. Michael E. Porter, "The Competitive Advantage of the Inner City," *Harvard Business Review*, vol. 73, no. 3 (1995), pp. 55–71. See also Michael E. Porter, *The Michael E. Porter Trilogy: Competitive Strategy, Competitive Advantage of Nations* (New York: Free Press, 1998).

37. Michael J. Piore and Charles F. Sabel, *The Second Industrial Divide: Possibilities for Prosperity* (New York: Basic Books, 1984).

38. Bennett Harrison, *Lean and Mean: The Changing Landscape of Corporate Power in the Age of Flexibility* (New York: Basic Books, 1994). Also see Dale Belman, Erica L. Groshen, Julia Lane, and David Stevens, *Small Consolation: The Dubious Benefits of Small Business for Job Growth and Wages* (Washington, D.C.: Economic Policy Institute, 1998).

39. David Segal, "Small Business: For Entrepreneurs, Hopeful Days at Center Stage," *The Washington Post Business*, 12 June 1995, p. 13.

40. David Birch, *Who's Creating Jobs?* (Cambridge, Mass.: Cognetics, Inc., 1995); and Case, "The Wonderland Economy," pp. 14–29. Birch defines gazelles as companies that averaged at least 20 percent sales growth in the 1990s. According to his analysis of the 9 million companies that have sales and employment data on file with Dun & Bradstreet, only about 3 percent qualified as gazelles between 1990 and 1994. Significantly, he noted that gazelles were overrepresented in manufacturing and underrepresented in services; only about 2 percent of gazelles were hitech companies.

41. Small Business Administration, op. cit.

42. National Association of Women Business Owners, *1999 Facts on Women-Owned Businesses: Trends in the Top 50 Metropolitan Areas* (Rockville, Md.: National Association of Women Business Owners, 2000). Reports are available at www.nfwbo.org.

43. National Association of Women Business Owners, *Women-Owned Businesses: Breaking the Boundaries* (Rockville, Md.: National Association of Women Business Owners, 1995); and U.S. Bureau of the Census, *Women-Owned Businesses, 1992 Economic Census* (Washington, D.C.: U.S. Government Printing Office, 1995), pp. 2–4. It is important to note that the increase in female entrepreneurship mirrors the greater labor participation rates of women since the 1960s and the increased pressures for dual incomes in order to maintain the middle-class lifestyle of American families; another factor has been job discrimination in the workplace.

44. National Association of Women Business Owners, *1999 Facts on Women-Owned Businesses.*

45. Ibid.; and U.S. House of Representatives, Committee on Small Business, *New Economic Realities: The Rise of Women Entrepreneurs,* Report no. 100-736 (Washington, D.C.: U.S. Government Printing Office, 1988).

46. Ellie Winninghoff, "Crashing the Glass Ceiling," *Entrepreneurial Woman,* vol. 1, 1990, pp. 66–70; Dorothy P. Moore, E. Holly Buttner, and Benson Rosen, "Stepping Off the Corporate Track: The Entrepreneurial Alternative," in Uma Sekaran and Fred Leong (eds.), *Womanpower: Managing in Times of Demographic Turbulence* (Newbury Park, Calif.: Sage, 1991), pp. 85–110; E. Holly Buttner, "Female Entrepreneurs: How Far Have They Come?" *Business Horizons,* March-April 1993, pp. 59–63; and Gayle Sato Stodder, "Girls Rule: Women Entrepreneurs Are Getting Rich . . . So Why Aren't They Getting Famous?" *Entrepreneur's Business Start-Ups,* December 1999, pp. 42–47.

47. National Association of Women Business Owners, *Women-Owned Businesses: Breaking the Boundaries.*

48. Davis Bushnell, "More Women Taking Charge," *Boston Globe,* 7 May 1995, p. 9; D'Vera Cohen and Kirstin Downey Grimsley, "Women-Owned Firms' Surge Mirrored in D.C.," *The Washington Post,* 6 March 1996, pp. D1–2; Elizabeth Kadetsky, "Small Loans, Big Dreams," *Working Woman,* vol. 20, no. 2 (February 1995), pp. 46–49; and U.S. Bureau of the Census, *Women-Owned Businesses, 1992 Economic Censuses,* p. 5.

49. Jackie Spinner, "Women Do Well in Business, but Not as Well at the Bank," *The Washington Post,* 27 July 1995, p. B10.

50. Quoted from National Association of Women Business Owners, op. cit. See also National Association of Women Business Owners, *Women Business Owners of Color: Challenges and Accomplishments* (Rockville, Md.: National Association of Women Business Owners, 1998). The study reports that between 1987 and 1996, the number of minority women-owned firms increased by 153 percent, employment grew by 276 percent, and revenues rose by 318 percent. During this period, the respective increases by racial and ethnic group were Latinos (206 percent), Asians/Native Americans (138 percent), and African Americans (135 percent). Significantly, the proportion with bank credit ranged from African Americans (38 percent), Native Americans (42 percent), and Asians (45 percent) to Latinos (50 percent) and whites (60 percent).

51. National Association of Women Business Owners, *1999 Facts on Women-Owned Businesses;* and U.S. Bureau of the Census, *Women-Owned Businesses, 1992 Economic Census.*

52. Pam Black, "A 'New-Girl' Network Starts to Take Root," *Business Week,* 15 September 1995, pp. 29–30.

53. David L. Birch, *Job Generation in America* (New York: Free Press, 1987); Mark Granovetter, "Small Is Bountiful: Labor Markets and Establishment Size," *American Sociological Review,* vol. 49 (June 1984), pp. 323–334; George Gilder, *The Spirit of Enterprise* (New York: Basic Books, 1984); Steven Pearlstein, "Fleet-Footed Firms Reshape Economy: 'Gazelles' Represent a Business Revolution," *The Washington Post,* 4 July 1994, pp. A1, A11; and Steven Solomon, *Small Business USA: The Role of Small Companies in Sparking America's Economic Transformation* (New York: Crown Publishers, 1986).

54. Quotes from Ken Western, "Company Cashes in on Coupons: Ideas Bring Fast Growth," *Arizona Republic,* 7 September 1997, p. D1.

55. Case, "The Wonderland Economy," pp. 9–10.

56. Case, *From the Ground Up,* pp. 223–224.

57. For a brief review of the leading trends and websites on small business in the United States, see Robert W. Price (ed.), *Entrepreneurship, 1999–2000* (Guilford, Conn.: Dushkin/McGraw-Hill, 1999).

58. Manning, op. cit., chap. 5.

59. Stanley, op. cit.

60. A fundamental flaw of Piore and Sabel (1984) and Harrison (1994) is their method-ological bias toward the manufacturing sector with its older and larger firms and neglect of small, "informal-sector" firms and various forms of self-employment.

61. The increasing use of credit cards has led to creative acceptance procedures by self-employed and small-business people on the fringe of the cash economy. Increasingly, self-employed entrepreneurs develop business networks whereby a credit card merchant account of a member is "borrowed" in order to accept noncash transactions. In return, a much higher merchant fee (typically 8–15 percent) is charged by the member with the account, which helps to defray the costs of the processing system.

62. "How to Use Credit Cards to Make Big Ca$h," Internet solicitation.

Chapter 9

1. The American Association of Retired Persons (AARP) commissioned a national survey in 1998 that was designed to measure its members' awareness of privacy issues and their atti-tudes regarding privacy of personal and financial information. The study concluded that "ir-respective of age, gender, education, income, or political views, a high proportion of AARP members believe that existing consumer protections are not strong enough to protect infor-mation privacy, and they strongly believe that companies, government agencies, and Web sites should not sell information about them to other companies." See Kristin Moag, "AARP Members' Concerns About Information Privacy," *Data Digest,* no. 39 (Washington, D.C.: AARP Public Policy Institute, February 1999).

2. For a discussion of credit discrimination against older adults, see AARP's "Credit Dis-crimination" at www.aarp.org/ontheissues.

3. Population projections are based on medium-growth assumptions for fertility, mortal-ity, and immigration. See Frank B. Hobbs with Bonnie L. Damon, *65+ in the United States,* Current Population Reports, P23-190 (Washington, D.C.: U.S. Government Printing Of-fice, 1996), p. 1. Also see Samuel H. Preston and Linda G. Martin (eds.), *Demography of Aging* (Washington, D.C.: National Academy of Sciences Press, 1994); Harry Moody, *Aging: Concepts and Controversies* (Thousand Oaks, Calif.: Pine Forge Press, 1997); and Paul John-son and Jane Falkingham, *Aging and Economic Welfare* (Newbury Park, Calif.: Sage, 1992).

4. Peter G. Peterson, "Will America Grow Up Before It Grows Old?" *Atlantic Monthly,* May 1996, pp. 55–86, available at www.theatlantic.com.

5. The most current data are available from the U.S. government's Administration on Aging at www.aoa.dhhs.gov. For historical trends and other important information on U.S. seniors, see the comprehensive website of Indiana University's Institute on Aging at www.iupui.edu. These include the rising median age of the U.S. population, life expectancy by gender, geographic distribution of older adults, and health care expenditures by age group.

6. Frances Fox Piven and Richard Cloward, *Regulating the Poor: The Functions of Public Welfare* (New York: Vintage, 1997).

7. Peterson, op. cit., pp. 55–86; Hobbs with Damon, op. cit.; Kevin Kinsella and Yvonne J. Gist (eds.), *Older Workers, Retirement, and Pensions,* IPC/95-2 (Washington, D.C.: U.S. Government Printing Office, December 1995); Olivia S. Mitchell (ed.), *As the Workforce Ages: Costs, Benefits, and Policy Challenges* (Ithaca, N.Y.: Cornell University Press, 1993); and Moody, op. cit.

8. Chapter 4 includes a discussion on the moral imperative that underlies the "cognitive connect" between earning/savings and credit/debt in formulating an appropriate household standard of living in the age of the consumer culture. Also see Lendol Calder, *Financing the American Dream: A Cultural History of Consumer Credit* (Princeton, N.J.: Princeton Univer-sity Press, 1999); David M. Tucker, *The Decline of Thrift in America* (New York: Praeger,

1991); and Daniel Horowitz, *The Morality of Spending: Attitudes Toward the Consumer Society in America, 1975–1940* (Baltimore: Johns Hopkins University Press, 1985).

9. Unpublished data from the 1995 Survey of Consumer Finance, cited in table 823, *1998 Statistical Abstract of the United States* (Washington, D.C.: U.S. Government Printing Office, 1999), p. 524.

10. CardWeb, "Profit Squeeze," CardTrak, October 1999. CardTrak is the most comprehensive and reliable source for current information on the credit card industry. It is available at www.cardweb.com/cardtrak/pastissues. The difference between the statistics reported by the 1995 Survey of Consumer Finance and CardTrak is that the former are self-reports of consumers' general behavior, whereas the latter measure consumers' actual payment history as reported by the credit card companies.

11. The promotion of cobranded frequent-flier credit cards is designed to appeal to the work ethic of earning free airline tickets simply by remembering to charge all personal expenses to the cardholder's account. Unfortunately, with membership fees typically ranging from $40 to $60 per year, the modest annual charge volume of most seniors means that the "free" ticket may cost as much as a normally discounted fare. Indeed, no-annual-fee credit card cash-back programs are usually a better financial choice. See Robert D. Manning, "So Many Credit Card Choices, So Little Time: How to Choose the Best Deal for You," at www.creditcardnation.com.

12. Board of Governors of the Federal Reserve System, *Federal Reserve Bulletin,* April 1998, cited in "Debt Status of Homeowners," table 1220, *1998 Statistical Abstract of the United States* (Washington, D.C.: U.S. Government Printing Office, 1999), p. 728.

13. U.S. Congressional Budget Office, *Baby Boomers in Retirement: An Early Perspective* (Washington, D.C.: U.S. Government Printing Office, September 1993), p. 29. For a comprehensive review of the social and economic issues confronting America's senior citizens, see Lois A. Vitt and Jurg K. Siegenthaler (eds.), *Encyclopedia of Financial Gerontology* (Westport, Conn.: Greenwood Press, 1996). Also see Table 9.3 in Chapter 9; and Joseph Anderson, *American Family Wealth: Analysis of Recent Census Data* (Washington, D.C.: Consumer Federation of America, 1999).

14. U.S. Bureau of the Census, *Current Population Reports,* P60-198 (Washington, D.C.: U.S. Government Printing Office, 1998), cited in "Persons Below Poverty Level," table 759, *1998 Statistical Abstract of the United States* (Washington, D.C.: U.S. Government Printing Office, 1999), p. 478. In 1997, the poverty rates by racial/ethnic group were whites, 9.4 percent; Asians and Pacific Islanders, 9.7 percent; Latinos, 20.7 percent; and African Americans, 25.3 percent. Overall, 13.6 percent of women and 6.8 percent of men over 64 years old were living in poverty in 1997.

15. U.S. Bureau of Labor Statistics, "Employment and Earnings," reported in table 645, *1998 Statistical Abstract of the United States* (Washington, D.C.: U.S. Government Printing Office, 1999), p. 403; and U.S. Congressional Budget Office, *Baby Boomers in Retirement: An Early Perspective* (Washington, D.C.: U.S. Government Printing Office, September 1993).

16. Daniel Bell, *The Cultural Contradictions of Capitalism* (New York: Basic Books, 1976); Witold Rybczynski, *Waiting for the Weekend* (New York: Viking Press, 1991); Victoria de Grazia and Ellen Furlough (eds.), *The Sex of Things: Gender and Consumption in Historical Perspective* (Berkeley: University of California Press, 1996); and Calder, op. cit., chap. 5.

17. Robert D. Manning, *Credit Cards on Campus: The Social Consequences of Student Debt* (Washington, D.C.: Consumer Federation of America, 1999), at www.creditcardnation.com; and American Association of Retired People (AARP), "Credit Marches On," *Horizons,* February 1995, p. 6.

18. Diane Crispell and William Frey, "American Maturity," *American Demographics,* March 1993, pp. 31–42; Alan Greco, "Representation of the Elderly in Advertising: Crisis or

Consequence?" *Journal of Services Marketing,* vol. 2 (Summer 1988), pp. 27–33; and H. Lee Meadow, Stephen C. Cosmas, and Andy Plotkin, "The Elderly Consumer: Past, Present, and Future," in Kent Munroe (ed.), *Advances in Consumer Research,* vol. 8 (Ann Arbor: Association for Consumer Research, 1981), pp. 742–747.

19. AARP, "Credit Marches On," p. 6; and unpublished data from the 1995 Survey of Consumer Finance, cited in table 823, *1998 Statistical Abstract of the United States* (Washington, D.C.: U.S. Government Printing Office, 1999), p. 524.

20. Robert D. Manning, *Credit Cards on Campus: Current Trends and Informational Deficiencies* (Washington, D.C.: Consumer Federation of America, 1999), at www.creditcard nation.com; and 1995 Survey of Consumer Finance.

21. James Langdon, "Shopping and Killing," *Sunday Telegraph,* 27 December 1998, p. 2; Robert Ruth, "Attorney Charged with Federal Felonies in Separate Cases," *Columbus Dispatch,* 10 December 1998, p. D3; Ace Atkins, "Prosecutors Target Fraud Against Elderly," *Tampa Tribune,* 11 April 1999, p. 9; "Ex-Stockbroker Pleads Guilty," *Boston Globe,* 25 October 1997, p. F1; and "Pair Arrested in Credit Card Scheme Totaling More Than $4 Million," *Tampa Tribune,* 22 May 1996, p. 3.

22. Tanya Rivenburg, "Charge, Granny, Charge!" unpublished manuscript, Department of Sociology, American University, 1994. In 1994, AARP received $8.7 million in revenues from Bank One for its Visa and MasterCard affinity credit cards, which were used by 1.2 million AARP members. See David S. Hilzenrath, "AARP's Nonprofit Status Comes Under Scrutiny," *The Washington Post,* 22 May 1995, p. A1.

23. George Ritzer, *Expressing America: A Critique of the Global Credit Card Society* (Thousand Oaks, Calif.: Pine Forge Press, 1995).

24. Teresa A. Sullivan, Elizabeth Warren, and Jay Lawrence Westbrook, *The Fragile Middle Class: Americans in Debt* (New Haven: Yale University Press, 2000); Robert Pollin, *Deeper in Debt: The Changing Financial Conditions of U.S. Households* (Washington, D.C.: Economic Policy Institute, 1990); Frederick R. Strobel, *Upward Dreams, Downward Mobility* (Lanham, Md.: Rowman & Littlefield, 1992); Teresa Sullivan, Elizabeth Warren, and Jay Westbrook, *As We Forgive Our Debtors: Bankruptcy and Consumer Credit in America* (New York: Oxford University Press, 1989); and Katherine Newman, *Falling from Grace: The Experience of Downward Mobility in the American Middle Class* (New York: Free Press, 1988).

25. Kim Wessel, "Two Plead Guilty in Ballroom-Dancing Fraud Case," *The Courier Journal,* 26 March 1999, p. B5; Thayer Scott, "Scam Cost 77-Year-Old $20,000," *St. Petersburg Times,* 12 July 1997, p. 1; J. Harry Jones, "Charmer Took Their Love and Their Loot," *San Diego Union-Tribune,* 16 December 1996, p. A1; and "Woman Says Firm Duped Her for Credit Card Number," *St. Petersburg Times,* 1 August 1999, p. 3.

26. Steve Strunsky, "77-Year Old Is Charged in Armed Robbery," *The New York Times,* 8 March 1998, p. 6; "Rockville Woman Is Charged with Purse-Snatchings," *The Washington Post,* 11 February 1998, p. B5; "Man Found Guilty of Killing Mother," *Arizona Republic,* 28 February 1998, p. B1.

27. U.S. Bureau of Labor Statistics, "Employment and Earnings," reported in table 645, *1998 Statistical Abstract of the United States* (Washington, D.C.: U.S. Government Printing Office, 1999), p. 403; U.S. Congressional Budget Office, *Baby Boomers in Retirement: An Early Perspective* (Washington, D.C.: U.S. Government Printing Office, September 1993), pp. 19–22; Vitt and Siegenthaler (eds.), op. cit., pp. 151–163; Joseph F. Quinn and Richard V. Burkhauser, "Retirement and Labor Force Behavior of the Elderly," in Preston and Martin (eds.), op. cit., pp. 50–101; Douglas Holtz-Eakin and Timothy M. Smeeding, "Income, Wealth, and Intergenerational Economic Relations of the Aged," in Preston and Martin (eds.), op. cit., pp. 102–145; and Greg J. Duncan and Ken R. Smith, "The Rising Affluence of the Elderly: How Far, How Fair, How Frail," *Annual Review of Sociology,* 1989, pp. 261–289.

28. Ronald D. Lee, "The Formal Demography of Population Aging, Transfers, and the Economic Life Cycle," in Preston and Martin (eds.), op. cit., pp. 8–49; Beth J. Soldo and Vicki A. Freedman, "Care of the Elderly: Division of Labor Among the Family, Market, and State," in Preston and Martin (eds.), op. cit., pp. 195–216; and U.S. Congressional Budget Office, op. cit., pp. 19–22.

29. Wu, op. cit., p. 5; Paul Ryscavage, "Trends in Income and Wealth of the Elderly in the 1980s," U.S. Bureau of the Census, *Current Population Reports*, P-60, no. 183 (Washington, D.C.: U.S. Department of Commerce, 1992); and Robyn Stone, "The Feminization of Poverty Among the Elderly," *Women's Studies Quarterly*, vol. 17 (1989), pp. 20–34.

30. Rivenburg, op. cit. Also see Shirley Shim and Mary Mahoney, "The Elderly Mail Order Catalog User of Fashion Products," *Journal of Direct Marketing*, vol. 6 (Winter 1992), pp. 49–58; and Kim I. Dempsey, "Capturing the Nation's Largest Consumer Group," *Best's Review*, February 1994, p. 54.

31. Beth H. Hess, "Stereotypes of the Aged," *Journal of Communication*, Autumn 1974, p. 79. See also John B. Mason and William Beardon, "Profiling the Shopping Behavior of Elderly Consumers," *Gerontologist*, vol. 18 (1978), pp. 454–461; Eric Sherman and Patricia Claper, "Life Satisfaction: The Mission Focus of Marketing to Seniors," *Journal of Health Care Marketing*, vol. 8 (March 1988), pp. 69–72; and Robert D. Manning and Brett Williams, "Credit Cards," in Vitt and Siegenthaler (eds.), op. cit., pp. 102–107.

32. Robert D. Manning, "Multiculturalism in America: Clashing Concepts, Changing Demographics, and Competing Cultures," *International Journal of Group Tensions*, Summer 1995, pp. 117–168; and Robert D. Manning, "Washington, D.C.: The Social Transformation of the International Capital City," in Silvia Pedraza and Ruben G. Rumbaut (eds.), *Origins and Destinies: Race, Immigration, and Ethnicity in America* (New York: Wadsworth Press, 1995), pp. 373–389.

33. U.S. Bureau of the Census, *Current Population Reports*, P60-197 (Washington, D.C.: U.S. Government Printing Office, 1998), cited in "Married-Couple Families—Number and Median Income," table 751, *1998 Statistical Abstract of the United States* (Washington, D.C.: U.S. Government Printing Office, 1999), p. 474, at www.census.gov.

34. U.S. Congressional Budget Office, op. cit., pp. 27–31.

35. The capital gains allowance for homeowners was raised from $125,000 to $300,000 ($600,000 for joint ownership) in 1999. Overall, homeownership rates for married-couple families headed by someone 30–34 years old fell from 71.9 percent in 1982 to 66.6 percent in 1991, whereas 40 percent of all home mortgages between 1983 and 1992 were adjustable rate mortgages. Also, housing prices over the next two decades are projected to range from about the rate of inflation to a decline of as much as 47 percent. See U.S. Bureau of the Census, Current Housing Reports, Series H121-90-2, *Homeownership Trends in the 1980s* (Washington, D.C.: U.S. Government Printing Office, 1991); Peter Saunders, *A Nation of Home Owners* (London: Unwin Hyman, 1990); N. Gregory Mankiw and David N. Weil, "The Baby Boom, the Baby Bust, and the Housing Market," *Regional Science and Urban Economics*, May 1989; Patrick H. Henderschott, "Are Real House Prices Likely to Decline by 47 Percent?" *Regional Science and Urban Economics* (December 1991); and Joyce M. Manchester and James M. Poterba, "Second Mortgages and Household Saving," *Regional Science and Urban Economics*, May 1989. Overall, homeownership rates rose from 64.1 percent in 1991 to 65.7 percent in 1997. Significantly, homeownership rates among the late baby boomers did not improve during this period, remaining essentially constant for age groups 35–39 (62.6 percent) and 40–44 (69.7 percent). Although the homeownership rate of older adults (aged 60–74) improved only slightly, it was substantially higher at over 81 percent. See U.S. Bureau of the Census, *Current Population Survey/Housing Vacancy Survey*, cited in "Homeownership Rates by Age of Householder," in table 1215, *1998 Statistical Abstract of the United*

States (Washington, D.C.: U.S. Government Printing Office, 1999), p. 726, at www.census.gov.

36. U.S. Congressional Budget Office, op. cit., pp. 27–31.

37. Anderson, op. cit., pp. 21–23, at www.consumerfed.org.

38. Pollin, op. cit.

39. Anderson, op. cit., pp. 21–23.

40. Wu, op. cit., pp. 5–10.

41. U.S. Congressional Budget Office, op. cit., pp. 27–31.

Chapter 10

1. Ann Landers, syndicated advice column, *The Washington Post,* 15 November 1995, p. D8.

2. George Ritzer, *Expressing America: A Critique of the Global Credit Card Society* (Thousand Oaks, Calif.: Pine Forge Press, 1995), pp. 71–72.

3. "Marketing Brief—1995 Citibank College Advertising Awards," corporate memo, Citibank, Spring 1995, p. 2 (author's emphasis).

4. Patricia Drentea and Paul J. Lavrakas, "Over the Limit: The Association Among Health, Race, and Debt," *Social Science and Medicine,* vol. 50 (2000), pp. 517–529. For statements by Janne O'Donnell and Tisha Johnson regarding the credit card debt–related suicides of their children, Sean and Mitzi, respectively, see "Credit Card Debt Imposes Huge Costs on Many College Students," 9 June 1999, available in the "Press Releases" section at www.consumerfed.org.

5. Robert D. Manning and Anita Butera, "Global Restructuring and U.S.-Mexican Economic Integration: Rhetoric and Reality of Mexican Immigration Five Years After NAFTA," special issue "Globalization, Transnationalism, and the End of the American Century," *American Studies,* vol. 41, nos. 2–3 (Summer/Fall 2000), pp. 183–209; and Dale Maharidge, *Journey to Nowhere: The Saga of the New Underclass* (New York: Hyperion Press, 1996).

6. Daniel Bell, *The Cultural Contradictions of Capitalism* (New York: Basic Books, 1976), pp. 3–30, 54–84.

7. Stephen Biggar, "Industry Surveys, Banking," *Standard & Poor's,* vol. 166, no. 24, sec. 1 (11 June 1998), pp. 2–3.

8. Book value is typically defined as the dollar value of the company's net assets as stated in its accounting books. See Gary A. Dymski, *The Bank Merger Wave: The Economic Causes and Social Consequences of Financial Consolidation* (Armonk, N.Y.: M. E. Sharpe, 1999); and Biggar, op. cit., pp. 6–8.

9. Dymski, op. cit., p. 271; and Biggar, op. cit., pp. 6–8.

10. Lewis Mandell, *The Credit Card Industry: A History* (Boston: Twayne Publishers, 1990), p. 37; and CardWeb, "Market Power," CardTrak, February 2000, available at www.cardweb.com.

11. Quoted in Associated Press, "Visa, MasterCard in Antitrust Trial, U.S. Argues That Firms Block Rivals," *The Washington Post,* 13 June 2000, p. D3.

12. CardWeb, "Profit Squeeze," CardTrak, October 1999, pp. 2–3, available at www.cardweb.com.

13. Citigroup, "Citigroup Reports Record Core Income for the Fourth Quarter and for 1999," Citigroup news release, 18 January 2000, available at www.citibank.com.

14. The forecast model is based on conservative assumptions, since it does not presume a sharp increase in unemployment or percentage of revolvers (57 percent) over the decade. First, the model assumes that revolving consumer debt will increase at a rate 25 percent slower than the preceding decade's annual average growth rate of 10.5 percent (1990–1999).

Second, the spread is based on the 1989 baseline rate of 8.8 percent, which is closest to the annual average for the decade (1980–1989) excluding the extraordinarily low 1.4 percent of 1981. The excessive spread rate is based on the current 11.2 percent, which produces a net consumer rip-off spread of 2.4 percent (11.2 percent – 8.8 percent). With an estimated growth of consumer revolving credit from $519 billion in January 2000 to $1,107.4 billion in January 2009, this yields an estimated credit card interest rip-off of $193.4 billion. For estimates of excessive penalty fees, the annual average increase for 1990–1995 of 5.65 percent was doubled for 1996, 1997, 1998, and 1999. This figure was then subtracted from the amount charged by the industry for each of these years. In 1999, the difference is $10.1 billion, and this amount is held constant over the forecast decade for a total of $101.0 billion. Together, a very conservative estimate of the decade's excessive charges imposed on credit card revolvers by card issuers will be at least $294.4 billion.

15. Citigroup, "Citigroup Reports Record Core Income for the Fourth Quarter and for 1999," Citigroup news release, 18 January 2000, available at www.citibank.com.

16. Market information from industry websites at www.visa.com and www.mastercard.com.

17. Ritzer, op. cit., p. 22.

18. Ibid, p. 157.

19. Citigroup, "Citigroup and Taiwan's Fubon Group Announce a Powerful Strategic Partnership," Citigroup news release, 6 May 2000; "Citigroup Grants $1 Million for Low-Income Loans in Asia," Citigroup news release, 24 March 2000; "Citigroup Strengthens Core Consumer Business with Three Acquisitions," Citigroup news release, 23 March 2000; "Citibank Announces $200-Million Loan Facility with OPIC for Caribbean and Central America," Citigroup news release, 10 February 2000; "Citibank Acquires Portions of Argentine Bank," Citigroup news release, 30 December 1998; and "Citicorp Completes Acquisition of Hungarian Bank," Citigroup news release, 10 August 1998, available at www.citibank.com.

20. Kevin Sullivan and Mary Jordan, "In Japan, Cash Registers, Many Merchants Start Accepting Credit Cards at Urging of Olympic Officials," *The Washington Post,* 8 February 1998, p. E2.

21. Gabriel Torres, "The El Barzón Debtors' Movement: From the Local to the National in Protest Politics," in Wayne A. Cornelius and David Myhre (eds.), *The Transformation of Rural Mexico: Reforming the Ejido Sector* (La Jolla, Calif.: Center for U.S.-Mexican Studies, 1998), pp. 133–151.

22. Talbot Stevens, "Make High-Interest Debt a Top Priority," *The London Free Press,* 10 July 2000, p. 7; Amy Cartmall, "Plastic Not So Fantastic Once Bills Start Mounting Up," *Evening Chronicle,* 13 July 2000, p. 32; "Help—My Credit Cards Are Costing Me a Fortune," *The Observer,* 2 July 2000, p. 9; "Consumer Credit Hits High," *Edinburgh Evening News,* 29 June 2000, p. 5; Magadalen Chow, "Credit Card 'Extortion' Rapped," *South China Morning Post,* 11 July 2000, p. 1; "Hong Kong Lenders Expected to Embrace Credit Card Securitization," *The Asian Banker Journal,* 7 July 2000, p. 1; Nick Bruining, "Don't Overlook Revolving Credit as a Risk to Wealth," *Australasian Business Intelligence,* 3 July 2000, p. 41; and Mary Teresa Bitti, "Almost Home: Before Sonia and Barbara Can Buy a Condo, They Have to Pay Off Those Bills," *National Post,* 1 May 2000, p. 21.

23. Patricia Lamiell, "Citigroup Plans 10,400 Job Cuts," *The Washington Post,* 15 December 1998, p. E1.

Bibliography

ABC *Nightline.* "Americans in the Red." 29 December 1998, www.abc.com.

Abraham, Jed H. "'The Divorce Revolution' Revisited: A Counter-Revolutionary Critique." *Northern Illinois Law Review,* vol. 9 (1989), pp. 251–298.

Ace Cash Express, Inc. "General Information," 2000, www.acecashexpress.com.

_____. *1999 Annual Report.* SEC Form 10-K.

AFL-CIO. "Worker Fact Sheet," 2000.

Alger, Horatio, Jr. *Ragged Dick.* Edited by Carl Bode. New York: Penguin Books, 1985.

Allen, Frederick Lewis. *Only Yesterday: An Informal History of the 1920s.* New York: Harper & Row, 1931.

Allen, John. "Fordism and Modern Industry." In *Modernity: An Introduction to Modern Societies,* edited by Stuart Hall, David Held, Don Hubert, and Kenneth Thompson. Cambridge: Basil Blackwell, 1996.

Allen, Kathi S., and Gloria Flynn Moorman. "Leaving Home: The Emigration of Home-Office Workers." *American Demographics,* October 1997, pp. 57–61.

"Ames CIA Mole." *The Washington Post,* 8 March 1993, p. A1.

Amin, Ash, ed. *Post-Fordism: A Reader.* London: Basil Blackwell, 1996.

Anders, George. *Merchants of Debt: KKR and the Mortaging of American Business.* New York: Basic Books, 1992.

Anderson, Joseph M. *American Family Wealth: Analysis of Recent Census Data.* Washington, D.C.: Consumer Federation of America, 1999.

Arensen, Karen W. "Columbia's Colossal Student Center, Designed by Dean of Architecture, Is to Open in September." *The New York Times,* 28 July 1999, p. B8.

Associated Press. "Visa, MasterCard in Antitrust Trial, U.S. Argues That Firms Block Rivals." *The Washington Post,* 13 June 2000, p.D 3.

_____. "Three-Year-Old Gets Gold Credit Card." *Boston Globe,* 10 August 1999, p. A17.

_____. "$70 Billion Deal: Citicorp, Travelers to Merge." *Seattle Times,* 6 April 1998.

_____. "Citicorp Gets Gold Mine of Choice Sales Targets." *Ottawa Citizen,* 19 December 1997, p. D9.

Atkins, Ace. "Prosecutors Target Fraud Against Elderly." *Tampa Tribune,* 11 April 1999, p. 9.

AT&T. "Citibank Acquires AT&T Universal Card Services." AT&T news release, 18 December 1997, www.citibank.com.

Ausubel, Lawrence M. "Personal Bankruptcies Begin Sharp Decline: Millennium Data Update." University of Maryland: Department of Economics, 2000.

_____. "A Self-Correcting 'Crisis': The Status of Personal Bankruptcy in 1999." Unpublished manuscript, Department of Economics, University of Maryland, College Park, January 2000.

_____. "The Failure of Competition in the Credit Card Market." *American Economic Review,* vol. 81, no. 1 (March 1991), pp. 50–81.

Babcock, Charles R. "Rising Tuitions Fill Loan Firm Coffers." *The Washington Post,* 27 October 1997, p. 1.

Baer, Herbert L., and Larry R. Mote. *The U.S. Financial System.* Chicago: Federal Reserve Bank, 1990.

Baker, Dean, Gerald Epstein, and Robert Pollin, eds. *Globalization and Progressive Economic Policy.* Cambridge: Cambridge University Press, 1998.

Baldassare, Mark. "Suburban Communities." *Annual Review of Sociology,* vol. 18 (1992), pp. 475–495.

Bankcard Holders of America. *Bankcard Consumer News,* vol. 15, no. 6 (November–December 1995), pp. 1–2.

"The Bankruptcy Express Slows Down." *Business and Industry,* August 1998, p. 2.

Barber, Benjamin R. *Jihad vs. McWorld: How Globalism and Tribalism Are Reshaping the World.* New York: Ballantine Books, 1995.

Barlett, Donald I., and James B. Steele. *America: What Went Wrong?* Kansas City: Andrews and McMeel, 1992.

Barron, John M., and Michael E. Staten. *Personal Bankruptcy: A Report on Petitioners' Ability to Pay.* Washington, D.C.: Credit Research Center, Georgetown University, October 1997.

Barsky, Neil. "Trump to Ask Bondholders for Debt Relief." *The Wall Street Journal,* 26 July 1990, p. A3.

Barth, James, Dan R. Brumbaugh, and Robert E. Litan. *The Future of American Banking.* New York: M. E. Sharpe, 1992.

Bartlett, Sarah. *The Money Machine: How KKR Manufactured Power and Profits.* New York: Warner Books, 1991.

Baum, Sandy, and Diane Saunders. "Life After Debt: Results of the National Student Loan Survey." In *Student Loan Debt: Problems and Prospects.* Washington, D.C.: Institute for Higher Education Policy, 1998.

Beale, Lewis. "Now It's 'Blair's' Bewitching Hour, Low-Budget Flick Set to Scare Up Big Box-Office Bucks." *New York Daily News,* 29 July 1999, p. 46.

Beaupre, Becky. "$10,000 Tip Rejected by Credit Firm." *Chicago Sun-Times,* 8 June 2000, p. 1.

Beck, Rachel. "Venator to Trim Jobs, Shut 358 Stores." *The Washington Post,* 26 January 2000, p. E3.

Behr, Peter. "Wave of Merges, Takeovers Is a Part of Reagan Legacy." *The Washington Post,* 30 October 1998, p. H1.

Bell, Daniel. *The Cultural Contradictions of Capitalism.* New York: Basic Books, 1996.

Belman, Dale, Erica L. Groshen, Julia Lane, and David Stevens. *Small Consolation: The Dubious Benefits of Small Business for Job Growth and Wages.* Washington, D.C.: Economic Policy Institute, 1998.

Bensman, David, and Roberta Lynch. *Rusted Dreams: Hard Times in a Steel Community.* Berkeley: University of California Press, 1988.

Berger, Joseph. "The Pain of Layoffs for Ex-Senior I.B.M. Workers." *The New York Times,* 22 December 1993, p. B1.

Bergman, Dennis, and Jeremy Quittner. "Credit Cards: Entrepreneurs Are Tapping Them More Than Ever." *Business Week,* 14 December 1998, p. 42.

Bernstein, Aaron. *Grounded: Frank Lorenzo and the Destruction of Eastern Airlines.* New York: Simon & Schuster, 1990.

Berry, John M. "Takeovers Eroding Corporate Equity, Increasing Debt." *The Washington Post,* 28 October 1988, p. H1.

Bianco, Anthony. "Charles Wang, Software's Tough Guy." *Business Week,* 6 March 2000, pp. 132–144.

Biggar, Stephen. "Industry Surveys, Banking." *Standard & Poor's,* vol. 166, no. 24, sec. 1, 11 June 1998, pp. 11–12.

Birch, David. *Who's Creating Jobs?* Cambridge, Mass: Cognetics, Inc., 1995.

————. *Job Generation in America.* New York: Free Press, 1987.

Bird, Edward J., Paul A. Hagstrom, and Robert Wild. "Credit Card Debts of the Poor: High and Rising." Unpublished paper, Department of Public Policy, University of Rochester, 1998.

Bitti, Mary Teresa. "Almost Home: Before Sonia and Barbara Can Buy a Condo, They Have to Pay Those Bills." *National Post,* May 2000, p. 21.

Black, Pam. "A 'New-Girl' Network Starts to Take Root." *Business Week,* 15 September 1995, pp. 29–30.

Black, Robert L., Don L. Boroughs, Sara L. Collins, and Kenneth Sheets. "Heavy Lifting: How America's Debt Burden Threatens the Economic Recovery." *U.S. News & World Report,* 6 May 1991, pp. 51–54.

Block, Fred L. *The Origins of International Economic Disorder.* Berkeley: University of California Press, 1977.

Bloomberg News. "Rent-Way Will Offer Gateway's Computers." *Los Angeles Times,* 22 April 2000, p. C2.

————. "Rent-to-own Customers Satisfied, Survey Shows." *Arizona Republic,* 10 April 2000, p. D1.

————. "Bond Sales Boost Berkshire." *Montreal Gazette,* 4 August 1998, p. C3.

Bluestone, Barry, and Bennett Harrison. *The Deindustrialization of America: Plant Closings, Community Abandonment, and the Dismantling of Basic Industry.* New York: Basic Books, 1982.

Borjas, George J. *Heaven's Door: Immigration Policy and the American Economy.* Princeton: Princeton University Press, 1999.

"Borrowing Loophole: Some Loans Better to Be Outlawed in Texas." *Houston Chronicle,* 16 March 1999, p. A18.

Boshara, Ray. *Federal and State Individual Development Accounts (IDA) Overview.* Washington, D.C.: Corporation for Enterprise Development, October 1999.

Bostic, Raphael, and Glenn B. Canner. "Consolidation in Banking: How Recent Changes Have Affected the Provision of Banking Services." *Neighborworks Journal,* vol. 18, no. 1 (2000), pp. 22–25.

Boswell, Terry, and Albert Bergesen, eds. *America's Changing Role in the World System.* New York: Praeger Press, 1987.

Bouvier, George. *Free Trade Fraud.* New York: St. Martin's Press, 1991.

Bowe, Christopher. "The Americas: Fed Rules over APR Rates for Payday Loans." *Financial Times,* 27 March 2000, p. 3.

Bowles, Samuel, David M. Gordon, and Thomas E. Weisskopf. "Power and Profits: The Social Structure of Accumulation and the Profitability of the Postwar U.S. Economy." *Review of Radical Political Economics,* vol. 18 (1986), pp. 132–167.

Boyd, John H., and Mark Gertler. "U.S. Commercial Banking: Trends, Cycles, and Policy." Working Paper no. 4404. Cambridge, Mass.: National Bureau of Economic Research, 1993.

Braun, Denny. *The Rich Get Richer: The Rise of Income Inequality in the United States and the World*. Chicago: Nelson-Hall, 1997.

Breen, T. H. *Tobacco Culture: The Mentality of the Great Tidewater Planters on the Eve of Revolution*. Princeton: Princeton University Press, 1985.

Broadway, Bill. "The Bishop Who Wasn't: Atlanta Diocese Loses Faith in Episcopal Priest." *The Washington Post*, 4 March 2000, p. B9.

Brobeck, Stephen. "Expanding Credit Card Debt: The Role of Creditors and the Impact on Consumers." Washington, D.C.: Consumer Federation of America, 16 December 1997.

Bruining, Nick. "Don't Overlook Revolving Credit as a Risk to Wealth." *Australasian Business Intelligence*, 3 July 2000, p. 41.

Burgess, John. "1999 Trade Gap Hits Record $271 Billion." *The Washington Post*, 19 February 2000, p. E1.

Burkett, Larry. *Debt-Free Living: How to Get Out of Debt and Stay Out*. Gainesville, Ga.: Christian Financial Concepts, Inc., 1995.

Burrough, Bryan. "Barbarians in Retreat." *Vanity Fair*, March 1993, pp. 190–230.

Burrough, Bryan, and John Helyar. *Barbarians at the Gate*. New York: Harper-Collins, 1990.

Burtless, Gary, and Timonthy Smeeding. "America's Tide: Lifting the Yachts, Swamping the Rowboats." *The Washington Post*, 25 June 1995, p. C3.

Bushnell, Davis. "More Women Taking Charge," *Boston Globe*, 7 May 1995, p. C9.

Business Week. "Corporate Scoreboard." 16 March 1992, pp. 64–92.

————. "Corporate Scoreboard." 18 March 1991, pp. 52–93.

————. "Corporate Scoreboard." 20 March 1989, pp. 62–116.

————. "Corporate Scoreboard." 16 March 1987, pp. 125–146.

Butler, Katy. "The Great Boomer Bust." *Mother Jones*, June 1989, pp. 33–42.

Buttner, Holly. "Female Entrepreneurs: How Far Have They Come?" *Business Horizons*, March–April 1993, pp. 59–63.

Buttner, Holly, and Rosen Benson. "Entrepreneurs' Reactions to Loan Rejections." *Journal of Small Business Management*, vol. 1 (1992), pp. 59–66.

Calder, Lendol. *Financing the American Dream: A Cultural History of Consumer Credit*. Princeton: Princeton University Press, 1999.

Calleo, David P. *The Bankrupting of America: How the Federal Budget Is Impoverishing the Nation*. New York: Basic Books, 1992.

————. *Beyond American Hegemony: The Future of the Western Alliance*. New York: Basic Books, 1987.

Canner, Glenn B., Arthur B. Kennickell, and Charles A. Luckett. "Household Sector Borrowing and the Burden of Debt." *Federal Reserve Bulletin*, April 1995, pp. 323–328.

Canner, Glenn B., and Charles A. Luckett. "Payment of Household Debts." *Federal Reserve Bulletin*, April 1999, pp. 218–229.

Caplovitz, David. *The Poor Pay More: Consumer Practices of Low-Income Families*. New York: Free Press, 1963.

CardWeb. "Rates Stand Still." CardTrak, June 2000, www.cardweb.com.

————. "Market Power." CardTrak, February 2000, www.cardweb.com.

————. "Credit Card U.S. Brand Marketshare." CardTrak, October 1999, www.cardweb.com.

————. "Profit Squeeze." CardTrak, October 1999, www.cardweb.com.

Cartmall, Amy. "Plastic Not So Fantastic Once Bills Start Mounting Up." *Evening Chronicle*, 13 July 2000, p. 32.

Case, John. "The Wonderland Economy." In *The State of Small Business.* Boston, Mass.: Goldhirsh Group, Inc., 1995.

———. *From the Ground Up: The Resurgence of American Entrepreneurship.* New York: Simon & Schuster, 1992.

Cash America International Inc. *1999 Annual Report.* SEC Form 10-K, 14 May 2000.

Caskey, John P. *Beyond Cash-and-Carry: Financial Savings, Financial Services, and Low-Income Households in Two Communities.* Washington, D.C.: Consumer Federation of America, 1997.

———. *Lower-Income Americans, Higher-Cost Financial Services.* Madison, Wis.: Filene Research Institute, Center for Credit Union Research, 1997.

———. *Fringe Banking: Check-Cashing Outlets, Pawnshops, and the Poor.* New York: Russell Sage, 1994.

Cavanaugh, Joanne P., Sue De Pasquale, Melissa Hendricks, and Dale Keiger. "Scrambling for Dollars: Why Is a Hopkins Education So Expensive?" *Johns Hopkins Magazine,* September 1998, pp. 12–27.

CBS News. "Bankrupt in Florida." *60 Minutes,* 28 November 1993.

Chang, Angela, Shubham Chaudhuri, and Jith Jayaratne. "Rational Herding and the Spatial Clustering of Bank Branches: An Empirical Analysis." Federal Reserve Bank of New York, Research Paper no. 9724, August 1997.

Chapman, Dennis. "Bill Would Alter Regulation of Rent-to-Own Firms." *Milwaukee Journal Sentinel,* 29 March 2000, p. 3B.

Chea, Terence. "Providian Agrees to Restitution and Fine." *The Washington Post,* 29 June 2000, p. E1.

Cherlin, Andrew. *Marriage, Divorce, Remarriage: Social Trends in the United States.* Cambridge: Harvard University Press, 1992.

Chevy Chase Bank. *Community Lending Performance.* 14 May 1994.

Chow, Magadalen. "Credit Card 'Extortion' Rapped." *South China Morning Post,* 11 July 2000, p. 1.

Citibank. "Marketing Brief—1995 Citibank College Advertising Awards." Corporate memo, Citibank, Spring 1995.

Citicorp Annual Report 1998. New York: Citicorp, 1999.

Citicorp Annual Report 1993. New York: Citicorp, 1994.

Citicorp Annual Report 1992. New York: Citicorp, 1993.

Citicorp Annual Report 1989. New York: Citicorp, 1990.

Citigroup. "Citigroup Declares 4-3 Stock Split" July 19, 2000.

———. "Citigroup and Taiwan's Fubon Group Announce a Powerful Strategic Partnership." Citigroup news release, 6 May 2000.

———. "Citigroup Grants $1 Million for Low-Income Loans in Asia." Citigroup news release, 24 March 2000.

———. "Citigroup Strengthens Core Consumer Business with Three Acquisitions." Citigroup news release, 23 March 2000.

———. "Citibank Announces $200-Million Loan Facility with OPIC for Caribbean and Central America." Citigroup news release, 10 February 2000.

———. "Citigroup Reports Record Core Income." Citigroup news release, 18 January 2000, www.citibank.com.

———. "Citibank to Acquire Mellon Bank's Credit Card Business." Citibank news release, 23 March 1999, www.citibank.com.

———. "Citibank Acquires Portions of Argentine Bank." Citigroup news release, 30 December 1998.

———. "Citicorp Completes Acquisition of Hungarian Bank." Citigroup news release, 10 August 1998.

_____. "Citicorp and Travelers Group to Merge." Citigroup news release, 6 April 1998, www.citibank.com.

Citizens for Tax Justice. *It's Working, but . . . The Resurgence of Business Investment and Corporate Income Taxes.* Washington, D.C.: Citizens for Tax Justice, 1989.

"Clinton's Credit Card Not Accepted: Expired American Express Forces President to Ask Aide for Help." *Houston Chronicle*, 2 March 1999, p. A3.

CNN Financial Network News. "Charging Your Business: More Owners Than Ever Are Relying on Credit Cards to Finance Their Businesses." 19 November 1998.

Coffey, Raymond R. "Even Benny Is on Payday Loan Act." *Chicago Sun-Times*, 23 March 1999, p. E1.

Cohen, D'Vera, and Kirstin Downey Grimsley. "Women-Owned Firms' Surge Mirrored in D.C.*" The Washington Post*, 6 March 1996, pp. D1–2.

Conley, Dalton. *Being Black, Living in the Red: Race, Wealth, and Social Policy in America.* Berkeley: University of California Press, 1999.

"Consumer Credit Hits High." *Edinburgh Evening News,* 29 June 2000, p. 5.

"Consumer Debt Rises at Weak Pace," *Los Angeles Times*, 9 July 1998, p. D3.

Consumer Federation of America. "Large Banks Increase Charges to Americans in Credit Counseling: New Practices Will Hurt Consumers on the Brink of Bankruptcy." 28 July 1999, www.consumerfed.org.

_____. "Credit Card Debt Imposes Huge Costs on Many College Students." 9 June 1999, available at www.consumerfed.org.

_____."Banks Expand Card Marketing and Credit Extension While Seeking to Restrict Consumer Access to Bankruptcy." 8 July 1998.

Consumer Reports, vol. 63, no. 7 "Special Report: Poverty Inc." (July 1998), pp. 28–35.

Conwell, Vikki Ramsey. "Church Business." *New Vision in Business,* vol. 1, no. 3 (September 1999), p. 19.

Craver, Charles B. *Can Unions Survive?* New York: New York University Press, 1995.

Crenshaw, Albert B. "Options for Parents As College Costs Climb." *The Washington Post*, 18 October 1998, p. H1.

Crispell, Diane, and William Frey. "American Maturity." *American Demographics,* March 1993, pp. 31–42.

Crowley, J. E. *This Sheba, Self: Conceptualization of Economic Life in Eighteenth-Century America.* Baltimore: Johns Hopkins University Press, 1979.

Danzinger, Sheldon, and Gregory Acs. "Educational Attainment, Industrial Structure, and Male Earnings, 1973–1987." Madison, Wis.: Institute for Research on Poverty, 1990.

David, Martin, and Thomas Flory. "Changes in Marital Status and Short-Term Income Dynamics." In *Individuals and Families in Transition,* edited by H. V. Beaton, D. A. Ganni, and D. T. Frankel. Washington, D.C.: U.S. Bureau of the Census, 1989.

Decker, Jonathan P. "Bankruptcies Drop, but Not by Much." *Christian Science Monitor,* 20 March 2000, p. 16.

de Grazia, Victoria, and Ellen Furlough, eds. *The Sex of Things: Gender and Consumption in Historical Perspective.* Berkeley: University of California Press, 1996.

Delaney, Kevin J. *Strategic Bankruptcy: How Corporations and Creditors Use Chapter 11 to Their Advantage.* Berkeley: University of California Press, 1992.

Dempsey, Kim. "Capturing the Nation's Largest Consumer Group." *Best's Review,* February 1994, p. 54.

Diggins, John P. *Thorstein Veblen: Theorist of the Leisure Class.* Princeton: Princeton University Press, 1999.

Dow Jones News. "Merger: Who's Next." 13 April 1998.

_____. ."Citicorp Buyback: Analyst Sees Other Bank Buyback This Year." 20 June 1995.

_____. "Citicorp Gets First World Bank Investment Guarantee." 19 June 1995.

_____. "Citicorp 1st Quarter Operating Net." 19 April 1995.

_____. "U.S. Banks Fourth Quarter Derivatives Activity Remains at $15 Trillion." 31 March 1995.

_____. "Citicorp Suspends Expansion Plans in Mexico." 24 March 1995.

_____. "Citicorp, Citibank: Disciplined Strategy Cited." 2 February 1995.

Drentea, Patricia, and Paul J. Lavrakas. "Over the Limit: The Association Among Health, Race, and Debt." *Social Sciences and Medicine,* vol. 50 (2000), pp. 517–529.

D'souza, Dinish. "The Billionaire Next Door." *Forbes,* 11 October 1999, pp. 51–60.

Dubofsky, Melvyn. *The State and Labor in Modern America.* Chapel Hill: University of North Carolina Press, 1994.

Dugas, Christine. "Going from Debt-Ridden to Debt-Free: Credit Cards Hard to Control." *USA Today,* 18 September 1998, p. B3.

Dumenil, G., M. Glick, and J. Rangel. "The Rate of Profit in the United States." *Cambridge Journal of Economics,* vol. 11 (1987), pp. 331–359.

Duncan, Greg, and Ken R. Smith. "The Rising Affluence of the Elderly: How Far, How Fair, How Frail." *Annual Review of Sociology,* 1989, pp. 261–289.

DuRivage, Virginia L., ed. *New Policies for the Part-Time and Contingent Workforce.* New York: M. E. Sharpe, 1992.

Dymski, Gary A. *The Bank Merger Wave: The Economic Causes and Social Consequences of Financial Consolidation.* Armonk, N.Y.: M. E. Sharpe, 1999.

_____. "The Theory of Credit-Market Redlining and Discrimination: An Exploration." *Review of Black Political Economy,* vol. 23, no. 3 (Winter 1995), pp. 37–74.

Dymski, Gary A., and John M. Veitch. "Financial Transformation and the Metropolis: Booms, Busts, and Banking in Los Angeles." *Environment and Planning,* vol. 28, no. 7 (July 1996), pp. 1233–1260.

The Economist. 2 November 1991, p. 69.

The Economist Newspaper. "After the Deal." 9 January 1999, p. 21.

Editorial Staff. "Controlling Loan Sharks." *St. Petersburg Times,* 29 February 2000, p. A16.

_____. "Crack Down on Those Payday Loans." *Tampa Tribune,* 5 February 2000, p. 10.

Education Resources Institute (ERI) and Institute for Higher Education Policy. *Credit Risk or Credit Worthy? College Students and Credit Cards: A National Survey.* Boston: ERI, 1998.

Ehrenreich, Barbara. *Fear of Falling.* New York: HarperCollins, 1987.

Einzig, Paul. *Primitive Money.* London: Erie and Spottiswoode, 1949.

Eisler, Kim I. "Say Uncle: Chevy Chase Bank Decided Not to Fight Back." *Washingtonian Magazine,* July 1995, pp. 47–53.

Elle. March 1992, p. 58.

Employee Benefit Research Institute (EBRI). "The Savings Paradox?" June 1999, at www.ebri.org/facts.

"Ex-Stockbroker Pleads Guilty." *Boston Globe,* 25 October 1997, p. F1.

Faludi, Susan C. "The Safeway LBO Yields Vast Profits but Exacts a Heavy Human Toll." *The Wall Street Journal,* 16 May 1990, p. 1.

Family Circle. 19 May 1978, p. 221.

Farhi, Paul. "Getting a Grip on Debt, Time Warner Owes $18.5 Billion." *The Washington Post,* 25 June 1995.

Federal Reserve Bulletin. www.bog.frb.fed.us/releases/G19/current.

Federal Reserve Statistical Release. "Consumer Credit." June 2000, www.bog.frb.fed.us.

Feldman, Amy. "Shareholders Embrace Citi/Travelers Pairing." *Daily News,* July 1998.

First USA. "Affinity Group Bankcard Agreement" with University of Tennessee at Knoxville. 28 June 1998.

Flint, Troy. "Students Graduate to Huge Debts." *The Times-Picayune,* 22 November 1998, p. 1.

Forbes. "Forbes Richest People in America—1999." www.forbes.com.

———. "The Billionaires." 17 July 1995, pp. 110–223.

———. "America's Highest-Paid Bosses." 22 May 1995, pp. 180–182.

The Forbes 400. "A Century of Wealth." *Forbes,* 11 October 1999, p. 169.

Foster, Stephen. *Their Solitary Way: The Puritan Social Ethic in the First Century of Settlement in New England.* New Haven: Yale University Press, 1971.

Fox, Jean Ann. *States Grant Payday Lenders a Safe Harbor from Usury Laws.* Washington, D.C.: Consumer Federation of America, 1999.

———. *Payday Lenders Charge Exorbitant Interest Rates to Cash-Strapped Consumers.* Washington, D.C.: Consumer Federation of America, 1998.

———. "The Growth of Legal Loan Sharking: A Report on the Payday Loan Industry." Washington, D.C.: Consumer Federation of America, 1998.

Fox, Richard W., and T. J. Jackson Lears. *The Culture of Consumptionism: Critical Essays in American History.* New York: Pantheon Books, 1983.

Frank, Robert H., and Philip J. Cook. *The Winner-Take-All Society.* New York: Free Press, 1995.

"Fraud Costs." *The Washington Post,* 31 March 1994, p. D12.

Frean, Alexandra, and Karen Wolfson. "Poor Using Alternative Bank System." *The Times,* 22 March 1999, p. A1.

Freedman, Alix M. "Peddling Dreams." In *Merchants of Misery: How Corporate America Profits from Poverty,* edited by Michael Hudson. Monroe, Maine: Common Courage Press, 1996, pp. 153–167.

Friedman, Benjamin M. *Day of Reckoning: The Consequences of American Economic Policy.* New York: Vintage Press, 1989.

Friedman, Jon. "Travelers Group–Citicorp Merger May Mean Higher Prices." *Bloomberg News,* 7 April 1998, p. 1.

Fromson, Brett D. "Warren Buffett, Taking Stock: Berkshire Hathaway's Chairman Rides a Bull Market to the Top of the Billionaires' Club." *The Washington Post,* 4 September 1993, p. B1.

Furlong, Frederick T., and Michael C. Keeley. "Capital Regulation and Bank Risk-Taking: A Note." *Journal of Banking and Finance,* November 1989, pp. 883–891.

Gallert, David J., Walter S. Hilborn, and Geoffrey May. *Small Loan Legislation: A History of the Regulation of the Business of Lending Small Sums.* New York: Russell Sage Foundation, 1932.

Gandel, Stephen. "Is American Express Headed for a Fall?" *Individual Investor,* November 1999, pp. 76–79.

Garland, Greg. "Payday Loans Exact High 'Fees' from the Desperate." *Baltimore Sun,* 19 September 1999, p. A8.

Gazel, Neil R. *Beatrice: From Buildup Through Breakup.* Chicago: University of Illinois Press, 1990.

Gelb, Betsy D. "Selling Your Service Business." *Business Horizons,* November–December 1995, pp. 71–76.

Gentlemen's Quarterly, August 1987, p. 21.

————. August 1985, p. 37.

Gilder, George. *The Spirit of Enterprise.* New York: Basic Books, 1984.

Glasberg, Davita Silfen, and Dan Skidmore. *Corporate Welfare Policy and the Welfare State: Bank Deregulation and the Savings and Loan Bailout.* New York: Aldine de Gruyter, 1997.

Glickman, Norman J., and Douglas P. Woodward. *The New Competitors: How Foreign Investors Are Changing the U.S. Economy.* New York: Basic Books, 1989.

Goldsmith, Raymond W. *A Study of Savings in the United States,* vol. 1. Princeton: Princeton University Press, 1955.

Goodnough, Abby. "The Day the Jobs Got Up and Moved Away." *The New York Times,* 23 July 1995, p. A13.

Gordon, David M. *Lean and Mean: The Corporate Squeeze of Working Americans and the Myth of Managerial Downsizing.* New York: Free Press, 1996.

————. "The Global Economy: New Edifice or Crumbling Foundations?" *New Left Review,* March–April 1988, pp. 24–64.

Gordon, Marcy. "Credit Cards at 50: The Problems of Ubiquity." *The New York Times,* 12 March 2000, p. A11.

————. "More Consumers Show Credit Card Restraint." *Boston Globe,* 19 January 2000, p. C2.

Gordon, Sara L., and Francis A. Lees. *Foreign Multinational Investment in the United States: Struggle for Industrial Supremacy.* New York: Quorum Books, 1986.

"A Grand Tip in Oregon Ignites a Grand Dispute." *The Washington Post,* 14 March 1996, p. A5.

Granovetter, Mark. "Small Is Bountiful: Labor Markets and Establishment Size." *American Sociological Review,* vol. 49 (June 1984), pp. 323–334.

Greco, Alan. "Representation of the Elderly in Advertising: Crisis or Consequence?" *Journal of Services Marketing,* vol. 2 (Summer 1988), pp. 27–33.

Greven, Philip. *The Protestant Temperament.* New York: Alfred A. Knopf, 1977.

Grimsley, Kirstin Downey. "Revenge of the Temps: Independent Contractors' Victory in Microsoft Case May Have Wide Impact." *The Washington Post,* 16 January 2000, p. H1.

————. "Temporary Workers Win in Lawsuit." *The Washington Post,* 11 January 2000, p. E3.

————. "After Closing Many Doors, RTC Shuts Its Own." *The Washington Post,* 29 December 1995, p. D1.

Halberstam, David. *The Fifties.* New York: Ballantine Books, 1994.

Halvorsen, Donna. "Rent-A-Center Customers Are Getting Refund Checks." *Star Tribune,* 8 March 2000, p. B1.

Hamilton, Martha M. "Coke to Cut 6,000 Jobs in Major Reshuffling." *The Washington Post,* 27 January 2000, p. E1.

Hardy, Charles O., ed. *Consumer Credit and Its Uses.* New York: Prentice-Hall, 1938.

Harney, Kenneth R. "The Portrait of a Homeowner Who Is Debt-Free." *The Washington Post,* 31 October 1998, p. E1.

Harper, Marla. "Not a Doctor Either." *The Washington Post,* 8 March 1993, p. B3.

Harrison, Bennett. *Lean and Mean: The Changing Landscape of Corporate Power in the Age of Flexibility.* New York: Basic Books, 1994.

Harrison, Bennett, and Barry Bluestone. *The Great U-Turn: Corporate Restructuring and the Polarizing of America.* New York: Basic Books, 1988.

Harvey, David. *The Condition of Postmodernity.* Cambridge: Basil Blackwell, 1989.

Hedgpeth, Dana, and Ariana Eunjung Cha. "Amazon Announces Layoffs." *The Washington Post,* 29 January 2000, p. E1.

Heinze, Andrew R. *Adapting to Abundance: Jewish Immigrants, Mass Consumption, and the Search for American Identity.* New York: Columbia University Press, 1990.

Heitmiller, David. *Getting a Life.* New York: Viking Press, 1997.

"Help—My Credit Cards Are Costing Me a Fortune." *The Observer,* 2 July 2000, p. 9.

Henderschott, Patrick H. "Are Real House Prices Likely to Decline by 47 Percent?" *Regional Science and Urban Economics,* December 1991.

Henderschott, Patrick, and Edward Kane. "Office Market Values During the Past Decade: How Distributed Have Appraisals Been?" Working Paper no. 4128. Cambridge, Mass.: National Bureau of Economic Research, 1992.

Henderson, Rex. "1040 Blues: For the Impatient Taxpayer, Refund Anticipation Loans—At a Stiff Price." *Tampa Tribune,* 14 February 1999, p. 1.

Hendricks, Gary, and Kenwood C. Youmans, with Janet Keller. *Consumer Durables and Installment Debt: A Study of American Households.* Ann Arbor, Mich.: Institute for Social Research, 1973.

Henry, Shannon. "Venturing onto TV for Capital." *The Washington Post,* 3 June 1999, p. E1.

Hilzenrath, David S. "AARP's Nonprofit Status Comes Under Scrutiny." *The Washington Post,* 22 May 1995, p. A1.

Hobbs, Frank B., with Bonnie L. Damon. *65+ in the United States.* Current Population Reports, P23-190. Washington, D.C.: U.S. Government Printing Office, 1996.

Hoffman, Saul, and Greg Duncan. "What Are the Economic Consequences of Divorce?" *Demography,* vol. 25 (1988), pp. 641–645.

Hogarth, Jeanne M., and Kevin H. O'Donnell. "Banking Relationships of Lower-Income Families and the Governmental Trend Toward Electronic Payment." *Federal Reserve Bulletin,* vol. 85 (July 1999), pp. 459–473.

Holtz-Eakin, Douglas, and Timothy M. Smeeding. "Income, Wealth, and Intergenerational Economic Relations of the Aged." In *Demography of Aging,* edited by Samuel H. Preston and Linda G. Martin. Washington, D.C.: National Academy of Sciences Press, 1994.

Homer, Sidney, and Richard Sylla. *A History of Interest Rates.* New York: Rutgers University Press, 1996.

"Hong Kong Lenders Expected to Embrace Credit Card Securitization." *Asian Banker,* vol. 7, July 2000, p. 1.

Hoover's Inc. Hoover's Online. 11 December 1999, www.hoovers.com.

Horowitz, Daniel. *The Morality of Spending: Attitudes Toward the Consumer Society in America, 1875–1940.* Baltimore: Johns Hopkins University Press, 1985.

Hosansky, David. "Potent Forces Brace for Battle on Bankruptcy Law Overhaul." *Congressional Quarterly,* 18 October 1997, p. 2536–2539.

HSN Consultants, Inc. "Credit Cards—Holders, Numbers, Spending, and Debt." *The Nilson Report.* Quoted in *1998 Statistical Abstract of the United States.* Washington, D.C.: U.S. Government Printing Office, 1999.

Huck, Paul, and Lewis Sepal. "New Data on Mortgage Lending." Federal Reserve Bank of Chicago, *Chicago Fed Letter,* no. 119 (July 1997), pp. 1–4.

Hudson, Michael, ed. *Merchants of Misery: How Corporate America Profits from Poverty.* Monroe, Maine: Common Courage Press, 1996.

Hutchinson, Robert A. *Off the Books.* New York: William Morrow and Company, 1996.

International Monetary Fund (IMF). *Direction of Trade Statistical Yearbook.* Washington, D.C.: International Monetary Fund, 1999.

Jackovics, Ted. "Cash Crunch: People Are Flocking to Payday Advance Shops." *Tampa Tribune,* 21 November 1999, p. 1.

Jackson, Jesse L., Sr., and Jesse L. Jackson Jr., with Mary Gotschall. *It's About the Money: The Fourth Movement of the Freedom Symphony.* New York: Times Books, 2000.

Jackson, Kenneth T. *Crabgrass Frontier: The Suburbanization of the United States.* New York: Oxford University Press, 1985.

Jacobs, Eva, and Stephanie Shipp. "How Family Spending Has Changed in the U.S." *Monthly Labor Review,* March 1990, pp. 20–27.

Jo, Steven. "Financing Your Business: The Uphill Battle." *New Vision in Business,* vol. 1, no. 3 (September 1999), p. 18.

Johnson, Paul. *Saving and Spending: The Working-Class Economy in Britain 1870–1939.* Oxford: Clarendon Press, 1985.

Johnson, Paul, and Jane Falkingham. *Aging and Economic Welfare.* Newbury Park, Calif.: Sage, 1992.

Jones, Harry. "Charmer Took Their Love and Their Loot." *San Diego Union-Tribune,* 16 December 1996, p. A1.

Jordon, Steve. "Quick Cash, High Fees: More Are Using Loans to Make It to New Payday." *Omaha World-Herald,* 9 April 2000, p. M1.

Judge, Elizabeth. "Briton Comes Home to Face Music over $10,000 Tip," *The Times,* 10 June 2000, p. 5.

Kadetsky, Elizabeth. "Small Loans, Big Dreams," *Working Woman,* vol. 20, no. 2 (February 1995), pp. 46–49.

Kalogerakis, George. "Going Broke." *People Magazine,* 24 February 1997, p. 7.

Kaplan, Steven N. "Taking Stock of the RJR Nabisco Buyout." *The Wall Street Journal,* 30 March 1995, p. 1.

Karp, Richard. "The Donald's CFO." *Financial World,* 14 May 1991, pp. 27–29.

Katsanos, Stephen. "FDIC Board Proposed Rule on Privacy of Consumer Information." Federal Deposit Insurance Corporation, Washington, D.C., spring 2000, at www.fdic.gov/news/press/2000.

Katz, Michael B. *Improving Poor People: The Welfare State, the "Underclass," and Urban Schools as History.* Princeton: Princeton University Press, 1997.

Kaufman, Bruce E. *The Origins and Evolution of the Field of Industrial Relations in the United States.* Ithaca: Industrial and Labor Relations Press, 1993.

Kellerman, Vivien. "A Credit Card with a Little Bonus for Retirement." *The New York Times,* 11 June 1994, p. A36.

Kelly, Kevin. "The Airline Industry's Haves and Have-Nots." *In These Times,* 1–7 May 1991, p. 2.

Kempson, Elaine, and Claire Whyte. *Understanding and Combating Financial Exclusion.* London: Policy Press, 1999.

Kennedy, Paul. *Preparing for the Twenty-First Century.* New York: Vintage Books, 1993.

Kennickell, Arthur B., and Myron L. Kwast. "Who Uses Electronic Banking? Results from the 1995 Survey of Consumer Finances." Finance and Economics Discussion Series, 1997, no. 35. Washington, D.C.: Board of Governors of the Federal Reserve System, 1997.

Kennickell, Arthur, and Janice Shack-Marquez. "Changes in Family Finances from 1983 to 1989: Evidence from the Survey of Consumer Finances." *Federal Reserve Bulletin,* January 1992, pp. 1–18.

Kennickell, Arthur B., and Martha Starr-McCluer. "Changes in Family Finances from 1989 to 1992: Evidence from the Survey of Consumer Finances." *Federal Reserve Bulletin*, October 1994, pp. 861–882.

Kennickell, Arthur B., Martha Starr-McCluer, and Brian J. Surette. "Recent Changes in U.S. Family Finances: Results from the 1998 Survey of Consumer Finances." *Federal Reserve Bulletin,* January 2000, www.bogfrb.fed.us.

Keynes, John Maynard. *How to Pay for the War*. London: Macmillan, 1940.

————. *The General Theory of Employment, Interest, and Money.* London: Macmillan, 1936.

————. *A Treatise on Money.* London: Macmillan, 1930.

Kilborn, Peter T. "New Lenders with Huge Fees Thrive on Workers with Debts." *The New York Times*, 18 June 1999, p. A1.

Kinsella, Kevin, and Yvonne J. Gist, eds. *Older Workers, Retirement, and Pensions*, IPC/95-2. Washington, D.C.: U.S. Government Printing Office, December 1995.

Kirchhoff, Bruce A. *Entrepreneurship and Dynamic Capitalism*. Westport, Conn.: Praeger Press, 1994.

Knox, Noelle. "Banking Titans Bury Hatchet in $35 B Deal." *USA Today*, 14 September 2000, p. B1.

Kossan, Pat. "Quick Cash, Easy Credit." *Arizona Republic*, 14 February 1999, p. A1.

Kroll, John J. "Getting the Goods on Rent-to-Own." *The Plain Dealer,* 3 April 2000, p. C1.

Labaree, Leonard W., ed. *The Autobiography of Benjamin Franklin*. New Haven: Yale University Press, 1964.

————. *The Papers of Benjamin Franklin,* vol. 7. New Haven: Yale University Press, 1963.

Laird, Pamela Walker. *Advertising Progress: American Business and the Rise of Consumer Marketing*. Baltimore: Johns Hopkins University Press, 1998.

Lamiell, Patricia. "Citigroup Plans 10,400 Job Cuts." *The Washington Post*, 15 December 1998, p. E1.

Landers, Ann. Column in *The Washington Post*, 15 November 1995, p. D8.

Langdon, James. "Shopping and Killing." *Sunday Telegraph*, 27 December 1998, p. 2.

"The Latest Round of Finger Pointing." *Credit Card Management*, June 1999, p. 5.

Lavoie, Denise. "Xerox to Cut Payroll by 5,200." *The Washington Post*, 1 April 2000, p. E8.

Leach, William. *Land of Desire: Merchants, Power, and the Rise of a New American Culture.* New York: Pantheon Books, 1993.

Lears, Jackson. *Fables of Abundance: A Cultural History of Advertising in America.* New York: Basic Books, 1994.

Lee, Matthew. "The First Comment ICP Filed with the Federal Reserve Board Opposing the Citicorp-Travelers Merger." *Inner City Press*, www.innercitypress.org.

Lee, Ronald D. "The Formal Demography of Population Aging, Transfers, and the Economic Life Cycle." In *Demography of Aging*, edited by Samuel H. Preston and Linda G. Martin. Washington, D.C.: National Academy of Sciences Press, 1994.

Leibovich, Mark. "The High-Tech Homeless: In Silicon Valley, a Dark Side to the Booming Economy." *The Washington Post*, 12 February 2000, p. A13.

————. "AOL Deal Could Weaken Market's Love for Online Stocks." *The Washington Post*, 15 January 2000, p. E1.

————. "Amazon.com, Service Workers Without a Smile." *The Washington Post*, 22 November 1999, p. G1.

_____. "Computer Associates Backs Off on Bid." *The Washington Post*, 6 March 1998, p. G1.

Lenin, V. I. *Imperialism, the Highest Stage of Capitalism.* New York: International Publishers, 1939.

Levy, Frank. *The New Dollars and Dreams: American Incomes and Economic Change.* New York: Russell Sage Press, 1998.

_____. *Dollars and Dreams: The Changing American Income Distribution.* New York: W. W. Norton, 1988.

Lewis, Michael. *The Money Culture.* New York: Penguin Books, 1992.

_____. *Liar's Poker: Rising Through the Wreckage on Wall Street.* New York: W. W. Norton, 1989.

Liebenson, Donald. "Will Blair Witch Project's Marketing Spell Continue?" *Los Angeles Times,* 18 October 1999, p. F2.

Light, Ivan H., and J. Steven Gold. *Ethnic Economies.* New York: Academic Press, 2000.

Linstedt, Sharon. "No Credit, No Problem." *Buffalo News,* 25 April 2000, p. E1.

Lissakers, Karin. *Banks, Borrowers, and the Establishment: A Revisionist Account of the International Debt.* New York: Basic Books, 1991.

Lloyd, Nancy. *Simple Money Solutions: Ten Ways You Can Stop Being Overwhelmed by Money and Make It Work for You.* New York: Times Books, 2000.

Lowenstein, Roger. *Buffett: The Making of an American Capitalist.* New York: Random House, 1995.

"Low-Income Banking Programs." *Milwaukee Journal Sentinel,* 8 May 2000, p. D1.

Lynd, Robert S., and Helen Merrell Lynd. *Middletown: A Study in Contemporary American Culture.* New York: Harcourt, Brace & Co., 1929.

Macey, Jonathan R., and Geoffrey P. Miller. *Banking Law and Regulation.* New York: Aspen Publishers, 1997.

Maharidge, Dale. *Journey to Nowhere: The Saga of the New Underclass.* New York: Hyperion Press, 1996.

Maloney, Eileen, and George Gregorash. "Banking 1989: Not Quite a Twice-Told Tale." *Economic Perspectives,* Federal Reserve Bank of Chicago, July-August 1990.

"Man Found Guilty of Killing Mother." *Arizona Republic,* 28 February 1998, p. B1.

Manchester, Joyce M., and James M. Poterba. "Second Mortgages and Household Saving." *Regional Science and Urban Economics,* May 1989.

Mandell, Lewis. *The Credit Card Industry: A History.* Boston: Twayne Publishers, 1990.

_____. *Credit Card Use in the United States.* Ann Arbor, Mich.: Institute for Social Research, 1972.

Mankiw, Gregory, and David N. Weil. "The Baby Boom, the Baby Bust, and the Housing Market." *Regional Science and Urban Economics,* May 1989.

Manning, Robert D. "Poverty, Race, and the Two-Tiered Financial Services System." In *Challenges to Equality: Poverty and Race in America,* edited by Chester Hartman. New York: M. E. Sharpe, 2000 forthcoming.

_____. "Credit Cards on Campus: Are Colleges Responsible for the Social Consequences?" Unpublished manuscript, Department of Sociology, Georgetown University, Washington, D.C., 2000, at www.creditcardnation.com.

_____. *Credit Cards on Campus: The Social Consequences of Student Debt.* Washington, D.C.: Consumer Federation of America, 1999, at www.creditcard nation.com.

_____. *Credit Cards on Campus: Current Trends and Informational Deficiencies.* Washington, D.C.: Consumer Federation of America, 1999, at www.credit cardnation.com.

_____. "[Financial] Reality Bytes: New Tax Relief for Recent Graduates and Parents of College Students," 1999, at www.creditcardnation.com.

_____. "So Many Credit Card Choices, So Little Time: How to Choose the Best Deal for You," 1999, at www.creditcardnation.com.

_____. "Multicultural Washington, D.C.: The Changing Social and Economic Landscape of a Post-Industrial Metropolis." *Ethnic and Racial Studies*, March 1998, pp. 328–355.

_____. "Multiculturalism in America: Clashing Concepts, Changing Demographics, and Competing Cultures." *International Journal of Group Tensions*, Summer 1995, pp. 117–168.

_____. "Washington, D.C.: The Social Transformation of the International Capital City." In *Origins and Destinies: Race, Immigration, and Ethnicity in America*, edited by Silvia Pedraza and Rubén G. Rumbaut. New York: Wadsworth Press, 1995.

_____. "U.S. Industrial Restructuring, Immigrant Workers, and the American State: The Political Economy of Mexican Migration." Ph.D. dissertation, Department of Sociology, Johns Hopkins University, Baltimore, 1989.

Manning, Robert D., and Anita Butera. "Global Restructuring and U.S.-Mexican Economic Integration: Rhetoric and Reality of Mexican Immigration Five Years After NAFTA." Special issue "Globalization, Transnationalism, and the End of the American Century," *American Studies*, vol. 41, nos. 2–3 (Summer/Fall 2000), pp. 183–209.

Manning, Robert D., and Liana Prieto. "I Have to Pawn to Pay My Credit Cards: The Social Stratification of American Pawnshops." Unpublished manuscript, Department of Sociology, Georgetown University, 2000.

Mannix, Margaret. "Goodbye to Debt." *U.S. News & World Report*, 27 April 1998.

Marchak, Patricia. *The Integrated Circus: The New Right and the Restructuring of Global Markets*. Montreal: McGill University Press, 1993.

Marchand, Ronald. *Advertising the American Dream: Making Way for Modernity, 1920–1940*. Berkeley: University of California Press, 1985.

Marketdata Enterprises. *Check-Cashing and Money Transfer Services*. New York: Marketdata Enterprises, 1999.

_____. *The U.S. Pawnshops Industry*. New York: Marketdata Enterprises, 1999.

Marshall, Gordon. *In Search of the Spirit of Capitalism*. London: Hutchinson, 1982.

Matthews, Arlene Modica. *Your Money, Your Self*. New York: Simon & Schuster, 1991.

McCartney, Robert J., and Kathleen Day. "Huge Fees May Have Blinded Trump's Lenders." *The Washington Post*, 26 June 1990, p. C1.

McIntry, Robert S., Douglas P. Kelly, Bruce L. Fisher, David Wilhelm, and Helen Luce. *It's Working but . . . The Resurgence of Business Investment and Corporate Income Taxes*. Washington: D.C.: Citizens for Tax Justice, 1989.

Meadow, H. Lee, Stephen C. Cosmas, and Andy Plotkin. "The Elderly Consumer: Past, Present, and Future." In *Advances in Consumer Research*, vol. 8, edited by Kent Munroe. Ann Arbor, Mich.: Association for Consumer Research, 1981.

Medoff, James, and Andrew Harless. *The Indebted Society: Anatomy of an Ongoing Disaster*. Boston: Little, Brown, 1986.

Meehan, John. "All That Plastic Is Still Fantastic for Citibank." *Business Week*, 28 May 1990, p. 90.

Meehan, John, and Leah Nathans Spiro. "Wanted: $5 Billion, Contact Citicorp." *Business Week*, 11 February 1991, pp. 64–65.

Mellan, Olivia. *Overcoming Overspending.* New York: Walker Press, 1995.

"Merger Mania, Sobering Statistics." *The Economist,* 20 June 1998, p. 89.

Merisotis, Jamie P., and Ernest T. Freeman. "A Look at the Rising Cost of College." *The Washington Post,* 3 November 1996, p. 3.

Metro Chicago Information Center. *1999 Metro Survey.* Chicago: MCIC, 1999.

Michelman, Irving S. *Consumer Finance: A Case History in American Business.* New York: Frederick Fell, 1966.

Miller, Kay. "Charging into Debt Triggers Student Anxiety." *Minneapolis Star Tribune,* 12 September 1999, p. 1A.

Miller, Richard. *Citicorp: The Story of a Bank in Crisis.* New York: McGraw-Hill, 1993.

Milton Bradley Company. "Mall Madness, Store Directory and Instructions," 1990.

Minutaglio, Robert. "Prince of Pawns." In *Merchants of Misery: How Corporate America Profits from Poverty,* edited by Michael Hudson. Monroe, Maine: Common Courage Press, 1996, pp. 58–70.

Mishel, Lawrence, Jared Bernstein, and John Schmitt. *The State of Working America.* Ithaca, N.Y.: Cornell University Press, 1999.

Mitchell, Olivia, ed. *As the Workforce Ages: Costs, Benefits and Policy Challenges.* Ithaca, N.Y.: Cornell University Press, 1993.

Moag, Kristin. "AARP Members' Concerns About Information Privacy." *Data Digest,* no. 39. Washington, D.C.: AARP Public Policy Institute, February 1999.

Moody, Harry. *Aging: Concepts and Controversies.* Thousand Oaks, Calif.: Pine Forge Press, 1997.

Moody's Handbook of Common Stock. New York: Moody's Investor Services, 1976–1996.

Moore, Dorothy P., Holly Buttner, and Benson Rosen. "Stepping Off the Corporate Track: The Entrepreneurial Alternative." In *Womanpower: Managing in Times of Demographic Turbulence,* edited by Uma Sekaran and Fred Leong. Newbury Park, Calif.: Sage, 1991.

Moore, Michael. "Campus Curbs on Card Eyed in Two States." *American Banker,* 20 May 1997, p. 7.

_____. *Downsize This!* New York: HarperCollins, 1996.

Morgan, Edmund S. "The Puritan Ethic and the American Revolution." *William and Mary Quarterly,* vol. 24 (January 1967), pp. 3–15.

Morgan, Leslie A. *After Marriage Ends.* Newbury Park, Calif.: Sage, 1991.

Moss, David, and Gibbs Johnson. "The Rise in Consumer Bankruptcy: Evolution, Revolution, or Both." *American Bankruptcy Law Journal,* Spring 1999.

Mundis, Jerrold. *How to Get Out of Debt, Stay Out of Debt, and Live Prosperously.* New York: Bantam Books, 1990.

Murphy, Anne. "Do-It-Yourself Job Creation." *Inc.,* January 1994.

Murphy, Jarrett. "Don't Bank on It." *City Limits,* December 1999, www.citylimits.org/lores/archives.

Murray, Teresa Dixon. "The Choice Is Yours." *The Plain Dealer,* 3 April 2000, p. C1.

_____. "Maxing Out Credit Cards Is Way to Get Started in Small Business." *The Plain Dealer,* 31 January 1999, p. H1.

Myers, Greg. *Ad Worlds: Brands, Media, Audiences.* New York: Edward Arnold, 1998.

Myles, John, and Jill Quadagno. *States, Labor Markets, and the Future of Old-Age Policy.* Philadelphia: Temple University Press, 1991.

Nader, Ralph. "Banking Jackpot." *The Washington Post*, 5 November 1999, p. A33.

Natale, Richard. "The Summer's Other Hitting Streak." *Los Angeles Times,* 31 August 1999, p. F1.

Natapoff, Sam. *Defenseless? Or Less Defense? A Comparison of U.S., German, and Japanese Public Expenditure.* Washington, D.C.: Campaign for New Priorities, 1992.

National Association of Women Business Owners. *1999 Facts on Women-Owned Businesses: Trends in the Top 50 Metropolitan Areas.* Rockville, Md.: National Association of Women Business Owners, 2000.

_____. *Women Business Owners of Color: Challenges and Accomplishments.* Rockville, Md.: National Association of Women Business Owners, 1998.

_____. *Women-Owned Businesses: Breaking the Boundaries.* Rockville, Md.: National Association of Women Business Owners, 1995.

National Directory of Advertisers. New Providence, N.J.: National Register Publishing, 1995 and 1998 editions.

National Republican Committee. "A Strategy for Growth: The American Economy in the 1980s." 1980.

National Science Foundation. *Research and Development Expenditures in the United States.* Washington, D.C.: U.S. Government Printing Office, 1991.

"New Jersey Board Gives Trump Slight Nod." *The Washington Post,* 18 June 1991, p. C5.

Newman, Katherine. *Declining Fortunes: The Withering of the American Dream.* New York: Basic Books, 1993.

_____. *Falling from Grace: The Experience of Downward Mobility in the American Middle Class.* New York: Free Press, 1988.

Newton, Charlotte. "Students' Credit Good." *USA Today,* 8 June 1998, p. A11.

Nightline. 31 August 1999 program, www.abcnews.com.

Nocera, Joseph. *A Piece of the Action: How the Middle Class Joined the Money Class.* New York: Simon & Schuster, 1994.

_____. "The Day the Credit Card Was Born." *Washington Post Magazine,* 4 December 1994, pp. 15–43.

Norman, Jan. "Business Incubators." In *Entrepreneurship 1999–2000,* edited by Robert W. Price. Guilford, Conn.: Dushkin/McGraw-Hill, 1999.

Nugent, Rolf. *Consumer Credit and Economic Stability.* New York: Russell Sage Foundation, 1939.

O'Brien, Timothy L., and Joseph B. Treaster. "Shaping a Colossus: Citicorp Plans Merger with Travelers Group." *The New York Times,* 7 April 1998, p. A1.

O'Connell, Vanessa. "New Risk in Credit Cards: Punitive Rates." *Dow Jones News,* 13 July 1995.

O'Harrow, Robert, Jr. "Consumer Advocates Fear Pitches by Companies Will Breach Personal Privacy." *The Washington Post,* 31 October 1999, p. H1.

Oliver, Melvin L., and Thomas M. Shapiro. *Black Wealth, White Wealth: A New Perspective on Racial Inequality.* New York: Routledge, 1997.

Olney, Martha L. *Buy Now, Pay Later: Advertising, Credit, and Consumer Durables in the 1920s.* Chapel Hill: University of North Carolina Press, 1991.

_____. "Demand for Consumer Durable Goods in 20th Century America." *Explorations in Economic History,* vol. 27 (July 1990), pp. 322–349.

Oppenlander-Eberle, Nan. *Good Fairy Thrift.* Swarthmore: Chatauqua Association of Pennsylvania, 1917.

Orman, Suze. *The 9 Steps to Financial Freedom.* New York: Crown, 1998.

Orser, Dean. "Citicorp Buyback Seen Paving Way for Dividend Increase." *Dow Jones/News Retrieval*, 20 June 1995.

Pacelle, Mitchell. "Trump to Give Up Plaza Stake to Saudi Prince, Hotel Firm." *Dow Jones/News Retrieval*, 12 April 1995.

"Pair Arrested in Credit Card Scheme Totaling More Than $4 Million." *Tampa Tribune*, 22 May 1996, p. 3.

Palen, John. *The Suburbs*. New York: McGraw-Hill, 1995.

Parker Brothers. "Official Monopoly Game Rules." Beverly, Mass.: Parker Brothers Company, 1995.

Parker, Robert E. *Flesh Peddlers and Warm Bodies: The Temporary Help Industry and Its Workers*. New Brunswick, N.J.: Rutgers University Press, 1994.

Parsons, John E. "Bankers and Bargaining: The Eastern Airlines Case." *Economic Notes*, April–May 1986, pp. 6–8.

Passaro, Vince. "Who'll Stop the Drain? Reflections on the Art of Going Broke." *Harper's*, August 1998, pp. 38–39.

Passell, Peter. "A Mystery Bankers Love: How Do Credit Cards Stay So Profitable?" *The New York Times*, 17 August 1995, p. D2.

"A Payoff to Loan Sharks." *St. Petersburg Times*, 8 March 1999, p. A8.

Peacham, Henry. *The Worth of a Penny or a Caution to Keep Money*. London: S. Griffen, 1664.

Pearlstein, Steven. "U.S. Finds Productivity, but Not Pay, Is Rising." *The Washington Post*, 11 January 1995, p. A1.

_____. "Fleet-Footed Firms Reshape Economy: 'Gazelles' Represent a Business Revolution." *The Washington Post*, 4 July 1994, pp. A1, A11.

Perrucci, Carolyn C., Robert Perrucci, Dena B. Targ, and Harry R. Targ. *Plant Closings: International Context and Social Costs*. New York: Aldine de Gruyter, 1988.

Peterson, Peter G. "Will America Grow Up Before It Grows Old?" *Atlantic Monthly*, May 1996, www.theatlantic.com.

Peterson, Richard R. "A Re-Evaluation of the Economic Consequences of Divorce." *American Sociological Review*, vol. 61 (1996), pp. 528–536.

_____. *Women, Work, and Divorce*. Albany: State University of New York Press, 1989.

Phelps, William Clyde. *The Role of Sales Finance Companies in the American Economy*. Baltimore, Md.: Commercial Credit Company, 1952.

Phillips, Kevin. *Boiling Point: Democrats, Republicans, and the Decline of Middle-Class Prosperity*. New York: Random House, 1993.

_____. *The Politics of Rich and Poor: Wealth and the American Electorate in the Reagan Aftermath*. New York: HarperCollins, 1991.

Pianin, E., and John M. Berry. "The Clinton Budget: A Sobering Surplus Scenario." *The Washington Post*, 8 February 2000, p. A1.

Piore, Michael J. *Birds of Passage: Migrant Labor and Industrial Societies*. New York: Cambridge University Press, 1979.

Piore, Michael J., and Charles F. Sabel. *The Second Industrial Divide: Possibilities for Prosperity*. New York: Basic Books, 1984.

Piven, Frances Fox, and Richard A. Cloward. *Regulating the Poor: The Functions of Public Welfare*. New York: Vintage Press, 1997.

Pizzo, Stephne, Mary Fricker, and Paul Muolo. *Inside Job: The Looting of America's Savings and Loans*. New York: HarperCollins, 1991.

Poggi, Giafranco. *Calvinism and the Capitalist Spirit: Max Weber's Protestant Ethnic*. Amherst: University of Massachusetts Press, 1983.

Pollak, Oliver B. "Gender and Bankruptcy: An Empirical Analysis of Evolving Trends in Chapter 7 and Chapter 13 Bankruptcy Filings, 1967–1997," *Commercial Law Journal* 102 (Fall 1997), pp. 333–338.

Pollin, Robert. *Deeper in Debt: The Changing Financial Conditions of U.S. Households.* Washington, D.C.: Economic Policy Institute, 1990.

Porter, Michael E. *The Michael E. Porter Trilogy: Competitive Strategy, Competitive Advantage of Nations.* New York: Free Press, 1998.

————. "The Competitive Advantage of the Inner City." *Harvard Business Review,* vol. 73, no. 3 (May–June 1995), pp. 55–71.

Portes, Alejandro, and Robert D. Manning. "The Immigrant Enclave: Theory and Empirical Examples." In *Ethnicity: Structure and Progress,* edited by Joan Nagel and Susan Olzak. New York: Academic Press, 1986.

Powers, Evelyn Tan. "Just How Did They Get Rich?" *USA Today,* 22 February 2000, p. 4B.

Pressler, Margaret Webb. "At Giant, a New Meaning for 'Paper, or Plastic?'" *The Washington Post,* 14 March 1996, p. D11.

Preston, Samuel H., and Linda G. Martin, eds. *Demography of Aging.* Washington, D.C.: National Academy of Sciences Press, 1994.

Price, Robert, ed. *Entrepreneurship, 1999–2000.* Guilford, Conn.: Dushkin/McGraw-Hill, 1999.

Public Interest Research Group (PIRG). *The Campus Credit Card Trap.* Washington, D.C.: PIRG, 1998.

Public Interest Research Group (PIRG) and Consumer Federation of America (CFA). *Show Me the Money! A Survey of Payday Lenders and Review of Payday Lender Lobbying in State Legislatures.* Washington, D.C.: PIRG, 2000.

Punch, Linda. "Citicorp: Where Does the Giant Go from Here?" *Credit Card Management,* October 1991, p. 42.

Purdy, Mathew, and Joe Sexton. "Short of Banking Services, the Poor Are Improvising." *The New York Times,* 11 September 1995, p. A1.

Quadagno, Jill. *The Transformation of Old-Age Security: Class and Politics in the American Welfare State.* Chicago: University of Chicago Press, 1988.

Quinlan, Michael. "Committee Kills Rules for Rental Stores." *The Courier-Journal,* 4 February 2000, p. B1.

————. "Title-Loan Firms Extinct in State." *The Courier-Journal,* 28 April 1999, p. B1.

Quinn, Jane Bryant. "Little Loans Come at Staggering Cost." *The Washington Post,* 13 June 1999, p. H2.

————. "New Tax Credits May Bring Cuts in Student Aid." *The Washington Post,* 31 August 1997, p. H2.

Ramsey, Dave. *Financial Peace: Restoring Financial Hope to You and Your Family.* New York: Viking Press, 1998.

Reich, Kenneth. "Son's Debt Plagues Dad for 7 Years." *Los Angeles Times,* 17 January 1999, p. 4.

Reid, Margaret G. *Consumers and the Market.* New York: F. S. Crofts, 1938.

Rent-A-Center, Inc. *1999 Quarterly Report.* SEC Form 10-K, 12 May 1999.

Riley, Richard W. "Give the Middle Class a Break on Education." *The Washington Post,* 24 April 1997, p. 25.

Ritzer, George. *Expressing America: A Critique of the Global Credit Card Society.* Thousand Oaks, Calif.: Pine Forge Press, 1995.

Rivenburg, Tanya. "Charge, Granny, Charge!" Unpublished manuscript, Department of Sociology, American University, 1994.

Robinson, Louis N., and Rolf Nugent. *Regulation of the Small Loan Business.* New York: Russell Sage Foundation, 1935.

"Rockville Woman Is Charged with Purse-Snatchings." *The Washington Post,* 11 February 1998, p. B5.

Rodgers, Will. "Car Title Lenders Say Rates Cheap." *Tampa Tribune,* 25 August 1999, p. 1.

Romell, Rick. "Title Loans Provide a Fast Lane to Cash, Debt." *Milwaukee Journal Sentinel,* 30 November 1999, p. 1.

Roska, John. "How High Can the Finance Companies Go? With Interest Rates, the Sky Is the Limit." *St. Louis Dispatch,* 16 July 1998, p. 4.

Rowan, Roy. "The Maverick Who Yelled Foul at Citibank." *Fortune,* 10 January 1983, pp. 46–56.

Ruth, Robert. "Attorney Charged with Federal Felonies in Separate Cases." *Columbus Dispatch,* 10 December 1998, p. D3.

Rybczynski, Witold. *Waiting for the Weekend.* New York: Viking Press, 1991.

Ryscavage, Paul. "Trends in Income and Wealth of the Elderly in the 1980s." U.S. Bureau of the Census, *Current Population Reports,* series P-60, no. 183. Washington, D.C.: U.S. Department of Commerce, 1992.

Salt Lake Tribune. "Rent-to-Own." Reprinted in *The Plain Dealer,* 3 January 2000, p. C3.

Samuelson, Robert J. "The Hypocrisy Scholarship." *The Washington Post,* 12 February 1997, p. A23.

Sanchez, Rene. "5% College Tuition Increase Still Outpacing 2% Inflation." *The Washington Post,* 25 September 1997, p. A3.

Sanders, Edmund. "Banking Takes Interest in Check-Cashing Industry." *Los Angeles Times,* 16 March 2000, p. A1.

Saunders, Peter. *A Nation of Home Owners.* London: Unwin Hyman, 1990.

Schlesinger, Allison. "College Students Urged to Avoid Credit-Card Debt." *St. Louis Post-Dispatch,* 31 August 1998, p. 5.

Schneider, Greg. "Lockheed to Reorganize, Cut 2,800 Jobs." *The Washington Post,* 28 January 2000, p. E3.

Schor, Juliet B. *The Overspent American: Upscaling, Downshifting, and the New Consumer.* New York: Basic Books, 1998.

Schurenberg, Eric. "Getting on Top of Your Debt." *Money,* April 1987, pp. 95–99.

Scott, Kenneth. "The Future of Bank Regulation." In *To Promote Prosperity: U.S. Domestic Policy in the Mid-1980s,* edited by John Moore. Stanford, Calif.: Hoover Institution Press, 1984.

Scott, Thayer. "Scam Cost 77-Year-Old $20,000." *St. Petersburg Times,* 12 July 1997, p. 1.

Securities Data Company. "Merger and Corporate Transactions Database Reported in Table 884," in *1998 Statistical Abstract of the United States.* Washington, D.C.: U.S. Government Printing Office, 1999, p. 556.

Segal, David. "Small Business: For Entrepreneurs, Hopeful Days at Center Stage." *The Washington Post Business,* 12 June 1995, p. 13.

Sexton, Patricia Cayo. *The War on Labor and the Left.* Boulder: Westview Press, 1991.

Shammas, Carole. "Explaining Past Changes in Consumption and Consumer Behavior." *Historical Methods,* vol. 22 (Spring 1989), pp. 61–67.

Shapiro, Isaac, and Robert Greenstein. *The Widening Income Gulf.* Washington, D.C.: Center on Budget and Policy Priorities, 1999.

Shenk, Joshua Wolf. "In Debt All the Way up to Their Nose Rings." *U.S. News & World Report,* 9 June 1999, p. 38.

Shilling, Gary. *The World Has Definitely Changed.* New York: Lakeview Press, 1986.

Shim, Shirley, and Mary Mahoney. "The Elderly Mail Order Catalog User of Fashion Products." *Journal of Direct Marketing,* vol. 6 (Winter 1992), pp. 49–58.

Shostak, Arthur. *Robust Unionism.* Ithaca, N.Y.: Industrial Relations Press, 1991.

Siklos, Richard, and Catherine Yang. "Welcome to the 21st Century." *Business Week,* 24 January 2000, pp. 36–44.

Silverman, Gary, and Leah Nathans Spiro. "Citicorp and Travelers: Is This Marriage Working?" *Business Week,* 7 June 1999, pp. 127–134.

Silvestri, George, and John Lukasiewicz. "Outlook: 1990–2005, Occupational Employment Projections." *Monthly Labor Review,* November 1991, pp. 64–94.

Skocpol, Theda. *Protecting Soldiers and Mothers: The Political Origins of Social Policy in the United States.* Cambridge: Harvard University Press, 1995.

Slaughter, Louise. "Why We Need HR-3142." *Rochester Democrat,* 31 August 1999, www.creditcardnation.com.

Sloan, Allen. "How You Can Invest with Revlon's Ronald Perelman." *Money,* July 1994, pp. 19–20.

———. "Airlines That Are Loaded Down with Debt Will Have Struggle to Stay Afloat." *The Washington Post,* 30 October 1990, p. D3.

Smith, Adam C. "Price of Fast Car Cash Can Put Unwary on Foot." *St. Petersburg Times,* January 1999, p. A1.

Smith, Joyce. "When Luck Runs Out." *Kansas City Star,* 9 January 2000, p. A1.

SMR Research Corporation. *The Personal Bankruptcy Crisis, 1997: Demographics, Causes, Implications, and Solutions.* Hackettstown, N.J.: SMR Research Corporation, 1997.

Snathmary, Richard. "Credit Card Offers Hit Record Volume." *DM News,* 31 July 1995, p. 5.

Soldo, Beth J., and Vicki A. Freedman. "Care of the Elderly: Division of Labor Among the Family, Market, and State." In *Demography of Aging,* edited by Samuel Preston and Linda Martin. Washington, D.C.: National Academy of Sciences Press, 1994.

Solomon, Steven. *Small Business USA: The Role of Small Companies in Sparking America's Economic Transformation.* New York: Crown Publishers, 1986.

Soyer, Daniel. *Jewish Immigrant Associations and American Identity in New York, 1880–1939.* Cambridge: Harvard University Press, 1997.

Spinner, Jackie. "Women Do Well in Business, but Not as Well at the Bank." *The Washington Post,* 27 July 1995, p. B10.

Spiro, Lee Nathans, and Ronald Grover. "The Operator: An Inside Look at Ron Perelman's $5 Billion Empire." *Business Week,* 21 August 1995, pp. 54–59.

Squires, Gregory D., ed. *From Redlining to Reinvestment: Community Responses to Urban Disinvestment.* Philadelphia: Temple University Press, 1992.

Squires, Gregory D., and Sally O'Connor. "Fringe Banking in Milwaukee: The Rise of Check-Cashing Businesses and the Emergence of a Two-Tiered Banking System." *Urban Affairs Review,* vol. 34, no. 1 (1998), pp. 126–163.

Stanback, Thomas. *The New Suburbanization: Challenge to the Central City.* Boulder, Colo.: Westview Press, 1991.

Stanley, Frances D. *Accessing Capital: Start to Finish.* Richmond, Va.: Federal Reserve Bank of Richmond, September 1998.

Stanley, Thomas J., and William D. Danko. *The Millionaire Next Door: The Surprising Secrets of America's Wealthy.* Atlanta: Longstreet Press, 1996.

Staten, Michael E. "A Profile of Debt, Income, and Expenses of Consumers in Bankruptcy." Testimony before the national Bankruptcy Review Commission, Washington, D.C., 17 December 1996.

Stein, Benjamin J. *A License to Steal: The Untold Story of Michael Milken and the
Conspiracy to Bilk the Nation.* New York: Simon & Schuster, 1992.

Stein, Ruthe. "A Haunting Tale of Success." *San Francisco Chronicle*, 11 July 1999,
p. 29.

Stevens, Talbot. "Make High-Interest Debt a Top Priority." *The London Press*, 10
July 2000, p. 7.

Stewart, James B. *Den of Thieves.* New York: Simon & Schuster, 1992.

Stodder, Gayle Sato. "Girls Rule, Women Entrepreneurs Are Getting Rich . . . So
Why Aren't They Getting Famous?" *Entrepreneurs' Business Start-Ups*, December
1999, pp. 42–47.

Stone, Robyn. "The Feminization of Poverty Among the Elderly." *Women's Studies
Quarterly*, vol. 17 (1989), pp. 20–34.

Strasser, Susan. *Satisfaction Guaranteed: The Making of the American Mass Market.*
Washington, D.C.: Smithsonian Institution Press, 1994.

Strasser, Susan, Charles McGovern, and Matthias Judt, eds. *Getting and Spending:
European and American Consumer Societies in the Twentieth Century.* Cambridge:
Cambridge University Press, 1998.

Strobel, Frederick R. *Upward Dreams, Downward Mobility: The Economic Decline of
the Middle Class.* Lanham, Md.: Rowman & Littlefield, 1993.

Strunsky, Steve. "77-Year-Old Is Charged in Armed Robbery." *The New York Times*,
8 March 1998, p. 6.

Sugawara, Sandra. "Merger Wave Accelerated in 1999." *The Washington Post*, 31
December 1999, p. E1.

Sullivan, Kevin, and Mary Jordan. "In Japan, Cash Registers, Many Merchants Start
Accepting Credit Cards at Urging of Olympic Officials." *The Washington Post*, 4
February 1998, p. E2.

Sullivan, Teresa, and Elizabeth Warren. "The Changing Demographics of Bankruptcy." *Norton Bankruptcy Law Advisor*, no. 10 (October 1999), pp. 1–7.

Sullivan, Teresa A., Elizabeth Warren, and Jay L. Westbrook. *The Fragile Middle
Class: Americans in Debt.* New Haven: Yale University Press, 2000.

_____. "Bankruptcy and the Family." *Marriage and Family Review*, vol. 21, nos.
3–4 (1995), pp. 194–215.

_____. "Consumer Debtors Ten Years Later: A Financial Comparison of Con-
sumer Bankrupts, 1981–91." *American Bankruptcy Law Journal*, vol. 68 (1994).

_____. *As We Forgive Our Debtors: Bankruptcy and Consumer Credit in America.*
New York: Oxford University Press, 1989.

Surowiecki, James. "Mindless Merging." *The Motley Fool Slate Archives*, 23 April
1998, www.slate.msn.com/motleyfool.

Susswein, Ruth. Testimony before the U.S. House Subcommittee on Consumer
Credit and Insurance, 10 March 1994.

Tapas, Tina D. "Issuers Graduate to the Risky, but Lucrative, College Market." *Card
Marketing*, July/August, pp. 12–15.

Taub, Stephen, and David Carey. "The Wall Street 100." *Financial World*, 5 July
1994, p. 33.

Teck, Alan. *Mutual Saving Banks and Savings and Loan Associations.* New York: Columbia University Press, 1968.

Thernstrom, Stephan. *Poverty and Progress: Social Mobility in a Nineteenth-Century
City.* Cambridge: Harvard University Press, 1964.

Thompson, E. P. "Time, Work-Discipline, and Industrial Capitalism." *Past and Present*, vol. 38 (December 1967), pp. 88–91.

Thurow, Lester. *Head to Head: The Coming Economic Battle Among Japan, Europe, and America*. New York: William Morrow, 1992.

Tigges, Leann. "On Dueling Sectors: The Role of Service Industries in the Earning Process of the Dual Economy." In *Industries, Firms, and Jobs*, edited by George Farkas and Paula England. New York: Aldine de Gruyter, 1994.

Tilly, Chris. *Half a Job*. Philadelphia: Temple University Press, 1996.

Tolchin, Martin, and Susan Tolchin. *Buying into America: How Foreign Money Is Changing the Face of Our Nation*. New York: Times Books, 1988, pp. 133–151.

Torres, Gariel. "The El Barzón Debtors' Movement: From the Local to the National in Protest Politics." In *The Transformation of Rural Mexico: Reforming the Ejido Sector*, edited by Wayne A. Cornelius and David Myhre. La Jolla, Calif.: Center for U.S.-Mexican Studies, 1998, pp. 131–155.

Tucker, David M. *The Decline of Thrift in America: Our Cultural Shift from Saving to Spending*. New York: Praeger, 1991.

Ullmann, Owen. "Billionaire and Activist Give the Same Advice: Avoid Credit Cards." *USA Today*, 12 October 1999, p. A5.

United Credit National Bank. "Disclosure of Terms." Visa Credit Card Contract, 1999.

U.S. Bureau of the Census. "Current Population Reports." *1998 Statistical Abstract of the United States*. Washington, D.C.: U.S. Government Printing Office, 1999. At www.census.gov/hhes/income/histinc.

———. *Current Population Survey/Housing Vacancy Survey*, cited in "Homeowner-ship Rates by Age of Householder," *1998 Statistical Abstract of the United States*. Washington, D.C.: U.S. Government Printing Office, 1999.

———. "Money Income of Families," reported in table 746, *1998 Statistical Abstract of the United States*. Washington, D.C.: U.S. Government Printing Office, 1999, p. 472.

———. "Per Capita Money Income," reported in table 755, *1998 Statistical Abstract of the United States*. Washington, D.C.: U.S. Government Printing Office, 1999, p. 476.

———. *Women-Owned Businesses, 1992 Economic Census*. Washington, D.C.: U.S. Government Printing Office, 1995.

———. "Current Housing Reports." *Homeownership Trends in the 1980s*. Washington, D.C.: U.S. Government Printing Office, 1991.

———. "Historical Income Tables." At www.census.gov/hhes/income/histinc/f07.html.

U.S. Bureau of Economic Analysis. "Gross Saving and Investment: 1990 to 1997." Cited in *1998 Statistical Abstract of the United States*. Washington, D.C.: U.S. Government Printing Office, 1999.

———. *Survey of Current Business*. "International Investment Position." Reported in *1998 Statistical Abstract of the United States*. Washington, D.C.: U.S. Government Printing Office, 1999.

U.S. Bureau of Labor Statistics. "International Comparisons of Hourly Compensation Costs for Production Workers in Manufacturing." Washington, D.C.: U.S. Government Printing Office, September 2000, at www.stats.bls.gov.flshome.

———. *Employment and Monthly Earnings*, vol. 47, no. 1, January 2000, p. 219, at www.stats.bls.gov.

———. "Employment and Earnings." Reported in *1998 Statistical Abstract of the United States*. Washington, D.C.: U.S. Government Printing Office, 1999.

_____. "Monthly Labor Review." *1998 Statistical Abstract of the United States.* Washington, D.C.: U.S. Government Printing Office, 1999.

_____. *News*, USDL 96-446. *1998 Statistical Abstract of the United States.* Washington, D.C.: U.S. Government Printing Office, 1999.

_____. *Handbook of Labor Statistics.* Washington, D.C.: Government Printing Office, 1993.

U.S. Bureau of the Public Debt, U.S. Department of Treasury. "The Public Debt to the Penny." At www.house.gov.

U.S. Congress, Congressional Budget Office. *The Budget and Economic Outlook: Fiscal Years 2001–2010.* Washington, D.C.: U.S. Government Printing Office, 2000.

_____. Memorandum, "Estimates of Federal Tax Liabilities for Individuals and Families by Income Category and Family Type for 1995 and 1999." Washington, D.C., 1998.

_____. *The Economic and Budget Outlook: Fiscal Years 1996–2000.* Washington, D.C.: U.S. Government Printing Office, 1995.

_____. *The Changing Business of Banking: A Study of Failed Banks from 1987 to 1992.* Washington, D.C.: U.S. Government Printing Office, 1994.

_____. *Assessing the Decline in the National Saving Rate.* Washington, D.C.: U.S. Government Printing Office, 1993.

_____. *Baby Boomers in Retirement: An Early Perspective.* Washington, D.C.: U.S. Government Printing Office, September 1993.

_____. *Displaced Workers: Trends in the 1980s and Implications for the Future.* Washington, D.C.: U.S. Government Printing Office, 1993.

U.S. Department of Commerce. "Foreign Direct Investment in the United States," reported in table 1309, *1998 Statistical Abstract of the United States.* Washington, D.C.: U.S. Government Printing Office, 1999, p. 791.

_____. "U.S. Balances on International Transactions," reported in table 1303, *1998 Statistical Abstract of the United States.* Washington, D.C.: U.S. Government Printing Office, 1999, p. 788.

_____. "U.S. International Transactions by Type of Transactions," reported in table 1302, *1998 Statistical Abstract of the United States.* Washington, D.C.: U.S. Government Printing Office, 1999, p. 786.

_____. "U.S. Total Trade Balances with Individual Countries, 1991–98." 1999, at www.ita.doc.gov/industry.

_____. "International Investment Positions: 1980 to 1992," reported in table 1309, *1994 Statistical Abstract of the United States.* Washington, D.C.: U.S. Government Printing Office, 1995, p. 807.

_____. "U.S. International Transactions: 1980 to 1992," reported in table 1306, *1994 Statistical Abstract of the United States.* Washington, D.C.: U.S. Government Printing Office, 1995, p. 804.

U.S. Department of Commerce, Bureau of Economic Analysis. *Survey of Current Business*, summarized in "U.S. Personal Savings Rate 1929–1998," at www.bea.doc.gov.

U.S. Department of Commerce, Small Business Administration. *The Facts About Small Business.* Washington, D.C.: U.S. Government Printing Office, 1997.

U.S. Department of Labor. *Handbook of Labor Statistics 1975.* Washington, D.C.: U.S. Government Printing Office, 1976.

U.S. Employment Standards Administration. "Federal Minimum Wage Rates," cited in table 699, *1998 Statistical Abstract of the United States.* Washington, D.C.: U.S. Government Printing Office, 1999, p. 438.

_____. "Flow of Funds Accounts," reported in *1998 Statistical Abstract of the United States*. Washington, D.C.: U.S. Government Printing Office, 1999.

_____. *Annual Statistical Digests*.

_____. *Federal Reserve Bulletins*.

U.S. Federal Reserve System. *Federal Reserve Bulletin*, April 1998, cited in "Debt Status of Homeowners," *1998 Statistical Abstract of the United States*. Washington, D.C.: U.S. Government Printing Office, 1999.

U.S. General Accounting Office. *High-Yield Bonds: Nature of the Market and Effect on Federally Insured Institutions*. Washington, D.C.: U.S. Government Printing Office, May 1988.

U.S. General Accounting Office. "Personal Bankruptcy: Analysis of Four Reports on Chapter 7 Debtors' Ability to Pay." GAO/GGD-99-103, June 1999.

U.S. House of Representatives, Committee on Small Business. *New Economic Realities: The Rise of Women Entrepreneurs*. Report no. 100-736. Washington, D.C.: U.S. Government Printing Office, 1988.

U.S. House of Representatives, Subcommittee on Oversight, Committee on Ways and Means. Transcript of "Federal Tax Payments by U.S. Subsidiaries of Foreign-Controlled Companies." 9 April 1992.

U.S. News & World Report. "Heavy Lifting: How America's Debt Burden Threatens the Economic Recovery." 6 May 1991, pp. 52–61.

_____. "The Vanishing Dream: Upward Mobility Is No Longer Possible for Millions of American Workers." 22 April 1991, pp. 39–43.

U.S. Office of Management and Budget. *Historical Tables*. "Federal Budget Outlays," reported in *1998 Statistical Abstract of the United States*. Washington, D.C.: U.S. Government Printing Office, 1999.

Vaughan, Roger, and Edward Hill. *Banking on the Brink*. Washington, D.C.: Washington Post Company, 1992.

Veblen, Thorstein. *The Theory of the Leisure Class*. New York: Macmillan, 1899.

Vickers, Marcia. "Big Cards on Campus." *Business Week*, 20 September 1999, p. 136.

_____. "A Hard Lesson on Credit Cards." *Business Week*, 15 March 1999, p. 107.

Violino, Bob. "Banking on E-Business." *Information Week*, 3 May 1999, pp. 1–6.

Vitt, Lois A., and Jurg K. Siegenthaler, eds. *Encyclopedia of Financial Gerontology*. Westport, Conn.: Greenwood Press, 1996.

Vogelstein, Fred. "How High Can It Go?" *U.S. News & World Report*, 18 March 1998, www.usnews.com/usnews/edu.

Waldman, Mark S. *The Way of Real Wealth*. New York: HarperCollins, 1993.

Waldman, Michael, and Public Citizens Congress Watch Staff. *Who Robbed America? A Citizen's Guide to the Savings and Loan Scandal*. New York: Random House, 1990.

Warren, Elizabeth. "Consumer Bankruptcy: Issues Summary." Unpublished paper, Harvard Law School, Cambridge, Mass., April 1999.

_____. "The Bankruptcy Crisis." *Indiana Law Journal*, vol. 73, no. 4 (1998), at www.law.indiana.edu.

Watson, Jamal E. "Banking on a Costly Alternative, Low Earners Turn to Check-Cashing Stores." *Boston Globe*, 28 February 2000, p. A1.

Weber, Max. "Class, Status, Power." In *Essays in Economic Sociology*, edited by Richard Swedberg. Princeton: Princeton University Press, 1999.

_____. *The Protestant Ethic and the Spirit of Capitalism*. London: Unwin Hyman, 1930.

Weinberg, Jean. "GU to Submit Plans for New MBNA Performing Arts Center." *The Hoya*, 17 September 1999, p. 1.

Weitzman, Lenore J. *The Divorce Revolution: The Unexpected Social and Economic Consequences for Women and Children in America.* New York: Free Press, 1985.

Wessel, Kim. "Two Plead Guilty in Ballroom-Dancing Fraud Case." *The Courier Journal,* 26 March 1999, p. B5.

Western, Ken. "Company Cashes in on Coupons: Ideas Bring Fast Growth." *Arizona Republic,* 7 September 1997, p. D1.

White, Gayle. "Diocese Cancels Bishop's Appointment." *Atlanta Journal-Constitution,* 26 February 2000, p. B1.

White House Office of the Press Secretary. "President Clinton Unveils 'First Accounts': Bringing the 'Unbanked' into the Financial Mainstream." May 2000, at www.whitehouse.gov/WH.

Williams, Monci Jo. "The Great Plastic Card Fight Begins." *Fortune,* 4 February 1985, pp. 18–23.

Winninghoff, Ellie. "Crashing the Glass Ceiling." *Entrepreneurial Woman,* vol. 1 (1990), pp. 66–70.

Wolff, Edward B. *Top Heavy: A Study of the Increasing Inequality of Wealth in America.* New York: A Twentieth Century Fund Report, 1999.

"Woman Says Firm Duped Her for Credit Card Number." *St. Petersburg Times,* 1 August 1999, p. 3.

Woodstock Institute. "Community-Bank Partnerships Creating Opportunities for the Unbanked." *Reinvestment Alert,* no. 15, June 2000, at www.woodstockinst.org.

Wu, Ke Bin. *Income and Poverty in 1993: How Did Older Americans Do?* Washington, D.C.: American Association of Retired Persons, 1995.

Yip, Pamela. "RALs Can Be Quick Money, but There's a Price to Be Paid for Getting Tax Refund in a Hurry." *San Diego Union-Tribune,* 5 March 2000, p. 12.

Zeimer, Richard C. "Impact of Recent Tax Law Changes." *Survey of Current Business,* vol. 65 (April 1985), pp. 28–31.

Zey, Mary. *Banking on Fraud: Drexel, Junk Bonds, and Buyouts.* New York: Aldine de Gruyter, 1993.

Zremski, Jerry. "End Wrongful Penalties for Paying on Time." *Buffalo News,* 19 August 1998, p. 2B.

Zuckerman, Gregory. "U.S. Boom: Living on Borrowed Dime?" *The Wall Street Journal,* 31 December 1999, p. 1.

Index